STOCKING UP III
America's Classic Preserving Guide

Carol Hupping
and the staff
of the Rodale
Food Center

D0926896

MJF BOOKS
NEW YORK

RECIPE DEVELOPMENT:
Judith Benn Hurley, with assistance from Nancy J. Zelko, Nancy Ayers,
    Susan Burwell, Frances J. Fry, Linda C. Gilbert, and Debra Deis Johnson
RESEARCH AND RECIPE TESTING:
Anita Hirsch, JoAnn Brader, Rhonda Diehl, Fran Wilson, Marilen Reed,
    Natalie Updegrove, Beth Pianucci, Marie Harrington, and Tom Ney
EDITORIAL COORDINATION:
Cheryl Winters Tetreau
DESIGN:
Glen Burris, Pat Pennington, Anita Patterson
ILLUSTRATIONS:
Kathi Ember
MANUSCRIPT COORDINATION:
Barbara Emert

Published by MJF Books
Fine Communications
Two Lincoln Square
60 West 66th Street
New York, NY 10023

Library of Congress Catalog Card Number 94-76048
ISBN 1-56731-073-7

Printed by arrangement with Rodale Press.

Manufactured in the United States of America

MJF Books and the MJF colophon are trademarks of Fine Creative Media,
Inc.

10 9 8 7 6 5 4 3 2 1

Contents

Meats, Poultry, and Fish

Nuts, Seeds, Grains, and Sprouts

Introduction

Revising this book for the second time has meant many months of concentrated work for me. But it's been a labor of love. After all, how often in life do you have the chance to redo something you've already done and make it better? I've had that opportunity not once, but twice now.

There was lots of room for change this third time around. For instance, we know more about the science of food safety than we did then: We know that not all tomatoes are high enough in acid content to be canned in the traditional way. New kitchen equipment can make certain procedures a whole lot easier: Food processors are godsends, and microwave ovens give you the first legitimate alternative to steam and water blanching. Now you can have wonderful pickles and cheeses that contain not a drop of added salt, and you can make jams and jellies with a non-nutritive sweetener if you wish.

Most of the recipes here are brand new; those that come from the last edition have all been retested and in many cases improved. We've held on to the good, old traditional elements you'd expect to find in a reliable food preserving book, like recipes for catsup and old-fashioned cucumber chunks, and directions for drying apples and making fruit leathers. But we've kept up with the times by adding new ones that reflect new food interests: sun-dried tomatoes, spiced mustards, new herb vinegars, and fruit sherbets.

There is now an Appendix with sources of information and supplies that we recommend. And the hints, tips, and boxes highlight important, updated information and advice for easier, quicker food handling.

MANY THANKS

When the original *Stocking Up* was written back in 1973, we had no home economists, no culinary artists, no food technologists, no product researchers on staff. But somehow we got by, thanks to the personal energy, practical experience, and tremendous enthusiasm of a handful of people.

By 1977, we had come a long way. It was then that the first revision of *Stocking Up* was written, and for that project we could call upon the expertise of the staffs of two of our newest departments: the Rodale Test Kitchen and our Product Testing Department.

But that growth of experience and expertise cannot come close to matching the resources that came together for *Stocking Up III*. Our Test Kitchen has mushroomed into the Rodale Food Center, with a staff of 14, devoted to food research and recipe development and testing. And our Product Testing Department is now called Technical Services. I can't imagine now how I ever got by without their help.

Judith Benn Hurley, Supervisor of Culinary Arts, is the brains behind most of the new recipes in this edition and the person whom I most depended upon to help me with baffling food questions. Once the recipes left Judith's hands, they then had to meet the careful scrutiny of Anita Hirsch, N.S., Test Kitchen Supervisor, who tested them not only for taste and eye appeal but also for how well they kept in storage. (And let me add that Anita now knows more about homemade cheeses than anyone else at Rodale.)

But there is much more to this team of food experts, and many more people to whom I owe much thanks. Linda C. Gilbert, now Director of the Rodale Food Consultants, got this revision off the ground in the Food Center and set priorities and pace for it there. Tom Ney, Director of the Food Center, not only showed us the proper way to shuck a clam but also gave his staff the support they needed to do their job so well.

Recipe developers Nancy J. Zelko, Nancy Ayers, Susan Burwell, Frances J. Fry, and Debra Deis Johnson did a masterful job in working along with Judith Hurley. Hats off, too, to home economists JoAnn Brader, Rhonda Diehl, Fran Wilson, Marilen Reed, and Natalie Updegrove, food technologist Marie Harrington, and research assistant Beth Pianucci.

On the editorial side, the prize goes to Cheryl Tetreau. Cheryl stayed with me through thick and thin; through dozens of illustrations that needed research, review, and captions; through endless questions from designers and copy editors. Barbara Emert, the wizard of the word processor, taught me more than just a thing or two about its magic, and rescued me more times than I care to confess when I got caught in its maze.

Then there's the artistic flair of Pat Pennington and Glen Burris who worked under Jerry O'Brien's direction to provide the good taste and design of this book. Kathi Ember, directed by Anita Patterson, created the light and lovely illustrations.

Let me not forget the many other people who helped us with information, equipment, and ideas: Elizabeth Andress, Research Assistant, and Dr. Gerald Kuhn, professor of food science, both at Pennsylvania State University; James B. Magee, Technical Director for Mrs. Wages Light Home Jell; Joan Randle, Manager for Consumer Affairs for Ball Corporation; Connie Sumberg and Brian Summer, both at Pomona's Universal Pectin; Ken Houser of Emmaus Seafood; Ricki and Bob Carroll of New England Cheesemaking Supply Company; Dr. Frank Thomas at Agricultural Extension Service at North Carolina State University; and Bob Spotts, Diane Maquire, and Adam S. Butz.

Carol Hupping

Vegetables and Fruits

Choosing Vegetable
and Fruit Varieties

As you page through any seed catalog, you'll discover that each vegetable and fruit is usually available in a number of varieties. Some may be particularly good for freezing; others maintain their quality best when canned. Certain varieties dry better than others, and some hold their flavor and texture well in underground storage. If you're planning to preserve a good part of your harvest, you'd do well to decide how you will be storing your garden surplus before you order your seeds, and then choose those fruit and vegetable varieties accordingly.

We've made that process a little easier for you here, by listing in the charts that follow those vegetables and fruits that are generally recognized as being best for freezing; canning; drying; pickling; juicing; turning into a sauce; making jam, jelly, and preserves; and keeping in some kind of cold storage, be it in a root cellar, basement, or outdoor storage area (noted here as "good keeper").

After each variety you'll find the name of seed companies that sell that variety. If your favorite seed company is not listed, forgive us. It does not necessarily mean that the company doesn't carry the variety in question; it merely means that we have only noted the larger and more popular seed companies that we are most familiar with. We know that some small companies sell some of the same varieties, and we also know that they may offer other varieties just as good for particular storage methods.

This is the third edition of *Stocking Up,* and the third time that we have extensively revised these charts. Each time we went back to the seed catalogs we were amazed at how much had changed since the last time, which only goes to show that the seed business is far from a static one. New varieties and hybrids are being developed all the time, so keep a lookout for varieties too new to make this present chart.

Vegetable Varieties

Artichokes

Globe	good pickler	Gurney
Jerusalem	good keeper	Burpee, Gurney

Asparagus

Brock Imperial Hybrid	good canner, freezer	Burpee, Gurney, Harris, Park
California 500	good freezer	Field
Lorella	good freezer	Thompson & Morgan
Martha Washington	good freezer	Harris, Thompson & Morgan
Mary Washington	good canner, freezer	Burpee, Field, Gurney, Park, Stark, Twilley
Roberts	good freezer	Gurney

Beans, bush, green

Blue Crop	good canner, freezer	Harris, Stokes
Blue Lake	good canner, freezer	Burpee, Field, Gurney, Harris, Park, Stokes, Twilley
Burpee's Tenderpod	good canner	Burpee
Constanza	good freezer	Thompson & Morgan
Cyrus	good freezer	Thompson & Morgan
Early Contender	good canner, freezer	Field, Gurney, Park, Stokes, Twilley
Empress	good freezer	Gurney
Frenchie	good canner	Stokes
Greencrop	good freezer	Burpee, Field
Green Ruler	good freezer	Thompson & Morgan
Greensleeves	good freezer	Burpee
Improved Tendergreen	good canner, freezer	Burpee, Field, Gurney, Park, Stokes, Thompson & Morgan
Joy	good canner, freezer	Field, Gurney
Jumbo	good freezer	Johnny's, Thompson & Morgan
Kentucky Wonder	good canner, freezer	Field, Gurney, Harris, Park, Twilley
Limelight	good freezer; dry	Johnny's, Thompson & Morgan
Provider	good freezer	Harris, Johnny's, Stokes, Twilley
Remus	good freezer	Thompson & Morgan

Roma	good canner, freezer; dry	Burpee, Gurney, Harris, Park
Roma II	good canner	Twilley
Romano	good canner, freezer	Field, Gurney, Stokes
Royal Burgundy	good freezer	Burpee, Gurney, Park, Thompson & Morgan, Twilley
Royalty Purple	good freezer	Johnny's
Slenderette	good canner, freezer	Gurney, Park
Spartan Arrow	good freezer	Field
Speculator	good canner, freezer	Stokes
Tendercrop	good canner, freezer	Burpee, Field, Gurney, Harris, Park
Tenderette	good canner, freezer	Field, Gurney, Park
Topcrop	good canner, freezer	Burpee, Field, Gurney, Park, Twilley
White Half Runner	good canner, freezer	Burpee, Park

Beans, bush, yellow

Brittle Wax	good canner, freezer	Burpee
Cherokee Wax	good freezer	Field, Gurney, Harris, Stokes
Earliwax	good canner, freezer	Gurney
Eastern Butter Wax	good canner, freezer	Gurney
Goldcrop	good canner, freezer	Burpee, Park, Stokes, Twilley
Golden Rod	good freezer	Harris, Stokes
Golden Wax	good canner, freezer	Field, Gurney, Park
King Horn Wax	good canner, freezer	Burpee, Gurney
Pencil Pod Wax	good canner	Burpee, Field, Gurney
Sungold	good freezer	Harris, Stokes

Beans, lima

Baby Bush	good canner, freezer	Burpee, Field, Gurney, Stokes
Burpee's Best	good freezer	Burpee
Eastland	good freezer	Harris
Fordhook 242	good canner, freezer	Burpee, Field, Gurney, Harris, Johnny's, Park, Stokes, Twilley
Henderson	good canner, freezer	Burpee, Field, Johnny's, Twilley
Improved Giant Bush	good freezer	Burpee

continued

Vegetable Varieties—*continued*

Beans, lima—*continued*

Jackson Wonder	good canner, freezer; dry	Field, Park
King of the Garden	good canner, freezer, dry	Field, Park, Stokes, Twilley
Kingston	good freezer	Burpee
Prizetaker	good freezer	Burpee
Thorogreen (baby lima)	good canner, freezer	Field, Gurney, Park

Beans, pole

Blue Lake	good canner, freezer; dry	Burpee, Field, Gurney, Park, Stokes
Burpee Golden	good freezer	Burpee
Enorma	good freezer	Thompson & Morgan
Erecta	good freezer	Thompson & Morgan
Goliath	good freezer	Thompson & Morgan
Kentucky Wonder (Old Homestead)	good freezer	Burpee, Field, Gurney, Harris, Johnny's, Stokes, Twilley
Purple Pod	good canner, freezer	Field, Gurney, Thompson & Morgan
Romano	good freezer	Burpee, Gurney, Harris, Park, Thompson & Morgan
Scarlet Emperor	good freezer	Thompson & Morgan
Selma Star	good canner, freezer	Park
Selma Zebra	good freezer; dry	Park

Beans, for drying

Black Turtle		Field, Gurney, Johnny's
Dwarf Horticultural		Twilley
Dwarf Taylor		Field, Gurney
Fava		Burpee, Field, Gurney, Johnny's, Thompson & Morgan
Garbanzo (chick-peas)		Burpee, Field, Gurney, Park
Great Northern		Burpee, Field, Gurney
Maine Yellow Eye		Johnny's
Mung		Burpee
Navy		Field, Gurney
Pinto		Burpee, Field, Gurney, Park
Red Kidney		Burpee, Field, Gurney, Johnny's, Park, Stokes

Redkloud		Harris
Soldier		Gurney, Johnny's
Swedish Brown		Gurney
White Kidney		Harris
White Marrow		Burpee, Stokes

Beets

Avenger	good freezer	Harris
Baby Canning (Gladiator)	good canner, pickler	Gurney
Badger Baby	good canner	Field
Burpee's Golden	good pickler	Burpee, Gurney, Stokes, Thompson & Morgan
Dark Red Canner	good pickler	Field
Detroit Dark Red	good canner, freezer, keeper	Burpee, Field, Gurney, Harris, Park, Stokes, Twilley
Early Wonder	good canner, pickler	Field, Gurney, Johnny's, Park, Twilley
Formanova	good canner, pickler, keeper	Johnny's, Stokes
Forono	good keeper	Gurney
Golden Beet	good pickler	Field, Park
Hybrid Red Ace	good pickler	Field, Gurney, Johnny's
Little Ball	good canner, pickler	Twilley
Little Mini Ball	good pickler	Stokes
Long Season	good keeper	Gurney, Harris, Stokes
Lutz Greenleaf	good keeper	Johnny's
Pacemaker	good canner, freezer	Stokes, Thompson & Morgan, Twilley
Perfected Detroit	good pickler	Gurney
Red Ball	good canner, freezer	Burpee, Stokes
Spinel	good canner, pickler	Thompson & Morgan
Ruby Queen	good canner, pickler	Field, Gurney, Harris, Park, Stokes, Twilley
Sweetheart	good canner, freezer, keeper	Johnny's
Warrior	good freezer	Harris

Broccoli

Bonanza Hybrid	good freezer	Burpee
De Cicco	good freezer	Johnny's, Park
Goliath	good freezer	Burpee, Stokes

Vegetable Varieties—*continued*

Broccoli—*continued*

Green Comet Hybrid	good freezer, keeper	Burpee, Gurney, Harris, Park, Thompson & Morgan, Twilley
Italian Green Sprouting	good freezer	Gurney, Park, Stokes, Thompson & Morgan
Paragon	good freezer	Stokes
Premium Crop Hybrid	good freezer	Burpee, Harris, Johnny's, Park, Stokes, Twilley
Raab 7 Top	good freezer	Thompson & Morgan
Romanesco	good freezer	Thompson & Morgan
Spartan Early	good freezer	Field, Gurney, Stokes
Waltham 29	good freezer	Harris, Johnny's

Brussels sprouts

Achilles F1	good freezer	Thompson & Morgan
Cambridge No. 5	good freezer	Thompson & Morgan
Citadel F1	good freezer	Thompson & Morgan
Jade Cross E Hybrid	good freezer	Burpee, Field, Gurney, Harris, Johnny's, Park, Stokes, Twilley
Long Island Improved	good freezer	Harris, Stokes
Prince Marvel Hybrid	good freezer	Harris, Stokes, Twilley

Cabbage

Amager Green Storage	good keeper	Johnny's
Blue Ribbon	good keeper	Twilley
Burpee Hybrid (Chinese)	good keeper	Burpee
Canada Kraut	kraut	Stokes
Copenhagen Market	good keeper; kraut	Burpee, Field, Gurney, Stokes
Danish Ballhead or Roundhead	good keeper; kraut	Burpee, Gurney
Emerald Cross Hybrid	good keeper	Burpee, Field, Stokes
Falcon	kraut	Stokes
Golden Acre	kraut	Field, Gurney, Johnny's
Gourmet Hybrid	kraut	Stokes
Green Boy	kraut	Twilley
Gurney's Giant	good keeper; kraut	Gurney
Hercules Hybrid	good keeper; kraut	Gurney

Hybrid King Cole	kraut	Field, Stokes
Hybrid Stonehead	kraut	Park, Stokes, Thompson & Morgan, Twilley
KK Cross Hybrid	kraut	Burpee
Lariat	good keeper	Johnny's
Late Flat Dutch	good keeper; kraut	Field, Gurney
Marion Market	kraut	Field
Michihli (Chinese)	good keeper	Park
Penn State Ballhead	good keeper; kraut	Stokes
Quick-Green Storage	good keeper	Stokes
Rio Verde	good keeper	Twilley
Roundup	kraut	Stokes, Twilley
Safekeeper	good keeper	Stokes
Savoy Ace Hybrid	good keeper	Burpee, Harris, Park
Savoy King	slaw	Park, Stokes, Thompson & Morgan, Twilley
Shamrock F1 (Big Apple)	kraut, slaw	Thompson & Morgan
Superslaw	good keeper; kraut	Stokes
Surehead	good keeper; kraut	Burpee
Two Seasons Hybrid (Chinese)	good keeper	Burpee
Winterkeeper	good keeper; kraut	Stokes
Wisconsin All Season	good keeper; kraut	Gurney, Park

Cabbage, red

Lasso	kraut	Johnny's
Mammoth Red Rock	good pickler, keeper	Gurney, Park, Stokes
Red Acre	good keeper	Burpee, Field, Gurney
Red Danish	good keeper	Stokes
Red Drumhead	good pickler	Thompson & Morgan
Red Rock	good pickler, keeper; kraut, relish	Gurney
Ruby Ball Hybrid	good keeper	Burpee, Harris, Johnny's

Carrots

Baby Orange	good freezer	Stokes
Camden	good canner	Stokes
Coreless (Scarlet Nantes)	good freezer, keeper; juice	Gurney, Harris
Danvers Half Long	good keeper	Burpee, Field, Gurney, Park
Danvers 126	good canner	Stokes, Twilley

continued

Vegetable Varieties—*continued*

Carrots—*continued*

Gold Pak	good canner, freezer, keeper; juice	Burpee, Field, Gurney, Stokes, Twilley
Juwarot Double Vitamin A	good freezer, keeper; juice	Thompson & Morgan
Kundulus	good canner, freezer	Thompson & Morgan
Mokum F1	good canner, freezer	Thompson & Morgan
Nantes Express	good canner, freezer	Thompson & Morgan
Nantes Fancy	good keeper	Johnny's
Nantes Half Long	good canner, freezer	Burpee
Oxheart	good keeper	Gurney
Pioneer	good freezer	Harris
Processor II	good canner	Stokes
Redca	good canner, freezer; juice	Thompson & Morgan
Red-Cored Chantenay	good freezer, keeper	Burpee, Field, Gurney, Stokes, Thompson & Morgan
Royal Chantenay	good canner, freezer	Burpee, Field, Gurney, Harris, Park, Stokes
Royal Cross Hybrid	good freezer	Park
Scarlet Nantes	good keeper; juice	Field, Johnny's, Stokes
Six-Pak	good freezer, keeper	Harris
Special Nantes 616	good keeper	Stokes
Suko	good canner, freezer	Thompson & Morgan
Tendersweet	good freezer	Field, Park
Trophy	good freezer	Harris

Cauliflower

Burpeeana	good freezer	Burpee
Dok Elgon	good freezer	Thompson & Morgan
Early White Hybrid	good freezer, pickler	Burpee
Imperial 10-6	good freezer	Harris
Purple Cape	good freezer	Thompson & Morgan
Purple Head	good freezer	Burpee, Stokes
Royal Purple	good freezer	Harris, Park
Self-Blanche	good freezer	Field, Harris, Stokes, Twilley
Snow Crown	good freezer	Burpee, Harris, Johnny's, Park, Stokes, Twilley
Snow King F1	good freezer	Thompson & Morgan
Super Snowball	good freezer	Field, Park, Twilley

Celery

Fordhook	good keeper	Burpee
Giant Pascal	good keeper	Gurney, Park
Golden Self-Blanching	good keeper	Burpee, Gurney, Johnny's

Corn

Bantam Evergreen	good freezer	Johnny's
Bellringer	good freezer	Harris
Blitz	good freezer	Harris
Burpee's Sugar Sweet	good freezer	Burpee
Butter and Sugar	good freezer	Harris, Park, Stokes, Twilley
Butterfruit	good freezer	Park
Butter Imp	good freezer	Thompson & Morgan
Candystick	good freezer	Gurney, Park
Concord	good freezer	Harris
Country Gentleman	good canner, freezer	Field, Gurney, Johnny's
Earliglo	good freezer	Thompson & Morgan
Earliking	good freezer	Thompson & Morgan, Twilley
Early Sunglow Hybrid	good freezer	Field, Gurney, Park, Twilley
Early Xtra Sweet	good canner, freezer	Field, Johnny's, Park, Thompson & Morgan, Twilley
Florida Staysweet	good freezer	Harris, Park
Golden Beauty	good canner, freezer	Gurney, Stokes
Golden Cross Bantam	good canner, freezer	Burpee, Field, Gurney
(Golden) Jubilee	good canner, freezer	Johnny's, Stokes, Twilley
Golden Midget	good freezer	Gurney, Johnny's, Park
Harmony	good freezer	Harris, Twilley
Honey and Cream	good freezer	Gurney
Hybrid Early Giant	good freezer	Gurney
Illini Chief	good canner, freezer	Twilley
Illini Xtra Sweet	good freezer	Burpee, Field, Gurney, Park
Iochief	good canner, freezer	Burpee, Field, Gurney, Park
Kandy Korn E.H.	good canner, freezer	Burpee, Field, Gurney, Stokes, Twilley
Marcross Hybrid	good canner, freezer	Gurney
Miracle	good freezer	Burpee, Stokes
Polar Vee F1	good freezer	Thompson & Morgan

continued

Vegetable Varieties—*continued*

Corn—*continued*

Quicksilver	good freezer	Thompson & Morgan
Silver Queen	good freezer	Burpee, Field, Gurney, Harris, Johnny's, Stokes, Twilley
Spring Gold	good freezer	Harris
Spring White	good freezer	Harris
Sprite	good freezer	Harris
Stowell's Evergreen	good canner, freezer	Field, Gurney, Johnny's
Stylepak	good canner, freezer	Stokes
Sugar Loaf	good freezer	Harris
Sundance	good freezer	Harris
Sweet Sal	good freezer	Harris
Sweet Sue	good freezer	Harris
Symphony	good freezer	Harris
Tendertreat EH	good keeper	Field, Twilley
Tokay Sugar F1	good freezer	Thompson & Morgan
White Magic	good freezer	Harris
Wonderful	good freezer	Harris

Cucumbers, for pickling

Bush Pickle		Harris, Park
Calypso		Harris, Twilley
Double Yield Pickling		Stokes
Hokus Original		Johnny's
Lemon		Stokes
Liberty Hybrid		Park, Twilley
Northern Pickling		Johnny's
Patio Pick		Stokes
Peppi		Stokes
Pickle-Dilly Hybrid		Park
Pioneer Hybrid		Park, Stokes
Salvo		Johnny's
Spartan Dawn Hybrid		Park, Stokes

Eggplant

Little Fingers	good pickler	Harris

Kale (keep in garden—dig as needed)

Blue Knight Hybrid	good keeper	Twilley
Cottagers	good freezer	Thompson & Morgan

Dwarf Blue Curled Vates	good keeper	Burpee, Field, Harris, Park, Twilley
Dwarf Curled (Borecole)	good keeper	Gurney, Thompson & Morgan
Dwarf Siberian	good keeper	Burpee

Kohlrabi

Early Purple Vienna	good freezer	Burpee, Field, Stokes
Early White Vienna	good freezer	Burpee, Field, Harris, Park, Stokes
Grand Duke	good freezer	Thompson & Morgan
Purple	good freezer	Gurney
White	good freezer	Gurney

Leeks (keep in garden—dig as needed)

Alaska	good keeper	Stokes
American Flag	good keeper	Park
Broad London	good keeper	Burpee
Catalina	good keeper	Twilley
Electra	good keeper	Harris
Splendid	good keeper; dry	Stokes
Titan	good keeper	Burpee, Stokes
Unique	good keeper	Stokes

Onions

Ailsa Craig	good keeper	Thompson & Morgan
Barletta	good pickler	Stokes
Bermuda White Hybrid	good keeper	Burpee, Park
Burpee Yellow Globe Hybrid	good keeper	Burpee
Canada Maple	good keeper	Stokes
Carmen (red)	good keeper	Stokes, Thompson & Morgan
Chieftain	good keeper	Stokes
Copra	good keeper	Johnny's
Crystal Wax	good pickler	Burpee, Park
Downing Yellow Globe	good keeper	Gurney, Johnny's
Ebenezer	good keeper	Burpee, Gurney, Harris, Park
Eclipse	good canner, freezer, pickler	Johnny's
Enterprise	good keeper	Stokes
Fiesta Hybrid	good keeper	Harris, Park, Stokes

continued

Vegetable Varieties—*continued*

Onions—*continued*

Giant Red Hamburger	good keeper	Burpee, Park
Hybrid Yellow Sweet Spanish	good keeper	Burpee, Field, Gurney, Harris, Park, Twilley
Improved Buccaneer	good keeper	Harris
Northern Oak	good keeper	Stokes
Orbit	good keeper	Johnny's
Owa	good keeper	Gurney
Quicksilver	good canner, freezer, pickler	Johnny's
Rijnsburger	good keeper	Thompson & Morgan
Riverside Sweet Spanish	good keeper	Stokes
Russet	good keeper	Stokes
Silver Queen	good pickler	Stokes
Snow White Hybrid	good keeper	Park
Southport Red, White, and Yellow Globes	good keeper	Burpee, Field, Gurney, Harris, Johnny's, Stokes
Spanish Yellow Hybrid	good keeper	Burpee
Spartan Sleeper Hybrid	good keeper	Gurney, Stokes
Stokes Exporter	good keeper	Stokes
Stuttgarter	good keeper	Harris, Johnny's, Stokes
Tamarack	good keeper	Stokes
Torpedo	good keeper	Field, Gurney, Thompson & Morgan
White Portugal	good pickler	Field, Stokes
White Sweet Spanish	good keeper	Field, Stokes

Parsnips (keep in garden—dig as needed)

All America	good keeper	Gurney, Harris
Gladiator F1	good freezer	Thompson & Morgan
Harris Model	good keeper	Harris, Johnny's, Stokes, Twilley
Hollow Crown	good keeper	Burpee, Park, Stokes

Peas

Alaska	good canner; dry, split	Burpee, Gurney, Park
Alderman	good canner, freezer	Harris
Blue Bantam (Laxtonian)	good freezer	Burpee, Gurney

Burpeeana Early	good freezer	Burpee
Dark-Skin Perfection	good canner, freezer	Field
Early Frosty	good freezer	Twilley
Feltham First	good freezer	Thompson & Morgan
Freezonian	good canner, freezer	Burpee, Harris
Fridget	good freezer	Harris
Frosty	good freezer	Harris, Johnny's
Green Arrow	good canner, freezer	Burpee, Field, Gurney, Johnny's, Park, Stokes, Twilley
Kelvedon Wonder	good freezer	Thompson & Morgan
Laxton's Progress (No. 9)	good canner, freezer	Field, Gurney, Park, Stokes
Lincoln	good freezer	Gurney, Harris, Stokes
Little Marvel	good canner, freezer	Burpee, Gurney, Harris, Stokes, Thompson & Morgan, Twilley
Maestro	good canner, freezer	Field, Johnny's, Park
Midseason Freezer	good freezer	Park
Novella	good freezer	Twilley
Oregon Sugar Pod	good freezer	Thompson & Morgan
Pacemaker	good canner	Gurney
Patriot	good freezer	Stokes
Perfection Dark Green	good canner, freezer	Gurney
Progress No. 9	good freezer	Burpee
Sparkle	good freezer	Harris, Johnny's
Tall Telephone	good freezer	Stokes
Thomas Laxton	good freezer	Field, Johnny's
Victory Freezer	good canner, freezer	Field, Gurney
Wando	good canner, freezer	Burpee, Field, Gurney, Harris, Johnny's, Twilley
Winfrida	good freezer	Thompson & Morgan
Peas, snap		
Sugar Ann	good canner, freezer	Gurney, Harris, Johnny's, Park, Stokes, Thompson & Morgan, Twilley
Sugar Bon	good freezer	Burpee, Field, Park, Twilley
Sugar Daddy	good freezer	Burpee, Field, Gurney, Johnny's, Park, Stokes
Sugar Snap	good freezer	Burpee, Field, Gurney, Harris, Johnny's, Park, Stokes
Sweet Snap	good freezer	Burpee, Field

continued

Vegetable Varieties—*continued*

Peppers, hot

Anaheim Chili	good pickler; dry	Harris, Park
Anaheim (TMR 23)	good pickler; dry	Burpee, Field, Twilley
Ancho	dry	Gurney
Big Jim	dry	Thompson & Morgan
Cayenne Long Slim	good canner; dry, sauce	Field, Gurney, Park, Thompson & Morgan
Crimson Hot	good pickler; catsup	Stokes
Cubanelle	good pickler	Johnny's
El Cid	dry	Thompson & Morgan
Fresho Chili	good pickler	Gurney
Hungarian Wax	good canner, pickler	Burpee, Field, Gurney, Harris, Johnny's, Park, Stokes, Twilley
Jalapeño	good pickler	Burpee, Field, Gurney, Harris, Johnny's, Park, Stokes, Twilley
Large Red Hot	good pickler	Twilley
Long Red Cayenne	good pickler; dry, sauce	Burpee, Stokes, Twilley
Pepperoncini	good pickler; dry	Field, Gurney
Red Chili	good pickler; dry	Gurney
Serrano	dry	Field
Small Red Chili	good pickler; dry	Field, Gurney
Zippy Hybrid	dry	Burpee

Peppers, sweet

Ace Hybrid	good freezer	Burpee, Johnny's, Stokes
Big Bertha F1	good freezer	Thompson & Morgan
Burpee's Early Pimento	good freezer	Burpee
Canada-Cheese Pimento	good pickler	Stokes
Cherry Sweet	good pickler	Burpee, Gurney, Harris, Park, Stokes, Twilley
Golden Belle	good freezer	Harris, Park, Twilley
Naples (Italian)	good canner	Stokes
Romanian	good pickler	Stokes
Spartan Garnet	good canner	Gurney
Super Shepherd (Italian)	good canner	Stokes
Sweet Pickle	good pickler	Park
Twiggy	good freezer	Thompson & Morgan

Potatoes

Kennebec	good keeper	Burpee, Field, Gurney
Norgold Russet	good keeper	Field, Gurney
Red Pontiac	good keeper	Burpee, Field, Gurney
Sangre	good keeper	Park

Pumpkins

Big Max	good canner	Field, Park, Twilley
Big Moon	good canner	Field, Park, Twilley
Bushkin	good keeper	Burpee
Connecticut Field (Big Tom)	good canner	Burpee, Field, Gurney, Harris, Johnny's, Stokes, Twilley
Early Sweet Sugar	good canner	Gurney
Funny Face	good keeper	Twilley
Howden	good keeper	Harris
Jack O'Lantern	good canner	Burpee, Gurney, Park, Stokes, Twilley
Small Sugar	good canner, keeper	Burpee, Park, Stokes
Spirit	good keeper	Twilley
Spookie	good canner	Stokes
Triple Treat	good keeper	Burpee
Winter Luxury	good canner, keeper	Gurney

Radishes

Black Spanish	good keeper	Gurney
Burpee White	good keeper	Burpee, Stokes
Champion	good keeper	Field, Johnny's, Park, Stokes
Cherry Belle	good keeper	Burpee, Field, Gurney, Harris, Park, Stokes, Thompson & Morgan, Twilley
Chinese Rose	good keeper	Field, Gurney, Stokes
Comet	good keeper	Stokes
Round Black Spanish	good keeper	Burpee, Harris, Stokes
Snow Belle	good keeper	Gurney, Twilley
White Chinese (Celestial)	good keeper	Burpee, Stokes

Rutabagas

Altasweet	good keeper	Stokes
American Purple Top	good keeper	Field, Gurney, Harris, Park, Twilley
Burpee's Purple-Top Yellow	good keeper	Burpee

continued

Vegetable Varieties—*continued*

Rutabagas—*continued*

Champion Purple Top	good freezer, keeper	Thompson & Morgan
Fortune	good keeper	Stokes
Laurentian	good keeper	Johnny's, Stokes
Pike	good keeper	Johnny's
York Swede	good keeper	Stokes

Soybeans

Edible Prize	good canner, freezer; dry, flour, grits, sprouts	Burpee, Field, Gurney
Envy	good canner, freezer; dry	Johnny's
Frostbeater	dry, sprouts	Burpee
Hodgson	dry, sprouts	Harris
Maple Arrow	tempeh, tofu	Johnny's

Spinach

America	good freezer	Burpee, Gurney, Stokes, Twilley
Bloomsdale	good freezer	Burpee, Field, Gurney, Harris, Johnny's, Park, Stokes, Twilley
Early Smooth Hybrid	good canner	Park
Giant Nobel	good canner	Field
Hybrid No. 7	good canner, freezer	Gurney
King of Denmark	good freezer	Thompson & Morgan
Melody F1	good freezer	Thompson & Morgan
Northland	good canner, freezer	Gurney

Squash, fall and winter

Baby Hubbard	good keeper	Gurney, Stokes
Banana Squash	good keeper	Field, Gurney
Blue Hubbard	good freezer, keeper	Gurney, Harris, Johnny's, Park, Stokes
Burpee's Butterbush	good keeper	Burpee, Stokes
Bush Acorn Table King	good keeper	Burpee, Stokes, Twilley
Butter Boy Hybrid	good keeper	Burpee
Buttercup	good freezer, keeper	Burpee, Field, Gurney, Harris, Johnny's, Stokes, Twilley
Butternut	good keeper	Burpee, Gurney, Johnny's, Stokes
Delicata	good keeper	Field, Gurney, Johnny's, Stokes

Early Acorn Hybrid	good keeper	Burpee
Early Butternut Hybrid	good keeper	Field, Gurney, Harris, Park, Twilley
Gold Nugget	good keeper	Gurney, Johnny's, Park, Stokes
Golden Delicious	good canner, freezer	Gurney, Harris, Stokes
Golden Hubbard	good canner, freezer, keeper	Stokes
Hubbard (True or Warted)	good keeper	Burpee, Gurney, Stokes, Twilley
Hungarian Mammoth	good canner, freezer	Stokes
Jersey Golden Acorn	good keeper	Johnny's, Park, Stokes, Twilley
Royal Acorn	good keeper	Stokes, Twilley
Sweet Mama Hybrid	good keeper	Burpee, Park, Twilley
Sweet Meat Squash	good keeper	Harris
Table Ace	good keeper	Field, Gurney, Harris, Park, Stokes, Twilley
Table Queen	good keeper	Burpee, Field, Gurney, Harris, Johnny's, Stokes
Vegetable Gourd	good keeper	Gurney
Vegetable Spaghetti	good keeper	Field, Harris, Johnny's, Stokes, Thompson & Morgan, Twilley
Waltham Butternut	good keeper	Burpee, Field, Gurney, Harris, Park, Stokes, Twilley

Squash, summer. See Zucchini and Summer squash.

Sweet potatoes

Centennial	good keeper	Field, Park
Jewell	good keeper	Field, Gurney
Nancy Hall	good keeper	Field
New Jewel	good keeper	Park
Vineless Puerto Rico	good keeper	Field, Park

Swiss chard

Burpee's Rhubarb Chard	good freezer	Burpee, Park, Stokes, Twilley
Fordhook Giant	good freezer	Burpee, Field, Johnny's, Stokes, Twilley
Lucullus	good freezer	Gurney, Park, Thompson & Morgan
Perpetual	good freezer	Burpee, Thompson & Morgan

continued

Vegetable Varieties—*continued*

Tomatoes

Beefmaster VFN	good canner	Gurney
Beefsteak	good canner	Gurney, Park, Stokes, Twilley
Bellarina	catsup, paste purée, sauce	Gurney
Bellstar	good canner; juice, paste, sauce	Stokes
Better Boy	good canner	Field, Park, Stokes, Twilley
Bonnyvee	good canner, keeper; catsup	Stokes
Burpee's Long Keeper	good keeper	Burpee
Campbell's 1327 VF	good canner, freezer	Gurney, Stokes, Twilley
Cold Set	good canner	Stokes
Climbing Trip-L-Crop	good canner	Field, Park
Crimsonvee	good canner; catsup	Stokes
Delicious	good keeper	Gurney
Earlirouge	good canner	Johnny's
Early Cascade	good canner; sauce	Johnny's
Early Girl	good canner; sauce	Gurney, Park
Early Pear	good canner; paste	Field, Gurney
Easy Peel	good canner	Park
Fantastic	good canner, keeper	Gurney, Park
Floramerica	good canner; juice	Twilley
Glamour	good canner	Harris, Stokes
Golden Sunray	juice	Field, Twilley
Harvestvee	good canner, keeper; juice	Stokes
Heinz 1350	good canner	Burpee, Harris, Stokes
Heinz 2653	good canner; paste, sauce	Johnny's
Hybrid Big Red Champion	good canner	Field
Hybrid Juice	juice	Field
Hybrid Surprise	good canner	Field
Marglobe	good canner	Burpee, Field, Johnny's, Park, Twilley
Moira	good canner; juice	Johnny's, Stokes
Mr. Stripey	catsup, juice	Thompson & Morgan
Nova	good canner; paste, sauce	Johnny's, Stokes
Pik-Red	good keeper	Harris

Ponderosa Pink	good canner	Field, Park, Stokes
Red Cherry	good pickler; preserves	Burpee
Red Pear	good canner; preserves	Field, Gurney
Roma VF	good canner; catsup, juice, paste, sauce	Burpee, Field, Harris, Stokes, Thompson & Morgan, Twilley
Royal Chico	good canner; catsup, paste	Gurney, Johnny's, Twilley
Rutgers	good canner; juice	Burpee, Field, Harris, Park
San Marzano	good canner; paste, purée	Burpee
Snowball	good pickler	Field
Sprinter	good canner	Twilley
Sub-Arctic Plenty	good canner, pickler	Gurney, Johnny's, Thompson & Morgan
Veeroma	catsup, paste	Stokes
White Beauty	good canner; juice	Gurney
Yellow Husk	preserves	Gurney
Yellow Pear	good canner, pickler; preserves	Burpee, Field, Gurney

Turnips

Early Purple	good keeper	Burpee
Milan	good keeper	Gurney
Ohno Scarlet	good pickler	Johnny's
Purple-Top White Globe	good keeper	Burpee, Gurney, Harris, Johnny's, Park, Twilley
Toyko Cross Hybrid	good keeper	Burpee, Park, Thompson & Morgan, Twilley

Zucchini and Summer squash

Aristocrat F1 Zucchini	good freezer	Thompson & Morgan
Black (Satin) Zucchini	good keeper	Gurney, Twilley
Burpee's Fordhook Zucchini	good freezer	Burpee
Early Golden Summer Crookneck	good freezer	Burpee, Field
Green Magic Zucchini	good keeper	Park
Grey Zucchini	good keeper	Johnny's

Fruit Varieties

Apples

Anoka	good keeper	Field, Gurney
Blushing Golden	good keeper	Stark
Chieftain	good keeper	Field
Dolgo Crab	good pickler; jelly, sauce	Gurney
Fireside	good keeper	Gurney
Granny Smith	good keeper	Burpee, Field, Gurney, Stark
Grimes Golden	sauce	Burpee, Field, Gurney, Stark
Haralson	good keeper	Field, Gurney
Jonathan	good freezer, keeper; cider, juice, sauce	Burpee, Field, Gurney
Lodi	cider, sauce	Stark
McIntosh	good keeper; cider, juice, sauce	Burpee, Field, Gurney
Mutsu	good keeper; cider, juice, sauce	
Northwest Greening	good keeper	Gurney
Prairie Spy	good keeper	Gurney
Red Baron	good keeper	Gurney
Red Duchess	sauce	Gurney
Red June	cider, sauce	Gurney
Red Rome	good keeper; cider, juice, sauce	Burpee
Red Winesap	good keeper; juice,	Burpee, Field, Gurney, Stark
Rome Beauty	good keeper	Stark
Shenandoah	good keeper	Field
Starkspur	good keeper	Stark
Stayman Winesap	good freezer, keeper; cider, juice, sauce	Burpee
Wealthy	sauce	Gurney
Whitney Crab	good pickler; jelly, sauce	Field, Gurney
Yellow (Red) Delicious	good keeper; sauce	Burpee, Field, Stark
Yellow Transparent	sauce	Burpee

Apricots

Chinese Golden	good canner; dry, preserves	Burpee
Early Golden	jam	Field

Goldcot	jam, jelly, preserves	Field, Gurney, Stark
Hardy Iowa	good canner; jam, jelly	Field
Henderson	good canner; jelly, sauce	Field
Hungarian Rose	dry	Stark
Manchu	good canner; preserves	Gurney
Moongold	good canner; preserves	Gurney
Moorpark	good canner; dry, preserves	Burpee
Scout	jam, sauce	Gurney
Stark Earli-Orange	good canner, freezer; dry	Stark
Sungold	good canner, freezer	Gurney
Wilson Delicious	good canner, freezer; dry	Stark

Blackberries

Black Satin	good canner, freezer; jam, preserves	Field, Park, Stark
Darrow	good canner, freezer; jam, preserves	Burpee, Field, Gurney, Stark
Ebony King	good canner, freezer	Gurney
Rosborough	jam	Stark
Snyder	jam, preserves	Field
Thornfree	good canner; preserves	Burpee, Gurney, Stark

Blueberries

Berkley	good canner	Gurney
Bluecrop	good canner, freezer	Stark
Blueray	good canner	Gurney
Coville	good canner	Field, Gurney
Earliblue	good freezer	Burpee, Stark
Jersey	good freezer	Burpee, Park
Pemberton	good canner, freezer	Field
Saskatoon	preserves, sauce	Gurney
Woodard	good canner, freezer; preserves	Stark

Boysenberries

Thornless	good canner, freezer; preserves	Burpee, Field, Gurney, Stark

continued

Fruit Varieties—*continued*

Cherries, bush

Golden Boy	good canner; jam	Field
Hansen	good canner; jelly, preserves, sauce	Field, Gurney
Nanking	good canner; preserves	Burpee, Field, Gurney

Cherries, sour

Early Montmore	good canner; preserves	Field, Gurney
Early Richmond	good canner; preserves	Field
Meteor	good canner; preserves, sauce	Gurney, Stark
Montmorency	good canner, freezer; preserves	Burpee, Field, Gurney, Stark
North Star Dwarf	good canner, freezer; preserves, sauce	Burpee, Field, Gurney, Stark
Suda Hardy	good canner, freezer	Stark

Cherries, sweet

Bing	good canner, freezer	Burpee, Field, Gurney, Stark
Black Tartarian	good canner, freezer; sauce	Burpee, Field, Gurney
Kansas Sweet	good canner, freezer; sauce	Burpee, Field
Royal Ann or Napoleon	good canner; sauce	Gurney, Stark
Stark Gold	good canner, freezer	Stark
Stark Lambert	good canner, freezer	Stark
Van	good canner, freezer	Stark
Yellow Glass	good canner, freezer	Burpee

Currants

Red Lake	jelly, preserves	Field, Gurney, Stark
Wilder	jelly, preserves	Field, Gurney

Gooseberries

Pixwell	jelly, preserves	Field, Gurney, Stark
Welcome	jelly, preserves	Field, Gurney

Grapes

Beta	jelly, juice	Gurney
Blue Lake	jelly, juice	Stark
Buffalo	jelly, juice	Field
Carlos	jam, jelly, juice	Burpee
Catawba	jam, jelly, juice	Burpee, Field, Stark

Concord	jam, jelly, juice	Burpee, Field, Gurney, Park, Stark
Delaware	jelly	Stark
Fredonia	jelly	Field, Gurney
Golden Muscat	juice	Stark
Himrod Golden	good keeper under refrigeration	Field
Niagara	jelly, juice	Burpee, Field, Gurney, Stark
Red Caco	jelly	Field, Gurney
Scuppernong	jam, jelly, juice	Burpee, Field, Stark
Stark Blue Boy	jelly, juice	Stark
Steuben	jelly, juice	Burpee, Field, Gurney
Suffolk Red Seedless	jelly	Stark
Valiant Blue	jelly, juice	Gurney
Venus Seedless	jam, jelly	Stark
Melons		
Allsweet Watermelon	good keeper	Twilley
Big Daddy	good keeper	Field, Gurney
Crenshaw	good freezer	Burpee, Gurney, Twilley
Crimson Sweet Watermelon	good keeper	Field, Twilley
Golden Beauty Casaba	good keeper	Burpee
Harvest Queen	good keeper	Twilley
Honey Dew	good keeper	Burpee, Twilley
Star Performer	good keeper	Twilley
Triple Sweet Watermelon	good keeper	Twilley
Peaches		
Balmer	good canner, pickler	Field
Belle of Georgia	good canner, freezer	Burpee, Field, Stark
Burbank July Elberta	good canner	Stark
Cresthaven	good canner, freezer	Stark
Elberta	good canner, freezer	Burpee, Field, Gurney, Stark
Golden Jubilee	good canner, freezer, pickler	Burpee
Hale Haven	good canner, freezer	Burpee, Field, Gurney
Madison	good canner	Stark

continued

Fruit Varieties—*continued*

Peaches—*continued*

Polly	good canner	Field, Gurney
Red Haven	good canner, freezer	Burpee, Field, Gurney, Stark
Reliance	good canner, freezer	Burpee, Field, Gurney, Stark
Stark EarliGlo	good canner, freezer; preserves	Stark
Stark Encore	good canner	Stark
Stark Hal-Berta Giant	good canner	Stark
Stark Summer Pearl	good canner; preserves	Stark
Starking Delicious	good canner, freezer	Stark

Pears

Bartlett	good keeper	Burpee, Field, Gurney, Stark
Colette	preserves	Field
Duchess	good canner; preserves	Stark
Kieffer	good canner, keeper; preserves	Field, Stark
Moonglow	good canner	Burpee, Field, Stark
Red D'Anjou	good keeper	Gurney
Red Sensation	good canner	Field
Seckel	good canner; preserves	Burpee, Field, Stark
Stark Honeysweet	good canner	Stark
Starking Delicious	good canner; preserves	Stark
Turnbull Giant	good canner	Field
Tyson	good canner	Stark

Persimmons

Hardy	preserves	Gurney

Plums

Abundance	good canner; preserves	Burpee
Allred	good canner; jelly	Field
Blue Damson	good canner; jam, jelly, preserves	Burpee, Field, Stark
Burbank	good canner; preserves	Burpee

Ember	good canner; preserves	Stark
Fellenberg	good canner; dry, preserves	Burpee
Monitor	good canner; preserves	Burpee
Ozark Premier	good canner; sauce	Field, Stark
Redheart	good canner; jelly, preserves	Stark
Santa Rosa	good canner; jelly	Field
Sapa	jam, jelly	Gurney
Shiro	good canner; preserves	Gurney, Stark
South Dakota	jam, jelly	Gurney
Stanley Prune	good canner; dry	Burpee, Field, Gurney, Stark
Superior	jam, jelly, preserves	Field, Gurney
Tecumseh	jam, jelly, sauce	Gurney
Underwood	good canner	Field, Stark
Waneta	jam, jelly	Field, Gurney
Raspberries, black		
Black Hawk	good canner, freezer	Field, Gurney, Stark
Bristol	good freezer	Stark
Cumberland	good canner; jam, preserves	Burpee, Field, Gurney
Raspberries, purple		
Brandywine	jam, jelly	Gurney
Royalty	good freezer; jam, preserves, sauce	Burpee, Field, Park, Stark
Sodus	good canner, freezer; preserves	Field
Raspberries, red		
Augustred	jam	Field
Canby	good freezer	Gurney
Dormanred	good freezer	Stark
Fall Gold	juice	Park
Fall Red Everbearing	good canner, freezer	Gurney, Field
Indian Summer Everbearing	good canner, freezer; preserves	Burpee, Gurney
Latham	good canner, freezer	Burpee, Gurney, Stark
September Red Everbearing	good freezer; jam, jelly, preserves	Burpee, Gurney

continued

Fruit Varieties—*continued*

Rhubarb

Canada Red	good canner, freezer; sauce	Field
Cherry Red	good canner; sauce	Park
Flare	good freezer; sauce	Field, Gurney
Starkrimson	good canner	Stark
Victoria	good freezer	Burpee, Park, Stark
Victoria Tenderstalk	good freezer	Field

Strawberries

All-Star	good canner	Field, Stark
Cardinal	good freezer, keeper; preserves	Field, Stark
Cyclone	good freezer	Field, Gurney
Guardian	good freezer; preserves	Burpee, Field
Jerseybelle	good freezer	Burpee
Midway	good freezer; preserves	Burpee, Stark
Ogallala (everbearing)	good freezer; preserves	Field, Gurney, Stark
Ozark Beauty (everbearing)	good canner, freezer; preserves	Burpee, Field, Gurney, Stark
Pocahontas	good canner, freezer; preserves	Burpee
Premier	good canner; preserves	Burpee
Red Chief	good freezer; preserves	Burpee
Red Honey	preserves	Field
Scott	good freezer; preserves	Burpee
(Senator) Dunlap	good freezer, canner; preserves	Field, Gurney, Stark
Sparkle	good canner, freezer	Burpee, Gurney
Streamliner (everbearing)	good freezer; preserves	Gurney
Sunburst	good canner; preserves	Park
Sunrise	preserves	Stark
Superfection	good canner, freezer; preserves	Burpee, Gurney
Surecrop	good canner, freezer	Burpee, Field, Stark
Trumpeter	good canner, freezer	Gurney

Harvesting Vegetables and Fruits

If you grow your own food, you've got it made over those who must rely on the grocery store or the supermarket for their daily sustenance, because you can pick and process the food that grows from your soil when its quality is at its very best. This means that you can harvest fruits and vegetables when they have reached just the right stage of maturity for eating, canning, freezing, drying, or underground storage, and you don't have to lose any time in getting the food from the ground into safekeeping, either.

Whether you want your vegetables or fruits very ripe or just barely so at the time you harvest them depends upon the specific food and what you intend to do with it. In most cases, vegetables have their finest flavor when they are still young and tender: peas and corn while they taste sweet and not starchy; snap beans while the pods are tender and fleshy, before the beans inside the pods get plump; summer squash while their skins are still soft. Carrots and beets have a sweeter flavor, and leafy vegetables are crisp but not tough and fibrous, when they are young. This is the stage at which you'll want to preserve their goodness.

Fruits, on the other hand, are usually at their best when ripe, for this is when their sugar and vitamin contents are at their peak. If you're going to can, freeze, dry, or store them, you'll want them fully mature. But if you plan to use your fruits for jellies and preserves, you will not want them all at their ripest because their pectin content—which helps them to gel—decreases as the fruit reaches maturity. In order to make better jellies, some of the guavas, apples, plums, or currants you are using should be less than fully ripe.

With the exception of perhaps a few gardening wizards, it is impossible to control just when your peaches, pears, apples, and berries will be mature. Once planted, fruit trees and berry plants will bear their fruit year after year when the time is right. You're at their mercy and must be prepared to harvest just when the pickings are ready if you want to get the fruit at its best.

Vegetables are a different story. Because most are annuals and bear several weeks after they are planted, you can plan your garden to allow for succession plantings that extend the harvesting season for you and furnish you with a continuous supply of fresh food. This means that you can eat fresh vegetables over several smaller harvests if you wish (and your weather cooperates) and be able to preserve small batches at a time as vegetables ripen.

By planting three smaller crops of tomatoes instead of one large crop, you won't be deluged with more tomatoes than you can possibly eat and process at one time. Space your three pea plantings ten days apart in early spring and you'll have three harvests of peas and still plenty of time to plant a later crop of something else in the same plots after all the peas are picked. Vegetables like salad greens that do not keep well should be planted twice. Plant early lettuce about a month before the last frost and follow it with cauliflower. After the onions are out of the ground, put some fall lettuce in their place for September salads. If corn is one of your favorites and you've been waiting out the long winter for the first ears to come in, by all means, eat all the early-maturing corn you want, but make sure that enough late corn has been planted for freezing later on.

Vegetables that keep well in underground storage, like cabbage, squash, and the root crops, should be harvested as late in the season as possible so you won't have to worry about keeping vegetables cool during a warm September or early October. Some vegetables, like carrots, parsnips, and Jerusalem artichokes, can be left right in the ground over the winter, so it is wise to plant some late crops of these vegetables just for this purpose. Green and yellow beans, planted in early May, can be followed by cabbage in mid-July for a fall harvest. Beets planted in the beginning of April may be followed by carrots in July that can be stored right in the ground over the winter and into the early spring.

The charts that follow will tell you when and how specific vegetables and fruits should be harvested for good eating and best keeping.

HARVESTING VEGETABLES

ARTICHOKES

If you're raising the perennial kind, don't harvest any artichokes until the second year, to give the plants time to establish themselves. When ready to harvest, the buds will be full but the bracts still closed. Once the bracts turn purple and flowers begin to form, the buds will be too tough to eat. The large central bud will probably mature first; then the side buds. Some of the stem—4 to 6 inches of it—will be edible, so cut some of the stem as well when harvesting.

ASPARAGUS

Usually not until third year after planting. Spears should be 6 to 10 inches above ground, and heads should still be tight. Harvest only for a 6- to 8-week period to allow for sufficient top growth after harvest. Cut off spears slightly below soil level.

BEANS, GREEN AND YELLOW

Before pods are full size and while the seeds are about one-quarter developed, or about 2 to 3 weeks after first bloom. Snap pole beans just below the stem end and you will be able to pick another bean from the same spot later in the season. Bush beans yield only one harvest, so it doesn't matter where you snap the pod from the bush. If you want to dry your beans, delay the harvest until the beans are dry on their stems.

BEANS, LIMA

When the seeds are green and tender, just before they reach full size and plumpness. If you intend to store your beans dry, harvest them when they are past the mature stage, when they are dry.

BEETS

When $1\frac{1}{4}$ to 2 inches in diameter.

BROCCOLI

Before dark green blossom clusters begin to open and display yellow flowers. Side heads will continue to develop after central head is removed, until frost kills the plant.

BRUSSELS SPROUTS

When full size and firm, before sprouts get yellow and tough. Lowest sprouts generally mature first. Sprouts may be picked for many months, even if temperatures go below freezing.

CABBAGE

When heads are solid and don't give when you push on them, but before they split. Splitting can be prevented by cutting or breaking off roots on one side with a spade after a rain. If a head splits, eat it within a few days or make sauerkraut from it, since it won't keep very long.

■ The outer leaves of cabbage, and the leaves around the florets of broccoli and cauliflower, are richer in vitamin C than the rest of the plants. Serve some of the undamaged leaves along with the rest of the vegetable.

CARROTS

Any time when 1 to 1½ inches in diameter.

CAULIFLOWER

Before heads are ricey, discolored, or blemished. Tie outer leaves above the head when curds are 2 to 3 inches in diameter; heads will be ready 4 to 12 days after tying. Check the heads every few days so that you can harvest the heads before the curds begin to loosen.

CELERIAC

Harvest any time the root crowns are 2 to 4 inches around. Cut the plant right below the soil surface.

CELERY

Blanch self-blanching celery 2 to 3 weeks before harvest in warm weather. If to be used immediately, cut plant root right below soil surface. For underground storage, lift plants with roots intact.

CHINESE CABBAGE

After heads form, cut as needed. For underground storage, pull up plants with roots attached.

COLLARD GREENS See Kale and Collard greens.

CORN

When kernels are fully filled out and in the milk stage (break a kernel open and check to see if corn milk flows when the kernel is pressed). Use before kernels get doughy. Silks should be dry and brown and tips of ears filled tight.

For popcorn, let the corn mature thoroughly on the ears. Husks should be brown and dry.

CUCUMBERS

When fruits are slender and dark green, before color becomes lighter. Harvest daily at season's peak. If large cucumbers are allowed to develop and ripen, production will be reduced. For pickles, harvest when fruits have reached the desired size, but don't let them get too big; many varieties develop large seeds and get watery when too large. Pick with a short piece of stem on each fruit.

EGGPLANT

When fruits are half-grown, before color becomes dull.

ENDIVE

To remove bitterness, blanch by tying outer leaves together when plants are 12 to 15 inches in diameter. Make sure plants are completely dry when this is done to prevent rot. Leave this way for 3 weeks before harvest. For underground storage, pull up plant with roots intact before a hard freeze.

GARLIC

Pull when tops are dry and bent to the ground. Cure as you do onions.

HERBS

Herb leaves should be harvested just before they are ready to blossom, because then their oils are at their peak. Cut them early in the morning, after dew has evaporated but before the sun is strong.

continued

Herb seeds should be picked when the seed pods have changed color but before they begin to shatter.

Herb flowers should be cut the first day they bloom.

Herb roots should be cut off during the plant's dormant stage—usually the fall and winter months—so that there is sufficient food stored in the plant to withstand the loss of some roots. Remove tender roots, and never cut more than just a few at a time.

For more on harvesting and preparing herbs for storage, see page 164.

JERUSALEM ARTICHOKES

Dig tubers any time after the first frost and any time throughout the winter.

KALE AND COLLARD GREENS

Pick early in the day when they are most crisp. Both are best tasting after a light frost in fall.

KOHLRABI

When balls are 2 to 3 inches in diameter. If bulbs are close together, cut them off below bulb in order not to cut off tangled roots of an adjacent bulb.

LEEKS

Dig or pull up the entire plant when it is 1 to 2½ inches in diameter.

LETTUCE

Pick early in the day to preserve crispness caused by the cool night temperatures. Wash thoroughly but briefly as soon as harvested, then towel or spin dry to prevent vitamin loss. Loose-leaf types, if cut off at ground level without disturbing roots, will send up new leaves for a second crop.

OKRA

Pick a few days after flowers fall, while still young and not woody. Pods will be 1 to 4 inches long, depending upon variety. Freeze, can, or dry at once because okra quickly becomes woody once mature.

ONIONS

For storage, pull when tops fall over, shrivel at neck of the bulb, and turn brown. Allow to mature fully but harvest before a heavy frost. Do not let them sit in the garden after their tops have fallen because the necks will get sunburned. If that happens, the onions can lose some of their outer scales which protect them, making them more susceptible to disease and early sprouting in storage. Bring them inside and cure them (let their outer scales dry) for about 2 weeks out of direct light.

PARSNIPS

Delay harvest until a heavy frost. Roots may be safely left in ground over the winter and used the following spring before growth starts. (Contrary to folklore, they are not poisonous if left in ground over winter.)

PEANUTS

Harvest when leaves begin to yellow and a sampling of dug-up nuts are mature and have light pink, papery thin skins. Peanuts may be dug up after frost, because frost shouldn't bother them if they're still underground. For a more complete discussion of harvesting peanuts, see page 543.

PEAS

For podded peas, when pods are firm and well filled, but before the seeds reach their fullest size. For drying, allow them to dry on the bush.

For sugar or snow peas, any time before the pods fill out. If peas have developed in the pods before you have harvested them, shell them just as podded peas.

PEPPERS

When fruits are solid and have almost reached full size. For red peppers, allow fruit to become uniformly red, but watch them carefully, since they can overripen and develop soft spots before they turn entirely red.

POTATOES

When tubers are large enough. Tubers continue to grow and their protective skins toughen until the vine dies. Skin on unripe tubers is thin and easily rubs off. For storage, potatoes should be mature and vines dead. Leave in the ground for about 2 weeks after vines die to make sure skins have toughened up.

■ If you want your potatoes to mature all at the same time so that you can harvest and store them together, cut or beat the vines with a shovel or stick to kill them. Then follow the usual advice, which says to leave the tubers in the ground for 2 weeks.

PUMPKINS AND WINTER SQUASH

Winter squash (with the exception of patty pan) and pumpkins should be well matured on the vine. Skin should be hard and not easily punctured with the thumbnail. Cut fruit off the vine with a portion of the stem attached. Harvest before heavy frost, but after light frost, if possible, because a light frost may actually increase the sugar content.

Patty pans may be picked any time when 1 to 4 inches in diameter. Skin should be soft enough to break easily with press of finger. If picked in this early stage, the vines will continue to bear.

RADISHES

Pull summer radishes as soon as they reach a good size. Leaving them in the ground after maturity causes them to become bitter. Winter radishes may be left in the ground until after frost.

RHUBARB See Harvesting Fruits.

RUTABAGAS

After exposure to frost but before a heavy freeze.

SALSIFY

Leave until after frost, as freezing of the roots improves flavor. Also may be dug out in spring.

SOYBEANS

Pick the green beans when the pods are almost mature, but before they start to yellow. Harvest period lasts for only about a week. For dry soybeans, allow to dry on the vines and pick just as they are dry, while stems are still green; otherwise the shells will shatter and drop their beans.

SPINACH

May be cut off entirely when fully mature (when 6 or more leaves are 7 inches long) or outer leaves can be cut from plant as they mature, leaving inner leaves on to ripen. Pick frequently, as spinach matures rapidly and bolts easily, especially as weather warms up.

SWEET POTATOES

Harvest on a mild day right before or right after the first fall frost. Sweet poatoes are affected adversely by temperatures of 55°F or lower, but the soil can reach this temperature even before the first frost. So, if your first frost comes late, but you have several cool days and cooler nights, you would be wise to harvest your potatoes then. (Serious sweet potato growers use a soil thermometer to make sure they harvest before the soil temperature dips to 55°F.)

Since the skins of the potatoes are thin at harvesttime, dig gently, removing the soil around the potatoes by hand. Get them out of the sun within half an hour of digging up to prevent sunburn. Then cure them for 1 to 2 weeks so that the skins can toughen up and the wounds at either end of the potatoes seal over; otherwise you'll be inviting disease and a ruined crop. They are best cured at warm temperatures of 85° to 90°F and a humidity of 80 to 90 percent. You can probably best achieve these conditions by laying the potatoes in a single layer on the ground and covering them with black plastic. The sun heating the plastic should keep them warm and cozy. Be careful, though, if nighttimes are cool; it should not get below 55°F. Once cured, they should be put in storage as soon as possible.

TOMATOES

When fruits are a uniform red, but before they become soft. Green and pink tomatoes can be picked if frost threatens; wrap them in newspaper or place in a paper bag and store at room temperature until they ripen. Ripening them on a sunny windowsill is not a good idea because it can cause sunburn damage. The tomatoes may never get a beautiful vine-ripened red, but they should get red enough to eat and enjoy.

■ When fall frost is nearing and it's apparent that new tomato fruit sets won't have sufficient time to mature, pinch off all flower clusters and new fruit sets. By doing this you're allowing the plant to direct all its energy to maturing existing fruit. Also, remove any leaves that are shading this ripening fruit.

TURNIPS

When 2 to 3 inches in diameter. Larger roots are coarse and bitter.

ZUCCHINI AND SUMMER SQUASH

Harvest zucchini and yellow summer squash in early immature stage when skin is soft and before seeds ripen, before squash are 8 inches long. Zucchini is a notoriously fast grower, so take care to pick it frequently. The smaller the better in taste and texture.

HARVESTING FRUITS

APPLES

Pick summer apples when ripe and use or preserve at once. They usually do not store well for more than a few days. Pick fall and winter apples at peak ripeness for best storage. Pick with the stems; if stems are removed, a break in the skin is left which will let bacteria enter and cause rot. When picking apples, be careful not to break off the fruiting spur, which will bear fruit year after year if undamaged.

APRICOTS

Leave on the tree until fully ripe, because once they are picked they do not increase their supply of sugar. For drying, they should be ripe but firm.

BLACKBERRIES AND BOYSENBERRIES

Berries are ripe when they fall readily from the bush into the hand, a day or two after they blacken. Pick berries in the cool of the morning, keep out of the sun, and refrigerate or process as soon as possible.

BLUEBERRIES

Leave on the bush several days to a week after they turn blue. When fully ripe they are slightly soft, come easily from the bush, and are sweet in flavor.

CANTALOUPES See Melons.

CHERRIES

In order not to damage the fruiting twigs, pick cherries without the stems. But this will leave a break in the fruit; therefore the picked cherries must be processed at once or else spoilage will begin. If sour cherries are protected from birds with netting, allow fruit to ripen on tree for 2 to 3 weeks. The longer it hangs, the sweeter it becomes.

■ To pit cherries quickly and easily, use a plastic drinking straw to push through each cherry where the stem was attached. The edge of the straw is sharp enough to cut right through the cherry, but since the straw is a little smaller than a cherry pit, it pushes the pit out, leaving the cherries firm with most of the juices in them and not on you.

CURRANTS

The longer currants hang, the sweeter they become, so leave on bush for 4 to 6 weeks, unless you plan to make jelly from them. For jelly, pick some of them when still a little green because they lose their pectin content as they ripen.

DATES

In dry weather leave dates on the trees until they are thoroughly ripe. If the weather becomes wet, pick them before any rain touches them. Then finish ripening them indoors.

GOOSEBERRIES

Because gooseberries of one variety all mature at the same time, they may be harvested in one day. With heavy leather gloves on, strip the branches of their fruit by running your hand along the whole branch, catching the berries in an open container such as a bushel basket. The small pieces of leaf and stem may be separated by rolling the fruit down a gentle incline made by tipping a piece of wood or cardboard. The leaves and stems will be left on the incline and the moderately clean fruit rolls to the bottom.

GRAPES

Pick when fully ripe. The fruit will be aromatic and sweet, and the stem of the bunch will begin to show brown areas. Pick grapes that are to be stored in the coolest part of the day. Clip the bunches from the stems with sharp shears and handle them by the stems rather than by the fruit.

GUAVAS

Guavas ripen in a period of about 6 weeks. If they are to be used for jelly or juice, some of them may be picked before they are quite ripe.

HONEYDEW MELONS See Melons.

LEMONS

Lemons are harvested when ripe and ready to eat, which is year-round in Southern California, where most are grown. Fall- and winter-harvested lemons usually keep better than spring and summer ones.

LIMES

Like lemons, many varieties should be picked ripe from the tree, although the West Indian lime will drop from the tree when it's ripe. Acid limes are harvested mainly in winter, although there will be some ready for picking year-round. Sweet limes mature only in winter.

MELONS

Get to know the smell of a ripe melon when cut, and you'll have a clue to when to pick them from the garden: just put your nose to their stem end and smell.

Muskmelons or cantaloupe will usually have a yellow tinge behind the netting of their skin when mature. You can also test them by putting pressure on the stem. It should separate easily from the fruit.

Winter melon and honeydew stems will not crack or fall away from the fruit when ripe; they must be cut away. When the blossom ends are springy and the stem ends smell sweet, winter melons are ready to eat. Honeydews will have changed from green to cream colored and they will no longer have their waxy look. They make a dull sound when thumped.

NECTARINES See Peaches and Nectarines.

ORANGES

Color is not always a sign of maturity in oranges. Their skin contains a mixture of pigments: green, orange, and yellow. In the fall the green predominates until the weather turns cool enough to check their growth; then the green fades out and the other pigments predominate. But in the spring when growth begins, green pigments will again appear in perfectly ripe fruit as it hangs on the tree. Pick Navel, Valencia, and other varieties with tight skins by pulling away from the stem. Pick those with loose skins, like mandarins, Temples, and tangerines, with clippers which cut the fruit with about $\frac{1}{2}$ inch of the stem remaining. Once clipped from the tree, cut off the remaining stub.

PEACHES AND NECTARINES

Peaches and nectarines are ripe when the fruit is yellow. Fully tree-ripened fruit will have more sugar and less acid than fruit which is picked when half ripe. Don't pull the fruit directly from the tree because it will cause a bruise which will make the fruit spoil quickly. Rather, remove the fruit from the tree by tipping and twisting it sideways.

PEARS

Harvest when they have reached their full size and the skins change to a lighter green. Seeds will be starting to turn brown at this stage, and the stems separate easily from the tree when lifted. The quality of the pears will be much better if they are picked before stony granules are formed through the flesh, during the last few weeks of ripening. Then allow them to ripen fully at room temperature. Better yet, place them in a closed paper bag and keep at room temperature. Keep them together because they give off gases which aid each other in completing the ripening process. Ripe pears you want to eat fresh should be stored for a short time in the refrigerator so that they're slightly chilled.

PERSIMMONS

When fully ripe, persimmons are very soft and very sweet. Harvest persimmons just before they are ripe, or leave them hanging on the tree into the winter months. Fruit left hanging through January, even though it is frozen on the tree, retains its flavor when picked and thawed.

PLUMS

For canning and jelly making, harvest plums as soon as they have developed their bloom. At this point they are slightly soft, but still retain some of their tartness and firmness. Leave those prune varieties that are to be dried hanging on the tree long after they are ripe. They will develop more sugar as they hang.

POMEGRANATES

Pick in the fall after they have changed color. They will ripen in cold storage. You can also let ripen on the tree, so long as they do not split.

QUINCES

Quinces may hang on the bush until after the first fall frost. If they are to be stored, you can pick them a few weeks earlier.

RASPBERRIES

Because they become soft when fully ripe, pick raspberries every day, or at least every other day during harvesting time. Rain at harvesttime causes berries to become moldy. Therefore, pick them immediately after a rain and process at once before they mold. If moldy berries are left on the plant the mold will spread to green berries and destroy them.

RHUBARB

Start picking stems only after the second year so that the plant has time to establish itself. The roots and leaves are toxic, so take care to harvest the stems only. Harvest stems in spring for 8 to 10 weeks, before the leaves are fully grown. The stems should be at least 12 inches long, and any stems longer than 24 inches are probably too tough to eat. Pull the stems by twisting them sideways from the crown.

ROSE HIPS

Pick when they are fully mature in late fall. At this time the rose hips will be deep in color, have a mellow, nutlike taste, and the vitamin C content will be at its peak.

STRAWBERRIES

Pick early in the morning when the fruit is still cool. Gently twist the fruit off its stem; do not pull it off. Fruits washed without their stems will lose more vitamins than fruits which are destemmed after washing.

WATERMELONS

Watermelons must ripen on the vine because they do not develop more sugar or better color after they have been taken from the vine while still green. Most melons are fully ripe when the tendril accompanying the fruits dies, but this is not always the case with all varieties. A ripe melon has a hollow sound and a green one has a metallic ring when knocked with the knuckles.

HANDLING FOOD AFTER HARVEST

Making sure that you harvest your food at the right time is only half the key to great-tasting fruits and vegetables kept through the winter months. Handling the food after the harvest—during the time between picking and processing—is just as important.

Although the actual growth of fruits and vegetables stops when they are plucked and cut off from their food supply, respiration and activity of enzymes continue. The physical and chemical qualities of the plants deteriorate rapidly. Not only will there be a degradation of appearance and flavor as the freshness of food fades, there will also be a loss of nutrients, particularly of the fragile vitamin C.

Fruits and vegetables should be prepared and canned, put into the freezer, dried, or placed in cold storage as soon as is humanly possible after harvest. But despite our best intentions, distractions and delays are a part of life. If you find some of them getting in the way of your garden-to-storage routine, at least take these precautions: Cool your food right after you pick it. Do not keep it at room temperature, or, even worse, expose it to the sun. The quickest way to cool it is to immerse the food in ice water.

After draining, keep the food cool, preferably between 32° and 40°F. Covering the produce with cracked ice is another means of cooling and thereby slowing down the loss of quality. These aids will help, but get back to the task of processing the food as soon as time allows.

■ If you've got a delicate harvest, like spinach, lettuce, or any of the other vegetable greens, you can carry a bucket of ice water into the garden with you and put your pickings right in the bucket, rather than leave them out in the hot sun.

Fruits and vegetables are at their best when first picked. And no storage technique, no matter how good it is, will make a great food out of just a so-so one. The most that you can expect is for it to preserve most of the goodness that the food first started with. If you've taken the effort to grow good food, you owe it to yourself to make the extra effort to harvest it at the right time and get it into proper storage as soon as you can.

Freezing Vegetables and Fruits

For many people freezing is the best way of preserving the prides of their gardens. Cost can be a factor—a new freezer will cost you at least $300, and then there is the electricity to keep it running. But nothing will preserve most foods the way freezing does. When you consider food flavor, color, texture, and nutrients, the flexibility you have in freezing food combinations, and the time you save by freezing rather than canning or drying your vegetables and fruits, the money is well spent.

A general rule to remember is that those vegetables most suited for freezing are those that are usually cooked before serving. These include asparagus, lima beans, beets, beet greens, cauliflower, broccoli, Brussels sprouts, peas, carrots, kohlrabi, rhubarb, squash, sweet corn, spinach, and other vegetable greens. Vegetables that are usually eaten raw, such as celery, cucumbers, lettuce, onions, and radishes, are least suited for freezing, at least all by themselves. Cabbage and peppers freeze moderately well. Almost all fruits, especially berries, freeze very well. The charts about preparing vegetables and fruits for freezing that come a little later show you the freezing potential—and limitations—of specific foods.

If you're concerned about preserving the vitamin C content of your harvest, then you should choose freezing over canning or drying. While no method of storage is going to save all of that fragile vitamin, freezing will save you the most, if you're careful as you go about the job.

Vegetables and fruits will lose some nutrients, most notably vitamins (with vitamin C being the most vulnerable) during freezer storage, but you can minimize the loss in a number of ways:

- Prepare your food as soon after you've harvested it as possible; keep it at 40°F or lower (no longer than 24 hours) before it is prepared and frozen.

43

- Blanch your vegetables, and, for maximum nutrient retention, steam blanch them rather than blanching them in boiling water. (See a more complete discussion of this on page 49.)

- Take care when blanching and cooling your foods before you freeze them; the quicker you work, the less time your food has to combine with the oxygen of the air and go through a process called oxidation, which will result in some nutrient loss.

- Abide by the old inventory rule that says first in, first out. In other words, try to take from your freezer those foods that have been in there the longest, so that nothing sits in there longer than need be. Most vegetables and fruits are good for 8 to 12 months, some even longer. Other foods vary, so check specific charts and recommendations you'll find throughout the book.

- When thawing foods, do so in the refrigerator and not on the kitchen counter, for the cooler refrigerator temperatures will thaw the food more slowly and mean less cellular breakdown and less "drip," which occurs during thawing.

CONTAINERS TO USE FOR FREEZING

You can use any containers that will exclude air and prevent contamination and loss of moisture. Plastic containers are ideal, providing the lids form a good seal. Refrain from recycling the thin plastic containers that yogurt and cottage cheese come in. These become brittle at cold temperatures and can crack, exposing your food to the cold drying air in the freezer and causing freezer burn.

There are boxes made especially for freezing that are initially cheaper than plastic containers, but probably more expensive in the long run because they can't be reused. Canning jars and other recycled jars can be used for freezing, but be sure not to fill them to within more than an inch of the top. That space will allow room for the normal expansion of the food during freezing without breaking the glass. Choose straight-sided glass jars over those with narrow necks and shoulders. Jars can get jostled around in the freezer when you're hunting for something, and those with straight sides are more stable, minimizing the chance of breakage. Even more importantly, since food expands upward as it freezes, it may cause jars with shoulders to break.

Fruits that are to be packaged dry and all vegetables can be placed in heavy plastic bags, closed tightly with a wire or rubber band at a point

Save freezer space by storing only the food and not the container it's in. To do so, press aluminum foil into a pan or bowl. Add the food, then use a second piece of foil on top or simply gather the foil to cover. Freeze until hard, then lift the wrapped food out of the container and return it to the freezer. For cooking, remove foil and slip food into its original container.

as close to the contents as possible so that there is a minimum of air in the package. Don't be tempted to use for freezing thin plastic bags like the kind you get at the supermarket produce counter; they just aren't strong enough and are more likely to rip or tear. Oxygen entering frozen food through tears in packaging can ruin the best quality foods. To test for rips and holes, fill the bag with water. If you discover a leak, don't use the bag for freezer storage. Even the smallest hole can allow oxygen to enter and moisture to escape.

■ It is a good idea to overwrap plastic packages, especially those with meat that has protruding bones, with another plastic bag or stockinette (which is a net bag, usually made of plastic, or even an old, clean stocking) to prevent the plastic material from tearing once inside the freezer.

There is nothing to stop you from recycling sturdy bags, so long as they are in good shape and haven't picked up any strong odors (watch out for bags that once housed strong-smelling foods like peppers or onions, for instance).

■ If you bag your vegetables and fruit for freezing, you wind up with unevenly shaped bags. Since bags have no shape of their own, they take the shape of what's in them. For nice, neat, square bags, lay filled bags on baking sheets and shape them into squares with your hands. Allow them to freeze hard, remove them from the cookie sheets, and stack.

Boilable bags have gotten better with time. Rodale used to object to them because there was reason to believe that the plastics used broke down during boiling and left traces on the food. But the plastics used now—polyester to help the bag withstand the high temperatures of boiling, and polyethylene to make them seal easily—are great improvements.

Their high price and the fact that they can't be reused for freezing may not make them practical for storing and cooking plain vegetables, but you might find them handy for sauced vegetables, entrées, and other combination foods, especially since you can take foods from freezer to pot without thawing. No pots or freezer containers to wash! Use only heavy-duty, vacuum seal bags. And seal only with a special sealing machine, following directions closely to get a good seal.

While the food stays in better shape for a longer time when frozen in boilable bags because there is no air inside, the environment is just right for the growth of that bacteria that causes botulism, *Clostridium botulinum*. If you are vacuum-sealing your freezer foods, take some precautions: Make sure low-acid vegetables, meats, and combination foods are clean and fresh when you bag them. And don't leave them sitting around, either before or after sealing them. Your best bet is to put them in the freezer as soon as you've sealed them, and then cook them without thawing first.

■ You can wash old quart milk cartons and save them all year to use as freezer containers. Fill them with food and put the tops back into their original position. Then fold down the "roof" flat toward one side, and seal well with a big piece of freezer tape.

All freezer containers should be marked before they are put into the freezer. The type of food and the date it was frozen should be marked so that you can pick out the fruit or vegetable that you want at a glance and can use up those that are oldest first. If you are freezing different varieties of the same food, mark the variety on the label as well, so that you'll be able to determine for the next season which varieties freeze best. If you don't already have them, go out and invest in some freezer tape and a freezer marker for writing labels. Unlike regular tape, freezer tape won't lose its stickiness, and the special marker won't smudge or fade, as felt tip and ballpoint pens are apt to do.

FREEZER ORGANIZATION

The organizational skills of many of us meet their match when it comes to the freezer, especially the chest freezer. Even a well-marked bag of snow peas can get buried under a frozen quiche and rest in peace there well after next year's harvest is blanched and frozen away.

One solution to this all-too-common problem is to conduct a quarterly inventory of your freezer's contents. Another, probably more rational, strategy is to keep an inventory log. A big blackboard on the wall next to your freezer is nice, but a clip pad is almost as good. List each

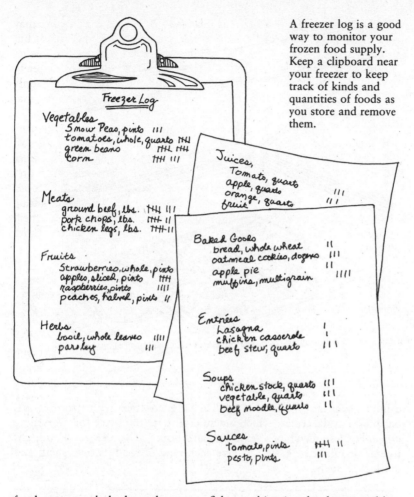

A freezer log is a good way to monitor your frozen food supply. Keep a clipboard near your freezer to keep track of kinds and quantities of foods as you store and remove them.

Freezer Log

Vegetables
Snow Peas, pints |||
tomatoes, whole, quarts ||||
green beans |||| ||||
Corn |||| |||

Meats
ground beef, lbs. |||| |||
pork chops, lbs. |||| ||
chicken legs, lbs. ||||||

Fruits
Strawberries, whole, pints |||
apples, sliced, pints ||||
raspberries, pints ||||
peaches, halved, pints ||

Herbs
basil, whole leaves ||||
parsley |||

Juices
Tomato, quarts
apple, quarts
orange, quarts |||
fruit, quarts ||

Baked Goods
bread, whole wheat ||
oatmeal cookies, dozens |||
apple pie ||
muffins, multigrain ||||

Entrées
Lasagna |
chicken casserole |
beef stew, quarts |||

Soups
chicken stock, quarts |||
vegetable, quarts |||
beef noodle, quarts ||

Sauces
tomato, pints |||| ||
pesto, pints |||

food category: baked goods, meats, fish, combination foods, vegetables, fruits, grains, nuts, etc. And then add specific foods to each category as you store them away, and subtract them as you take them out. If you're like most people, you'll forget to put some foods on your log, so you may have to verify your lists by doing an inventory occasionally. But at least you'll have a pretty good idea of what's in there at all times, making it easy to plan meals ahead and replenish the freezer periodically.

Knowing what's in your freezer is one thing; knowing where in your freezer is another matter. To lick that problem, draw yourself a freezer map and keep that nearby, too. Assign one section of your freezer to each food category. Since frozen packages tend to slip and slide around a lot in chest freezers, especially when you're hunting for something in

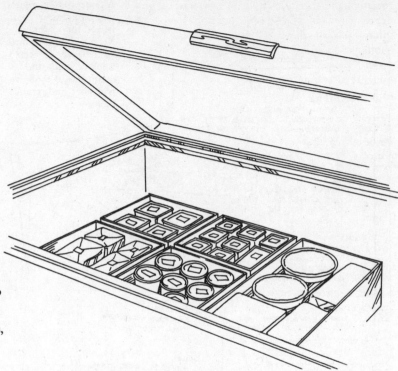

Cardboard boxes, wire baskets, and plastic milk crates help to keep frozen foods organized neatly by food group: vegetables, fruits, meats, baked goods, and so forth.

a hurry, you may want to formalize assigned areas with wire baskets, big plastic milk crates (which are sold all over the place for everything but milk these days), or even cardboard boxes. If you've got an upright freezer, it might be easiest to give each type of food its own shelf, and mark it as such.

■ If your frozen vegetables are mushy, you may have blanched them too long. If they're mushy and they have big ice crystals on them, then they froze too slowly, due either to the fact that your freezer isn't cold enough, or you packed them in too tightly when first freezing them.

THAWING VEGETABLES AND FRUITS

Freezing is not a method of sterilization as is heat processing in canning. While many microorganisms are destroyed by blanching, there are some, most notably molds, that continue to live even though their growth is retarded and their activity rate is slowed down by freezing. When foods are removed from freezer storage, their temperatures rise and the dormant microorganisms begin to multiply. Even during thawing, the process of spoilage sets in, and the higher the thawing temperature, the faster the growth of spoilage microorganisms. Thus, the microbial population will increase at a slower rate if food is thawed at a low temperature, such as in a refrigerator, rather than at room temperature.

■ Corn on the cob is the only vegetable that should be thawed before cooking for best flavor and texture. But steam or roast instead of boiling so that it does not come in contact with water.

Frozen foods that need to be thawed, like those that will be eaten raw or mixed with other foods for casseroles, should be thawed in their original containers in the refrigerator and not on the kitchen counter or in hot water, whenever possible, to best retain nutritive value, appearance, and flavor. Because decomposition of thawed foods is more rapid than that of fresh foods, they should be used as quickly as possible after thawing. Of course, if frozen food is to be cooked, there is often no reason at all to thaw it first. The quality of many foods, most notably vegetables, is best when they are not thawed before cooking. Just remove the food from the freezer and immediately place it in or over boiling water or in a preheated oven or a microwave oven and cook it frozen, before microorganisms become active. Fruit should be eaten or cooked before it is entirely thawed or immediately after it has thawed.

■ Foods still partially frozen or even those that are completely thawed but appear to be edible may be refrozen. Refrozen foods may lose some of their quality, but they will be safe to eat. Don't, however, refreeze any food that shows any signs of off-odor, off-color, or other indication of bacterial change. Mark foods that have been refrozen and use them as soon as you can.

FREEZING VEGETABLES

How and Why to Blanch Vegetables

If you have ever tried to freeze vegetables without first blanching them, you may have discovered the horrible cardboard flavor they acquire after a few months in the freezer. They bear no relation to the succulence of the products you so hopefully packed away last summer. This is the work of enzymes.

Vegetables, as they come from the garden, have enzymes working in them. These break down vitamin C in a short time and convert sugar into starch. They are all slowed down (not stopped) by cold temperatures, but they are inactivated by heat—by blanching.

■ Because blanching and then freezing soften tissues and change the texture of vegetables, frozen vegetables need only be cooked one-third to one-half as long as fresh vegetables.

Instead of blanching root vegetables like carrots and turnips, you can sauté them in butter or oil, just until they have softened a bit. Then pack and freeze. When ready to cook, thaw the vegetables in a buttered or oiled pan in a 350°F oven.

The blanching idea isn't new. Methods for scalding or steaming fresh produce in preparation for freezing were introduced over 50 years ago. Since then, however, researchers have been discovering more about the unrealized and subtle effects of using this pre-cold-storage process. They have found that blanched vegetables are somewhat softened, so that they can be packed more easily and solidly into freezer containers. But more importantly, they've discovered that blanching makes certain enzymes inactive so that they cannot cause unnatural colors and disagreeable flavors and odors to develop while the foods remain frozen.

The Rodale Food Center's taste tests of blanched versus unblanched freezer vegetables confirmed the fact that blanching is worth the effort. It asked taste testers to sample blanched and unblanched green beans, corn, and broccoli after 3 months in the freezer. The vote was unanimous: All the testers chose the blanched vegetables because their colors were brighter and they tasted fresher and had more crunch. The unblanched broccoli was the big loser; it had developed an unpleasant smell and an aftertaste.

Some of the best research done on the "to blanch or not to blanch" issue comes from the University of Illinois. Researchers there froze a variety of vegetables, blanched and unblanched, and tested batches of each several times over the course of a year. Those that had been blanched rated 4.0 to 4.4 on taste, texture, and looks, which translates into good to high good, after as long as 9 months in the freezer. On the other hand, unblanched samples that had been stored for only 1 month received general acceptability scores of 2.4 to 2.9, which corresponds to ratings between poor and fair. Strong off-flavors developed and unblanched products lost color during the first month in the freezer.

Over the longer storage periods, the vegetables that were not blanched deteriorated still further, some of them so much that they were considered inedible. Most became faded, dull, or gray; all became tough or fibrous; and some, broccoli especially, developed an objectionable haylike flavor.

There is another benefit to blanching besides taste, texture, and looks. Experiments have shown that nutrients are retained in greater amounts in many of those vegetables blanched before freezing. Studies published by the North Dakota Cooperative Extension Service show that if foods are prepared and frozen properly, they retain much of their original food value:

- Carbohydrates show no change with the exception of the sugar (sucrose) being reduced to simple sugars (glucose and fructose) during long storage. This is of no importance. Minerals might be lost in solution during the blanching and cooking of vegetables, but this loss is usually no greater than when cooking fresh vegetables.

- Vitamin A is lost only when vegetables are not blanched.

- B vitamins, such as thiamine and riboflavin, are lost by over-storage and through solution in cooling and blanching because they are water soluble. However, a greater loss is suffered if the vegetables are not blanched. Some thiamine is lost by heat in cooking.

- Vitamin C is easily lost through solution as well as oxidation. Vegetables lose some of their vitamin C through blanching, but without this process, the loss would be much greater. The same amount of vitamin C is lost in cooking fresh vegetables.

Another study conducted by the University of Illinois shows us that blanching makes a dramatic difference in the vitamin C content of frozen foods:

- The blanched vegetables kept more of their vitamin C, and the longer they were stored, the bigger the difference in vitamin retention.

- After only 1 month, blanched peas kept 11 percent more vitamin C than unblanched peas. By 3 months, the blanched samples had 36 percent more, and after 9 months in the freezer, 89 percent more.

- Time was even more of a factor with green beans. After 9 months, the blanched beans had 1,300 percent more vitamin C than the unblanched ones.

- When comparing steam-blanched vegetables to boiling-water blanching, researchers have found that steam is more gentle on flavor, color, and water-soluble nutrients like vitamins B and C. The differences range from 9 to 23 percent more vitamins in those that were steam blanched, with the biggest savings in vitamin C.

Steps to Follow for Freezing Vegetables

Specific guidelines for freezing vegetables and fruits follow these general directions.

1. Pick young, tender vegetables for freezer storage; freezing doesn't improve poor-quality produce. As a rule, it is better to choose slightly immature produce over any that is fully ripe; avoid bruised, damaged, or overripe vegetables. Harvest in early morning. Try to include some of the tastiest early-season crops; don't wait only for later ones.

2. Line up everything needed for blanching and freezing first. Nothing counts more than speed in holding on to freshness, taste, and nutritive value. If you have a lot to freeze at once, plan a family operation deep-freeze; have all hands on deck to help quickly, and arrange equipment and containers in advance for a smooth production.

3. Blanch with care and without delay. Vegetables should be thoroughly cleaned, edible parts cut into pieces if desired, then blanched to stop or slow down enzyme action. For water blanching, use at least a gallon of water to each pound of vegetable, preheated to boiling point in a covered pot. If you're steaming, use a wire-mesh holder over 1 inch of boiling water in an 8-quart pot. The same wire-mesh holder is handy for plunging vegetables into boiling water, 1 pound at a time. Start timing when water resumes boiling, following the recommended time in the charts that follow. If you live in a high altitude area, add $\frac{1}{2}$ minute to blanching time for each 2,000 feet above sea level.

4. Cool quickly to stop cooking when time is up and to chill vegetables for the freezer. The extra time it takes your freezer to freeze warm vegetables results in bigger ice crystals and limper food. Vegetables not chilled quickly to stop the cooking are

It's important to prepare and freeze foods quickly for optimum flavor and nutritive value. Start by setting up your workspace so it's neat and efficient; everything has its place.

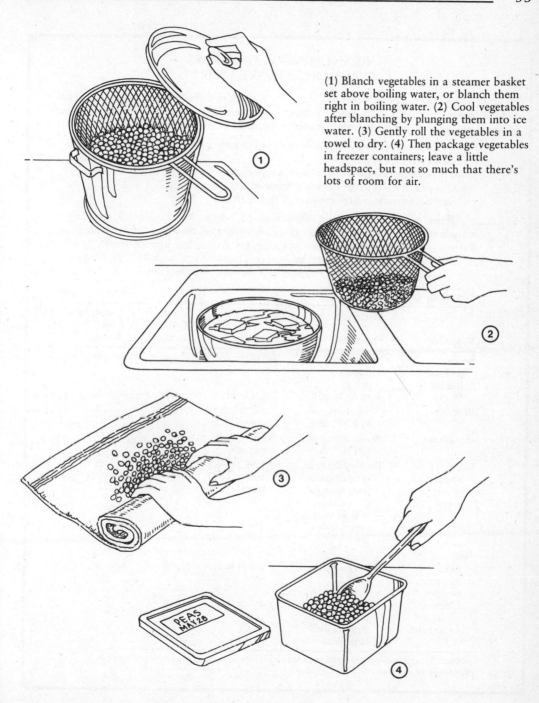

(1) Blanch vegetables in a steamer basket set above boiling water, or blanch them right in boiling water. (2) Cool vegetables after blanching by plunging them into ice water. (3) Gently roll the vegetables in a towel to dry. (4) Then package vegetables in freezer containers; leave a little headspace, but not so much that there's lots of room for air.

BLANCHING VEGETABLES
IN A MICROWAVE OVEN

While using a microwave to blanch your vegetables before you freeze them doesn't reduce the blanching time, microwaving also doesn't contribute to the heat in your kitchen—a definite benefit in the heat of summer. For best results, follow these guidelines:

- Limit the amount of your vegetable to 4 cups of leafy green vegetables or 2 cups of all other prepared vegetables.
- Use a 1-quart round glass casserole or similar microwave container.
- Add ¼ cup of water to the casserole *before* adding the vegetables.
- Cover the container with microwavable plastic film.

If your microwave is a 650- or 700-watt model, is larger than 1 cubic foot, and has a mode mixer or a revolving table, use the recommended blanching times for high-wattage ovens. Otherwise, use the times recommended for low-wattage ovens.

Air-cool your blanched vegetables by spreading them in a single layer on a large tray. They can be packaged and frozen after 5 minutes of cooling time.

Blanching Timetable

Vegetable	Preparation	Piece Size	Minutes at High Wattage	Minutes at Low Wattage
Beans podded Italian Snap	Snap ends, remove strings	Small beans	3	4
	Snap to length	Large beans	3	5
Broccoli	Wash, trim, cut to 1"-2" dice	Small or large pieces	5	8
Cauliflower	Wash, trim, cut to 1"-2" dice	Small or large pieces	5	7
Corn, sweet whole kernel	Remove kernels; scrape tips and juice from cob to combine with kernels for cream-style corn	Whole cut kernels	4	6
Peas Black-eye and green sweet	Wash pods, shell, rinse	Small or large peas	4	6
Chinese, snow, and sugar snap	Wash pods, snap ends, remove strings, shell large peas	Small or large pods	4	6

SOURCE: These guidelines are recommended by Dr. Gerald Kuhn of the Department of Food Science at the Pennsylvania State University.

overblanched and show a loss of color, texture, flavor, and nutritive value. Plunge blanched vegetables into cold water, ice water, or cold running water.

5. Package at once in suitable containers. Glass jars require a 1- to 1½-inch headspace; paper and plastic containers call for leaving a ½-inch headspace, except for vegetables like asparagus and broccoli that pack loosely and need no extra room. Work out air pockets by gently pressing on the food and its packaging, if it's flexible. Then seal tightly.

6. Label all frozen food packages; indicate vegetable, date of freezing, and variety. Then store with other foods of its type in the freezer for easier retrieval later on.

■ For chilling vegetables after blanching, use blocks of ice instead of cubes; they won't melt so fast or get mixed up with the vegetables. Early in the season freeze blocks of ice in any extra containers you have around so that you've got plenty when you need them.

BLANCHING IN A PRESSURE CANNER

Pressure canner blanching is quick and easy, so long as you watch the pot very carefully and take it off the heat just as soon as the recommended pressure is reached. Leave it on longer, and you'll wind up with cooked vegetables that have lost all their crispness and are hardly worth freezing.

Prepare your vegetables and put them on the bottom rack of the canner with 4 cups water. Don't fill the canner over two-thirds full. Then fit the lid on tightly and cook until the gauge reads the recommended pressure. Remove the canner from the heat, and run cold water over the top of the canner. When the gauge reads zero, remove the lid and cool the vegetables right away in ice water. Here are recommended times for some popular vegetables, from the people at National Presto Industries:

Vegetable	Blanch until Gauge Reads (in pounds)
Asparagus, spears	10
Beans, green	5
Beans, yellow	5
Broccoli	10
Carrots	10
Corn, off or on the cob	15
Squash, winter	5

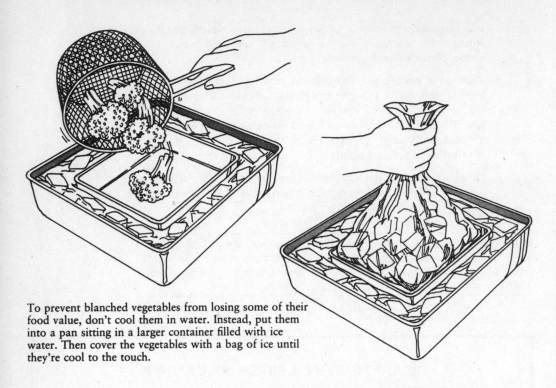

To prevent blanched vegetables from losing some of their
food value, don't cool them in water. Instead, put them
into a pan sitting in a larger container filled with ice
water. Then cover the vegetables with a bag of ice until
they're cool to the touch.

■ You can also try cooling your vegetables with a fan. You won't have the mess
of melting ice and water, and a fan dries the food as it cools. Put your vegetables
1 layer deep on mesh racks or towels and blow a fan right on them. If the day
is very hot and humid, this method may not work; then ice is still best.

Although all the vegetables listed in the following table can be
frozen, there will most likely be some here that you will prefer to store
in other ways. If your freezer space is limited or if you want to do as
little slicing and blanching as possible, think about root cellaring or in-
the-garden storage of carrots and other root crops. Potatoes, for the most
part, don't freeze well, but they keep fine in a root cellar if you cure them
properly first. The same is true for onions. Beets are preferred canned by
most people, as is sauerkraut and other pickled vegetables. Dried beans
and grains can be kept in a cool, dry place if they are wrapped properly.
And the list goes on. Your best bet when getting ready to store a new
vegetable is to look it up in the Index in the back of this book and check
out all the recommended methods before you assume freezing will be
best for you.

■ When trimming vegetables for freezing or canning, save the clean, undamaged scraps and store them in a plastic bag in your freezer. This is your stock bag, and its contents get emptied into your stockpot when you make soup.

If you like to freeze mixed vegetables, cut and blanch each vegetable separately. Then mix and freeze them. Since blanching times vary according to the type of vegetable, blanching separately for the required time assures you that each vegetable is sufficiently—but not overly—precooked.

See the recipes starting on page 307 for prepared foods and combination dishes for the freezer.

PREPARING VEGETABLES FOR FREEZING

ARTICHOKES

Select small artichokes or artichoke hearts. Cut off the top of the bud and trim the thorny end down to a cone. Wash and blanch for 8 minutes in boiling water or 8 to 10 minutes in steam.

ASPARAGUS

Use young, green stalks. Rinse and sort for size, then cut into convenient, equal lengths to fit your containers. Blanch in boiling water for 4 minutes or in steam for 3 minutes.

AVOCADOS See page 68.

BEANS, DRIED

Freeze dried beans in bags.

BEANS, GREEN AND YELLOW

Pick when pods are of desired length, but before seeds take a shape that you can see through the pod. Wash in cold water and drain. Snip ends and cut, if desired. Blanch in boiling water for 3 minutes or in steam for 4 minutes.

BEANS, LIMA

Pick when pods are slightly rounded and bright green. Wash and blanch in boiling water for 2 minutes or in steam for 4 minutes. Drain and shell. Rinse shelled beans in cold water.

BEETS

Beets are usually better canned, but they may be frozen if they are thoroughly cooked first. Harvest while tender and mild flavored. Wash and leave ½ inch of the tops on. Cook whole until tender (about 30 to 45 minutes for small beets and 45 to 70 minutes for large ones). Cool, then skin and cut or leave whole. No further blanching is necessary.

BROCCOLI

Select well-formed heads. Buds that show yellow flowers are too mature and should not be frozen (or canned). Rinse, peel, and trim. Split broccoli lengthwise into pieces not more than 1½ inches across. If there is a chance that the tiny green cabbage worm has invaded the buds, soak in cold salt water for 10 to 15 minutes. Then rinse well and pick over. Blanch in boiling water for 2 to 4 minutes or in steam for 3 to 5 minutes, depending upon size.

BRUSSELS SPROUTS

Pick only green buds. Like broccoli, heads that are turning yellow are too mature to process. Rinse and trim, cutting off outer leaves. Blanch in boiling water for 4 minutes or in steam for 6 minutes.

CABBAGE

Trim off outer leaves. You can shred for tight packing, or cut into wedges. Blanch the shredded cabbage in boiling water 1½ minutes or in steam 2 minutes. Wedges should be blanched in boiling water for 3 minutes or in steam for 4 minutes.

CARROTS

Root cellar storage is usually preferred, but they can be frozen. Harvest while still tender and mild flavored. Trim, wash, and peel. Small carrots may be frozen whole. Cut others into ¼-inch cubes or slices. Blanch in boiling water 2 minutes for small pieces, 3 minutes for larger pieces, and 5 minutes for whole carrots; or blanch in steam 4 minutes for small pieces and 5 minutes for larger ones.

CAULIFLOWER

Select well-formed heads free of blemishes. Wash and break into florets. Peel and split stems. If there is a chance that the tiny green cabbage worm has invaded the head, soak in cold salt water for 10 to 15 minutes. Then rinse well and pick over. Blanch in boiling water for 3 minutes or in steam for 5 minutes.

CELERIAC

Wash and trim. Cut into rounds or cubes. Blanch in boiling water for 4 minutes or in steam for 5 minutes.

CELERY

Root cellaring is preferred, but it may be frozen and used in soups and casseroles where a crisp texture is not that important. Select crisp stalks. Clean well and cut across the rib into ¼-inch pieces. Blanch in boiling water for 3 minutes or in steam for 4 minutes.

CORN

Pick ears as soon as they ripen. The natural sugars in corn turn to starch quickly after ripening, so good timing is critical. Husk, desilk, and wash the ears.

If you are freezing whole cobs, it is best to choose varieties that

To cut corn kernels off the cob more easily, place the cob on a nail embedded in a block of wood, or push the cob into the hole of a tube pan. Either method will hold the cob firmly while you work.

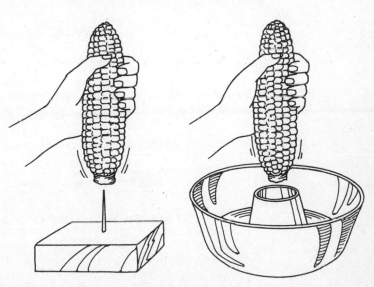

have small ears. Blanch 3 ears at a time in steam or boiling water for 6 to 8 minutes. Cool and pack separately, or pack together enough for one meal. Ears can be wrapped in freezer paper, a double layer of aluminum foil, or in plastic freezer bags.

If you are freezing cut corn, it is still easier to blanch with kernels on the cob first. Follow above blanching directions. Then cool and remove the kernels from the cob with a sharp knife or corn cutter. If you prefer to blanch the kernels after they have been cut from the cob, put about a pound of cut corn at a time in boiling water for 4 minutes or in steam for 6 minutes.

CUCUMBERS

Cucumbers don't freeze very well; they are much better stored as pickles. But they can be frozen for soups and casseroles where a crisp texture is not important. To prepare them for freezing, peel, core, and remove the seeds. Cut into chunks, grate, or purée. Freeze without blanching.

EGGPLANT

Eggplant is best frozen when it is partially prepared (sautéed or roasted) first. Select firm, heavy fruit of uniform dark purple color. Harvest before skin loses its gloss and when seeds are tender. Wash and peel, since skin toughens in storage. Cut into $\frac{1}{3}$- to $\frac{1}{2}$-inch slices or cubes. To prevent darkening, dip in a solution of 1 tablespoon lemon juice to 1 quart water. Blanch in boiling water for 4 minutes or in steam for 6 minutes. Dip again in lemon solution after cooling.

GARLIC

Garlic may be frozen as unpeeled cloves or you can peel and chop it.

■ You can purée garlic, shape it into a log, and wrap in plastic wrap for freezing. Cut off as much as you need at a time while still frozen, and refreeze the rest.

GREENS See Spinach and Other greens.

HERBS See pages 73 and 164.

KALE See Spinach and Other greens.

FREEZING GRAPE LEAVES

Grape leaves for stuffing are at their tenderest in spring. Choose large, flat leaves that are pale green in color. The deeper the green, the tougher the leaves. While some people freeze leaves without blanching, we've found blanched leaves are far superior.

Bring a large pot of water to a boil. With tongs, hold about 8 leaves at a time by their stems and swish them around in the boiling water until their color dulls. This should take about 2 minutes. Cool immediately in cold water and towel dry. Pack in convenient quantities in freezer bags and freeze.

To use, thaw in the refrigerator or in a bowl of warm water.

KOHLRABI AND RUTABAGAS

Harvest while tender and mild flavored. Avoid any that are overmature. Wash and trim off trunk. Peel and slice or dice into ½-inch pieces or smaller. Blanch in boiling water for 3 minutes or in steam for 4 minutes.

LEEKS

Harvest while still tender. Wash and trim off outer leaves, tops, and base. Leeks need not be blanched before freezing unless you plan to freeze them for more than 9 months. Just slice and freeze. For longer keeping, blanch in steam 2 minutes for sliced leeks and 3 minutes for whole leeks.

LETTUCE See Spinach and Other greens.

MUSHROOMS

Most mushrooms are best sautéed or steamed before freezing. But procini mushrooms are better dried. Water blanching drowns their delicate flavor. Select firm, tender mushrooms, small to medium size. Wash or cut off the lower part of the stems and cut large mushrooms into pieces. Steam or sauté 3 minutes for small mushrooms and 5 minutes for larger ones. Most frozen mushrooms can be added directly to recipes without thawing. All, except for morels (which lose their texture), can be thawed before preparation.

OKRA

Select tender, young pods. Wash and cut off stems so as not to rupture seed cells. Blanch in boiling water for 2 to 3 minutes or in steam for 5 minutes. Freeze whole or slice crosswise.

ONIONS

Like leeks, onions need no blanching before freezing, unless you plan to freeze them for over 9 months. Just peel, slice if they are regular-size onions, and freeze. For longer keeping, blanch in steam 2 minutes for sliced onions and 3 minutes for small, whole onions.

PARSNIPS

Root cellaring is preferred, but parsnips may be frozen. Choose smooth roots; woody roots should not be chosen for freezing because they will be tough and tasteless. Remove tops, wash, and peel. Cut into slices or chunks. Blanch in boiling water for 3 minutes or steam for 5 minutes.

PEAS

For podded peas, pick when seeds become plump and pods are rounded. Shell but do not wash. Freeze the same day they are harvested, as sugar is rapidly lost at room temperature. Discard immature and tough peas. Sugar or snow peas can be harvested any time before the pods fill out. Blanch both types of peas in boiling water for 2 minutes or in steam for 3 minutes.

PEPPERS, SWEET AND CHILI

Select when fully ripe, either green, red, or yellow. Skin should be glossy and thick. Wash, halve, and remove seeds and whitish membrane. Peppers do not require blanching but you may blanch for 2 minutes in boiling water or steam to make for easier packing.

POTATOES

Store these in a root cellar; they don't freeze well, with just a couple of exceptions. Pan-fried cubed potatoes, often called home fries, freeze reasonably well. For home fries, choose a waxy or all-purpose potato; baking potatoes will disappoint you because they lose their shape when cooked this way. Scrub well, then bake or steam potatoes until partially softened. Cool and chop into ¼-inch cubes. Put a few tablespoons of vegetable oil in a frying pan, heat to medium, and add potatoes. Turn the heat to medium low and cover pan. Turn potatoes when browned on one side. Brown on the other side, then cool and pack for freezing. Cook the potatoes while still frozen; if you thaw them first, they will become watery and grainy.

You may also freeze whole baked potatoes, although don't expect them to be as good as the fresh ones. Cool after baking and wrap in aluminum foil or plastic freezer bags. Cook without thawing.

PUMPKINS AND WINTER SQUASH

Harvest when fully colored and when shell is hard. Wash, pare, and cut into small pieces. Bake at 375°F or steam until soft and completely cooked. Then pack for freezing.

RHUBARB See page 72.

RUTABAGAS See Kohlrabi and Rutabagas.

SOYBEANS, GREEN

Pick when pods are well rounded, but still green. Yellow pods are too mature for processing. Even 2 or 3 days too long in the garden will result in overmaturity. Wash. Blanch in boiling water or steam for 5 minutes before shelling. Cool and shell; rinse in cold water. Pack for freezing.

SPINACH AND OTHER GREENS (AMARANTH, BEET, COLLARD, DANDELION, KALE, LETTUCE, MUSTARD, SORREL, SWISS CHARD, TURNIP, ETC.)

Harvest while still small and tender. Harvest entire spinach plant so long as it is not overly mature. Use only tender center leaves from old mustard and kale plants. Select beet, turnip, and dandelion leaves from young plants. Rinse well and trim off large midribs and leaf stems. Blanch in boiling water for 2 minutes or in steam for 3 minutes. Stir a few times while blanching to prevent leaves from matting. Cool and chop, if desired, before freezing.

SWEET POTATOES

Use smooth, firm sweet potatoes. Wash and steam or bake at 350°F until soft. Cool and remove skins, if you wish. Pack whole, sliced, or mashed. To retain bright color, to each 3 cups of pulp mix in 2 tablespoons lemon or orange juice, or dip whole or sliced potatoes in ½ cup lemon juice.

SWISS CHARD See Spinach and Other greens.

TOMATOES

Tomatoes can better than they freeze, although they may be frozen. They do not need to be blanched first. To save space and preparation time later, you may also stew tomatoes. Peel and then cut into quarters and simmer slowly in a covered heavy pot until tomatoes are soft and release their juices. Then remove lid and cook as long as you'd like. You can cook the tomatoes down into a paste, but be sure to keep heat low and stir frequently to prevent burning.

■ To peel tomatoes, submerge them in boiling water for 30 seconds, then plunge into cold water and drain. The skins will slip right off. You can also run the dull side of a knife over the skin until it wrinkles, and then peel the skin away.

■ Here's a quick way to freeze whole tomatoes; it's an especially good trick in the middle of hot August, when you're inundated with a bumper crop: Freeze whole tomatoes on baking sheets and, when frozen, store them in plastic bags. The skins will conveniently crack during freezing, making it easy to remove them once the tomatoes have thawed.

To get a big tomato harvest into the freezer and out of the way fast, place whole, unpeeled tomatoes on a baking sheet and freeze until hard. Then transfer them from the sheet to a plastic freezer bag. Take out as many as you need at a time and run them under warm water for faster thawing and easy removal of the skin.

TURNIPS

Use only young, tender roots. Cut off tops, wash, and peel. Slice length-wise into strips or chop into small cubes. Blanch in boiling water for 2½ minutes.

WINTER SQUASH See Pumpkins and Winter squash.

ZUCCHINI AND SUMMER SQUASH

Most everyone is tempted to freeze zucchini, not because it's a good freezer food, but because there's always so much of it! Eat as much fresh as you can, because it's never the same once out of the freezer.

Harvest before skin becomes dull and hard. Pick zucchini frequently since it grows so fast; the smaller the better. It can be frozen as cubes or shredded. If cubed, peel if you wish and blanch it in boiling water or steam for 2 to 3 minutes. Shredded zucchini need not be peeled or blanched.

Other summer squash is best cubed or sliced. Peel first, then blanch in boiling water or steam for 3 to 4 minutes.

Both will become somewhat watery when thawed, so strain in colander or strainer to drain off liquid if using in a mixed dish. Thawing is not necessary when reheating for eating as is.

■ One of the best ways to freeze zucchini is to cook it with a small amount of water, some onions, and herbs. Then purée it in a food processor and freeze in containers as an instant soup base. When ready to prepare, thaw and mix with chicken broth and vegetables, or thin with milk and heat but do not boil. Season with more herbs, if desired, and pepper.

■ Here's a good way to rid yourself of some of the guilt you feel when you discover the remains of last year's garden in the corner of your freezer as you're getting ready for this year's harvest: Make soup stock. Pour all those bags of green beans, spinach, and carrots in a pot, add a few bay leaves and peppercorns, cover with cold water, and slowly simmer for an hour or two. If you've got some soup bones, so much the better. You can use the stock right then, or you can slip it back into the freezer in its now-condensed form for later soup making. Freeze in usable quantities, be it ice cubes or quart sizes.

FREEZING FRUITS

Fruits lend themselves to freezing better, in most cases, than do vegetables, because fruits do not need to be blanched before they are frozen. There are certain changes that occur in fruits during freezer storage, particularly in texture, resulting from a cellular breakdown or softening of the fruits' tissues. These changes are similar to the changes that take place when fruits are cooked. Some fruits, such as papayas, pears, mangoes, watermelons, and avocados, are more subject to the loss of texture than others and for this reason don't freeze very well. However, when you can put a fruit in the freezer and be reasonably sure that you'll have a pleasant product to thaw later, you'll find it to be a plus over canning and drying. There's less work involved, and you'll be saving more vitamins using this method. Fruits can sit in the freezer for up to a year without sacrificing a good deal of their looks and flavor to the cold temperatures.

Freezing Fruits with Honey

Fruits are usually frozen in one of two ways—dry or floated in a sweet syrup. Most information on freezing fruits recommends freezing them with dry sugar or mixing them in a syrup of water and sugar. Fruits held at freezing temperatures will keep without the aid of a sweetener, but they may lose some of their flavor, texture, and color when packed alone. If you want to add something to preserve the taste and appearance of your frozen fruit, you can use honey, and that's what we recommend here.

In general, you can substitute honey for sugar in recipes for freezing fruit. Just cut down the amount of sweetener you use by one-half. This means that when the recipe calls for $\frac{1}{2}$ to 1 cup sugar for each pint of dry fruit, use $\frac{1}{4}$ to $\frac{1}{2}$ cup honey instead. The honey will coat fruit best when the fruit is at room temperature, and the honey is slightly warm.

A thin syrup can be made by blending 1 cup honey with 4 cups very hot water. A medium syrup can be made by blending 2 cups honey with 3 cups very hot water. Let the syrup cool to room temperature before using it, and use enough syrup to completely cover the fruit. If the fruit is packed tightly enough, $\frac{1}{2}$ cup chilled honey syrup should be sufficient for pint containers and 1 cup should be enough for quart containers.

Because honey has a flavor of its own while sugar does not, it is important to use mild-flavor, light honeys for freezing—unless you enjoy the taste of light, fruit-flavor honey instead of sweet frozen fruit! Early summer and spring honeys are generally milder than those collected in the fall. Clover, locust, orange blossom, and alfalfa honeys are certainly more suitable for freezing with fruit than dark honeys like buckwheat.

For the Best Frozen Fruits

There are a few simple steps that you can take to make sure that you're preserving as many of the qualities of fresh fruit as possible:

- Freeze only mature fruit. Immature fruit is usually higher in tannins and other substances involved in darkening; some contain compounds which become bitter during freezer storage and thawing.

- Handle fruits and fruit products quickly during preparation for freezing, packing, partial thawing, and serving to minimize exposure to air.

- Cut directly into syrup any fruit that is likely to discolor, and place crumpled wax paper or foil on top to keep fruit under the syrup.

- Apples, pears, peaches, nectarines, apricots, sweet and sour cherries, and figs darken easily during freezing and thawing, so the addition of ascorbic acid is recommended to help prevent discoloration. A tablespoon or two of lemon juice or rose hips concentrate in liquid or powder form may be added to pure honey or a honey syrup before it is poured over the packed fruit. You can also add ½ teaspoon of ascorbic acid powder, crystals, or crushed tablets to a quart of water and dip each piece of fruit into the solution before packing. Ascorbic acid is bitter, so use sparingly.

■ You can also freeze peaches and other fruits in orange juice. Slice your fruit into thawed orange juice concentrate, making sure the slices are thoroughly coated to keep them from darkening. Two large cans of concentrate will easily do for a crate of peaches.

PREPARING FRUITS FOR FREEZING

APPLES

To freeze in slices, peel, core, and slice apples. Pack them dry or mix with 2 to 4 tablespoons honey, combined with lemon juice or rose hips concentrate to prevent browning.

For sauce, core (but leave skins on) and either grind whole in blender or cook until soft in open kettle and put through food mill. Add honey and lemon juice or rose hips concentrate to taste, if desired.

APRICOTS

Skins tend to toughen during freezing; peel them before freezing. Dip a few of them at a time into boiling water for 15 seconds or until skins loosen. Chill quickly in ice water and peel. Cut in half and remove pits. Add a few pits to each container for flavor. Trickle honey thinned with warm water over fruit. Add lemon juice or rose hips concentrate to prevent browning. Apricots may also be packed in syrup.

AVOCADOS

Choose those that are ripe and perfect. Peel, halve, and remove pits. Scoop out the pulp and mash it, adding lemon juice or rose hips concentrate to prevent browning. Pack and freeze.

BANANAS

Peel and freeze in chunks or as a purée. For chunks, freeze loose on baking sheets and then bag when frozen. For a purée, mash with a fork or potato masher, or use a food processor or blender, adding lemon juice or rose hips concentrate to prevent browning.

BERRIES (BLACKBERRIES, BLUEBERRIES, BOYSENBERRIES, GOOSEBERRIES, MULBERRIES)

Pick out leaves and debris, wash, and then drain. Pack dry or trickle small amount of honey over the berries in the container. Seal and shake until well mixed.

CARAMBOLA

Wash and slice. The tough rind is not softened by freezing, so it is best used as a garnish. Pack in syrup.

CHERRIES, SOUR

Wash and chill in ice water before pitting to minimize loss of juice. Stem and pit. Mix and pack.

CHERRIES, SWEET

Wash and chill in ice water before pitting to minimize loss of juice. Add lemon juice or rose hips concentrate to hold color. Light varieties need more lemon juice or rose hips concentrate to retain color.

COCONUT

Drain out milk. Cut away the hull and skin. Leave in large pieces or grate in blender, food processor, or meat chopper. Pack fresh or toast on a baking sheet in a 350°F oven for 20 to 30 minutes and then pack.

CRANBERRIES

Choose plump, glossy berries. Sort, wash, and drain. Pack dry or make a purée by cooking berries in 1 cup water to each pint of berries until skins burst. Put in blender or food processor or through food mill and add syrup. Pack and freeze.

CURRANTS

Choose the larger varieties for freezing. Stem and wash. Pack dry or add honey to taste.

DATES

Choose ripe, firm fruit. Wash and remove pits. Pack whole or purée dates in blender, food processor, or food mill.

FIGS

Wash, sort, cut off stems, peel, and leave whole or slice. Cover with syrup, adding lemon juice or rose hips concentrate to prevent browning.

For crushed figs, wash and coarsely grind in blender or food processor. Add honey if desired. Add lemon juice or rose hips concentrate to prevent browning.

GRAPEFRUIT

Peel and remove sections from heavy membrane. Smaller membranes may be left on; they contain important vitamins. Pack dry or add honey to taste.

GRAPES

Wash and stem. Leave seedless grapes whole. Cut in half and remove seeds from others. Pack dry or in syrup.

■ Frozen grapes make a great frozen snack. Just lay them out on a baking sheet in your freezer so that they freeze separately, and then bag them for snacking later.

■ To peel frozen grapes, dip one at a time into cool water while still frozen hard. The skins will slip right off.

GUAVAS

Freeze as a purée or in slices. For purée, remove seedy portion and strain to remove seeds. Sweeten with honey, if desired. For slices, pare, halve, and slice. Cover with syrup.

KIWI FRUITS

Peel, slice, and pack in syrup; do not pack dry because they will lose their liquid and become astringent.

LEMONS AND LIMES

Peel and remove sections from heavy membrane. Pack dry or add honey to taste.

■ If you have whole lemons that you won't use within a few weeks, you can freeze them. The skins will get soft when thawed, but the insides will be fine. Do this with limes and key limes, too.

LYCHEES

Wash. Leave about ¼-inch stem on fruit. Pack dry.

MELONS

Cut flesh in slices, cubes, or balls. Add honey and lemon juice or rose hips concentrate, if desired. The texture of the melon can best be captured if the fruit is served before entirely thawed.

■ You can purée cantaloupes and honeydew melons with ¼ cup lemon juice for each quart, then freeze. Thaw and stir in a couple of cups chopped fruit, top with some yogurt, and you've got a lovely fruit dessert soup.

NECTARINES

Freeze like peaches since they are really a fuzzless peach. Their disadvantage is that their skins aren't as easy to peel. Peel with a vegetable peeler or small, sharp knife.

ORANGES

Peel and remove sections from heavy membrane. Pack dry or add honey to taste.

PEACHES

Peaches are better canned, but they may be frozen. Use ripe fruit; to avoid browning, prepare only enough fruit for one container at a time. Wash, skin, pit, and freeze in halves or slices. Add honey mixed with a small amount of lemon juice or rose hips concentrate, if desired.

■ Peaches and nectarines can be frozen whole. This is good to know when time is short and you want to get the fruit into storage quickly, without peeling and slicing it first. Freezing them whole also preserves the color. To use, put frozen fruit in a strainer and pour boiling water over them until the skins crack. Then peel, pit, and slice as usual.

PEARS

Pears retain better appearance and texture when they are canned. If you wish to freeze them, choose ripe but firm (not hard) fruit. Wash, peel, and remove cores. Prepare only enough fruit at one time to fill one container to avoid unnecessary browning. Slice pears directly into a syrup mixed with a small amount of lemon juice or rose hips concentrate.

PERSIMMONS

Sort and wash. Slice and freeze or press through a food mill or blend in a food processor or blender for purée. Add lemon juice or rose hips concentrate to prevent browning. Sweeten to taste, if you wish, with honey.

PINEAPPLE

Use ripe fruit. Pare, trim, core, and slice or cut in wedges. Pack in its own juice or in syrup.

PLUMS

If freestone, wash, peel, and pit; halve or quarter. If clingstone, pit and crush slightly, heat just to boiling, cool, and purée in a food mill. Or remove pits and skin, then purée in a blender or food processor. Add lemon juice or rose hips concentrate to prevent browning. Sweeten with honey or add syrup.

POMEGRANATES

The tasty seeds of this fruit are what you really eat. Cut a slice halfway into the fruit and then break it apart at this cut. Pop out the seeds, taking care not to bruise them. Pack in bags and freeze. Sprinkle, still frozen, over fruit salad, cottage cheese, or whatever. They'll thaw quickly.

QUINCES

Best used as jelly, jam, or sauce, but may be frozen in chunks. Peel, quarter, and core. Cut into chunks and blanch in water for 2 minutes or steam for 4 minutes. Cool by plunging into ice water, drain, and pack.

RASPBERRIES

Clean and remove stems. Pack dry or fill containers and trickle small amount of honey over the berries. Seal and shake to mix.

RHUBARB

Choose crisp, tender red stalks. Early spring rhubarb freezes best. Remove leaves and discard any woody ends. Wash and cut into 1-inch pieces. Blanch for 1½ minutes in steam or boiling water and pack dry; or pack fresh and cover with syrup or a favorite sauce.

STRAWBERRIES

Wash and slice, cut in half, or freeze whole. Sweeten to taste with honey or pack in syrup. Strawberries may also be packed dry so long as you are freezing fully ripe berries. To pack dry, freeze on baking sheets and bag when frozen.

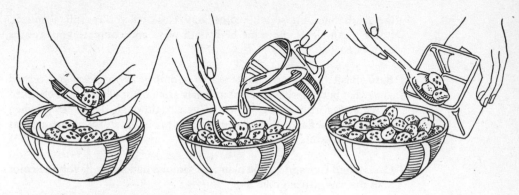

Strawberries can be frozen whole or in a
honey syrup. To freeze them in syrup, first
slice them into a bowl, then toss gently with
honey syrup and pack in freezer containers.

To freeze whole strawberries, simply place
them on a baking sheet and freeze until hard.
Then transfer the berries to freezer bags.

FREEZING HERBS

How fortunate are those who can get fresh herbs year-round. Dried herbs
are distant cousins to their fresh counterparts, and even those that are
frozen are a disappointment if you're used to using herbs right from the
garden. The Rodale Food Center did some experimenting with preserving
herbs and discovered that you can improve upon frozen herbs by blanching them before freezing. While they still won't taste and look quite like

the fresh ones, most will come very close. If you're still skeptical, freeze a sample of the same herb both ways and compare your results with ours:

Basil. Basil frozen raw darkened to a drab grayish-green and turned somewhat bitter, losing much of its lovely aroma. But when it was blanched in water before freezing, it stayed green (although darker than when fresh) and was flavorful and aromatic. Surprisingly, steam blanching was not as successful.

Chervil and Coriander. The blanched samples had better flavor and color than the raw, frozen ones.

WHAT TO DO WHEN THE FREEZER STOPS RUNNING

If for any unfortunate reason (like a power failure or a freezer breakdown) your freezer stops functioning, don't run to it and open the door to check the contents. This is probably the worst thing you can do. First, try to approximate how long the freezer will be out of service. This may mean calling the electric company or the repairman. Do it as soon as possible after you discover the problem. If your freezer will be off for 48 hours or less and it is packed full, you have nothing to worry about. The food will stay frozen, so long as you don't open the door and let warm air enter. A freezer packed less than half full should cause more concern; it may not keep food frozen for more than 24 hours.

If you expect the food to start thawing before the freezer resumes operation, place dry ice (with gloves on—dry ice "burns") inside the freezer, out of direct contact with food. Place pieces of cardboard or wood on top of the food packages and put the dry ice on top of these. Close the freezer door and open only to add more ice. If the dry ice is placed in the freezer soon after it has stopped running, 25 pounds should keep the food frozen 2 to 3 days in a half-full 10-cubic-foot freezer and 3 to 4 days in a fully loaded 10-cubic-foot freezer.

If it is necessary to remove some food to make room for the ice, store it in the refrigerator and cook the food as it thaws. Some foods moved to the refrigerator may be frozen again if your freezer starts operating sooner than you expected. Foods that have thawed may be refrozen as long as they show no signs of spoilage. Mark refrozen foods appropriately and use them before you pull other foods from the freezer. Foods that have been removed from the freezer and then cooked may be frozen again, so long as they are frozen soon after cooking.

If no dry ice is available, you can always move your frozen food to a commercial locker plant or to a friend's freezer. Pack the food in ice chests or wrap it in thick layers of newspaper to prevent thawing during transportation.

Chives. Raw, frozen chives tasted oniony and were dull looking, while the blanched ones stayed bright green and were sweet and mild.

Dill. The blanched sample was far superior to the raw, frozen one: It was more tender, brighter green, and more flavorful.

Lovage. There was little difference in the flavor of lovage frozen raw or blanched, but the blanched version stayed bright green, while the raw, frozen herb turned drab.

Sorrel. The sample frozen raw had an acceptable flavor, but it was tough; blanching improved the flavor and kept the leaves tender. Both frozen samples were dull compared to fresh.

Thyme. Blanched thyme stayed fragrant and attractive, with a flavor different from the fresh, but still good. The sample that went into the freezer raw came out with a strange, medicinal flavor.

Because herbs are so delicate, they need only be blanched for a few seconds. Wash them if visibly dirty. Then hold them by their stems with tongs and dip them in boiling water briefly, swishing them around a bit. When their color brightens, remove them from the water. Then cool them, either by holding them under running water and then blotting them dry with towels, or by placing them on towels after taking them from the boiling water to let them air cool. (We found little difference between the two cooling methods.) Then remove the stems, chop if you wish, or leave in whole leaves to chop later. To make separating herbs easier when they're frozen, lay the dried herbs out in a single layer on wax paper, and roll or fold the paper so that there is a layer of paper separating each layer of herbs. Then pack, paper and all, in freezer bags or wrap in freezer-rated plastic wrap. To use, break off as much as you need, and chop, if you didn't earlier. Use frozen. They may also be thawed in the refrigerator, where they will keep in good shape for a week.

See page 168 for a chart on the best ways to preserve different herbs and page 164 for information on drying herbs.

■ You can also freeze individual portions as ice cubes. Herb ice cubes are particularly good if you make a lot of soups and stews—just pop one or two cubes in as your dish is cooking. To make herb ice cubes, merely prepare your herbs by removing the stems and chopping, and then pack them into ice cube trays, cover with water, and pop into the freezer. When frozen, remove the cubes from the trays and store in freezer bags. If you use boiling water, you're not only covering them to protect them from exposure to air, you're also blanching them at the same time.

Ice cube trays are wonderful for freezing small quantities of any food, such as minced herbs. When they're frozen, pop into plastic bags.

Herb Pastes and Butters

Instead of covering your herbs with water for ice cubes, you may want to cover them with oil to make a paste, or chop and mix them with butter. You can spoon herb butter into ice cube trays, too, or you can roll the prepared butter into a log and wrap first in wax paper and then in freezer wrap. Herb pastes are good for making pasta sauces, herb breads much like garlic breads, and for use in casseroles. Butters can be used similarly; they also make wonderful spreads for seasoning fish, grains, and vegetables.

See page 363 for some herb butter recipes.

Canning Vegetables
and Fruits

Compared to the ease of freezing, canning is so old-fashioned, so cumbersome, so much more work: hovering over the kitchen stove processing jars filled with food. And why does canning always seem to have to be done during the hottest days of summer and early fall? Many people who used to can now feel that way and have traded in their canning jars for freezer containers.

But tradition dies hard, and in the case of canning, for good reason. Canning still has its advantages. An obvious one is that there is hardly any storage space problem. You may can until your basement bulges, whereas your freezer space is definitely limited. You need only invest in canning jars and a large pot for water-bath canning and a pressure canner for pressure canning, all of which can be used over and over again through many harvests. Another plus for canning is that some foods are much better canned than frozen. Sauerkraut doesn't freeze well at all; it loses its crispness. The same goes for most other pickled foods. Pears get somewhat soft when frozen, but not when they're canned. And canned beets are much preferred over frozen ones.

STERILIZING FOOD

In simple terms, canning food means sterilizing it and keeping it sterile by sealing it in glass containers or in tin cans. Sterilization is achieved by heating the food and the canning container sufficiently to kill all pathogenic and spoilage organisms that may be present in raw food. The duration of the processing time and the temperature at which the food and its container are held during processing depend upon the food being canned.

High-acid foods, like pickled vegetables, fruits, and tomatoes, are vulnerable only to heat-sensitive organisms. Boiling temperatures, achieved in *boiling-water-bath processing*, are sufficient to sterilize these foods, killing off molds and yeasts. These temperatures are not high enough to destroy botulism-causing bacteria, but this lethal bacteria cannot survive in high-acid foods with a pH of 4.6 or less anyway.

Low-acid foods, like vegetables, meats, poultry, and fish, however, are not only susceptible to heat-sensitive organisms but also to bacteria that can withstand temperatures above the boiling point of water. *Clostridium botulinum* forms a dangerous toxin that causes botulism, and this may be present in low-acid foods even after long boiling. This bacteria is so toxic that even the tiniest taste can kill. In order to assure that there are no possible traces of *Clostridium botulinum*, food must be processed at 240°F. Temperatures above the boiling point of water (212°F) cannot be reached under ordinary conditions. Pressure is necessary to reach such temperatures, and this is where *pressure canning* comes in. It must be used to process low-acid foods. (Some people have tried to avoid the extra effort of pressure canning low-acid foods by raising their acidity

THE TOMATO CONTROVERSY

If you've been keeping up with food scientists at the U.S. Department of Agriculture or your State Extension Service, you know that in the last few years there has been a good deal of controversy about whether or not all tomatoes are acidic enough to be canned by the traditional boiling-water-bath method. This is because tomatoes, while generally considered high-acid foods, have a pH range of 4.05 to 4.77. Since any food that has a pH over 4.4 is considered low-acid for canning purposes, tomatoes are pretty close to the borderline. Overripe tomatoes or those that are damaged in some way could actually have an even higher pH. Be sure to use only prime, properly ripened fruit. Do not use overripe

fruit. Add bottled lemon juice; use 2 tablespoons for each quart and half that amount for each pint.

In the 9 years since the last edition of *Stocking Up* was published, the U.S. Department of Agriculture has changed its tomato canning recommendation after considering recent research on various spoilage organisms, and we have followed suit. Pickled foods and relishes are still fine for cold packing, but we advise that you can all tomatoes, tomato sauce, and tomato juice in the hot pack, eliminating the raw-pack option altogether for these foods. And process for a longer time, as the canning timetable on page 109 indicates.

with lemon juice, vinegar, or citric acid. Don't attempt it; there is no way for you to be sure that the food you're treating will become acid enough to eliminate the risk of botulism.)

Sealing the container immediately after heat processing, be it water-bath or pressure canning, makes it impossible for destructive organisms to invade the food and reinfect it. In addition, sealing creates a vacuum

CANNING COMBINATION FOODS

Tomato sauce isn't tomato sauce once it's spiced up with lots of peppers, onions, mushrooms, or other vegetables—at least as far as canning procedures are concerned. That's because vegetables other than tomatoes are low-acid, and if you add enough of them to your tomatoes, you can bring the acid content down dangerously low. To avoid any risk, just follow this rule: When you're canning mixed-ingredient foods like sauces, soups, mixed vegetables, and juice combinations, follow the directions for the ingredient that needs the most processing time. If one ingredient would normally be canned in the pressure canner, process the combination food that way for the full time. Don't make the mistake of assuming that you should follow the guidelines for the food that is in the greatest quantity. Rather, follow the guidelines for the food with the lowest acidity.

To give you some examples, the following combination foods are high-acid and can generally be processed in a boiling-water bath, unless a specific recipe advises otherwise and so long as it contains no more than 3 cups of any combination of finely chopped celery, onions, carrots, or sweet peppers for each 18 pounds of tomatoes and it contains no meats:

- stewed tomatoes
- tomato purées

- meatless tomato sauces
- barbeque sauces
- mincemeats (which contain no meats)

And here is a sampling of foods that should be processed under pressure because they contain low-acid foods:

- tomato-celery combinations
- tomato-pepper sauces (such as Mexican sauces)
- vegetable soups (even if they have a tomato base, like minestrone)
- tomato-bean combinations
- tomato-zucchini combinations
- chili (with or without meat, beans, or tomatoes)

You will notice that in a few of our recipes using combination foods, we recommend processing in a boiling-water bath. In these particular recipes lemon juice or vinegar is one of the ingredients, which increases the acidity. These recipes have been tested for pH levels by the Rodale Food Center and were found to be acceptable.

If in doubt about any of your own recipes, play it safe and pressure can; if you don't want to pressure can, then freeze.

inside the container. This vacuum protects the color and flavor of the product, helps to retain the vitamin content, and prevents rancidity due to oxidation.

You can see why the success of preserving the taste, appearance, flavor, nutritional value, and safety of foods depends on the complete sterilization of foods and their containers and upon perfect seals. We can't stress enough the importance of following the canning instructions presented later in this chapter.

CHOOSING AND PREPARING YOUR VEGETABLES AND FRUITS

Although it may seem obvious, it deserves repeating: As when freezing, use only fresh food in tip-top condition. Sort foods for size and maturity so that they will heat up evenly and pack well. Don't bring hot food into contact with copper, iron, aluminum, or chipped enamel. If possible, use soft water (as opposed to hard water) for syrups. Some foods darken or develop a gray tinge during the canning process; this is often a chemical reaction between the food and the minerals in hard water or in metal utensils. Although such a discoloration does not mean that the food is unfit to eat, it may make your canned food unattractive.

For best results, food should be canned quickly, preferably on the day it is harvested. There should be no time lag between steps, so have all equipment clean and at hand before you begin. Food spoilage called "flat sour" can result if vegetables, particularly starchy ones like corn, have stood too long between steps. The canned food may look all right and smell fine, but it has an unpleasant, sour taste. It is not fit to eat, even though it is not poisonous.

HEADSPACE

Headspace is the space between the contents and the top of the jar. You want to leave enough headspace so that the food can swell and move about as it's heated without running up and over the sides of the jar, but not so much that there's an unnecessarily large quantity of air to exhaust to create a good vacuum during processing. The problem with food being forced out of the jar because of insufficient headspace is more than just the mess it makes in the canner. Food that winds up outside on the rim

SHORTCUTS FOR MAKING TOMATO PASTE, CATSUP, AND THICK SAUCES

Most recipes for pastes, catsups, and thick sauces direct you to cook the purée slowly in a heavy pot over a low burner, stirring frequently so that the bottom of the purée doesn't burn. This is a fine method, so long as you have the time and patience to watch your pot carefully. But if patience isn't one of your virtues, try one of these alternative methods:

- Use a slow cooker during the final cooking-down stage when making tomato paste or catsup. Cook down your tomatoes and spices in a heavy pot on the stove and purée according to the recipe in a food mill, blender, or food processor. Cook down some more if necessary to thicken a bit, then pour the mass into your slow cooker and set it on high. Keep the lid off so that water can evaporate. Hours later your purée will be nice and thick. No stirring and no burned bottom.

- Use a colander or sieve. Wash and quarter your tomatoes and other vegetables, and, without chopping or

squeezing, simmer slowly in a heavy pot with spices. Don't stir. You'll notice that the water separates out of the tomatoes and rises to the top. When this has happened, gently pour the contents of the pot through a colander or sieve, saving the light liquid for soup stock. The pulp that's left can be run through a food mill, blender, or food processor. If not quite thick enough, cook down over low heat, stirring frequently.

- Use your oven instead of the stove, following a standard recipe. Make a large batch and cook it all in a roasting pan, first with the lid on until the tomatoes break down. Process into a purée and bake again, this time with the lid off, so that the water can evaporate and the purée can thicken. Set the oven at about 350°F for the first stage, and lower it to 300°F for the last cooking-down stage.

of the jar can interfere with a good, tight seal. And food that winds up around the lid and is not entirely washed can harbor mold, which in turn can grow its way right into the jar and break a seal.

Most vegetables and fruits—either in pint or in quart jars—need about ½-inch headspace, but don't assume that this is standard for them all. Headspace requirements change with the density, shape, and cooking characteristics of individual foods. Always follow headspace requirements in a recipe, and for individual foods, check the processing timetables that come later. If you're a high-altitude cook, you'll have to remember to leave a bit more headspace in your jars, about an extra ⅛ inch for each 1,000 feet above sea level.

CANNERS

The Boiling-Water-Bath Canner

As we've already explained, high-acid foods, which include all fruits, tomatoes, and pickled vegetables, should be processed in a boiling-water bath, usually just called a water bath. (But this is not the same as a simmering-water bath; the water should be boiling rapidly the entire processing time.) With a few exceptions, these foods can be packed either hot or raw (sometimes called cold) in jars before processing. See the discussion of hot and raw packs a little later on.

Any large vessel will do for a water-bath canner, so long as it meets these requirements: It should be deep enough to have at least 1 to 2 inches of water over the top of the jars and 1 to 2 inches of extra space for boiling. It should be large enough so that you can fit in enough jars to make it worth your while (at least 5 jars). And the jars should fit in so that none of them are touching any others; you need room for the water to circulate freely among them. If you wedge them in too tightly, there is a good chance they will crack as they push against one another and the sides of the canner when they expand with the heat. The canner should have a snug-fitting cover. And there should be a metal rack to keep the jars from touching the bottom of the pot. Plan on a second rack between layers of jars if you're planning double-decker canning in your pot.

A large stockpot will do nicely; so will a pressure canner. A pressure cooker, though, probably won't be big enough. There's no reason to go out and buy a special pot if one you already have can serve double duty. If you're using your pressure canner for water-bath canning, just set its

Any large pot can be used for water-bath canning provided that it's deep enough to hold water to cover the jars, has some extra space for boiling, and is large enough to hold at least 5 jars without touching. It should have a snug lid and some sort of rack to hold jars off its bottom.

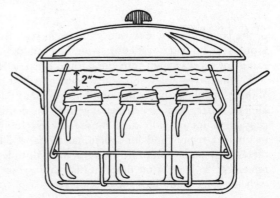

cover in place without fastening it. Be sure to have the petcock open wide (if yours has a dial gauge) or remove the weighted gauge so that the steam escapes and no pressure is built up.

The Pressure Canner

All vegetables, except tomatoes, are low-acid foods and must be processed in a pressure canner because they require temperatures higher than that of boiling water for sterilization. There's a difference between a pressure canner and a pressure cooker. While we have heard that some people do can in a pressure cooker, we don't advise it. A pressure cooker isn't as reliable at maintaining proper pressure, and besides, it's not big enough to hold most canning jars. You should have a canner especially made for pressure processing. It must be in good working condition, and it must contain a rack to keep the jars up off the bottom of the pot. The safety valve and petcock opening on the canner should be checked regularly to make sure that they are not stopped up with food or dirt. They can be cleaned by drawing a string or piece of cloth through them.

Your canner will probably have a weighted gauge, although some canners have dial gauges. Weighted gauges have three markings: 5 pounds, 10 pounds, and 15 pounds pressure. They are usually more reliable for indicating the correct pressure than dial gauges, which have markings to indicate pounds of pressure from 5 to 15 pounds.

The advantage of the dial gauge is most appreciated by those who live in high-altitude areas, where it's necessary to increase the pressure

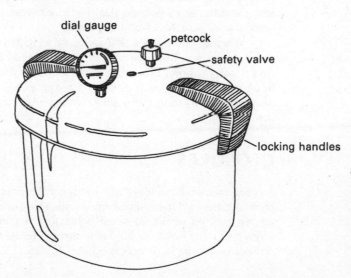

dial gauge   petcock   safety valve   locking handles

Get into the habit of checking and cleaning your pressure canner each year before you start canning. Make sure your gauge is accurate and clean out the safety valve and petcock.

OPEN-KETTLE CANNING—
OLD-FASHIONED AND DANGEROUS

Lots of people used to do it, and some people still do it, but that doesn't make it safe. Open-kettle canning has fallen out of favor for good reason. In theory, food is sterilized by bringing it to a boil and then kept sterile by placing it immediately in sterile jars covered with sterile lids. When the screw band or cap or bailed wire is tightened over the lid, a vacuum is created, sealing the food and keeping it safe from spoilage.

That's the theory. In reality, there is a chance that bacteria, spores, or mold can get into the food after it's been heated through but before it's been covered with that sterile lid, by means of a less-than-sterile piece of equipment, hand, or even the air. We don't take chances, and we don't think that you should either. Forget tradition in this case, and stick with the boiling-water or pressure-canning methods, depending upon your food. And this even goes for most jams and jellies, the last hold-out for the open-kettle method. As you'll see in the chapter Jams, Jellies, and Fruit Butters, we no longer recommend that you paraffin-seal jellies, jams, and preserves because paraffin can only be used with open-kettle canning.

by $\frac{1}{2}$ pound for each 1,000 feet above sea level. With a weighted gauge all that you can do is increase the pressure by the next mark, which means that if your food requires 5 pounds of pressure at sea level (which is how most charts are figured) and you live high in the mountains, process at 10 pounds instead; if it calls for 10 pounds, process at 15 pounds, and if it calls for 15 pounds, then increase the pressure a bit so that the marker goes past the 15-pound point.

Whether yours has a dial gauge or weighted gauge, check it each year for accuracy. Instructions for checking should come with the canner. And if not, the home economist at your County Extension Office should be able to help you find a place to get your gauge checked. A weighted gauge needs only to be thoroughly cleaned; make sure the canner is clean before using it.

CLOSURES

Ask for canning jars today, and you'll get the ones with the common 2-piece closure—a flat metal disk lined with a ring of rubber that fits snugly against the rim of the jar when processing is done right, and a metal screw band that holds the lid down during processing and that is usually removed once the jar is processed and cooled.

But there are other kinds of jars with different closures still around, left over from the days when freezers hadn't yet captured the fancy of so many people who canned. You can't buy these other types of jars and closures anymore, but you might have some good ones sitting around, perfectly fine and ready to be used. Go ahead and use them, so long as they really are perfectly fine, and so long as you get new rubber rings to use with them. Luckily, rubber rings are still for sale. They come in both narrow and wide-mouth sizes.

Be sure that all jars, lids, and bands are in perfect condition. Discard any with cracks, nicks, or chips. Even slight imperfections may prevent proper sealing. Last year's metal rings are fine to use again, so long as they are in perfect shape and have no rust on them. Use new metal lids each time you can. Jars need not be sterilized, but they should be washed in hot soapy water and scalded well with boiling water. Closures must also be washed in hot soapy water and rinsed well. Place lids and screw bands in water and bring to a simmer. Remove from heat and leave in hot water until ready to use. Porcelain-lined zinc caps that have previously been used must be boiled in water for 15 minutes. Wash rubber rings in hot soapy water and rinse well. Keep rings in hot water until ready to use. When using rubber rings, place them on jars while they are still wet, stretching only enough to fit over the shoulder of the jar.

Two-Piece Caps

When people speak about canning jars today, these are the ones they mean. Use the metal lid only once; buy new ones for next season's canning. The metal screw band can be used over and over again, so long as it's not rusted. It is needed only during processing and cooling. Screw this band on snugly over the lid before processing, and do not tighten it after taking the jar from the canner, for it provides no seal itself; its only purpose is to hold the lid down in place. When processing is successful, a vacuum in the jar will seal the lid. Remove the band after the contents of the jar are cold, usually after 24 hours. (But don't force the band off; you might just break the seal if you do.) If it doesn't come off easily, store it with the band in place but be sure to check the food carefully before you're ready to use it. (See the box Signs of Spoilage—Throw It Out on page 94.) If you leave the screw bands on during storage, there is a good chance that they will rust. The only reason you'd want to leave them on is if you have to move the sealed jars and want extra protection for the seals.

Porcelain-Lined Zinc Caps

These aren't being made anymore, but you might be able to find some usable ones at a flea market or in grandma's attic. The jars themselves are probably okay; it's the caps you need to check out carefully. If the porcelain lining is cracked, broken, or loose, or if there is even a slight dent at the seal edge, discard the cap. Opening these jars by thrusting a knife blade into the rubber and prying ruins many good covers. The caps are reusable, but the rubber rings are not. Use new ones each time. If the jars are in good shape, but the caps aren't, you can probably replace the caps with the 2-piece caps; jar sizes are pretty standard.

Unlike the 2-piece caps, these zinc caps should not be screwed on snugly before processing, since there must be some room for the air to exhaust itself to form the vacuum. After filling the jars, begin by screwing these caps on all the way, just so you know how tight is tight. Then unscrew them slightly, just a fraction of an inch. Then can. As you're taking them out of the canner, while they are still hot, screw down the caps all the way. Do this slowly, so as not to disturb the rubber ring, and hence the seal. This tightening is what is meant when it says to complete the seals in the directions for canning that come later.

Bailed Wire Caps

The common 2-piece cap is by far the most popular canning jar closure but there are others, like those shown here, that are fine to use, too.

These are the oldest of them all. Unless they have been stored carefully in a dry place, there is a very good chance that the wire bail is either rusted or bent and therefore quite unreliable. Again, check both the jar rims and the lids for cracks or nicks, and give the wire bail close scrutiny. Don't try to bend the wire back into shape, or wedge anything between it and the glass to create a tight seal. If in doubt, don't use these antiques

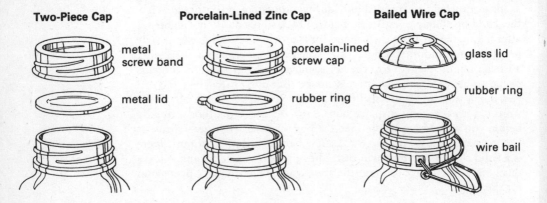

Two-Piece Cap   **Porcelain-Lined Zinc Cap**   **Bailed Wire Cap**

metal screw band   porcelain-lined screw cap   glass lid

metal lid   rubber ring   rubber ring

wire bail

RECYCLING JARS FOR CANNING

Officially, we recommend using only jars made especially for canning. But unofficially, we acknowledge the fact that some people do use other jars for canning; mayonnaise, peanut butter, and jelly jars are particularly popular. When we tested recycled mayonnaise jars for canning, they didn't do badly. Only 3 out of 100 broke. Their biggest disadvantage is that only 6 mayonnaise jars fit into a 7-jar canner. So, unofficially, we say go ahead and use these jars, but use them *only for boiling-water processing* and only with new 2-piece caps.

It should go without saying that no matter what jars you use, be sure they are in good condition, clean, and sterile before packing food in them. Be sure there are no chips along the rim.

for canning; save them for storing grains, nuts, and other dry foods in your cupboard.

If you do have some perfectly good bailed wire jars, get yourself new rubber rings. Fill the jar, put on the wet rubber ring, and then the glass lid. Clamp the longer wire over the glass lid, leaving the short piece up and loose; then can. As you remove the jars from the canner, snap the short wire down against the shoulder of the jar so the wire bail is tight. Again, this tightening is what we mean when we say complete the seals in the directions that come later.

TIN CANS

You won't find many tin cans being used today for home canning; most are used at community canning centers, which are equipped with industrial equipment. Tin cans are more difficult to find than canning jars, and you need a special piece of equipment that seals the lid to the can itself after the food inside the can has been heated to 170°F, but before it has been processed in a boiling-water bath or in a pressure canner. Cans cannot be used for processing jams and jellies, fish, or pickles and relishes. And cans cannot be used over again.

Tin cans come in two sizes: No. 2, which holds about $2\frac{1}{2}$ cups of food, and No. $2\frac{1}{2}$, which holds about $3\frac{1}{2}$ cups. And they come in two types: plain tin and tin coated inside with a protective enamel. Meats, vegetables, and many fruits can be processed in plain tin cans, but certain fruits will react with the metal and therefore are better canned in the enamel-lined cans, called R-enamel. (A C-enamel can exists as well, but it's really not necessary to stock any of these; any foods recommended for canning in these cans also can be canned in plain tin.) The reaction of these fruits with the metal is not dangerous; it won't affect the taste, texture, or safety of the food, but it will affect the color. The foods that are most susceptible to this color change are those deep-colored, high-acid foods like all berries, cherries, dark grapes, plums, and rhubarb. We'll remind you of what type can to use with what foods in the canning timetables that come later. We'll also give you instructions for how to use them.

Even though you won't be using recycled tin cans or lids, it's still a good idea to check your new ones for damage. There's a small chance they were banged around in transport and have some dents or scratches, or that they sat too long in a damp place and developed some rust. Throw out any that are not perfect. And test your sealer before you use it each year. You can do this simply by filling a can halfway with water and then sealing it. Now drop it in a pot of boiling water. Wait a few seconds and then look for air bubbles rising out of the can; if you see any, you know that the seal wasn't tight enough. Check the instructions that came with your sealer and follow them for adjusting it so that you have a tight seal at the seam where lid meets can.

RAW PACKS AND HOT PACKS

Raw packing means putting your sliced or diced carrots or your pitted cherries right into their canning containers fresh and cold. Hot packing means simmering them first in a separate pot and spooning them while still hot into your jars or cans. Which method is better? In some cases the decision is up to you; in others, stick with the recommendations on the canning timetables that come later.

The advantages of *packing hot* are that hot foods tend to pack into jars or cans more easily because they are not so rigid. They've also already shrunk slightly during the initial heating, which means that you can usually pack more of them into one container. And because foods are already hot, they need less processing time in the boiling-water bath. If you need to pressure can the food, you won't save any time using the hot pack; it takes about the same length of time for both hot and raw packed foods to reach the proper pressure. A disadvantage of hot packing is that foods may lose some of their food value when they are hot packed because of the additional heating. And some foods with delicate texture may break down more readily when hot packed because their tissues are softer and more vulnerable to damage as they are being put into the jars or cans.

The plus of *raw packing* is that there's one less step to bother with, and one less pot to clean, which can be a big advantage when your kitchen counters are covered with dozens of jars and lids and vegetables and fruits in different stages of cleaning, prepping, and processing.

Caution: Raw-packed jars go into a canner that's filled with *hot* water; put them into one filled with boiling water and there's a good chance the cool jars will crack.

As we explained in the box The Tomato Controversy (see page 78), we don't recommend that tomatoes be canned by raw packing, and neither does the U.S. Department of Agriculture, for fear that these borderline high-acid vegetables will not reach high enough internal temperatures.

CHECKING SEALS

After processing and cooling canned foods, check their seals.

Two-Piece Caps. Press down on the center of the lid. If it does not "give" when you press on it, the jar is sealed properly.

Bailed Wire Caps. Tilt the jar so that the food in it is up against the rim. If bubbles don't appear there or in the contents as you tilt it and no liquid leaks out, you have a good seal.

Porcelain-Lined Zinc Caps. Follow the procedure above for bailed wire caps; no bubbles and no leaking mean a good seal.

Tin Cans. Examine all seams and seals. Properly sealed cans should have flat, not bulging, ends, and the seams should be smooth with no buckling. If you suspect a container of having a faulty seal, either discard the food or open the container and process the food over again for the required time, or freeze. If you suspect a faulty seal after the food has been in storage for a while, check the box Signs of Spoilage—Throw It Out on page 94. If you're still suspicious, throw the food out where no person or animal can get at it.

LABELING CONTAINERS

After you process and cool the jars or cans and remove the screw bands from the 2-piece caps, mark the type of food and the canning date on the top of the containers. If you have canned different varieties of the same food, the variety of the food (for example: Peaches—Elberta, or Peaches—Hale) should be marked on the label. This extra effort will give

continued on page 92

COMMUNITY CANNING CENTERS

During the World War II years there were literally millions of "Victory Gardens." From these backyard vegetable plots more than 3,800 community canning centers developed. The theory behind the centers was similar to an old-fashioned barn raising, quilting bee, or cornhusking party: When people work together using the proper equipment, a lot of work gets done quickly and fairly easily. With backyard gardens becoming popular again as a means of producing food, community canning centers began a revival in the 1970s.

Canning centers are modern units designed to preserve foods using the same methods you use at home, only they enable you to do large amounts of food at a time, greatly reducing the total time and labor involved in large-scale food preservation. The Ball Corporation began a community canning program in the early 1970s. In 1980 Ball donated the program to the Church of the Brethren and the church funded the program, under the name of Food Preservation Systems (FPS), for 5 years. FPS is now run by Joel Jackson. There are 111 active community canning centers in the United States, heavily concentrated in the Southeast, with Tennessee, Kentucky, Mississippi, Florida, North Carolina, Arkansas, and Alabama having the most centers per state. The other centers are scattered across 30 states, including Michigan, New York, and Maryland. There are centers in 12 countries, including Canada and Mexico. (See the Appendix for the FPS address.)

FPS provides all the equipment and spare parts needed to start a canning center. They will help set up and inspect the equipment, and they will provide planning and technical advice, as well as training programs, for center supervisors. FPS acts as a clearinghouse for information on canning centers across the country and throughout the world.

The basic community canning center has the capacity to process from 200 to 2,400 quarts a day. Although estimates vary, the consensus holds that a canning center is about twice as fast as home canning. The FPS centers are equipped with 4 pressure canners with a capacity of 16 quarts or 24 pints each, an atmosphere cooker, a blancher/sterilizer, a 10-gallon, steam-jacketed kettle, a pulper/juicer, a cooling tank, table carts, and miscellaneous equipment. Many centers have a large variety of options, from meat-cutting saws and sausage stuffers to slicing/dicing/cutting machines and pea shellers to temperature-monitoring devices that record exact temperatures at which food is processed. (Without such a temperature-recording device, low-acid foods cannot be processed for resale.)

It is sometimes necessary to make an appointment to use the facilities, but many centers operate on a first-come basis. The disadvantage of lugging your produce over to the center may be more than offset by the opportunity to use first-rate equipment under ideal conditions, and, often, to have a good sociable time, and possibly get some good advice while processing your food.

To cover the yearly operating costs at a

typical center, 500 families would need to spend about $13 per year at the center. Fees at canning centers vary widely. Some centers charge 10¢ to 15¢ per quart and 7¢ per pint for all items processed, while others are free; some charge by the amount of food canned, while others charge by the number of machines used; some give discounts based on financial need.

Finding a means of finance is one of the main topics of discussion among people trying to establish a center. In most cases, it is sponsored by a cooperative, a nonprofit organization, a school, a church, or other neighborhood group. Because of recent cutbacks in federal spending, churches, community development groups, and county governments provide most of the funding. In some states, Extension Services have taken over centers. In most cases a canning center will serve from 50 to 500 families. Recently, the New Windsor, Maryland, FPS center was licensed by the state to can for soup kitchens.

The Dixie Canner Equipment Company also provides low-volume canning equipment (actually a small-scale commercial cannery) to schools and other groups through their Nutrition Education and Food Conservation (NEFCO) centers. A fully equipped center costs about $87,000 to set up. (See the Appendix for the NEFCO address.)

NEFCO centers are capable of a much higher volume than the FPS system and have monitoring equipment to make resale of processed foods possible. A typical NEFCO cen-

ter provides cans, jars, cookers, can sealers, pea and bean shellers, juice makers, pulping machines, washers, blanchers, exhausters, meat grinders, and kettles. Many NEFCO centers are funded and operated by community service organizations, local governments, school boards, cooperatives, community action agencies, and the like. Often, local county agents, high school vocational-agriculture teachers, and representatives of the local Extension Service act as instructors and help run the centers. The centers are then opened to all community residents for use. The states of Virginia and Georgia both have extensive school programs with the canning centers, with their use dating back to the early 1930s.

The other main use of the NEFCO centers is for privately owned custom canneries, or cooperatively owned canneries. These operations are usually owned either by growers, consumers, or community groups. Their goal is to have more local produce sold and processed in their area instead of selling to brokers, having the food processed in large factories, and resold in the area at a higher price.

Although canning centers are formed for different reasons, the basic goal is always the same. By setting up a small food-processing center, you are able to can a great quantity of food that you either grow yourself or buy directly from a grower, without a large personal investment in canning equipment.

you useful information for next year, because you'll be able to compare different varieties and decide which you liked best. By marking down the date on the label, you'll be able to use the foods in the order in which they were canned.

■ Permanent pens can write directly on canning lids; no stick-on labels are necessary.

STORING CANNED FOODS

Once canned, fruits and vegetables should be stored in a cool, dry, dark place for best keeping. The higher the temperature of the storage area, the more chance of vitamin loss in the canned product. The U.S. Department of Agriculture tells us in the *Handbook of Agriculture* (1959) that canned fruits and vegetables will lose insignificant amounts of vitamin C when stored at 65°F or lower. Losses are about 2 to 7 percent after 4 months and increase slowly to about 10 percent after 1 year's time. When canned fruits and vegetables are stored at 80°F, however, 15 percent of the vitamin C value can be lost after 4 months, 20 percent after 8 months, and up to 25 percent after 12 months.

You don't want to store the food in a place so cold that it freezes. Food expands when it freezes, which could break the seals.

Dryness is important, because humidity can corrode canning lids. And darkness prevents the food from losing its color due to fading in sunlight or artificial light.

Don't Discard the Liquid

The liquid in canned fruits and vegetables is an important source of food value. If you discard it, you're throwing out a good part of the vitamins and minerals found in the can or jar. Normally, fruit and vegetable solids make up about two-thirds of the total contents of the container; the rest is water. Soon after canning, the water-soluble vitamins and minerals distribute themselves evenly throughout the solids and liquid. It follows, then, that about one-third of the water-soluble nutrients are in the liquid portion.

SPOILED FOOD

If, when opening canned food for use, you suspect that it has spoiled, do not test it by tasting it. The botulism bacteria is so toxic that a taste may be fatal. Boil the suspected food rapidly for a few minutes. If you notice an unusual and unappetizing odor developing, you can be certain that the food is not safe to eat. Burn the food or bury it deep enough so that no animal can uncover it and eat it. There's a chance that you could contaminate the water supply by flushing it down the toilet or kitchen drain or garbage disposal, so boil it rapidly for 15 minutes beforehand.

SAFE, BUT UNSIGHTLY

Cauliflower that develops a pinkish hue in the jar during storage might look a bit odd, but it's safe to eat. The color change means that it was overly mature when it was canned. Pickled cauliflower may change color because some varieties react with the vinegar.

Garlic added to vegetables before canning has a tendency to turn blue and may share its new color with the rest of the can. No harm done.

It's not unusual for the pulp in canned tomatoes or tomato juice to separate from the liquid during storage. The culprit is an enzyme in the vegetable that breaks down the peeled tomatoes if the tomatoes sit too long before being processed. Unsightly, but safe.

The pinkish color of some canned pears is caused by heating the natural tannins in the fruit. It's harmless.

A newly canned jar that has a lid with a "buckle" in it should be refrigerated and eaten within a few days, or it may be reprocessed, using a new lid, even if the buckled lid is sealed tightly on the jar. The buckling means that there is still some air inside the jar; all air must vent from the jar during processing to create a vacuum seal.

Dark smudges on the underside of the lid is a black, powdery deposit that forms when some vegetables react with the metal on the lid. It's harmless, so long as you processed the food according to directions. Such deposits are more likely to occur with raw-packed foods than with hot-packed ones.

Canned fruit that floats is safe to eat. It floats because it's lighter than its syrup. You can prevent the problem next time by trying a few different things: Heat the fruit first to drive out some of its air, switch to a lighter syrup, or try rolling the jar on its side after it's been canned and the jar is cool; this may cause the fruit to reabsorb some of the liquid it lost during the vacuum process of canning, making the fruit heavier.

Sometimes the liquid level in canned food drops during processing, leaving the jar with a big headspace. To avoid this problem next time, try one of the following:

- Be sure to remove all air bubbles by carefully running a nonmetallic spatula around the inside of your jar and adding more liquid as necessary to reach headspace level.

- Don't pack the food too tightly, or the jar too full; if this happens, the food can boil over and take with it some of the liquid.

- Be sure that the lids are centered on the jar and the bands are screwed down evenly and firmly so that you get a good seal; partial seals allow liquid to escape. If liquid loss occurs during pressure canning, be sure that the pressure is held constant and that the jars are allowed to cool slowly.

SIGNS OF SPOILAGE—THROW IT OUT

Glass Jars

- A jar that is soiled or moldy on the outside indicates that food has seeped out during storage, which means that air and bacteria, yeasts, and molds could have seeped in. (Jars right out of the canner might be a bit soiled from some of the liquid that was exhausted out with the air; this is okay, so long as half the contents of the jars aren't floating outside in the canning water! If you've wiped the jars as you should have done, the jars would have gone clean into storage and any food on the outside of the jars now is *not* okay.)

- A significant change in color, most notably a much darker color, can mean spoilage. Some brown, black, or gray discoloring may be due to minerals in the water or in the cooking utensils; while it may detract from the looks of the food, there is no harm done otherwise.

- A change in texture, especially if the food feels slimy, is a sure sign that the food isn't fit to eat.

- Mold in the food or inside the lid— sometimes nothing more than little flecks—is not a good sign.

- Small bubbles in the liquid or a release of gas, however slight, when you open the can means foul play. Sometimes you get a strong message: Liquid actually spurts out when you release the seal; other times the gas is more subtle.

Tin Cans

- Bulging ends or liquid leaking from the seam, where the lid meets the can, spells trouble.

Be particularly careful about sterilizing jars, screw bands, and any other equipment that might have come in contact with the food. Wash your hands with soap and hot water and rinse well.

CANNING FRUITS

How to Prevent Fruits from Discoloring

Fruits have a tendency to darken in the canning process. To keep apples, apricots, figs, nectarines, peaches, and pears from darkening, place fruit, as soon as they are washed and sliced, in a solution of 1 tablespoon lemon juice or ascorbic acid powder, crystals, or crushed tablets to 1 gallon of water. Or place fruit in a solution of 2 tablespoons vinegar to 1 gallon water and let fruit soak no longer than 20 minutes. Then rinse fruit in cold water before packing.

Fruit Syrups

Most people who can fruits pack them in a sweet syrup. However, fruit may be canned without sweetening. It may be packed in juice made from the fruit itself (by blenderizing or extracting), in purchased juice (apple, orange, etc.), or in water. Sugar helps canned fruit hold its shape, color, and flavor, but it is not needed to prevent spoilage. Unsweetened fruit should be processed just as sweetened fruit.

You can also make a honey syrup. A very satisfactory syrup can be made by blending 2 cups honey with 4 cups very hot water. Just as when freezing fruit with honey, choose a light-flavor honey for making your syrup so that the honey taste will not overpower the flavor of the fruit.

Do not substitute an artificial sweetener for honey or sugar. Saccharin products develop an off-taste under the high temperatures of canning, and aspertame—otherwise known by its brand names, Nutrasweet and Equal—loses its sweetness.

■ The clean pear, apple, and peach peelings left over at canning time can be cooked down and put through a food mill or food processor to make a fine pear, apple, or peach sauce.

■ The delicious fruit syrup left in your home-canned jars is wonderful for freezing into Popsicles.

STEP-BY-STEP DIRECTIONS
FOR PROCESSING FRUITS, TOMATOES,
AND PICKLED VEGETABLES
IN A BOILING-WATER BATH

1. Fill boiling-water canner over half full, deep enough to cover containers completely. There should be about 2 inches of water over the tops of the jars and at least 2 inches of headspace in the canner above the water. Turn on the heat so water can heat up. If you're raw packing, be careful not to let the water boil. Raw-packed jars should go into hot, but not boiling, water to prevent a chance of jars cracking from the sharp temperature difference.

2. If you are using jars, wash and rinse them and put them into hot water until needed. Place lids and screw bands in water and bring to a simmer. Remove from heat and leave in hot water until ready to use. If you are using closures that have

rubber rings, wash rings in hot water and rinse well. Keep rings in hot water until ready to use.

If you are using tin cans and lids, have new ones ready and have a sealer at hand.

3. Prepare syrup, if it is to be used.

4. Prepare fruit, pickled vegetables, or tomatoes for canning.

5. If you are using jars, pack fruit, either raw or hot, into jars. If you haven't read it already, go back and read the section that talks about hot and raw packs. You'll see that with some foods you can pack either way, but with others you have no choice and must follow specific recipe directions or directions in the timetable that comes a little later.

Then add hot syrup, juice, or water to fill jars, leaving recommended headspace as noted in the timetable or in the specific recipe. Remove the air from the jars by running a nonmetallic spatula along the inside, pressing the food as you do so. Add more liquid, if necessary; the correct amount of liquid helps to create a good vacuum. Wipe the jars, paying particular attention to any food or liquid that might have spilled onto the lid; any food left there could ruin your chances of a good seal. Then close jars (see the section Closures on page 84).

■ Use a nonmetallic spatula, not a knife or other sharp utensil, for removing air bubbles, because a knife sliding around the inside of a canning jar will make tiny scratches or nicks in the glass. The dramatic temperature swings of canning stress the glass, and it could break along these weak spots.

If you are using tin cans, fill the cans with raw or hot food and cover the food with syrup or water. To exhaust the air in cans, the food must be heated to at least 170°F. Place the open, filled cans in a large pot with boiling water about 2 inches below the tops of the cans. Cover the pot and bring the water back to boiling. Boil until the food reaches 170°F (about 10 minutes). To be sure that the food is heated enough, test the temperature with a dairy or candy/jelly thermometer, placing the bulb in the center of one of the cans. Remove the cans from the water one at a time. Replace any liquid spilled from the cans by filling them with *boiling* syrup or water. Put a clean lid on each can and seal at once with a sealer.

6. Place the closed jars or sealed cans upright on a rack in the canner so that none of them are touching any others, allowing the water to circulate freely. If there is room for 2 layers of

jars, place a rack between the 2 levels and stagger the containers so that none are directly over any of those below. Cans may be staggered without a rack between layers. Water should be 2 inches over the tops of the containers. Add water, if needed (boiling water if hot packing, and hot water if raw packing). Be careful not to pour water directly on the containers. Allow 2 inches headspace in canner for water to boil without running over.

7. Put the lid on the canner and bring the water to boiling.

8. *Begin to count time as soon as the water starts to boil* and process for time recommended for each specific food in the timetable. The processing times given on the chart are for altitudes less than 1,000 feet above sea level. For high-altitude areas, increase the processing time 2 minutes for each 1,000 feet above sea level. For example, if you live 3,000 feet above sea level, process 6 minutes longer than the recommended time. Leave the lid on the canner, but remove it periodically to make sure the water is boiling gently and steadily. Add more boiling water as needed to keep containers covered.

9. As soon as the processing time is up, remove the containers from the canner. Place them upright, out of drafts, on wood racks, a wooden board, or several thicknesses of a dry towel so that they are not in direct contact with anything cold, like a countertop or metal rack, or anything damp, like a wet towel or sink, either of which might cause very hot jars to crack. Be sure that the jars are not touching so that air can circulate under, over, and around each one. Let them cool by themselves; don't tamper with them until they are cool.

   Tin cans should be cooled quickly in cold water, using as many changes of water as is necessary. Remove cans from the water while they are slightly warm so that they will dry in the air.

10. In jars, the last bit of air is exhausted as the food cools, creating that vacuum you want. The common 2-piece lid is self-sealing; you'll hear a reassuring high-pitched sound of the metal lid snapping down on the glass rim when the vacuum is complete and the jar seals itself. You can tell if the 2-piece lid is sealed by pressing down on the center of the lid. If it is down already or stays down when pressed, the seal is good. If it fails to stay down, reprocess the jar, place in the refrigerator and use within the next few days, or freeze the jar.

    If you're using caps that don't self-seal, complete the seals as soon as you take them out of the canner (see the section
    continued on page 100

98

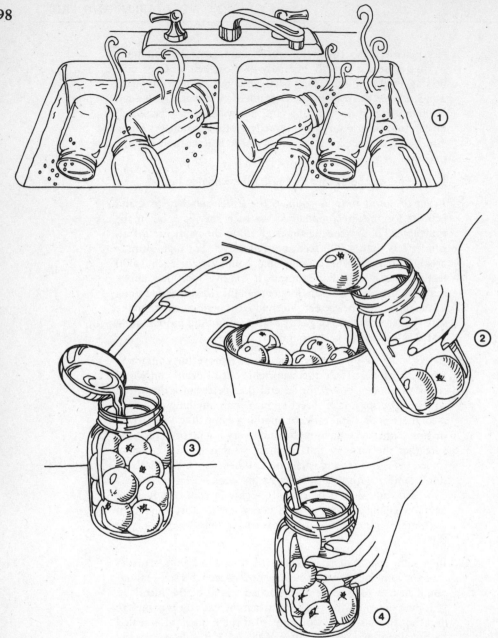

(1) For boiling-water-bath processing, wash and rinse your jars and keep them in hot water until you need them. (2) Pack the fruit into jars. (3) Add hot syrup or juice, leaving recommended headspace. (4) Remove air from the jars by running a nonmetallic spatula along the inside of the glass.

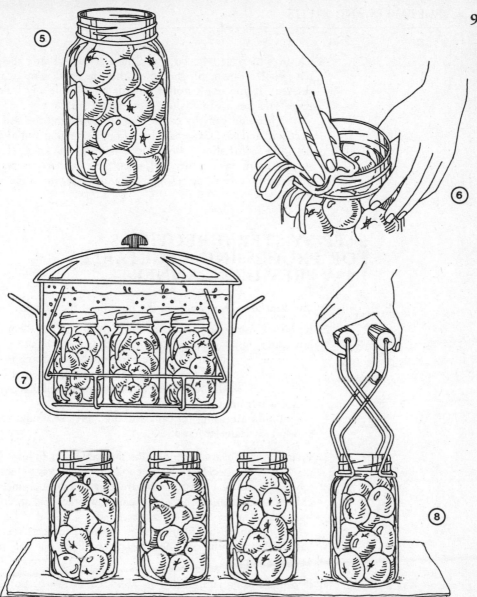

(5) Add more liquid if necessary, making sure all jars have the correct headspace. (6) Wipe the jar rims to pick up any spilled food or liquid, then close jars. (7) Place the jars on a rack in the canner, making sure none are touching. There should be at least 2 inches of water above the jars. (8) When processing time is up, remove the jars and place them on a folded towel or wooden rack. Be sure the jars aren't touching so air can circulate around them and hasten cooling.

Closures on page 84). To check for a good seal after the jars have cooled down, tilt the jar so that the food is up against the seal. If you don't notice any air bubbles or any leakage there, you can assume you've got a good seal.

Check tin cans by examining all seams and the seal between lid and can. Can ends should not be bulging, but almost flat, and seams should be smooth with no buckling. If you suspect a can has a faulty seal, open the can and reprocess it, or place the can in the refrigerator and use it within the next few days.

STEP-BY-STEP DIRECTIONS FOR PROCESSING VEGETABLES IN A PRESSURE CANNER

1. Put 2 inches of hot water in the bottom of the canner.

2. If you are using jars, wash and rinse them and put them into hot water until needed. Place lids and screw bands in water and bring to a simmer. Remove from heat and leave in hot water until ready to use. If you are using closures that have rubber rings, wash rings in hot water and rinse well. Keep rings in hot water until ready to use.

   If you are using tin cans and lids, have new ones ready and have a sealer at hand.

3. Prepare vegetables for canning as timetable that follows suggests. It is not necessary to precook or blanch vegetables intended for canning as you do for freezing and drying, since the enzymes that would otherwise break down the food are killed by the heat in the canning process.

   Vegetables should be packed unsalted for best texture. Salt used in canning does not prevent spoilage; it is only used as a seasoning.

4. If you are using jars, pack vegetables, either raw or hot, into jars, leaving recommended headspace, as noted in the timetable. Pour in enough boiling water to cover the vegetables. Run a nonmetallic spatula around the inside of the jar to remove any air bubbles from the jar. Add more liquid if necessary to bring up to headspace level. Wipe tops and rims of jars, paying particular attention to any food or liquid that might have spilled onto the lid; any food left there could ruin your chances of a good seal. Then close jars (see the section Closures on page 84).

If you are using tin cans, fill the cans with raw or hot vegetables and cover them with water. To exhaust the air in the cans, the food must be heated to at least 170°F. Place the open, filled cans in a large pot with boiling water about 2 inches below the tops of the cans. Cover the pot and bring the water back to boiling. Boil until the food reaches 170°F (about 10 minutes). To be sure that the food is heated enough, test the temperature with a dairy or candy/jelly thermometer, placing the bulb in the center of one of the cans. Remove the cans from the water one at a time. Replace any liquid spilled from the cans by filling them with *boiling* water. Put a clean lid on each and seal at once with a sealer.

5. Set the closed jars or sealed cans on a rack in the canner so that steam can circulate around them freely. If there is room for 2 layers of jars, place a rack between the 2 levels and stagger the containers so that none are directly over any of those below. Cans may be staggered without a rack between layers.

6. Fasten the cover of the canner securely so that no steam escapes except at the open petcock (if your canner has a dial gauge) or weighted gauge opening.

7. Allow steam to escape from the opening for 10 minutes so all the air is driven out of the canner. Then close the petcock (if your canner has a dial gauge) or put on the weighted gauge and let the pressure rise. When the pressure climbs close to the pressure you need (see the timetable), turn the heat down a bit and let it rise a bit more slowly to where you want it. (If you live in a high-altitude area, you need to increase the pressure by ½ pound for each 1,000 feet above sea level. See page 83, The Pressure Canner, for a discussion of adjustments for high altitudes.)

8. Start counting time as soon as 10 pounds pressure is reached, and process for the required time on the timetable. When the proper pressure is reached, turn the heat down a bit, since all you need to do now is maintain that temperature (which affects the pressure), not raise it. Watch the gauge carefully to be sure it stays at the right pressure. Avoid changing the heat suddenly because it will affect the pressure. Don't leave the kitchen even though you might be using a timer; you'll want to be close by to check the gauge frequently.

Fluctuating pressure can cause liquid to be pulled from the jars, which might affect the seals. (If this happens, check the seals after the jars have cooled. If the liquid level is low, but the seals are good, no need to worry.)

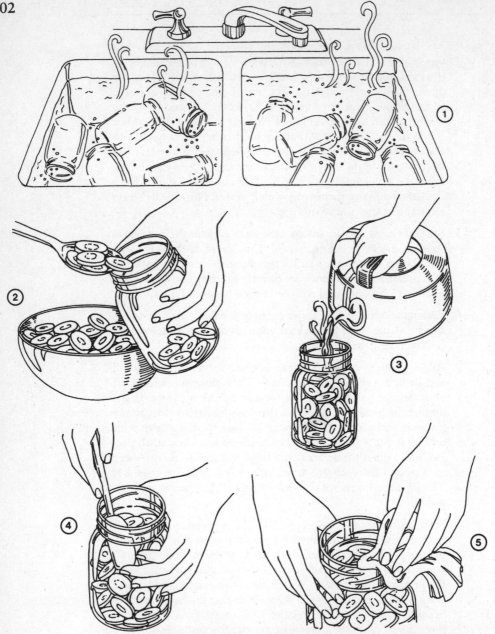

(1) To pressure can vegetables, first wash and rinse jars and keep them in hot water until you need them. (2) Pack the vegetables into jars, leaving the recommended headspace. (3) Pour in enough boiling water to cover the vegetables. (4) Remove air from the jars by running a nonmetallic spatula along the inside of the glass. (5) Wipe the jar rims, then close jars.

(6) Put the jars on a rack in the canner. Jars can be staggered in 2 rows with a rack between them. (7) Fasten the cover on the canner and allow steam to escape for 10 minutes. (8) When processing time is up, remove the canner from the heat and let it stand until the pressure returns to zero. (9) Remove the cover by tilting it so that the steam doesn't rise up in your face. (10) Take the jars out and place them on a folded towel or wooden rack. Be sure the jars aren't touching so air can circulate freely and hasten cooling.

If you do leave the kitchen and return to find that the pressure has dropped, start timing from the beginning again.

9. At the end of processing time, gently remove the canner from the heat.

10. If you are using jars, let the canner stand until pressure returns to zero. Do not try to bring the pressure down quickly by running cold water over the canner in the sink. The shock could be enough to crack the jars. Wait a minute or two, but no more, then slowly open the petcock (if your canner has a dial gauge) or remove weighted gauge.

11. Wait 2 minutes, then unfasten the cover and tilt it so the stream doesn't hit you in the face. As you take jars from the canner, complete the seal if the jars are not the self-sealing lids (see the section Closures on page 84). Set jars upright on a wooden rack or board or several layers of dry toweling so that you keep them off cold and wet surfaces. Keep them out of a draft. You want them to cool gradually. Place them far enough apart so that the air can circulate around all of them.

   If you are using tin cans, release steam in the canner at the end of processing time by slowly opening the petcock or taking off the weighted gauge. When no more steam escapes, remove the cover. Cool tin cans in cold water, changing water often enough to cool them quickly. Take cans out of cooling water while still slightly warm so they can air-dry.

12. In jars, the last bit of air is exhausted as the food cools, creating that vacuum you want. The common 2-piece lid is self-sealing; you'll hear a reassuring high-pitched sound of the metal lid snapping down on the glass rim when the vacuum is complete and the jar seals itself. You can tell if the 2-piece lid is sealed by pressing down on the center of the lid. If it is down already or stays down when pressed, the seal is good. If it fails to stay down, reprocess the jar, place in the refrigerator and use within the next few days, or freeze the jar.

   If you're using caps that don't self-seal, complete the seals as soon as you take them out of the canner (see the section Closures on page 84). To check for a good seal after the jars have cooled down, tilt the jar so that the food is up against the seal. If you don't notice any air bubbles or any leakage there, you can assume you've got a good seal.

   Check tin cans by examining all seams and the seal between lid and can. Can ends should not be bulging, but almost flat, and seams should be smooth with no buckling. If you suspect a can has a faulty seal, open the can and reprocess it, or place the can in the refrigerator and use it within the next few days.

Timetable for Processing Fruits, Tomatoes, and Pickled Vegetables in a Boiling-Water Bath

If raw pack and hot pack work well for a specific food, we give directions for both. Otherwise, we describe the preferred method only. The same is true for canning in tin cans. Our step-by-step directions, page 95, will give you the basic procedure for canning in a boiling-water bath; read them before you follow the directions here. They're also a good refresher course if you haven't canned since last year.

Put filled jars into canner containing hot or boiling water. For raw pack have water in canner hot but not boiling; for hot packs have water boiling. Add boiling water to bring water about 2 inches over tops of jars, but don't pour boiling water directly on glass jars. Put cover on canner. Begin to count processing time when water in canner comes to a rolling boil. Note for high-altitude canners: If processing time is 20 minutes or more, increase it by 2 minutes for every 1,000 feet above sea level. Directions for relishes and other pickled foods can be found in the chapter Pickles and Relishes, page 193.

| | | Processing Time | | | |
| | | Glass Jars | | Tin Cans | |
Product	Directions	Pints (min.)	Quarts (min.)	#2 (min.)	#2½ (min.)
Apples	HOT PACK. Peel, core, and cut into pieces. To keep from darkening, place in water containing lemon juice, ascorbic acid, or vinegar (see page 94). Drain, then boil 5 minutes in syrup, juice, or water. Pack apples in jars to ½ inch of top. Cover with boiling syrup, juice, or water, leaving ½ inch at top.	15	20	10*	10*
Applesauce	HOT PACK. Make applesauce according to your recipe or one that appears on page 330; pack hot to ¼ inch of top.	20	20	20*	20*
Apricots	See Peaches.				
Beets, pickled (For other pickled products, see the chapter Pickles and Relishes, page 193.)	Unpickled beets need pressure canning; see Timetable for Processing Low-Acid Vegetables, page 111. HOT PACK. Cut off beet tops, leaving 1 inch of stem and root. Wash beets, cover with boiling water, and cook until tender. Remove skins and slice. For pickling syrup use 2 cups vinegar to 1 cup honey. Heat to boiling. Pack beets in jars to ½ inch of top. Cover with boiling syrup, leaving ½ inch at top.	30	30	–	–

continued

Timetable for Processing Fruits, Tomatoes, and Pickled Vegetables in a Boiling-Water Bath—*continued*

		Processing Time			
		Glass Jars		Tin Cans	
Product	Directions	Pints (min.)	Quarts (min.)	#2 (min.)	#2½ (min.)
Berries, except Strawberries	Berries, because of their delicate texture and flavor, are better frozen than canned.				
	RAW PACK. This is preferred for raspberries, blackberries, boysenberries, dewberries, and loganberries. Wash berries and drain well. Fill jars to ½ inch of top, shaking berries down gently. Cover with syrup, juice, or water, leaving ½ inch at top.	15	20	15†	20†
	HOT PACK. This is preferred for firmer berries: blueberries, cranberries, currants, elderberries, gooseberries, and huckleberries. Wash berries and drain well. Add ¼ cup honey to each quart fruit. Cover pan and bring to boil. Pack berries to ½ inch of top. If the berries haven't made enough of their own juice, cover them with syrup.	15	20	15†	20†
Cherries	RAW PACK. Wash; remove pits in sour or pie cherries. Sweet cherries need not be pitted, but do prick their skins with a pin or tip of a knife so that they don't burst during processing. Fill jars to ½ inch of top, shaking cherries down gently. Cover with boiling juice, syrup, or water, leaving ½ inch at top.	25	25	20†	25†
	HOT PACK. Wash; remove pits if desired (see raw pack). Add ¼ cup honey to each quart of fruit. Add a little water to unpitted cherries. Cover pan and bring to a boil. Pack hot to ½ inch of top.	15	20	15†	20†
Figs	HOT PACK. Use ripe figs only. Wash, but do not remove skins or stems. Cover with boiling water and simmer for 5 minutes. Pack hot figs and add 1 tablespoon lemon juice to each pint. Add boiling syrup, juice, or water to ½ inch of top. If lemon juice is not used, jars must be pressure canned at 5 pounds pressure for 10 minutes for pints.	45	50	85†	90†
Fruit purée	HOT PACK. Use sound, ripe fruit. Wash; remove pits if desired. Cut large fruit in pieces. Simmer until soft; add a little water if needed. Put through strainer or food mill. Add honey to taste. Heat to simmering and pack to ¼ inch of top.	15	15	20†	20†

Product	Directions	Processing Time			
		Glass Jars		Tin Cans	
		Pints (min.)	Quarts (min.)	#2 (min.)	#2½ (min.)
Grapefruits, Oranges, and Tangerines	RAW PACK. Remove fruit segments, peeling away the white membrane that could develop a bitter taste in the canning process. Seed carefully. Pack fruit in jars and cover with boiling syrup, juice, or water. Leave ½ inch at top.	10	10	–	–
Grapes	RAW PACK. Wash and stem seedless grapes. Pack tightly, but be careful not to crush. Add boiling syrup, juice, or water, leaving ½ inch at top.	15	20	20*†	25*†
	HOT PACK. Prepare as for raw pack. Bring to a boil in syrup, juice, or water. Pack without crushing. Add boiling syrup, juice, or water to ½ inch of top.	10	10	20*†	25*†
Juices	See the chapter Juicing Your Harvest, page 287.				
Mixed fruit	HOT PACK. Prepare pineapples, pears, and peaches by peeling and cutting into uniformly sized pieces. Add slightly underripe seedless grapes if you wish. Cook in syrup, juice, or water for 3 to 5 minutes, until slightly limp. Pack hot into jars and cover with boiling syrup, juice, or water to within ½ inch of top. Do not use tin cans if pineapple is included.	20	25	15*	20*
Peaches, Apricots, and Nectarines	RAW PACK. Wash fruit and remove skins. About 20 seconds in boiling water makes skins easier to remove. Remove pits. To keep from darkening, place in water containing lemon juice, ascorbic acid, or vinegar (see page 94). Drain. Pack fruit in jars to ½ inch of top. Cover with boiling syrup, juice, or water, leaving ½ inch at top.	25	30	30*	35*
	HOT PACK. Prepare fruit as for raw pack. Heat fruit through in hot syrup, juice, or water. If fruit is very juicy, you may heat it with ½ cup honey to 1 quart raw fruit, adding no liquid. Pack fruit to ½ inch of top.	20	25	15*	20*

continued

Timetable for Processing Fruits, Tomatoes, and Pickled Vegetables in a Boiling-Water Bath—*continued*

Product	Directions	Processing Time			
		Glass Jars		Tin Cans	
		Pints (min.)	Quarts (min.)	#2 (min.)	#2½ (min.)
Pears	RAW PACK. Peel, halve, and core. To keep from darkening, place in water containing lemon juice, ascorbic acid, or vinegar (see page 94). Drain. Pack fruit in jars to ½ inch of top. Cover with boiling syrup, juice, or water, leaving ½ inch at top.	–	–	30*	35*
	HOT PACK. Prepare fruit as for raw pack. Heat fruit through in hot syrup, juice, or water. If fruit is very juicy, you may heat it with ½ cup honey to 1 quart raw fruit, adding no liquid. Pack fruit to ½ inch of top.	20	25	15*	20*
Pineapple	HOT PACK. Peel, core, and cut into uniformly sized chunks or slices. Simmer fruit in syrup, juice, or water for about 10 minutes. Pack hot and cover with syrup, juice, or water to within ½ inch of top.	15	20	–	–
Plums and Italian prunes	RAW PACK. Wash. To can whole, prick skins. Freestone varieties may be halved and pitted. Pack fruit in jars to ½ inch of top. Cover with boiling syrup, juice, or water, leaving ½ inch at top.	20	25	15†	20†
	HOT PACK. Prepare as for raw pack. Heat to boiling in syrup, juice, or water. If fruit is very juicy, you may heat it with honey, adding no liquid. Pack hot fruit to ½ inch of top. Cover with boiling syrup, juice, or water, leaving ½ inch at top.	20	25	15†	20†
Rhubarb	HOT PACK. Wash, trim, and peel only if stalks are not young and tender. Discard all leaves—they are poisonous. Cut into ½-inch pieces. Add ¼ cup honey to each quart rhubarb and let stand 3 to 4 hours to draw out juice. Bring to boiling. Pack hot to ½ inch of top.	15	15	10†	10†

		Processing Time			
		Glass Jars		Tin Cans	
Product	Directions	Pints (min.)	Quarts (min.)	#2 (min.)	#2½ (min.)
Sauerkraut (For other ways to keep sauerkraut, see the chapter Pickles and Relishes, page 193.)	**HOT PACK.** Heat well-fermented sauerkraut to simmering (185° to 210°F). Pack hot kraut to ½ inch of top. Cover with boiling juice, leaving ½ inch at top.	15	20	20*	25*
Strawberries	Strawberries don't can as well as they freeze. We recommend freezing them or making jams and preserves instead, when possible.				
	HOT PACK. To can, wash and hull berries. Using ¼ to ½ cup honey for each quart of berries, spread berries one layer deep in pans and drizzle honey over them. Cover and let stand at room temperature for 2 to 4 hours. Then place berries and the juice that they've weeped in saucepan and simmer for 5 minutes, stirring to prevent sticking. Pack without crushing and cover with extra boiling syrup if berries didn't produce enough juice of their own. Leave ½ inch at top.	10	15	15†	20†
Tomatoes (For sauces and combination foods, see the box on page 79, and recipes starting on page 307.) See also the chapter Juicing Your Harvest.	Because tomatoes are borderline low-acid foods, we no longer recommend raw packing them. Hot pack only.	35	45	45*	45*
	HOT PACK. Wash tomatoes. Place a few at a time in boiling water just long enough to loosen skins. Then dip in cold water. Leave tomatoes whole or cut into quarters. Bring to boil and pack to ½ inch of top, adding extra boiling water or juice if tomatoes have not made enough juice of their own to cover.				

*Use plain tin cans for apples, apricots, light grapes, peaches, pears, sauerkraut, and tomatoes.
†Use R-enamel cans for berries, cherries, figs, dark grapes, plums, and rhubarb.

Timetable for Processing Low-Acid Vegetables

If raw pack and hot pack work well for a specific food, we give directions for both. Otherwise, we describe the preferred method only. The same is true for canning in tin cans. Our step-by-step directions, page 100, will give you the basic procedure for pressure canning; read them before you follow the directions here. Work rapidly.

Raw pack or hot pack foods following directions. Place jars or cans on rack in pressure canner containing 2 inches of boiling water. Fasten canner cover securely. Let steam escape for 10 minutes before closing petcock (on dial gauge canners) or putting on weighted gauge. Note for high-altitude canners: For each 1,000 feet above sea level, increase the pressure by $\frac{1}{2}$ pound. For more specific directions, see the section The Pressure Canner, page 83.

| | | Processing Time at 10 Lbs. Pressure (unless otherwise noted) | | | |
| | | Glass Jars | | Tin Cans | |
Product	Directions	Pints (min.)	Quarts (min.)	#2 (min.)	#2½ (min.)
Artichokes	HOT PACK. Trim and wash artichokes. Be sure that you trim enough so that the chokes can fit into a wide-mouth jar. Cook for 5 minutes in a solution of $\frac{3}{4}$ cup vinegar to 1 gallon water. Then discard the solution and pack chokes to $\frac{1}{2}$ inch of top. Cover with a brine made from $\frac{3}{4}$ cup lemon juice and 3 tablespoons salt to 1 gallon water, leaving $\frac{1}{2}$-inch headspace. (To make pulling the chokes out of the jar easier and prevent them from falling apart when you do, tie a string firmly around the petals.)	25	30	–	–
Asparagus	RAW PACK. Wash asparagus; trim off scales and tough ends and wash again. Cut into 1-inch pieces. Pack asparagus as tightly as possible without crushing to $\frac{1}{2}$ inch of top.	30	40	20*	20*
	HOT PACK. Prepare as for raw pack; then cover with boiling water. Boil 2 or 3 minutes. Pack asparagus loosely to $\frac{1}{2}$ inch of top. Cover with boiling water, leaving $\frac{1}{2}$ inch at top.	30	40	20*	20*
Beans, dried, with Spiced Tomato Juice (see page 306) or molasses sauce	HOT PACK. Sort and wash dried beans. Cover with boiling water; boil 2 minutes, remove from heat, and let soak for 1 hour. The beans should expand to twice or a bit more in volume after soaking. Heat to boiling and drain, saving liquid for molasses sauce if desired. Fill jars $\frac{3}{4}$ full with hot beans. Fill to 1 inch of top with Spiced Tomato Juice or molasses sauce. To make molasses sauce, mix 1 quart liquid from beans, 3 tablespoons dark molasses, 1 tablespoon vinegar, and $\frac{3}{4}$ teaspoon dry mustard. Heat to boiling.	65	75	65*	75*

		Processing Time at 10 Lbs. Pressure (unless otherwise noted)			
		Glass Jars		Tin Cans	
Product	Directions	Pints (min.)	Quarts (min.)	#2 (min.)	#2½ (min.)
Beans, lima	RAW PACK. Shell and wash beans. Pack the small type loosely to 1 inch of top of jar for pints and 1½ inches for quarts; for large beans fill to ¾ inch of top for pints and 1¼ inches for quarts. Cover with boiling water.	40	50	40*	40*
	HOT PACK. Shell the beans, then cover with boiling water and bring to a boil. Pack beans loosely in jar to 1 inch of top. Cover with boiling water, leaving 1 inch at top.	40	50	40*	40*
Beans, green and yellow	RAW PACK. Wash beans. Trim ends and cut into 1-inch pieces. Pack tightly in jars to ½ inch of top. Cover with boiling water, leaving ½ inch at top.	20	25	25*	30*
	HOT PACK. Prepare as for raw pack. Then cover with boiling water and boil 5 minutes. Pack beans in jars loosely to ½ inch of top. Cover with boiling cooking liquid and water, leaving ½ inch at top.	20	25	25*	30*
Beets (For pickled beets, see timetable, page 105.)	HOT PACK. Sort beets for size. Cut off tops, leaving a 1-inch stem and root to prevent color bleeding. Then wash. Boil until skins slip off easily. Skin, trim, cut, and pack into jars to ½ inch of top. Cover with boiling water, leaving ½ inch at top.	30	35	30†	30†
Broccoli	Not recommended for canning because the processing intensifies the strong flavor and discolors the vegetables. It is much better frozen.				
	HOT PACK. Cut off woody, tough stems and old leaves and yellowing blossoms. Soak in cold, salt water for 10 to 15 minutes to drive out any clinging bugs. Rinse well and pick over. Cut into 2-inch pieces. Cover cut vegetables with boiling water and boil for 3 minutes. Drain, reserving liquid. Pack tightly and cover with boiling liquid, leaving 1 inch at top.	25	30	30‡	30‡
Brussels sprouts	Not recommended for canning because the processing intensifies the strong flavor and discolors the vegetables. It is much better frozen.				

continued

Timetable for Processing Low-Acid Vegetables—*continued*

Product	Directions	Glass Jars		Tin Cans	
		Pints (min.)	Quarts (min.)	#2 (min.)	#2½ (min.)
Brussels sprouts —*continued*	HOT PACK. Choose small sprouts that fit easily into jars. Avoid using larger sprouts that need to be cut in half because once cut into wedges or slices there is more chance that they will fall apart during boiling. Cover vegetables with boiling water and boil for 3 minutes. Drain, reserving liquid. Pack tightly and cover with boiling liquid, leaving 1 inch at top.	25	30	30‡	30‡
Cabbage	Not recommended for canning, except for sauerkraut, which is described in the boiling-water-bath processing timetable, page 109. Fresh cabbage is much better kept in cold storage.				
	HOT PACK. Clean, cut up into small wedges. Cover cut vegetables with boiling water and boil for 3 minutes. Drain, reserving liquid. Pack tightly and cover with boiling liquid, leaving 1 inch at top.	25	30	40‡	40‡
Carrots	RAW PACK. Wash and scrape carrots. Slice, dice, or leave whole. Pack tightly in jars to 1 inch of top. Cover with boiling water, leaving 1 inch at top.	25	30	20*	25*
	HOT PACK. Prepare as for raw pack, then cover with boiling water and bring to boil. Pack carrots in jars to ½ inch of top. Cover with boiling liquid and water, leaving ½ inch at top.	25	30	20*	25*
Cauliflower	Not recommended for canning. Much better pickled or frozen.				
	HOT PACK. Clean, cut up into small wedges. Cover cut vegetables with boiling water and boil for 3 minutes. Drain, reserving liquid. Pack tightly and cover with boiling liquid, leaving 1 inch at top.	25	30	30‡	30‡
Celery	Not recommended for canning. Because of its high moisture content, celery does not can well.				
	HOT PACK. Wash and trim off tough leaves and woody bottoms. Cut into 1-inch pieces. Cover with boiling water and boil for 3 minutes. Drain, reserving liquid. Pack jars and cover with boiling liquid, leaving 1 inch at top.	30	35	30*	30*

Processing Time at 10 Lbs. Pressure (unless otherwise noted)

Product	Directions	Processing Time at 10 Lbs. Pressure (unless otherwise noted)			
		Glass Jars		Tin Cans	
		Pints (min.)	Quarts (min.)	#2 (min.)	#2½ (min.)
Corn, cream style	RAW PACK. Husk corn and remove silk. Wash. Cut corn from cob at about center of kernel and scrape cobs. Pack corn loosely in pint jars to 1 inch of top. Cover with boiling water.	95	—§	105‡	—
	HOT PACK. Prepare as for raw pack. Add 1 pint boiling water to each quart of corn. Heat to boiling. Pack hot corn and liquid to 1 inch of top.	85	—§	105‡	—
Corn, whole kernel	RAW PACK. Husk corn and remove silk. Wash. Cut corn from cob at about ⅔ the depth of kernel. Pack corn loosely to 1 inch of top with mixture of corn and liquid.	55	85	60‡	—
Eggplant	Not a particularly good canner or frozen food by itself. Eggplant is better pickled or frozen in a casserole.				
	HOT PACK. Wash and peel, then slice or cube. To draw out the bitter juice, line a colander with eggplant, sprinkle with salt, put over that another layer of eggplant, then salt, and so on. Let stand for 1 hour. Then press the eggplant against the sides of the colander before taking out and rinsing off well. Boil in fresh water for 5 minutes. Drain, reserving liquid. Pack into jars and cover with hot liquid, leaving 1 inch at top.	30	40	35*	40*
Mushrooms	Not recommended for canning. Much better frozen or dried.				
	HOT PACK. Select tender, young mushrooms. Discard any that have opened. Wash thoroughly and trim off tough stalks. Cut in slices or leave small mushroom caps whole. Steam mushrooms for 4 minutes. Pack into hot jars, leaving 1 inch at top. You may add ½ teaspoon salt. Cover mushrooms with boiling water.	45	—	—	—
Okra	HOT PACK. Choose young, tender pods only. Wash and trim stems. Leave whole or cut into 1-inch slices. Cover with boiling water and	20	40	25*	35*

continued

Timetable for Processing Low-Acid Vegetables—*continued*

Product	Directions	Glass Jars		Tin Cans	
		Pints (min.)	Quarts (min.)	#2 (min.)	#2½ (min.)
Okra —*continued*	boil for 1 minute. Drain, reserving liquid. Pack into jars and cover with hot liquid, leaving 1 inch at top.				
Onions, small white	HOT PACK. Choose onions of uniform size, about 1 inch in diameter. Peel, trim off roots and stalks, and wash if necessary. Cover with boiling water and cook gently for 5 minutes. Pack hot onions loosely in jar and cover with boiling liquid to within ½ inch of top.	25	30	–	–
Peas, green	RAW PACK. Shell and wash peas. Pack peas loosely in jars to 1 inch of top. Cover with boiling water, leaving 1 inch at top.	40	40	30*	35*
	HOT PACK. Prepare as for raw pack. Cover with boiling water and bring to a boil. Pack peas loosely in jars to 1 inch of top. Cover with boiling water, leaving 1 inch at top.	40	40	30*	35*
Peas, snow or sugar, whole pods	RAW PACK. Trim, wash, and pack loosely in jars to 1 inch of top. Cover with boiling water, leaving 1 inch at top.	20	25	–	–
Peppers, hot	Hot peppers are not good canned alone. Either pickle and then can, or freeze. For pickling, see the chapter Pickles and Relishes, page 193.				
Peppers, sweet	HOT PACK. Remove stem, core, and remove seeds and inner white membrane. Remove skins by first plunging in boiling water for a few minutes, then running under cold water, and finally taking off the now-split skins with a sharp knife or potato peeler. Slice peppers or flatten whole halves and pack carefully in layers. Cover with boiling water to within ½ inch of top. You can add ½ tablespoon of lemon juice or 1 tablespoon of vinegar per pint if you wish.	35	–	–	–
Potatoes	HOT PACK (cubed). Wash, peel, and cut into ½-inch cubes. Dip cubes in brine (1 teaspoon salt to 1 quart water) to prevent darkening. Drain. Cook for 2 minutes in boiling water. Pack hot and cover with boiling water to within 1 inch of top.	35	40	–	–

Processing Time at 10 Lbs. Pressure (unless otherwise noted)

Product	Directions	Processing Time at 10 Lbs. Pressure (unless otherwise noted)			
		Glass Jars		Tin Cans	
		Pints (min.)	Quarts (min.)	#2 (min.)	#2½ (min.)
Potatoes —*continued*	HOT PACK (whole). Use potatoes 1 to 2½ inches in diameter. Wash, peel, and cook in boiling water for 10 minutes. Pack hot and cover with hot cooking liquid or boiling water to within 1 inch of top.	30	40	–	–
Pumpkins and Winter squash	Because puréed squash is so dense, it's difficult to get good heat penetration. Can only cubes and freeze purée. HOT PACK. Wash pumpkin or winter squash, remove seeds, and peel. Cut into 1-inch cubes. Steam until tender (about 25 minutes). Pack hot and cover with hot cooking liquid or boiling water to within ½ inch of top.	55	90	50	75
Salsify	HOT PACK. To prevent from discoloring, scrub roots and slice. Immediately drop each slice into ½ gallon of water to which 1 tablespoon of vinegar and 1 tablespoon of salt have been added. When all have been cut and set in this solution, rinse quickly but well, place in a pot, and cover with boiling water. Boil for 2 minutes; drain, reserving liquid. Pack in jars and cover with hot liquid, leaving 1 inch at top.	30	35	30	30
Soybeans, green	HOT PACK. Shell beans, then cover with boiling water and bring to a boil. Drain, reserving liquid. Pack beans loosely in jar and cover with hot liquid, leaving 1 inch at top.	55	65	50*	60*
Spinach and other greens	HOT PACK. Pick over and wash thoroughly. Cut out tough stems and midribs. Place about 2½ pounds of spinach in cheesecloth bag and steam for about 10 minutes or until well wilted. Pack loosely to ½ inch of top. Cover with boiling water, leaving ½ inch at top.	70	90	65*	75*
Sweet potatoes	HOT PACK. Wash and sort for size. Boil or steam for 20 to 30 minutes to facilitate slipping of skins. Cut into uniform pieces. Pack hot sweet potatoes lightly, pressing gently to fill air spaces to within 1 inch of top. Cover with boiling water, leaving 1 inch at top.	55	90	–	–
Tomatoes	See boiling-water bath processing timetable, page 109.				

continued

Timetable for Processing Low-Acid Vegetables—*continued*

		Processing Time at 10 Lbs. Pressure (unless otherwise noted)			
		Glass Jars		Tin Cans	
Product	Directions	Pints (min.)	Quarts (min.)	#2 (min.)	#2½ (min.)
Turnips, Parsnips, and Rutabagas	Not recommended for canning. These are much better kept in cold storage. HOT PACK. Wash and peel. Cube or slice. Do not can mashed. Cover with boiling water and boil for 3 minutes. Drain, reserving liquid. Pack into jars and cover with hot liquid, leaving 1 inch at top.	25	30	30‡	30‡
Vegetable mix (carrots, green beans, celery, lima beans, etc.)	HOT PACK. Use almost any mixture. Prepare each separately. Mix vegetables together; boil for 3 minutes. Pack hot and cover with boiling water to within 1 inch of top.	Process pints and quarts for the time needed for the food requiring the longest processing. Pay particular attention if mixture contains any meat at all. If so, see the tables in the chapter Canning and Drying Meats and Poultry, page 479, for necessary processing times.			
Vegetable soups (vegetable, dried bean, meat, poultry)	Prepare according to your favorite recipe but cook only half or less the time suggested; let the soup do most of its cooking during processing. Pack to within 1 inch of top.	60	75	–	–
	Caution: Process 100 minutes if soup contains seafood.				
Zucchini and Summer squash	None of these are particularly good canned or frozen, but you can do both. You can also pickle zucchini, and you'll find a good recipe for such pickles on page 217.				
	RAW PACK. Wash and slice; do not peel unless squash is large and skin is tough. Cut into ½-inch slices and halve or quarter slices that are extra large in diameter. Pack tightly in jars and cover with boiling water, leaving 1 inch at top.	25	30	20*	20*
	HOT PACK. Prepare as for raw pack. Cover with boiling water and bring to a boil. Drain, saving liquid. Pack loosely and cover with hot liquid, leaving ½ inch at top.	30	40	20*	20*

*Use plain tin cans.
†Use R-enamel cans.
‡Use C-enamel cans.

Drying Vegetables and Fruits

When you're drying food, you're removing a good part of its moisture through evaporation. Air movement is the key. But the drier and, up to a point, the warmer the air is, the faster and more complete the evaporation of the water. At its simplest, drying is incredibly basic: Small pieces of food are placed out in the warm sun on a dry day. Warm, dry air passing over, under, and around the food pulls moisture from it. And that's it. If the air is dry enough, and if the sun is hot but not scorching, and if the food is cut properly, and if there are no insects or dust or other pollutants, you'll get a pretty good dried food for hardly any effort at all.

As we found out in our food drying tests, those conditions are not always easily met and hardly ever simple to control all the time. But there are ways to take the chance out of the process. One step up from placing food out in the sun is to place it in a solar food dryer that helps to protect food from insects and pollution and concentrates the sun's warmth right where you want it without sacrificing good ventilation. Or, you can bring the drying indoors for even more control and use your oven to do the work. Very low, steady temperatures and good air circulation might take a little practice to get right, but at least you don't have to worry about having enough sun. Oven drying can even be done at night and on the rainiest of days. If that's not good enough, you can take almost all of the guesswork out of the process and use an electric dryer designed to provide just the right amount of heat and maximum air movement all the time. Rodale researchers found this to be by far the most convenient method, and it gave them consistently good dried foods.

We discuss all these food drying options, and a few others, in this chapter. And we give you some techniques for treating the food before

117

and after it is dried to retain as much flavor, color, food value, and texture as possible.

WHY DRYING WORKS

When foods are properly dried, they can't support the growth of spoilage organisms: Bacteria, yeasts, and molds can only live in foods that have a certain amount of moisture in them. Well-dried fruits have roughly 80 percent of their water removed, and vegetables almost 90 percent, creating an environment hostile to bacteria, molds, and yeasts.

Enzymes in low-acid foods like vegetables speed up the natural deterioration of foods by breaking down complex substances within the foods, changing them into simple ones, and thereby changing their color, texture, and flavor. While the temperatures for food drying are high enough to inactivate these enzymes, it's not high enough to destroy them. But there is something you can do to destroy these enzymes before the drying process starts, and this is blanching—the same kind of blanching that you do to vegetables before you freeze them.

This precooking also helps to set color and flavor and it softens tissues so that water is more readily released during drying. And in our experiments at the Rodale Food Center, we found that blanched foods rehydrated quicker than those we didn't blanch. And they tasted better.

NUTRITIONAL VALUE OF DRIED FOOD

The nutritional value of dried food is about equal to that of frozen food. While there is some loss of vitamins A and C during the drying process itself, the major losses don't happen while the food is drying, but rather when it is being blanched. And it is this same blanching that is responsible for the majority of the mineral and vitamin loss in frozen food. As far as nutrients are concerned, drying is superior to canning, because canning's high processing temperatures can destroy as much as 65 percent of the original food value, particularly vitamin C, thiamine, and riboflavin.

Four pounds of fresh food will give you approximately 1 pound of dried food. Since it's mainly water that's missing, you wind up with a highly concentrated food that contains more food value on a pound-for-pound basis than fresh food. Of course, if you reconstitute your dried food, as you will for many uses, you're putting that water right back, so the concentrated food value won't really mean that much to you. But those foods that you eat dried—like many fruits—are nutritional powerhouses.

PREPARING FOOD FOR DRYING

The bigger the piece of food, the longer it's going to take to dry. Within reason, the smaller, the better. So keep all pieces that will be dried together in the same batch about the same size so that they'll dry at the same rate.

Both fruit and vegetables should be perfect for drying. Blemished or bruised fruit will not keep as well and may turn a whole tray of drying fruit bad. Fruit must be fully ripe so that its sugar content is at its peak. However, it should not be overripe. Overripe fruit can be saved for making fruit leathers—see page 159.

Blanching

Most vegetables and some fruits should be blanched or precooked in steam or boiling water after they are sliced for drying. This blanching sets the color, hastens drying by softening the tissues, checks the ripening process, and prevents undesirable changes in flavor during drying and storage. Vegetables blanched before drying require less soaking before they are cooked for eating and have a better flavor and color when served. Blanching vegetables by steaming is preferable to blanching by boiling because nutrients are dissolved in the boiling water, and the water adds extra moisture, which is hardly what you need when you're getting ready to remove as much moisture from the vegetables as possible.

DRYING MEATS AND FISH

The principles are the same, and so is much of the equipment. But meats and fish require different preparation and constant drying temperatures of 140° to 150°F, which is higher than those needed for fruits or vegetables. So read the basic drying instructions in this chapter, and then turn to page 492 for specifics on drying meats and page 514 for specifics on drying fish.

Vegetables should be blanched before drying to set color, stop ripening, and prevent changes in flavor. Put vegetables in a steamer basket over boiling water or blanch directly in boiling water. When blanching time is up, gently roll the vegetables in a towel to soak up moisture.

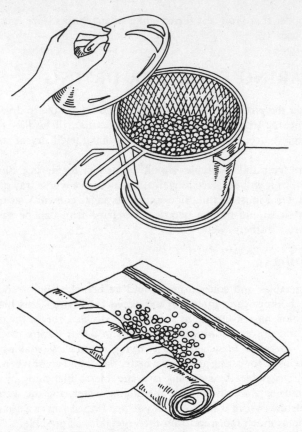

The recommended blanching time for foods to be dried is shorter than for other types of processing since pieces of food cut for drying are exceptionally small and thin. Likewise, the chilling step used for foods to be frozen or canned can be skipped because foods are heated somewhat during drying.

A pressure cooker or a large, heavy pot makes a good steamer. Place a shallow layer of vegetables, not over 2½ inches deep, in a vegetable steamer, in a wire basket with legs or one that rests on the inner rim of the pot so that it doesn't let the vegetables sit in the water, or put them in a stainless steel or enamel colander. Have 2 or more inches of boiling water in the pot, and set the steamer, basket, or colander in the pot. Cover tightly, and keep the water boiling rapidly. Steam for the required time, as shown in the charts below.

If there is no convenient way of steaming, boiling is second best. Use a large amount of boiling water and a small amount of food so that the temperature of the water will not be appreciably lower when the food is added. About 3 gallons of water to every quart of vegetables is good. Place the vegetables in a wire basket and immerse them in the boiling water for the required time, as shown in the charts below.

Vegetables can also be blanched in a microwave oven. Follow the directions on page 54.

DRYING VEGETABLES

ASPARAGUS

Use only the top 3 inches of the spear. Blanch until tender and firm, about 5 minutes. When dry, asparagus will be very tough to brittle.

BEANS, GREEN AND YELLOW

Use tender beans only. Cut them, if you wish, and blanch 6 minutes. When dry, they will be brittle and crisp. See also page 126 for more information on drying beans, peas, and corn.

■ Soaking and then cooking dried beans take several hours, but you can plan ahead and have presoaked beans ready for dinner cooking. Soak a couple of pounds of dried beans at a time. Rinse and drain them very well and freeze in bags. When ready to cook, bang the bag against a hard surface to separate them and pour the amount you want into boiling water. The beans will cook a little more quickly than if they had not been frozen. Leftover cooked beans can also be frozen, but they tend to fall apart when they're cooked again. This hardly matters, though, if you're making a soup with them.

BEANS, LIMA

Shell and blanch 5 minutes. When dry, limas will be hard and brittle. See also page 126 for more information on drying beans, peas, and corn.

BEETS

Remove tops and roots and blanch about 45 minutes or until cooked through. The time will depend upon the size of the beets. Cool, peel, and cut into $\frac{1}{4}$-inch cubes or slice very thin. When dry, beets will be tough to brittle.

BROCCOLI

Trim and slice into small ½-inch strips. Blanch 4 minutes. When dry, broccoli will be crisp and brittle.

BRUSSELS SPROUTS

We don't recommend drying.

CABBAGE

Cut into long, thin slices and blanch 2 to 3 minutes. When dry, cabbage will be brittle.

CARROTS

Wash and slice thinly. Blanch 4 minutes. When dry, carrots will be tough to brittle.

CAULIFLOWER

Use only the florets. Remove them from the core and split the stems. Blanch 3 minutes. When dry, cauliflower will be crisp and slightly browned.

CELERY

Remove leaves and cut stalks into small pieces. Blanch about 1 minute. When dry, celery will be very brittle.

CORN

Husk and remove the silk, then blanch the whole cob 10 minutes to set the milk. Cut the cob deeply enough to obtain large kernels, but be careful not to cut so deeply as to include any cob. When dry, corn will be dry and brittle. See also directions for drying corn on the cob without blanching on page 127.

CUCUMBERS

Peel and slice. Blanch 1 minute. When dry, cucumbers will be crisp.

EGGPLANT

Peel and cut into ½-inch slices. Blanch about 4 minutes. When dry, eggplant will be leathery to brittle.

GARLIC

Peel and cut into thin pieces. No blanching is necessary. When dry, garlic will be crisp.

HERBS See page 164.

HORSERADISH

Trim tops off and grate or slice root. No blanching is necessary. When dry, horseradish will be brittle.

KALE See Spinach, Kale, and Swiss chard.

LEEKS See Onions and Leeks.

LETTUCE

We don't recommend drying.

MUSHROOMS

Peel and cut off stems if they are tough. Cut into ½-inch slices. Blanch 3 minutes. When dry, mushrooms will be leathery to crisp.

OKRA

Cut off tips and slice. Blanch 5 minutes. When dry, okra will be tough to brittle.

ONIONS AND LEEKS

Peel and dice. No blanching is necessary. When dry, onions and leeks will be brittle.

PARSNIPS

Trim off tops, peel, and slice. Blanch 5 minutes. When dry, parsnips will be tough to brittle.

PEANUTS See page 543.

PEAS

Shell and blanch 3 minutes. When dry, peas will be wrinkled and brittle. See also directions for drying peas in the pod on page 126.

PEPPERS, CHILI

If possible, do not pick until they are mature and fully red. However, if frost threatens, harvest your crop even if some are still green; many should ripen while drying. If using a food dryer, dice, wearing rubber gloves. No need to blanch.

You may also string the peppers by running a needle and thread through the thickest part of the stem. Hang them outdoors or in a sunny window to dry. They will shrink and darken considerably and will be leathery when they are dry. Although dried chilies can be kept in storage containers, they are best left hanging in a dry place.

PEPPERS, SWEET

Clean and slice into thin strips. No blanching is necessary. When dry, peppers are leathery to brittle.

POTATOES

Wash and slice into $\frac{1}{4}$-inch rounds. Peeling is optional. Blanch 5 minutes and then soak in $\frac{1}{2}$ cup lemon juice and 2 quarts cold water for about 45 minutes to prevent potatoes from oxidizing during drying. When dry, they are brittle.

PUMPKINS

Clean and cut into 1-inch strips and then peel. Blanch 3 minutes, until slightly soft. When dry, pumpkin will be very tough to brittle.

RADISHES

We don't recommend drying.

RHUBARB

Cut into thin strips about 1 inch wide and blanch 3 minutes. When dry, rhubarb will be tough to crisp.

SPINACH, KALE, AND SWISS CHARD

Cut very coarsely into strips. Blanch spinach and Swiss chard about 2 minutes and kale about 4 minutes. Spread not more than ½ inch thick on trays. When dry, they will be crisp and crumble easily.

SQUASH, WINTER

We don't recommend drying.

SWEET POTATOES

Wash and then grate, slice, or dice. Peeling is optional. Blanch 3 minutes. When dry, potatoes are tough to brittle.

SWISS CHARD See Spinach, Kale, and Swiss chard.

TOMATOES

Slice and blanch 3 minutes. When dry, tomatoes will be leathery. See the box Sun-Dried Tomatoes on page 128.

TURNIPS

Trim off tops and roots and slice. Blanch 5 minutes. When dry, turnips will be very tough to brittle.

ZUCCHINI AND SUMMER SQUASH

Do not peel, but slice into thin strips and blanch 3 minutes. If you're making zucchini chips to eat right away, you needn't bother blanching. When dry, squash is leathery to brittle.

SPECIAL TECHNIQUES
FOR DRYING PEAS, BEANS, AND CORN

Drying Right in the Garden on the Vine or Stalk

This is often the easiest way to dry peas, lima beans, soybeans, and other dried beans, provided you have the following:

1. A long growing season, so that the food can remain on the vine or stalk until the pods are thoroughly dry, but before frost hits.

2. Dry weather, not wet, which might cause some beans and peas to sprout right in their pods and shatter.

3. Good timing, so that you get out and collect your dried food before the pod splits open and scatters what it's holding all over the ground. Limas and soybeans should be watched quite carefully as they near the dry stage because their pods split easily once dry.

Air-Drying Beans and Peas

You can also pick bean and pea pods when mature and spread them out in shallow layers in an attic, covered porch, or in a spare room to dry. Green or yellow beans should be blanched before drying. We tried drying ours both blanched and fresh from the garden, and found that the blanching was really worth it. The unblanched ones didn't rehydrate well and were tough.

You can make "leather britches" by stringing the beans on heavy thread or string, about one-third of the way down from one end. Then blanch the whole string for 6 minutes, and hang in a dry, warm place, like under a porch or on attic rafters. If they're hung indoors you can just keep them there until you're ready to use them, so long as the air is dry and warm enough.

You can also cut the whole bean or pea plant when most of the pods are mature and hang it upside down in a dry, well-ventilated place, allowing the beans or peas to dry. Ours took 5 days to dry completely. We found that pinto beans are hard to dry this way because they cling so tightly to the poles on which they climb.

Shelling Dried Beans and Peas

To shell dried beans and peas, place them in cloth bags and beat them with a mallet, or else stomp on them. This rough treatment cracks the pods and makes it easy for you to sort the beans or peas from their shells. Soybeans and chick-peas have much tougher pods and must be shelled by hand.

Dried beans and peas can also be shelled by putting them in a clean pillowcase. Tie it shut and put in a clothes dryer on low for about $\frac{1}{2}$ hour. The heat and tumbling encourage the pods to break open.

Extra Assurance before Storing

Before storing beans or peas, place them on shallow trays in a 175°F oven for 10 to 15 minutes to kill any insect eggs they may contain. Oven heating also assures that the beans or peas are thoroughly dry. If they aren't completely dry when they are put into storage, they will build up a great deal of heat and either smolder or crumble. You can put them in paper bags and then pack these inside plastic bags and seal with wire twists. But to rodent- and insect-proof your dried goods, put the paper bags in metal cans with tight-fitting lids instead. Recycled coffee cans work fine for small quantities. Or store the beans or peas plain in sterilized glass jars with tight

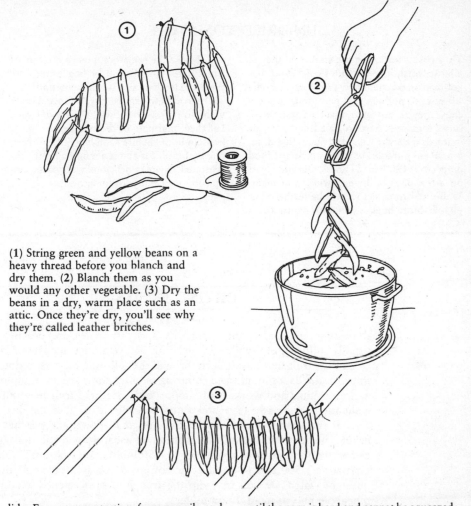

(1) String green and yellow beans on a heavy thread before you blanch and dry them. (2) Blanch them as you would any other vegetable. (3) Dry the beans in a dry, warm place such as an attic. Once they're dry, you'll see why they're called leather britches.

lids. For extra protection from weevils and other insects, try putting a dried chili pepper in with your food.

Drying Corn

The husk covering corn won't allow the kernels to dry completely on the stalk, so you'll have to pick the corn and remove this outer husk. Then sun- or oven-dry the corn cob until the corn is hard and cannot be squeezed. Corn can be stored on the cob, but it will take up much less space and be more convenient for later use if it is shelled, pasteurized or heat-treated (see page 146), and stored like beans and peas. The easiest way to shell dried corn is to hold the cob between both hands and twist in opposite directions, allowing the kernels to fall into a container underneath.

SUN-DRIED TOMATOES

They cost a fortune in the store, and they're almost worth it because they're so good. But you can make sun-dried tomatoes at home for next to nothing. Use paste tomatoes because they're meatier and will dry faster than salad tomatoes. Slice in half lengthwise, or in thirds if they're huge, and place cut-side up on screens outdoors or put in an electric food dryer set at 120°F for 24 hours. Outside, count on a few days of drying; bring in at night. Well-dried tomatoes should be leathery but pliable. Store in glass jars with tight lids.

To use the tomatoes, pour a mixture of equal parts vinegar and boiling water over them and let them sit a few minutes until they soften to a chewy consistency. Drain and cover with olive oil seasoned with a sliver of garlic. Let them marinate in the refrigerator for at least 24 hours before sampling. They'll keep fine in this oil for about a month. Their concentrated flavor is delicious with pasta, antipasto, or mixed with tomato sauce.

DRYING FRUITS

In most commercial drying operations, apricots, apples, and peaches are usually sulfured, but while sulfured fruit will retain more of its original color than fruit that hasn't been through the sulfuring process, it doesn't improve the flavor at all. And sulfuring requires some special equipment and extra time and work. More importantly, sulfured fruit may impart a slightly sour or acid taste and a questionable chemical to the diet.

If you wish to pretreat fruits like apricots, apples, and peaches for drying, we suggest that you dip them in an ascorbic acid solution. You can prepare a solution by crushing 3 or 4 500-milligram vitamin C tablets, or stirring 1,500 to 2,000 milligrams of powdered ascorbic acid, into 1 quart of water. Or you may dip the fruit into unsweetened lemon or pineapple juice instead if you prefer.

You'll probably be slicing most and peeling some fruits before you dry them. But there are some fruits—perhaps grapes, berries, and cherries, to name a few—that you'll only be pitting or slicing in half. Before you put these fruits out to dry, it's best to crack their skins so that moisture inside the fruit can readily escape. There are two ways to do this.

The first is to blanch them in either steam (1 to 2 minutes, depending upon the thickness of the skin and the size of the fruit) or boiling water

($\frac{1}{4}$ to 1 minute), following the directions on page 119. Then quickly plunge them into cold water. The skins should crack with the shock of the temperature change.

The second way to crack their skins is to make several nicks in the skin with a sharp knife.

APPLES

Use firm fruit. Peel, core, and cut into thin slices or rings. Don't peel unless the apples have been heavily sprayed. Blanch 4 minutes. When dry, apples will be soft and pliable and slightly tough.

APRICOTS

Cut in half, remove pit, and slice. Dip in ascorbic acid solution. Blanch 4 minutes. When dry, apricots will be soft and pliable.

BANANAS

Peel and slice thinly. No blanching is necessary. When dry, bananas will be pliable to crisp.

BLACKBERRIES

We don't recommend drying.

BLUEBERRIES

Remove stems and blanch quickly to break skins. When dry, blueberries will be leathery and pliable, something like raisins.

CHERRIES

Cut in half, pit, and remove stems. (If you don't pit them, the dried cherries will taste like all seed.) Blanch 1 minute. When dry, cherries will be pliable and leathery, something like raisins.

CITRUS PEELS

Wash well and scrape out the white bitter pith inside. When dry, the peel will be crisp.

COCONUT

Punch a hole in one end and drain the milk. Then cut in half and remove meat from the shell. Grate or slice. When dry, coconut will be leathery to crisp.

DATES

No pretreatment is necessary. When dry, dates will be leathery and a deep russet color.

FIGS

Cut in half. When dry, figs will be leathery.

GRAPES

Use seedless grapes only. Remove stems and crack skins by blanching quickly or nicking with a knife. When dry, grapes are raisins.

LEMON PEEL
See Citrus peels. See also the recipe on page 131 for Dried Lemon or Orange Zest.

NECTARINES See Peaches and Nectarines.

ORANGE PEEL
See Citrus peels. See also the recipe on page 131 for Dried Lemon or Orange Zest.

PAPAYAS

Remove seeds, peel, and slice. When dry, papayas will be leathery to crisp.

PEACHES AND NECTARINES

Quickly blanch to crack skins, then remove them. Pit, slice, and dip in ascorbic acid solution. When dry, peaches and nectarines will be soft, pliable, and leathery.

PEARS

Peel and cut into slices or rings. Blanch 2 minutes. When dry, pears will be soft, pliable, and leathery.

PINEAPPLE

Peel and core. Cut into slices. Blanch 1 minute. When dry, pineapple will be leathery and no longer sticky.

PLUMS

Pit and cut into thin slices. When dry, plums will be pliable and leathery.

RASPBERRIES

We don't recommend drying.

STRAWBERRIES

Remove stems and cut in halves or thirds. Blanch 1 minute. When dry, strawberries will be pliable and leathery.

Dried Lemon or Orange Zest

Lightly grate lemon or orange zest, being careful not to grate the bitter white pith. Using a home food dryer, lay grated zest on racks. You may need to cover the racks with cheesecloth to prevent zest from falling through the slats in the racks. Dry zest according to food dryer manufacturer's directions, or follow oven drying directions below. Zest should be crisp in 1 to 2 hours.

> Yield: 1 orange yields 2 teaspoons dried zest
> 1 lemon yields 1 teaspoon dried zest

Variation

Oven Drying: Dry with oven door slightly open and oven temperature at 145°F. Use an oven thermometer to regulate the heat and keep it at 145°. You will need to turn the trays if one area of the tray is drying more than another. Zest will be crisp in 1 to 1¼ hours.

Candied Ginger

This is wonderful sprinkled on ice cream or on cakes.

1 cup thinly sliced peeled ginger
    root
1 cup water
½ cup maple syrup

In a small saucepan stir together the ginger, water, and maple syrup. Place over medium heat and simmer until liquid completely evaporates, about 20 to 30 minutes. Watch carefully during the last 10 minutes of cooking to prevent syrup from burning.

Separate pieces and place on a lightly greased cooling rack. Dry in a 200°F oven until all syrup is absorbed and pieces snap when broken, about 2 hours.

Yield: 1½ cups

TEMPERATURE AND VENTILATION

Maintaining a good, steady temperature is of critical importance when it comes to a good dried food. Too high a temperature and your food can quite literally cook. What usually happens is that the food cooks on the outside, forming a dry skin that traps inside moisture. This is called case hardening, and it's best prevented by making sure temperatures don't get too hot, especially in the first few hours of drying. High temperatures, up near 145°F, will kill off significant amounts of vitamins. Lower temperatures save more vitamins, but if drying gets too low, down near 90°F (and especially if conditions are humid), there's a greater chance of bacteria and mold growth. Most commercial dryers are designed to keep food at a low-medium temperature of 95° to 130°F, and this is a good target for homemade dryers and oven drying as well.

For fast, efficient drying, good ventilation is essential, too. The aim is not to heat the food, but to remove moisture from it. The more warm, dry air moving over the maximum surface area the better. This is why the best drying trays are those that let air through, top and bottom, and also why dryers should be well ventilated, and why some commercial dryers have small fans built into them.

DRYING OUTDOORS

The cheapest and usually easiest way to dry is to let the sun do all the work. But drying outdoors works well only if you live in an area that enjoys long, hot, sunny days of low humidity—and only if you live in an area that has clean, unpolluted air. If you can't depend upon about 3 good drying days in a row or if you live in an industrial area or near a heavily traveled highway—both of which usually mean poor air quality—perhaps you ought to move on to the next section and read about indoor drying.

If drying is to be done outdoors, plan to set the food out early in the morning, but after the dew has dried, so that the food will have a full day to dry and not be too wet the first night. Place the trays in a comparatively dust-free location, on racks raised above the ground. Raising the racks permits air to circulate freely under as well as over the food.

This free air movement under the racks is very important if you're covering the racks with a solid material, like glass or polyethylene sheeting. Although glass and plastic don't allow for much air circulation above the food, they are good in that they allow you to take advantage of the greenhouse effect; that is, capturing heat from the sun's radiation and holding it in. You'll find that drying under glass or polyethylene is good in areas of higher humidity and lower temperatures where you need all the help you can get. Be careful, however, when using glass or polyethylene in hot, dry areas, as the excessive heat buildup around your food could actually cook or burn it!

To prevent any unhappy surprises, test the temperature in such a setup first with a minimum/maximum thermometer before you attempt to dry any food. Such a thermometer records the highest and the lowest temperatures reached over any given time period and will let you know if you've got a good temperature range for drying your foods. You'll want the space to stay within 95° to 130°F. If heat buildup is a problem, you can increase air circulation when using glass or polyethylene by raising the cover slightly with blocks. Then cover the space you've just created with screening or netting to keep bugs out.

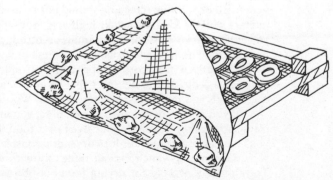

If you live in an area that enjoys hot, sunny days and low humidity, you've got the best weather for outdoor food drying. A wooden frame with nylon mesh stretched across it makes a good tray. The cheesecloth keeps out dirt and insects.

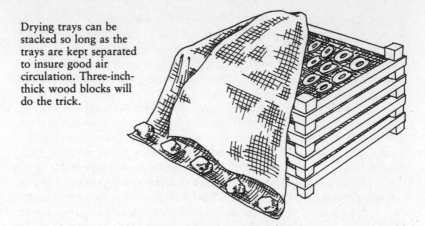

Drying trays can be stacked so long as the trays are kept separated to insure good air circulation. Three-inch-thick wood blocks will do the trick.

If the trays are not protected by polyethylene or glass, they must be covered at night to prevent dew from settling on the food. Put them in a sheltered place or cover them with cardboard (cartons are fine), heavy towels, an old shower curtain, or anything that will keep moisture out. Obviously, if you expect rain, make sure the cover is really waterproof. And cover tightly, as many insects are nocturnal and will try to get into the food after the sun goes down. Be sure to exclude insects and animals from the drying area during the day, too. Turn the food often, and dry only on sunny days. When the food is dry enough to bring in, try to do it in the heat of the day on a hot day, to make sure that surface moisture has evaporated.

Trays

Just about anything that has a good-size flat surface can work as a drying tray, but the best trays are those that have ventilated bottoms made of cheesecloth, nylon screening, or fine wooden slats. Although convenient, wire mesh or window screening should not be used alone. The metal can interact with the food (especially high-acid foods like fruits and tomatoes) and either destroy some of the vitamins or introduce a questionable metal onto the food itself. If you're using wire mesh or window screening, cover it with tightly woven cotton fabric, brown or freezer paper, or clean grocery bags opened inside out. Paper should be replaced each time and cheesecloth and mesh or screening washed. Wood should be scrubbed.

If you plan to dry your food outdoors, you may want to make your trays so that they'll fit into your oven or a food dryer, too, just in case you hit a rainy spell and decide to dry indoors instead or become impatient with the sun and want to speed things up with extra, controlled heat. Trays made especially for drying food may be purchased, but they are

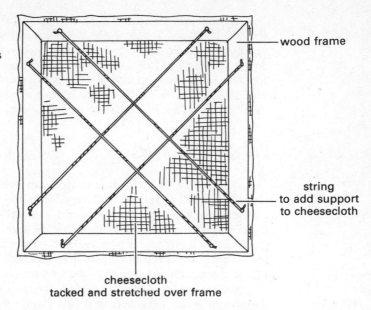

This drying tray is simple to make, perhaps from materials you already have at home.

wood frame

string to add support to cheesecloth

cheesecloth tacked and stretched over frame

easy to make. Construct wooden frames and stretch nylon mesh, cotton sheeting, or cheesecloth over them. If you're using cheesecloth, make the frames at least an inch or two under 36 inches, as most cheesecloth comes in 3-foot widths. The mesh or cheesecloth should be reinforced underneath with string that is tacked diagonally between the corners of each frame as shown in the illustration above.

Put food on the tray one piece deep. If one side of your piece of food is covered with skin, put that side down on the tray. By the time it's ready to be turned, the side without the skin will be dry enough to have lost its stickiness. Then place a piece of cheesecloth, other fine-meshed material, wire mesh, or window screening over (but not touching) the food, keeping it slightly above the food with blocks of wood or clean stones. When done out in the open, carefully lay strips of wood or stones on the edges of the cheesecloth or other screening material to prevent the material from blowing off. When you're finished drying a batch, remove the material, wash it well, and let it dry before you set out more food. Scrub any sticky wooden surfaces as well.

DRYING INDOORS

Many parts of the country are not blessed with many warm and dry days on a consistent basis. If such is the case where you live, you'll probably have more luck if you do your drying indoors.

Drying with controlled heat in a kitchen oven or in a dryer has several advantages. The drying goes on day and night, in sunny or cloudy weather. Controlled-heat dryers shorten the drying time and extend the drying season to include late-maturing varieties. Vegetables dried with controlled heat cook up into more appetizing dishes than do sun-dried vegetables and have a higher vitamin A content and a better color and flavor. And you have no insects to worry about.

OVEN DRYING

Each square foot of shelf space in either an oven or a food dryer will hold about 1 to 2 pounds of produce, which comes out to be, for instance, a little more than a quart of peas or 4 medium-size apples. Of course, the poundage depends upon how thick the slices of fruit or vegetables are. Place food directly on oven racks, one piece deep, or, if the slats are too far apart, cover them first with finer wire cooling racks, cotton sheeting, or cheesecloth and then place the food on top. Regular baking sheets can be used, but because they are solid, they will not expose the food to drying heat on all sides. Special drying trays, either purchased or made of mesh or wooden slats for drying food in the sun (see page 134), may also be used in the oven.

It's very difficult to give more than general guidelines for time and temperature. Set your oven no higher than 145°F. This will be tricky with most ovens since the lowest setting is often 200°F. If this is the case with yours, set it to "warm" and use an oven thermometer to check the real temperature inside. If you can't get the temperature to stay below

Drying trays are much better than baking sheets for oven drying because air can circulate more freely around the food. Separate the trays by placing small blocks of wood at each corner when stacking them.

145°F, you ought to consider other ways to dry food. Food drying in the oven should be checked often, especially during the end of the drying time, and the trays should be rotated periodically for more even drying. If your oven isn't vented (and many electric ones aren't), leave the oven door slightly ajar to get good air circulation. Propping the door open just a bit with a folded towel or hot mat works well. Move the trays or oven racks from time to time. Don't place any food closer than about 6 inches from either the top or bottom of your oven. Turn your oven on bake; do not broil. Some ovens use their broiling element even on bake, and if this is so with yours, then deflect the broiler's heat away from your food by placing a baking sheet or a sheet of aluminum foil on the uppermost shelf and keeping all your food on the shelves underneath this one.

Don't overload your oven in an attempt to save energy. Extra food just means extra drying time, and it might mean even longer drying time because of poor air circulation from crowded food. Sliced fruits and vegetables and small whole berries can take from 4 to 12 hours to dry in a warm oven.

As when drying outside, put skin-side down. By the time you're ready to turn the fruit, the moister, exposed side should have dried out a bit and lost some of its tackiness, and there's less chance that it will stick to the tray.

An oven is a handy place to dry food, and if you can keep the temperature below 145°F, a perfectly acceptable place. However, it's not usually an economical means of drying big batches of food, since keeping the oven on with the door ajar for several hours at a time can use up a lot of energy. But for an occasional batch of food, ovens are more reliable than drying outdoors and certainly cheaper than going out and buying a food dryer.

DON'T MICROWAVE YOUR FOOD DRY

Microwaves are good for many things, like blanching vegetables before you freeze or dry them. But they are not particularly good for actually drying foods. They are too hard to control, and there's a good chance you'll cook your food instead of dry it.

HOME DRYERS

There was a surge of interest in home food drying in the late '70s, and with it came a new generation of food dryers, mostly indoor ones, but a few solar dryers as well. Because there were so many new home drying units suddenly on the market, Rodale Technical Services decided to do some comparative testing on several different kinds of dryers. Hopefully their observations and generalizations will help you select the most appropriate unit for your particular needs.

Drying techniques fall into 3 categories: electrical, stovetop, and solar. Electrical units tend to be more expensive, but we think that the shorter drying time and the higher dependability are worth the price if you're serious about drying food. Stovetop dryers are of 2 varieties: those requiring a primary heat source (electric coil, gas flame, or hot stove surface), and those requiring heat convected from the corner of a wood-burning stove. Most solar drying is of the build-it-yourself type. It's often less costly, but more risky. We say often, not always, considering the price of building materials these days.

Electrical Units

Size and Appearance. First decide what the greatest volume is you plan to dry at any one time and convert that volume into drying space. Figure that each square foot of shelf space will hold 1 to 2 pounds of sliced vegetables or fruit. To determine the drying space of any dryer, follow this formula:

$$\frac{\text{shelf length} \times \text{width (in.)} \times \text{no. of shelves}}{144} = \text{sq. ft. of drying space}$$

It's important to know where you want to put the dryer when balancing cost, size, and drying space factors. Some models are made with a wood veneer or colored porcelain finish to match any kitchen decor. These tend to be the more compact, deluxe units ranging in price from $150 to over $250. They're costly but attractive and handy to your work area.

You'll find a greater selection of dryers open to you if you don't confine yourself to the kitchen. With thermostatic temperature control and an electrically safe unit, there's no need to keep the dryer under constant surveillance.

Several of the dryers are noisy. This might not be much of a problem for you if you keep yours in the basement or pantry, but it will be annoying if it's around you all the time. In that case look for a quiet model.

Unit Construction. Among the units Rodale tested were dryers made of particle board, Masonite, aluminum, and sheet metal. Wood, acting as a good insulator, confines heat within the dryer while the exterior remains cool and safe to touch. Such efficient heat utilization keeps the running cost down. Some competitors complain of wood's tendency to warp and absorb odors, but we didn't notice these problems during our short testing period.

As far as efficiently utilizing heat, both sheet metal and aluminum dryers can get as hot as an oven door after the turkey's been roasting a few hours. But on the positive side, metal won't warp, it is easy to clean, and it won't absorb odors. The difference in weights of comparable wooden and metal dryers is surprisingly insignificant.

Thermostat. Don't bother with a dryer that doesn't have a thermostat. Not only does a thermostat let you dry at the proper temperature, it lets you keep it there, and that is a help. One dryer we worked with didn't have a thermostat. The temperature was controlled by leaving the dryer drawers open a bit. Twice the temperature soared to a scorching 176°F and burned the food. Even after the testers got used to the unit they still found they couldn't walk away from the dryer for more than 2 hours at a time. The recommended drying temperatures are 100°F for herbs, 120° to 130°F for fruits and vegetables, 140° to 150°F for meats (see page 494), and 140° to 150°F for fish (see page 514).

Fans and Air Flow. For fast, efficient drying, a fan to improve ventilation is a must. Your aim in drying is not to heat the food but to remove moisture from it. The way to do that is to get warm, dry air moving across as much surface area of the food as possible. Dryers without fans may have hot spots, which can lead to cooked or burned food. You will find basically 2 air flow systems to choose from: vertical and horizontal. Dryers with vertical air flows have their heat source on the bottom of the unit, and dryers with horizontal air flows have their heat on one side. We preferred the horizontal air flow because it keeps air moving across both the top and underside of the food (provided you don't use solid shelves) instead of up through the dryer between the pieces of food. But with both types of dryers we found it important to rotate trays for the best heat distribution. Not only does moving the trays around prevent hot spots, it can also cut down on drying time by as much as 2 hours.

You'll find some manufacturers emphasizing air flow recycling systems as a big selling point on their dryers; they claim that they cut down on the amount of air allowed to leave the unit, retain more heat, put less strain on the heating unit, conserve energy, and improve drying efficiency. Instead of blowing it out, it's blown around the food. We found little advantage to such a system, because the recycled air has already picked up a lot of moisture from the food, and blowing it over the food repeatedly doesn't mean it's going to be able to remove more moisture from it. Our tests showed that air recycling systems use about as much heat as other dryers.

Shelf Construction. You'll find almost as many different types of shelves available as there are dryers. A popular style uses an aluminum frame to support a thin mesh nylon screening without support underneath. Easy to clean and lightweight, these are hot to handle fresh out of a hot dryer. If consistently overloaded with moist, heavy fruits, they will stretch.

Some shelves are made of expanded metal or heavy plastic and have a pattern such as you'd find on a radiator cover. The great thing about these is their sturdiness, but the holes are so big that some foods will fall through. Covering the shelf with cheesecloth, cotton sheeting, or nylon netting is a big help in such cases.

Other shelves are made of solid wood or metal and are the least desirable. Air has no way of getting to the underside of the food so the drying process is slowed and the food needs to be turned. Most shelves of this type don't have turned-up edges to keep things like peas and grapes from rolling off.

When buying any kind of plastic shelf, make sure it is FDA food-quality approved and that it will withstand high temperatures. Hardware cloth and aluminum screening will lose some of its metallic finish to the food.

Miscellaneous. Don't let cute little extras cloud your evaluation. On-off switches mean nil. Timers are nice, but remember, you are drying by the hour, not the minute. Warranty times are not indicative of the product's quality. A new manufacturer will put a 1-year warranty on its unit to make it look as good as the rest, while a big-money company will gladly replace a few rejects for the added sales a 5-year warranty will bring in.

Stovetop Dryer

This is the kind of dryer that was popular about 50 years ago. It was originally designed to sit on top of the old wood cook stove and make use of the ever-present heat it generated. If you don't have a wood stove, you'll have to use some other primary source of heat like an electric or gas burner. You can improvise such a dryer by placing a baking sheet over a roasting pan filled with water.

A water reservoir 3 inches deep below a stainless steel drying surface is used to temper direct heat from the stove so that moisture may be gently driven from the food. The unit we tested had 3 square feet of

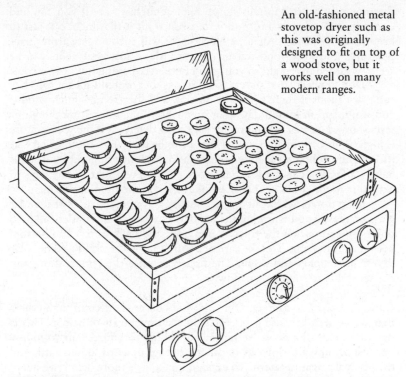

An old-fashioned metal stovetop dryer such as this was originally designed to fit on top of a wood stove, but it works well on many modern ranges.

drying space, small compared to electric dryers but certainly enough for drying odds and ends.

It'll take a little time until you know just how to regulate heat under the dryer. On our first trial run, the testers forgot to grease the top and applied enough heat to cook the food in an hour. After that disaster it didn't take them long to catch on.

No gadgets are provided with stovetop dryers to improve ventilation, but then the food isn't confined within a box either. Left exposed, moisture is carried away by air currents rising from the heat of the stove and by the dry breeze coming in a nearby window.

Solar Dryers

Your selection in solar dryers is not nearly as large as it is in dryers that run on electricity. The balance between temperature and air flow is a delicate one, and success depends a lot on the operator. The frame should be airtight except for vents so you can direct air flow through the dryer. It will be useful to have a thermometer installed inside. A regular outdoor thermometer doesn't usually go up high enough, so see if you can find one to handle at least 150°F (not that you want it that high, but just to keep track if it does). Again, a black cover will encourage warmer temperatures and keep food out of the sun. Make sure that vents can be securely closed overnight so you aren't bothered moving trays in and out.

Don't expect solar dryers to do things they weren't meant to. They can't dry foods if there's little or no sun, and they're not much good if you use them on humid days that aren't hot. One interesting thing our tests showed us was that humidity isn't a big deterrent if the temperature is high. If air coming into a solar dryer can be heated to 100°F or higher, its moisture-robbing capacity is so high that relative humidity outside is hardly a factor. This means that if you pick a few bright, sunny days to dry your food, you'll probably be okay even if the humidity is high.

Solar dryers act like little greenhouses, trapping the sun's heat under glass or plastic and warming the air that flows over and under the food that is spread out on the trays. Vents front and back or top and bottom keep the air moving. To take care of nature's unpredictability, some solar dryers have lights and a fan. The first is to raise the temperature, and the second is to increase air flow.

Rodale's Solar Food Dryer. Our solar food dryer is different than others that we've seen because it operates on the downdraft principle. This is due to an extra baffle we've put in our design that forces air to follow not just an upward flow, as in others, but an upward, downward, and then upward again pattern. To explain it in a little more detail, we quote from *Solar Food Dryer,* a book in the Rodale Plans series (edited by Ray Wolf and published in 1981, and, unfortunately, now out of print):

> Solar dryers traditionally depend on the fact that as air is heated it rises. Thus, they have a collector which heats air and then allows the air to rise through the food trays and exit the top of the unit. In working with dryers we found that this technique actually works against some other laws of nature. For when the air begins to dry the food, it cools as it absorbs moisture. Even though moist air is lighter than dry air, the fact that it is cool overpowers everything else, and it wants to sink, not go up, creating a slow air-movement pattern in the food area of the dryer.
>
> [Rodale's food dryer solves this problem with baffles and its exhaust chimney.] As the dryer gets warmer, the air in the exhaust chimney begins to be heated. As the air in the chimney is heated, it rises and exits the chimney. This creates a negative pressure at the bottom of the cabinet that draws warm air down, through the food trays. As air passes over the food, it cools and falls to the bottom of the cabinet. At that point, the air is still warmer than the outside ambient air and flows up the chimney to exit. As it goes up the chimney, it is reheated to speed up its flow.
>
> Thus, air starts moving through the dryer somewhat slowly, but quickly gathers momentum and becomes a natural type of flywheel, pulling air

OUR SOLAR FOOD DRYER

The dryer shown here has 3 basic parts to it: a collector, a food cabinet, and a stand.

The collector, which is hinged in the middle for easier storage, is made from black painted plywood. There's a layer of black aluminum wire mesh between the outside plastic glazing and the back of the box to help transfer heat. (Comparison tests showed us that the mesh doubled the amount of heat that traveled from collector to food cabinet.)

The plywood food cabinet holds simple food trays made from wood frames that have been screwed together. Fiberglass window screen was stretched and stapled over the frames. A vent door closes over the chimney in the cabinet so that no moisture enters at night, and the entire cabinet back opens to give access to the food trays.

The stand is not needed if you have a standard-size picnic table on which to place the dryer.

A backup system—a light tray made from 4 40-watt bulbs, and a fan that moves 50 cubic feet of air per minute—is nice to help you control heat and air movement, especially if you don't have regular warm and sunny days with low humidity, or you're planning to dry meat or fish, both of which need higher drying temperatures than fruits and vegetables.

The Rodale solar food dryer operates on the downdraft principle: air inside the dryer is forced upward, downward, then upward again. The result is that large quantities of food are readily exposed to warm air that carries moisture away with it, drying the food efficiently.

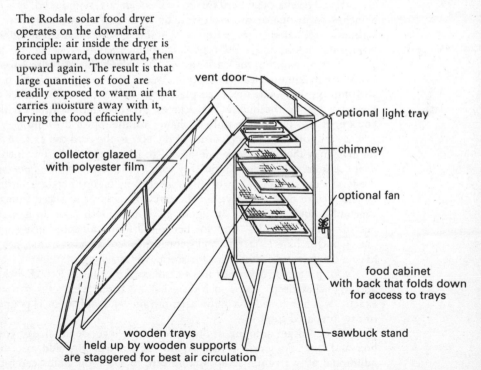

vent door

optional light tray

chimney

optional fan

collector glazed with polyester film

food cabinet with back that folds down for access to trays

wooden trays held up by wooden supports are staggered for best air circulation

sawbuck stand

from the collector in, over the food, and out the chimney, much faster than dryers that rely on natural convection. That is what allows Rodale's Solar Food Dryer to handle such large loads of food using only solar energy.

That explanation wasn't intended as a pitch for our dryer. There's no dryer to sell, and, as we said, the book with the instructions and plans is out of print anyway. It was, rather, just to explain the principle to you, so that the illustration on page 143 would make a bit more sense and so that, if you were handy, you could figure out how to build one of these with the sparse information we've been able to include here. (You could check the library for a copy of the book, though.)

A Low-Cost Indoor Dryer

If you only want to dry small batches of food at a time or wish to experiment with preparing and using dried foods, a simple, inexpensive dryer built by Rodale Technical Services may interest you.

You'll need a cardboard carton or wooden box, without lid, at least 8 inches deep; one or more 60-watt bulbs; a socket base and cord; a stainless steel baking sheet or piece of stainless steel sheet cut to fit the box; some tinfoil; and a few brushfuls of black paint.

Start by painting the back side of the baking sheet or metal sheet black for maximum heat absorption. While it's drying, line your box with tinfoil, shiny side up. Then place your bulb setup in the center of the box, angling the bulb at 45 degrees. (To help diffuse heat evenly, you might also put a little tinfoil "shade" on the top of the bulb.)

After notching the top corner of the box so the cord can exit, place the tray over the box (black side down) so it is suspended a few inches over the light bulb. Then coat the tray with a little vegetable oil to prevent the food from sticking to it (or put a layer of nylon or fiberglass netting or cheesecloth over the tray), fill the tray with a layer of sliced fruit or vegetables, and plug it in. In about 12 hours (more time on a high-humidity day; much less time for herbs and foods cut into fairly small pieces; and perhaps longer for high-moisture foods like most fruits), you'll have a trayful of dried goodies for storage or snacking.

Our prototype dryer features a cardboard fruit box 12 × 18 inches and 8¼ inches deep. The 1-inch-deep baking sheet, which fits the top exactly, was purchased at a hardware store and will hold about 1½ pounds of raw prepared food.

To dry larger amounts at one time, simply increase the size of your box and tray. For every 2 to 3 square feet of tray you add, use one additional 60-watt-bulb setup, taking care to space the bulbs carefully for even heating. This should keep your surface tray temperature at about

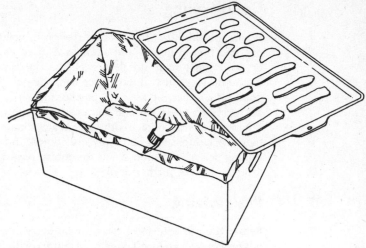

This indoor dryer is simplicity itself. While not very large or sophisticated, it costs practically nothing to build and will quickly give you a sense of the food-drying principle in action.

125° to 130°F—"cool" enough so you can just bear to touch it, but hot enough to dry your harvest slowly and surely without scorching or experiencing the kind of nutrient loss that begins at around 145°F.

■ This cardboard dryer has other uses, too. You can put pans of bread on top of it to provide low heat for rising dough. You can also put your milk and yogurt starter mixture inside and use the gentle heat to make yogurt. It will liquefy crystallized honey, make limp crackers crisp again, and soften butter.

WHEN YOUR FOOD IS DRY

Drying is finished when fruit feels dry and leathery on the outside, but *slightly* moist inside. It should still be pliable. Beans, peas, and corn should be very hard; leafy and thin vegetables should be leathery. See the directions for drying specific vegetables and fruits, pages 121–31, for what the finished dried food should feel like. If in doubt, leave the food on the trays a little longer, but reduce the temperature if you're drying with an oven or indoor dryer. Fruit seems to be more moist when it is hot, so remove a few pieces from the tray occasionally and allow them to cool before you determine if they are dry. Since some pieces of food will dry faster than others, it is important to remove pieces as they dry rather than wait until every piece of fruit or vegetable is totally dehydrated to stop the drying process. Food that overheats near the end of drying will scorch easily. Remember to cut up or slice a particular fruit or vegetable as uniformly as possible, so the pieces will take approximately the same time to dry.

Conditioning

When you think the food is dry, store it in open containers in a warm, dry area free of insects and animals. A glass, enamel, or crockery bowl or pot is fine; so is stainless steel. But don't use an aluminum one if you're drying fruits. It can react with the acid in them. Wood's not a good idea, either, because it's porous and can retain moisture. For 7 to 10 successive days stir the contents thoroughly each day to bring the drier particles in contact with some that are more moist. In this way the moisture content will be evenly distributed. If, at the end of this conditioning period, the food seems too moist, return it to the dryer or leave it in the sun for further drying.

Pasteurizing

Before you put your food away for storage you might want to pasteurize it. Our Food Center isn't convinced that food that has been dried properly under sanitary conditions needs pasteurizing. But if you didn't use an electric food dryer or other indoor dryer, but dried outdoors where insects might have landed on your food and possibly left their microscopic eggs, or where it might have picked up some spoilage organisms, pasteurizing isn't a bad idea. The reasons for pasteurizing increase if you plan to keep the food for more than 6 months.

You can pasteurize your food by either heating it or freezing it. To pasteurize with heat, spread dried food 1 inch thick on baking sheets or trays, and heat for 10 to 15 minutes in a 175°F oven. Then cool thoroughly. To freeze-pasteurize it, place it in plastic bags or food containers and hold it *below 0°F* for a minimum of 48 hours. Freezing is preferable because it destroys fewer vitamins than heating, but impossible to do if you don't have a freezer that stays below zero. Only chest or upright freezers will get so cold; don't expect a freezer-refrigerator to be able to do the job.

Storing

When thoroughly and uniformly dry and pasteurized, pack the food for storage. Promptness is important here, because dried food will immediately start to pick up moisture from the air. Dried food that's not in an airtight container should never be stored in the refrigerator. Refrigerators are humid, and the moisture in that cool air will rehydrate that food you worked so hard to get dry. Store in airtight, sterilized glass jars, in heavy-duty plastic bags, or in metal cans (with tight-fitting lids) that are lined with new brown paper bags to keep food out of contact with the metal. Using brown paper bag liners isn't a bad idea for plastic bags and glass jars, too, because they keep the light out. If you don't use such a liner to shield food from the light, then make sure the storage area is dark. And if storing in paper bag-lined plastic bags, make sure the area is rodent-proof! Squeeze excess air out of plastic bags or pick jars that are just big enough to hold your food. Half-filled jars are also half filled with air, and it's air and the natural moisture in it that you want to avoid.

Store only one type of food in each container, even if each is wrapped in separate plastic bags within that container, so that flavors and smells don't mix. It's generally preferable to package small quantities—enough, say, for one meal. Then if one package spoils, only a small amount of food will be wasted. Several brown paper bags of dried food can be stored inside one larger heavy-duty plastic bag.

After your food is packaged, place a label on each container indicating the kind of food and the date it was packaged so that you can use your foods in the order in which you dried them. First in, first out. Then store in a dark place in a cool (below 60°F), dry basement or pantry. During warm, humid weather dried foods retain their quality best if they are kept under refrigeration.

The chart here shows you how long you can keep specific foods at room temperature (70°F) and at a cooler temperature, close to the temperature of unheated basements (52°F). You can see that dried foods store considerably longer at the lower temperature.

It is a good idea to examine dried food occasionally for mold. If you find any, the food's a loss; throw it out. The food probably wasn't dried sufficiently in the first place. Live and learn. If, on the other hand,

Storage Time of Dried Foods

Food	Months Stored at 70°F	Months Stored at 52°F
Vegetables		
Asparagus	2	4 to 6
Beans, green	4	8 to 12
Beans, lima	4	8 to 12
Beets	4	8 to 12
Broccoli	1	2 to 3
Cabbage	1	2 to 3
Carrots	6	12 to 18
Cauliflower	1	2 to 3
Celery	2	2 to 3
Corn	4	8 to 12

continued

Storage Time of Dried Foods—*continued*

Food	Months Stored at 70°F	Months Stored at 52°F
Vegetables—*continued*		
Cucumbers	2	4 to 6
Eggplant	2	4 to 6
Garlic	4	8 to 12
Horseradish	4	8 to 12
Mushrooms	2	4 to 6
Okra	4	8 to 12
Onions, Leeks	4	8 to 12
Parsnips	4	8 to 12
Peas	4	8 to 12
Peppers, chili	8	16 to 24
Peppers, sweet	8	16 to 24
Potatoes, white	4	8 to 12
Pumpkins	1	2 to 3
Rhubarb	4	12 to 16
Spinach, Kale, Swiss chard	2	4 to 6
Sweet potatoes	1	2 to 3
Tomatoes	3	6 to 9
Turnips	2	4 to 6
Zucchini, Summer squash	1	2 to 3
Fruits		
Apples	6	18 to 24
Apricots	8	24 to 32
Bananas	4	12 to 16
Blueberries	6	18 to 24
Cherries	12	36 to 48
Citrus peels	6	18 to 24
Coconut	1	3 to 4
Dates	12	36 to 48
Figs	6	18 to 24
Grapes	6	18 to 24
Papayas	6	18 to 24
Peaches, Nectarines	6	18 to 24
Pears	6	18 to 24
Pineapple	8	24 to 32
Plums	8	24 to 32
Strawberries	6	18 to 24

FREEZE-DRYING—GOOD, BUT NOT AT HOME

Freeze-drying seems to be an excellent way to store foods. The foods are substantially reduced in weight and volume and they will keep for about 2 years without much loss of nutrients, color, or flavor. Unfortunately, freeze-drying is a sophisticated process that requires special equipment not available to most people. It is not a technique that can be carried out under normal home situations.

Freeze-drying is, simply, a drying method in which water is removed from frozen foods. The food is first sliced, diced, powdered, granulated, or liquefied. Then it is frozen.

Once frozen it is spread out on trays and placed in a vacuum cabinet. The door is closed and the pressure is lowered, creating a vacuum. Heat is applied, and the ice within the food disappears in the air and is taken out of the cabinet with a pump. Drying takes about 10 hours (during drying the food is kept frozen) and almost all of the water is removed from the food. The moisture content is usually 2 percent or lower. The food is taken from the drying chamber and tightly packaged in a can so it will stay dry until used.

upon examination you find that it is more limber and moist than you remember, but there's no mold at all, you can stick it in the oven or food dryer to dry it out. Use it sooner rather than later.

Dried foods keep well for a month to 2 years, depending upon the food and how well they were stored, and at what temperature they were stored. You can see by the chart that cooler temperatures substantially increase safe storage times. Dried foods will keep even longer if you put them in the freezer. If you're ultimately going to put the food in the freezer you obviously could have done so right at the start, without drying it first. True, but dried food takes up nearly no space compared to what fresh-frozen food requires—something to keep in mind if freezer space is at a premium in your home.

If you discover just a few bugs in your food, don't throw it out. Spread it in shallow pans and put it in your oven for about 20 to 25 minutes at 300°F. The heat will take care of the insects and eggs and sterilize your food at the same time.

Rehydrating

Water is taken out of fruits and vegetables for preservation, and, in many cases, you will want to put the water back in before you eat the food. Dried fruits are quite good eaten just as they are, by themselves or chopped up in cereals and desserts. And vegetables that you plan to use in soups and stews do not need to be rehydrated first. But vegetables used alone, and fruits intended for baked products and compotes, should be rehydrated.

At our Food Center we found that in most cases it was better to rehydrate foods by soaking them in boiling water and covering them with a lid. Soaking in cold water was not nearly so successful. As usual, there are always exceptions, and in this case it's carrots and all beans other than green beans. They tasted and looked better to us when reconstituted in cold water.

In some cases, the boiling water not only reconstituted the food, it more or less cooked it as well so that no further cooking was necessary. Dried spinach is so fine that it need not be reconstituted. Just steam it as if cooking it fresh without soaking it first.

To rehydrate vegetables and fruits, place the food in a pot and pour boiling water over it. Don't add the food to the water; it's not the same. Cover the pot immediately and turn the heat quite low, so that the food stays hot but doesn't boil, not even simmer. The water should just cover the food. Too much water will take a lot of the flavor out of the food. You can always add more boiling water if it needs more, so it's better to add too little at the start than too much. Check the charts starting on page 151 for the suggested amount of water you should pour over each food; they all don't need the same amount. Do not add salt to rehydrating vegetables or sugar to fruits; both cause food to absorb less water than they normally would.

The charts also give suggested soaking times. But the times are only suggestions. If this is your first time rehydrating a certain food, you might want to lift the lid now and then and check to see how things are coming. Taste it after a while to see how you like it and see how it looks. Remember that the rehydrated food should look pretty much like the fresh after it has been cooked. When done correctly, all the water will be soaked up.

Cooking Dried Vegetables and Fruits

In taste tests we conducted at our Food Center, we found that the majority of tasters preferred dried vegetables over those that had been canned, second only to fresh and frozen vegetables. We also discovered that the best way to use dried vegetables is to cook them in soups and stews. The color and aromas are appetizing, the textures are soft, and the flavor is delicious. What's more, dried vegetables don't need to be rehydrated before cooking them this way. For stew, use 1 cup water for every cup dried vegetables. For soup, use 2 cups, or more, water for every cup vegetables. Combine ingredients, bring to a boil, cover, and reduce heat to low. Simmer for about 20 minutes. The vegetables that we like best for soups and stews are green beans, lima beans, beets, broccoli, cabbage, carrots, cauliflower, celery, corn, eggplant, garlic, mushrooms, onions, peas, chili peppers, sweet peppers, potatoes, spinach, and summer squash.

■ Make yourself a thermos of soup by adding 5 tablespoons mixed dried vegetables, 1 tablespoon macaroni or other small pasta, some spices or herbs, and a few drops soy sauce to 2 cups boiling hot stock (vegetable, chicken, beef, or whatever). Cap the thermos and let it sit to "cook" for a few hours. We tried other ingredients like lentils, brown rice, and split peas, but were disappointed with the results; they were undercooked.

To cook dried vegetables not intended for soups and stews, and to cook fruits, put them and the water they did not absorb in a pot so the extra water just covers the bottom of the pot. Cover and quickly bring the vegetables or fruits to a boil. Reduce the heat and simmer until the vegetables are plump and tender. If the vegetables are still tough after about 5 minutes of cooking or all the water is quickly absorbed by the cooking vegetables, they have not been soaked long enough. Next time, extend the soaking time so that the vegetables are fully rehydrated before cooking.

Rehydrated vegetables can also be steamed, and some sauté very nicely.

Soybeans need special attention. Soak them overnight in the refrigerator, throw out their soaking water, then cook for 1 to 2 hours in fresh liquid before using in recipes. Soybeans contain an antinutritional enzyme and should be eaten only after they are completely cooked.

When measuring out dried foods to use in place of fresh in recipes, keep in mind that 1 part dried vegetable or fruit equals about 2 to 4 of the same fresh food.

USING DRIED VEGETABLES

The recommendations below are based on our experiences in the Rodale Food Center. Unless otherwise noted, pour boiling water over the vegetable to rehydrate it as described on page 149.

As we've said before, there are no hard-and-fast rules for using dried foods. Use our recommendations as a starting point, and experiment from there.

ASPARAGUS

Use enough water to cover the asparagus; soak for 15 to 20 minutes. The tips become tender and plump up well, but the stems remain tough.

BEANS, GREEN AND YELLOW

French-cut beans are better than regular-cut beans. Dried green and yellow beans tend to lose some of their flavor, but they can be successfully dried if you follow instructions carefully.

BEANS, LIMA

Soak 1 cup beans in 2 cups cool water for 2 hours. Some beans remain wrinkled but most puff up nicely and have a bright, light green color like raw, fresh lima beans. Cook before eating as you would cook fresh or frozen lima beans.

BEETS AND PARSNIPS

Use equal amounts of vegetables and water; soak for about 1 hour. They have good flavor and color, and are tender but limp; the grain is pronounced.

BROCCOLI

Simply steaming broccoli may be the best method. Use equal amounts of broccoli and water. After 30 minutes the florets are reconstituted, but the stems remain woody and tough. Color is good.

CABBAGE

Use 1½ cups water for 1 cup cabbage; soak for 50 minutes. Reconstituted cabbage has the green and white color of fresh cabbage; flavor and texture are like lightly steamed cabbage. There is none of the strong odor that usually accompanies cooked cabbage. Can also be reconstituted by soaking in cool water for 15 minutes. Has good flavor and texture. Sauté or use in a baked dish; steaming dried cabbage causes it to turn brown and become soggy.

CARROTS

For results close to fresh-cooked carrots, either soak carrots in an equal amount of cool water for 30 minutes, and then steam for 5 minutes; or combine equal amounts of carrots and water, bring to a boil, cover, reduce heat to low, and simmer for 10 minutes. Both methods have very good results: good color retention, great flavor and texture. For results close to raw carrots, combine equal amounts of carrots and water and soak for 30 minutes. The color is bright, the flavor fresh; they are crunchy though not crisp; the edges may be curled.

CAULIFLOWER

Use equal amounts of cauliflower and water; soak for 15 to 20 minutes.

CELERY AND RHUBARB

Use equal amounts of vegetables and water; soak for 20 minutes.

CORN

Combine corn with twice as much water in a saucepan. Bring to a boil, cover, reduce heat to low, and simmer for 30 minutes or until all water is absorbed. The flavor is good and similar to cooked frozen corn; the color is fresh and the texture good.

CUCUMBERS

Use equal amounts of cucumbers and cool water; soak for 1 hour. These retain color but are not very good; they are tough and have a bland flavor. Recommend using in a marinade, dip, or spread.

EGGPLANT

Use equal amounts of eggplant and water; soak for 30 minutes. Flavor is a bit strong, the texture is somewhat leathery, and the color a bit darker than that of fresh, but reconstituted eggplant is good tasting.

GARLIC

Need not be reconstituted. Use in dried form in cooking.

HERBS See page 164.

HORSERADISH

Does not need to be reconstituted for cooking, but can be reconstituted for dips and spreads by soaking in an equal amount of warm water for 30 minutes.

KALE See Spinach, Kale, and Swiss chard.

LEEKS See Onions and Leeks.

MUSHROOMS

Dried mushrooms should be used in stews, soups, or casseroles, or for pot roasts. None of these uses requires reconstituting before cooking.

OKRA

Use twice as much water as okra, bring to a boil, cover, reduce heat to low, and simmer for 30 minutes.

ONIONS AND LEEKS

Use equal amounts of vegetables and water; soak for 15 minutes. Results are like steamed fresh vegetables. Do not reconstitute well in cool water.

PARSNIPS See Beets and Parsnips.

PEAS

Dried peas are a surprisingly good snack. To reconstitute, use twice as much water as peas, bring to a boil, cover, reduce heat to low, and simmer for 30 minutes.

PEPPERS, CHILI

Use in dried form for seasoning.

PEPPERS, SWEET

Use equal amounts of peppers and water; soak for 20 minutes. Flavor is like a cooked pepper; flesh is soft; skin remains a bit tough; good color.

POTATOES, SWEET AND WHITE

Use equal amounts of potatoes and water; soak for 25 minutes. Flavor is like raw potatoes; texture is more like that of raw than that of cooked potatoes. There is no discoloration if they are dipped in lemon juice before drying.

PUMPKINS

Use equal amounts of pumpkin and water; soak for 30 minutes and then steam for 5 minutes. Or combine with an equal amount of water and bring to a boil, cover, reduce the heat to low, and simmer for 10 minutes.

RHUBARB See Celery and Rhubarb.

SPINACH, KALE, AND SWISS CHARD

Steam leaves for 5 to 6 minutes. Good flavor; tender; color is good but dulled.

SWEET POTATOES See Potatoes, sweet and white.

SWISS CHARD See Spinach, Kale, and Swiss chard.

TOMATOES

Use equal amounts of tomatoes and water; soak for 30 minutes. Flavor is like that of tomato paste; flesh is mushy; skin is tough; color is duller and darker than fresh-cooked tomatoes. See the box Sun-Dried Tomatoes on page 128.

TURNIPS

Use equal amounts of turnips and water; soak for 1 hour. Good color and flavor; tender but limp; grain is pronounced.

ZUCCHINI AND SUMMER SQUASH

Soak equal amounts of squash and water for 15 minutes, then steam for 8 minutes. Good flavor and color; limp but not mushy.

USING DRIED FRUITS

The recommendations below are based on our experiences in the Rodale Food Center. Unless otherwise noted, pour boiling water over the fruit to rehydrate it as described on page 149.

As we've said before, there are no hard-and-fast rules for using dried foods. Use our recommendations as a starting point, and experiment from there.

APPLES

Use equal amounts of apples and water; soak for 10 minutes. Reconstituted apples are very similar to baked apples. The flavor is good, and the flesh is soft but holds its shape. Although more flavor will be lost this way, you can also reconstitute apples by soaking in cool water. Keep the apple surfaces in contact with the water. It will take 10 to 30 minutes to rehydrate, depending upon the size of the slices. Excellent eating dried.

APRICOTS, DATES, AND FIGS

Use equal amounts of fruit and water; soak for 15 minutes. The flavor is good. Apricot flesh is soft but has body; color darkens a bit. Apricots do not reconstitute well in cool water. Excellent eating dried.

BANANAS

Use equal amounts of bananas and water; soak for 10 minutes. Reconstituted bananas are very soft, limp, and sweet; they have the dark color of very ripe bananas. They do not reconstitute well in cool water. Excellent eating dried.

BLUEBERRIES

Use equal amounts of berries and water; soak for 10 to 15 minutes. Do not reconstitute in cool water. Good eating dried.

CHERRIES

Use equal amounts of cherries and water; soak for 10 minutes. They'll be dark in color and soft, with almost a mushy texture, but they'll hold their shape. Rehydrated cherries taste sweet like cooked cherries. They do not reconstitute well in cool water; much flavor is lost and it takes over an hour for them to become tender. Good eating dried.

CITRUS PEELS

Use in dried form. Grind coarsely and use for flavoring or cook with honey to prepare candied fruit rinds.

COCONUT

Use in dried form in cooking or sprinkle on foods.

DATES See Apricots, Dates, and Figs.

FIGS See Apricots, Dates, and Figs.

GRAPES

Dried grapes are raisins and can't be reconstituted back to grapes.

NECTARINES See Peaches, Nectarines, and Papayas.

PAPAYAS See Peaches, Nectarines, and Papayas.

PEACHES, NECTARINES, AND PAPAYAS

Use equal amounts of fruit and water; soak for about 5 minutes. Flavor is good; flesh becomes soft but holds its shape. Tasty when eaten dried.

PEARS

Use equal amounts of pears and water; soak for 10 minutes. Flavor is good; the flesh is soft, but it darkens in color a bit. Pears also reconstitute well in cool water; soak for 10 minutes.

PINEAPPLE

Use equal amounts of pineapple and water; soak for 10 minutes. Good in all respects; it is a bit mushy, but it holds its shape. Does not reconstitute well in cool water. Excellent eating dried.

PLUMS

Dried plums are prunes. To reconstitute, use equal amounts of plums and water, and soak for 20 minutes. Plums reconstitute well in cool water. Flavor and color are good, but they're a bit slimy. Different kinds of plums give very different results.

STRAWBERRIES

Use equal amounts of strawberries and water; soak for 10 minutes. Strawberries do not reconstitute well in cool water. Good eating dried.

FRUIT PURÉE

Dried fruits can be reconstituted as a purée and used as sweeteners in baked goods and confections. When preparing fruit purée from a tart fruit, as shown in the chart, add some sweet fruit to sweeten, rather than honey. Apple is ideal for this, as it blends well with other fruits.

Fruit purées can be used as toppings, added to yogurt for homemade fruit yogurt, or used as a fruit filling in baked goods. The beauty is that you get fresh fruit flavor but only have to reconstitute as much as you need at the time.

To prepare fruit purée, coarsely chop the desired fruit alone in a blender. In a saucepan, combine the fruit with water to cover. Cook uncovered, over low heat, for about 30 minutes or until the fruit is tender. Stir frequently. Return the fruit to the blender and purée to the desired consistency. Berries should be puréed well or they will be gritty. Softer fruits such as apples, peaches, or pears can be left with some chunks.

Sweet and Tart Fruits

Sweet		Tart
Apples	Figs	Apricots
Bananas	Grapes	Cherries
Blackberries	Pears	Nectarines
Blueberries	Pineapple	Peaches
Cherries	Plums	Plums
Coconut	Raspberries	
Dates	Strawberries	

FRUIT AND VEGETABLE FLOUR

Fruits and vegetables dried extra dry so they are crisp can be ground in a dry blender or coffee mill to a flourlike consistency. This flour can then be used in breads, cookies, cakes, pancakes, fritters, crackers, etc.

For every cup flour called for in your original recipe, you can add up to ½ cup fruit or vegetable flour. Depending upon the recipe and the type of flour used, it may be necessary to add 1 to 2 tablespoons additional liquid to the recipe. Mix the fruit or vegetable flour with the other dry ingredients.

Custards and puddings can also be prepared using fruit or vegetable flours. For custard, use about 1 cup fruit or vegetable flour to 4 cups milk and 3 eggs. In pudding, use about 1 cup fruit or vegetable flour to 4 cups milk and 6 tablespoons cornstarch.

FRUIT LEATHER

Fruit leathers are wonderful, natural sweets. With few exceptions, fruit leathers have a full, fruity flavor and the texture of chewy candy. They're called leathers because they feel (but not taste!) something like leather— soft and pliable. You make them by drying cooked puréed fruit on a baking sheet until a good part of the moisture and stickiness is gone and you're left with a thin sheet of fruit. Any single fruit is good, and combinations can be quite delicious. Spices and sweetening are optional.

Fruit leathers are usually dried in a very low oven (see the recipes starting on page 160), but you can also dry them in a food dryer. To prevent sticking, pour the purée on oiled trays or those lined with freezer paper or plastic wrap, so that it is ¼ inch thick. If it is much thicker than ¼ inch, it will take very long to dry. Don't use wax paper or aluminum foil; the leather will stick to it. It'll take about 6 to 8 hours to dry in an electric food dryer. You know the leather is done when the center is no longer sticky, and you'll know it's overdried if it's brittle. Once it's dry, remove it from the tray, place on a cake rack, and leave it there for a few hours so that you're sure both sides are dry. Then dust with cornstarch or arrowroot powder before you roll it up or stack it in layers with wax paper, freezer paper, or plastic wrap between each sheet. Store fruit leathers in a cool, dry place.

Apricot, Peach, or Nectarine Leather

1 gallon pitted apricots,
    peaches, or nectarines
1½ cups unsweetened pineapple
    juice
¼ cup mild-flavor honey (or
    more to taste)
3 teaspoons almond extract
    (optional)

Place the pitted fruit and pineapple juice in a large, heavy pot. Cover the pot and set it over low heat. Cook the fruit until it is soft. Drain off the juice well, lifting the fruit from the sides of the strainer to allow all the juice to run out freely. The more juice strained out, the quicker the process of "leather making." The juice is too good to discard. Can or freeze it for later or drink it fresh.

Run the fruit through a blender, food processor, or food mill, removing the skins if you prefer a smooth product, or use the skins as part of the pulp for the leather. A food processor will purée the skins right along with the pulp. Sweeten the pulp to taste with honey and add the almond extract if you wish. The pulp should be as thick as a thick applesauce or more so. Spread it on lightly oiled baking sheets or baking sheets covered with freezer paper or plastic wrap, so that it is ¼ inch thick.

Place the baking sheets in a low oven or food dryer. If using an oven, turn the control to warm (120°F) and leave the oven door slightly

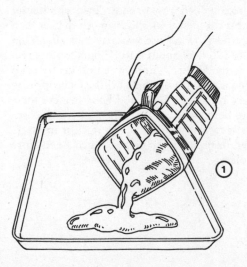

(1) To make fruit leather, purée the cooked fruit in a blender, then pour the purée onto an oiled baking sheet.

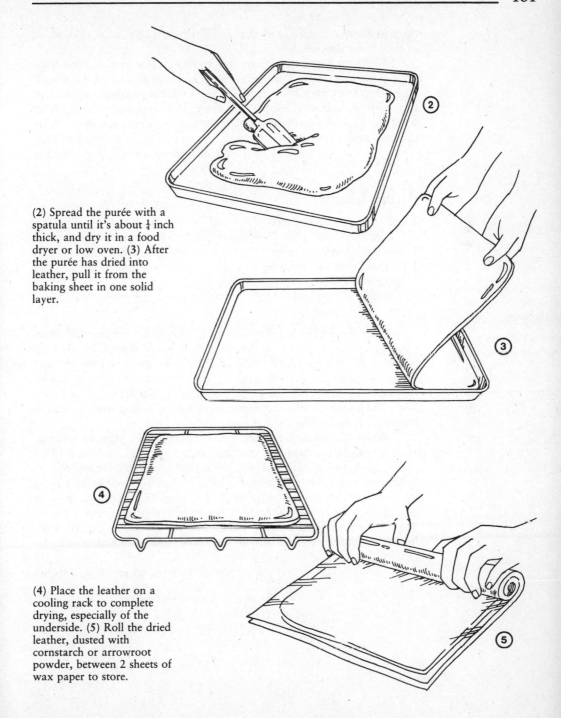

(2) Spread the purée with a spatula until it's about ½ inch thick, and dry it in a food dryer or low oven. (3) After the purée has dried into leather, pull it from the baking sheet in one solid layer.

(4) Place the leather on a cooling rack to complete drying, especially of the underside. (5) Roll the dried leather, dusted with cornstarch or arrowroot powder, between 2 sheets of wax paper to store.

open to allow moisture to escape. It will dry in 12 hours in an oven set at the lowest temperature.

When the leather is dry enough to be lifted or gently pulled from the baking sheets, put the leather on cake racks so that it can dry on both sides. Dust the leather lightly with cornstarch or arrowroot powder to absorb any stickiness left in the leather. Then stack the leather in layers with wax paper, freezer paper, or plastic wrap between each sheet. Cover the stack with freezer paper or plastic wrap and store in a cool, dry place.

Yield: 4 sheets, about 10 × 5 inches

Apple Leather

1 gallon apples, peeled and
    cored
1 cup apple cider (or more)
½ to 1 cup mild-flavor honey
    ground cinnamon, cloves,
        and/or nutmeg, added to
        taste (optional)

Place the apples and their juice in a large, heavy pot and add 1 cup apple cider. (Apples are drier than other fruit and will scorch as they are heated if no liquid is added to the pot.) Place the pot over low heat and bring the apples to a boil. Add more cider if needed to prevent the apples from sticking to the bottom of the pot. If the apples are tart, add honey when the mixture looks somewhat clear and is boiling well. Then add the spices if you wish.

When the mixture reaches the consistency of a very thick sauce, remove it from the heat and run through a food mill, blender, or food processor. Return to heat and cook to the consistency of thick applesauce. Spread the pulp, about ¼ inch thick, on oiled baking sheets or on baking sheets lined with freezer paper or plastic wrap. Dry this apple pulp as described in the recipe for Apricot, Peach, or Nectarine Leather, above. Then place it on cake racks so that it can dry on both sides. Dust the leather with cornstarch or arrowroot powder and wrap and store as for other leathers.

Yield: 4 sheets, about 10 × 5 inches

Quince Leather

1 pound quinces
   water
1 stick of cinnamon, 2 inches
   long
2 whole cloves
1 whole nutmeg
½ cup mild-flavor honey

    Peel, core, and grind quinces. In a pressure cooker, pour quince and add water to cover; add a cheesecloth bag with cinnamon, cloves, and nutmeg. Process for 20 minutes. Remove cheesecloth bag. Drain quinces and reserve juice for jelly making. Add honey to quince and heat again, stirring constantly, for 20 minutes or until you have a thick purée.

    Then spread the pulp, about ¼ inch thick, on a baking sheet that is oiled or lined with freezer paper or plastic wrap. Dry, dust, wrap, and store the pulp as the other leathers above.

Yield: 1 sheet, about 10 × 7 inches

Prune Leather

1 gallon pitted prunes
   (6 pounds)
1½ cups water
3 teaspoons almond extract
2 tablespoons mild-flavor
   honey (optional)

    Place the fruit and water in a large, heavy pot and cook over low heat until the fruit is tender, about 25 minutes. Drain off any remaining juice and save it for a breakfast drink or punch. (It can be diluted with equal parts or more of water.) Run the pulp through a food mill or a food processor and purée, using pulp and skins. Add the almond extract and honey to taste. Then spread the pulp, about ¼ inch thick, on 3 baking sheets that are oiled or lined with freezer paper or plastic wrap. Dry, dust, wrap, and store the pulp as the other leathers above.

Yield: 3 sheets, about 10 × 7 inches

PREPARING HERBS FOR DRYING

Storing herbs in dried form is so popular because it is such a simple means of preservation. Dried herbs can be taken from their jars just as they are needed, to be mixed with foods while they are cooking or just before they are served. However, the fresh quality of the just-picked herb is lost in the drying process. Although marjoram, mint, oregano, rosemary, and thyme dry well, basil, borage, salad burnet, chervil, chives, cilantro (coriander), dill, and parsley are disappointing. For this reason, some people prefer to preserve some of their herbs by other methods, like freezing (see page 73), preserving in vinegar (see page 299), freezing as an herb butter (see page 363), or mincing and keeping under oil in the refrigerator.

Harvesting and Drying Herb Leaves

Herb leaves are cut when the plant's stock of essential oils is at its highest. In the leafy herbs—basil, chervil, marjoram, and savory—this occurs just before blossoming time. Basil, lemon balm, parsley, rosemary, and sage can be cut as many as 4 times during the outdoor growing season. Cutting should be done on the morning of a day that promises to be hot and dry. As soon as the dew is off the plants, snip off the top growth—perhaps 6 inches of stem below the flower buds.

If the leaves are clean, do not wash them; some of the oils will be lost in the rinsing process. Naturally, if the leaves are dusty or have been thickly mulched, wash them briefly under cold water. Shake off any excess water and hang the herbs, tied in small bunches, in the sun, just until the water evaporates from them.

Before the sun starts to boil them, take them in and hang them in a warm, dry place which is well ventilated and free from strong light. Traditionally, herbs were hung above the mantels of kitchen fireplaces or in attics. Tie herbs and hang their leaves down so that the essential oils in the stems will flow into the leaves. Don't hang them above the stove you cook on, as grease and odors can damage the delicate texture, flavor, and aroma of the herbs. To prevent dust from accumulating on the drying leaves, put them in a brown paper bag that you've punched some holes in to increase the air circulation.

But there are other ways to air-dry herbs—any way that keeps air circulating freely around the herbs and keeps them out of sunlight, dust, grime, and moisture will do. If you don't want to hang them up, remove their stems and dry them on baking sheets, window screens covered with clear sheeting or cheesecloth, or even on a towel.

Or dry them in a food dryer. Be certain, though, that the screen or netting on the tray is very fine so that no leaves can fall through its

You can dry herbs in a brown paper bag that has holes punched in it for air circulation. Place the bunch stems up and gather the bag at the stems; close it with string, a rubber band, or wire twist. The paper bag will shade the leaves from direct light that would otherwise darken them unnecessarily. Basil, horehound, lemon balm, marjoram, mint, oregano, sage, and savory are some good herbs to dry in this fashion.

openings. You may have to line your racks with sheeting or cheesecloth. For best flavor, the temperature inside the dryer should stay under 105°F. When thoroughly dry, remove leaves from stems, but don't crush them unless you plan to use them right away. There's no sense releasing precious oils and have them degenerate in storage.

Harvesting and Drying Herb Seeds

To harvest seeds, gather anise, caraway, coriander, cumin, dill, and fennel plants when the seed pods or heads have changed color, but before they begin to shatter. You may spread the pods one layer thick on drying trays just as you do the leaves. When they seem thoroughly dry, rub the pods between the palms of your hands, and the seeds should fall out easily. You can also dry the seeds by hanging the whole plant upside down inside a paper bag to dry. As the seeds dry and fall from the pods, the paper bag will catch them. You can give the dried seeds, especially dill seed, a light-duty threshing to separate pods from seeds. Rub the seeds between your palms. Then pick a day when there is a light breeze and pour the seeds slowly from a 2-foot height into a large bowl, bucket, or any container big enough for the job. Put a clean sheet under the bucket in case the breeze is too strong and carries a lot of the seeds with it. Because pods are lighter than seeds, the breeze should blow them away while the seeds fall in the container below. You will probably need to repeat this a few times until the seeds are clear of pods.

To separate seeds from the plants, you can rub the dried stems between your palms and let the seeds drop into a bowl. Once you've harvested the seeds, go outdoors on a slightly breezy day and slowly pour the seeds from a height of about 2 feet into a container below. Pods are lighter than seeds, so the wind will blow them away while the seeds fall into the container. While this simple technique works pretty well, you will probably have to repeat it a few times to eliminate all the pods.

Harvesting and Drying Herb Flowers

Cut flowers that you plan to use in cooking on the first day they are open. If petals alone are used, remove them from the calyx and spread them on a tray. Rose petals should have their claws—the narrow white portions at the base of each petal—removed. Flower heads used for tea, like camomile, are dried whole.

Harvesting and Drying Herb Roots

The roots of certain plants, particularly angelica, burdock, comfrey, ginger, and ginseng, are highly aromatic and can be dried and cut for candy, teas, and cold beverages. These roots are much thicker than the delicate seeds, flowers, and leaves of other plants, and the drying process is a long one. So as not to injure the plant, roots should be dug out and cut off during the plant's dormant stage, when there is sufficient food stored in the plant cells. This is usually during the fall and winter months. Cut off tender roots—never more than a few from each plant. Scrub them with a vegetable brush to remove all dirt. If the roots are thin, they may be left whole, but thick roots should be sliced lengthwise and possibly cut into even thinner slices if they are really thick. Place them one layer deep in a food dryer or low-temperature oven to dry.

(Do not dig the roots of the sassafras tree for harvesting; we now know that it's not safe to eat, because it contains safrole, a substance found to cause cancer in laboratory rats. While the tea made from sassafras contains very little toxin because safrole is not water soluble, there's no need to take chances. There are plenty of other nice herbs for making teas that do not present even this small health hazard.)

Storing the Herbs

Leaves may be crushed before being stored away, but they retain their oils better if they are kept whole and are crushed right before they are used. Seeds should not be ground ahead of time because they deteriorate quickly when the seed shell is broken. If the seeds are kept whole and stored properly, they will keep several years although flavor will gradually diminish. Store leaves, seeds, flowers, and roots in tightly sealed jars in a warm place for about a week. At the end of that time, examine the jars. If there is moisture on the inside of the glass or under the lid, remove the contents and spread out for further drying. Checking the jars is especially important if you are storing dried roots because it is difficult to know when they are completely dry. If further drying is not done, there is a good chance that mold will develop, and the leaves, seeds, flowers, or roots will not be fit to use. Do not store herbs in cardboard or paper containers, because these materials absorb the oils and leave the dried herbs tasteless. Ideally, herbs should be stored in a cool place, out of strong light, either in dark glass jars, in tins, or behind cabinet doors. Herbs deteriorate after a while in storage. It's best to throw them out after a year and restock with fresh ones.

While herbs are usually stored separately, you might like to make some herb blends. During storage, the distinct aromas and flavors of the different herbs are given a chance to meld together and form delightful herb mixtures that can be sprinkled on foods or tied in cheesecloth and plunged in soups and stews while they are simmering. Below you'll find some recipes for popular herb combinations.

■ When substituting dried herbs for fresh ones in recipes, remember that 1 tablespoon of fresh herbs equals ½ teaspoon of dried herbs or ¼ teaspoon of dried powdered herbs.

Ways to Preserve Herbs

Common Name	Drying	Freezing	Herb Vinegar	Blended with Butter or Oil[1]	Minced, under oil[2]
Angelica	■	■			
Anise	■				
Anise hyssop	■	■			
Basil, sweet	■	■	■[3]	■	■
Bay, sweet	■				
Bergamot (Bee Balm)	■				
Blackberry	■	■			
Boneset	■				
Borage	■				
Burdock, great	■				
Burnet, salad	■	■			
Camomile, German	■				
Caraway	■				
Catnip	■				
Chervil	■				
Chicory	■				
Chives	■		■[4]		
Comfrey	■	■			
Coriander	■				
Costmary	■				
Dandelion, common	■	■			
Dill	■		■[3]	■	
Fennel, sweet	■	■			
Garlic	■		■[3]	■	■
Geranium, scented	■				
Germander	■				
Horehound	■				
Hyssop (Blue flower)	■				

Fines Herbes

Traditionally fines herbes is a mixture of finely ground *fresh* herbs that is sprinkled on food in the last few minutes of cooking or added to the food just before it is served. Fines herbes are usually served in or on sauces, soups, cheese dishes, and egg entrées. Fines herbes can be made from equal parts of any of these herbs: basil, chervil, chives, marjoram, mint, parsley, rosemary, sage, sweet savory, tarragon, and thyme.

Common Name	Drying	Freezing	Herb Vinegar	Blended with Butter or Oil[1]	Minced, under oil[2]
Lamb's-quarters	■	■			
Lavender	■				
Leek	■				
Lemon balm	■				
Lovage	■				
Mallow (Marshmallow)	■				
Marjoram	■				
Mint family	■	■	■[3]		
Mustard	■				
Nasturtium	■		■[3]		
Oregano	■				
Parsley	■	■			
Plantain	■	■			
Purslane	■				
Rosemary	■			■	
Rue	■				
Safflower	■				
Sage	■			■	
Savory	■	■			
Shepherd's purse	■				
Tarragon	■		■[3]		■
Thyme	■				■
Woodruff, sweet	■				
Yarrow	■				

1. Blend 2 cups packed leaves with ½ cup light oil (not olive), or cream ½ cup softened butter with ½ cup minced herbs. Freeze up to 6 months.

2. Refrigerate up to 6 months.

3. See Index for recipe.

4. Use flowers only.

Bouquet Garni

Bouquet garni is a mixture of *fresh or dried* herbs and sometimes spices which are tied in a cheesecloth sack or put in a spice ball and plunged into a stew or soup to be left in the food while it is cooking. The sack and the herbs are removed when the stew or soup is taken from the heat. Bouquet garni can be made from almost any herbs, but we recommend the combinations below for starters. Traditionally bouquet garni includes one fresh herb. If a dried bouquet is used, a few sprigs of fresh parsley should be added to it at the time of cooking.

For meat and vegetable soups and stews, mix together:

1 part thyme	2 parts marjoram
2 parts savory	1 part sage
2 parts rosemary	

For fish stews and soups, mix together:

½ part dill	½ part thyme
1 part lemon balm	¼ part oregano
1 part basil	1 part savory

Herb Tea Combinations

While you can certainly blend any herbs you wish to make your own teas, here are some suggestions for mixes. Some herbs and spices are going to seem more exotic to you than others, but we checked and found them all to be available at our local natural food stores. Hopefully they are available at yours, too.

- blueberry, camomile, and spearmint
- peppermint and camomile
- spearmint and orange peel
- strawberry leaf and almond extract
- orange peel, cinnamon, and clove
- hibiscus, lemon grass, and alfalfa
- orange peel and chicory
- camomile, hops, and valerian (sedative)
- rose hips, ginger, and orange peel (for congestion)
- rosemary, lemon peel, and cinnamon
- cardamom and nettle
- fennel and dandelion root
- peppermint, spearmint, and lemon peel
- blackberry leaves and orange peel
- camomile, rosemary, and borage
- lemon balm, lavender, and rosemary
- wood betony and orange peel
- lemon grass and clove
- pineapple, sage, and ginger
- sage, cinnamon, and nutmeg
- thyme, bergamot, and ginger

Underground Storage

Cold storage, cool storage, underground storage, or root cellaring—they all mean the same thing: storing fruits and vegetables usually in a cool, humid place for anywhere from a couple of weeks to the entire winter, depending upon the food and storage conditions. With the exception of in-the-ground storage, you've got to check the food regularly to adjust temperature and humidity and remove those vegetables and fruits that show signs of spoilage. This is especially true if you're new at keeping food this way and don't have your own particular system down right yet. Even then, you can't be sure that food is just fine without some checking every so often, since outside weather plays a big role, and no two winters are exactly the same.

The importance of quality is at least as significant here as it is with other methods of storage, and in some cases even more important. You know what they say about one rotten apple spoiling the whole bunch. Store only sound fruits and vegetables; diseased or injured ones may be used early in the fall or preserved in some other way by cutting out bad sections and freezing, canning, or drying. Harvesting, in most cases, should be delayed as long as possible so that you have cold weather to help you keep the food cool once it's out of the garden or orchard. All vegetables and fruits to be stored must be handled with great care to avoid cuts and bruises. Food that is really dirty, usually just the root crops, should not be washed, but rather rubbed lightly with a soft cloth or glove or rinsed under gently running water. (Let excess water evaporate before storing.) Do not bring warm-from-the-garden food right into the storage area. Try to chill it first because it'll take a long time for warm food to cool down once in storage, risking the chance of spoilage in the process.

171

To help you determine what cold storage methods will suit you best, let us show you what gets stored how first. Then you can choose from several storage techniques described later in the chapter.

VEGETABLES IN UNDERGROUND STORAGE

Storage times will vary. Times noted here assume constant recommended temperature and humidity, which can best be achieved in a root cellar, either underground or built into a basement. Storage times in other storage areas—like cellar steps, buried boxes and barrels, mounds, and hay bale storage—will vary. Vegetables not listed here do not keep well in underground storage. Refer to the chapters on canning, freezing, drying, and juicing for other methods of preservation.

BEANS, DRIED (LIMA, SOYBEANS, ETC.)

These should be shelled and dried; see the chapter Drying Vegetables and Fruits. To eliminate fumigation, which is practiced by commercial growers in order to kill weevils, simply heat the crop in an oven for 30 minutes to an hour at a constant temperature of 135°F. Spread the beans in pans for this treatment, and do not let the temperature drop or rise significantly. Alternatively, you can freeze the beans at below 0°F for at least 48 hours. After drying thoroughly, place in jars or bags for storage. The temperature of the storage area is not important, but it must be dry.

They will keep indefinitely. For more on drying beans, see page 126.

BEETS

Beets should be harvested in late November, after 30°F nights. Remove most of the greens, which might otherwise rot, but leave a 2-inch stubble. Never cut off the greens right at the root; you might very well cut the vegetable, inviting quick decay. Do not wash. Then pack in containers surrounded by straw or in moist sand for keeping in any outdoor storage pit or root cellar. Place them in an area just above freezing, with 95 percent humidity.

They may also be left in the garden where they grew. If you choose in-the-garden storage, make winter digging easier by covering the rows with leaves or straw, then a layer of plastic, and then another layer of leaves or straw. The plastic keeps the bottom layer of mulch dry so that you won't have a bottom layer of frozen leaves or straw to hack away at when you want to dig up some beets. Make the top cover of mulch a foot deep, and weight it down with chicken wire or rocks.

Beets stored at 32°F will keep 4 to 5 months.

BRUSSELS SPROUTS

Brussels sprouts can be kept in the garden a remarkably long time, sometimes right up to New Year's in areas that enjoy moderate winters. If you are not blessed with such weather, create a basement "garden" of Brussels sprouts so that you can pick them as they mature. To do so, don't pick the sprouts off the stem, but dig up the plants carefully, keeping the roots intact with soil clinging to them. Plant the whole plants upright by burying the roots in a box of soil. Water slightly and pick sprouts as they are ready.

CABBAGE AND CHINESE CABBAGE

Choose a late cabbage variety. Prepare these for storage by removing loose outer leaves. If produce is to be wrapped with newspaper, burlap, or some other material, roots and stems should be removed; otherwise, leave these in place (they will stay crisper longer if you do). Wrapped cabbages should be stored in boxes or bins at a temperature just above freezing in a damp area. When roots and stems are left on, any of the outdoor storage areas that are made all or in part of damp sand or soil are effective. Cabbage emits a strong odor during storage that is usually not welcome in the house, so most people prefer to store it in one of the many outdoor storage arrangements.

Late cabbage stored at 32°F will keep 3 to 4 months. Early cabbage stored at 32°F will keep only a few weeks.

■ Smooth, green cabbage stores better than savoy or red cabbage. Red cabbage tends to store the worst, but savoy is the most cold resistant of them all and therefore is best kept in the garden, not the root cellar, as long as possible in the fall.

CARROTS

Store like beets. Carrots stored at 32°F will keep 6 months.

CELERY

Celery is best maintained by pulling the crop, leaving the roots intact. Do not cut off at ground level. Leave the tops dry; do not wash. The roots should be placed in slightly moist sand or soil, and the plant kept at 32° to 34°F. To avoid odor contamination, do not store with cabbage or turnips. In areas without very severe winters, celery may be left in the ground, covered with a thick layer of leaves or straw.

Celery stored at 32°F will last through the winter.

ENDIVE OR ESCAROLE

This lettuce, which goes under both names, should be kept like celery, with its roots in slightly moist sand or soil.

Stored at 32°F, it will keep 2 to 3 months.

GARLIC

Just like onions, garlic must be cured before storing. Dry garlic thoroughly, making sure bulbs are not in the direct rays of the sun. For large quantities, garlic may be cured in the garden with its tops covering the bulbs. (Small quantities may be bunched and tied or braided and hung in a well-ventilated cool room to store and dry.) Remove tops and roots with knife or shears, leaving 1 inch of root on the bulb, and store like onions, in a cool, slightly humid (60 to 75 percent) area.

Stored in a dry place at 40°F, garlic will keep through the winter.

Garlic should be cured and stored in a cool, dry place. Braiding them in small bunches as shown here keeps them neat and makes it easy to cut off bulbs as you need them.

wrap together three long-stemmed garlic bulbs with twine

begin to braid the stems

work in another bulb every inch or so along the braid

HORSERADISH

Dig out the whole roots and store in a root cellar in damp sand in a bucket or in a plastic bag. They will keep 1 to 2 months this way.

They can also be left in the ground throughout the winter. To make digging easier, cover the rows with about 1 foot of leaves or straw before the ground has frozen. Horseradish roots are thin skinned and do not keep well once dug up, so dig up no more than a 2 weeks' supply at a time.

JERUSALEM ARTICHOKES

Store like horseradish.

KOHLRABI

Remove leaves and roots and store in an area with about 95 percent humidity. Stored at 32°F, kohlrabi will keep 2 to 3 months.

ONIONS

Pull the vegetable when its top falls over, shrivels at the neck of the bulb, and turns brown. Do not leave the vegetable on the ground after pulling because the necks will get sunburned and lose some of their protective outer scales, making them more susceptible to disease and early sprouting in storage. Rather, keep them off the ground in the shade, or bring them inside out of direct sun for about 2 weeks before storing. Then remove the tops and place in bins or string bags, or braid their tops together and store at temperatures ranging from 33° to 45°F in an area with about 60 to 75 percent humidity. Attics often prove to be good storage areas so long as they are cool.

Onions stored in a cool, dry place will keep throughout the winter.

■ Old, clean stockings may look a bit silly filled with onions or garlic, but they do a fine job of keeping them organized and well ventilated. Add an onion (or garlic bulb) or two and then tie a knot in the stocking. Continue to add and tie until the stocking is full, and hang up. Cut off a piece of stocking each time you need an onion; the knot you made above will hold the rest in place.

PARSLEY

This leafy herb is best kept right in the garden, protected from frosts by a layer of mulch 1 to 2 feet deep. You can also cover it with an inverted basket or pail that has been stuffed with chopped cornstalks, leaves, or hay.

PARSNIPS

Store like beets. Stored at 32°F, parsnips will keep 4 to 5 months.

PEAS, DRIED

Store liked dried beans.

PEPPERS, CHILI

If mature, they should be picked just before frost. Chili peppers store best if they are dried first and then stored in a cool, dry place. Do not store them in cellars because they are too damp. To dry chili peppers, pull the plants from the ground and hang them up until dried, or harvest the peppers and string them up on thread or lightweight string to dry.

Once dry, they will keep throughout the winter and maybe longer.

POTATOES

Leave tubers in the ground for about 2 weeks after the vines have died to make sure that the potato skins have toughened up for storage. Then dig the potatoes and store in a dark, humid place at about 40°F. Lower temperatures tend to turn starch to sugar and change the flavor. Never store with apples, which give off ethylene gas, promoting sprouting.

Stored at 40°F at 95 percent humidity, potatoes will last throughout the winter.

PUMPKINS AND WINTER SQUASH

Be sure that they are well matured on the vine before picking. Skin should be hard and not easily punctured with your nail. Cut the fruit off with a portion of the stem attached. Then leave them in the field for 2 weeks after picking if the days are not cold. If weather is near freezing, cure squash instead in a room with a temperature of about 80°F for several days. After curing, place them gently on shelves, separated from each other, in a 50° to 60°F dry place. Examine them every few weeks for mold. If you find some, wipe the squash carefully with a cloth made slightly oily with vegetable oil.

Stored at 50° to 60°F in a dry place, pumpkins and winter squash will keep throughout the winter.

RADISHES, WINTER

Store like beets. Winter radishes stored at 32°F will keep up to 4 months.

RUTABAGAS

Store like beets. You can also wrap them well in plastic wrap that clings tightly to protect their skins and keeps their strong odor contained. Rutabagas stored at 32°F will keep up to 4 months.

SALSIFY

Store like beets. If kept at 32°F, salsify will keep 4 to 5 months.

SWEET POTATOES

Sweet potatoes should be free from injury, and need to be cured for 1 to 2 weeks before final storage in a place that's warm (85° to 90°F) and humid (80 to 90 percent), until the skins toughen and the wounds at either end grow a protective, corky coating.

Stored in a warm, 50° to 60°F room which is well ventilated, with moderate humidity (up to 75 percent), sweet potatoes will keep throughout the winter.

TOMATOES

Ripe tomatoes do not store well, but green ones can be held in storage and be encouraged to ripen there. Harvest all tomatoes that are of good size, be they ripe or still green, just before the first killing frost. Remove tomatoes from plants, wash, and allow to dry before storing. If you remove the stems, there is less likelihood that the tomatoes will puncture one another. Separate green tomatoes from those that show red, and pack green tomatoes no more than 2 deep in shallow boxes or trays for ripening. Green mature tomatoes will ripen in 4 to 6 weeks if held at 55° to 70°F in moderate humidity.

TURNIPS

Store like beets. As with rutabagas, you can wrap turnips in plastic wrap that clings tightly to protect their skins and keeps their odor contained. Turnips stored at 32°F will keep up to 4 months.

FRUITS IN UNDERGROUND STORAGE

Many major fruits do not store well for extended periods of time. Of the ones that do—most notably apples and pears—the varieties vary in keeping quality, and it is best to plan to grow good-keeping varieties if you know that you will be storing many of them.

If you've got a root cellar, partition off a section for fruits, or at least make sure that they are in separate bins, away from vegetables. Fruits should never be stored with potatoes, turnips, or cabbage. The ethylene gas released from apples and pears during respiration can cause potatoes to sprout. Cabbage and turnips can transmit their odor to apples and pears. (Wrapping apples and pears in paper or packing them in maple leaves in barrels is recommended if these fruits must be stored with cabbage and turnips, because these materials will prevent absorption of such odors.)

If the fruit you wish to store is not listed here, refer to the chapters on canning, freezing, drying, and juicing for alternative preservation methods.

APPLES

These are among the better-keeping fruit. The Granny Smith is among the best apples, frequently lasting up to 6 months in cold storage. Next in keeping quality are the Stayman-Winesap and Rome Beauty. Normal storage ranges from 4 to 6 months with these varieties. Jonathan, McIntosh, and Delicious (red or yellow) can be kept for shorter periods. There are other factors that influence keeping qualities of different apple varieties, such as locality (McIntosh apples grown in New England store better than those grown in the Middle Atlantic states), seasonal conditions, maturity when picked, and length of time between picking and storing.

Good keeping qualities are increased with careful handling to prevent bruising. Storage at 32°F and 85 to 90 percent humidity is preferred for most varieties. Wrapping in oiled paper or in shredded paper helps prevent storage scald (a general texture breakdown and browning of the fruit), acknowledged to be the most serious disorder.

GRAPES

Grapes should be cooled to 50°F as soon as possible after picking and spread out in single layers. Allow the fruit to remain in this condition until the stems shrivel slightly. Then place the grapes in trays no more than 4 inches deep in a cellar which is slightly humid and has a temperature of about 32°F. Try to keep separate from other foods, as they can absorb odors, especially from vegetables.

Stored this way, grapes will keep 1 to 2 months. If you have some left over at this point, you can turn them into jams and jellies.

ORANGES

Florida oranges may be kept 4 to 6 weeks at 30° to 32°F with 85 to 90 percent humidity. California oranges can be kept 6 to 8 weeks at 35° to 37°F; they are subject to rind disorders at lower temperatures.

PEACHES

Peaches are fairly perishable and may be stored only several days to 2 weeks in a cool cellar.

PEARS

These can be held from 8 weeks to several months, depending upon variety. Winter Nelis, Anjou, and Easter Beurre keep better than Bosc, Kieffer, Bartlett, Comice, and Hardy.

Pears should be harvested in a condition that would seem to the amateur to be immature. If allowed to begin to yellow on the tree, pears develop hard, gritty cells in the flesh. They should be harvested when the dark green of the skin just begins to fade to a yellowish green, and the fruit begins to separate more or less readily from the tree.

Pears ordinarily do not ripen as satisfactorily at storage temperatures as apples. For highest eating quality they should be removed from storage while they are still comparatively hard and green and ripened at room temperature with a high relative humidity. Pears often keep somewhat better in home storage if wrapped in newspaper or other paper. This fruit, like apples, should be stored at a temperature as close to 32°F as possible and with a high relative humidity, ranging from 85 to 90 percent.

QUINCES

This fruit will keep 2 to 3 months if picked before it is thoroughly ripe and if held in a cool, moist storage area.

GOOD STORAGE CONDITIONS

As you'll see as you read on, you've got a lot of options when it comes to cold storage places: barrels buried underground, straw- and soil-covered outside mounds, Styrofoam chests in unheated garages, basement root cellars, and more. Essentially the storage area can be any convenient place where temperature and humidity are held to the proper level for keeping produce. This means lower-than-usual household or basement temperatures, ranging from 32° to 40°F, and higher-than-usual humidity of 80 percent or more.

Temperature

With the exception of a few fruits and some vegetables, you want to keep your food as close to freezing as possible, without letting any of it freeze. The proper range, as we've said, is 32° to 40°F. Take advantage of cold outside temperatures by not putting up any food for cold storage until temperatures drop outside. And then use those cold temperatures to cool your stored food. In a basement you can do this by opening up a window or vent when you need to lower the temperature, and by insulating the space to keep warmer indoor air out.

If you're storing in a covered trash can or barrel buried outside, you'll want just enough soil over and around the container to keep it cold but not freezing. Styrofoam chests are their own insulators.

Humidity

Most vegetables shrivel rapidly unless stored in a moist atmosphere where the humidity is between 80 and 95 percent. Shriveling may be prevented in barrel and Styrofoam chest storage by layering and covering the food in moist burlap or sphagnum moss. In a storage room you can keep the humidity up either by keeping the air quite moist throughout the room or just by keeping the food itself moist by containing it in rustproof cans, pails, or barrels, and layering and covering it in moist sphagnum moss or something similar.

To keep the air in the storage room moist, you can spray water regularly right on the cement floor or dirt floor. (If you've got a dirt floor, think about building a floor over it made from slats so that you won't be walking around in wet dirt, otherwise known as mud. Better yet, because of the extra surface area it provides, lay down a layer of coarse, well-washed gravel 3 inches thick, and keep that moist.) Whenever the cellar air gets too dry (a hygrometer will tell), sprinkle the floor with water from a watering can. Be careful not to water so much that puddles collect; these could easily encourage the growth of molds and bacteria. You'll have to sprinkle each time the relative humidity of the air falls below 80 percent, which could be quite often. You can also get large shallow pans, place them around the room, and keep them filled with water.

If you can't or don't want to go through the trouble of keeping the entire storage room humid, you can store vegetables particularly likely to shrivel in closed rustproof containers layered between sand, burlap, or sphagnum moss that you have dampened. Large crocks, metal cans, tight wooden boxes, and barrels are all suitable.

Ventilation

Good ventilation is important in keeping airborne bacteria and molds that like humid conditions from thriving. This is not so important when you're just storing a small amount of food in a mound or buried barrel as it is when you're storing a large amount in a storage room. Letting in fresh, cold outside air is also necessary when you want to bring your storage room temperature down to 32° to 40°F.

Light

Keep your fruits and vegetables in the dark. Light will hasten the food's deterioration.

Regular Inspections

Regardless of the method, you've got to check your food to avoid loss from decay, growth, or excessive shriveling. Decaying food should be taken out as soon as noticed. If vegetables start to sprout and grow, the temperature is too high. Foods that begin to shrivel a great deal should be wrapped, placed in closed containers, or sprinkled with water.

WHERE TO STORE YOUR STASH

Before you opt for partitioning off your basement to build a cold storage room there, take a look at some other, simpler ideas. A basement root cellar is lovely to have because it is so convenient to use, but it can be expensive to build and may just cancel out any savings you'd realize from storing your harvest instead of buying fresh from the grocery during the winter. Cold storage areas can be fashioned from anything that will meet the temperature, humidity, ventilation, and no-light requirements. If, after reading about these ingenious ideas for smaller storage spaces, you want a basement storage area, you'll find some information about constructing one at the end of this chapter.

The Cellar Steps

You can make a small but simple and inexpensive storage area by taking advantage of the steps that lead from your basement to the outside basement door. Install an inside door to keep out basement heat at the bottom of the steps. If you want to create an even larger storage area,

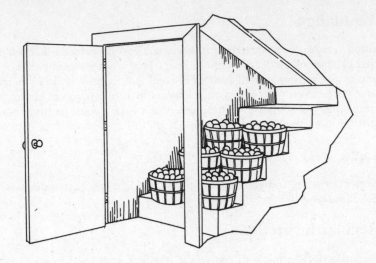

An outside basement entrance can second as a produce storage area. Set baskets of fruits and vegetables on the steps, with those that need the coolest storage conditions at the top, closest to the outdoors.

build inward into the basement, but take care to insulate this extra interior wall space from the rest of the basement. Temperatures in the stairwell will go down as you go up the steps, and a little experimenting will help you determine the best levels for the different crops you are storing. If the air is too dry, set pans of water at the warmest level for extra humidity.

Window Wells

In a pinch, window wells can hold bushels of food over part or all of the winter. Because they are adjacent to the house and below ground level, the temperatures inside them should remain fairly constant throughout the winter, although not nearly as constant as temperatures in the basement or cellar steps that lead to any outside entrance.

Cover the wells with screening and wood. To raise the temperature in very cold weather, open the basement windows and allow some house heat to enter. When the temperature in the window well gets too high, remove food from the top of the well to permit the cold outside air to cool the area. If your basement windows open inward or are the sliding type, you might find it easier to use them to get access to your food, rather than going outside and uncovering the window well.

Styrofoam Chests

Styrofoam picnic chests may be all you need to store a few root crops for a short period of time, so long as you have an unheated space that does not freeze, such as a garage or porch. Prepare vegetables just as you

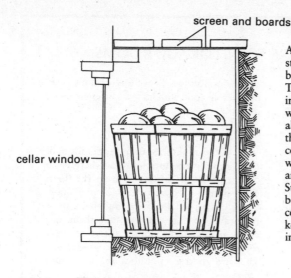

screen and boards

cellar window

Another handy food storage area is a basement window well. The ground acts as an insulator, keeping the window well cold, but above freezing except in the colder parts of the country. Cover the wells with screening and wooden boards (or Styrofoam insulation boards if you have very cold winters) to help keep the temperature inside constant.

would for any other storage area and put a different one in each chest. Put the lid in place and keep out of the sun, which might heat up the chest. Vegetables kept this way will probably be good for several weeks.

Recycling an Old Chest Freezer

We know a few of *Rodale's Organic Gardening* readers who have resurrected out-of-service home chest freezers for cold storage by outfitting them with a vent stack and a slatted floor. Fresh air enters the freezer if you keep the lid open a bit, and the vent stack—if it opens into the freezer near the bottom, under the slatted floor—sucks stale air up and away.

From Truck Body to Storage Room

Many years ago the manager of the Rodale farm built himself a cold storage room from an old truck body. He reinforced the roof with pipes, built in two vent stacks, and buried it into an embankment on a bed of crushed stone. A concrete block entrance finished it off.

Simple, In-the-Ground Storage

When we speak about in-the-ground storage we mean burying or partially burying containers filled with food, preferably a different food in each container. The earth provides insulation and humidity control, and it keeps out light. But it doesn't keep out rodents and other animals; only a secure container can do that. And it's a good idea to provide some

STORAGE CONTAINERS FOR STORAGE ROOMS

Containers need to be clean and easy to clean and air out again after the storage season is over, but they don't have to be new. Here's a great opportunity to put your recycling creativity to work.

Wooden Boxes

Boxes that were originally designed to store and ship apples and other fruits make ideal storage units for root cellars or larger storage areas. Interior packing for stuffing between food may be leaves (dry and crisp), hay, straw, sphagnum moss, or crumpled burlap.

Pails, Baskets, and Watertight Barrels

These can be used just as boxes are. Layer packing material and produce alternately, finishing with 2 inches or more of packing at the top. These containers are used in pit storage areas as well as in larger units.

Plastic and Metal Garbage Cans, Large Pails, and Barrels

Metal cans and pails are fine, so long as they are rustproof. Even diaper pails can be re-cycled for storage. Leave any of these open or cover the food with leaves, sphagnum moss, or straw.

Storage Bins

What we're talking about here are bins built right into storage areas so that there is no chance of water seeping in from the floor. They should be constructed for permanent use 4 inches off the floor. But make them removable so that you can take them outdoors at the end of storage season to wash them thoroughly and give them a good airing. They are good for potatoes and other root crops.

Styrofoam Ice Chests

With their lids removed, these make fine containers. A crack or two will do no harm.

Orange Crates and Mesh Bags

These are excellent for storage of onions and other foods that need good air circulation.

When stacking wooden boxes for storage, be sure to place furring strips between the boxes and the floor and between individual boxes to permit good air circulation.

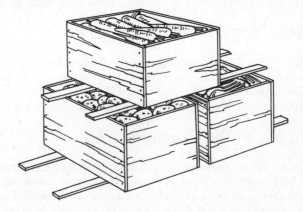

kind of drainage so that water doesn't seep into the container and create problems.

Areas of the country that have moderate winters without extreme temperature swings are the best for this kind of cold storage. The earth acts as a pretty good insulator, but there's no guarantee that it's going to keep out subzero temperatures that will freeze your food, or springlike temperatures that could cause food to spoil.

Buried Box

The box for this storage idea is nothing more than a wooden box, made from 2 × 4s, that is 3 feet wide, 6 feet long, and 2 feet deep. The inside is lined entirely with $\frac{1}{4}$-inch hardware cloth, carefully kept tight—as it *must* be—to keep out rodents. The top is a neat wooden lid. It sits on sloping ground so that excess water promptly drains away.

At harvesttime in late autumn, select beets, carrots, parsnips, potatoes, turnips, and the like. Wash them free of soil, but be careful not to bruise the skin. (Let excess water evaporate before storing.) Put a layer of clean, sharp builder's sand (washed sand) on the pit bottom. Then place a layer of root vegetables on top of this, resisting the temptation to just dump vegetables into the pit. Cover this first layer of root crops with a layer of sand, then continue layering like this until you fill the pit, finishing with a layer of sand. Try to keep different vegetables separate from one another. (A map is mighty helpful in keeping account of where different vegetables are to be found.) For insulation, close the lid and

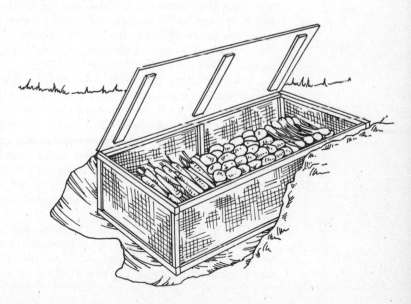

One type of in-ground storage is this buried box. Made of 2 × 4s and hardware cloth, it holds several layers of vegetables, packed in sand to help stabilize humidity and temperature.

Another type of in-ground storage is the barrel pit, made by partially burying a barrel with earth and covering it with straw and wooden boards.

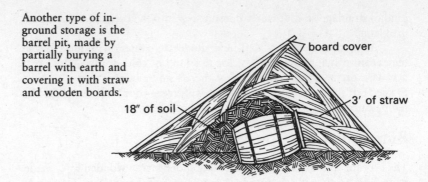

board cover

3′ of straw

18″ of soil

cover it with bales of straw, and then cover this with a plastic sheet to keep out rain and snow.

Once all food is gone from the box, clean everything out and let in sunshine and ventilation over the summer.

Storing with Hay

Building top-of-the-ground areas is quite simple, and the materials used may be turned into mulch or compost after the storage season. They are so quickly and simply made that a number of them can be constructed each storage season. Just lay 2 bales of hay end-to-end, and about 14 inches across from them, place 2 more bales end-to-end parallel to the first 2 (see the illustration). Do this on a well-drained spot, of course. (If you have drainage problems or anticipate problems, play it safe and dig a shallow trench alongside the bottom bales to carry away rain.) Close the ends off by placing a bale across each end. Then put a thin layer of hay in the bottom of the resulting "box."

Do not dump the produce in, and don't mix types of fruits or vegetables. Careless handling will cause bruising, which will quickly cause rot. Cover the top with loose hay and place hay bales across the opening. Then put a stone under each of the top bales to create a litle air space and keep them from completely sealing the opening.

Wait until freezing weather sets in, then remove the stones so that the top bales may completely seal the opening to keep out freezing temperatures. When the weather warms up a bit, you should lift 1 bale and place a stone under it to permit some ventilation. Close again when colder temperatures set in.

The great thickness of the hay bales makes excellent insulation against cold. And enough air seeps through to create ventilation without permitting freezing cold to enter when the stones are removed and the bales on top sit tightly against one another.

Top-of-the-ground storage is suitable for most root crops in most climates, except the coldest ones. Here, a "box" is made from bales of hay, with a hay bale "lid" to cover the food in the center.

No soil is heaped up around them as in most other methods of storage each fall. Access to the stored produce is quickly and easily gained.

Hay Insulation around Tomato Plants

A number of gardeners we know keep their tomatoes ripening on their vines long after frosts have invaded. How to do this is quite simple and highly effective. Make sure you stake your tomatoes, because the stake is necessary to support the hay that you'll be using to insulate the plants from frost. Remove all small tomatoes that have no chance of ripening and keep on the vine only those showing signs of even the faintest blush color. Then tie the vine as compactly as possible to the stake.

Next, push up old hay around and over each tomato plant like the skirt around the waist and legs of a hula dancer. Keep this hay wrap loose and 3 or 4 inches thick, and secure it by wrapping with twine around the tomato plant and its stake. The stake makes a support for the entire arrangement. To pick tomatoes, carefully part the hay without pulling it free. Remove the ripened fruit and replace the hay.

Storing in Garbage Pails

Ten-gallon garbage pails can be converted into storage bins by burying them in holes, leaving their rims above ground. In addition to being inexpensive and readily accessible, the garbage-pail storage bins are water-proof and rodent-proof and store easily over the summer as a compact stack of pails. Here is how to do it.

Wait for several 30°F nights and then start harvesting your root crops. Pull them up and shake off the loose dirt, cut the tops off, and place them in cans *without washing them.* Put a different vegetable in each can. If the skins of the vegetables are dry, you can sprinkle them with water as you put them in the cans, being careful not to form a pool

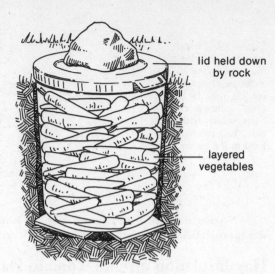

Garbage pails will do for inexpensive in-ground vegetable storage. Bury the pails with the rims at ground level and make layers of one kind of vegetable.

lid held down by rock

layered vegetables

of water at the bottom. Then put the lids on the cans. In colder regions you may want to cover everything with 6 inches of straw, adding more when the ground freezes. During the winter, especially if it is dry, it is a good idea to sprinkle a little water over the vegetables once in a while.

Instead of emptying one pail at a time, take a little from each in turn, so that the level in each can is lowered as the winter progresses. The lower the contents are, the less chance of damage from frost. If the vegetables are 6 to 8 inches below the bin cover, it will take a very severe freezing to cause frost damage because the heat from the earth below the frost line will move into the bins.

Mound Storage

Other gardeners have had success storing root crops and pears and apples right on the ground in a mound storage construction. To make a mound storage, place straw, hay, or dry leaves on the ground, place a particular fruit or vegetable on top of this, and cover with more mulch. Cover the mound with soil, then boarding. A ventilating pipe can be added by placing stakes or a pipe through the center of the pile. This should be capped in freezing weather to prevent cold temperatures from entering. A trench is then dug around the mound for drainage.

Once the pit is opened, all the food should be removed. For this reason it's a good idea to build a few of these, each containing a different vegetable or fruit. It's a good idea to construct your mounds in different places every year, because leftovers in used mounds are usually spoiled.

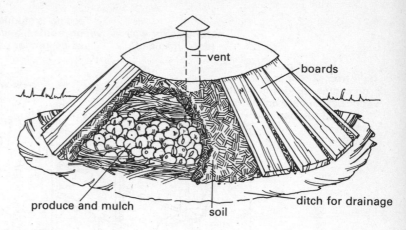

Build several small mound storage areas to hold your produce—just enough in each to last your family 1 or 2 weeks. All food inside should be removed once a mound is opened.

vent

boards

produce and mulch

soil

ditch for drainage

A Built-In Basement Storage Room

The cellars in old houses didn't have dirt floors just because they were cheap and easy to construct. These dirt floors made cellars excellent food storage areas; they helped to keep food cool and moist. These old root cellars have long been used for storage in the colder parts of our country, and some new country houses that have wood-burning stoves or solar heating instead of basement-located central heating are now being built with dirt floor cellars for just this reason. These cellars usually have an outside entrance which can be opened to ventilate the cellar and regulate the temperature inside. Many have insulating material on the ceiling of the cellar to prevent cold air in there from chilling the whole house.

Centrally heated homes with concrete floor basements are generally too warm to be used just as they are for food storage, since most vegetables and many fruits require temperatures between 33° and 40°F. But with a little ingenuity and a little investment, part of just about any basement can be converted into a storage room.

With few exceptions, the most desirable temperature is at or very near 32°F. Except for potatoes, vegetables are not injured at this temperature, and many fruits prefer it. Such temperatures cannot be reached and kept there except in a room that is separated from the rest of the basement, is reasonably well insulated, and has a window or other means of allowing cold outside air in on occasion to cool the space.

A storage room 8 × 10 feet is going to be large enough for most families who plan to store both vegetables and fruits. A room this size will hold 60 bushels of produce. Where practical, the storage room should be located either in the northeast or northwest corner of the basement

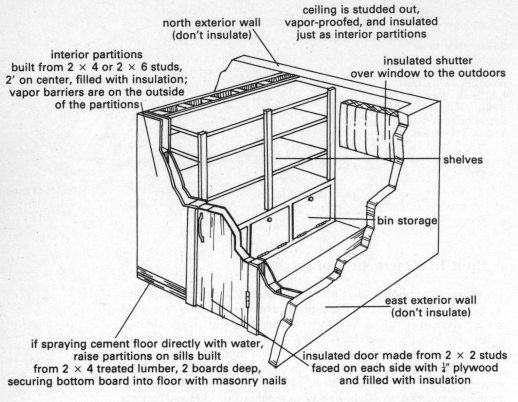

ceiling is studded out,
vapor-proofed, and insulated
just as interior partitions

north exterior wall
(don't insulate)

interior partitions
built from 2 × 4 or 2 × 6 studs,
2' on center, filled with insulation;
vapor barriers are on the outside
of the partitions

insulated shutter
over window to the outdoors

shelves

bin storage

east exterior wall
(don't insulate)

if spraying cement floor directly with water,
raise partitions on sills built
from 2 × 4 treated lumber, 2 boards deep,
securing bottom board into floor with masonry nails

insulated door made from 2 × 2 studs
faced on each side with ¼" plywood
and filled with insulation

The basement often provides needed space for fruit and vegetable storage, but too much heat and too little humidity—frequently found in basements of centrally heated homes—often cancel out its usefulness. A cellar storage room can be constructed by blocking off and insulating a corner of the basement.

and away from the chimney and heating pipes. The northeast corner takes advantage of the two coldest walls of a house; the northwest corner is second best. You have the added advantage when building into a corner of only having to construct 2 interior walls to enclose your storage space.

Ability to maintain a desirable temperature range of 32° to 40°F in the basement storage room depends largely on outside weather conditions. In both early fall and late spring, day temperatures are likely to be higher than you want in the storage area. It stands to reason, then, that during these times you'll keep windows closed. As a general rule, windows should be opened whenever the outside temperature is lower than that in the storage room and the inside temperature is above 40°F. When the temperature in the storage room drops to 32°F, windows should be closed. Place one reliable thermometer inside and another outside the window for guidance.

Since light must be excluded from stored vegetables and fruits, cover the windows with opaque material. Wide wooden louvers fitted to the outside of the window frame aid in excluding light if the window is opened for ventilation in the daytime. Cover louvers, or open windows if louvers are not used, with screening to keep out insects and animals.

You've got a real potential breeding ground for bacteria and molds, and keeping the room clean is going to minimize your chances of spoilage. The walls, ceiling, and floor should be made of a smooth material so that it can be cleaned easily. Built-in bins should be removable. Remove dead leaves, stalks, and the like from under shelves and planking. Spring cleaning is obligatory, and it is best done during dry summer days. Brush shelves, crates, baskets, and other containers in the open air or in the storage room when you have all windows open.

Pickles and Relishes

While the Chinese are said to have invented pickling, it's the Pennsylvania Dutch who made pickles popular in the United States. Every Pennsylvania Dutch cookbook contains dozens of recipes for both fruit and vegetable pickles, and every meal served by the Pennsylvania Dutch is supposed to contain the "seven sweets and seven sours."

Unfortunately, a long history does not necessarily mean a nutritious one. In traditional pickles, the long brining or fermenting process may indeed preserve cucumbers and other foods, but it does nothing to preserve their food value. Water-soluble nutrients leach out into the brine, never to be heard from again. Vitamin B losses can be as high as 75 to 85 percent; and forget the vitamin C—almost 100 percent of it is lost during brining.

But honestly, no one eats pickles to get their daily minimum allowance of any vitamin or mineral. Pickles are hardly mainstays, only condiments, so food loss isn't a big concern. Of bigger concern than food value, however, is the amount of salt in pickles. A raw cucumber contains about 6 milligrams of sodium; a large dill pickle boasts close to 2,000 milligrams. Eat one big pickle, and you're eating all the salt you should eat in an entire day.

With so many people so salt-conscious these days because of the link between salt and high blood pressure, we've added a whole bunch of new recipes to this edition of *Stocking Up* that calls for no salt or just a little of it. We've taken out some of the very high-salt recipes found in the last edition, leaving in our favorites and those that we consider to be pickle classics. The ones we took out were good, but not worth their weight in salt. Because our brined pickles are soaked in brine for a short time, compared with traditional, long-brine pickles, preparation time is often shorter and nutrient loss may be lessened.

193

SALT-FREE PICKLES

A brined pickle needs the salt to control spoilage microorganisms while it soaks in brine for days before canning. But saltless pickles aren't soaked in a brine at all. Rather, they're canned immediately (hence the name, quick pickles). And they're canned in a strong vinegar solution. It's this vinegar that does the preserving; the salt, if any is used, is there for flavor and texture only. Saltless pickles can be just as crunchy as salt pickles if you take care to pick your vegetables when they make the best pickles, which is not necessarily when they are best for fresh eating. Cucumbers and peppers should be underripe—no yellowness on cucumbers, and no tinge of red on peppers. Tomatoes pickle best when they're green, but corn is best pickled when it's mature enough to eat. The secret is getting to know just when each vegetable is ready to be turned into pickles.

The variety you pick can also affect the crunch of your pickles. Take cucumbers for example. The seedless cucumbers that are longer and lighter than the others—often called burpless—stay crunchier be-

---

THERE ARE PICKLES, AND THERE ARE PICKLES

We call any food that's preserved with vinegar or some other acidic solution a pickle or pickled product, but there are actually four distinct kinds of pickled products.

Brined pickles are so-called because they are cured or aged in salt. They are the old-fashioned, traditional pickle. The salt encourages fermentation, or the growth of friendly lactic acid-producing bacteria naturally found on the food. This lactic acid raises the acidity high enough to prevent the growth of any not-so-friendly bacteria that would otherwise cause the food to spoil while it is curing, before it's canned. The scum that sits on top of the brine must be skimmed off each day, making the brining process one that needs daily attention. Sauerkraut is actually a brined pickle and so is the Korean version of sauerkraut, Kim Chee.

Fresh-pack or quick-process pickles are the easiest to prepare. They are sometimes soaked in a low-salt brine for several hours or overnight. If so, they're then drained and processed with boiling-hot vinegar, spices, herbs, or other seasonings, or they are cooked with the spiced vinegar and packed and processed right away. Unlike brined pickles, vinegar, not lactic acid, provides the acidity in these pickles.

Fruit pickles are usually prepared from whole fruits—pears and peaches are good choices—or watermelon rind simmered in spicy, sweet-sour vinegar syrup, then packed and processed.

Relishes are mixed fruits and vegetables which are chopped, seasoned, and then cooked, packed, and processed. Relishes may be hot and spicy or sweet and spicy. Familiar ones include piccalilli, chutneys, corn relish, catsup, and Pennsylvania Dutch chow chow.

cause there is no loss of texture around the seed section. And small, whole cucumbers stay crunchier than larger ones that are cut into spears or slices.

■ Grape leaves and horseradish can give pickles more crunch. To each quart of pickles, add 1 or 2 clean grape leaves *and/or* 1 3 × 1½-inch stick of horseradish; can as usual.

INGREDIENTS

Fruits and Vegetables

Use only tender fruits or vegetables that are in prime condition. Produce should not be more than 24 hours old and should be refrigerated or cooled immediately after picking to keep the food in good shape and to preserve the microorganisms found on fresh food that is crucial for good fermentation during the brine pickling process. Freshness is especially important for cucumbers, which deteriorate rapidly after picking. They should be green and solid and not the least bit yellow. Yellow coloring is a sign that they are overripe; their skin gets tough, seeds grow and hollow areas develop inside.

You may, if you wish, sort the produce for uniform size. Meticulous canners—those who win prizes at county fairs—always sort for uniformity. By using vegetables or fruits of the same size, you can be sure that all the food will cook and cure evenly.

Do not use for pickling whole fruits or vegetables that have mold damage or are injured. Damaged ones can be cut up for relishes or, in the case of cucumbers, sliced for bread and butter pickles, with the injured or moldy part being cut out and discarded. Although proper processing does kill the spoilage organisms in moldy parts, an off-flavor will develop from the mold growth that cannot be masked by spices or herbs.

Fruits and vegetables should be washed thoroughly under running water. Scrub the food with a soft brush or with the palms of your hands. Rinse well so that all soil drains off. It is important that the food be handled gently so that it does not become bruised; this is especially important for cucumbers or for soft fruits like peaches or pears (although the latter two may be picked slightly underripe for pickling). Be sure to remove the blossom ends from cucumbers—the blossoms may be a source of spoilage enzymes.

Produce should never be picked for canning after a heavy rain because it will be waterlogged and therefore not crisp. Wait 12 hours after the rain to pick your fruits and vegetables.

When picking cucumbers, *cut* them from the vines, leaving a short bit of stem on the fruit. If pulled off the vines, they are likely to rot where the stem was broken from the skin.

Drain your produce on a tea towel or on a dish drain. Wipe them dry if you wish, but be careful not to bruise them.

Vinegar

As practical and self-satisfying as it might be to use your own homemade vinegar in your pickles, *don't*. Vinegar should be a good grade of 40 to 60 grain strength (4 to 6 percent acetic acid). The vinegar you make may be some of the best you've ever had, and it is fine for your salads and other cooking. But homemade vinegars vary in acidity, so you'll never know what the acidity of your vinegar is unless you test it, or have it tested. It is much safer to rely on commercial vinegar for your pickles. The only exception to this rule might be when making a pickle that uses 100 percent vinegar as its pickling liquid; in other words, when the vinegar is not diluted with water or any other liquid.

If you'd like to know how to make your own vinegar, turn to page 297.

Cider vinegar has a good flavor and aroma, but it is not good for white pickles such as onion or cauliflower because it may discolor them. Distilled vinegar is clear so there is no chance of discoloration. The fact that it is slightly more acidic than cider vinegar makes little difference.

Honey

Light honeys, such as clover, orange blossom, and alfalfa, are very mild in flavor and for that reason are good to use for canning or pickling. If you use dark, stronger-flavor honeys (like wildflower and buckwheat) in pickling, you might find that their flavor will overpower the flavors of the other ingredients. But, no matter what kind of honey you are using, we suggest that you taste your syrup as you add the honey to it. If you think that the syrup is sweet enough, stop adding honey, although you may not have reached the amount suggested in the recipe. Those amounts are intended to be guidelines only, not hard and fast rules. Your best guides are your taste buds.

Unlike jams and jellies, you can alter a recipe to replace the sugar with honey because in pickles, honey or sugar is added just for taste, not for texture or keeping quality. Pickling recipes in most cookbooks suggest that you boil the syrup, consisting of vinegar, spices, and sugar, for a certain amount of time. This allows the sugar to dissolve completely and also allows the spices to flavor the syrup. If you are altering a recipe that you've found in another book because you want to use honey in it rather than sugar, remember that the heating of honey tends to break down the sugars in honey and cause a change in flavor. Honey can be heated to high temperatures for short periods without causing too much damage, but it will not stand sustained boiling. For this reason, never add the honey to the syrup *before* it is boiled. Instead, boil the vinegar and spices together for the stated time; then add the honey, tasting the syrup as you add it to determine sweetness. (As a rule of thumb, if you are substituting honey for sugar, cut the amount of sweetener by one-half.) Bring the syrup to a boil and pour it over the pickles. Process as directed.

Seasonings

Always use whole, fresh spices or herbs; ground herbs and spices tend to darken pickles. Whole spices or herbs should be tied in a cheesecloth or muslin bag, called a spice bag, or in a stainless steel spice ball and removed before the pickles are packed. Some whole spices, if left in the jar after the pickles are canned, may cause an off-flavor in the product.

Make a habit of tasting the pickling liquid before you can it. You'll find that spices vary considerably in strength, and you can usually correct the seasoning by adding more spices. Unused spices should be kept in airtight jars in a cool place, as heat and humidity tend to sap their quality.

Water

For the best-looking pickles, we recommend that you use soft water. Iron or sulfur in hard water will darken pickles; calcium and other salts can interfere with the fermentation process. If you have especially hard water running from your tap, you might find that one of the bottled waters you can buy in the supermarket is softer water. But be careful, as many

Don't use chlorinated water when making fermented pickles because the chlorine will discourage friendly microbial growth. You can dechlorinate tap water either by leaving it in an uncovered bowl or pot overnight or whizzing it in an uncovered blender for 10 minutes so that the chlorine can oxidize.

OR

bottled waters have a very high mineral content; look for one marked distilled water.

You also shouldn't use chlorinated water in fermented pickles because the chlorine will discourage good friendly microbial growth. Again, bottled water is good to use; none that we know of contain chlorinated water. But you needn't buy your water in bottles just to remove the chlorine. You can dechlorinate your own tap water either by whizzing the water in a blender for 10 minutes, or by leaving a bowl or pot of water uncovered on the kitchen counter overnight.

Salt

You should use plain salt that does not contain iodine or non-caking agents such as those found in regular, iodized table salt. Buy pickling or canning salt. Iodine can cause darkening, and the non-caking agent sometimes causes a cloudy brine. Kosher salt is pure and contains no iodine, but it needs to be measured by weight rather than volume because it is a coarse salt that doesn't pack down in a measuring cup. We don't recommend you use sea salt because it's high in minerals and can darken and discolor foods. And don't use rock salt or any other salt meant to melt ice on sidewalks and driveways; this is not sold for human consumption and shouldn't be used for anything but its intended purpose.

EQUIPMENT

You shouldn't need any more specialized equipment for pickling than you already have to do your other canning chores. Use unchipped enamel or stainless steel for heating liquids you may be using in your pickling. Do not use copper, brass, galvanized iron, or aluminum utensils. These metals react with acids and salts in the liquids and may cause undesirable color changes in the finished product.

For fermenting or brining, use a crock, stone jar, plastic container, unchipped enamel pan, or large glass jar, bowl, or casserole. Use a heavy plate or large glass lid that fits right inside the circumference of the crock and a weight to hold the vegetables in the brine. Clean rocks or a glass jar filled with water can be used as a weight, or a large plastic bag filled with water can serve as both weight and cover (so long as it completely covers the food and is tight against the circumference of the brining container).

If you are using recipes that specify ingredients by weight, a small household scale is a necessity. It is best to use a scale to make large quantities of sauerkraut to insure the proper proportion of salt and cabbage.

To hold down pickles in a crock, use a heavy plate that fits right inside the circumference of the crock and weight it down with a clean rock or other heavy object. You can also fill a large plastic bag with water and set it into the crock. Just be sure the bag completely covers the food and is tight against the mouth of the crock.

CANNING PICKLED FOODS

Pickles are high-acid foods and are therefore canned in a boiling-water bath. Jars should be filled as recommended in the recipes, leaving the necessary headspace. Pack jars firmly and uniformly, but avoid packing so tightly that there's no room for the brine or syrup to fit around and over the food; the brine or syrup is necessary for flavor and good keeping. Wipe the rims and threads of the jar with a clean, hot cloth, and cap. Be careful not to overprocess the pickles; they'll get soft if you do.

In the chapter Canning Vegetables and Fruits, you'll find detailed information on canning jars and boiling-water canners. Turn back to page 82 to refresh your memory. We repeat here for your convenience the steps to follow when boiling-water-bath canning your pickles.

STEP-BY-STEP DIRECTIONS FOR CANNING IN A BOILING-WATER BATH

1. Fill boiling-water canner over half full, deep enough to cover containers completely. There should be about 2 inches of water over the tops of the jars and at least 2 inches of headspace in the canner above the water. Turn on the heat so water can heat up.

2. If you are using jars, wash and rinse them and put them into hot water until needed. Place lids and screw bands in water and bring to a simmer. Remove from heat and leave in hot water until ready to use. If you are using closures that have rubber rings, wash rings in hot water and rinse well. Keep rings in water until ready to use.

continued on page 202

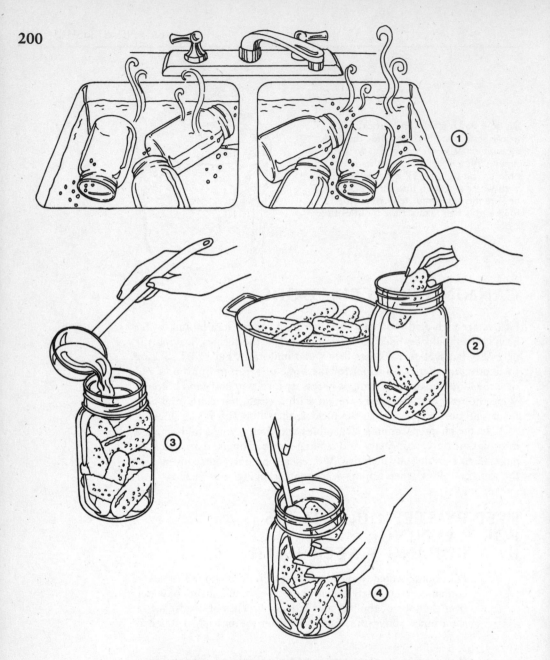

(1) For boiling-water-bath processing of pickles, wash and rinse your jars and keep them in hot water until you need them. (2) Pack the pickles into jars. (3) Add hot syrup or other liquid, leaving recommended headspace. (4) Remove air from the jars by running a nonmetallic spatula along the inside of the glass.

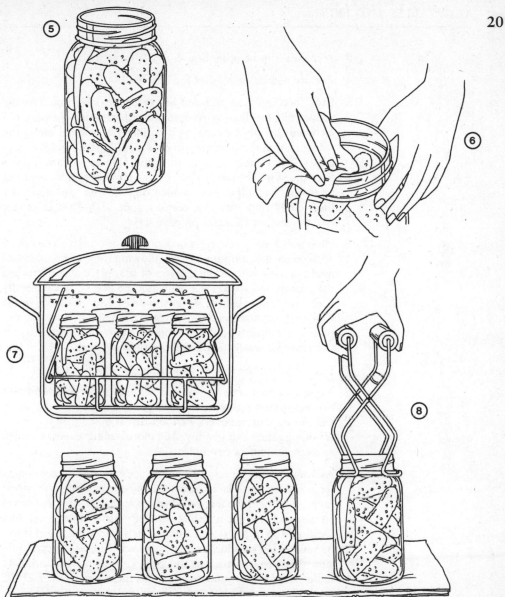

(5) Add more liquid if necessary, making sure all jars have the correct headspace. (6) Wipe the jar rims to pick up any spilled food or liquid, then close jars. (7) Place the jars on a rack in the canner, making sure none are touching. There should be at least 2 inches of water above the jars. (8) When processing time is up, remove the jars and place them on a folded towel or wooden rack. Be sure the jars aren't touching so air can circulate around them and hasten cooling.

3. Prepare syrup or other liquid, if it is to be used.

4. Prepare pickles or relishes for canning.

5. Pack food into jars and add hot syrup or other liquid as the recipe calls for, leaving recommended headspace. Remove the air from the jars by running a nonmetallic spatula along the side, pressing the food as you do so. Add more liquid, if necessary; the correct amount of liquid helps to create a good vacuum. Wipe the jars, paying particular attention to any food or liquid that might have spilled onto the lid; any food left there could ruin your chances of a good seal. Then close jars (see the section Closures on page 84).

6. Place the closed jars upright on a rack in the canner so that none of them are touching any others, allowing the water to circulate freely. If there is room for 2 layers of jars, place a rack between the 2 levels and stagger the containers so that none are directly over any of those below. Water should be 1 to 2 inches over the tops of the containers. Add water, if needed. Be careful not to pour water directly on the containers. Allow 2 inches headspace in canner for water to boil without running over.

7. Put the lid on the canner and bring the water to boiling.

8. *Begin to count time as soon as the water starts to boil* and process for time recommended in your recipe. Leave the lid on the canner, but remove it periodically to make sure the water is boiling gently and steadily. Add more boiling water as needed to keep containers covered.

9. As soon as the processing time is up, remove the containers from the canner. Place them upright, out of drafts, on wood racks, a wooden board, or several thicknesses of a dry towel so that they are not in direct contact with anything cold, like a countertop or metal rack, or anything damp, like a wet towel or sink, either of which might cause very hot jars to crack. Be sure that the jars are not touching so that air can circulate under, over, and around each one. Let them cool by themselves; don't tamper with them until they are cool.

10. The last bit of air is exhausted as the food cools, creating that vacuum you want. The common 2-piece lid is self-sealing; you'll hear a reassuring high-pitched sound of the metal lid snapping down on the glass rim when the vacuum is complete and the jar seals itself. You can tell if the 2-piece lid is sealed by pressing down on the center of the lid. If it is down already or stays down when pressed, the seal is good. If it fails to stay down,

reprocess the jar, place in the refrigerator and use within the next few days.

If you're using caps that don't self-seal, complete the seals as soon as you take them out of the canner (see the section Closures on page 84). To check for a good seal after the jars have cooled down, tilt the jar so that the food is up against the seal. If you don't notice any air bubbles or any leakage there, you can assume you've got a good seal.

Storing Pickles

Pickled products should be stored in cool, dark, dry places. Extreme fluctuations of temperature may cause a breakdown of texture, resulting in an inferior product. It might also cause enough expansion of the product to break the jar or the seal. Light causes products to fade and become less appetizing in appearance. This does not mean that the product is spoiled, however.

A storage area in a basement is fine if it is cool, dry, and dark. Do not store canned products like pickles in a root cellar or in a place where you're storing whole vegetables or fruits that need to be kept moist. Dampness may rust enclosures and cause spoilage.

We found that our canned pickles kept fine for a year, but after that their flavor started to suffer. Most spices tended to lose their punch, and a few, notably ginger, got stronger.

BRINE CURING

To refresh your memory, brined pickles are those that have been held in a salty solution anywhere from overnight to a number of weeks before they are eaten or canned. Just about any vegetable can be cured this way: cabbage, green or yellow beans, cucumbers, cauliflower, onions, broccoli, green tomatoes, Jerusalem artichokes, and carrots.

By covering such foods with a brine and keeping them in a moderately warm room, you can create ideal conditions for the lactic acid-forming bacteria existing on the food surface to feed upon the sugar naturally present in the food. The lactic acid will continue to grow (or ferment) until enough has formed to kill any bacteria present that would otherwise cause the food to spoil. Lactic acid, which aids digestion and helps to kill harmful bacteria in the digestive tract, gives the brine food a slightly acid, tangy flavor.

You'll find a couple of recipes later in this chapter that use such a brine cure. Euell Gibbons's dill crock and our version of it also use the brining technique. We have also added a salt-free dill crock recipe.

EUELL GIBBONS'S DILL CROCK

Nationally known author and expert on wild foods Euell Gibbons wrote in *Organic Gardening and Farming* a number of years ago about his own adventures with pickled vegetables, using his "dill crock." This method has great appeal because it not only brines the vegetables, but flavors them as well. Gibbons wrote:

Naturally, I got started at this tasty sport with wild foods. A nearby patch of wild Jerusalem artichokes had yielded a bumper crop, and I wanted to preserve some. I used a gallon-size glass jar, getting all of these jars I wanted from a nearby school cafeteria.

Packing a layer of dill on the bottom of the jar, I added several cloves of garlic, a few

Nearly any kind of firm, crisp vegetable is good in a dill crock. Use your imagination along with whatever's on hand, fresh from the garden. Euell Gibbons's dill crock is made with dill, garlic, red tabasco peppers, Jerusalem artichokes, winter onions, cauliflower, sweet red peppers, and nasturtium buds in a brine, covered with a weighted lid, and left to sit for 2 weeks before eating.

red tabasco peppers, then some cored and peeled Jerusalem artichokes, plus another layer of dill. With room still left, I looked around for other things to add. The winter onions had great bunches of top sets, so I peeled a few and made a layer of them. Then I dug up some of the surplus onions and used the bottom sets—shaped like huge cloves of garlic—to make still another layer. I then put in a layer of cauliflower picked apart into small florets, and added some red sweet pepper cut in strips, along with a handful or so of nasturtium buds.

This was all covered with a brine made by adding three-fourths of a measure of salt to 10 measures of water. I added some cider vinegar too, but only $\frac{1}{4}$ cup to the whole gallon. I topped the whole thing with some more dill, set a small saucer weighted with a rock on top to keep everything below the brine, and then let it cure at room temperature.

After 2 weeks I decided it must be finished. The Jerusalem artichokes were superb, crisp and delicious. The winter onions, both the top and bottom sets, were the best pickled onions I ever tasted. The cauliflower florets all disappeared the first time I let my grandchildren taste them, while the nasturtium buds make better capers than capers do.

The next summer I determined to get started early and keep a huge dill crock running all season. Any size crock can be used, from 1 gallon up. I use a 10-gallon one and wish it were bigger. Never try to use a set recipe for a dill crock, but rather let each one be a separate and original "creation." I plant plenty of dill, and keep planting some every few weeks so I'll always have some on hand at just the right stage.

What is good in a dill crock? Nearly any kind of firm, crisp vegetable. Green beans are perfect, and wax beans also very good. These are the only two things cooked before being added to the brine, and they should be cooked not more than about 3 minutes. And small green tomatoes are great. Nothing else so nice ever happened to a cauliflower. Just break the head up into small florets, and drop it into the dilled brine. In a week or two—the finest dilled cauliflower pickle ever tasted.

If you have winter onions, clean some sets and put them in the crock. It's a tedious job, but the results are worth it. Not only do they add to the flavor of all the rest of the ingredients in the jar, but the little onions themselves are superb. If you don't have winter onions, you can sometimes buy small pickling onions on the market and use them. If not, just take ordinary onions and slice them crosswise into three or four sections. These will come apart after curing, but so what? They are simply great pickled onion rings. I've even cut off the white part of scallions and thrown them in the brine, with some success, and one late-fall dill crock was flavored with white sections of leek, which did it wonders.

To preserve these pickles, pack them in hot, scalded quart jars along with some fresh dill. Strain the brine, bring to a boil, and pour over pickles, leaving $\frac{1}{2}$-inch headspace. (You can also make new brine using $\frac{1}{2}$ cup salt and 4 cups vinegar to 1 gallon water, but the old brine is much more flavorful.) Seal and process in a boiling-water bath for 15 minutes.

Brine-Cured Dill Crock
(with salt)

4 handfuls fresh dill
1 gallon glass jar or crock
3 cloves garlic, peeled
3 hot chili peppers, washed, slit, and seeds removed
1 pound Jerusalem artichokes, sliced into ½-inch rounds
6 scallions, cut in half; use tops also
½ head cauliflower, broken into florets

½ pound green beans, whole
3 medium-size carrots, cut in diagonal slices
3 stalks celery, cut in diagonal slices
10 small pickling onions
⅓ cup salt
8 cups white vinegar, approximately

Place 1 handful of dill on the bottom of a 1-gallon glass jar or crock. Add garlic and peppers. Top with the Jerusalem artichokes. Add a layer of dill. Place scallions on the dill. On top of this place a layer of cauliflower. Next, add a layer of beans. Next, a layer of dill. The carrots are the next layer, followed by the celery, topped with whole small onions. Top all with remaining dill.

Combine salt with 2 cups vinegar. Mix to dissolve salt. Pour into jar or crock. Add remaining 6 cups vinegar to cover ingredients. Be sure all vegetables are covered with vinegar solution. Crunch up clear plastic wrap to push vegetables down and cover with a weight.

Let stand on kitchen counter 4 to 6 days, then refrigerate. It will keep up to a week. Drained, it will keep 2 to 3 months. Drain before serving.

Yield: 1 gallon

Dill Crock
(without salt)

The rice bran in this recipe helps to keep the vegetables crisp without salt. Judith Hurley, at the Rodale Food Center, came across the use of rice bran, or *nuka*, in a book on Japanese food preservation and tried it. It worked! Rice bran is sold in many natural food stores. You might also check in an Asian market.

4 handfuls fresh dill
1 gallon glass jar or crock
3 cloves garlic, peeled
3 hot chili peppers, washed, slit, and seeds removed
4 tablespoons rice bran (*nuka*)
1 pound Jerusalem artichokes, peeled and quartered
9 grape leaves
6 spears horseradish root, 3 × 1½ inches

6 scallions, cut in half; use tops also
½ head cauliflower, broken into florets
½ pound green beans, whole
3 medium-size carrots, cut in diagonal slices
3 stalks celery, cut in diagonal slices
10 small pickling onions
1 gallon cider vinegar

Place 1 handful of dill on the bottom of a 1-gallon glass jar or crock, add garlic, peppers, and 1 tablespoon rice bran. Top with Jerusalem artichokes, 3 grape leaves, and 2 of horseradish root spears. Next, add the scallions, a handful of dill, and 1 tablespoon rice bran. On top of this place a layer of cauliflower, then a layer of beans. Now another layer of 3 grape leaves, 2 horseradish root spears, and 1 tablespoon rice bran. The carrots are the next layer. Then a layer of dill, 3 grape leaves, and 2 horseradish root spears. Add the celery in a layer, and top with the small onions. Complete with a handful of dill and the remaining tablespoon rice bran. Cover with vinegar.

Place a plastic bag filled with water on top of jar or crock to keep ingredients immersed for 9 days.

Drain and refrigerate. It will keep for 2 to 3 months.

Yield: 1 gallon

IF YOUR PICKLES FAIL

If for some reason your pickles don't turn out the way you'd like them to, too bad this year. Hopefully you can learn from your mistakes and not do the same thing wrong next year. Here are some common causes of pickle failure and how you can correct them:

If your pickles are *shriveled*, you may have used too strong a vinegar or salt solution at the start of the pickling process. Shriveling may also be caused by overcooking or overprocessing. Pickles may not look too good, but they're okay to eat.

Hollowness in cucumber pickles usually results from one or several of the following: poorly developed cucumbers, cucumbers that were too ripe, holding the cucumbers too long before pickling, too rapid fermentation, or too strong or too weak a brine during fermentation. Again, such pickles are safe to eat.

SIGNS OF SPOILAGE—THROW IT OUT

- A jar that is soiled or moldy on the outside indicates that food seeped out during storage, which means that air and bacteria, yeasts, and molds could have seeped in. (Jars right out of the canner might be a bit soiled from some of the liquid that was exhausted out with the air; this is okay, so long as half the contents of the jars aren't floating outside in the canning water! If you've wiped the jars as you should have done, the jars would have gone clean into storage and any food on the outside of the jars now is *not* okay.)

- A significant change in color, most notably a much darker color, can mean spoilage. Some brown, black, or gray discoloring may be due to minerals in the water or in the cooking utensils; while it may detract from the looks of the food, there is no harm done otherwise. For instance, pickled cauliflower may turn pink; this is a result of a red pigment in the vegetable released by the acid in the vinegar. Commercially, the bleaching agent sulfur dioxide is used to prevent the problem. It's not harmful to eat such cauliflower, and not all varieties turn pink in vinegar.

- A change in texture, especially if the food feels slimy, is a sure sign that the food isn't fit to eat.

- Mold in the food or inside the lid— sometimes nothing more than little flecks—is not a good sign.

- Small bubbles in the liquid or a release of gas, however slight, when you open the can means foul play. Sometimes you get a strong message: Liquid actually spurts out when you release the seal. Other times the gas is more subtle.

Dark pickles are not spoiled pickles; however, if you pride yourself on the looks of your home-canned products, darkening can be annoying. Darkening may result from the use of too much spice, iodized salt, overcooking, hard water containing lots of minerals (especially iron), iron utensils, or cider vinegar instead of white (distilled) vinegar. Go ahead and eat the pickles, but make adjustments next time.

Soft or slippery pickles are spoiled pickles. *Do not eat them.* This condition is generally a result of microbial action which caused the spoilage; it is irreversible. Proper processing should halt microbial activity, but if it happens, here are some things you might have done wrong: used too little salt or acid, failed to cover your cucumbers with brine during fermentation, allowed scum to scatter through the brine during fermentation, processed the pickles for too short or too long a time, did not seal the jar airtight, or used moldy garlic or spices. Also, if you failed to remove the blossoms from the cucumbers before fermentation, they may have contained fungi or yeasts responsible for the softening action.

And then there are improper canning or storage procedures that can result in spoiled canned food of any kind. We discussed such problems back in the chapter Canning Vegetables and Fruits, but we repeat the box here. If you notice any of these conditions in your pickles or relishes, *do not eat the food; destroy it.* Burn the food or bury it deep enough so that no animal can uncover it and eat it. There's a remote chance that you could contaminate the water supply by flushing it down the toilet or kitchen drain or garbage disposal, so boil it rapidly for 15 minutes beforehand. Be particularly careful about sterilizing jars, screw bands, and any other equipment that might have come in contact with the food. Wash your hands with soap and hot water and rinse well.

SAUERKRAUT

Sauerkraut used to be one of the only winter sources of vitamin C and was used as a cure for scurvy on sea voyages. In addition, like other cured vegetables, sauerkraut contains beneficial lactic acid.

Sauerkraut is cured in salt, but it is packed in a dry salt, not covered in a saltwater solution, because the cabbage contains a great deal of water and forms its own brine when the salt draws out water from its shredded leaves.

After fermentation, sauerkraut can either be canned in a boiling-water bath or stored in the container in which it was made. It cannot be frozen. If you're just keeping it in the container, be sure to keep it in a cool place. Temperatures just above freezing are best. Low temperatures will discourage the growth of surface scum. Still the kraut should be checked periodically and scum should be removed.

Tight-forming head lettuces can be used instead of cabbage to make a milder form of "sauerkraut," and although we've never made it ourselves, we have heard of people who have used shredded carrots and turnips instead of cabbage.

Sauerkraut

This recipe is based on one prepared by the U.S. Department of Agriculture. White winter cabbage should be used.

15 pounds cabbage
9 tablespoons pickling salt

Harvest winter cabbage and let sit at room temperature for one day. Remove outer leaves and any undesirable portions from firm, mature heads of cabbage; wash and drain. Cut into halves or quarters; remove the core. Use a shredder or sharp knife to cut cabbage into thin shreds about the thickness of a dime.

In a large container, thoroughly mix 3 tablespoons salt with 5 pounds shredded cabbage. Let the salted cabbage stand for several minutes to wilt slightly; this allows packing without excessive breaking or bruising of the shreds.

Pack the salted cabbage firmly and evenly into a large, clean crock. Using a wooden spoon, tamper, or your hands, press down firmly until the juice comes to the surface. Repeat the shredding, salting, and packing of cabbage until the crock is filled to within 3 or 4 inches of the top.

Cover cabbage with a clean, thin white cloth (such as muslin) or a piece of plastic wrap and tuck the edges down against the inside of the container. Cover with a plate that just fits inside the container so that the cabbage is not exposed to the air. Put a weight on top of the cover so the brine comes to the plate but not over it. Two glass jars or two heavy-duty plastic bags filled with water make a good weight. The amount of water in the plastic bag or jars can be adjusted to give just enough pressure to keep the fermenting cabbage covered with brine.

Formation of gas bubbles indicates fermentation is taking place. A room temperature of 68° to 72°F is best for fermenting cabbage. Fermentation is usually completed in 4 to 6 weeks.

What You Did Wrong
If Your Sauerkraut Spoiled

Spoilage of sauerkraut is indicated by undesirable color, off-odors, and soft texture. If your kraut has spoiled, here's what you might have done wrong:

Soft sauerkraut may be due to insufficient salt. Try using more salt the next time. High temperatures during fermentation may cause softness, too. Uneven distribution of salt may also be a cause of softness—be sure that your salt is well mixed with the kraut next time. Air pockets caused by improper packing may make your kraut soft. Your crock or jar may have had air spaces that caused poor fermentation; this can be remedied by packing the jar or crock tightly and being sure to weight it properly.

Pink kraut is caused by the growth of certain types of yeast on the surface of the kraut. These yeasts may grow if there is too much salt, if there is an uneven distribution of salt, or if the kraut is improperly covered or weighted during fermentation.

Rotted kraut is usually found at the surface where the cabbage has not been covered sufficiently to exclude air during fermentation. This

Darkness in kraut may be caused by improperly trimmed cabbage. It may also be caused by insufficient brine in the fermenting process. Be sure that the brine completely covers the fermenting cabbage. Exposure to air or a long storage period in the crock after fermentation is complete may also result in darkened kraut. Another cause of darkening may be high temperatures during fermentation, processing, or storage.

PICKLES

Kosher Dills

These no-salt dills use grape leaves and horseradish to retain their crispness.

4½ cups white vinegar
4½ cups water
14 cloves garlic
7 grape leaves
7 spears horseradish root,
   3 × 1½ inches
4 pounds cucumbers 4 inches
   long, washed, dried, and
   cut in half lengthwise
14 sprigs fresh dill
7 teaspoons mustard seeds
21 peppercorns
7 whole cloves

In a medium-size enamel or stainless steel saucepan boil together the vinegar, water, and garlic. Reserve garlic.

Meanwhile, place 1 grape leaf and 1 horseradish spear into each hot, scalded pint jar. Place cucumbers into jars. (Cutting the cucumbers in half instead of into spears insures a crisp pickle. If you want spears, cut them further at serving time.) To each jar add 2 sprigs dill, 1 teaspoon mustard seeds, 3 peppercorns, and 1 clove. Pour boiling liquid into jars, allowing ¼-inch headspace. Add 2 cloves reserved garlic to each jar. Cover and turn once to disperse spices. Seal and process in a boiling-water bath for 15 minutes.

Yield: 7 pints

Variation

Use extra vinegar instead of a vinegar-water mixture for liquid, and processing can be cut to 10 minutes.

Old-Fashioned Cucumber Chunks

These pickles shouldn't be canned but rather kept in the refrigerator for up to 2 months.

1 gallon cucumbers, washed,
      dried, and cut into 1-inch
      pieces
1½ cups salt
1 gallon and 3 cups water
5 cups vinegar
2 tablespoons Rodale's Whole
      Pickling Spice (see below)
1 cup honey

Put cucumbers into a crock or large enamel or stainless steel container. Dissolve salt in 1 gallon water and pour over cucumbers. Cover with plate to weight down so that cucumbers remain submerged in brine. Let stand overnight.

Drain and rinse. Place cucumbers in large enamel or stainless steel pot. Pour vinegar and remaining 3 cups water over cucumbers, add cheesecloth bag containing pickling spice, and bring to a boil. Simmer 10 minutes. Remove spice bag. Add honey and stir well. Bring to a boil.

Pack pickles into hot, scalded jars and pour hot syrup over them. If there is not enough liquid to cover pickles, add more vinegar.

Yield: 3 quarts and 1 pint

Rodale's Whole Pickling Spice

2 tablespoons bay leaves
1 tablespoon cardamom seeds
1 tablespoon dried ginger root
1 stick of cinnamon
1½ whole dried chili peppers (more can be
      used if you like it hot)
2 tablespoons mustard seeds
1 tablespoon whole allspice
1 tablespoon coriander
1 tablespoon peppercorns

Crush bay leaves. If you have cardamom in the pod, pound it with a mortar and pestle to extract seeds. Also pound dried ginger root and break cinnamon stick into small pieces to distribute flavors. Dried chilies can be broken or crushed into small pieces.

Combine bay leaves, cardamom seeds, ginger, cinnamon, chili peppers, mustard seeds, allspice, coriander, and peppercorns. Blend, and store in an airtight container. Use as directed in recipes.

Yield: 4 ounces

Cucumber Oil Pickles

1 tablespoon peppercorns	2 medium-size onions, thinly sliced
2 tablespoons mustard seeds	
2 tablespoons celery seeds	1 cup honey
8 cups vinegar	$\frac{1}{2}$ cup olive oil
2 quarts ice cubes	
25 medium-size cucumbers, washed, dried, and thinly sliced	

Place peppercorns, mustard seeds, and celery seeds in a cheesecloth bag and put in a stainless steel or enamel pot with vinegar and ice cubes. Add cucumbers and onions. Let stand all night in a cool place. Next day drain, reserving liquid.

Place liquid in a kettle, add honey and oil; add drained cucumbers and onions. Simmer until cucumbers change color. Bring to a boil.

Pack cucumbers into hot, scalded pint jars. Pour hot liquid over cucumbers, leaving $\frac{1}{4}$-inch headspace. Seal and process for 10 minutes in a boiling-water bath.

Yield: 7 to 8 pints

Crisp Lime Pickles

This is a no-salt bread and butter variation.

$3\frac{1}{2}$ pounds cucumbers, sliced $\frac{1}{2}$ inch thick	3 cups honey
1 cup pickling lime*	6 teaspoons Rodale's Whole Pickling Spice (see page 212)
1 gallon water	
6 cups white vinegar	

In a large enamel, stainless steel, or glass bowl, soak cucumbers in lime and 1 gallon water overnight. Stir occasionally to disperse lime. Wash cucumbers thoroughly in cold running water. Soak 4 hours in ice water, then drain completely.

In a medium-size enamel or stainless steel saucepan bring vinegar and honey to a boil. Meanwhile, pack cucumbers into hot, scalded pint jars, and place one teaspoon pickling spice in each jar. Pour the hot vinegar mixture over cucumbers, leaving $\frac{1}{2}$-inch headspace. Seal and process in a boiling-water bath for 10 minutes.

Yield: 6 pints

*Pickling lime is a fine white powder otherwise known as calcium hydroxide. It's used in commercial pickles to keep them crisp without salt.

Salt-Free Bread and Butter Pickles

15 medium-size cucumbers	2 teaspoons ground ginger
5 medium-size onions	½ cup honey
5 cups vinegar	1 teaspoon turmeric
2 teaspoons celery seeds	2 teaspoons mustard seeds

Thinly slice cucumbers and onions.

Make a spiced vinegar using vinegar, celery seeds, ginger, honey, turmeric, and mustard seeds. Let spiced vinegar come to a boil in an enamel or stainless steel saucepan, add cucumbers and onions, and bring to boiling point.

Pack cucumbers and onions in hot, scalded pint jars. Then pour hot vinegar over them, leaving ¼-inch headspace. Seal and process 10 minutes in a boiling-water bath.

Yield: 11 pints

Fresh-Pack Dill Pickles
(unsweetened)

These pickles should not be canned but should be kept in the refrigerator for up to 2 months.

5 pounds cucumbers	12 teaspoons mustard seeds
6 cups vinegar	18 sprigs fresh dill (you may
9 cups water	substitute 9 tablespoons
2 tablespoons Rodale's Whole	dried dill or 6 tablespoons
Pickling Spice (see page	dill seeds)
212)	

Wash cucumbers and drain. Cover with cold water and ice cubes. Weight down with heavy plate to keep cucumbers covered with water. Refrigerate overnight.

Combine vinegar, water, and pickling spice tied in cheesecloth bag. Heat to boiling.

Pack cucumbers in hot, scalded quart jars. Add 2 teaspoons mustard seeds and 3 sprigs fresh dill or 1½ tablespoons dried dill or 1 tablespoon dill seeds to each jar. Cover with boiling liquid.

Yield: 6 quarts

Sour Pickles

2 quarts and 1 cup vinegar
8 spears horseradish root,
   3 × 1½ inches
½ cup honey
2 tablespoons whole allspice
2 tablespoons mustard seeds
1 small blade of mace or ½
   teaspoon powdered mace

4 pounds cucumbers, washed,
   trimmed, and cut into
   2-inch lengths
4 sticks of cinnamon
4 bay leaves
12 peppercorns
8 cloves garlic

Combine vinegar, horseradish spears, and honey in a medium-size enamel or stainless steel saucepan. Place allspice, mustard seeds, and mace in a cheesecloth bag. Drop spice bag in vinegar mixture and simmer, covered, for 15 minutes.

Distribute cucumber chunks, cinnamon sticks, bay leaves, peppercorns and garlic evenly among hot, scalded 4-quart canning jars. Remove horseradish spears from vinegar mixture and divide evenly among jars. Pour the simmered mixture into the jars, taking care to cover all pieces of cucumber, but leaving ½-inch headspace. Seal and process 10 minutes in a boiling-water bath.

Yield: 4 quarts

Note: For half-sour pickles, use ¾ cup honey.

Freezer Pickles

2 pounds cucumbers, washed
   and thinly sliced
1 large onion, thinly sliced
½ cup vegetable oil
1½ cups white vinegar

½ cup honey
½ cup water
2 cloves garlic, crushed
8 sprigs fresh dill

Layer cucumbers and onions in 2 1-quart freezer containers.

In a medium-size bowl whisk together oil, vinegar, honey, water, and garlic. Blend well.

Place dill on top of cucumbers. Pour liquid into containers leaving 2-inch headspace.

Cover and place in freezer. These pickles will keep 3 months in the freezer; they may also be stored 1 week in the refrigerator.

Yield: 2 quarts

Refrigerator Sun Pickles

The sun "cooks" these quick dills, allowing the vinegar and spices to work more quickly to spice them.

cucumbers to fill a 1-gallon
  wide-mouth glass jar
2 to 3 quarts vinegar (white
  or cider)*
2 sprigs fresh dill
3 cloves garlic, chopped

Wash cucumbers. Any size cucumbers can be used, so long as they are not overripe. Prepare cucumbers by cutting ¼ inch off each end. If the cucumbers are large, use a sharp paring knife and slice through the cucumber, making deep slashes beginning ¼ inch from one end to within ¼ inch of the other end. These slashes through the cucumber enable the vinegar to penetrate the cucumber and also make it easier to divide the pickle into spears.

Pack prepared cucumbers into jars vertically. Don't overpack. Add vinegar, dill, and garlic until the vinegar completely covers the cucumbers.

Expose the jar to sunlight for 2 days for a total of at least 14 hours of sunlight. Chill and eat.

These pickles must be stored in the refrigerator.

Yield: 1 gallon

*If you wish to use salt, add 3 tablespoons salt to 2 quarts water and decrease vinegar to 1 quart.

Mixed Mustard Pickles

4⅔ cups white vinegar
1 cup honey
3 tablespoons celery seeds
4 tablespoons mustard seeds
½ teaspoon turmeric
4 pounds pickling cucumbers,
  3 to 4 inches long, washed
  and cut into chunks
1½ pounds small onions, peeled
  and halved

2 cups celery, cut into 1½-inch
  pieces
2 cups carrot sticks
½ pound green beans, whole
2 cups sweet red peppers, cut
  into 1-inch squares
2 cups cauliflower florets

In an enamel or stainless steel pot combine vinegar, honey, celery seeds, mustard seeds, and turmeric. Heat to boiling. Add cucumbers, onions, celery, carrots, beans, peppers, and cauliflower; heat just to boiling.

Fill hot, scalded pint jars with vegetables. Then cover with the hot liquid, leaving ½-inch headspace. Process for 5 minutes in a boiling-water bath.

Yield: 10 pints

Sweet Gherkins

6¼ pounds immature cucumbers, 1½ to 3 inches long
6 cups cider vinegar
¾ teaspoon turmeric
2 teaspoons celery seeds
2 teaspoons Rodale's Whole Pickling Spice (see page 212)
8 sticks of cinnamon, 1 inch long
½ teaspoon fennel seeds
2 cups honey

Wash cucumbers, place in a large container, and cover with cold water and ice cubes. Refrigerate 5 hours. Drain.

Place cucumbers in a large enamel or stainless steel pot. Add vinegar, turmeric, and cheesecloth bag containing celery seeds, pickling spice, cinnamon, and fennel seeds. Bring to a boil. Add honey. Bring to a boil again.

Pack cucumbers into hot, scalded pint jars. Cover with boiling liquid, leaving ¼-inch headspace. Seal and process 10 minutes in a boiling-water bath.

Yield: 10 to 11 pints

Refrigerator Zucchini Pickles

4 pounds small zucchini
1 pound small white onions
1 quart cider vinegar
½ cup honey
2 teaspoons celery seeds
2 teaspoons turmeric
2 teaspoons dry mustard
2 teaspoons mustard seeds

Cut unpeeled zucchini into thin slices, like cucumbers. Peel onions and slice thin. In an enamel or stainless steel saucepan combine remaining ingredients. Bring to a boil and pour over vegetables. Let stand 1 hour.

Return to heat, bring to a boil, and cook 3 minutes. Pour into hot, scalded jars. Cover tightly and refrigerate.

Yield: 4 pints or 2 quarts

PICKLED VEGETABLES

Pickled Beets

1 gallon small beets
2 tablespoons whole allspice
2 sticks of cinnamon, 2 inches
   long
1½ quarts vinegar
½ cup honey

   Cook beets with roots and about 2 inches of stem left on in water to cover. When tender, dip beets in cold water and slip off skins. If beets are very small, keep whole; if not, slice thickly or cut in quarters.

   Put beets in large enamel or stainless steel pot. Combine the allspice, cinnamon, and vinegar, pour over beets and bring to a boil. Then add honey. Pack into hot, scalded pint jars. Cover beets with boiling syrup, leaving ¼-inch headspace. Seal and process 30 minutes in a boiling-water bath.

Yield: 9 pints

Dilled Brussels Sprouts

2 pounds Brussels sprouts,
   cleaned and trimmed
2 cups water
2 cups vinegar
1 cup lemon juice
½ to 1 teaspoon cayenne pepper
9 sprigs fresh dill
4 cloves garlic
1 teaspoon mustard seeds

   Steam whole Brussels sprouts until just tender. Combine water, vinegar, lemon juice, cayenne, and 5 sprigs of dill in an enamel or stainless steel pot and boil 5 minutes. Pack Brussels sprouts into hot, scalded pint jars. Place 1 clove garlic, 1 sprig dill, and ¼ teaspoon mustard seeds in each jar. Pour hot vinegar solution over Brussels sprouts, leaving ¼-inch headspace.

   Seal and process 10 minutes in a boiling-water bath.

Yield: 4 pints

Cooked Dutch Spiced Red Cabbage

4 pounds red cabbage
3 quarts red wine vinegar
½ cup water
1 teaspoon celery seeds
1 teaspoon ground pepper
1 teaspoon ground mace
1 teaspoon ground allspice
1 teaspoon ground cinnamon
½ cup honey

Shred cabbage; you should have 12 cups.

In an 8-quart enamel or stainless steel pot, boil vinegar for 8 minutes with water, celery seeds, ground pepper, mace, allspice, and cinnamon. Add honey. Add cabbage and simmer for 15 minutes.

Drain cabbage, saving liquid. Pack cabbage in hot, scalded pint jars. Pour hot liquid over cabbage, leaving ¼-inch headspace. Seal and process in boiling-water bath for 15 minutes.

Yield: 6 to 7 pints

Pickled Cauliflower

1 tablespoon whole allspice
1 tablespoon mustard seeds
1 tablespoon celery seeds
2 quarts white vinegar
2 heads cauliflower
18 carrot strips

Prepare a cheesecloth bag containing allspice, mustard seeds, and celery seeds. Place spice bag in enamel or stainless steel saucepan with vinegar. Simmer together for 15 minutes.

Meanwhile, wash cauliflower, cut away all leaves, and break into small, uniform florets. Blanch in boiling water for 2 minutes. Drain. Put cauliflower into hot, scalded pint jars. Add 3 carrot strips to each jar. Pour hot liquid over the cauliflower, leaving ½-inch headspace. Seal and process for 10 minutes in boiling-water bath.

Yield: 6 pints

Note: Some varieties of cauliflower may turn pink when pickled. The red color is a result of the red pigment being released when the cauliflower reacts with the vinegar.

Pickled Eggplant

This is a great salad and antipasto addition.

6 eggplants, peeled and cut into thick sticks, 2 inches long

2 medium-size or 1 large onion, coarsely chopped

½ teaspoon whole allspice

½ teaspoon white peppercorns

1 stick of cinnamon, 1 inch long

3½ cups red wine vinegar

½ cup honey

1 cup water

Boil eggplants and onions in water for 5 minutes; drain, cover with cold water; drain again.

Meanwhile, place allspice, peppercorns, and cinnamon in a cheesecloth bag and cook it with vinegar, honey, and water to boiling in an enamel or stainless steel saucepan. Simmer until syrup is thick. Add eggplants and onions. Heat through. Remove spice bag; pour into hot, scalded pint jars, leaving ¼-inch headspace. Seal and process 15 minutes in a boiling-water bath.

Yield: 4 to 5 pints

Penang Pickled Garlic

Pickled garlic adds character to many Southeast Asian recipes. Use it in other recipes as you would plain garlic, or stuff it between chicken meat and skin before roasting. Strain the liquid to make a wonderfully fragrant vinegar for marinades and salad dressings.

4 ounces fresh cloves garlic (about 1 cup)

1½ cups rice vinegar

2 tablespoons Rodale's Whole Pickling Spice (see page 212)

Peel garlic and blanch for 30 seconds. Drain.

In a small enamel or stainless steel saucepan, combine vinegar and pickling spice and bring to a boil. Pack garlic in 2 hot, scalded half-pint jars. Pour hot liquid over garlic, leaving ½-inch headspace. Seal and process for 10 minutes in a boiling-water bath.

Refrigerate after opening.

Yield: 2 half-pints

Japanese Pickled Ginger

Use this as a garnish for sushi, sashimi, and other Asian foods. It's also a delightful condiment for Western meals such as roast poultry and cold meat platters.

1½ cups (about ¼ pound) peeled
    ginger root, cut into very
    thin (2 × ⅛-inch) slivers
1¼ cups rice vinegar
1 teaspoon honey
1 teaspoon red miso

    Soak ginger in ice water, covered, overnight. Drain.

    In a small enamel or stainless steel saucepan, combine vinegar, honey, and miso. Bring to a boil. Pack drained ginger in 2 half-pint jars. Pour hot liquid over ginger, leaving ½-inch headspace.

    Seal and process in a boiling-water bath for 10 minutes.

Yield: 2 half-pints

Hot Spiced Jerusalem Artichokes

Serve as a condiment or with salad greens.

1 to 1¾ pounds Jerusalem
    artichokes
3 cups white vinegar
¼ cup honey
2 teaspoons turmeric
4 dried red peppers
4 cloves garlic, peeled
20 peppercorns
4 bay leaves
1 tablespoon mustard seeds

    Scrub artichokes and slice to ¼-inch thickness.

    In a small enamel or stainless steel saucepan, bring vinegar, honey, and turmeric to a slow boil, while you fill each of 4 hot, scalded pint jars with 1 pepper, 1 clove garlic, 5 peppercorns, and 1 bay leaf. Divide the mustard seeds among them and add the artichokes. Fill each jar with the hot liquid, seal, and process 10 minutes in a boiling-water bath.

Yield: 4 pints

Dilled Green Beans

4 pounds green beans	4 teaspoons dill seeds
8 dried chili peppers, 2 inches long	8 cloves garlic
	5 cups vinegar
4 teaspoons mustard seeds	5 cups water

Cut beans into lengths to fill pint jars. Pack beans into hot, scalded jars; add 1 chili pepper, ½ teaspoon mustard seeds, ½ teaspoon dill seeds, and 1 clove garlic to each jar.

Combine vinegar and water in enamel or stainless steel pan; heat to boiling. Pour boiling liquid over beans, filling jars, leaving ¼-inch headspace. Seal and process in a boiling-water bath for 5 minutes.

Yield: 8 pints

Horseradish in Vinegar

1 pound horseradish roots
1½ cups white vinegar
   (approximately)
¼ teaspoon crystalline ascorbic
   acid (optional)

Horseradish cannot be canned in the standard fashion because the flavoring oils are heat sensitive. It is best to hold the horseradish roots in cold storage or in the ground, and prepare ground horseradish in amounts that can be used within 1 month. Horseradish can be ground with a special tool with fine teeth that tears it apart. The flavor is best released when the horseradish is well ground or shredded. If cut into tiny chunks, as a blender will do, the flavor does not develop as well. Place ground horseradish in a jar and pour vinegar on top. Then add ascorbic acid. Keep in refrigerator or other cool place.

By Food Processor

Scrub horseradish, peel, and scrub again. Using a fine shredding disk, shred without pressing down on horseradish. (This makes finer shreds.) Then, replace shredding disk with metal knife blade and process in pulses until moistened and finely pulverized.

By Hand

Scrub horseradish, peel, and scrub again. Use a very fine shredder or a coarse grater. Shredding is the more pleasant technique because grating causes more eye irritation. In either case, set grater in a shallow bowl to catch all the fluid. Work at arm's length from the horseradish and avoid breathing the fumes.

By Blender

Rodale taste testers found that using a blender resulted in a slightly inferior, but still good, product. Scrub horseradish, peel, scrub again, and chop into small pieces. Place in a blender with just enough vinegar to process. Then blend until very finely chopped.

Pickled Nasturtium Buds
(false capers)

If you pride yourself on your gourmet cooking, one recipe you can't afford to pass up is the following. As Euell Gibbons said, "Nasturtium buds make better capers than capers do." Nasturtium buds should be gathered while they're still green—yellow ones are useless. So are those that have opened.

Place the nasturtium buds in a 10 percent brine—made by adding 1 cup salt to 2 quarts water—to cover. Weight them, if necessary, to hold them in the brine. Allow them to cure in brine for 24 hours.

Remove from brine, and soak in cold water for an hour. Drain the buds. Bring vinegar to a boil in an enamel or stainless steel pot. Pack nasturtium buds in hot, scalded pint jars and cover with boiling vinegar, leaving ½-inch headspace. Seal and process 10 minutes in a boiling-water bath.

It is best to let your "capers" stand for 6 weeks before you use them, as they will be more flavorful.

Okra Pickles

3 cups white vinegar
5 cups water
3 teaspoons celery seeds
3 pounds small okra pods, washed, with stems removed

⅔ pound baby onions, peeled
6 cloves garlic
6 small hot chili peppers (optional)
6 pieces green pepper, 1-inch square

Make a brine with vinegar, water, and celery seeds. Boil in an enamel or stainless steel pot.

Meanwhile, pack okra firmly in hot, scalded pint jars. In each jar put 4 onions, 1 clove garlic, 1 chili pepper, and 1 square of green pepper. Pour boiling brine over okra, leaving ¼-inch headspace. Seal and process for 15 minutes in a boiling-water bath.

Let ripen several weeks before using.

Yield: 6 pints

Onion Pickles

2 pounds small white onions
2 tablespoons mustard seeds
2 tablespoons celery seeds
4 spears horseradish root,
    3 × 1½ inches
6 cups white vinegar
6 teaspoons honey
4 small hot chili peppers (fresh
    or dried)

To make peeling easier, drop onions in boiling water, and after about 2 minutes, remove and plunge into cold water, then peel. Drain.

In an enamel or stainless steel pot, combine mustard seeds, celery seeds, horseradish root, and vinegar and simmer 15 minutes. Add honey. Remove and reserve horseradish root.

Pack onions into hot, scalded pint jars, leaving ¼-inch headspace. Add 1 chili pepper and 1 piece of reserved horseradish root to each jar. Seal and process 10 minutes in a boiling-water bath.

Yield: 4 pints

Marinated Daikon Radish

Halfway between a pickle and a salad, this delightful Japanese pickle is gently hot with an addictive crunchy texture.

2 daikon radishes, about 1½
    pounds
2 medium-size carrots
2¾ cups rice vinegar
1 cup water
2 tablespoons honey
2 teaspoons finely chopped
    fresh ginger root
2 cloves garlic, minced
4 small dried hot chili peppers,
    2 to 3 inches long
2 tablespoons soy sauce

Scrub radishes and carrots and cut crosswise into lengths that fit pint jars. Quarter each section lengthwise, then slice (again lengthwise) into thin slivers. Combine vinegar, water, honey, ginger, garlic, chili peppers, and soy sauce in an enamel or stainless steel saucepan. Bring to a boil. Meanwhile, pack radishes and carrots loosely into 4 hot, scalded pint jars. Pour hot vinegar mixture into jars, leaving ¼-inch headspace. Seal and process 10 minutes in a boiling-water bath.

Yield: 4 pints

Pickled Sweet Peppers

3 pounds green peppers,
      cleaned and sliced
      lengthwise
1 quart cider vinegar
¼ cup honey

Blanch pepper strips in steam for 2 minutes. Drain.

Combine vinegar and honey in an enamel or stainless steel saucepan. Bring to a boil. Meanwhile, pack pepper strips in hot, scalded pint jars. Cover with the hot vinegar solution, leaving ¼-inch headspace. Seal and process for 10 minutes in a boiling-water bath.

Yield: 4 to 5 pints

Green Tomato Pickles

9   cups white vinegar
1¼ cups honey
5   pounds green tomatoes, cut
      into ½-inch-wide slices
10 medium-size onions, cut into
      ½-inch-wide slices
10 teaspoons celery seeds
5   teaspoons mustard seeds
5   teaspoons dill seeds
15 peppercorns
5   cloves garlic

In an enamel or stainless steel pot, bring vinegar and honey to a boil. Meanwhile, layer tomatoes and onions in 5 hot, scalded quart jars. To each jar add 2 teaspoons celery seeds, 1 teaspoon mustard seeds, 1 teaspoon dill seeds, 3 peppercorns, and 1 clove garlic.

Pour boiling vinegar mixture into jars, allowing ¼-inch headspace. Seal, then turn jars once to disperse spices. Process in a boiling-water bath for 15 minutes.

Yield: 5 quarts

Kim Chee (Korean Pickled Vegetables)
(for refrigerator storage)

This crisp and spicy-hot condiment can be eaten with other dishes, or chopped and added to other foods in need of some zip.

1 pound celery cabbage stalks
1 large carrot
¼ pound white Oriental radishes (about 3)
2 scallions, thinly sliced
¼ cup soy sauce
½ cup water

2 tablespoons honey
3 tablespoons cider vinegar
1 teaspoon minced fresh ginger root
4 cloves garlic
2 to 4 dried peppers, 2 inches long, split

Slice the cabbage, carrot, and radishes lengthwise and then into 2 ½-inch-long strips. Toss with the scallions and soy sauce and water. Cover loosely and let stand overnight.

Drain the liquid from the vegetables into a bowl. Add honey and vinegar to the liquid and stir well to dissolve honey.

Add ginger, garlic, and peppers to the vegetables and pack them into a sterilized quart jar. Pour liquid into the jar. If more liquid is needed to cover vegetables, add water.

Cover loosely with a lid and let sit at room temperature for 3 to 5 days to ferment. The liquid will bubble and the flavor will become sour. The Kim Chee should then be refrigerated. In 3 or 4 days the cabbage will become translucent and will be ready to serve.

Kim Chee can be stored in the refrigerator for 2 months.

Yield: 1 quart

RELISHES

Chow Chow

3 cups cauliflower, cut in small florets
3 cups sliced celery
1 pound onions, sliced, or 1 pound pearl onions
2 cups sliced green peppers
4 cups green beans, cut in pieces
12 ears of corn, kernels removed

4 cups chunked carrots
6 cups sliced cucumbers
1 tablespoon mustard seeds
1 tablespoon peppercorns
1 tablespoon whole cloves
1 stick of cinnamon, broken
7 cups cider vinegar
2 cups honey

Cover cauliflower, celery, onions, peppers, beans, corn, carrots, and cucumbers with water and ice. Let stand in refrigerator 24 hours. Drain.

Place mustard seeds, peppercorns, cloves, and cinnamon in a cheese-cloth bag. Add bag to vinegar and honey in a stainless steel or enamel kettle. Bring to a boil; add vegetables and again bring to a boil.

Pack in hot, scalded jars, leaving ½-inch headspace. Seal and process 10 minutes in a boiling-water bath.

Yield: 12 pints

Corn Relish

8 cups whole-kernel corn (use
        16 to 20 medium-size ears
        of fresh corn or 6 10-ounce
        packages of frozen corn)
2 cups diced green peppers
2 cups diced sweet red peppers
4 cups chopped celery
8 to 10 small onions, or 3
        medium-size onions,
        chopped or sliced
1 cup honey
3 cups vinegar
1 cup lemon juice
2 teaspoons celery seeds
2 tablespoons dry mustard
1 teaspoon turmeric

For fresh corn, remove husks and silk. Cut corn from cob. Do not scrape cob.

For frozen corn, defrost overnight in refrigerator or for 2 to 3 hours at room temperature.

Combine green peppers, red peppers, celery, onions, honey, vinegar, lemon juice, and celery seeds in an enamel or stainless steel pot. Cover until mixture starts to boil, then simmer uncovered for 5 minutes, stirring occasionally. Mix mustard and turmeric and blend with mixture. Add corn. Heat to boiling and simmer for 5 minutes, stirring occasionally.

Bring to a boil. Pack loosely while boiling into hot, scalded pint jars, leaving ¼-inch headspace. Adjust seals and process in a boiling-water bath for 10 minutes.

Yield: 8 pints

Pepper-Onion Relish

4 cups finely chopped onions
2 cups finely chopped sweet red
   peppers
2 cups finely chopped green
   peppers
½ cup honey
4 cups vinegar

Combine all ingredients and bring to a boil. Cook until slightly thickened (about 45 minutes), stirring occasionally. Pack the hot relish into hot, scalded pint jars; fill to top of jar. Seal tightly. Cool and store in refrigerator.

If extended storage without refrigeration is desired, process in a boiling-water bath. Pack the hot relish into hot, scalded pint jars, leaving ¼-inch headspace. Seal and process in a boiling-water bath for 5 minutes.

Yield: 4 pints

Piccalilli

4 cups chopped green tomatoes
1 cup diced sweet red peppers
1 cup chopped green peppers
1½ cups chopped onions
5 cups chopped cabbage
2 tablespoons salt
2 tablespoons Rodale's Whole
   Pickling Spice (see page
   212)
3 cups vinegar
½ cup honey

Combine tomatoes, red peppers, green peppers, onions, and cabbage. Mix with salt and let stand overnight. Drain to remove all liquid possible.

Tie pickling spice in a cheesecloth bag and combine with vinegar. Bring mixture to a boil in an enamel or stainless steel pot. Add honey. Add vegetables, bring to a boil, and simmer about 30 minutes, or until there is just enough liquid to moisten vegetables. Remove spice bag. Pack hot relish into hot, scalded pint jars, leaving ¼-inch headspace. Seal and process in a boiling-water bath for 5 minutes.

Yield: 4 pints

Pickled Garden Relish

For best results, use freshly picked vegetables.

1	small head cauliflower, cut into florets	9	baby carrots, pared
2½	cups white wine vinegar	2	stalks celery, cut into 1-inch pieces
1½	cups water	2	green peppers, cut into 2-inch strips
½	teaspoon dried oregano		
1	bay leaf	½	pound pearl onions
½	teaspoon crushed red pepper	3	cloves garlic
¼	teaspoon turmeric	½	cup honey
1	tablespoon mustard seeds	12 to 15 fresh basil leaves	

In a large saucepan, cook cauliflower in boiling water 5 minutes; drain.

In an 8-quart enamel or stainless steel saucepan, combine vinegar, water, oregano, bay leaf, red pepper, turmeric, and mustard seeds; heat to boiling. Add carrots, celery, green peppers, onions, and garlic; simmer 2 minutes. Add honey. Keep warm.

Arrange 3 basil leaves in each hot, scalded pint jar. Pack vegetables into jar; add liquid to cover, leaving ½-inch headspace. Seal and process 5 minutes in a boiling-water bath.

Yield: 4 to 5 pints

Red Pepper Relish

12	medium-size sweet red peppers, stems and seeds removed	2	cups chopped onions
		2	cups white vinegar
		3	cups honey
4	teaspoons whole allspice	4	teaspoons salt
½	teaspoon ground ginger	1	lemon, sliced

Cover peppers with boiling water; let stand 5 minutes; drain. Repeat, and drain well. Put through coarse blade of food chopper. The mixture should measure about 4 cups.

Tie allspice and ginger in a cheesecloth bag. In an enamel or stainless steel saucepan, combine with other ingredients. Boil 30 minutes, stirring occasionally. Let stand overnight.

Next day, bring mixture to a boil in large saucepan and simmer 10 minutes. Ladle boiling hot into hot, scalded half-pint jars. Seal and process in a boiling-water bath for 10 minutes.

Yield: about 6 half-pints

PICKLED FRUITS

Pickled Bramble Berry

Use these tangy berries to garnish poached chicken and fish. The liquid is a fragrant fruit vinegar that makes a lovely mayonnaise for chicken salads.

3½ cups blackberries
¾ cup white vinegar
¾ cup cider vinegar
1 teaspoon ground ginger
½ teaspoon ground cinnamon
¼ teaspoon ground cardamom
¼ teaspoon ground allspice
1 bay leaf
1 blade of mace

Wash and pick over blackberries.

In a small enamel or stainless steel saucepan, bring white vinegar, cider vinegar, ginger, cinnamon, cardamom, allspice, bay leaf, and mace to a boil. Remove bay leaf and mace. Meanwhile, place blackberries in hot, scalded half-pint jars. Pour hot vinegar mixture over berries. Seal and process in boiling-water bath for 5 minutes.

Yield: 4 half-pints

Spiced Sweet Cherries

Serve with roast pork or game meats such as venison.

6 to 7 cups sweet cherries
juice of 1 lemon
3 cups cider vinegar
½ cup honey
2 sticks of cinnamon, 2 inches long
24 whole cloves
2 slices of ginger root, ⅛ inch thick
2 bay leaves

Wash and pit cherries and chill in ice water plus juice from half the lemon.

In a saucepan with remaining lemon juice, simmer vinegar, honey, cinnamon, cloves, ginger, and bay leaves for 15 minutes.

Drain cherries. Fill 4 hot, scalded pint jars three-quarters full with cherries. Strain hot liquid, and pour over cherries, leaving ½-inch headspace. Seal and process in boiling-water bath for 10 minutes.

Yield: 4 to 5 pints

Spiced Crabapples

6 pounds crabapples
1 stick of cinnamon
1 tablespoon whole cloves
1 teaspoon whole allspice
1 teaspoon whole mace
1 cup honey
6 cups vinegar

Wash crabapples well; be sure to remove blossom ends.

Place cinnamon, cloves, allspice, and mace in a cheesecloth bag and add it to the honey and vinegar. Bring the mixture to a boil.

When this syrup is cool, add the crabapples and heat slowly so as not to burst the fruit. Sometimes it is best to prick each apple to avoid bursting. Bring to a boil. Allow to cool overnight.

Remove spice bag. Heat slowly to boiling point. Pack crabapples in hot, scalded pint jars. Fill with hot syrup, leaving ¼-inch headspace. Seal and process 10 minutes in a boiling-water bath.

Yield: 6 to 8 pints

Sweet Spiced Pickled Peaches

8 pounds peaches
2 cups apple juice
1 quart cider vinegar
⅛ cup honey

21 whole cloves
3½ sticks of cinnamon
7 slices of ginger root, ¼ inch long

Rinse, peel, halve, and pit peaches. Reserve 7 pits and set peaches aside.

In a large kettle, combine apple juice, vinegar, and honey. Bring to a boil and add peaches. Simmer for 5 minutes.

Place a peach pit in each hot, scalded pint jar along with 3 whole cloves, ½ stick of cinnamon, and slice of ginger. Distribute peaches among the jars. Pour liquid over peaches to cover, adding more vinegar if necessary and leaving ¼ inch headspace.

Seal and process for 10 minutes in a boiling-water bath.

Yield: 7 pints

Notes:

The peach pits will help keep the peaches from turning brown.

If you want a sweet pickled peach, double the honey.

Use peelings and pits to make Peach Vinegar, page 301.

When you have opened and enjoyed your peaches, reserve the syrup. Pour it over ham when baking.

Pear Pickles

8 pounds pears	6 cups red wine vinegar
10 sticks of cinnamon, 2 inches long	½ to 1 cup honey, depending on sweetness of fruit
2 tablespoons whole allspice	

For Seckel Pears

Wash the pears and remove the blossom ends only. Boil pears for 5 minutes in enough water to cover. Drain. Prick the skins. Tie cinnamon and allspice in cheesecloth and combine with vinegar and honey. Boil for 5 minutes. Add pears; simmer for 5 minutes or until pears are tender. Do not overcook. Let stand overnight.

In the morning, remove the spice bag. Drain syrup from pears and heat syrup to boiling. Pack pears in hot, scalded pint jars. Pour hot syrup over pears, leaving ¼-inch headspace. Seal and process 10 minutes in a boiling-water bath.

For Kieffer Pears

Wash the pears, pare, cut in halves or quarters, remove hard centers and cores. Boil 10 minutes in enough water to cover. Drain. Boil, for 5 minutes, 5 cups vinegar, the honey, and cinnamon and allspice in a cheesecloth bag. Add pears; simmer for 5 minutes or until tender. Let stand overnight. Proceed as for Seckel pears.

For Bartlett Pears

Use 4 pounds pears instead of 8 pounds since this variety is so large. Wash, cut out centers and cores, and cut into quarters. Tie cinnamon and allspice in a cheesecloth bag and boil in vinegar and honey for 10 minutes. Add pears to hot liquid and boil for 2 minutes. Immediately pack pears in hot, scalded pint jars. Pour hot syrup over pears, leaving ¼-inch headspace. Seal and process 10 minutes in a boiling-water bath.

Yield: about 8 pints

Plum Delicious

This tangy purée is very versatile. Use it as a filling for a pie, as a fruit preserve for bread, or freeze it for rich fruit Popsicles.

5 pounds plums (overripe is okay)	¼ teaspoon ground cinnamon
¼ cup and 1 tablespoon honey	1 stick of cinnamon
1 apple, chopped	1½ tablespoons pure maple syrup
5 tablespoons currants	
½ tablespoon lemon juice	1 to 2 tablespoons cornstarch (optional)
½ teaspoon lime juice	

Put a few plums into a wire basket. Dip plums in boiling water about 30 seconds until skins split. Rub off skins and squeeze out pits. Put plums into a large enamel or stainless steel pot on low heat. Finish preparing the remaining plums. Add ¼ cup honey and apple. Simmer 15 minutes. Drain off excess juice and save for a drink or part of a compote. Add currants, lemon juice, lime juice, cinnamon, cinnamon stick, and remaining 1 tablespoon honey. Simmer 10 minutes. Test. If you like it tart, add more lemon and lime juice. Balance with cinnamon. Simmer again. Test. Add maple syrup. If you like it sweeter, add 2 teaspoons honey to 1 teaspoon maple syrup until it is sweet enough.

Prepare as you normally do for preserves *or* mix 2 tablespoons cornstarch into ½ cup plum juice. Pour half of cornstarch mix into plums. Stir until back to original color. When nice and thick, pour one-third of the mixture into a 9-inch pie shell, cool in refrigerator, and top with ice cream. *Or* pour into ice cube tray with toothpick in each square. Freeze.

Yield: 3 pints

Note: This recipe can be doubled if you have a large crop of plums.

Gingered Watermelon Rind

Serve as a relish, or drain it for use in Gingered Sour Cream Fruitcake, page 337.

7   cups 1-inch-square peeled
      watermelon rind
6   cups white vinegar
1   cup honey
4   strips lemon peel
1   stick of cinnamon, 2 inches
      long
12 whole cloves
4   thin slices ginger root

Blanch watermelon rind just until the tines of a fork will pierce the flesh. Don't overcook. Drain rind.

Make syrup by simmering vinegar, honey, lemon peel, cinnamon, cloves, and ginger for 10 minutes.

In a large bowl, pour hot syrup over rind, cover, and chill overnight. Remove rind and put into 4 hot, scalded pint jars, filling three-quarters full. Bring syrup to a boil and pour over rind in jars, leaving ½-inch headspace. Seal and process 10 minutes in a boiling-water bath.

Yield: 4 pints

CHUTNEYS

Apricot Chutney

Serve as a condiment with Indian meals, or with roast meats and poultry.

½ cup honey
½ cup cider vinegar
½ cup coarsely chopped onions
½ teaspoon ground allspice
1 tablespoon chopped raisins
1 tablespoon crushed and
    minced peeled ginger root
2 pounds fresh apricots, pitted
    and quartered

    In a large enamel or stainless steel saucepan, combine honey, vinegar, onions, allspice, raisins, and ginger. Simmer for 10 minutes. Add apricots and simmer for 30 minutes, or until thick, stirring occasionally.

    Pour into 4 hot, scalded half-pint jars. Seal and process 10 minutes in a boiling-water bath.

Yield: 4 half-pints

Currant and Green Tomato Chutney

This recipe can be used as green tomato mince meat pie filling. Instead of chopping tomatoes and apples, just put them through a meat grinder. You also can substitute raisins for the currants.

3 cups currants
4½ cups finely chopped green
    tomatoes
4½ cups peeled and chopped tart
    apples
2 lemons, seeded, quartered,
    and sliced thin
2 cups minced onions

2 cloves garlic
½ cup honey
1 cup vinegar
1 cup water
2 tablespoons mustard seeds
½ teaspoon cayenne pepper
2 teaspoons ground ginger

    Combine all ingredients. Simmer for 20 minutes or until fruit is soft. Pack into hot, scalded pint jars, leaving ¼-inch headspace. Seal and process for 5 minutes in a boiling-water bath.

Yield: 6 pints

Mango Chutney

3 cups cider vinegar
¾ cup lime juice
5 tablespoons honey
6 large ripe mangoes, peeled
    and sliced
1 cup currants
1 cup and 2 tablespoons
    raisins
¾ cup minced onions
1½ cups chopped green peppers

1 cup slivered almonds
1 piece ginger root, 3 inches
    long, peeled and finely
    chopped
1½ tablespoons crushed mustard
    seeds
1½ tablespoons minced hot chili
    pepper, or 1 dried chili
    pepper, ground

Combine all ingredients. Bring to a boil, then turn heat down and simmer for 30 minutes. Drain off juice and boil it down to half of its volume. Add it to chutney and ladle into hot, scalded pint jars, leaving ¼-inch headspace. Seal and process for 5 minutes in boiling-water bath.

Yield: 6 pints

Quince Chutney

Serve this as a relish with roast meats or poultry.

2 pounds quinces, peeled,
    cored, and quartered
1½ cups apple juice
⅓ cup honey
⅓ cup cider vinegar
⅓ cup coarsely chopped onions
⅓ teaspoon ground coriander
⅓ teaspoon ground cardamom
⅓ cup raisins
1 tablespoon crushed and
    minced peeled ginger root

In a medium-size enamel or stainless steel saucepan, combine all ingredients. Bring to a boil and simmer for 45 minutes. Pour into hot, scalded pint jars, leaving ½-inch headspace. Seal and process in a boiling-water bath for 10 minutes.

Yield: 3 pints

MUSTARDS

Honey Mustard

Serve with sandwiches, in salad dressings, to glaze meats and poultry. Also wonderful with cold shrimp and fish.

⅓ cup honey
¾ cup dry mustard
1 cup cider vinegar
3 eggs

In the top of a double boiler combine all ingredients, stirring until smooth. Continue to simmer for 8 to 10 minutes, or until thick and smooth. Pour into hot, scalded half-pint jars, leaving ¼-inch headspace. Seal and process in a boiling-water bath for 10 minutes.

Yield: 2 half-pints

Hunter's Mustard

Spread on sandwiches and on roast meats before cooking.

1 medium-size onion, peeled
4 whole cloves
2 cloves garlic, thinly sliced
1¼ cups cider vinegar
1 cup dry mustard
1 bay leaf
1 teaspoon honey
¼ teaspoon dried basil

¼ teaspoon ground marjoram
¼ teaspoon turmeric
⅛ teaspoon tarragon
   dash each of cayenne pepper
   and white pepper
1 teaspoon homemade
   horseradish (see page 222)
   (optional)

Stick onion with cloves. In a medium-size bowl, combine onion, garlic, and vinegar; cover and refrigerate 2 to 3 hours. Pour off liquid and reserve. Discard onion and garlic.

In a medium-size bowl, slowly stir ½ cup reserved vinegar into the dry mustard. In an enamel or stainless steel saucepan, boil remaining vinegar and bay leaf, covered, 3 minutes. Add honey, basil, marjoram, turmeric, tarragon, cayenne, and white pepper. Add this mixture to the mustard. Return to pan and bring to a boil; cook, stirring constantly, 6 minutes. Pour into hot, scalded half-pint jar, leaving ¼-inch headspace. Seal and process in a boiling-water bath for 15 minutes. If you're not going to process, cool mustard before pouring into jar. Refrigerate after opening.

Yield: about 1 half-pint

Spicy Mustard

A zippy condiment to serve plain or to add to sauces.

1 cup cider vinegar	1 teaspoon honey
4 whole cloves	¼ teaspoon ground ginger
4 peppercorns	¼ teaspoon ground allspice
1 bay leaf	¼ teaspoon ground cinnamon
1 small onion, thinly sliced	⅛ teaspoon ground mace
1 clove garlic, thinly sliced	¼ teaspoon turmeric
1 cup dry mustard	pinch of tarragon

In a small enamel or stainless steel saucepan, combine vinegar, cloves, peppercorns, bay leaf, onions, and garlic. Bring to a boil over medium heat; lower heat and simmer, covered, 5 minutes. In a blender container, combine remaining ingredients.

Strain vinegar mixture, pressing down on vegetables to release flavorings. Add to mustard mixture. Process 1 minute; scrape down contents; process 30 seconds. Pour into top of double boiler. Place over simmering water. Cook until thick. Pour into hot, scalded half-pint jar, leaving ¼-inch headspace. Seal and process in a boiling-water bath for 15 minutes. If you're not going to process, cool mustard before pouring into jar. Refrigerate after opening.

Yield: about 1 half-pint

Jams, Jellies, and Fruit Butters

Look at almost any book on food preservation and you'll probably find that the chapter on making jams and jellies is the largest section in the entire book. This is because jam and jelly making offer a chance to be truly creative. As long as you follow some basic rules, you can explore some interesting flavor combinations of fresh fruits, dried fruits, and nuts.

Making jellied fruit products—jams, jellies, preserves, conserves, marmalades, and fruit butters—is an excellent way of using up fruits and berries that can't be used for other types of canning. When you size your fruit for canning or freezing, you'll most likely have some fruit that is too small or too large. Some pieces may be rejected because they have imperfections, like soft spots or insect damage. Other pieces may be too ripe or not ripe enough for canning. All these fruits can be used for jam and jelly making, and all of them can make a definite contribution to the finished product. Ripe fruit adds to the flavor of the product and should always be used when you are using commercial pectins. Slightly underripe fruit contains more natural pectin and acid than you'll find in the same fruit that is just ripe or overripe, and a small proportion of it in a recipe can help the fruit gel. And, of course, size or blemishes that can be trimmed away won't matter because all the fruit is going to be cut up and peeled anyway.

MAKING JAMS AND JELLIES WITH HONEY

As you read on in this section you'll find that the directions and recipes here are quite different from those in jam and jelly chapters of other

IS IT A JELLY, JAM, PRESERVE, CONSERVE, MARMALADE, OR FRUIT BUTTER?

For the sake of brevity, we refer to jellies, jams, preserves, conserves, and marmalades as jellies and jams in this chapter, but there's a fine line separating each of them.

Jellies are made from fruit juice squeezed from the fruit, which is sometimes cooked first. It is a clear or translucent gel. *Jams* are purées made with fruit; they are thick, but not as firm as jellies.

Preserves, conserves, and marmalades are made with bits of fruit, cooked until translucent with sweetening and pectin. *Preserves* are generally made from a single kind of fruit (strawberry preserves contains only strawberries); *conserves* are made with fresh fruits and dried fruit or nuts, or both; and *marmalades* are made most often from one or many kinds of citrus fruits.

Cooked-down jams and jellies rely upon the natural pectin found in fruits that naturally contain a lot of it: tart apples and crabapples, blackberries, Concord grapes, lemons and oranges, Damson plums, quinces, and raspberries. No extra pectin is added. Both jams and jellies are *boiled* with a sweetener and sometimes lemon juice or citric acid to raise the acidity, until a gel forms. *Pectin jams and jellies* have extra pectin added to them to form a good gel. This pectin may be natural pectin, such as that made from tart apples, or it can be a commercial pectin or low-methoxyl pectin. The fruit is boiled with pectin and a sweetener and sometimes lemon juice or citric acid. *Uncooked jams and jellies* are often called refrigerator jams and jellies because they are not sterilized by boiling and will spoil unless they are refrigerated or frozen. These jams and jellies use no pectin, but either gelatin or agar (a natural thickening agent made from seaweed) to form a gel.

Fruit butters are fruits cooked down until they form a very thick purée. They often—but not always—have added sweeteners and spices. Because fruit butters fall into a category of their own, we discuss them separately beginning on page 266.

books. Recipes for jams and jellies elsewhere call for great quantities of sugar, but you won't find any sugar in our recipes. Some amount and type of sweetener is necessary to create a good gel if you're relying on the natural pectin found in some fruits or regular commercial powdered or liquid pectin. The sweetening that's most often used is sugar, but in *Stocking Up* it's honey.

We stress healthful foods in this book, and jams and jellies loaded with sugar don't make for particularly healthy eating. To provide you with a more healthy alternative, we've worked very hard in our Food Center to come up with an assortment of delicious, original recipes that use honey instead of sugar. A number work with regular pectins, and a host of them were developed for use with low-methoxyl (LM) pectin. LM pectin reacts not with sugar or honey, but with calcium salts to form a gel, so sweetening can be cut way back without affecting the consistency of the finished product. You use as much or as little as you want for flavor only. The same is true for jams and jellies made with gelatin or agar; neither need sweetening for gelling, but just for flavor.

Our recipes use honey in smaller amounts than the sugar equivalent—for a few good reasons. One is that honey has a taste of its own, and the less used, the more opportunity for the good fruit flavor to come through. Second, honey, while it does contain some vitamins and minerals (sugar contains none whatsoever), is still a highly refined sweetener that adds calories but not a great deal more to our diets. We'd much rather cut back on the honey and make more room for the fruit. We also cut back on the amount of honey because we just don't like our jams and jellies so sweet. Commercial and traditional homemade jams and jellies, in our opinion, taste way too sweet. And we don't think we're the only ones that feel this way. Taste buds are changing; we're beginning to appreciate real foods for their own flavors, not for the salt, sugar, or other "flavor enhancers" that are often so liberally added to them. If you haven't had some strawberry jam or raspberry preserves that really zing with a fruity taste not bolstered by lots of sugar, that are more fruity than sweet, you're in for a very pleasant surprise when you taste ours.

Although sorghum, molasses, and maple syrup are all natural sweeteners, we don't recommend you use them in jams and jellies. They have a strong flavor of their own and will overpower or at least affect the flavor of the fruit. And they don't generally work as well with pectin to make a good gel. We made one exception and have included a very good apricot jam (which calls for no pectin) that uses maple syrup as its sweetener.

Before we discuss making jams and jellies with honey, we'll tell you right out that they are a bit trickier to make than the conventional jams and jellies made with sugar. In order for the traditional cooked-down and pectin products to gel, they have to be cooked longer than they would if made with sugar—about 8 to 10 minutes for pectin jellies and jams and even longer for the cooked-down ones that have no extra pectin added. But don't go over 20 minutes because the pectin will break down.

■ A few words of warning: We suggest that you don't fool around with recipes, trying to replace the sugar with honey or artificial sweeteners. All are very different foods that have their own special characteristics and reactions when they are combined with other ingredients and with heat. And don't try to double or triple a recipe. Quantities don't multiply proportionately. We know. We had enough failures in our Food Center when we were developing our own recipes! Rather, make several batches of the same recipe if you want to make larger quantities.

If you have a little patience and follow the recipes carefully, you should be able to make some fine jelly products this way. The only real problem with using pectin for the cooked-down method is that the long cooking time required will lessen the food value of both honey and the fruit and alter their flavor and color. If you're concerned about such things, you may prefer to make jellies and jams with LM pectin, gelatin, or agar, none of which require sweetening or long cooking to gel. Discussions of all these methods of making jams and jellies follow.

COOKED-DOWN AND PECTIN JAMS AND JELLIES

The traditional cooked-down method of jam and jelly making simply uses fruit, some liquid like water or fruit juice, and a sweetening. It should be used only with fruits that have a good amount of natural pectin in them. (These include tart apples and crabapples, blackberries, Concord grapes, lemons and oranges, Damson plums, quinces, and raspberries.) There is usually some guesswork involved in making jams and jellies this way because how the pectin responds and makes a gel is dependent upon the amount of acids and sugar in the mixture, and the ripeness of the fruit. The fruit must contain a sufficient amount of acid to achieve a gel. If the fruit you're working with is low in acid, recipes will call for the addition of lemon juice or citric acid. When using this method, select your fruit carefully. A batch of fruit should contain one-quarter just-ripe fruit and three-quarters fully ripe fruit for best pectin and flavor content. (Pectin levels drop in many fruits as they ripen.)

Extra pectin—be it commercial pectin or those fruits naturally high in pectin—should be added to fruits that don't have much natural pectin in them, like strawberries and apricots. Pectin can also be added to other fruits in order to cut down on the cooking time necessary to get them to form a gel. When using honey instead of sugar, added pectin can be especially helpful in cutting down on this cooking time. Jellies made with added pectin also require less fruit than the cooked-down type to make the same amount of finished product.

Commercial pectin is made from either citrus fruit or apples and is available in most supermarkets under several different brand names. It's available in both liquid and powdered forms. You can also make your own pectin from apples and use it instead of the commercial kind (see page 244).

EXTRACTING THE JUICE FOR JELLIES

Before you make jelly, you must first extract juice from your fruit. Different fruits require slightly different procedures; we describe them below.

Before you begin, there are a few things you should know. You will need to procure a jelly bag, which is a cloth bag used to extract the

The clearest jelly comes from juice that has dripped through a jelly bag without being squeezed. However, if you do not have a jelly bag, you may use cheesecloth instead. Dampen several thicknesses of cheesecloth, and place your fruit pulp in the cheesecloth and gather the cloth with string. Loop the string around a kitchen-cabinet knob and suspend the bag over a bowl and allow the juice to drip into the bowl overnight.

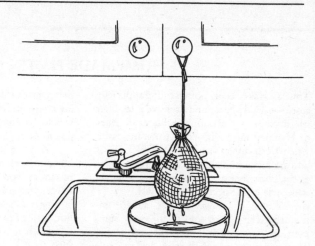

juice from fruit. (If you cannot obtain a jelly bag, you may use a fruit press or several thicknesses of dampened cheesecloth.) Your jelly bag should be dampened before you use it. The clearest jelly comes from juice that has dripped through a jelly bag without squeezing it, but you can get more juice by twisting the jelly bag slightly and squeezing the juice out. Pressed juice should be re-strained through a damp jelly bag or a double thickness of cheesecloth without squeezing. If the juice yield is slightly short and you need a bit more for your recipe, add a little water to the pulp in the jelly bag and let it drain through. When you're finished with the jelly bag, wash it out well. The last thing you want is for your next batch of fruit to pick up a sour or musty taste from a jelly bag that had bits of old fruit or juice fermenting in it.

As an alternative to fresh fruit juice, you can use your own canned or frozen fruit juice or any commercial unsweetened fruit juices, so long as you use a recipe that calls for added pectin.

Use an 8-quart saucepan to heat all the fruit when using the directions here.

For Apples (5 pounds). Remove blossoms and stem ends. Chop coarsely. Add 5 cups water; cover and simmer 10 minutes, stirring occasionally. Then crush and simmer 5 more minutes. Pour into jelly bag and drain. Yield: about 10 cups.

For Grapes and Fruits with Pits, such as Cherries, Plums, and Peaches (3 pounds). Remove pits (this isn't necessary for grapes) and chop finely. Add ½ cup water, cover and simmer 5 to 10 minutes, stirring occasionally. Pour into jelly bag and drain. Yield: about 5½ cups.

For Berries (2½ quarts). Purée or mash. Pour into jelly bag and drain. Yield: about 5½ cups.

HOMEMADE PECTIN

You can make pectin—often called apple jelly stock—ahead of time and preserve it for later use if you enjoy making combination jellies or blending them with other fruits in season when fresh apples are not available. Or, if you are lucky enough to have the fresh apples at the same time as the other fruits, you can make use of the pectin immediately.

"Apple thinnings"—those small, immature green apples sold in the early summertime—are rich in both acid and pectin. They will make good jelly stock and will give a snappy tartness to your jelly. However, if you prize the clarity of the jelly product, be warned that such apples will not produce as clear and transparent a jelly as pectin made from fully mature apples.

If you happen to have a bumper crop of apples, you will like the idea of using some of the surplus to make apple stock. It represents one more good use for that large supply. You can use imperfect fruit, even with insect damage, bird peckings, bruises, or cuts from dropping from the tree. Merely cut away the imperfect sections and use the sound parts.

Wash the apples carefully, but don't peel or core them, as pectin is concentrated just under the skins and in and around the seeds. Trim off bad parts and cut pieces into thin slices. Measure 1 pint water for every pound of apples. Place the slices in a kettle and boil for 15 minutes.

Strain off the free-running juice through one thickness of cheesecloth, without attempting to squeeze the pulp. Return the pulp to the kettle, and add the same measure of water again. This time, cook the mixture at a lower temperature for 15 minutes. Allow it to stand for 10 minutes, then strain the second batch of juice through one thickness of cheesecloth. Again, do not attempt to squeeze the pulp. Allow it to cool enough so

that you can handle it. Squeeze out the remaining juice, and combine all you have. There should be about 1 quart of juice for every pound of apples you used.

You can use this stock immediately for blending with other fruit juices to make jelly or jam, or you can preserve it for future use. If you wish to can the stock, heat it to the boiling point and pour it immediately into hot, scalded canning jars. Seal, and invert the jars to cool. No further processing is necessary.

If you prefer to freeze the stock, allow it to cool and then pour into freezer containers. Allow 1-inch headspace for expansion.

Four cups of homemade pectin replaces approximately one-half bottle or 3 ounces of commercial liquid pectin in most recipes.

If you have a bumper crop of apples, you can use some of the surplus to make your own pectin—also called apple jelly stock. (1) Wash the apples, but don't peel or core them. Cut into thin slices and boil in water. (2) Strain off the juice through cheesecloth and reserve. (3) Return the pulp to the kettle, add more water, and cook. (4) Strain the second batch of juice through cheesecloth, then allow the pulp to cool enough so you can handle the cloth. (5) Gather the cheesecloth into a ball and squeeze out the remaining juice into the bowl with the other juice. This is your pectin.

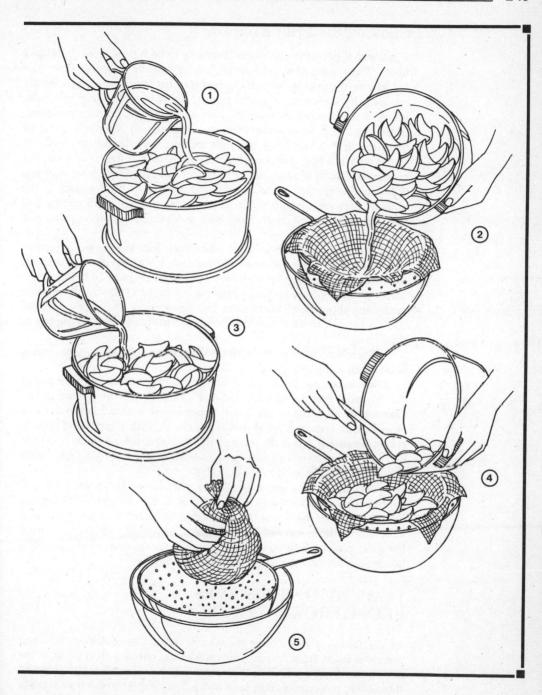

Cooking the Fruit Mixture

Commercial pectin is commonly available in both powdered and liquid form. When using powdered pectin, mix it with the unheated fruit juice for jelly or with the unheated, crushed fruit for jams or preserves before cooking. If you are using liquid pectin, add it to the boiling juice-and-honey mixture when making jelly, or, when making jams or preserves, to the cooked fruit-and-honey mixture immediately after it is removed from the heat. Then bring the fruit mixture with liquid or powdered pectin to a full boil and cook for the recommended length of time, but no longer. Pectin is activated by heat, but deactivated by long cooking. A full boil is reached when bubbles form over the entire surface of the jams or preserves, or when the jelly mixture reaches a full rolling boil that cannot be stirred down. Slow boils make for disappointing jams and jellies.

You know the jelly is done when your jelly thermometer reaches 220°F (subtract 2 degrees from that for each 1,000 feet above sea level), or when it passes one of the jelly tests described on page 248. Then skim off the foam. If you're making a preserve instead of a jelly, stir the mixture gently for about 5 minutes before ladling into jars so that the mixture cools a bit and there is less likelihood that fruit will float to the top of the liquid.

There's no need to do a jelly test for jams. You know your jam is done when a spoonful holds its shape in a cold bowl or spoon.

It is better to make a small quantity of jelly or jam at a time rather than a large one so that the mixture heats up fast and there is fast evaporation of some of the liquid. Since honey foams when it boils, a large kettle is required. An 8- or 10-quart kettle with a flat, broad bottom is best because it brings the mixture in contact with heat quickly. Do not use an aluminum or cast-iron pot, as acids in the fruit may react with the aluminum.

We suggest you use a light-color, mild-flavor honey for jams and jellies unless your family likes the taste of darker honeys. Dark honeys will impart a strong flavor to the product in which they are used, and although the taste will not be unpleasant, it probably will be too strong for most people. Clover, alfalfa, orange blossom, and other very light honeys are best for making jellied fruit products.

JAMS AND PRESERVES FROM FROZEN FRUIT

At the Rodale Food Center we were delighted to find that jams and preserves made from frozen fruit tasted and looked just as good as the ones made from fresh fruit. Knowing that you don't have to drop all those other projects to make jams and jellies right when the fruit is ready

(1) When using *powdered* pectin for jams and jellies, mix it with the unheated juice (for jelly) or crushed fruit (for jams and preserves) before cooking. If you're using *liquid* pectin, add it to boiling juice or to cooked fruit immediately after it is removed from the heat. (2) Bring the fruit-pectin mixture to a full boil and cook for recommended time.

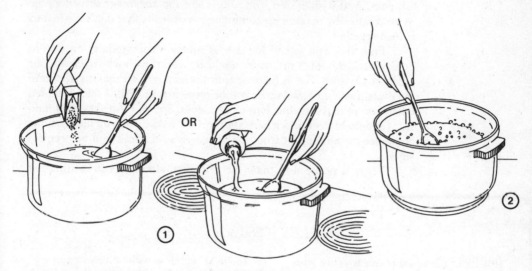

(3) If you're making jelly, remove it from the heat when it reaches 220°F on a jelly thermometer and do a jelly test. (4) Skim off the foam. (5) Ladle the mixture into jars set on a towel. Make sure there is space between the jars for air to circulate and speed cooling.

could really be a godsend. You'll still have the work of cleaning and slicing the fruit for the freezer, but you can postpone the cooking and mashing for another time so that you don't have to do it when you're also attempting to freeze your bumper crop of tomatoes and plant your fall peas. And with frozen fruit you've got the advantage of being able to be creative by making up combinations of fruits that don't come into season together.

Fruit that you intend for jam or preserve making later on should be dry-packed, which means it should be frozen without sweetening or syrup of any sort. This is because fruit thaws faster without a syrup, and the measurement of sweetener will be more precise if the honey is added when you're making your jam or preserves. Stems, blemishes, pits, and skins should be removed where appropriate. Make sure you mark on the container the amount of fruit you've frozen so the fruit will be premeasured.

There is no need to thaw the fruit first, although you can thaw it

JELLY TESTS

Jellies that use added pectin are done when they have been boiling rapidly for the time required by your recipe. But jellies without added pectin are less reliable. You can use a jelly thermometer to check for doneness; when it reads 220°F (subtract 2 degrees for each 1,000 feet above sea level), it's done. If you don't have a jelly thermometer, you can test for doneness by doing a jelly test. And if you're using LM pectin, a jelly test is really the only way you can tell if your jelly is ready.

While you're doing a jelly test, remove the jelly from the heat so that it doesn't continue to cook. There are a couple of different tests you can use.

The spoon or sheet test is the most traditional, but perhaps not the easiest. To make a spoon or sheet test, dip a cold metal spoon in the boiling jelly mixture. Raise it at least a foot above the kettle, out of the steam, and wait 20 seconds. Then turn the spoon so that the syrup runs off to one side. If the syrup forms 2 drops that flow together and fall off

the spoon as one sheet without breaking or dripping, the jelly should be done.

To do *the refrigerator test*, pour a small amount of boiling jelly on a cold plate and put it in the freezer compartment of a refrigerator for a few minutes. If the mixture has a good jellylike jiggle to it when you shake it, it's passed the test.

Then there's the method that the Rodale Food Center particularly likes. We call it *the metal bowl method*. Float a light metal mixing bowl in a larger bowl, pot, or basin filled with cold water or ice water. Drop a teaspoon of jelly mixture in the bottom of the metal bowl. Because metal conducts heat quickly, the jelly mixture will cool quickly. Once cool, run your finger through the jelly. It's ready if it doesn't run back together.

If the jelly test you conducted fails, cook the jelly mixture a little longer and try again. Keep cooking for a bit and testing until your jelly passes. Don't overcook, though. If you do, your jelly may get gummy.

if you wish. Browning may take place if the fruit is allowed to thaw normally, but you can prevent some of this if you thaw it quickly over heat in a saucepan.

Jams are made from fruit purées. You can purée the frozen fruit in a food processor. If you don't have a processor, then you're going to have to partially thaw it first and chop it in a blender or mash it with a fork, potato masher, or pastry blender. Measurements in our recipes are for whole, prepared fruits, that is, cups of whole berries, of sliced peaches, and so forth. After the fruit has been puréed, it will measure somewhat less. For instance, 1 cup strawberries will yield $\frac{3}{4}$ cup purée.

Preserves are made with chunks of whole fruit. To make them from frozen fruit, place the whole fruit, still frozen, in a saucepan. Add a little fruit juice—about $\frac{1}{4}$ cup to each quart of fruit. Cover the pan and warm it over very low heat until the fruit is softened and its juices have been released. You may then want to crush some of the fruit, particularly if the pieces are very large. Then proceed from here with any recipe, as if

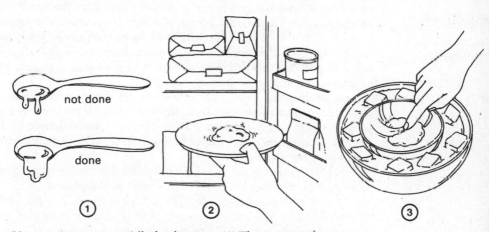

not done

done

① ② ③

Here are 3 ways to test jelly for doneness. (1) The spoon or sheet test: Dip a cold metal spoon in the boiling jelly, raise it a foot above the kettle, out of the steam, and turn the spoon so the syrup runs off. If the syrup forms 2 drops that flow together and fall off the spoon as one sheet, the jelly is done. (2) The refrigerator test: Pour a small amount of boiling jelly on a cold plate and put it in the freezer for a few minutes. Take it out and shake the plate. If the mixture jiggles, it's done. (3) The metal bowl method: Float a light metal mixing bowl in a larger bowl filled with ice water. Drop a teaspoon of the jelly mixture in the bottom of the small bowl. Run your finger through the jelly. If the jelly doesn't run back together, it's ready.

the fruit were fresh. More juice may drain from the frozen fruit than from fresh fruit, which is ideal for making preserves because it combines with the sweetener to make the clear, syrupy part of the preserves.

IF YOUR JELLIED FRUIT FAILS

Because there are many factors involved in making jellied fruit products, it's often hard to pinpoint one single factor that is responsible for a poor end product. Such is the challenge of making jellies and jams. A good grape jam or apple jelly of just the right firmness, with beautiful color and good fruit flavor, needs one special ingredient that you'll also find in a finely textured, light yeast bread, a fluffy soufflé, and a crisp home-made pickle—experience. And the best way to get experience is to learn from your mistakes and try again.

Jellies and jams made with honey tend to be softer than those made with sugar because honey contains so much more moisture. If your jelly was *too runny* and you used added liquid pectin, use the powdered kind next time. It generally gels better with honey than does the liquid kind. Maybe you didn't use enough pectin, be it liquid or powder. The problem could be caused by boiling the jelly too long or too slowly; you need a steady, rapid boil that can't be stirred down. Runny jams and jellies are still delicious. Just think of them as toppings for ice cream, yogurt, pancakes, waffles, and cereal instead of as jellies.

If, on the other hand, your jelly is *too stiff*, you may have used too much pectin. If you were making a jelly with fruit that required no extra pectin, perhaps you cooked it too long. (Perhaps some underripe fruit in the batch contributed extra pectin to the product.) If the jelly is *gummy*, it may have been overcooked.

If jelly is improperly sealed, *fermentation* may occur or mold may develop. Any jelly that has mold on it should be thrown out.

Jellied fruit products made with honey are generally a bit darker than those made with sugar; however, if your jellies or jams *darken at the top of the jar,* it might be because you stored them in too warm a place or because a faulty seal is allowing air to enter the jar. The color of jellied products can *fade* if they are stored in too warm a place or if kept in storage for too long a time. Red fruits, such as strawberries or red raspberries, are especially likely to fade.

If you've stirred your jams and preserves properly before jarring them, you should have no trouble with *fruit floating to the surface.* If you find fruit floating in your preserves, stir the preserve mixture gently for 5 minutes after removing it from the heat the next time you make them. Also, make sure that you've used fully ripe fruit, that it was cooked long enough, and that it was properly crushed or ground.

Sometimes *part of the liquid will separate* from the jellied mass during storage. This could be the result of too much acid in the fruit or keeping the preserves in too warm a place. Separation is more common in preserves made with honey or those that contain less sweetener than in preserves made using traditional recipes because sugar has a tendency to hold liquids and solids in the preserves together. If there is no evidence of mold or spoilage, the preserve is still safe to eat.

UNCOOKED JAMS AND JELLIES

If you miss the fresh flavor, color, and texture of fruit that is cooked away in most jams and jellies, you might like to try making some that are not cooked. These jellied products don't use pectin, but use gelatin or agar to gel, and they do it without a sweetener, so you can use as little honey as you'd like. They cannot be cooked, and certainly not boiled, because high temperatures affect the gelatin or agar that's used to create the gel. You won't find agar (which is a natural thickening agent made from seaweed) in many supermarkets, but you shouldn't have much trouble finding it in a natural food store, an Asian market, or one of the mail-order food companies listed in the Appendix.

All uncooked jams and jellies have to be stored in the refrigerator or freezer; they can't be canned. Pour them into sterilized jars with tight-fitting lids and refrigerate for no more than about 3 weeks, or store in the freezer for up to 6 months. If you're going to freeze them, remember to leave ½-inch headspace for expansion and let them cool in the refrigerator for at least 10 hours so that they can set up before being put in the freezer.

Uncooked Jam with Agar

This recipe was developed for agar flakes. Agar comes in other forms, but the flakes are the most convenient to use.

1 tablespoon lemon juice
3 cups of prepared mashed
    fruit, at room temperature
½ cup cold water
3 tablespoons plus 1½ teaspoons
    agar flakes
½ cup mild-flavor honey, such
    as clover (the amount of
    honey can be adjusted 3
    tablespoons either way,
    according to taste)

continued

Stir lemon juice into fruit and set aside. Place water in a small saucepan and stir in agar flakes. Without further stirring, wait 1 minute, then bring agar to a simmer over medium-low heat. Once it's simmering, stir for at least 2 minutes, or until the agar is completely dissolved. Then stir in the honey. Use a heatproof rubber spatula to scrape the sides and bottom of the pot.

Pouring with one hand and stirring with the other, add the agar mixture to the fruit (do not add the fruit to the agar). Continue stirring until it's completely mixed. Taste at this time and add more honey if desired. Pour into hot, scalded half-pint jars, leaving ¾-inch headspace, and seal.

Jam that will be used within 3 weeks can be kept in the refrigerator but freeze the rest. To freeze, leave ½-inch headspace and allow to cool in the refrigerator for 10 hours before freezing. Thaw jams in the refrigerator.

Yield: 4 half-pints

Unconventional Refrigerator Apricot Jam

We call this unconventional because it breaks all the rules we just gave you about what an uncooked jam or jelly should and should not do. Contrary to convention, this does not use gelatin or agar, and so, contrary to convention, it can be canned.

2 cups dried apricots
2 cups water
4 tablespoons lime juice
2 tablespoons maple syrup
½ teaspoon almond extract

Combine apricots and water, and simmer until apricots are soft and juice is almost gone. Purée in food processor. Return to saucepan and add lime juice, maple syrup, and almond extract; heat through. Can, refrigerate, or freeze. To can, pour into hot, scalded half-pint jars, leaving ¼-inch headspace, and seal. Process for 10 minutes in a boiling-water bath. To freeze, leave ½-inch headspace and allow to cool in the refrigerator for 10 hours before freezing.

Yield: 3 half-pints

Variation

Substitute prunes for apricots.

USING LOW-METHOXYL (LM) PECTIN

Regular jams and jellies gel through an interaction of pectin, acid, and sugar. Those made with added pectin are no different in this respect from cooked-down jellies, which gel with the aid of the natural pectin of fruits. LM pectin differs from both the commercial and natural pectin in fruits because it requires calcium salts, usually a dicalcium phosphate solution. (LM pectin is a natural product derived from the rind of citrus fruit. LM pectin can also be made from apples, but so far as we know, it's not yet available commercially.)

Naturalist Euell Gibbons discovered LM pectin through his brother, a diabetic who was experimenting with it for use in his own diet, and reported on his own experiments in *Organic Gardening and Farming* magazine back in the '60s. At that time, Gibbons's big problem was getting a small quantity of the pectin since it was only available wholesale. That problem was solved for him—and for all of us—since now many natural food stores and even some supermarkets carry it under a number of labels. If you can't find any, there are some sources listed in the Appendix.

LM pectin makes a wonderfully fruity jam or jelly that has a fresher fruit flavor than the longer-cooked products. And because it doesn't depend upon any sweetener to gel, be it honey or sugar, you need add only enough sweetener to enhance the fruit flavor and color.

There are several tricks to achieving a nice jam or jelly with this unique pectin. Because the calcium content of each type and batch of fruit will vary, a recipe cannot always be followed exactly, even if you've made the recipe before with great success. It's going to be necessary for you to test each batch before it's canned or frozen with a jelly test. If the jam or jelly passes the test, pour it into jars for storage or processing. But if it doesn't, then follow the procedures for correcting it in the general directions that introduce the charts; see page 255.

We've noticed that some of the LM pectin jams and jellies we've made have sometimes weeped or puddled, and when we checked with LM pectin suppliers we discovered that they, too, noticed this same condition in some of their jams and jellies. (You've got some weeping if you take out a spoonful of jelly or jam and the hole left fills up with liquid.) It seems that this weeping is caused by calcium. You can perhaps control weeping in subsequent batches by reducing the amount of calcium salts, but this is tricky because fruit itself contains some calcium, and this naturally occurring calcium will vary depending upon the variety of fruit, the season, and even the amount of calcium in the soil in which it grew. Console yourself with the fact that there's nothing wrong with a jam or jelly that weeps. It is fine to eat and will not affect the consistency. You can spoon out the liquid or absorb it with a paper towel.

Because they contain little sweetening, LM pectin jams and jellies don't keep as well as sugary ones. They should be canned in a boiling-water bath, or frozen. After they are opened, they must be refrigerated and used within 2 to 3 weeks.

USING ARTIFICIAL SWEETENER IN UNCOOKED JAMS AND JELLIES

Aspartame (which is sold in little packets under the name Equal and appears as Nutra-Sweet in sodas and other low-calorie products) is incredibly sweet—180 times as sweet as an equal amount of sugar. And it has no bitter aftertaste as does saccharin. Aspartame is a protein and not a sugar, which means that you can only use it in recipes that thicken without sugar. And because aspartame breaks down under heat, you can only use it in those sugarless recipes that don't rely upon any cooking, which rules out LM pectin recipes. All this means that you can only use it in uncooked jam and jelly recipes. Refer to the sweetener's package for the sugar equivalency and substitute in the recipe proportionately; or see the recipe here.

A few words about safety: Because we received requests for a recipe using aspartame from our magazine readers, we developed the one below for *Rodale's Organic Gardening* magazine. (Actually, this recipe was adapted from one that appeared in the last edition of *Stocking Up*. There it called for honey, and you can see that honey *or* aspartame can be used in it.)

At the time of this writing, we have no proof that aspartame is harmful, but we are listening very carefully to the debate. In 1985 the Centers for Disease Control (CDC) received a number of complaints from people with symptoms that appear whenever they eat anything with aspartame in it. These people "may be sensitive," says the CDC, and it is recommending that clinical studies be conducted that would concentrate on such symptoms as "headaches, mood alterations, and behavior changes." But Gerald Gaul, vice-president for nutrition and medical affairs for aspartame's manufacturer, says it is possible that "a few people may be allergic or sensitive to it. For these few people, the issue is not one of safety but rather of food selection." As far as we're concerned, the jury is still out on its safety.

Fresh Strawberry Preserves

1 cup water
1 envelope unflavored gelatin
2 cups coarsely chopped strawberries
   (about 1 quart whole berries)
1 teaspoon lemon juice
9 packets aspartame (Equal) or ⅓ cup honey

Pour water into a saucepan and sprinkle gelatin over it. Let stand 5 minutes.

Add berries, lemon juice, and honey, if you are using instead of the aspartame, to gelatin mixture and heat just to boiling, stirring all the while. If you are using aspartame in place of honey, remove fruit mixture from heat, add aspartame, and stir well.

Pour into hot, scalded containers, cool slightly, and refrigerate. If you plan to freeze, leave ½-inch headspace and allow to cool in the refrigerator for 10 hours before freezing.

Yield: about 4 half-pints

LM Pectin Jams and Jellies

The charts that follow give you the proper amounts and preparation directions for making LM pectin jams and jellies with specific fruits. Since the procedure is the same for all of them, we describe here just once.

(We tested more kinds of fruit than wound up in this chart. Those, like pears and rhubarb, that didn't taste good enough to us, we left out. So if you don't find a particular fruit here, you can assume that it doesn't make a good LM pectin jam or jelly.)

Stir pectin, 1 teaspoon at a time, into the honey until it's completely mixed. (Don't try adding the honey to the pectin or the pectin to the fruit. It will lump up and not dissolve.) In a large stainless steel or enamel saucepan, combine the fruit (for jam) or fruit juice (for jelly) and lemon juice (if called for in recipe). The wider the pot, the better, because a larger bottom surface area will allow the fruit or fruit juice to heat up faster than a tall, narrow pot. Bring to a full boil. Stir in the pectin-honey mixture and bring back to a full boil that cannot be stirred down. Immediately stir in the calcium solution (see below) and remove from the heat. Do this quickly. The pectin is activated by high heat, but overcooking weakens it.

Check the firmness with a jelly test (see page 248). If the jam or jelly is too loose, add more calcium solution, 1 teaspoon at a time, and test, repeating until it thickens nicely. (If the fruit or juice cools, as it

continued on page 262

DICALCIUM PHOSPHATE SOLUTION

This mineral solution works a kind of magic with LM pectin, enabling it to gel without sweetening. The powder comes with the pectin when you order it. Make up a batch of this solution to use when making any of the jams and jellies on the charts starting on page 256.

½ teaspoon dicalcium phosphate powder
1 cup water

In a small jar, shake together the dicalcium phosphate powder and water. Store in refrigerator. Shake well each time before using.

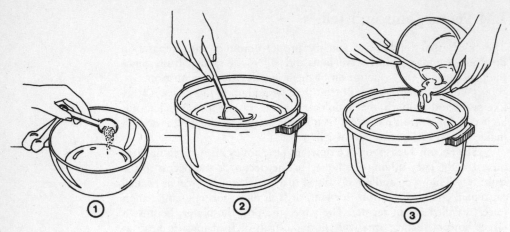

To make LM pectin jams and jellies, (1) stir pectin into the honey until completely mixed. (2) Combine the fruit or fruit juice and lemon juice (if called for in the recipe) in a large pot and bring to a boil. (3) Stir in the pectin-honey mixture and return to a boil.

Making LM Pectin Jam

Fruit	Quantity	Preparation	Prepared Fruit (cups)
Apricot (high acid)	3½ pounds	Pit (do not peel) apricots. Grind or finely chop fruit.	5
Blackberry or Red raspberry (low acid)	2 quarts	Crush berries one layer at a time. If desired, sieve half the pulp to remove some of the seeds.	5
Blueberry (low acid)	3 quarts	Remove stems from blueberries. Crush fruit one layer at a time or grind.	6½
Cherry, sour and sweet (sour—high acid) (sweet —low acid)	3 pounds	Remove stems and pits from cherries. Grind or finely chop fruit.	4
Grape (high acid)	4 pounds	Remove stems from grapes. Crush. Add 1 cup water. Cover and simmer 5 minutes, stirring occasionally. Sieve or put through food mill to remove seeds and skin.	6

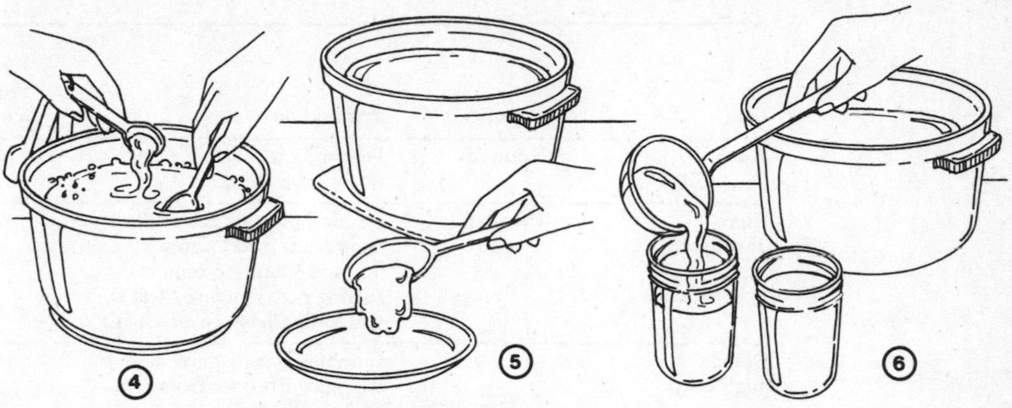

(4) Stir in the calcium solution and remove from the heat. (5) Check firmness with a jelly test. (6) Ladle into jars and seal.

Dry LM Pectin (teaspoons)	Honey (cups)	Lemon Juice (teaspoons)	Dicalcium Phosphate Solution (teaspoons)	Approx. Jam Yield (cups)
2½	⅔	—	6	5¾
2½	⅔	3 to 6	6	5¾
3¼	¾	6	6½	7½
2	½	6 (sweet only)	4	4½
3	¾	2	6	6¾

continued

Making LM Pectin Jam—*continued*

Fruit	Quantity	Preparation	Prepared Fruit (cups)
Peach (low acid)	3 pounds	Peel and pit peaches. Grind or finely chop fruit.	4
Plum (low acid)	4 pounds	Pit (do not peel) plums. Finely chop fruit. Add ½ cup water. Stir and simmer 5 minutes, stirring occasionally. (Peel if you wish a less tart product.)	6
Quince (high acid)	—	Combine 2 cups purée and 1 cup juice left over from quince jelly (below).	—
Raspberry, red. See Blackberry or Red raspberry.			
Strawberry (high acid)	2 quarts	Remove caps from strawberries. Crush berries one layer at a time.	5

Making LM Pectin Jelly

Fruit	Quantity	Preparation of Fruit to Extract Juice*	Juice (cups)
Apple or Crabapple (apple—low acid) (crabapple—high acid)	5 pounds	Remove blossom and stem ends from apples. Do not peel or core. Cut fruit into small chunks. Add 5 cups water. Cover and simmer 10 minutes, stirring occasionally. Crush, then simmer 10 minutes longer.	6
Blackberry (low acid)	2½ quarts	Crush berries one layer at a time.	3½
Cherry, sour (high acid)	3½ pounds	Remove stems and pits from cherries. Grind or finely chop fruit. Add ½ cup water. Cover and simmer 10 minutes, stirring occasionally.	3½

Dry LM Pectin (teaspoons)	Honey (cups)	Lemon Juice (teaspoons)	Dicalcium Phosphate Solution (teaspoons)	Approx. Jam Yield (cups)
2	$\frac{1}{2}$	6	4	$4\frac{1}{2}$
3	$\frac{3}{4}$ to 1	3	6	$7\frac{1}{4}$
1	$\frac{1}{4}$	1	3	2
$2\frac{1}{2}$	$\frac{2}{3}$	—	5	$5\frac{3}{4}$

Dry LM Pectin (teaspoons)	Honey (cups)	Lemon Juice (teaspoons)	Dicalcium Phosphate Solution (teaspoons)	Approx. Jelly Yield (cups)
3	1	6	6	8
$1\frac{3}{4}$	$\frac{1}{2}$	6 to 9	$3\frac{1}{2}$	4
$1\frac{3}{4}$	$\frac{1}{2}$	6	$3\frac{1}{2}$	4

continued

Making LM Pectin Jelly—*continued*

Fruit	Quantity	Preparation of Fruit to Extract Juice*	Juice (cups)
Currant (high acid)	4½ quarts	Remove large stems from currant clusters. Crush currants one layer at a time. Add 1½ cups water. Cover and simmer 10 minutes, stirring occasionally.	6½
Grape (high acid)	3½ pounds	Remove large stems from grapes. Crush fruit one layer at a time. Add 1 cup water. Cover and simmer 10 minutes, stirring occasionally.	4
Peach (low acid)	3½ pounds	Pit (do not peel) peaches. Grind or finely chop fruit. Add ½ cup water. Cover and simmer 5 minutes, stirring occasionally.	3
Plum (low acid)	5 pounds	Pit (do not peel) plums. Grind or finely chop fruit. Add 1½ cups water. Cover and simmer 10 minutes, stirring occasionally.	4
Quince (high acid)	3½ pounds	Wash, quarter, and core. Cut into large cubes. Cover with water. Bring to a boil and simmer 1 hour.	5 (reserve 1 cup for jam)
Raspberry, black (low acid)	3½ quarts	Crush berries one layer at a time. Heat gently until juice starts to flow. Cover and simmer 10 minutes, stirring occasionally.	4½
Raspberry, red (low acid)	2½ quarts	Crush berries one layer at a time. Heat gently until juice starts to flow. Cover and simmer 10 minutes, stirring occasionally.	4
Strawberry (high acid)	2½ quarts	Remove caps from strawberries. Crush fruit one layer at a time.	3½

*See page 242 for further information on extracting juice for making jelly.

Dry LM Pectin (teaspoons)	Honey (cups)	Lemon Juice (teaspoons)	Dicalcium Phosphate Solution (teaspoons)	Approx. Jelly Yield (cups)
3¼	¾	9	6½	7½
2½	½	2	4	5
1½	⅓	3	3	3⅓
2	¾ to 1	3	4	4¾
2	⅔	4	4	4⅔
2¼	½	4	4½	5
2	½	9	4	4½
1¾	½	—	3½	4

might during a second test, reheat it as quickly as possible.) If it is gummy, thin with juice, ½ cup at a time, and retest.

To can, pour into hot, scalded half-pint jars, leaving ¼-inch headspace, and seal. Process jams for 10 minutes and jellies for 5 minutes in a boiling-water bath.

LM pectin jams and jellies may also be frozen. Be sure to leave ½ inch headspace for expansion.

FILLING AND SEALING CONTAINERS

Cooked jellied fruit products should be sealed in glass canning jars. Some simple jellies that are made with sugar can be sealed safely using the open kettle method, but all the jellies and jams, preserves, conserves, marmalades, and fruit butters in this book must be canned in a boiling-water bath. The less sweetening you use, the more likely it is you should use boiling-water processing instead of the open kettle method, and since our recipes are lower in sweetening than traditional recipes, *we use only a boiling-water bath*. All LM pectin jams and jellies must be processed in a boiling-water bath, too.

We also do not recommend waxing jellies and jams as a means of sealing them. Until fairly recently, food preservation researchers thought that any jelly or jam firm enough could be sealed safely with paraffin. Such is no longer the case, no matter how much or what kind of sweetener you use. It's been discovered that wax seals fail more often than the common 2-piece lids, inviting molds and other contaminants. People used to just scrape off the top layer of food when they noticed mold, but this isn't advised anymore because we know that some molds produce toxins that can seep below the surface and go deep into the food.

In the chapter Canning Vegetables and Fruits, you'll find detailed information on canning jars and boiling-water canners. Turn back to page 82 to refresh your memory. We repeat here for your convenience the steps to follow when boiling-water-bath canning your jams and jellies.

STEP-BY-STEP DIRECTIONS
FOR CANNING IN A
BOILING-WATER BATH

1. Fill boiling-water canner over half full, deep enough to cover containers completely. There should be about 1 to 2 inches of water over the tops of the jars and at least 1 to 2 inches of headspace in the canner above the water. Turn on the heat so water can heat up.

2. Wash and rinse the jars and put them into hot water until needed. Place lids and screw bands in water and bring to a simmer. Remove from heat and leave in hot water until ready to use. If you are using closures that have rubber rings, wash rings in hot water and rinse well. Keep rings in water until ready to use.

3. Prepare jams or jellies for canning.

4. Spoon jam or jelly into jars, leaving recommended headspace. Remove the air from the jars by running a nonmetallic spatula along the side, pressing the food as you do so. (This step is necessary only if your jam or jelly has pieces of fruit in it.) Add more jam or jelly, if necessary; the correct amount of food helps to create a good vacuum. Wipe the jars, paying particular attention to any food or liquid that might have spilled onto the lid; any food left there could ruin your chances of a good seal. Then close jars (see the section Closures on page 84).

5. Place the closed jars upright on a rack in the canner so that none of them are touching any others, allowing the water to circulate freely. If there is room for 2 layers of jars, place a rack between the 2 levels and stagger the containers so that none are directly over any of those below. Water should be 2 inches over the tops of the containers. Add water, if needed. Be careful not to pour water directly on the containers. Allow 2 inches headspace in canner for water to boil without running over.

6. Put the lid on the canner and bring the water to boiling.

7. *Begin to count time as soon as the water starts to boil* and process for time recommended in your recipe. Leave the lid on the canner, but remove it periodically to make sure the water is boiling gently and steadily. Add more boiling water as needed to keep containers covered.

8. As soon as the processing time is up, remove the containers from the canner. Place them upright, out of drafts, on wood racks, a wooden board, or several thicknesses of a dry towel so that they are not in direct contact with anything cold, like a countertop or metal rack, or anything damp, like a wet towel or sink, either of which might cause very hot jars to crack. Be sure that the jars are not touching so that air can circulate under, over, and around each one. Let them cool by themselves; don't tamper with them until they are cool.

9. The last bit of air is exhausted as the food cools, creating that vacuum you want. The common 2-piece lid is self-sealing; you'll hear a reassuring high-pitched sound of the metal lid snapping

continued on page 266

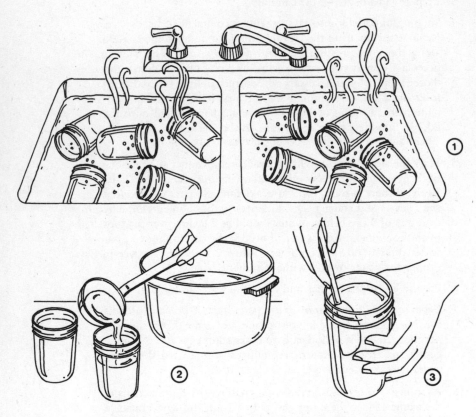

(1) Start the boiling-water–bath processing of jellies and jams by washing and rinsing your jars and lids; keep the jars in hot water until you need them. (2) Ladle the jelly or jam into the jars. (3) Remove air from the jars by running a nonmetallic spatula along the inside of the glass; this step is necessary only if your jelly or jam has pieces of fruit in it. (4) Add more jelly or jam if necessary, making sure all jars have the correct headspace. (5) Wipe the jar rims to pick up any spilled food or liquid, then adjust the caps. (6) Place the jars on a rack in the canner, making sure none are touching. There should be 2 inches of water above the jars. (7) When processing time is up, remove the jars and place them on a folded towel or wooden rack. Be sure the jars aren't touching so air can circulate around them and hasten cooling.

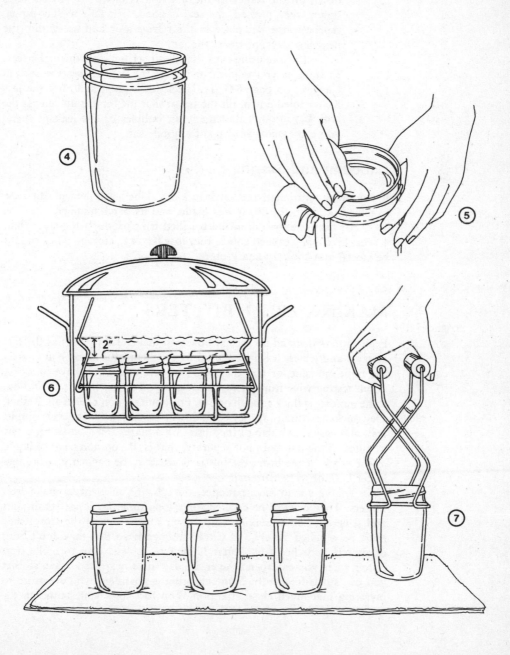

down on the glass rim when the vacuum is complete and the jar seals itself. You can tell if the 2-piece lid is sealed by pressing down on the center of the lid. If it is down already or stays down when pressed, the seal is good. If it fails to stay down, reprocess the jar, place in the refrigerator and use within the next few days, or freeze the jar.

If you're using caps that don't self-seal, complete the seals as soon as you take them out of the canner (see the section Closures on page 84). To check for a good seal after the jars have cooled down, tilt the jar so that the food is up against the seal. If you don't notice any air bubbles or any leakage there, you can assume you've got a good seal.

Labeling and Storing

If you make more than one batch in a day, label each jar with the type of jellied product, the day it was made, and its batch number.

For best quality, do not keep jellied fruit products for more than 1 year. Like many canned goods, they lose flavor in storage. They should be stored in a cool, dry, dark place.

MAKING FRUIT BUTTERS

Fruit butters demand no special knack to make. They aren't as delicate as jams and jellies. It isn't essential to get them off the stove at exactly the right moment for fear they will not gel. You won't have to worry about testing your fruit for pectin or acid, or do a jelly test to find out if the mixture is thick enough or not. Fruit butters don't gel at all. Rather, they thicken naturally as they cook down. Testing for thickness is simple, fast, and easy: Put a dab of the butter on a plate, and let it sit for a few minutes. If the dab does not separate, that is, if you don't notice liquid at the edges of the drop, the butter is ready to be canned in a boiling-water bath or to be frozen.

You've got to have patience, though, if you want to make fruit butters. They have to be cooked for a long time, far longer than jams and jellies. If you're making fruit butter on the top of the stove, they must be watched closely and stirred frequently so that they don't burn or scorch. Scorched fruit butter is next to useless. Plan to make fruit butter when you can spend the entire day in or near the kitchen so that you can stir it frequently. Some cheating is possible if you're not up to investing that much close attention. You can cook your butter in the oven or in a slow cooker; neither demands constant watching.

Equipment

A large kettle or pot with a heavy bottom is best for making fruit butters. Because they take so long to cook down and the quantity is considerably reduced after all that cooking, you'll probably want to start with a good amount of fruit to make it worth your while, so a big pot is essential. And it needs a heavy bottom because the thicker the butter gets, the more chance of scorching. Heavy bottoms don't mean you don't have to stir frequently, though, especially toward the end.

The Pennsylvania Dutch, who brought fruit butter with them when they came to this country from Germany, used cast-iron or copper pots slung on tripods over an open fire outdoors. If you're planning to make a great quantity of fruit butter, you may want to invest in a modern-day version of those big kettles—a stockpot. And make it stainless steel, not aluminum. Aluminum is going to cost you less, but don't be tempted by the lower price. The acids in your fruit may react with the aluminum and cause both a color and a flavor change. Stainless steel, despite its price, is best because the metal is stable and will not react with fruit acids.

If the bottom of the pot that you use is on the thin side—in other words, if it's just a regular pot, not an especially thick-bottomed one— we suggest that you buy an asbestos pad and place it under your pot, over the burner. It will spread heat evenly over the bottom of the pot, helping to prevent hot spots from developing which can otherwise lead to scorching.

A heavy pot is not nearly so important if you're making your butter in the oven. Use a large roasting pan so that as much surface area of the butter as possible is exposed to heat, encouraging good evaporation. Stay away from aluminum. Stainless steel is, of course, just fine. So are glass and enamel.

Any slow cooker is good, too. The bigger, the better. But slow cookers don't come in giant sizes, so you might find it more convenient to start your butter on top of the stove until it's cooked down to a loose purée, and then finish it off in the slow cooker. This way you can start off with a larger quantity in a big pot, but still take advantage of the slow cooking in the cooker toward the end, when the butter is more apt to burn on the stove. Because you want water to evaporate out of the pot, don't use the cooker's lid.

Additions to Fruit Butters

You will notice that in most of the recipes that follow we recommend adding honey to taste when the butter has finished cooking down, rather than adding honey while the fruit is still cooking. If fruit is ripe or slightly

To make apple butter, (1) simmer unpeeled and uncored apple slices in cider, stirring frequently. (2) After the butter has thickened, put it through a food mill, discarding the peels, seeds, and stems. (3) Put this puréed mixture back in the pot and simmer until thick. (4) The butter can also be cooked down in the oven. To do so, place the purée in a large roasting pan and cook, uncovered, until thick.

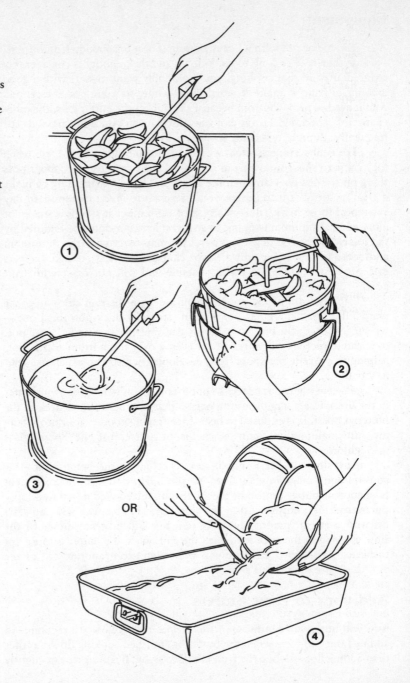

OR

overripe, the natural sugars in them are at their peak, and no extra sweetener may be necessary at all. You may spoil your butter by making it too sweet if you add honey without tasting the finished product first.

You can spice up your butter with cinnamon, cloves, allspice, and other flavorings near the end of the long cooking. Add stick cinnamon about 40 minutes before you suspect the butter will be finished, and add powdered spices about 15 minutes before the butter is done.

FRUIT BUTTERS

Apple Butter

Some people swear that the best apple butter is made from unpeeled and uncored apples. Others see no differences. If you are peeling and coring your apples, leave out the step that tells you to run your fruit through the food mill.

3 cups apple cider
5 pounds apples, unpeeled and
   uncored, sliced thin
   honey, to taste

ground cinnamon, to taste
ground allspice, to taste
ground cloves, to taste

Put cider in a big stainless steel or enamel pot and bring to a boil. Add apples slowly, being careful not to splatter yourself when you do. Allow the apples and cider to come to a boil, then simmer, stirring frequently to prevent sticking (and do remember to stir).

When the apple butter has begun to thicken considerably, the apple slices will start to fall apart as you stir the butter. At some point after the butter has thickened, remove it from the heat and put everything through a food mill, discarding the peels, seeds, and stems. Put the remaining soupy mixture back into the pot, put the pot back on the heat, and simmer until the apple butter is a thick, dark-brown mass. This will take approximately 4 to 5 hours. You can also cook down the butter in the oven or in a slow cooker. After puréeing it, put it in a large roasting pan and cook, uncovered, in the oven at 325°F until thick. Or use a slow cooker and cook on high for 10 hours, stirring occasionally and pushing the outer edges into the middle of the butter. Leave the lid off.

If you want to sweeten the apple butter, use honey and sweeten to taste. You may also want to add spices to your apple butter. If so, add spices, to taste. Bring the mixture to a boil, and jar the apple butter in hot, scalded half-pint jars, leaving a ½-inch headspace. Seal and process for 10 minutes in a boiling-water bath.

Yield: 4 half-pints

Grape Butter

1 gallon grapes
¼ cup water
  honey, to taste

Put grapes in stainless steel or enamel kettle with water. Heat and mash grapes. Continue cooking as the mixture thickens, about 30 minutes, stirring frequently. When thicker, put through a food mill and remove skins and seeds. Return to heat and cook 2 to 3 hours until thick.

If you want to sweeten your grape butter, add honey to taste, just before canning.

When thick, pack in hot, scalded half-pint jars, leaving ½-inch headspace, and seal. Process for 5 minutes in a boiling-water bath.

Yield: 3 half-pints

Prune Butter

1 pound pitted dried prunes
3 cups water
½ cup white or cider vinegar
¾ cup honey, or to taste
¼ teaspoon grated nutmeg
  (optional)
½ teaspoon ground allspice
  (optional)
¼ teaspoon ground cloves
  (optional)

Rinse prunes. Cover with water, bring to a boil in a stainless steel or enamel pot, and then reduce heat and simmer until tender, about 15 minutes. Cool slightly. Drain prunes and reserve liquid for another use, or use as a juice. Put the prunes through a sieve or blender to purée. Add vinegar and honey. Spices can be added at this time if desired. Cook over low heat for 10 to 15 minutes.

Pour into hot, scalded half-pint jars, leaving ½-inch headspace. Seal and process for 5 minutes in a boiling-water bath.

Yield: 4 half-pints

Variation

Substitute an equal amount of raisins for half the prunes.

Baked Peach Butter

12 cups peeled, pitted, and
      sliced peaches (about 8
      pounds)
4   cups water
3   tablespoons lemon juice
½   cup honey

Place sliced peaches and water in an 8-quart stainless steel or enamel pot and cook over medium heat until peaches are soft, about 20 to 25 minutes. Stir frequently to prevent peaches from sticking. When fruit is tender, add lemon juice and honey and stir to combine. Put the peach mixture through a food mill, blender, or food processor and blend until smooth. Pour and divide the purée into two shallow 9 × 13-inch baking pans or roasting pans and bake uncovered for 1 hour at 325°F. Continue baking, stirring every 15 to 20 minutes, until the butter is thick. This will take approximately 1 to 1½ hours. The peach butter will be thick, fine textured, and a rich reddish-amber color.

Ladle it into hot, scalded half-pint jars, leaving ½-inch headspace, and seal. Process for 10 minutes in a boiling-water bath.

Yield: 3 half-pints

Pear Butter

16 cups peeled, cored, and
      sliced winter pears
      (approximately 8 pounds)
1   cup pineapple juice
½   cup lemon juice
½   cup honey
3   sticks of cinnamon, 2 inches
      long
20 whole cloves, tied into a
      piece of cheesecloth

In a blender or food processor purée pears, in batches, adding some of the juices if needed to help purée them.

Pour pear purée into a large stainless steel or enamel kettle. Add juices, honey, cinnamon sticks, and cloves. Cook, partially covered, over low heat until thick, about 3 hours. Remove cinnamon sticks and bag of cloves and discard. Pour into hot, scalded half-pint jars, leaving ½-inch headspace, and seal. Process for 10 minutes in a boiling-water bath. Leave at room temperature to cool and check to be sure each is sealed before storing.

Yield: about 6 half-pints

Cranberry Butter

This very unusual fruit butter is a real treat when served with roast pork, beef, or turkey, or spread on spiced quick breads.

2½ pounds cranberries
⅔ cup apple juice
1 cup maple syrup
½ cup honey
½ teaspoon ground cinnamon

In a large stainless steel or enamel kettle, combine cranberries and juice and cook until cranberries have popped and are soft, about 20 minutes. Purée cranberries in a food processor.

Put cranberries back into kettle and add maple syrup, honey, and cinnamon. Cook until thick, 10 to 15 minutes.

Spoon into hot, scalded half-pint jars, leaving ½-inch headspace, and seal. Process for 5 minutes in a boiling-water bath.

Yield: 6 half-pints

JAMS

Concord Grape Jam

Concord grapes are the ultimate fruit from which to make jams. Their strong spicy flavor and high pectin content combine in a perfect jam with an aroma of crisp fall days. Only 40 minutes is needed from picking the grapes to ladling the jam into jars. Note that the initial cooking is done gently, at just over a simmer. After the honey is added, a vigorous boil is necessary to optimize the effects of the natural pectin.

3 pounds Concord grapes
1½ cups mild-flavor honey

Wash grapes and place in large stainless steel or enamel saucepan. Crush them with a potato masher or a wooden spoon, picking out whatever stems are easily extracted. When a little juice is released, cook grapes at a gentle boil until the center of the grape becomes tender enough to squash with a spoon. This point is reached about 10 minutes after the grapes come to a boil. Using a rubber spatula, force the grapes through a sieve to strain out the seeds. Press hard to extract all the pulp.

Return the strained pulp to the saucepan. Quickly bring to a boil and stir in honey. Stir frequently but slowly, scraping all parts of the bottom of the pot carefully. Keep the temperature as high as possible, regulating the heat so that the grapes do not splatter wildly but boil vigorously. After about 10 minutes you should not be able to stir down the boil. Begin testing for the gelling point. The jelly will darken slightly and begin to feel thicker as stirred. You can lower the heat slightly as the grapes thicken. The jam should reach the gelling point 15 to 20 minutes after it begins to boil. Ladle it into hot, scalded half-pint jars, leaving ¼-inch headspace, and seal. Process in a boiling-water bath for 10 minutes.

Yield: 4 half-pints

Peach Jam

4 pounds fully ripened fresh
    peaches, washed, peeled,
    and pitted
¼ cup fresh lemon juice
2 packages powdered fruit
    pectin
2 cups mild-flavor honey

Chop or coarsely grind peaches, blending with lemon juice. Measure prepared fruit, packing down in cup. You should have 4 full cups. Place fruit and lemon juice in a 6- to 8-quart stainless steel or enamel saucepan. Add pectin and mix well.

Bring to a boil over high heat, stirring constantly. When fruit is boiling, stir while slowly pouring in honey, blending well. Continue stirring and return to a full rolling boil. When boiling cannot be stirred down, boil for 4 more minutes. Remove from heat. Alternately stir and skim for 5 minutes to cool slightly.

Can or freeze. To can, pour into hot, scalded half-pint jars, leaving ¼-inch headspace, and seal. Process in a boiling-water bath for 10 minutes. To freeze, leave ½-inch headspace and allow to cool in the refrigerator for 10 hours before freezing.

Yield: 3 half-pints

Salvation Jam

This jam is a divine combination of nectarines and pineapple sage. The name comes from *salvia,* the Latin name for sage, and means "salvation."

4 cups peeled, pitted, and
   finely chopped nectarines
1 package powdered fruit
   pectin
2 tablespoons lemon juice

1 cup honey
12 large leaves pineapple sage,
   torn into small pieces and
   tied into a cheesecloth bag

In a large stainless steel or enamel saucepan combine the nectarines, pectin, and lemon juice. Heat over medium-high heat until fruit begins to soften. Mash fruit.

Bring to a rolling boil. Stir in honey. Place the pineapple sage leaves into the fruit mixture.

Bring again to a rolling boil. Cook, stirring constantly, until the mixture resembles a thick syrup, about 3 to 5 minutes.

Remove pineapple-sage bag. Pour jam into hot, scalded half-pint jars, leaving ¼-inch headspace, and seal. Process in a boiling-water bath for 5 minutes.

Yield: 3 half-pints

Spiced Blueberry Jam

This jam is spiced with cinnamon and cloves.

8 cups frozen or fresh
   blueberries, puréed
¾ cup apple juice
4 tablespoons plus 1½
   teaspoons lemon juice

1 cup honey
½ teaspoon ground cinnamon
¼ teaspoon ground cloves

Combine blueberries and apple and lemon juices in an 8-quart stainless steel or enamel saucepan. Place over high heat and stir until mixture comes to a boil. Add honey, cinnamon, and cloves. Continue stirring.

When mixture comes to a full boil again, begin timing for approximately 20 to 30 minutes. Jam is ready when it is thick, jamlike, and sticks slightly to the bottom of the pan.

Pour into hot, scalded half-pint jars, leaving ¼-inch headspace, and seal. Process in a boiling-water bath for 5 minutes.

Yield: 4 half-pints

Cherry-Berry Jam

Raspberry provides the predominant flavor in this multi-fruit jam, which can be made from all frozen fruits.

3 cups fresh or frozen blueberries, puréed
3 cups fresh or frozen cherries, puréed
2 cups fresh or frozen raspberries, puréed

¾ cup apple juice
4 tablespoons plus 1½ teaspoons lemon juice
1 cup plus 2 tablespoons honey

Combine blueberries, cherries, raspberries, apple juice, and lemon juice in an 8-quart stainless steel or enamel saucepan. Place over high heat and stir until mixture comes to a boil. Add honey and continue stirring.

When mixture comes to a full boil, begin timing for approximately 25 minutes. Jam is ready when it resembles thick, sticky syrup.

Pour into hot, scalded half-pint jars, leaving ¼-inch headspace, and seal. Process in a boiling-water bath for 10 minutes.

Yield: 4 half-pints

Tangelemono Jam

In this recipe the rinds of the fruits provide the pectin and the juice provides the acid. Only use tangelos (or oranges) at the height of the season. The older they are, the more bitter.

5 tangelos (or oranges)
2 lemons
1¼ cups honey

Cut one tangelo in half and remove seeds. Purée until pieces of rind are finely ground. Peel and seed the remaining tangelos and the lemons. Add to first tangelo and purée until smooth.

Pour into an 8-quart stainless steel or enamel saucepan, then stir in honey. Place over high heat, stirring frequently until it reaches a boil that cannot be stirred down. At this point, begin timing for approximately 9 minutes. Boil and stir until mixture resembles a thick syrup.

Pour into hot, scalded half-pint jars, leaving ¼-inch headspace, and seal. Process in a boiling-water bath for 10 minutes. Allow the jam to "age" for 2 weeks before tasting or the jam may be too bitter.

Yield: 3 half-pints

Honey-Strawberry Jam

This jam is not as stiff as those made with sugar. Its loose texture is a delightful change.

4   cups stemmed and
       thoroughly crushed
       strawberries (about 2 quarts
       whole berries)
2   tablespoons lemon juice
1   package powdered fruit
       pectin
1¾ cups honey

Combine the berries and lemon juice in a 6- to 8-quart stainless steel or enamel saucepan. Mix pectin into fruit.

Place over high heat and stir until mixture comes to a boil. Immediately add honey and stir until mixture comes to a full rolling boil that cannot be stirred down. Start timing at this point for approximately 10 to 12 minutes. Continue to stir slowly. Jam will foam at first, then subside and, when ready, will feel thick and sticky when stirred. The color becomes a deep garnet red.

Ladle into hot, scalded half-pint jars, leaving ¼-inch headspace, and seal. Process in a boiling-water bath for 5 minutes.

Yield: 4 half-pints

Hot Pepper Jam

This is not your usual jam by any means. It's hot and spicy—more of a condiment than a jam. Try it on hors d'oeuvres and canapés. It's especially nice on a cucumber slice with cream cheese and freshly snipped dill.

1   cup seeded and chopped
       green peppers
⅓   cup seeded and chopped
       jalapeño peppers
1½ cups cider vinegar
2   teaspoons low-methoxyl
       pectin
¾ to 1 cup honey
4   teaspoons dicalcium
       phosphate solution (see
       page 255)
5   drops natural green food
       coloring (optional)

Combine peppers with 1 cup vinegar in a blender or food processor until smooth.

Pour mixture into a heavy-bottom stainless steel or enamel saucepan. Rinse blender or processor with remaining vinegar and add to peppers. Dissolve pectin in honey, add all at once to peppers, and bring mixture to a rolling boil. Stir until pectin is completely dissolved. Remove pan from heat. Add dicalcium phosphate solution, stirring to blend in well. Set aside for 5 minutes.

Skim foam from top and discard. Add food coloring if desired. Spoon into hot, scalded half-pint jars, leaving $\frac{1}{4}$-inch headspace, and seal. Process for 10 minutes in a boiling-water bath. Or jar and refrigerate, where it will last for 2 months.

Yield: 3 half-pints

JELLIES

Cherry Citrus Jelly

3 cups sweet cherry juice
1 cup sour cherry juice
$\frac{2}{3}$ cup orange juice concentrate
2 tablespoons lemon juice

In a large stainless steel or enamel saucepan combine all ingredients. Boil for 12 minutes. Do a jelly test, and when firm enough, ladle into hot, scalded half-pint jars, leaving $\frac{1}{4}$-inch headspace, and seal. Process for 15 minutes in a boiling-water bath.

Yield: 2 half-pints

Lemon Honey Jelly

$\frac{3}{4}$ cup lemon juice
2 cups honey
$\frac{1}{2}$ cup liquid fruit pectin

In a stainless steel or enamel saucepan combine lemon juice and honey. Bring to a full rolling boil. Add pectin, stir vigorously, and boil about 2 minutes. Do a jelly test, and when firm enough, ladle into hot, scalded half-pint jars, leaving $\frac{1}{4}$-inch headspace, and seal. Process for 5 minutes in a boiling-water bath.

Yield: 2 half-pints

Wild Berry Jelly

Use elderberries, dewberries, loganberries, rowan (mountain ash), beach plums, rose hips, or youngberries, making sure they're not overly ripe. The riper the fruit, the lower the natural pectin content.

1¾ pounds berries, washed and
    stemmed
¾ pound green apples, halved
2½ cups water
1 cup honey
3 tablespoons lime juice

In stainless steel or enamel saucepans boil berries in half the water for 10 minutes while you boil the apples in the other half for 15 minutes. Combine and boil for 5 minutes more. Strain through a jelly bag. Add honey and lime juice and bring to a boil for another 5 minutes or until gelled. Do a jelly test, and when firm enough, ladle into hot, scalded half-pint jars, leaving ¼-inch headspace. Process for 5 minutes in a boiling-water bath.

Yield: 2 half-pints

Variation

Substitute halved cherries or plums for half the berries.

Notes:
    1. If using rowan, add a bay leaf to cooking mixture. Remove before jarring.
    2. If using beach plums, follow recipe, then measure strained liquid and add ⅓ that amount of honey.
    3. For rose hips, gather when deep red and firm, which is usually after the first frost. Slit and remove seeds and flesh with the thin handle-end of a fork. Omit apples and proceed with main recipe, making sure hips are soft before straining.

Paradise Jelly

1½ pounds quinces (about 4), cored and chopped (not peeled)
2 pounds tart apples, cored and chopped (not peeled)
1 cup cranberries, picked over and washed

1 tablespoon low-methoxyl pectin
1 cup honey
4 teaspoons dicalcium phosphate solution (see page 255)

In a stainless steel or enamel saucepan bring quinces to a boil in water to cover, about 30 minutes. Add apples and cranberries and simmer until fruit is soft, about 10 minutes. Strain through a colander that has been lined with dampened cheesecloth. Let juice drip through. Do not squeeze cheesecloth or pulp.

Bring 5 cups juice to a boil. Dissolve the pectin in honey and add all at once to boiling juice. Stir until pectin is completely dissolved. Remove from heat. Add dicalcium phosphate solution, stirring to blend in well.

Pour into hot, scalded half-pint jars, leaving ¼-inch headspace, and seal. Process for 5 minutes in a boiling-water bath.

Yield: 6 half-pints

Persimmon Jelly

3½ to 4 pounds ripe
    persimmons (about 50)
2 cups water
3 tablespoons lemon juice
1 package powdered fruit
    pectin
½ cup honey

Wash persimmons and remove blossom end. Place in a 6- to 8-quart stainless steel or enamel saucepan. Add water. Bring mixture to a boil. Mash persimmons. Reduce heat and simmer 10 minutes.

Remove from heat. Press pulp through strainer to remove pits. Measure 3 cups pulp. Stir in lemon juice and pectin. Bring mixture to a boil. Stir in honey all at once. Let mixture return to a full rolling boil that can't be stirred down. Boil for 1 to 2 minutes, stirring constantly. Do a jelly test, and when firm enough, ladle into hot, scalded half-pint jars, leaving ¼-inch headspace, and seal. Process for 5 minutes in a boiling-water bath.

Yield: 3 half-pints

Apple Jelly

The simplest of jellies, because apples make their own pectin.

5 pounds apples
    honey

Wash apples. Remove stems and dark spots and quarter apples, but do not pare or core. Add just enough water to half cover apples and cook in a stainless steel or enamel saucepan until the fruit is soft. Drain, using a jelly bag. You'll get more juice if you squeeze the bag, but it will make a cloudy jelly. Measure 6 cups juice. Add ½ cup honey for every cup juice. Boil until a good jelly test is obtained. Pour into hot, sterilized half-pint jars, leaving ¼-inch headspace, and seal. Process for 5 minutes in a boiling-water bath.

Yield: 5 half-pints
continued

Variations

Apple Mint Jelly—Just before removing apple jelly from the heat, add a few mint leaves that have been washed (about ¼ cup mint leaves to 1 quart juice) and a bit of natural green food coloring. Stir, remove the leaves, and process as above. This makes an attractive and delicious jelly to serve with lamb.

Apple Cinnamon Jelly—Drop a stick of cinnamon in each jar before processing.

Raspberry Jelly with Homemade Pectin

5   cups homemade apple pectin
    (see page 244)
1   cup raspberry juice
1½ cups honey

In a large stainless steel or enamel saucepan stir together the apple pectin, raspberry juice, and honey. Bring to a boil over high heat, stirring constantly until syrupy, about 18 minutes. Do a jelly test, and when firm enough, ladle into hot, scalded half-pint jars, leaving ¼-inch headspace, and seal. Process for 5 minutes in a boiling-water bath.

Yield: 6 half-pints

Cranapple Jelly

4   cups cranberries
3   cups water
8   cups green apples
1   cup cranberry juice
3   cups apple juice
½   cup honey
1   tablespoon lemon juice

In stainless steel or enamel saucepans boil cranberries in 1 cup water for 10 minutes while you boil the apples in the other 2 cups water for 15 minutes. Strain through a jelly bag. Combine cranberry juice, apple juice, honey, and lemon juice. Cook for 18 to 20 minutes. Do a jelly test, and when firm enough, ladle into hot, scalded half-pint jars, leaving ¼-inch headspace, and seal. Process for 5 minutes in a boiling-water bath.

Yield: 2 half-pints

PRESERVES

Strawberry Rhubarb Preserves

The famous strawberry-rhubarb pie combination in a tangy, sweet preserve.

⅔ cup honey
4 cups hulled, washed, and sliced strawberries
4 cups washed and diced unpeeled rhubarb

3½ teaspoons low-methoxyl pectin
3 tablespoons lemon juice
4 teaspoons dicalcium phosphate solution (see page 255)

Drizzle ⅓ cup honey over strawberries. Leave at room temperature for 3 to 4 hours.

Combine strawberries, their juice, and rhubarb in a medium-size stainless steel or enamel saucepan. Simmer over medium heat until rhubarb is tender, about 10 minutes. Dissolve low-methoxyl pectin in ⅓ cup honey and add all at once to simmering strawberry-rhubarb mixture. Stir until pectin is completely dissolved. Remove from heat. Add lemon juice and dicalcium phosphate solution, stirring it in well.

Pour into hot, scalded half-pint jars, leaving ¼-inch headspace, and seal. Process for 10 minutes in a boiling-water bath.

Yield: 6 half-pints

Peach Orange Preserves

1 orange
4 cups frozen peaches, puréed
¼ cup apple juice
1 tablespoon lemon juice
¾ cup honey

Cut orange in quarters and remove seeds. Purée until rind is finely chopped. Combine orange purée, peaches, apple juice, and lemon juice in an 8-quart stainless steel or enamel saucepan.

Place over high heat, stirring frequently, until mixture comes to a boil. Add honey and continue stirring. When mixture comes to a full boil, start timing for approximately 8 to 10 minutes. Jam is ready when it resembles thick syrup.

Pour into hot, scalded half-pint jars, leaving ¼-inch headspace, and seal. Process for 10 minutes in a boiling-water bath.

Yield: 7 half-pints

Plum Honey Preserves

Because plums are naturally high in pectin, no extra pectin is necessary.

2 pounds red or purple plums
      (not prune plums), slightly
      underripe, or a mixture of
      underripe and fully ripe
      fruits
1 cup mild-flavor honey (clover
      or orange blossom)

Use a heavy-bottom 6- to 8-quart stainless steel or enamel saucepan, preferably a pan that is wide in proportion to its depth. Work over the saucepan to catch the juice. Pit plums and cut them into large chunks.

Stir in honey. Bring to a boil over low heat, stirring frequently. When mixture looks soupy, increase heat and bring to a full rolling boil. Skim off the solid white froth.

Continue to stir slowly, not vigorously. After 15 to 20 minutes, the mixture will become translucent and slightly darker. It feels thicker when stirred and will thicken further as it cools.

Pour into hot, scalded half-pint jars, leaving ¼-inch headspace, and seal. Process for 10 minutes in a boiling-water bath.

2 half-pints

Red Tomato Preserves

Be sure to use a mild-flavor honey that won't upstage the delicate tomato taste.

10 cups cherry tomatoes,
       skinned and coarsely
       chopped
2 cups apple juice
2 cups honey
2 lemons, sliced
1 teaspoon ground cinnamon
½ teaspoon ground cloves
¼ teaspoon ground allspice

In a 6- or 8-quart stainless steel or enamel saucepan, stir together all ingredients.

Place over high heat and bring to a full rolling boil. Boil, stirring constantly, until very thick, about 20 minutes.

Pour into hot, scalded half-pint jars, leaving ¼-inch headspace, and seal. Process 10 minutes in a boiling-water bath.

Yield: 5 half-pints

Sunshine Preserves

Gently thickened by the sun, these preserves are chunks of fresh fruit in a jewellike syrup. Before you begin to prepare the fruit, note the special setup you'll need.

1 cup honey
4 cups prepared fruit—any
    single fruit or combination*

Begin early in the day to optimize sunny hours.

In a large stainless steel or enamel saucepan bring honey to a full boil. Add fruit and bring to a rolling boil over high heat, stirring slowly. Immediately pour onto stainless steel baking sheets, or some other type of tray fashioned from ceramic or glass, to a depth of no more than $\frac{1}{2}$ inch. (Do not use aluminum, as the metal will react with the acid in the fruit and discolor it.)

The trays have to be covered with glass or plastic, both to keep insects out and to increase the heat. However, since evaporation of excess liquid is a priority, it is important that the cover be well vented, which means that it shouldn't be right up against the tray.

If using glass, choose a framed piece (like a used window) and place it over the tray, sliding small blocks of wood or something similar at the four corners to raise it just a bit above the tray. You can use a rigid sheet of plastic in the same way, or you can stretch plastic wrap over a frame to give it rigidity.

Remove the glass or plastic covering and stir every 4 hours to keep the fruit coated with syrup. Bring preserves indoors when the sun goes down.

Preserves are done when the syrup is as thick as honey. With ideal conditions, the preserves will be ready after a total of 12 hours in the sun. Less-than-ideal conditions may require up to 3 days.

Pack into hot, scalded half-pint jars and refrigerate; use within 3 weeks.

Yield: 2 half-pints

*To prepare fruit, slice strawberries thinly; lightly crush smaller berries. Peel and finely chop peaches or apricots, bananas, raspberries, tropical fruit (guava, papaya). Pit and halve cherries.

CONSERVES

Ginger and Pear Conserve

3 pounds seckel or winter
   pears (about 21 to 24)
2 tablespoons grated orange
   rind
2 oranges, peeled, seeded, and
   chopped fine
1 tablespoon chopped, peeled
   ginger root or 1 piece about
   1½ inches square
½ cup honey
3 tablespoons lemon juice

Wash, peel, core, and slice pears. If desired to save time, chop half the amount of peeled and cored pears in a blender along with the orange rind and orange.

Put ginger into a cheesecloth bag. Combine pears, orange rind, orange, ginger bag, honey, and lemon juice and bring slowly to a simmer in a covered stainless steel or enamel saucepan. Cook until pears are tender, about 10 minutes. Remove cover and continue to cook, stirring occasionally, until desired consistency is reached.

Pour into hot, scalded half-pint jars, leaving ¼-inch headspace, and seal. Process for 15 minutes in a boiling-water bath.

Yield: about 3 half-pints

Black Cherry Conserve

2 medium-size navel oranges,
   peeled, seeded, and chopped
   (½ cup juice and pieces)
2 tablespoons grated orange
   rind
4 cups sweet cherries
½ cup honey
½ cup lemon juice
¾ teaspoon ground cinnamon
6 whole cloves

In a large stainless steel or enamel saucepan, combine oranges, rind, cherries, honey, lemon juice, and cinnamon. Put cloves into a cheesecloth bag and add to saucepan. Bring to a boil, then turn down and simmer for 20 minutes. Bring back to boil for 4 to 5 minutes or until thickened.

Pour into hot, scalded half-pint jars, leaving $\frac{1}{4}$-inch headspace, and seal. Process for 15 minutes in a boiling-water bath.

Yield: 3 half-pints

Concord Grape Conserve

7 cups grapes, washed and
    stemmed (about 2$\frac{1}{2}$ pounds)
$\frac{1}{2}$ cup honey
$\frac{1}{4}$ lemon, seeded and sliced
    very thin
$\frac{1}{2}$ cup raisins
$\frac{1}{2}$ cup pecans, coarsely chopped

Slip skins off grapes. Do not discard skins. Bring pulp to a boil in a stainless steel or enamel saucepan and simmer over low heat until seeds are loosened. Press pulp through colander and/or strainer to remove seeds.

Combine puréed pulp, grape skins, honey, lemon, raisins, and pecans. Simmer over low heat to plump raisins.

Pour into hot, scalded half-pint jars, leaving $\frac{1}{4}$-inch headspace, and seal. Process for 10 minutes in a boiling-water bath.

Yield: 4 half-pints

MARMALADES

Quince Marmalade

The name "marmalade" probably is derived from *marmelo,* the Portuguese word for quince.

2 pounds quinces, peeled,
    cored, and ground
1 cup chopped apples
$\frac{1}{2}$ cup honey
1 cup apple juice

In a large kettle combine all ingredients and boil gently, covered, for 2$\frac{1}{2}$ hours. Uncover and simmer 30 more minutes.

Pour into hot, scalded pint jars, leaving $\frac{1}{4}$-inch headspace, and seal. Process for 10 minutes in a boiling-water bath.

Yield: 2 pints

Bitter Orange Marmalade

An aromatic and delicious variation of the classic.

5 oranges
2 lemons
12 cups water
3 cups mild-flavor honey

Place oranges, lemons, and water in an 8-quart stainless steel or enamel saucepan. Cover and bring to a boil. Lower heat and simmer 2 hours. Remove fruit; seed and quarter. Chop fruit in food processor or by hand. Return to water. Bring fruit mixture to a boil. Stir in honey. Return to a full rolling boil, stirring constantly, until mixture resembles a thick syrup, 15 to 30 minutes. (Keep at a full rolling boil or it will take longer to reach the gel stage.)

Pour into hot, scalded half-pint jars, leaving ¼-inch headspace, and seal. Process for 10 minutes in a boiling-water bath.

Allow the marmalade to "age" for 2 weeks before tasting or it may be too bitter.

Yield: 5 to 6 half-pints

Juicing Your Harvest

You've canned carrots, pickled them, turned them into breads and cakes, and root cellared enough to last your family a year, but you've still got carrots coming out of your ears. You've made grape jelly, grape jam, grape preserves, grape leather, and frozen grapes, and the vines are still heavy with sweet fruit. There's a late bumper crop of tomatoes on the way, but you've already got more sauce, paste, catsup, and frozen tomatoes than you know what to do with. What to do? Juice 'em all.

Juice them and drink them. Don't give them the chance to lose any of their fresh flavor and concentrated nutrition by canning or freezing them. Vegetable juices don't can or freeze well, as we learned for ourselves in our Food Center. But some fruit juices and tomato juices freeze or can well, if you take some precautions, like blanching by gentle simmering most juices before freezing them, especially if you plan to keep them frozen for more than 6 months, or canning them in a *hot*-water bath rather than a *boiling*-water bath.

Theoretically, you can juice just about any crop. Fruits are easier, and some fruits are easier than others. Grapes and citrus fruits, for instance, are naturals. Bananas are another story; they turn into a mash rather than a juice and are best used to fortify other fruit juices. Tomatoes, of course, are the easiest of the vegetables to juice. Carrots, cabbage, and celery are classic vegetable juices, at their best when they're mixed with one another or with other juices. You need nothing more than a big pot and a food mill or strainer for tomato and fruit juices, but plan on getting a heavy-duty juicer if you want to juice carrots and most other vegetables.

With the pulp goes the bulk, reducing your fruits or vegetables to their very essence. A pound of carrots becomes an 8-ounce glass of juice. Seven medium tomatoes make a drink for two. The juice from a pound of spinach will fill a small juice glass half full. You're reducing your extra harvest without wasting it.

(The only thing you're leaving out is the fiber, which is a very valuable thing to have lots of each day, not only to keep yourself regular, but also for weight control and for lowering your chance of developing cancer and other serious health conditions, the experts tell us. So eat lots of your fruits and vegetables whole, reserving juice for when you've had all the whole fruits and vegetables you can eat.)

TOMATO AND FRUIT JUICES

These juices don't require any special kind of juicer to make. Lemon, lime, and orange juices can be squeezed on the familiar cone-shaped citrus juicer. You can even squeeze them by hand, cutting the fruit into quarters first. Other fruits—and tomatoes—are easy to juice once their tissues have been broken down with a little heat. Specific directions for some juices follow, but the procedure is just about the same for all of them. Basically all you do is simmer tomatoes or fruit in water or in its own juice in a stainless steel, glass, or enamel pot. Don't use aluminum because the metal can react with the food acid. The fruits may be smaller and less perfect than the ones you save for canning and freezing, but they must be very ripe.

When the fruit is tender, press it through two layers of cheesecloth, or through a food mill or colander. Straining through cheesecloth will give you the clearest juice.

The juice should not need sweetening if the fruit you started with was ripe. If you do wish to sweeten it, though, add honey to taste; usually ½ cup is sufficient for each gallon of juice. Lemon juice can also be added to peach and apricot nectar, as well as sweet cherry juice; it will add a little zing and help preserve the color.

Storing the Juice

Because these juices have already been heated, there's no need to blanch or heat them further before freezing them. Just pour into clean glass jars or freezer containers and leave ½-inch headspace (for quarts) for expansion. Seal and freeze right away. You can also pour the juice into ice cube trays, freeze, and then transfer to plastic bags.

Canning procedures for fruit juices vary from food to food, so check specific directions in the recipes later in this chapter. The delicate flavor of most fruit juices can be spoiled by the high temperatures of a long boiling-water bath. For this reason, directions state that some juices be poured boiling hot into scalded jars and sealed without processing, and

You don't need a fancy juicer to make tomato juice. Just simmer the tomatoes in water until tender, then put through a food mill.

other juices be processed in a *hot*-water bath, which means that the water is steadily *simmering* all the while and reads at 185° to 190°F on a candy/jelly thermometer. The flavor of tomato juice is not spoiled by high temperatures, and it can and actually *should* be canned in a *boiling*-water bath where the water is rapidly boiling all the while and reads 212°F on a thermometer. For more information on boiling-water canning, see page 82.

USING JUICERS FOR VEGETABLES AND FRUITS

There are lots of these to choose from. They're the only way you're going to get juice from your vegetables, and many people like them for juicing fruits as well, even though there are other ways to make fruit juice, as we've already explained. The nice thing about using one of these is that the juice never gets heated at all, so its flavor and vitamins stay intact. This is great if you're drinking juice fresh, but if you want to freeze fruit juice, then blanch it first to kill off the enzymes that would otherwise deteriorate the flavor.

Freezing and Canning the Juice

When fruit juices are frozen commercially, they are "flash pasteurized," which means that they're quickly heated to 185°F, cooled right away,

STEAM-JUICING FRUITS

A steam juicer makes the juicing process described on page 288 a whole lot easier because everything happens in one pot, and you don't need to mash and stir the fruit along the way. It looks something like a double boiler. The bottom holds boiling water. The top section is really 2 parts; there is a colanderlike basket that holds the fruit and a pan below it to catch the juice. As the water in the bottom boils, it creates steam which rises into the basket above. When exposed to the hot steam, the fruit easily yields its clear juice, which is caught in a pan below the colander that has an outlet for draining off juice into bottles. Take a look at the illustration to see just how this works. Thorough washing of the fruits or vegetables is the only preparation necessary except for cutting the larger or firmer foods for quicker extraction of the juice. This is a marvelous time-saver when juicing elderberries, cherries, or other small foods—fruits go into the juicer stems, seeds, pits, skins, and all.

Steam juicers have been around for some time, but until recently they were all made of aluminum, a metal we don't think much of for preparing foods, especially acid foods that are heated for some time, as juice is. Acids react with aluminum to form an aluminum salt that can then be transferred to food by the liquid. Now there are enamel and stainless steel steam juicers available, and we recommend them strongly. All come with direction booklets.

A steam juicer is a real time-saver for making juices. The juicer has 3 sections. As water boils in the bottom, steam rises up through the midsection to the top, which is perforated like a colander. The fruit sits in the top section and yields its juice as it gets steamed. The juice flows down into the midsection, where it drains out through a tube into a bottle or a bowl.

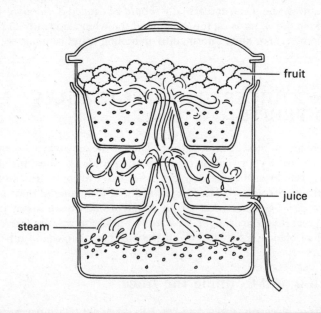

fruit

juice

steam

and frozen. You can flash blanch or pasteurize your juice similarly. The secret is to work in small quantities so that the heating and then cooling go fast. Heat about a quart at a time to 185°F, which is to simmering, not boiling. Use a candy/jelly thermometer to get an accurate reading of the temperature. Then pour the hot juice into freezer containers, leaving ½-inch headspace, and freeze. Don't let the juice cool down on the counter; you want to cool it quickly, and putting it in the freezer is the easiest and about the quickest way to do this.

Can fruit juice made with a juicer just the way you'd can juice made with a steam juicer or by heating, mashing, and then straining by hand.

We were disappointed when we froze vegetable juices other than tomato juice, even after blanching them first. And they suffered, too, under canning. We don't recommend that you freeze or can them.

Centrifuge Juicer. Most juicers on the market that are designed to extract juice from carrots, celery, and other vegetables, as well as fruits, are centrifuge juicers. They work by grinding the food with a bladed disc at high speeds. The juice is thereby released, and the whirling of the disc produces a centrifugal action that throws the juice off. The pulp is trapped on the strainer. The better models have an automatic pulp ejector that forces the pulp from the strainer into a separate compartment so that the strainer is free to accept more pulp. This is a nice feature because it means you don't have to continually stop the machine to clean off the strainer as you're juicing. We tested a half-dozen such juicers and found that they all have their strengths and weaknesses. You're making a hefty investment when you're buying one; they start at about $85 and go all the way up to $300. Get a personal recommendation or check a buyer's guide before you buy.

Liquefier or Pulverizer. We don't know what else to call this machine because it's not technically a juicer, although it does make juice. You may know it as a Vita-Mix, which is a brand name and the most popular of this kind of machine. It mashes fruits or vegetables—skin, seeds, and all—into a thick homogeneous liquid, which then gets strained through a strainer bag. This juicer isn't cheap; it costs more than most other types, but it does more than make juice. The Vita-Mix boasts many skills, including making ice cream, grinding grain, and kneading dough in addition to juicing.

Mechanical Juicer. If you'd rather spend muscle power than money, you can invest about $60 in an auger-type juicer. It looks a lot like an old-fashioned meat grinder. It's heavy because it's made of cast iron, and it clamps to a counter or tabletop. The auger breaks up your fruits or

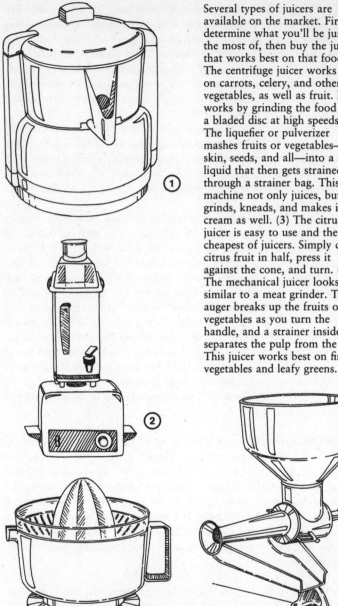

Several types of juicers are available on the market. First determine what you'll be juicing the most of, then buy the juicer that works best on that food. (1) The centrifuge juicer works best on carrots, celery, and other vegetables, as well as fruit. It works by grinding the food with a bladed disc at high speeds. (2) The liquefier or pulverizer mashes fruits or vegetables— skin, seeds, and all—into a thick liquid that then gets strained through a strainer bag. This machine not only juices, but grinds, kneads, and makes ice cream as well. (3) The citrus juicer is easy to use and the cheapest of juicers. Simply cut a citrus fruit in half, press it against the cone, and turn. (4) The mechanical juicer looks similar to a meat grinder. The auger breaks up the fruits or vegetables as you turn the handle, and a strainer inside separates the pulp from the juice. This juicer works best on firm vegetables and leafy greens.

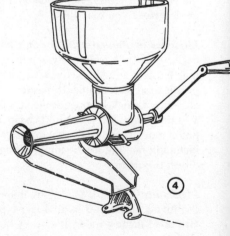

vegetables as you turn the handle, and a strainer inside the device separates the pulp from the juice. In our tests, we liked what we got from firm vegetables and leafy greens, but weren't too happy with the mush we got from apples and tomatoes. The only brand that we know of is The Chop Rite; it's been around for years and years, and the company is still making them new.

Citrus Juicer. And then there's the familiar cone-shaped lemon, orange, lime juicer that you'll find in almost every kitchen. Cut a citrus fruit in half and press it against the cone, turning as you do. Not the fastest way to make lots of juice, but certainly the simplest and cheapest.

APPLE CIDER

What Apples to Use

Apples for cider need not possess the flawless perfection we seek in table fruit. Here you can use the blemished, the bug-marred, the runts, the "drops," and the otherwise unchoice, mixing all apple varieties together or using only what you have. Just make sure you don't use any apples that have spoiled or those parts of them that are spoiled. Don't use apples in brown decay because their juice will ferment too rapidly and cause a prematurely "hard" cider. Highly flavored cider begins with a blend of suitable varieties. Apples should be firm-ripe, but not overripe. Peak ripeness is indicated by characteristic fragrance and spontaneous dropping from trees. Green, undermature apples cause a flat flavor when juiced. The best-flavored cider comes from a blend of sweet, astringent, tart, and aromatic apple varieties.

Juicing Apples by Hand

If you have no fruit press and only a little fruit, ordinary household gadgets will suffice. Juicing will be a bit awkward and not as easy as using a real cider press, but you can get by. Apples can be cored and cut and run through a food chopper, blender, or food processor.

Put your crushed pulp into a clean muslin sack—an old but clean pillowcase will do—and squeeze out all the apple juice possible. Now pour this juice into clean glass jugs or bottles and refrigerate, or, of course, just drink right away.

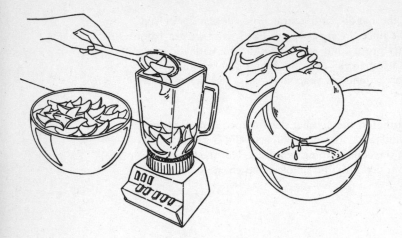

To juice apples by hand, core and cut the fruit and run through a food chopper, blender, or food processor. Then put the crushed pulp into a clean muslin sack or old pillowcase, hold it over a bowl, and squeeze out all of the juice that you can. Pour the juice into clean glass jugs or bottles and refrigerate.

Using a Fruit Press

Far easier and less messy, and a must for more than just a small basket of apples, is a fruit press. Be sure it is a *hard*-fruit press, with a cutting cylinder that minces the toughest apples with no strain at all. There are hand-operated and power-driven models.

Gather all your fruit together and pick over it for decayed or wormy specimens. This is especially important if you've picked a lot of your apples off the ground. Hose them down and allow to dry briefly. A bushel of apples, thoroughly squeezed, will yield 3 gallons of juice, so gauge your container needs accordingly. All jugs, bottles, and kegs should be scrupulously clean. You will also need a large tub—not aluminum or copper—to hold crushed pulp, a smaller one to catch juice runoff, and a clean muslin sack or clean panty hose with the legs tied for pressing the juice out of the pulp.

Set up your fruit press outdoors to facilitate easier handling and subsequent cleanup. If it's raining, or is too cold, work in a garage or shed. Apples should not be used when rain-wet. No need to peel or cut up fruit when using a hard-fruit model; the cutting cylinder takes the toughest whole apple in stride. But *be careful*; keep hands and fingers away from rotating blades. As the pulp receptacle fills up, transfer the mash into your tub and repeat until all fruit is ground up. Be sure the smaller vessel is placed where it will catch all escaping juice. Now fill the muslin sack with only enough pulp to fit the juicer well, which is usually built under the mash well. Crank the presser handle until no more juice runs, and repeat the process with the rest of the pulp. All squeezed juice may be temporarily contained in a wooden tub or a crock.

The rest of the work is a pleasure. Pour the apple juice through a

A cider press like this one makes an easy job of grinding and extracting juice from apples. Set up the fruit press outdoors for easier handling and cleanup.

straining cloth into your containers. Fill each almost to the brim, and let stand at room temperature for about 3 days before drinking so that flavors can blend and mellow out. As you siphon off the clear liquid from the sediment into new bottles, be sure to replace the loss of the settled portion—always keeping fermenting cider jugs full.

Settling and Racking Off Cider

If you want a very clear cider with a bit of a bite, let the bottled cider stand at room temperature. The bottles should be filled to just below the brim and stoppered with cotton wool rather than a regular lid or cap. Just in case pressure builds up inside because of the start of fermentation, the cotton wool will pop out, releasing the pressure. Put on a lid and the pressure can only go out one way—right through the glass.

After 3 or 4 days sediment will begin settling on the bottom as fermentation beads rise to the top. If you wish only a mild, sweet cider, this is the time to "rack off" the clear liquid from the sediment and store in a cold place for drinking soon; unpasteurized cider like this should be drunk within 4 or 5 days for best taste. "Racking off" is done by inserting one end of a rubber tube (about 3 feet in length) into the liquid and sucking at the other end with your mouth, as you would with a soda straw. As soon as you feel liquid in your mouth, pinch off this end with your fingers and insert the tube into an empty container which should

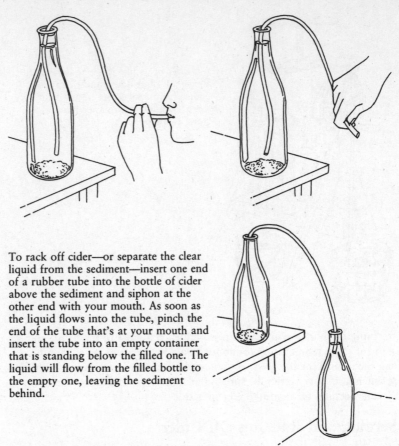

To rack off cider—or separate the clear liquid from the sediment—insert one end of a rubber tube into the bottle of cider above the sediment and siphon at the other end with your mouth. As soon as the liquid flows into the tube, pinch the end of the tube that's at your mouth and insert the tube into an empty container that is standing below the filled one. The liquid will flow from the filled bottle to the empty one, leaving the sediment behind.

stand well below the filled one. Naturally all this equipment should be scrupulously clean. Rack off only the clear liquid; do not disturb the sediment at the bottom.

Fermenting Cider

If you prefer a cider with more zip and on the dry side, allow the cider to stand longer at room temperature. Don't use cotton wool as your plug, but an airlock—a curlicue glass "cork" sold by home-brew suppliers. You can use as a substitute 3 thicknesses of clean muslin tightly stretched over the bottle opening and secured well around the neck. Be sure you use strong, sound glass, like cider jugs, or the bottle may burst with increasing fermentation. In about 10 days it will begin frothing and may foam over the top. Clean off the sides of the bottle, replace the muslin, if necessary, and let the frothing continue until fermentation subsides.

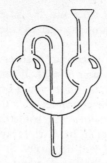

A glass or plastic fermentation lock fits into the neck of a wine jug or bottle and prevents air from contaminating your cider while allowing fermentation gases to escape.

Since this process turns all available sugars in the "must" or fermenting cider to alcohol, it stands to reason this brew will no longer be a sweet drink—it will become dry or hard cider. And the longer it stands, the harder it becomes.

■ Alcohol—which does not freeze—may be extracted from cider by allowing this drink to freeze solidly—remove corks first or the bottle may break. Once frozen, run a hot poker through the frozen cider until you reach the free alcohol, and then pour it off.

Storing Cider

Fresh, unpasteurized cider will keep in the refrigerator 4 or 5 days just as it is. If you want to keep it there longer, pasteurize it to stop all fermentation. You can pasteurize the cider just as you do other fruit juices before you freeze them. Heat it to 185°F, which is just to simmering. A candy/jelly thermometer will give you an accurate reading. Skim off the froth that will probably develop and pour the hot cider into clean plastic containers or glass jars that have been heated so that they won't crack with the shock of the hot cider. Refrigerate right away. Don't leave it on the counter to cool down because more flavor will be lost.

We found that fresh, unpasteurized cider freezes quite well, so long as you don't keep it for more than about 6 months. If you want to freeze it longer, then pasteurize it, following the directions in the paragraph above. While still hot, pour it into clean, hot glass jars or plastic freezer containers, leaving ½-inch headspace, and freeze.

TURNING APPLE CIDER INTO VINEGAR

The hard part of making apple cider vinegar is extracting the juice, and if you've followed the directions above, you've already done that. The rest is simple. It is just a matter of allowing the extracted apple juice to ferment past the stage of sweet cider and dry cider into the vinegar stage. (You can also use store-bought unpasteurized cider or juice to make your vinegar.)

Pour the strained apple juice into a crock, a watertight wooden container, dark-colored glass jars, or jugs. If you don't want your fermenting juice to run all over the floor, you'd better leave ample headspace—about 25 percent of the container—for the juice to foam during fermentation. Cover your container with something that will keep dust, insects, and animals out, but let air in. A triple layer of cheesecloth, clean sheet material, or a tea towel will do nicely. Stretch this material over your crock, jars, or whatever, and tie it tightly with string. Store your brew in a cool, dark place, like an unheated basement or garage. Now sit back and wait while the juice does all the rest of the work. Fermentation will take from 4 to 6 months. (Add a mother—see below—and fermentation will go a lot quicker.)

After about 4 months, remove the cover and taste the vinegar. If it is strong enough for your liking, strain it through a triple layer of cheesecloth, pour it into bottles, and seal with caps or corks. If the vinegar is too weak, let it work longer, testing it every week or so, until it is strong enough for you. If it doesn't get any stronger with time, add some store-bought kind. And if you mistakenly let it sit too long, and it turns out stronger than you'd like it, just dilute it with a little water.

The scum or, to put it more nicely, the layer that forms on top of the vinegar during fermentation and that sort of looks like a cloud is called the "mother." This is what you want to strain off when your vinegar is strong enough so that it stops working. You can use this mother

PICKLING
WITH HOMEMADE VINEGAR

It is a risky business pickling food with home-made vinegar because, unlike store-bought vinegar which has a controlled acid content, the acidity of homemade vinegar varies. If you wish to pickle with your own vinegar, we suggest that you make small batches at a time so that you won't stand the chance of ruining all your relish or chowchow. To play it safe, use 100 percent vinegar brines and add no water to them.

as a starter for your next batch of vinegar. Just pour your apple juice—
or any other fruit juice or wine—into a crock, wooden container, dark-
colored glass jars, or jugs, add the fresh mother, skimmed from the batch
of vinegar you just made, and let it ferment. In a little while you'll have
more vinegar.

HERB VINEGARS

While we don't advise pickling with homemade vinegar, there's nothing
wrong with adding herbs and spices to your home brew; as a matter of
fact, we encourage it! Herbed vinegars are delightful to use and lovely
to give as simple gifts. And they are so easy to make. Just add individual
herbs like tarragon or garlic, or a combination of your favorites. The
herbs mellow and blend together in the bottle, so you can use just about
any combination and not go wrong.

Louise and Cyrus Hyde, owners of Well-Sweep Herb Farm in Port
Murray, New Jersey, make herb vinegar for friends, visitors to their
organic farm, and of course for themselves. Although almost any herb
can be added to vinegar, they have found a few to be the most popular.
The favorites are tarragon vinegar, basil and tarragon vinegar, and basil
and garlic vinegar. Other popular kinds are dill vinegar (made from seeds
and leaves); rosemary vinegar, a purple-tinted vinegar made from opal
basil and sweet basil leaves; orange-mint vinegar for fruit salads; and
cucumber-flavored salad burnet vinegar.

The Hydes like the distinct flavor of apple cider vinegar, but find
that when used alone with herbs, its strong flavor masks the more subtle
flavor of the herbs. For this reason they prefer to mix apple cider vinegar
with the milder-tasting white distilled vinegar before they add herbs to
it.

Because the Hydes like to have herbs floating in their bottled vinegars, they add fresh sprigs of them—about a handful, or 3 or 4 sprigs—
to each quart of vinegar. Then they let the mixture sit at least 2 weeks
before they use it. They don't remove the herbs, but leave them in the
bottle because they look nice there and continue to flavor the vinegar.
As they use the vinegar, the herbs are poured onto the salad along with
the vinegar.

If you prefer herb vinegar without the leaves floating in it, crumble
about 3 tablespoons of dried leaves in a jar. If you're adding herb seeds,
such as dill or anise, crush them well first. Then warm your vinegar and
pour it over the herbs. The warm vinegar decomposes the leaves and
extracts oil from the herbs more quickly than cool vinegar. Let the vinegar
and herbs sit for 2 to 4 weeks in a covered bottle or crock. Stainless steel
and enamel containers are also fine, but never use any other metal because

the acid in vinegar will react with it and give your herb vinegar an undesirable appearance and taste. After a few weeks, test your vinegar to see if it is flavorful enough for you. When its flavor is right, strain it into sterilized jars and cap until you're ready to use it.

Here are a few herb and spiced vinegar recipes that you might like to try in addition to the Hydes' suggestions.

Dill and Nasturtium Bud Vinegar

This unusual vinegar has a clear, sharp flavor.

Bring 1 quart white vinegar to a boil. Place 1 tablespoon nasturtium buds and a sprig of fresh dill in a crock or stainless steel or enamel pot and pour the boiling vinegar over them. Cover and allow to steep for 1 week.

Then boil again briefly and filter while hot into a hot, scalded quart bottle. Cap or cork tightly.

Yield: 1 quart

Cucumber Vinegar

Clean and slice, but do not peel, 3 medium-size cucumbers. Place in clean crock, stainless steel or enamel pot, or large wide-mouth bottle. Add 1 teaspoon peppercorns. Bring 1 quart white vinegar to a boil and pour over the cucumbers and peppercorns. Cover and steep for 3 weeks in a cool place.

Then strain into a wide-mouth jar or other glass container and let the vinegar settle a few hours. Ladle or pour off the clear vinegar into a sterilized quart bottle. Cork or cap tightly.

Yield: almost 1 quart

Basil and Garlic Wine Vinegar

1   cup fresh basil leaves
2½ quarts cider vinegar
6   cloves garlic, peeled
1   cup fresh basil leaves (added
       after 2 weeks)
1   cup red wine vinegar (added
       after 3 weeks)
1   cup boiled water (added
       after 3 weeks)
3   sprigs fresh basil (added after
       3 weeks)

Place 1 cup basil leaves in a 4-quart stainless steel or enamel pot. Crush the leaves with your hands or a potato masher and add cider vinegar. Bring quickly to a boil over high heat. Remove from heat. Cover the pot or pour the mixture into a clean crock or wide-mouth bottle, add garlic, and then cover and allow to steep for 2 weeks.

After the steeping period, strain basil and garlic from vinegar. Place 1 cup basil leaves in the pot, crock, or bottle, and pour the strained vinegar into it, cover, and allow to steep for 7 more days. Strain the vinegar again and add red wine vinegar and water.

Sterilize 3 quart bottles, fill with vinegar, add a sprig of fresh basil to each bottle, and cap or cork tightly.

Yield: 3 quarts

Ruby Vinegar

The cranberries in this vinegar add zest to salad dressings and sauces.

12 ounces cranberries
$\frac{3}{4}$ cup cider vinegar
$\frac{1}{3}$ cup honey
1 stick of cinnamon 2 inches
   long

Rinse cranberries and pat dry.

In a medium-size stainless steel or enamel saucepan, combine cranberries with vinegar, honey, and cinnamon and bring to a boil. Simmer until cranberries burst, 5 to 10 minutes.

Strain, pour into hot, scalded half pint bottles, and seal. Store in refrigerator for up to 1 year.

Yield: 1$\frac{1}{2}$ half-pints

Hot Pepper Vinegar

4 hot chili peppers
4 cups apple cider vinegar

Wearing rubber gloves, wash peppers and make 2 to 3 small slits in each.

Place in sterilized quart jar. Pour vinegar over peppers. Cover tightly. Let stand 3 weeks before using. Remove peppers. Keep in the refrigerator for up to 1 year.

Yield: 1 quart

Note: For a hotter vinegar, split one of the peppers in half.

Peach Vinegar

Use peelings and pits from Sweet Spiced Pickled Peaches, page 231, to make this fruity vinegar. It's lovely as a marinade for chicken, duck, and pork; in salad dressings; or combined with mayonnaise and chicken for a delicious chicken salad.

Tie peelings and pits together in a double thickness of cheesecloth or in a jelly bag. Combine with 2 cups vinegar in a medium-size stainless steel or enamel saucepan and bring to a boil slowly, then simmer gently 15 minutes. Remove bag and let stand until cold.

Strain and pour into a hot sterilized pint bottle. Seal.

The vinegar keeps in the refrigerator for 1 year.

Yield: 1 pint

Variation

Add 1 to 2 tablespoons Rodale's Whole Pickling Spice (see page 212) to bag.

JUICES

Berry and Currant Juices
(all berries except cranberries; to can or freeze)

Do not add any water; just crush berries in a stainless steel or enamel pot and *simmer* them in their own juice, stirring occasionally, until they are soft. Add a small amount of water only if berries threaten to scorch. Strain by letting the liquid drip through a jelly bag or several thicknesses of cheesecloth for several hours, until the pulp releases no more liquid. Heat liquid to a simmer and add lemon juice and honey to taste. Freeze or can. To can, pour hot into hot, scalded jars, leaving ¼-inch headspace for half-pints and pints and ½-inch headspace for quarts. Seal and process pints and quarts in a *hot-water* bath for 30 minutes.

Yield: 4½ quarts fruit equals 1½ quarts juice

Cherry Juice
(to can or freeze)

Sweet cherries make a rather bland juice, so add some sour cherry juice to it if possible.

Prepare just as Berry and Currant Juices on page 302, adding a little water if necessary to prevent scorching. If desired, heat to a simmer and add lemon juice and/or honey to taste. Freeze or can. To can, pour hot into hot, scalded jars, leaving ¼-inch headspace for pints and ½-inch headspace for quarts. Seal and process pints and quarts in a *hot-water* bath for 30 minutes.

Yield: 3½ pounds or 2 quarts cherries equals 1 quart juice

Cranberry Juice
(to can or freeze)

For every cup berries add 1 cup water. Bring to a *boil* in a stainless steel or enamel pot and cook until berries burst. Strain through jelly bag or several layers of cheesecloth. Boil 1 minute, and add honey if desired. Freeze or can. To can, pour boiling juice into hot scalded pint or quart jars, leaving ¼-inch headspace for pints and ½-inch headspace for quarts. Adjust caps and seal immediately. No further processing is necessary.

Yield: 1 quart berries equals 1½ quarts juice

Grape Juice
(white or blue; to can or freeze)

Blue grapes will produce about twice as much juice as white grapes.

Place grapes in a stainless steel or enamel pot and cover them with boiling water (1 cup water for every 7 pounds grapes). Heat slowly to a simmer and continue to simmer until fruit is very soft (about 10 minutes). Do not boil. Strain through jelly bag or several thicknesses of cheesecloth.

Refrigerate for 24 to 48 hours and then strain once more to remove any sediment that remains. Because of the tartaric acid in it, the sediment lends to the juice a sharp taste that's not at all pleasant. Heat to a simmer and add honey to taste, if desired. Freeze or can. To can, pour hot juice into hot, scalded jars, leaving ¼-inch headspace for pints and ½-inch headspace for quarts. Process pints and quarts in a *hot-water* bath for 30 minutes.

Yield: 3½ pounds grapes equals 1½ quarts juice

Note: Fresh grapes can also be crushed and pressed in a juice press or through a strainer or cheesecloth for juice.

Peach, Apricot, or Nectarine Nectar
(to can or freeze)

Although the nectar can be thinned with water to make juice, it's more convenient to can it as is and then thin it with ice water when you serve it.

In a stainless steel or enamel pot add 1 cup boiling water to each quart ripe, pitted peaches, apricots, or nectarines. Cook until fruit is soft and press through sieve or food mill. Reheat and add honey to taste, remembering that the juice will be diluted later.

Freeze or can. To can, pour hot into hot, scalded jars, leaving ¼-inch headspace for half-pints and pints and ½-inch headspace for quarts. Process half-pints and pints for 15 minutes in a *boiling-water* bath.

Yield: 3½ quarts fruit and water equals 4½ quarts purée

Plum Juice
(to can or freeze)

For every cup cut-up, unpitted plums, add 1 cup water and gently simmer together in a stainless steel or enamel pot. Continue to simmer until fruit is soft, 10 to 15 minutes. Strain through jelly bag or several thicknesses of cheesecloth. Heat to a simmer and add honey to taste, if desired. Freeze or can. To can, pour hot juice into hot scalded jars, leaving ¼-inch headspace for pints and ½-inch headspace for quarts. Process pints and quarts in a *hot-water* bath for 5 minutes.

Yield: 5 pounds fruit equals 1 quart juice

Syrup for Lemonade
(to freeze)

⅓ cup honey
 juice of 8 lemons (about 1¼
   cups lemon juice)

In a small saucepan over medium heat, warm honey. Add lemon juice and cook, stirring, for another 30 seconds. Remove from heat and let cool.

This mixture can be frozen in ice cube trays (an ice cube is about 2 tablespoons).

To use, combine 4 tablespoons syrup or 2 frozen cubes with 1 cup water. Add more sweetening if desired. Garnish with a lemon slice or fresh mint.

Yield: 1½ cups syrup

Tomato Juice Cocktail
(to can or freeze)

For safety, this must be pressure canned or frozen.

12 pounds large, ripe tomatoes
4 medium-size carrots
2 large sweet green or red peppers
4 stalks celery, diced, leaves included
2 onions, diced
1 clove garlic, minced

¼ cup lemon juice
2 tablespoons honey (or to taste)
½ teaspoon black pepper
2 bay leaves
2 sprigs fresh basil, dill, or thyme (optional)

Wash umblemished tomatoes; remove stems and cores; cut in small pieces. Scrub and grate carrots. Core, seed, and mince peppers.

Combine all ingredients in large stainless steel or enamel kettle, and simmer over low heat 45 to 50 minutes, stirring occasionally, until vegetables are soft. Pick out herbs. Strain vegetables and juice.

Freeze or can. To can, return strained juice to kettle and bring to boil. Pour hot into hot scalded quart jars, leaving ½-inch headspace, and seal. Process for 30 minutes at 10 pounds pressure.

Yield: 4 quarts

Tomato Juice
(to can or freeze)

Varieties considered especially good for juice are Rutgers, Bellstar, Golden Sunray, and Moira. Italian plum tomatoes are good for a thicker juice. If your larger tomatoes are very juicy, adding Italian plum tomatoes gives body to the juice.

Method 1

Chop up clean tomatoes with ends cut out, and simmer slowly until soft (about 15 minutes). Press through fine sieve or food mill. Add spices or honey to taste if desired. Add 4 teaspoons lemon juice to each quart and half that amount to each pint to raise the acid content (see page 78).

Freeze or can. To can, reheat juice to just below boiling and pour hot into hot, scalded jars, leaving ¼-inch headspace for pints and ½-inch headspace for quarts. Process pints 35 minutes and quarts 35 minutes in a *boiling-water* bath.

Yield: 5 pounds tomatoes equals 2 quarts juice
continued

Method 2

Many people prefer the taste of juice made from tomatoes which are first puréed (raw) then strained. The yield is a little less, but for small quantities this method is practical. For large amounts of tomatoes, the first method is preferable even though it involves 2 heatings.

Wash tomatoes and cut off ends. Cut into chunks and purée in food processor or blender, then strain through fine sieve or food mill. Bring juice to a boil. Add 4 teaspoons lemon juice to each quart and half that amount to each pint to raise the acid content (see page 78).

Freeze or can. To can, pour into hot, scalded jars, leaving ¼-inch headspace for pints and ½-inch headspace for quarts. Seal and process pints 35 minutes and quarts 40 minutes in a *boiling-water* bath.

Yield: 5 pounds tomatoes equals 2 quarts juice

Spiced Tomato Juice
(to can or freeze)

For each 4 pounds tomatoes use ¾ cup chopped onions, 3 whole cloves, and 1 stick of cinnamon. Cook all ingredients by Method 1 for Tomato Juice (see page 305) and add 2 teaspoons honey and 4 teaspoons lemon juice to each quart and half those amounts to each pint before canning. Freeze or can as for Tomato Juice (see page 305).

Yield: 4 pounds tomatoes equals 3 pints juice

Spicy Hot Tomato Juice
(to can or freeze)

For each 15 tomatoes add 1 chopped green pepper, 1 small chopped onion, 3 cloves garlic, halved, and 2 fresh chili peppers, split and seeded. Cook all ingredients by Method 1 for Tomato Juice (see page 305). Add 2 tablespoons lemon juice to each quart and half that amount to each pint. This juice is particularly good if you add a dash of Worcestershire sauce and a spoonful of horseradish when serving. Freeze or can as for Tomato Juice (see page 305).

Yield: 4 pounds tomatoes equals 3 pints juice

Vegetable and Fruit Recipes

VEGETABLE DISHES

Marinated Artichokes
(to freeze)

The leftover marinade makes an excellent vinaigrette for green salads.

4 small fresh artichokes
1 quart cold water
3 tablespoons fresh lemon juice
½ teaspoon dried basil
⅓ cup peanut or olive oil
3 tablespoons white wine
  vinegar
1 clove garlic, minced
1 tablespoon minced onions

1 tablespoon minced green
  peppers
2 teaspoons finely chopped
  carrots
2 sprigs fresh parsley
⅛ teaspoon dried tarragon
⅛ teaspoon dried rosemary
½ teaspoon Dijon mustard
  dash of cayenne

Wash artichokes and trim loose leaves. Cut off 1 inch from top and bottom. Remove leaves and chokes.

Combine water and lemon juice in a large stainless steel or enamel saucepan. Add artichokes; let stand 10 minutes. Add basil.

Bring artichoke mixture to boil. Cover and cook gently 25 to 30 minutes or until tender. Drain. Cool. Cut in halves or quarters, or leave whole.

In a medium bowl, mix together remaining ingredients. Add artichokes. Marinate, covered, in refrigerator for 2 to 3 hours. Drain off marinade, remove parsley. Spoon artichokes into container. Label and freeze.

Yield: 4 servings

307

Baked Beans
(to freeze)

3 pounds (about 2 quarts)
   dried beans (navy, Great
   Northern, marrow, or pea)
3 medium-size onions
2½ cups dark molasses
3 teaspoons dry mustard

Wash and pick over beans. Soak overnight in water to cover. Discard soaking water the next day, and then cover again with water. Bring to a boil, then lower the heat and simmer gently until beans are tender. Drain, reserving liquid.

Preheat oven to 300°F.

Into each of 3 2-quart bean pots (with covers) place one whole onion. Divide the beans among the 3 pots. Combine the molasses and mustard with the reserved liquid, and divide the mixture among the 3 pots of beans. If there is not enough liquid to fill the pots to within 1 inch of the top, add more water.

Cover and bake for 6 hours, adding water if necessary. Don't allow the beans to dry out.

Cool and freeze. When ready to serve: Thaw overnight. Place in a saucepan and heat over low heat 15 to 20 minutes until hot. Or bake in a 350°F oven until heated through.

Yield: 5½ quarts

Note: During the last hour of baking, you may want to add 1 teaspoon ground cinnamon and ½ cup catsup to each pot.

Black Bean Soup
(to freeze)

1 cup dried black beans
4 cups water
3 bay leaves
2 cloves garlic
¼ teaspoon dry mustard
1½ teaspoons chili powder

4 whole cloves
2 onions, chopped
   soy sauce
   lemon slices (garnish)
   hard-cooked eggs, sliced
   (garnish)

Wash and pick over beans. Soak overnight in water to cover. Discard soaking water the next day.

Bring water to boiling. Add beans, bay leaves, garlic, mustard, chili powder, cloves, and onions. Simmer until beans are tender, about 1 to 1½ hours. Purée and serve. Add soy sauce to taste and garnish with lemon slices and sliced egg, or cool and freeze.

Yield: 4 servings or 5 cups

Hunter's Bean Stew
(to freeze)

3   tablespoons olive oil
1   large onion, chopped
1½ cups diagonally sliced carrots
    (½ inch thick)
2   stalks celery, cut into ½-inch
    lengths
1   clove garlic, minced
1   cup diagonally cut green
    beans (1-inch lengths)
2 to 3 cups reserved bean
    liquid, vegetable stock, or
    water

1   cup cooked dried white
    beans (navy or pea)
1   cup cooked dried kidney
    beans
2   cups peeled, seeded, diced
    tomatoes
¼   cup minced parsley
¼   teaspoon dried oregano
1   teaspoon dried basil
½   teaspoon ground rosemary
    dash of pepper
    chopped parsley (garnish)

Heat oil in large saucepan. Over medium heat sauté onions, carrots, celery, garlic, and green beans for 5 minutes. Add 2 cups of the reserved bean liquid, vegetable stock, or water. Bring to a boil over medium heat, cover, and simmer 20 minutes, stirring gently several times and adding more liquid if needed.

Add cooked white beans and kidney beans, tomatoes, parsley, oregano, basil, rosemary, and pepper. Simmer 20 minutes, covered, stirring occasionally. Add more liquid if necessary. Cool, then freeze.

Sprinkle with chopped parsley to serve.

Yield: 6 to 8 servings

Variations

Other vegetables can be added with the onions and sautéed; for example, diced turnips.

You can add 1 large potato (unpeeled and diced), chopped spinach, or chopped cabbage along with tomatoes.

Small cubes of browned beef or cooked pork or chicken provide extra nutrition and may be added along with tomatoes.

Harvard Beets
(to freeze)

1 tablespoon mochiko rice
   flour*
½ cup cider vinegar
½ cup water
⅓ cup honey
2 whole cloves
4 cups sliced boiled beets
   butter (for serving)

In a stainless steel or enamel saucepan stir together the rice flour, vinegar, and water. When smooth, place over low heat and stir in honey and cloves. Turn heat to medium and boil 5 minutes, until sauce is thick and clear. Add beets. Spoon into containers and freeze.

When ready to serve: Place frozen beets in saucepan, add 1 tablespoon butter for each cup beets, and simmer for about 20 minutes.

Yield: 2 pints

*Traditional thickeners such as wheat flour, potato flour, and cornstarch will curdle in the freezer. Mochiko rice flour is the exception; it thickens without curdling at freezer temperatures. Look for it in Asian food markets.

Baked Broccoli
(to freeze)

3 to 4 cups trimmed broccoli
1 cup pearl onions
2 eggs, beaten
1 cup ricotta cheese
1 tablespoon minced scallions
   pepper, to taste
½ cup grated cheddar cheese
¼ cup bread crumbs
   butter (optional)

Parboil broccoli and onions for 7 minutes, drain, and arrange in a 1½-quart, buttered casserole dish. Mix eggs, ricotta cheese, scallions, pepper, and ¼ cup grated cheese. Pour over broccoli and onions. Sprinkle bread crumbs and the rest of the grated cheese over casserole. Freeze.

When ready to serve, preheat oven to 350°F, dot frozen casserole with butter, if desired, and bake, uncovered, for 1½ hours. Or let thaw overnight in a casserole dish in the refrigerator and then bake at 350°F for 45 minutes.

Yield: 6 to 8 servings

Dried Sweet Corn

This is simply the basic recipe for serving dried sweet corn as a vegetable. It can be used in casseroles or omelets, mixed with other vegetables or in salads, and even used for desserts such as puddings. It has a nutty flavor.

1 cup dried corn
2 cups boiling water
1 tablespoon butter
1 tablespoon honey
   pepper, to taste

    Soak corn in water for 2 hours. Do not drain.
    Cover, bring to a boil, reduce heat, and cook slowly until the kernels are tender (30 to 35 minutes). Add butter, honey, and pepper. Serve, broth and all. Two tablespoons milk per serving may be added if you like.

Yield: 4 to 6 servings

Holiday Dried Corn

1 cup dried corn
2 cups cold water
½ cup milk
½ cup heavy cream
2 eggs, well beaten
2 tablespoons melted butter
2 tablespoons finely chopped
   sweet red peppers
1 tablespoon finely chopped
   sweet green peppers
3 tablespoons snipped chives
2 tablespoons minced parsley
⅛ teaspoon white pepper
1 teaspoon soy sauce

    In a medium saucepan, soak corn in water for 3 hours. Cover and cook over low heat until tender, about 1 hour. Drain any remaining liquid.
    Preheat oven to 350°F.
    Add milk, cream, eggs, butter, red and green peppers, chives, parsley, white pepper, and soy sauce. Pour into a buttered one-quart casserole. Bake for 40 minutes or until slightly browned and set.

Yield: 6 servings

East Indian-Style Black-Eyed Peas

Serve over cooked brown rice.

3 cups water
1 cup dried black-eyed peas,
    unsoaked
1 onion, chopped
2 tablespoons unsweetened
    shredded coconut
¼ teaspoon turmeric
1 teaspoon honey
¼ teaspoon cumin

Bring water to a boil. Add remaining ingredients to boiling water and simmer until most of the liquid is absorbed and beans are tender, about 1 hour and 10 minutes.

Yield: 4 servings

Vegetable Gumbo
(to freeze)

Gumbo is a corruption of the Bantu word for okra. This creole dish is a cross between a soup and a stew and could be served over cooked brown rice.

8 cups water
1 pound collard or mustard
    greens
1 pound fresh spinach
1 pound beet or turnip greens
6 sprigs fresh parsley
2 large bay leaves
¾ cup whole wheat pastry flour
½ cup olive oil
2 tablespoons vegetable oil
1 pound fresh okra, trimmed
    and cut into 1-inch pieces
1 tablespoon butter
1 cup finely chopped onions
½ cup finely chopped green
    peppers

1 cup finely chopped celery
½ cup finely chopped scallions
1½ cups coarsely chopped
    tomatoes
½ teaspoon ground thyme
½ teaspoon cayenne pepper
¼ teaspoon ground allspice
⅛ teaspoon freshly ground
    pepper
1 teaspoon Worcestershire
    sauce
fresh chopped tomatoes
(garnish)

In an 8-quart saucepan bring water to a boil. Drop in collard or mustard greens, spinach, beet or turnip greens, and parsley and bay leaves tied together. Reduce heat to low and simmer, partially covered, about

1 hour, or until greens are tender. Strain greens through a sieve over a bowl, pressing down on the greens firmly. Set aside liquid. Purée greens in a food processor or blender in 2 or more batches.

In a 6-quart heavy saucepan, combine flour and olive oil to make a roux. Cook over medium heat, whisking constantly, until flour turns brown and is cooked, about 15 to 20 minutes. Set roux aside.

In a heavy skillet, heat vegetable oil. Sauté okra for 5 to 10 minutes or until lightly browned and "roping" has stopped (white threads disappear). Remove okra. In same pan, melt butter. Add onions, green peppers, celery, and scallions; cook until vegetables are wilted. Add to the reserved stock.

Stir roux, and, if it has cooled, reheat over low heat, stirring constantly. Whisk stock and vegetables into warm roux and combine well. Add okra, tomatoes, thyme, cayenne, allspice, pepper, Worcestershire sauce, and reserved puréed greens. Bring to a boil, reduce heat to low, and simmer, partially covered, for about 5 minutes if freezing, or 30 minutes if eating immediately. Garnish with fresh chopped tomatoes. If frozen, thaw and cook over low heat for about 15 minutes.

Yield: 8 to 10 servings or 3½ quarts

Tuscan Minestrone
(to freeze)

Every region of Italy has its version of this hearty soup.

1 quart water	1 tablespoon chopped fresh thyme or 1 teaspoon dried thyme
½ cup dried white beans (marrow, navy, Great Northern)	
	1 tablespoon chopped fresh rosemary or 1 teaspoon dried rosemary
3 tablespoons olive oil	
1 cup chopped onions	
½ cup chopped leeks	1 tablespoon chopped fresh basil or 1 teaspoon dried basil
1 cup coarsely chopped carrots	
½ cup coarsely chopped celery	
2 cups coarsely chopped zucchini	⅛ teaspoon freshly ground pepper
1½ cups chopped escarole or Swiss chard	1½ cups canned Italian tomatoes, undrained and chopped
½ pound green beans, trimmed and cut into 1-inch segments	
	2 sprigs parsley
1 cup shredded cabbage	1 bay leaf
2 cloves garlic, minced	1 cup whole wheat elbows, shells, or ditalini, cooked

continued

Garnish

1 tablespoon chopped fresh
    basil or 1 teaspoon dried
    basil
1 tablespoon chopped fresh
    parsley or 1 teaspoon dried
    parsley
½ teaspoon finely chopped garlic

In a heavy 3- or 4-quart saucepan, bring 1 quart water to a boil. Add beans and boil briskly for 2 minutes. Remove from heat and let beans soak undisturbed for 1 hour. Then return pan to stove; over low heat simmer the beans uncovered for 2 hours or until barely tender. Drain beans thoroughly. Reserve liquid.

In a large heavy saucepan, heat oil. Sauté onions and leeks until soft and golden. Add carrots and cook for 2 to 3 minutes, stirring once or twice. Next add celery, zucchini, escarole or Swiss chard, and green beans and cook for 2 to 3 minutes. Then add cabbage and cook for about 5 minutes, stirring occasionally. Add garlic, thyme, rosemary, basil, and pepper and sauté 1 minute.

Stir in tomatoes, parsley sprigs and bay leaf tied together, and stock from beans (add water if needed to make 6 cups). Bring soup to a boil over high heat; reduce heat and simmer, partially covered, 30 minutes.

Remove and discard parsley sprigs and bay leaf. Add beans and cook until hot throughout. Cool rapidly by setting pan in ice-cold water. Pack in containers and freeze.

To reheat, place containers in warm water for 10 minutes. Hold containers over a 4-quart saucepan and let contents slide out. Reheat over low heat, adding water if necessary. Add cooked pasta and heat through. Taste the soup, adjust seasonings if necessary. Garnish with basil, parsley, and garlic.

Yield: 8 to 10 servings or 1½ quarts

Onion-Cheese Turnovers
(to freeze)

¼ pound butter
2½ pounds onions, sliced
2 tablespoons whole wheat
    flour
    paprika, to taste
    pepper, to taste

1 tablespoon poppy seeds
½ pound shredded cheddar
    cheese
    pastry for 2 Basic Rolled
    Piecrusts (see page 594)

Melt butter in a large, heavy pan, and add onions. Sauté until soft and juicy, and sprinkle with flour. Remove from heat and season with paprika, pepper, and poppy seeds. Fold in cheese.

Roll out the pastry to ⅛-inch-thick rectangle. Cut into 10 5-inch squares. Place 2 to 3 tablespoons of the onion mixture on half of each square. Moisten the edge and fold over the other half. Seal the edges with a fork.

Wrap and freeze immediately.

When ready to serve, thaw and place turnovers on a baking sheet and bake at 425°F for 20 minutes or until pastry is browned.

Yield: 10 turnovers

Variation

Onion Pie—Prepare double recipe of onion-cheese mixture. Roll pastry into 2 pieces. Line an 8-inch pie pan with 1 pastry and fill with onion-cheese mixture. Cover with top pastry. Bake at 425°F for 20 to 30 minutes or until top crust is lightly browned.

Potato-Cheese Casserole
(to freeze)

4 pounds all-purpose potatoes
¼ pound butter
¼ cup milk
½ pound cream cheese, at room
     temperature
½ cup shredded cheddar cheese
½ cup grated Romano or
     Parmesan cheese
1 green pepper, chopped
½ cup snipped chives
¼ cup minced pimiento
   pepper, to taste

Steam potatoes until tender. Peel and mash. Melt butter; add milk, cream cheese, cheddar cheese, Romano or Parmesan cheese, green pepper, chives, pimiento, and pepper, and combine with mashed potatoes. Beat until fluffy. Pour into casserole dishes and freeze.

To serve, thaw and bake uncovered in a preheated 350°F oven for about 1½ hours. Top should be browned and mixture bubbly.

Yield: 3 1-quart casseroles

Classic Ratatouille
(to freeze)

This is the perfect midsummer dish, when eggplants, tomatoes, peppers, and basil are so plentiful. Make a double batch and freeze the extra.

¼ cup olive oil
2 medium onions, chopped
2 cloves garlic, minced
2 small eggplants, cut into
　1-inch cubes
3 small zucchini, sliced
1 sweet red pepper, cored,
　seeded, and cut into ½-inch
　cubes
1 green pepper, cored, seeded,
　and cut into ½-inch cubes

2 stalks celery, sliced thin
4 plum tomatoes, seeded and
　quartered
1 tablespoon chopped fresh
　basil or ½ teaspoon dried
　basil
2 tablespoons packed minced
　fresh parsley
1 teaspoon dried oregano
¼ teaspoon dried thyme

In a heavy skillet, over medium heat, heat 2 tablespoons of the oil. Add onions and garlic. Cook until soft, but not browned. Add eggplants, zucchini, red peppers, green peppers, celery, and remaining oil. Cover and cook gently over low heat 30 minutes.

Add tomatoes, basil, parsley, oregano, and thyme. Cover and cook 10 minutes, or until most of the liquid has evaporated and mixture is thick. Pack in containers and freeze.

Yield: 8 to 10 servings or 2½ quarts

Note: Ratatouille serves up beautifully many ways. Reheat over low heat and:
1. Use as a topping for whole wheat pizza; top with grated mozzarella.
2. Use in an omelet: Make a 4-egg omelet (4 eggs, 1½ tablespoons cold water, 2 tablespoons butter). Let eggs sit a bit and then spoon ¾ cup heated ratatouille on top. Cook until omelet is almost set. Fold or serve flat.
3. Spoon heated ratatouille onto whole wheat toast and top with a poached egg. Garnish with chopped fresh tomatoes.
4. Serve as sauce over pasta.
5. Serve warm or at room temperature in hollowed-out eggplant or zucchini shells, or on crackers or pita bread.

Spinach Croquettes
(to freeze)

2 pounds young spinach leaves,
　stems removed
½ cup whole wheat bread
　crumbs
1 egg, beaten

1 small onion, chopped
½ teaspoon dried thyme
　dash of nutmeg
　vegetable oil

Wash spinach until free of sand. Place wet leaves in saucepan, cover, and cook over medium heat until tender, 4 to 6 minutes. Chop coarsely.

In a large bowl combine spinach, crumbs, egg, onions, thyme, and nutmeg. Mix together and shape into 3-inch round patties. Sauté briefly on each side in oil until light brown.

To freeze, place croquettes on tray in freezer. When frozen, wrap with double sheets of freezer wrap between patties.

When ready to serve, heat frozen croquettes in 325°F oven on baking sheet for about 25 minutes.

Yield: 2 servings or 5 croquettes

Spinach-Pasta Casserole
(to freeze)

2 large onions, chopped
2 cloves garlic, minced
¼ cup vegetable oil
3 pounds ground beef
1 pint canned tomatoes, with juice
½ teaspoon ground cinnamon
⅓ cup plus ¼ cup butter
¼ cup mochiko rice flour*
1 quart milk

dash of pepper
dash of nutmeg
½ cup grated Parmesan cheese
6 cups uncooked elbow macaroni
3 eggs, slightly beaten
2 pounds spinach, cooked
1 pound cheddar cheese, shredded

Sauté onions and garlic in oil until limp; add beef and brown. Pour off excess fat. Add tomatoes and cinnamon. Set aside.

Melt ⅓ cup butter, stir in flour, and cook, stirring, for several minutes. Add milk, pepper, nutmeg, and Parmesan cheese, and stir until thickened. Set aside.

Cook macaroni in boiling water. Drain and add remaining ¼ cup butter and the eggs.

To freeze: In each of 2 shallow baking dishes, layer one-quarter of the macaroni, half of the meat mixture, half of the spinach, one-quarter of the cheddar cheese, one-quarter of the macaroni, half of the sauce, and one-quarter of the cheddar cheese. Freeze.

When ready to serve, preheat oven to 375°F. Unwrap frozen casserole and bake until hot, about 1½ hours. Cover with foil after 15 minutes.

Yield: 2 13 × 9-inch casseroles, serving 8 people each

*Traditional thickeners such as wheat flour, potato flour, and cornstarch will curdle in the freezer. Mochiko rice flour is the exception; it thickens without curdling at freezer temperatures. Look for it in Asian food markets.

Giant Stuffed Squash
(to freeze)

1 egg
1 large clove garlic, crushed
½ cup whole wheat bread
    crumbs
1 giant zucchini, at least 1 foot
    long
1 tablespoon wheat germ
1 tablespoon vegetable oil
1 large onion, chopped
½ sweet red or green pepper,
    chopped
2 small carrots, diced
  any small amount (about ¼
    pound) vegetables on
    hand—mushrooms,
    kohlrabi, string beans,
    cucumbers
1 very ripe tomato, diced
3 tablespoons tomato paste
1 teaspoon ground oregano
1 teaspoon ground basil
¼ cup chopped walnuts
½ pound cheddar cheese,
    shredded

Preheat oven to 350°F.

Beat egg with garlic. Add bread crumbs.

Halve zucchini lengthwise, scrape out seed cavity, and sprinkle with wheat germ. Spread egg mixture over remaining cut surface. Place zucchini on a rack set over a pan of water and steam in the oven about 10 minutes.

Heat oil; sauté onions, peppers, carrots, and on-hand vegetables until onions are limp and transparent. Add tomatoes, tomato paste, oregano, and basil. Drain. Fill zucchini shells with the vegetable mixture, top with chopped walnuts, and cover with cheese.

To freeze, place filled squash halves on tray in freezer. When frozen, wrap and return to freezer.

When ready to serve, preheat oven to 350°F. Bake thawed squash on a rack over a baking sheet for about 35 minutes or until cheese melts and squash is tender. Cut into thick slices to serve.

Yield: 4 servings as a main dish or 8 servings as a side dish

Spiced Squash Purée
(to freeze)

This tasty alternative to applesauce enhances roast pork and lamb.

12 cups peeled, seeded, shredded squash (use yellow, acorn, crooked neck, or whatever you have on hand; 6 to 8 pounds)

12 ounces unsweetened frozen apple juice concentrate
1 teaspoon ground cinnamon
¼ teaspoon ground allspice
¼ teaspoon ground ginger

Combine all ingredients in a large, heavy-bottom saucepan and simmer until liquid is evaporated and squash is translucent.

Allow to cool, then purée in a food processor, blender, or food mill. Pack into containers and freeze.

When reheating, add 2 to 3 tablespoons water if consistency is too thick.

Yield: 3 pints

Variation

Substitute 1½ teaspoons Chinese Five Spice Powder (available in Asian food markets) for cinnamon, allspice, and ginger.

Succotash
(to can or freeze)

12 ears of fresh corn
6 cups lima beans or green snap beans
optional:
  butter
  paprika
  chopped parsley

Boil corn for 5 minutes. Cut kernels cleanly from cobs; do not scrape. Steam beans until tender. Mix hot corn with an approximately equal amount of beans.

To can, fill hot, scalded pint jars with the corn-bean mixture, leaving 1-inch headspace; seal. Process in a pressure canner at 10 pounds pressure for 60 minutes.

To freeze, season mixture with butter, paprika, or parsley, if desired. Pack in freezer containers.

When ready to serve, thaw if frozen, then reheat gently on top of stove.

Yield: 7 to 8 pints

Summer Vegetable Casserole
(to freeze)

2 tablespoons butter
1 cup corn
1 cup diced zucchini
1 cup diced fresh tomatoes
½ cup diced green peppers
½ cup diced onions
1 teaspoon dillweed

2 teaspoons dried parsley
⅛ teaspoon pepper
⅓ cup shredded cheddar cheese
¾ cup bread crumbs
1 tablespoon grated Parmesan
   cheese

Melt butter. Add corn, zucchini, tomatoes, peppers, and onions and sauté until tender (about 10 minutes). Season with dill, parsley, and pepper. Mix cheddar cheese and bread crumbs. Place one-third of the cheese mixture into the bottom of a 1½-quart casserole dish. Top with half of the vegetables. Repeat. Top with the remaining one-third of the cheese mixture. Sprinkle with Parmesan cheese. Freeze.

When ready to serve, thaw in refrigerator overnight. Bake at 350°F for 30 minutes or until top turns light golden brown and center is heated through.

Yield: 4 servings

Apricot-Glazed Sweet Potatoes
(to freeze)

4 large sweet potatoes or yams
½ cup maple syrup
⅓ cup apricot juice*
1 teaspoon lemon juice
3 tablespoons butter
½ teaspoon ground cinnamon
⅛ teaspoon ground nutmeg
   optional:
      1 cup crushed pineapple
      ½ cup raisins
      ¼ cup finely chopped nuts

Using a 3-quart saucepan, cook sweet potatoes in boiling water until just tender, about 25 minutes (or bake in a 400°F oven, about 45 minutes). Cool and peel. Slice, halve, or quarter potatoes, or leave whole. Arrange potatoes in a single layer in a 2½- or 3-quart casserole dish.

In a small saucepan, combine maple syrup, apricot juice, lemon juice, butter, cinnamon, and nutmeg. Bring to a boil; simmer 2 minutes.

Pour over potatoes. At this point you may freeze the casserole. Thaw when ready to use. Bake, uncovered, in a preheated 350°F oven for 50 minutes.

When reheating potatoes, you can add, if desired, crushed pineapple, raisins, or nuts 20 minutes before casserole has finished baking.

Yield: 8 servings

Variation

Cranberry-Glazed Sweet Potatoes—Instead of the apricot juice, use ⅓ cup cranberry juice and ½ cup fresh or frozen cranberries, heated in water until the skins pop.

*Prepare apricot juice by placing ½ cup dried apricots in ¾ to 1 cup water. Simmer for approximately ¾ hour. Reserve apricots for another use.

Roasted Sweet Peppers
(to freeze)

8 large green peppers

Set peppers 4 at a time on a broiler pan, so they are about 5 inches below broiler element. Broil, turning often, until peppers are well blistered and charred on all sides, about 25 minutes.

Place peppers in a paper bag; close bag tightly. Let rest 18 to 20 minutes to loosen skins on peppers. Remove peppers from bag and strip off skins. Cut peppers lengthwise into quarters. Remove and discard stems and seeds. Cut peppers into 1-inch strips.

To freeze, place peppers in a plastic container; label.

Note: Roasted peppers are delicious in so many ways:
 1. Use in green salads, or rice or pasta salads.
 2. Cook in a little olive oil. Toss with hot pasta and grated cheese.
 3. Add to an antipasto or appetizer tray; decorate with hard-cooked egg wedges.
 4. Purée peppers with tuna. Add olive oil. Use to garnish hot pasta, tomatoes, cold meats.
 5. The roasted peppers can be marinated in any vinaigrette. The ones on page 322 are very good. They will keep about three days refrigerated, and much longer in the freezer. Thaw desired quantity of frozen marinated peppers in the refrigerator overnight and then allow them to stand at room temperature until oil melts.

Basic Vinaigrette
1 clove garlic, minced
2 tablespoons white wine
    vinegar
¼ teaspoon Dijon mustard
8 tablespoons olive oil
    freshly ground pepper, to
        taste

In a small bowl, stir together garlic, vinegar, and mustard. Gradually whisk in oil. Add pepper. Pour over roasted pepper strips.

Yield: ½ cup

Lemon Vinaigrette
1 clove garlic, minced
2 tablespoons fresh lemon juice
8 tablespoons olive oil
¼ teaspoon ground cinnamon
¼ teaspoon paprika
    dash of cayenne pepper
    freshly ground pepper, to
        taste

In a small bowl, stir together garlic and lemon juice. Gradually whisk in oil. Add cinnamon, paprika, cayenne, and pepper. Pour over peppers.

Yield: ½ cup

Italian Vinaigrette
4 tablespoons olive oil
2 tablespoons white wine
    vinegar
1 clove garlic, minced
½ teaspoon oregano

Combine all ingredients and pour over peppers.

Yield: ¼ cup

Tomato Sauce
(to can or freeze)

5 pounds Italian plum tomatoes (about 25)	2 tablespoons finely chopped celery
1 tablespoon olive oil	2 tablespoons finely chopped parsley
1 onion, chopped	
1 clove garlic, crushed	1 teaspoon oregano
1 tablespoon chopped green peppers	1 bay leaf
	pepper, to taste
2 tablespoons finely chopped carrots	¼ cup lemon juice (if canning)

Loosen tomato skins by plunging tomatoes into boiling water for 1 minute, then under cold running water. Remove skins. Cut tomatoes into chunks.

Alternatively, you can just wash and core the tomatoes and purée them in a food processor. Although a bit messy, you save yourself the bother of skinning—and you save some of the tomatoes' nutrients, which are found in and right beneath the skin. If you like chunky sauce, spare a few skinned tomatoes from the processor.

Heat the oil in a large, heavy enamel or stainless steel kettle, and sauté onions and garlic. Stir in the green peppers, carrots, celery, and tomatoes; add parsley, oregano, bay leaf, and pepper. Simmer, uncovered, until thickened (1 to 2 hours), stirring occasionally. Remove bay leaf.

To can, add the lemon juice and pour into hot, scalded pint jars, leaving ½-inch headspace. Seal and process in a boiling-water bath for 35 minutes.

To freeze, pour into freezer containers.

Yield: 2 pints

Tomato Paste
(to freeze)

14 to 15 pounds tomatoes
¾ cup cider vinegar

Wash, peel, and chop tomatoes. In an 8-quart stainless steel or enamel saucepan, bring tomatoes to a boil and simmer gently, uncovered, 1 hour. Remove from heat. Put tomatoes through a food mill. Discard seeds and bring juice and pulp back to a boil. Boil until tomato mixture is thick and stays on a spoon (about 6 hours), stirring occasionally to prevent sticking. Stir in vinegar and remove from heat.

When cool, spoon into ice cube trays and freeze. When frozen, pop out cubes and place in plastic bags. Use as needed.

Yield: 3 half-pints

Catsup
(to can)

5 quarts tomatoes, sliced
1½ cups chopped onions
2 sticks of cinnamon, 3 inches long
2 large cloves garlic, chopped
1 teaspoon whole cloves

2 cups cider vinegar
¼ cup honey
¼ cup lemon juice
2 teaspoons paprika
dash of cayenne pepper

In a stainless steel or enamel saucepan, simmer together tomatoes and chopped onions for 20 to 30 minutes, until onions are soft. Put through a food mill. Boil tomato purée rapidly until one-half original volume, 1 to 2 hours. Stir frequently to prevent sticking.

While tomato mixture is cooking, tie the cinnamon, garlic, and cloves in a cheesecloth bag. Add to vinegar and simmer 30 minutes. Remove spices. Add spiced vinegar, honey, lemon juice, paprika, and cayenne to tomato mixture. Boil rapidly, stirring constantly, until slightly thickened (about 35 minutes).

To can, pour into hot, scalded half-pint jars, leaving ¼-inch headspace. Seal and process for 15 minutes in a boiling-water bath.

Yield: 3 half-pints

Note: If you want a somewhat sweeter catsup, add honey to taste just before you seal.

Tomato Junk
(to freeze)

This is easy and quick to make, especially when there's a dozen other things to do during tomato harvesttime. A good sauce in stews, meat loaf, Swiss steak, and various other dishes. If you want this sauce hot, leave the seeds in the chili peppers as you slice them.

8 quarts tomatoes, quartered
3 large onions, coarsely chopped
3 large green peppers, coarsely chopped

12 cloves garlic
4 hot chili peppers, sliced
3 stalks celery, chopped (optional)

Combine all ingredients in a large stainless steel or enamel pot and cook for 30 to 45 minutes until tender. Let cool, then freeze.

Yield: about 3 quarts

Mexican Tomato Salsa
(to freeze)

Keep a container in the freezer to serve with beans and tortillas, or as a spicy sauce for Spanish omelets. If you want this sauce hot, leave the seeds in the chili peppers as you mince them.

2 tablespoons olive oil
½ cup finely chopped onions
½ cup minced celery
2 tablespoons minced green or
    red sweet peppers
2 tablespoons minced hot chili
    peppers
1 clove garlic, finely chopped
4 medium tomatoes, seeded and
    chopped
2 tablespoons fresh lime juice
1 teaspoon honey
½ teaspoon dried basil or
    rosemary
¼ teaspoon dried coriander
¼ teaspoon cumin seeds
¼ teaspoon chili powder, or to
    taste

In a large skillet, heat oil. Add onions, celery, sweet and hot peppers, and garlic. Cook 5 minutes, stirring occasionally. Stir in tomatoes, lime juice, honey, basil or rosemary, coriander, cumin seeds, and chili powder. Bring to a boil. Reduce heat to low; cover and simmer 20 minutes.

Freeze in small containers. To reheat, place frozen salsa in saucepan, simmer over low heat, correcting seasoning.

Yield: 5 half-pints

Chili Sauce
(to can or freeze)

4 quarts peeled and chopped
   tomatoes
2 cups chopped sweet red
   peppers
2 cups chopped onions
2 cloves garlic, minced
2 dried hot chili peppers, finely
   chopped
1 teaspoon ground ginger

1 teaspoon ground nutmeg
2 tablespoons celery seeds
1 tablespoon mustard seeds
1 bay leaf
1 teaspoon whole cloves
2 sticks of cinnamon, 3 inches
   long
½ cup honey
3 cups cider vinegar

Combine tomatoes, sweet peppers, onions, garlic, hot peppers, ginger, and nutmeg in a large stainless steel or enamel pot.

Tie the celery seeds, mustard seeds, bay leaf, cloves, and cinnamon in a cheesecloth bag. Add to tomato mixture, and boil, uncovered, until volume is reduced to half, 2 to 3 hours. Stir frequently to prevent sticking. Remove the spice bag.

Add honey and vinegar. Bring to a rapid boil, stirring constantly. Allow to simmer about 5 minutes.

Can or freeze. To can, pour into hot, scalded pint jars, leaving ¼-inch headspace. Seal and process 35 minutes in a boiling-water bath.

Yield: 7 to 8 pints

Mexican Pepper Sauce
(to freeze)

This sauce freezes well, but be sure to adjust seasoning *after* freezing.

4 green peppers
6 sprigs fresh parsley or
   coriander
¼ cup finely chopped onions
1 clove garlic, minced
½ teaspoon chili powder, or to
   taste
½ teaspoon oregano
   freshly ground pepper, to
   taste
3 tablespoons peanut or
   safflower oil
1 cup tomato purée

In a stainless steel or enamel saucepan, simmer green peppers in boiling water 5 minutes; remove and cool. Remove stems and seeds. Coarsely chop peppers. In a blender, combine green peppers, parsley or coriander, onions, garlic, chili powder, oregano, and pepper. Blend 2 to 3 seconds. In a large skillet, heat oil. Add pepper mixture and tomato purée. Cook 5 minutes, stirring constantly.

Freeze in small containers. To reheat, place frozen sauce in a pan and simmer over low heat, correcting seasoning.

Yield: 3 half-pints

Red-Hot Sauce
(to can or freeze)

This may be used as a barbecue sauce and as a sandwich condiment.

24 long hot chili peppers (about
        1½ cups chopped)
12 large red, ripe tomatoes
        (about 8 cups chopped)
4   cups vinegar
2   tablespoons Rodale's Whole
        Pickling Spice (see page
        212)
½   cup honey

Wash and drain peppers and tomatoes. Remove seeds from peppers. You may want to wear gloves if your peppers are really hot. Core and chop tomatoes. Add 2 cups vinegar to the vegetables and boil in a stainless steel or enamel saucepan until soft. Press through sieve or food mill. Place pickling spice in a cheesecloth bag. Put this bag in a pot with the strained vegetables and boil until thick. Add remaining 2 cups vinegar and the honey. Boil 15 minutes, or until as thick as wanted.

Can or freeze. To can, pour into hot, scalded half-pint jars. Seal and process 15 minutes in a boiling-water bath.

Yield: 3 half-pints

Worcestershire Sauce

No need to can or freeze this, since it will keep in the refrigerator for as long as 6 months.

1 small onion, chopped
1 clove garlic, crushed
1 slice of ginger root, ¼ inch thick
2 tablespoons mustard seeds
1 teaspoon peppercorns
1 stick of cinnamon, 1½ inches long
½ teaspoon crushed red pepper
¼ teaspoon whole cloves
½ teaspoon cardamom seeds
½ teaspoon whole coriander
¼ teaspoon whole mace
2 cups cider vinegar
½ cup unsulfured molasses
½ cup soy sauce
4 tablespoons fresh lemon juice
2 tablespoons fresh lime juice
½ teaspoon curry powder
½ cup water
½ cup honey

Tie onions, garlic, ginger, mustard seeds, peppercorns, cinnamon, red pepper, cloves, cardamom, coriander, and mace together in a cheese-cloth bag. Set aside.

In a medium-size stainless steel or enamel saucepan, bring vinegar, molasses, soy sauce, and lemon and lime juices to a boil; simmer 5 minutes. Add spice bag; simmer, covered, 1½ hours.

Mix together curry powder and water. Add to the mixture. Cook over low heat 5 minutes, stirring occasionally.

In a small saucepan, over very low heat, bring honey to a boil. Boil 4 minutes or until thick and dark golden in color. (Be careful not to let honey burn.)

Add honey to the simmering mixture. Cook over low heat 2 minutes, stirring constantly.

Let mixture cool in refrigerator for 2 hours, keeping tightly covered. Occasionally press spice bag against sides of pan.

Remove spice bag. Strain sauce through a fine sieve. Pour into clean bottles and cap tightly. Store in refrigerator, where it will keep up to 6 months.

Yield: about 1½ pints

Sweet and Sour Sauce
(to freeze)

Use as a dipping sauce for appetizers, as a glaze for chicken, or as a sauce with stir-fried vegetables like green peppers, carrots, and onions. You can substitute apricot jam for the peach, or cherry jam for the plum.

¾ cup peach jam or preserves
¾ cup plum jam or preserves
½ cup plus 1 tablespoon cider
   vinegar
2 whole allspice berries, ground

    In a medium-size saucepan, combine all ingredients, stirring well. Bring to a boil and immediately turn down heat to simmer. Continue cooking until mixture thickens, about 10 minutes. The sauce may appear thin but will thicken as it cools. Freeze when cool.

Yield: ½ pint

Tomato-Zucchini Sauce
(to freeze)

This lovely vegetable pasta sauce freezes well.

2 tablespoons olive oil
1 tablespoon butter
¾ cup chopped onions
1 small red or green sweet
   pepper, seeded and chopped
¼ cup chopped carrots
¼ cup chopped celery
1 clove garlic, minced

2 cups crushed tomatoes
½ teaspoon crumbled rosemary
½ teaspoon ground marjoram
1 bay leaf
3 tablespoons chopped parsley
¼ cup chicken stock or water
3 medium zucchini, thinly sliced
   (about 1 pound)

    In a medium-size stainless steel or enamel saucepan, heat oil and butter. Add onions, peppers, carrots, and celery. Sauté until soft, 5 to 8 minutes. Add garlic and sauté 1 minute. Add tomatoes, rosemary, marjoram, bay leaf, parsley, and stock or water. Bring to a boil. Reduce heat, cover and simmer 25 to 30 minutes. Stir in zucchini. Cook, covered, 5 to 7 minutes. Remove bay leaf before freezing.

Yield: about 2½ cups

Vegetable Combinations
(to can or freeze)

No recipes here, just some suggestions for vegetables that go well together. For freezing, blanch vegetables separately and then package together. For canning, process for the time recommended for the vegetable requiring the longest processing time on the chart starting on page 111.

eggplant, tomatoes, onions, and garlic

zucchini, tomatoes, onions, and garlic

baby peas and mint

carrots, peas, and pearl onions

corn, lima beans, and scallions

green beans and cherry tomatoes

corn, red sweet peppers, green peppers, and onions

yellow squash and raisins

yellow squash, prunes, and carrots

julienne of carrots and zucchini with onion wedges

cauliflower, broccoli, and carrots

red beets and their tops with oranges and a stick of cinnamon

carrots, turnips, and peas

celery, carrots, and broccoli

sliced parsnips, carrots, and green beans

Brussels sprouts, carrots, and cloves

FRUIT DISHES

Applesauce or Pearsauce
(to can or freeze)

4 pounds apples or pears

1 cup water

$\frac{1}{4}$ cup lemon juice (optional)

$\frac{1}{2}$ cup honey

ground cinnamon, to taste (optional)

ground cloves, to taste (optional)

ground nutmeg, to taste (optional)

Wash and core apples or pears. Peel if desired. Cut into chunks or slices. In a large, heavy stainless steel or enamel kettle, cook the fruit with water, lemon juice, honey, cinnamon, cloves, and nutmeg until tender, about 20 minutes. Drain in a colander. Put through food mill or sieve, if desired.

Can or freeze. To can, pour into hot, scalded pint jars, leaving ½-inch headspace. Seal and process for 20 minutes in a boiling-water bath.

Yield: 2½ pints

Apricot-Nut Bars
(to freeze)

⅔ cup dried apricots
½ cup soft butter
¾ cup honey
1⅓ cups whole wheat pastry
    flour
½ teaspoon baking powder
2 eggs, well beaten
½ teaspoon vanilla extract
½ cup chopped walnuts

Preheat oven to 350°F.

Rinse apricots, cover with water, and boil 10 minutes. Drain, cool, and chop. Oil an 8 × 8-inch pan.

Mix butter, ¼ cup honey, and 1 cup flour. Press into prepared pan and bake for 20 to 25 minutes.

Meanwhile, sift remaining ⅓ cup flour and the baking powder together. In large bowl, with mixer at low speed, gradually beat remaining ½ cup honey into eggs; mix in flour mixture and vanilla extract. Stir in walnuts and apricots. Spread over baked layer. Bake 30 minutes or until done; cool in pan. Cut into bars. These freeze well.

Yield: 32 bars

Apricot-Prune Soufflé

¾ pound dried apricots and
    prunes
5 tablespoons honey
5 egg whites
   pinch of cream of tartar

Preheat oven to 300°F.

Place apricots and prunes in saucepan, cover with water, and bring to a boil. Reduce heat and simmer 5 minutes. Drain. Purée with food processor or blender. Add honey and mix thoroughly. Beat egg whites and cream of tartar until stiff, and fold gently into the fruit. Lightly oil a soufflé dish and put the fruit mixture into it. Bake until firm, about 45 minutes. Serve immediately.

Yield: 4 to 6 servings

Berry-Peach Coffee Cake
(to freeze)

Use ripe peaches because they're so sweet. If they're not available, add extra honey to taste in the topping.

Topping
½ cup butter
1 cup whole wheat pastry flour
2 tablespoons honey
3 tablespoons rolled oats
1 teaspoon ground cinnamon

Cake
2 cups blueberries
1 tablespoon whole wheat
    pastry flour
¾ cup butter, softened
½ cup honey
1¾ cups whole wheat pastry
    flour
2 teaspoons baking powder
⅛ teaspoon nutmeg
4 eggs
1 cup sliced peaches

To make the topping: In a small saucepan over medium heat, melt butter. Remove from heat. Stir in flour, honey, oats, and cinnamon. Set aside.

To make the cake: Preheat oven to 325°F. Grease and flour a 13 × 9-inch pan.

Clean and dry blueberries. Toss blueberries with 1 tablespoon flour.

In a large bowl with mixer at medium speed, beat butter and honey until light and fluffy. Reduce speed to low. Add 1¾ cups flour, baking powder, nutmeg, and eggs. Beat until just blended, scraping bowl occasionally. Increase speed to medium; beat until smooth. Fold in 1¾ cups blueberries.

Spread batter evenly in prepared dish. Drop topping by teaspoonfuls on top of batter. Bake cake 20 minutes. Meanwhile, cut each peach slice in half. Quickly top cake with remaining ¼ cup blueberries and peaches. Bake 25 to 30 minutes longer, or until cake tests done. Serve warm, or cool completely on a wire rack. Enjoy now or wrap and freeze.

To serve cake: Thaw at room temperature for one hour, then wrap in aluminum foil and heat in 350°F oven for 20 to 25 minutes.

Yield: 16 servings

Variation

For a more dramatic presentation, the cake can be baked in a Bundt pan. The batter is prepared without the blueberries and by substituting ¾ cup unbleached flour for ¾ cup whole wheat pastry flour. Omit the topping and bake the cake for 50 minutes or until a toothpick comes out clean. Remove cake from pan and cool on a wire rack. When ready to serve, top with sliced peaches and 1 cup blueberries. The fruit can be glazed by brushing with warmed honey.

Frozen Blackberry Pie

You can use blueberries for the blackberries if you wish.

1 8-inch graham cracker crust	1½ cups blackberries
3 egg whites	1 envelope unflavored gelatin
1 cup vanilla ice cream	½ teaspoon vanilla extract
½ cup cream cheese	¼ teaspoon ground cinnamon

Brush crust with 1 egg white. Bake at 425°F until lightly browned, about 5 minutes. Cool completely.

In a small bowl beat together ½ cup ice cream and the cream cheese with electric mixer until smooth. Pour into pie crust and freeze until set.

In a bowl beat together with wooden spoon the remaining ½ cup ice cream and ½ cup blackberries until combined. Pour into frozen pie crust and freeze until set.

In a saucepan place the remaining 1 cup blackberries. Cook over medium heat, mashing occasionally until juice is extracted, about 5 minutes. Pour through strainer to remove seeds. Place juice in refrigerator to cool.

Sprinkle gelatin over surface of cooled blackberry juice. Let soften 5 minutes. Then heat over medium heat until gelatin dissolves. When dissolved, stir in vanilla extract and cinnamon. Blend well. Place in freezer until cool but not jelled, about 5 to 10 minutes.

In a medium-size bowl beat remaining 2 eggs whites until stiff peaks form. Gently fold whites into cooled blackberry juice. Spread mixture evenly onto top of pie. Freeze at least overnight before serving.

Remove from freezer 15 minutes before serving.

Yield: 1 8-inch pie

Cherry-Almond Coffee Cake

Dough
5 to 5¾ cups whole wheat flour
2 tablespoons dry yeast
1 cup milk
½ cup apple juice
⅓ cup honey
½ cup butter
2 eggs (at room temperature)

Filling
1½ cups chopped almonds
1½ cups chopped sour cherries
½ teaspoon grated lemon peel
½ teaspoon ground cinnamon
3 tablespoons honey

Glaze
2 tablespoons nonfat dry milk
1 tablespoon honey
1½ teaspoons water
¼ teaspoon almond extract

To make the dough: In a large bowl thoroughly mix 2 cups flour and the yeast.

In a saucepan combine milk, apple juice, honey, and butter. Heat over low heat until liquids are very warm (120° to 130°F); do not boil. Gradually add to dry ingredients. Beat at medium speed 2 minutes, scraping bowl occasionally. Beat in eggs. Stir in enough flour to make a dough that's easy to handle. Knead for about 5 minutes. Place in greased bowl. Cover bowl with plastic wrap and a towel. Set aside 20 minutes.

To make the filling: Combine almonds, cherries, lemon peel, cinnamon, and honey. Set aside.

Punch down dough. Divide in half. Roll each half into a 14 × 10-inch rectangle. Spread with filling. Roll from long side as for a jelly roll. Pinch seam to seal. Place seam-side down on greased baking sheets. Cut diagonal slits 1 inch apart, cutting about two-thirds of the way through the dough. Pull pieces alternately right and left. Cover rolls with greased wax paper, then plastic wrap. Place in the refrigerator for several hours or overnight, where it will rise. When ready to bake, preheat oven to 375°F. Remove dough from refrigerator and uncover carefully. Let stand at room temperature 15 minutes. Bake for 25 to 30 minutes or until done. Cool on a wire rack.

To make the glaze: Combine glaze ingredients. Spread on cooled rolls.

Yield: 2 coffee cake rolls, 14 servings each

Golden Aura Compote

Serve on shortbread, as a cake topping, or on ice cream.

¾ cup dried pears, chopped
¾ cup dried apricots, chopped
¼ cup maple syrup
½ cup water
½ teaspoon ground nutmeg
½ cup yogurt
1 cup heavy cream
¼ teaspoon almond extract
  whole almonds (garnish,
    optional)
  whipped cream (garnish,
    optional)

In a small saucepan combine the pears, apricots, maple syrup, water, and nutmeg. Cook over low heat until fruit softens, about 5 minutes.

Purée until smooth, then cool completely. Gently fold yogurt into fruit purée.

In a medium-size bowl combine cream and almond extract. Whip cream until soft peaks form, about 3 minutes. Carefully fold whipped cream into fruit mixture. Chill completely.

Garnish with whole almonds and whipped cream, if desired.

Yield: 4 servings or 3¾ cups

Variation

Substitute dried apples and peaches for dried pears and apricots.

Fresh Fruit Salad Popsicles

Fill Popsicle container two-thirds full with fruit pieces such as strawberries, seedless grape halves, banana slices, kiwi fruit slices, sweet cherries, or crushed pineapple.

Fill container with fruit juice such as orange, grape (white, pink, or red), pineapple, apple, or any mixed fruit juice.

Cover container and freeze partially. Insert stick and freeze thoroughly and serve.

The Rodale Food Center Favorite Fresh Fruit Salad Popsicles

Of all 12 variations tested, this was our favorite:

½ cup chopped fresh pineapple
½ cup mashed bananas
½ cup chopped strawberries
½ cup orange juice

In a small bowl, stir together pineapple, bananas, strawberries, and orange juice. Spoon mixture into an ice cube tray. Cover with plastic wrap and freeze partially. Add sticks and freeze thoroughly before serving.

Yield: 14 Popsicles

Notes:

Use small pieces of fruit; large ones freeze too hard.

An equal proportion of heavy cream or yogurt can be mixed with the fruit juice or fruit purée before pouring over the fruit pieces for a creamy flavor.

Do not use water to bind fruit pieces; it freezes too hard.

Purée overripe bananas with the fruit juice for a creamier pop.

Remove pops from freezer about 5 minutes before serving for easier eating, unless the weather is really hot.

Fruit-Nut Bars
(to freeze)

2 cups nuts
1 cup dates or pitted prunes,
    raisins, or dried apricots
2 eggs, beaten
⅓ cup honey

Preheat oven to 375°F.

Grind nuts and fruit. Blend with eggs and honey. Place in lightly oiled 9 × 9-inch pan. Bake for about 20 minutes, until firm. Cut and serve, or freeze.

Yield: 2 dozen bars

Gingered Sour Cream Fruitcake
(to freeze)

The best you've ever tasted. It's the gingered watermelon rind that gives it its special flavor.

½ cup chopped dried peaches
½ cup chopped dried apricots
½ cup chopped dried apples
½ cup chopped dried pears
¼ cup chopped dried figs
¼ cup chopped prunes
1 cup coarsely chopped pitted dates
¼ cup golden raisins
½ cup seedless dark raisins
½ cup currants
½ cup chopped Gingered Watermelon Rind (see page 233)
½ cup coarsely chopped walnuts
½ cup coarsely chopped pecans, almonds, or hazelnuts
1½ cups whole wheat flour
½ cup wheat germ
2 teaspoons baking powder
1 teaspoon ground cinnamon
½ teaspoon ground nutmeg
¼ teaspoon ground cloves
¼ teaspoon ground allspice
⅛ teaspoon ground mace
4 eggs
3 tablespoons honey
3 tablespoons unsulfured molasses
1½ cups sour cream
⅓ cup butter, melted
1 teaspoon vanilla extract
¼ teaspoon almond extract chopped Gingered Watermelon Rind (garnish, optional)

Butter two 8 × 4 inch loaf pans. Line with wax paper; butter wax paper. Preheat oven to 325°F.

In a medium bowl, combine peaches, apricots, apples, pears, figs, prunes, dates, golden and dark raisins, currants, watermelon rind, walnuts, and pecans, almonds, or hazelnuts; set aside.

In a large mixing bowl, stir together flour, wheat germ, baking powder, cinnamon, nutmeg, cloves, allspice, and mace.

In a small mixing bowl, beat eggs until foamy. Add honey, molasses, sour cream, butter, vanilla extract, and almond extract. Mix well. Add egg mixture to flour mixture, then add fruit-and-nut mixture. Mix well. Turn batter into prepared pans. Bake at 325°F for 60 to 65 minutes, until cake tests done. Cool in pans 10 minutes. Turn cakes out onto a wire rack. Peel off wax paper. Cool completely. When cooled, wrap tightly in foil and store in refrigerator or freezer.

If desired, garnish with chopped watermelon rind before serving.

Yield: 2 loaves, 18 to 20 servings each

Peach Paradise
(to freeze)

This is a quick, tasty, and delicate cobbler that freezes well. You can substitute fresh cherries, plums, or berries for peaches.

1 egg, slightly beaten
¼ cup honey
3 tablespoons butter, melted
⅓ cup buttermilk
½ cup whole wheat pastry flour
2 teaspoons baking powder
3 cups peeled, sliced peaches
½ teaspoon ground cinnamon
⅛ teaspoon ground nutmeg
1 teaspoon cornstarch

Preheat oven to 375°F.

In a medium-size bowl, beat together egg, honey, butter, and buttermilk. Stir together flour and baking powder. Stir dry ingredients into egg mixture.

Combine peaches, cinnamon, nutmeg, and cornstarch in a medium bowl. Spread into a buttered 8 × 8-inch pan. Top fruit with batter, spreading to cover. Bake for 18 to 20 minutes until crisp and golden.

To freeze, cool and wrap pieces in freezer wrap. To thaw frozen cobbler: Place in oven-proof baking dish and heat covered in a 350°F oven for 20 to 25 minutes.

Yield: 8 to 9 servings

Prune Stuffing

This is a lovely stuffing for poultry and pork.

3 cups diced whole wheat bread
¼ cup butter, melted
1 cup prunes
1 cup cold water
2 tablespoons lemon juice
1 tablespoon honey
¼ teaspoon ground nutmeg
½ cup almonds, chopped

Preheat oven to 350°F.

Mix bread and butter. Place prunes in a pan with water, lemon juice, and honey. Bring to a boil, then simmer for 5 minutes. Drain, reserving ½ cup liquid, and mix the liquid with the bread. Pit the prunes, chop, and sprinkle with nutmeg. Mix prunes and almonds into bread.

Bake, covered, in a 1-quart casserole for 35 minutes, or stuff bird or pork chops and cook as directed.

Yield: about 2½ cups

Variation

Dried apples or peaches can be used instead of prunes.

Raspberry Almond Cobbler

If you don't want to pay a premium price for raspberries, frozen sour cherries will do nicely.

3   cups frozen raspberries
¾   cup water
5   tablespoons honey
2½ tablespoons quick-cooking
     tapioca
1   cup whole wheat pastry flour
1½ teaspoons baking powder
¼   cup and 2 tablespoons butter
¼   cup finely chopped almonds
¼   cup buttermilk
1   egg, slightly beaten
⅛   teaspoon almond extract

Preheat oven to 400°F.

In a medium-size saucepan, combine raspberries, water, 4 table-spoons honey, and tapioca. Set aside.

In a medium-size bowl, stir together flour and baking powder. Cut in ¼ cup butter. Stir in almonds. In a small bowl combine buttermilk, egg, and the remaining 1 tablespoon honey. Add to dry ingredients, stirring just to moisten.

Bring raspberry mixture to boil; cook, stirring constantly, 1 minute. Stir in remaining 2 tablespoons butter and the almond extract. Pour into a buttered 2-quart casserole. Drop dough by rounded tablespoonfuls on top of fruit. Bake for 20 to 25 minutes, or until lightly browned.

Yield: 6 servings

Apple-Ginger Syrup
(to can)

Use as is over poached pears or peaches; or mix with rice and raisins to serve with Indian curries.

½ cup sliced, peeled ginger root
2 cups apple juice
2 cups and 3 tablespoons water
2 tablespoons honey
2 tablespoons cornstarch

In a medium-size saucepan combine ginger, apple juice, 2 cups water, and honey. Bring to a boil over medium-high heat. Continue cooking, stirring occasionally, until the liquid is reduced by half.

Strain liquid through a jelly bag and return to saucepan. Stir cornstarch and remaining 3 tablespoons water together to make a paste. Blend into the mixture in the saucepan. Place over medium heat. Cook, stirring constantly, until thickened and less opaque, 2 to 3 minutes.

Pour into hot, scalded half-pint jars, seal, and process for 10 minutes in a boiling-water bath.

Use hot or cold. If using cold, thin with a small amount of boiling water to desired consistency.

Yield: 2 half-pints

Variation

Ginger Ale—Add 1 tablespoon apple-ginger syrup to sparkling water.

Halifax Blueberry Sauce
(to freeze)

Serve over cheesecake, custard pie, ice cream, or yogurt.

½ cup currant jelly
2 tablespoons water
2 tablespoons honey
2 teaspoons lemon juice
½ teaspoon ground cinnamon
    freshly grated nutmeg, to
        taste
2 tablespoons mochiko rice
        flour*
4 cups blueberries

In a medium-size saucepan combine jelly, water, honey, lemon juice, cinnamon, nutmeg, and flour. Place over medium heat and simmer, stirring constantly, until thick and syrupy, about 5 minutes.

Remove from heat. Stir in blueberries until coated. Pour into containers and freeze.

To prepare frozen sauce, partially thaw and place in a saucepan. Cook over low heat until mixture is heated throughout, about 15 minutes.

Yield: 4 half-pints

*Traditional thickeners such as wheat flour, potato flour, and cornstarch will curdle in the freezer. Mochiko rice flour is the exception; it thickens without curdling at freezer temperatures. Look for it in Asian food markets.

Jubilation Sauce
(to freeze)

Serve over cheesecake, custard pie, or ice cream.

2 tablespoons cranberry juice
   concentrate, thawed
2 teaspoons lemon juice
¼ cup honey
¼ teaspoon almond extract
   (optional)
2 tablespoons mochiko rice
   flour*
4 cups sour cherries

In a medium-size bowl whisk together cranberry juice concentrate, lemon juice, honey, almond extract, and flour. Blend well. Stir in cherries. Pour into small containers and freeze.

To serve, place partially thawed cherries in saucepan. Cook over medium heat, stirring occasionally, until cherries thaw and liquid resembles thick syrup, about 7 minutes.

Yield: 3 half-pints

*Traditional thickeners like wheat flour, potato flour, and cornstarch will curdle in the freezer. Mochiko rice flour is the exception; it thickens without curdling at freezer temperatures. Look for it in Asian food markets.

Spiced Pineapple Sauce
(to freeze)

¼ cup honey
½ cup Unconventional
    Refrigerator Apricot Jam
    (see page 252)
4 teaspoons lemon juice
½ to 1 teaspoon ground
    cardamom
¼ teaspoon ground ginger
⅛ teaspoon ground nutmeg
4 cups chopped fresh pineapple
    (1 whole fruit)

In a small bowl stir together honey, jam, lemon juice, cardamom, ginger, and nutmeg. Pour mixture over pineapple and toss. Freeze.

To prepare, thaw completely and spoon over cheesecake or custard pie, or heat gently and serve over ice cream.

Yield: 5 half-pints

Rhubarb Sauce
(to freeze)

A terrific topping for fresh fruit, ice cream, and cakes.

2 cups orange juice
1 cup honey
½ to 1 teaspoon ground
    cinnamon
4 cups sliced rhubarb (½-inch
    slices)
½ cup currants

Bring orange juice, honey, and cinnamon to boil in a large saucepan. Add rhubarb and currants. Cook, stirring, until rhubarb is tender and liquid is syrupy, 5 to 10 minutes. Pour into small containers and freeze.

Yield: 4 half-pints

YOGURT
MAKER

Dairy Foods

Storing Milk, Cream, and Eggs

The information here on freezing milk and cream will be of interest to you if you have a milk goat or cow because there are probably times when you've got more milk on hand than you and your family can use. You can make butter or cheese or yogurt with the extra, and the chapters that follow will give you instructions for making them at home. But you can also freeze the cream and milk for later use as you'll read about in this chapter.

Because eggs keep better longer in the refrigerator than the more perishable milk and cream, storage won't be as much of a problem. Figure 4 to 5 weeks in the refrigerator for eggs. If you want to keep them longer, then freeze them. Because shells will crack under freezing temperatures, eggs cannot be frozen whole. And all but the separated whites need to be stabilized, which is a simple process, as you'll find out later.

FREEZING MILK AND CREAM

To freeze, pour milk or cream into scrupulously clean glass jars or plastic containers, leaving 2-inch headspace for expansion. Glass is better than plastic because plastic, no matter how clean, often has traces of the flavor and smell of the last food stored in it. Seal tightly and place in the coldest part of your freezer so that it freezes quickly. Whole milk will keep safely in the freezer for 4 to 5 months; cream should not be stored frozen for more than 2 or 3 months.

At our Food Center we found a significant difference between cream stored for 2 months and that held in the freezer for 3. After 2 months, thawed heavy cream whipped very nicely. It tasted just like fresh whipped cream. But after 3 months in the freezer, the butterfat separated out. The cream still whipped, but it had a grainy texture and was much better used in frozen desserts like ice cream than in fresh ones. If you want to use it for cooking—in soups, sauces, gravies, custards, and the like—we suggest that you beat it a little first so that the butterfat is not floating on top.

Both milk and cream should be thawed for 3 to 4 hours at room temperature before using.

EGGS

Because each egg is intended by nature to house an unborn chicken, nature packages each one in its own protective shell. The shell is porous enough to permit oxygen and other gases to flow in and out through its wall, but its outer coating or membrane prevents bacteria and molds that would otherwise contaminate the egg from entering.

The shell of the egg will protect what's inside for a short time, providing it is kept cool. Brush, don't wash, dirt off eggs before you store them. People who vigorously wash off the dirt are also washing off the egg's protective membrane. If possible, store your eggs in a covered container to keep out objectionable odors that travel with gases through the shell's pores. The carton the eggs come in is the best place to keep them.

Eggs stored in their cartons will keep at refrigerator temperatures 4 to 5 weeks, but their freshness fades as time passes. Eggs lose carbon dioxide and water, which causes them to spread out more when they're broken open. The yolk of an old egg will usually break into the white when the shell is cracked open, making separating the yolk from the white of old eggs a difficult, if not impossible, task.

HOW MANY EGGS?

For large, grade A eggs, assume that:
12 yolks = 1 cup
12 whites = $1\frac{2}{3}$ cups
 5 whole eggs = 1 cup
 3 tablespoons whole scrambled eggs
    = 1 whole egg
 1 tablespoon yolk + 2 tablespoons white
    = 1 whole egg

fresh   not fresh

To determine the freshness of an egg, break it onto a plate. If the yolk stands high, the egg is fresh. If it breaks and runs into the white, the egg is safe to eat but past its prime.

■ Cracked eggs may contain harmful bacteria. They can be eaten, but only if they are cooked well first. Use cracked eggs for hardcooking, or in baked goods or casseroles.

Raw egg whites separated from the yolks will keep 7 to 10 days if refrigerated in a tightly covered container. The best way to store unbroken egg yolks is to cover them with water and keep refrigerated in a tightly covered container. Keep for no more than 2 to 3 days; they are much more perishable than the whites.

■ Very fresh eggs are good to use for everything but hardcooking because they are so difficult to peel afterwards, due to the fact that there is not much of an air layer separating the egg from its shell. If you must use very fresh eggs for hardcooking, let them sit at room temperature for a few hours first before peeling.

Old-Fashioned Storage Methods

Before farmers had access to freezers, they devised some simple (but not always successful) means of preserving their excess eggs. Some farmers relied solely on the use of salt to keep their eggs from rotting. After gathering their eggs, they packed them in a large barrel or crock with plenty of salt and stored them in a cellar or springhouse to keep them cool.

The majority, however, found some way to clog up the pores of the egg shells so that moisture would not escape and air could not enter. Eggs were rubbed with grease, zinc, or boric ointment, or submerged in a solution of lime, salt, cream of tartar, and water.

Probably the most popular way to seal egg shells was to waterglass them. By this method a chemical, sodium silicate, was mixed with water and poured into a crock filled with eggs that were about 12 hours old. The sodium silicate (which is used today to seal concrete floors and as an adhesive in the paper industry) would clog the pores in the shells and make them airtight.

Some people, even today, use waterglassing as a means of preserving eggs, but this storage method has its drawbacks. Eggs preserved this way are not good for boiling because their shells become very soft in the waterglass solution. The whites will not become stiff and form peaks, no matter how long they are beaten. No soufflés, eggnogs, or meringues can be made with waterglassed eggs. There is also a very good possibility that by consuming eggs stored in waterglass you would be consuming some of the undesirable chemical, sodium silicate.

If you keep roosters with your hens, waterglassing may not be a successful means of preservation for you. The life factor in fertilized eggs makes these eggs deteriorate more quickly than sterile, unfertilized eggs, and waterglassing may not be enough of a preventive against spoilage.

■ A blood spot is caused by a rupture of a blood vessel on the yolk surface during formation of the egg. Despite what some people think, it doesn't indicate that the egg is fertile. Such a spot in an egg is not harmful and actually is a sign that the egg is fresh. This is because as an egg ages the yolk absorbs water from the egg white, diluting the blood spot. The spot can be removed with the tip of a knife if you wish.

Freezing Eggs

Freezing is the only way to keep eggs safely at home for more than 4 to 5 weeks. Eggs, both fertile and unfertile, will keep as long as 6 months in the freezer, if you prepare and pack them properly. The rule for selecting the right food for freezing applies to eggs just as it does to fruits and vegetables: Choose only the very freshest. Only freeze eggs that you know are very fresh.

Eggs in their shell expand under freezing temperatures and split open. For this reason, they must be shelled and stored in appropriate containers. If you are storing eggs in rigid containers, leave a little headspace for expansion. You can separate the white from the yolk and freeze each separately, or you can store the eggs whole.

Substitutions for Large Eggs in Recipes

Large	Jumbo	X-Large	Medium	Small
1	1	1	1	1
2	2	2	2	3
3	3	3	3	4
4	3	4	5	5
5	4	4	6	7
6	5	5	7	8

If you are freezing egg whites alone, they can be frozen as is, in airtight containers. For convenience, pack as many eggs together as you will need for your favorite recipes. You can then thaw and use a whole container of egg whites at one time.

If you are packing yolks separately or are packing whole eggs, you will need to stabilize the yolks so that they won't become hard and pasty after thawing. To do this, add 1 teaspoon salt or 1 teaspoon honey to

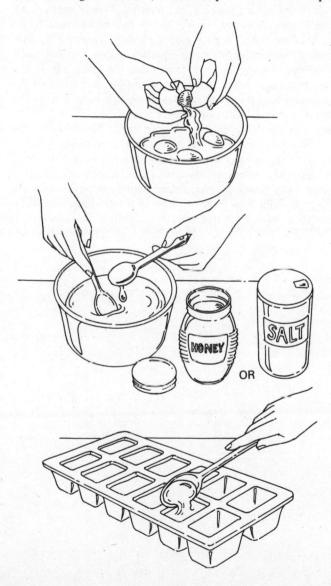

To freeze whole eggs, break them into a bowl and add a teaspoon of honey or salt for each cup of whole eggs, then scramble them. The scrambled eggs can be packed for freezing in one container or packed individually in plastic ice cube trays. Three tablespoons of the scrambled eggs equal 1 whole egg. To freeze separated eggs, see the text.

each cup of yolks. Twelve yolks make 1 cup. Break up the yolks and stir in the salt or honey. Mark on the container which was used as a stabilizer so that you won't ruin recipes by adding more salt or honey than you had intended.

If you are packing your eggs whole, you will also need to stabilize them with salt or honey. Add 1 teaspoon salt or honey to each cup of whole eggs. There are about 5 whole eggs in 1 cup. Scramble the eggs with the salt or honey before packing and freezing. Whole eggs can be packed together in one container, or they can be packed individually by using a plastic ice cube tray. To pack eggs separately, measure 3 table-spoons of whole scrambled eggs (which equals 1 whole egg) into each separate compartment of the ice cube tray. Place the filled tray in the freezer, and when the eggs have frozen, pop them out and store all the egg cubes in a freezer bag. By so doing you will be able to take from the bag and thaw just as many eggs as you need at one time.

Eggs should be thawed completely before using. They thaw in the refrigerator in about 9 hours and at room temperature in about 4 hours. If frozen properly, thawed eggs have the taste, texture, and nutritional value of fresh eggs and can be used successfully in all recipes calling for eggs. To make up 1 egg from separately frozen whites and yolks, measure out 1 tablespoon of yolk and 2 tablespoons of white. Eggs should be used soon after they thaw, as they deteriorate rapidly.

Homemade Butter

A time-honored way of preserving extra cream is to churn it into butter. Although butter is also a perishable food, it will keep longer than milk or cream under refrigeration if all the buttermilk is worked out of it. Because butter is a concentrated form of cream—1 gallon of cream will yield about 3 pounds of butter—it takes up a lot less refrigerator space than cream. And, like cream and milk, butter can be kept for a longer time in the freezer.

SEPARATING THE CREAM

The first step in butter making is separating the cream from the milk. This is easy to do if you're using cow's milk. The butterfat in cream is lighter in weight than the other ingredients in whole milk and will rise to the top naturally by gravity in 24 to 36 hours.

You can use a cream separator to separate the cream from the milk, but there are two fairly simple methods of separating the cream without using any special equipment: *the shallow-pan method* and *the deep-setting method*.

In the shallow-pan method, the milk is drawn from the cow and immediately poured into shallow pans or tubs. These pans or tubs are placed in a cool spot like a refrigerator or a basement for at least 24 hours. The cream that has risen to the top is then skimmed off with a flat dipper. Although this is certainly the easiest way to separate cream, some people object to this method because during the time it takes for the cream to rise, the surface of the milk is exposed to the air and frequently absorbs or develops objectionable odors and tastes.

A more satisfactory method of separating cream is by the deep-setting method. By this method, the milk is drawn from the cow and immediately poured into cans or buckets which are placed in cold water or, preferably, ice water for 12 hours. The quick cooling of the milk causes the cream to rise more rapidly and more completely. The cream can be skimmed in half the time required by the shallow-pan method, and its freshness and sweet flavor are retained.

Separating Goat's Milk

If it's goat's milk you're working with, the job is a little more difficult. The fat globules in goat's milk are small and well emulsified, which means that the cream will take much longer to separate out than it does in cow's milk. If you let goat's milk take its time to separate out, it may begin to develop a strong "goaty" flavor that most people find unappetizing. To separate the cream properly and quickly, a cream separator, which separates the cream from the skim milk by centrifugal force, is needed. Warm milk (about 90°F) is poured into the separator, where it is whirled around. The cream and skim milk are released through separate spouts in minutes, while both are still warm and fresh.

A cream separator is a delicate piece of equipment and should be cleaned and operated according to the manufacturer's directions. For best results, milk poured into the separator should be warm (about 90°F) and fresh. Most separators are left in the milk room or other unheated area. In winter, the cold temperatures can chill the instrument, and if the separator is cold enough, it will cool the first milk that is poured in to

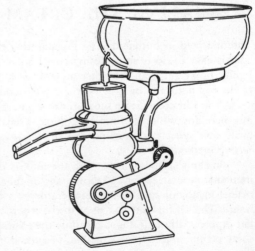

Separating the cream from the milk in cow's milk is relatively easy. The cream will rise to the top within 24 to 36 hours and can then be skimmed off. But the job is a bit more difficult with goat's milk. It takes a lot longer for the cream to separate out, thus imparting a "goaty" flavor to the milk. A quick way to separate the milk from the cream is with a cream separator, such as this one, which works by centrifugal force.

below 90°F. To prevent this from happening, warm the separator by running warm water through it before pouring in the milk.

The separator should be cleaned and sterilized immediately after each use. All parts should be rinsed in warm water and then scrubbed with a brush, warm water, and soda ash or a cleansing powder made especially for use in dairies. Soap should not be used because it is difficult to wash off completely and may leave a soapy film on the equipment. All the parts of the separator should be sterilized in a farm sterilizer or in boiling water for 5 minutes.

New cream separators aren't cheap. Used ones are cheaper, of course, but since the popularity of keeping goats for milk has increased in the last few years, the demand for used separators is growing and the supply diminishing.

CHILLING AND RIPENING THE CREAM

It is not very practical to churn a few cups of cream at a time, so many people who have just one or two milk-producing animals will collect cream over a few days, waiting until they have enough separated to make churning worthwhile. This is fine, but don't hold cream for more than 4 days before making butter. Butter made from old cream has an acidic, overripe taste, and it spoils quickly. If you are collecting cream over a few days' time, keep its temperature below 50°F and don't add it to any cream that is not cooled to at least this temperature. The addition of warm cream raises the temperature of the older cream and hastens souring. Mix all the cream together—after it is chilled—12 to 20 hours before you churn it, and stir it occasionally with a stirring rod (a smooth rod with a 4- to 5-inch-diameter disk on one end) or long-handled spoon so that it will have a uniform thickness.

The best way to cool cream rapidly is to cool it in a tub of ice water. Ice water will cool the cream more quickly than will refrigerator temperatures, providing the water is allowed to circulate on all sides as well as under the cream container. If ice water is not available, use plain water, but change it frequently.

When the cream has reached a temperature of 50°F, it can be placed in a cool spot until churning. (Get yourself a floating dairy thermometer, available at farm supply and some hardware stores, to measure temperatures accurately.) All cream should be kept at 52° to 60°F in the summer and 58° to 66°F in the winter while it is being churned. If the cream is too warm when it is churned, the butter develops too soon and is too soft and greasy. But if the cream is too cold when churned, not all of the butterfat will separate out to form butter. This results in creamy buttermilk and less butter.

Cow's cream which is allowed to ripen before it is churned will produce more flavorful butter than that which is made from sweet cream. You can ripen raw cream by allowing it to sit at room temperature (65° to 75°F) until it is thick and slightly sour. To ripen cream quickly, add about ½ cup cultured buttermilk (the kind you buy in the store is cultured; that which you take off your own homemade butter is not) or yogurt. Fresh cream should not be added after ripening begins. Once ripened, the cream should be cooled quickly in a container of ice water until it reaches churning temperature. It should be kept at churning temperature for at least 2 hours before it is churned. Don't try to ripen goat's cream before churning. The goaty or cheesy flavor it will acquire will produce an unpalatable butter.

CHURNING

The old wooden upright churn with its long dasher is rarely used for butter making anymore; most of these relics have found their way into antique shops. The wooden churn more commonly found in operation today is the barrel churn. You can also buy electrically powered and hand-operated glass churns. If you want to make just a small amount of butter, you don't even need a real churn. You can improvise with a blender, electric mixer, or food processor. Early Americans made butter by shaking cream in a deep, wooden, lidded bowl; you can improvise with a glass jar. This is a rather tedious way of making butter and it calls for a strong arm, but it does work.

Whatever device you use to churn butter, make sure it is thoroughly clean before any cream is poured into it. If you have a wooden churn that is used only occasionally, it is advisable to scrub it out well and then fill it with water 24 hours before you plan to use it so that the wood will swell and be watertight. After that, scald the wooden churn with boiling water and then chill it down to churning temperature by filling it with ice water or placing it in a refrigerator or cool basement before using. Glass churns, mixers, blenders, food processors, and glass jars should be sterilized in boiling water and cooled before using.

To make sure that there are no lumps in the cream before you begin, pour the cream through a strainer into your churn, blender, or whatever equipment you are using. Fill your churn only one-third full. Butter made from goat's cream is white. If you wish to color it, now is the time. Add a few drops of vegetable coloring to attain the desired shade of yellow. (Colonial housewives colored their butter with carrot juice.)

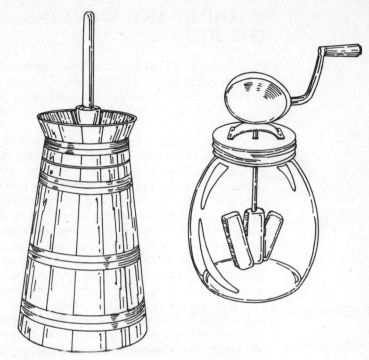

While the old-fashioned butter churn shown on the left is rarely used anymore, the hand-operated glass churn on the right is ideal for churning small amounts of butter. Electrically powered models are even more convenient, but a blender or food processor also does a fine job.

If you are using a hand-operated or electric churn, churn about 10 times and then lift up the lid or remove the plug to permit gas to escape. Churn 20 times more and allow gas to escape again. Then resume churning, at about 60 revolutions per minute, until beads of butter about the size of corn kernels form. The churning process should take about 30 to 40 minutes. Approximately 20 minutes will pass before you will hear the splash of the beads forming and feel the thickness of the butter.

TAKING OFF THE BUTTERMILK

When churning is finished, strain off the liquid. Don't throw it away. This is buttermilk. It won't be as thick as the commercial kinds because it is not cultured. It is lighter than regular milk and has a natural effervescence. It's the real, old-fashioned buttermilk that makes delicious pancakes, biscuits, and breads. What's left in the churn is mostly butter, with a little buttermilk mixed in. This remaining buttermilk must be removed to obtain the taste and texture of good butter. If it is not removed, the butter will have a shorter keeping quality and a slightly acidic or sour taste.

WASHING AND WORKING THE BUTTER

Wash the butter with clean water. Water temperature may vary according to the temperature of the butter that has formed, but it should be about 60°F. If your butter is too soft and warm, make your wash water cooler than 60°F; if it is too hard and cold, have your wash water a little warmer than 60°F.

The washing can be done right in the churn. Pour as much clean water as there is buttermilk into the churn after the buttermilk is poured off. Close the churn and churn it a few times to wash the butter. Pour off the cloudy water and repeat the washing process with fresh water. If this water is cloudy when poured off, wash again until the rinse water stays clear. Be patient—you may have to repeat this washing process as many as 10 times before all the buttermilk is out. If the butter gets too hard, wash with water that's a little warmer.

You can also take the butter out of the churn and wash it in a large, shallow bowl. Pour in clean water and knead or cut the butter to work out the milk. Don't spread the butter, though, or else it will get greasy.

Now pour your butter into a large, shallow bowl. Work out every drop of liquid by pressing and squeezing the butter against the sides and bottom of the bowl with a rubber spatula until no water can be poured off. Again, do not spread or thin the butter on the sides and bottom of the bowl; this makes the butter greasy.

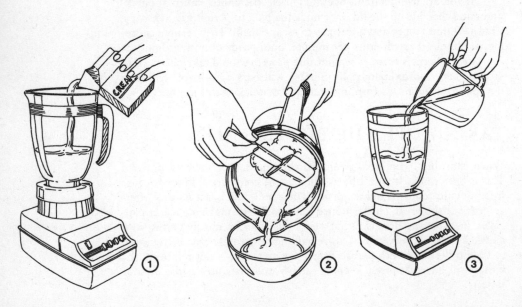

Making Butter in a Blender

If you're working with a food blender, pour in the heavy cream until it fills the container about one-third full. This should mean using 2 cups of heavy cream. Set your blender at its slowest speed. Once the blades begin, remove the cap and watch the cream. It will first get foamy and then begin to thicken. Yellow beads will start to form in about 5 to 8 minutes. Once they get to be the size of a kernel of corn and the liquid seems a bit watery (like skim milk), your butter has formed. Turn off the blender and pour off the buttermilk. Pour in the wash water, turn on the blender for a second or two, pour off the water, and repeat the washing until the wash water stays clear. Then place the butter in a large, shallow bowl and work all the liquid out in the manner described on page 358.

Making Butter in a Food Processor

Basically, this is the same as making butter in a blender, so read the paragraph above before you read the one here.

Pour 2 cups of heavy cream into the processor fitted with a steel blade. Put on the lid and process for 5 to 6 minutes. Pour off the buttermilk and pour in cool water. Process again for a few seconds. Continue this process, pouring off wash water and adding new cool water, until the wash water is clear. Then place the butter in a large, shallow bowl and work out the remaining liquid in the manner described on page 358.

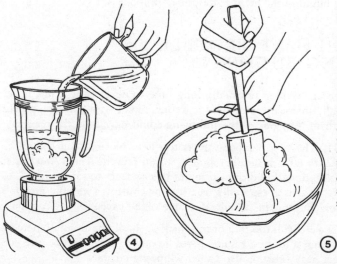

(1) To make butter in a blender, pour in the cream to fill the container about one-third full. (2) Blend on low for 5 to 8 minutes, then pour off the buttermilk. (3) Pour in the wash water, turn on the blender for a few seconds, and pour off the cloudy water. (4) Repeat this washing procedure until the wash water stays clear. (5) Pour the butter into a large bowl and work out all the liquid by pressing it against the sides of the bowl with a spatula.

Making Butter with an Electric Mixer

The end result is just fine, but getting there can be messy! Start off by pouring 2 cups heavy cream into a deep, chilled bowl. Use your mixer at its lowest speed. Increase the speed to medium and continue beating for 10 to 12 minutes, until the butter has formed. Then pour off the buttermilk and add an equal amount of clean water. Beat for 1 or 2 seconds and pour off the wash water. Repeat until the wash water pours off clear. Then place the butter in a large, shallow bowl and work out the remaining liquid in the manner described on page 358.

Making Butter in a Glass Jar

While not a practical way to make butter, it does do the job. Use it only if you have a small amount of cream to churn—and you have a strong arm.

Fill a glass jar with a tight-fitting lid one-third full of heavy cream. If you're using a quart jar, this means $1\frac{1}{4}$ cups of cream. Shake about 10 times, then remove the lid to allow the gas to escape. Screw on the lid and shake about 20 times more. Remove the lid and let the gas escape again. Replace the lid and resume shaking without stopping until lumps of butter form and the liquid takes on a thin and slightly watery appearance. It will take about 20 minutes to reach this point. Pour off buttermilk and replace with fresh water. Shake jar about 5 times, pour off the wash water, and wash again, until the wash water pours off clean. Place the lumps of butter in a large, shallow bowl and work out the remaining liquid in the manner described on page 358.

IF YOU HAVE TROUBLE MAKING BUTTER

If your butter takes an unusually long time to develop or it just never comes at all, obviously something is wrong, either with your equipment or your cream. Any one of the following could have been the reason:

1. The churning temperature is too low. Normally, it should be 52° to 60°F in summer and 58° to 66°F in the winter, but under exceptional conditions it might be necessary to raise it to 65° to 70°F. This is especially true if your churn is very cold and you are churning in an unheated area on an exceptionally cold day.

2. The cream is too thin or too thick. It should be about 30 percent butterfat for best results. If you're buying cream, make sure you get heavy cream, also called whipping cream.

3. The cream is too sweet. Very sweet cream will need to be churned longer than cream that has been ripened until it is thick and slightly sour. Ripening can be speeded up by adding about ½ cup of a starter, like *cultured* buttermilk or yogurt, to the fresh or sweet cream.

4. The churn is too full. The churn should not be more than one-third full, no matter what type of equipment you are using for churning. The extra space allows the butterfat to move about freely.

5. There's a ropy fermentation of the cream. This may be prevented by sterilizing all the utensils and producing milk and cream under sanitary conditions. If additional measures are needed, pasteurize the cream, being careful to keep it from contamination after pasteurization. Then ripen the cream with a starter before churning.

6. Individuality of the animal. The only remedy is to obtain cream from a dairy animal recently fresh or cream that is known to churn easily. If you want to use cream that you know is hard to churn, try mixing it with cream you know will churn easily. Mix them together before you ripen the cream.

7. The goat or cow being far advanced in the period of lactation. The effects may at least be partially overcome by adding, before ripening, some cream from another goat or cow that is not far advanced in the period of lactation.

8. Feeds that produce hard fat. Such feeds are cottonseed meal and timothy hay. Linseed meal, gluten feed, and succulent feeds such as silage and roots tend to overcome the condition and make churning the cream into butter easier.

9. Off-flavor of butter. Influenced by cow's feed. Refrain from giving cows strong-flavored and strong-odored foods like turnips. If off flavor persists, milk cows before, not after, feeding.

SALTING AND STORING THE BUTTER

Butter which is worked free of all its buttermilk and wash water may be eaten or stored as it is. This is unsalted, sweet butter. Salt, which enhances the flavor and lengthens butter's keeping quality, may be added at this time, if you wish. If you salt the butter, add ½ teaspoon salt for each pound (2 cups) of butter. Work the salt into the butter by pressing and

Dress up your
homemade butter by
shaping it into balls
with a butter baller, or
by pressing it into
butter molds like those
here.

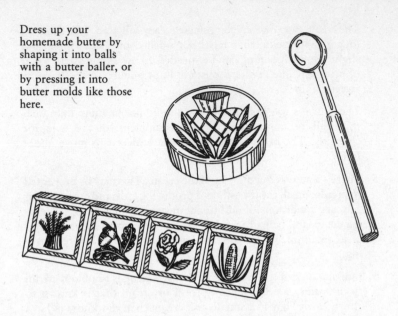

thinning the butter in the bowl with a rubber spatula, then adding a little
salt and folding the butter over. Repeat this process until all the salt is
worked in and the butter is firm and waxy. Don't spread the butter to
thin it; this causes the butter to become oily and lose its firm texture.

When the butter is "worked," it is ready to be placed in appropriate
containers and stored. You can roll your butter into a ball (or balls) and
wrap it in aluminum foil or heavy-duty plastic wrap and then in a freezer
bag. You can also press it into small bread pans and cover the pans with
wrap. Or you can put the butter into glass jars with lids. It is not a good
idea to store butter in plastic containers. These containers are porous
and will allow air and strong odors to penetrate their walls. The taste
of butter deteriorates more the longer it is stored in the refrigerator. Keep
it no longer than 2 weeks at refrigerator temperatures. If you wish to
keep your butter longer than 2 weeks, freeze it at temperatures of 0°F
or colder. Do not keep it frozen for more than 6 months. Thaw butter
for about 3 hours at refrigerator temperatures before using.

■ When mixing minced herbs with your butter to make herb butter, a little
lemon juice not only tastes good but seems to improve the butter's keeping
qualities.

■ For special occasions you can roll your butter into a log in wax paper and
either refrigerate or freeze it. Thaw out, if frozen, and cut off slices to serve on
vegetables, pasta and grains, fish, bread, or whatever.

FLAVORED BUTTERS

Garlic Dill Butter

This spread is lovely when used to make garlic bread or a sauce for fish, or when tossed with steamed vegetables.

6 cloves garlic
½ cup butter
1 tablespoon finely chopped
    fresh dill
dash of paprika

In a small saucepan combine garlic with water to cover. Bring to a boil, reduce heat and simmer for 10 minutes. Strain, let cool, and slip skins off garlic. Crush garlic through a press.

In a food processor, combine garlic, butter, dill, and paprika. Process until well combined. Refrigerate or freeze in portion-size packets.

Yield: ⅔ cup

Basil Butter

The lemon juice helps to keep the basil a nice green.

3 cups fresh basil leaves, finely
    chopped
½ cup butter
2 teaspoons lemon juice

Mix all ingredients together. Pack into small containers and freeze. This will keep 6 months in the freezer.

It's good on pasta, eggs, potatoes and other vegetables, and fish.

Yield: ⅔ cup

Dill Butter

3 tablespoons finely chopped
    fresh dill
2 tablespoons finely chopped
    scallions
1 tablespoon finely chopped
    parsley
¼ cup butter
1 teaspoon lemon juice

Mix all ingredients together. Pack into small containers and freeze. It will keep in the freezer up to 6 months.

It's good on potatoes, cabbage, fish, and pasta.

Yield: ⅔ cup

Chili Butter

Toss this seasoned butter with pasta and cheese or with green beans, or spread it on sandwiches or crackers.

½ cup finely minced onions
½ cup butter
1 tablespoon chili powder
2 tablespoons cider vinegar

In a small saucepan, sauté onions in 1 tablespoon of the butter. When golden, add chili powder and vinegar and mix.

Scoop chili mixture into the bowl of a processor and add remaining butter. Process until combined. At this point, the mixture may appear to be too thin, but will solidify when refrigerated. Be sure to stir before refrigerating or freezing, to keep onions from sinking to the bottom.

Yield: ⅔ cup

Apple and Spice-Flavored Butter

Warm muffins, pancakes, and toast are all enhanced by this unusual breakfast butter.

3 tablespoons grated green
  apples (with skin)
3 tablespoons grated red apples
  (with skin)
½ cup butter, cut into pieces
½ teaspoon ground cinnamon
2 teaspoons maple syrup

Combine all ingredients in the bowl of a food processor and process until smooth. Refrigerate or freeze.

Yield: ⅔ cup

Lite Butter

This butter blend tastes very much like the real thing, but contains fewer calories and less cholesterol.

¼ cup butter, softened
¼ cup corn oil

Combine butter and oil in a processor or blender until smooth. Use as you would regular butter.

Yield: ½ cup

Homemade Cheeses

Cheese is one of those foods that has a certain mystique associated with it. Perhaps this is because there are hundreds of kinds, so many of which come from foreign places: Roquefort, Brie, and Camembert from France; Emmenthal and Gouda from Switzerland; mozzarella and ricotta from Italy; and Stilton and cheddar from England. Incorporated into this mystique is the idea that cheesemaking is something not to be attempted by amateurs. This is just not so. There are many fine amateur cheesemakers around who make some wonderful cheeses.

Like wine making, cheesemaking is some science, some craft, and a little luck. No two cheeses taste exactly the same; they're a product of ingredients, technique, and environment. Make a change in any one of them—heat the curds a little higher, use a different starter, age it a little longer in a drier place—and you've got a slightly different cheese. It can be frustrating at times not knowing what you're going to wind up with, and disappointing when all that work and good milk doesn't yield the cheese you had expected. But it can be fun, too. There's the challenge of another day, another cheese, a new recipe, a new technique to try.

The simplest cheese to make is cottage cheese. Ricotta and cream cheeses are close seconds. The ingredients and equipment are pretty basic, and little time is involved. If you've never made any cheese before, we heartily suggest you start with one of these. Then move to the harder cheeses, which are more demanding to make, but which reward you with a wider range of flavors and textures.

365

EQUIPMENT

None of the soft cheeses require any fancy equipment, except for a *dairy thermometer*. The cheaper and simpler type is made of glass and floats on top of the milk. Fancier is a dial thermometer with a stainless steel rod that is set into the milk; it hooks onto the side of your pot so you can easily read the temperature. It's more responsive to heat than the glass model, so you can take a quicker reading. If you have a *big stainless steel pot*, a *long stainless steel knife* and *ladle or big spoon*, a *colander*, and some *cheesecloth*, you've got everything else you need.

When you move on to the semisoft and harder cheeses, you need more in the way of equipment. Count on needing those things just mentioned. Also, for cheddar cheeses, *a large pot* (which can be the same one you used to heat the milk and curds) with a bottom rack is necessary for cheddaring (meaning gently dry-heating the curds). *A cheese press*, while not absolutely essential, is nice for making the harder cheeses. The elaborateness and expense of your press should be in direct proportion to the amount of cheese you make. Presses can get pretty fancy—far too fancy for someone who's just dabbling. Some people improvise with rocks, books, or other heavy objects. (See David Page's improvisation in his recipe for Plain Semihard Cheese, page 378. But a press makes things much easier and much neater. Presses are fairly simple pieces of equipment, and you can make your own if you're handy. *The Complete Dairy Foods Cookbook*, by E. Annie Proulx and Lew Nichols (see the Appendix), has plans for a homemade press.

Some of the semisoft cheeses you'll find later in this chapter, like mozzarella and chèvre, call for a *cheese mold*. You can get yourself some of the lovely molds made just for cheesemaking, or you can make do quite nicely with plastic food containers, like those that cottage cheese comes in; just punch some holes in the bottom and the sides. *Cheese boards* are made from squares of hardwood that usually measure 6 inches

Cheesemaking requires just a few simple pieces of equipment, among them a dairy thermometer. One type is made of glass and floats on top of the milk. Another type is made of stainless steel, with a rod that sits in the milk and a dial that hooks onto the side of the pot.

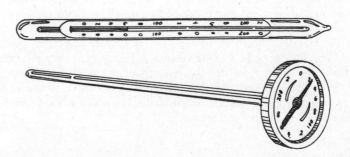

Cheese mats are made
from wooden reeds or
hard plastic. Mats are
sometimes used to drain
cheeses, such as Gouda,
after they've been pressed.

on each side. *Cheese mats* are made from wooden reeds or hard plastic.
Both boards and mats are sometimes used along with a cheese mold for
shaping and draining certain soft cheeses, like Coulommiers. And sometimes mats are used for draining cheeses after they've been pressed, as
with Gouda cheese.

If you don't have the right bacteria in your milk, you won't be able
to make cheese (see Ingredients, below), but if you've got the wrong kind
of bacteria, you won't get cheese either. Use clean, clean equipment, and
stick to glass and stainless steel. Aluminum and cast iron are especially
bad because they react so easily with the lactic acid produced during
cheesemaking, changing the flavor of the cheese.

INGREDIENTS

The main ingredient in cheese is, of course, *milk*—and you need lots of
it. To make 1 pound of hard cheese like cheddar, you'll need 5 quarts
of milk, and for about 1¾ pounds of cottage cheese or 3 cups of cream
cheese, you'll need 4 quarts of milk. While a pound or so of cottage or
cream cheese is an adequate amount to make at one time, there's not
much sense in making less than 3 to 5 pounds of a harder cheese at a
time because smaller cheese dries out too quickly, and just about the
same amount of work is involved, no matter how much you make. So
figure you'll need at least 15 quarts of milk to make one batch of one
of the harder cheeses.

You can make cheese out of fresh raw milk, or homogenized, pasteurized milk. Both will work and, unless it is so specified, you can use
raw or pasteurized milk in the recipes that follow. Raw milk, however,
gives a slightly firmer curd than pasteurized milk. If you're going to buy
homogenized, pasteurized milk at supermarket prices, your homemade
cheese can turn out to be mighty expensive. Your cheese will be a lot
more economical (and many people claim better tasting) if you have a
good source of fresh raw milk. It goes without saying that if you have
your own cow or goat, your milk will be the cheapest, freshest, and, in
milking season, most plentiful.

Most cheese recipes also call for a *starter or activator*; some call for two. This is a substance that contains beneficial bacteria that will make the milk clabber or, in other words, separate the curds from the whey. Raw milk contains the beneficial bacteria that are responsible for making milk clabber, so technically you don't have to use a starter with raw milk. But in most recipes a starter *is* used with raw milk because it speeds up the clabbering process and guarantees that the milk won't sour before it clabbers sufficiently. Pasteurized milk definitely needs a starter to clabber since the beneficial bacteria have been killed off in the heating process.

Cheese starter culture is a freeze-dried bacteria often used in cheese recipes to separate out the milk solids. There are different kinds, for different types of cheeses. Sometimes a starter is used alone, and it's often used along with rennet. You must always make up a batch of starter by mixing the freeze-dried culture with milk, following the directions that come with the starter. Although we don't use it in any of our recipes, it is called for in many cheesemaking directions in other books.

Cultured buttermilk also contains the activating bacteria, and some recipes call for it in place of a cheese-starter culture. Don't use the kind that you pour off your homemade butter because it doesn't have the beneficial bacteria. The kind to use is the thick supermarket kind—make sure it's fresh.

Yogurt also contains the right bacteria. If a recipe calls for it, use fresh, homemade yogurt or an unflavored commercial yogurt, so long as it's really yogurt and not a sweet yogurtlike custard which some "yogurts" are.

Rennet is a milk-clotting enzyme extracted from the lining of unweaned calves' stomachs. Cheese rennet is available in both liquid and tablet form. Rennet tablets used to be found in almost all grocery and drugstores, but that was when home cheesemaking was commonplace. You still might be able to find them in some such stores, but if you can't, check in a hobby store that sells cheesemaking equipment or in one of the cheesemaking catalogs. Be sure you completely dissolve the rennet in cold water before you add it to the milk.

There are some *herbs,* too, that have the milk-clabbering properties of rennet, yogurt, and buttermilk. They are sometimes packaged as *vegetable rennet.* Nettle, giant purple thistle, the sorrels (lemon and common), fermitory, and the sap of the unripe fig will all curdle milk. Vegetable rennet is not as good a clabberer as animal rennet.

■ Don't try to adjust a recipe to increase the yield, especially if the recipe calls for rennet. Rennet does not double as the recipe doubles.

Paraffin or cheese wax is used to protect the harder cheeses during their aging. Cheese wax does a better job than paraffin because it's more

SALTY CHEESES

Most cheeses are naturally quite salty. The saltiest common cheese is Parmesan. Two ounces contain 1,064 milligrams, almost a third of the maximum safe allowance for one day. That's more salt than 20 ounces of potato chips. Processed cheeses also have a lot of sodium; for example, American contains 817 milligrams in 2 ounces and processed Swiss has 783 milligrams. The sodium content in some other cheeses follows: blue (797 milligrams), Edam (551 milligrams), provolone (500 milligrams), Gouda (468 milli-grams), Monterey Jack (306 milligrams), Muenster (228 milligrams), and mozzarella (213 milligrams). The common hard cheese lowest in sodium is unpasteurized Swiss (150 milligrams), only 5 percent of the maximum daily allowance.

The cheeses featured in the recipes in this chapter use no salt with the exception of David Page's semihard cheese and cheddar cheese, and the Gouda and mozzarella which are soaked in salt brines.

pliable and will not crack, exposing some of the cheese to mold. Both should be melted and then brushed on the cheese in 2 or 3 coats after the cheese has been pressed, right before it gets put away for aging.

STORING CHEESES

You can generally figure that the softer a cheese is, the less likely it is to freeze well. Cottage cheese, ricotta, Brie, Camembert, and cream cheese get crumbly and deteriorate in flavor when frozen. They are best kept in the refrigerator and eaten within a week. You can freeze them, but plan on using them in cooking when they're thawed so you won't notice that they've lost much of the smooth texture. Parmesan and Romano cheese freeze quite nicely. They'll keep for 6 months in the freezer.

■ For easy use, shred your cheese before you freeze it and freeze in convenient quantities.

Cheeses in between, and there are many, get a bit crumbly when frozen and begin to lose some of their flavor in the freezer after a few months. This doesn't bother everybody, and if you've got an over-abundance of cheese, it's better to risk some change in texture and flavor than to let the cheese get moldy or dry out in your refrigerator. If you are going to freeze one of these semihard cheeses, like cheddar, Swiss, provolone, Gouda, or Monterey Jack, cut it into small pieces—about ½ pound each—and wrap each piece individually in freezer paper or place in a plastic freezer bag, squeeze out all of the air, and close with a wire twist. In small pieces like this, the cheese will thaw quickly when it's taken from the freezer, giving it less chance to get gritty. To thaw cheese properly, remove the wrapper when you take it from the freezer and then rewrap it, making sure the package is airtight. Let it thaw in the refrigerator. Such cheese will keep for at least 2 months without any noticeable change.

If your cheese gets some mold on it while it's in the refrigerator, either cut out all of the mold or throw the entire piece of cheese away. The mold is not one of the benign molds you'll find in blue, Stilton, and Roquefort cheeses, but something that could be more dangerous.

■ For extra protection against drying out or getting moldy in the refrigerator, wrap your cheddar and other semihard cheeses in clean cotton sheeting or cheesecloth that has been dipped in a weak vinegar solution. Check the cheese now and then and dampen the cloth in vinegar water when it dries out.

■ To prevent cut edges of a round of cheese from drying out, spread butter or a light-flavor oil on the cut ends before wrapping and refrigerating it.

To make cottage cheese with pasteurized milk, (1) add buttermilk, yogurt or rennet solution to a large potful of milk, cover, and let sit in a warm place until the milk clabbers. (2) After the milk has clabbered, you must cut the curd to separate out the whey. Cut the curd into 2-inch strips in one direction, then crosswise to make 2-inch squares. (3) Heat the curd over a pot that contains several inches of water. Gently stir the curd and heat it to 115°F. Hold it at this temperature for about 30 minutes.

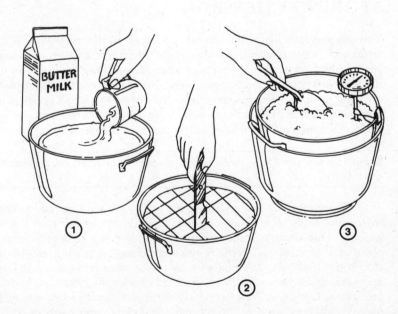

COTTAGE CHEESE

Cottage cheese got its name from the fact that it is a cheese that can easily be made in the home—or in the cottage. Traditionally, this soft, perishable cheese was made from the skim milk left after butter making. After the cream had been taken off the top, the remaining milk was poured into a good-size crock and set in a warm place (usually on the back of the wood stove in the kitchen) for 2 days or so, until the milk had clabbered and much of the whey had separated from the curd. Then the curd was cut into cubes and heated gently over a low fire to firm it up a little. The warm curd and whey were poured into a cheesecloth sack and hung up over a tub until all the whey had drained off and only the soft curds were left. The cheese was then chilled for a few hours and mixed with a little salt and fresh cream and stored in the springhouse, cellar, or ice chest, where it could be kept as long as 5 days without spoiling.

Cottage cheese made at home today is made in much the same way as it has always been made. You can make it with fresh, raw skim milk, but fresh pasteurized or raw whole milk will do, too.

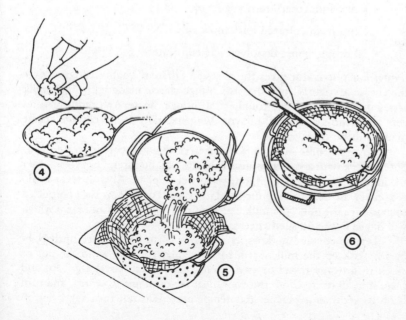

(4) Test the curd for firmness by spooning some from the pot and gently squeezing it between your fingers. The curd should feel slightly firm and rubbery. If it is dry and hard, it's been overcooked, and if it is very soft and moist, it isn't done. (5) Pour the curds into a cheesecloth-lined colander to strain out the whey. (6) When all the whey has drained out (about 3 to 5 hours), rinse the curds by placing the colander in a large pot of cold water and gently stirring.

Raw milk contains the beneficial bacteria that are responsible for making milk clabber. Pasteurized milk has been heated to temperatures that kill this bacteria, and it will not clabber by itself, no matter how long it sits in a warm place. If you're using pasteurized milk, you'll need to add something to activate the curd and start the milk clabbering. You can add a milk product that contains the necessary beneficial bacteria, like cultured buttermilk or plain, unsweetened yogurt, or you can use rennet tablets.

In addition to the milk and activator, you'll need an earthenware crock, glass casserole dish, or stainless steel or enamel pot. Also have on hand a dairy thermometer, a long spoon (preferably made from glass or stainless steel), a spatula or knife, a large pan or shallow pot that is larger than your crock, cheesecloth, and a colander. All your equipment should be scrupulously clean. Wash it with soap and water and rinse well with very hot water before bringing it in contact with the milk.

As we said before, cottage cheese is simple to make.

Clabbering the Milk

Pour 1 gallon of fresh raw or pasteurized skim or whole milk into a pot or crock. If the milk is cold, bring it to room temperature (70 to 80°F) over very low heat. If you are using pasteurized milk, whisk *one* of the following into the milk:

- $\frac{1}{2}$ cup unflavored fresh yogurt *or*
- $\frac{1}{2}$ cup fresh cultured buttermilk *or*
- 20 drops rennet dissolved in $\frac{1}{4}$ cup water

(Note: Each activator gives the cheese a different quality. Yogurt gives the cheese a yogurty, tart flavor. Cottage cheese made with buttermilk tastes and looks most like commercial cottage cheese. And rennet creates very large curds and a mild flavor. We personally prefer cottage cheese made with buttermilk.)

Cover the milk mixture with cheesecloth and secure it around your pot or crock with a string or large rubber band. Be careful not to smother the milk by covering it with a heavy towel or plate. All you want to do is to cover the milk to keep dust and insects out of it. If air isn't permitted to pass over the milk, the milk can acquire a musty odor and taste which will linger in the finished cheese.

Let the covered milk sit in a warm (75° to 85°F) place until clabbered. To keep the milk warm for this long, you can wrap the pot or crock in a heavy towel or two, taking care not to cover the top, and place it in an oven. Close the door, heat the oven just to warm, and turn it off as soon as it reaches this temperature. Do not turn the oven on again. Both the towels and the oven box will act as insulators, keeping the milk from cooling down.

It will take 16 to 24 hours for pasteurized milk activated with buttermilk or yogurt to clabber. The rennet clabbers the milk more quickly, and raw milk that has not had any of these three activators added to it may take as long as 48 hours to clabber. You can check the milk to see if it is clabbered by sticking the end of a knife into the curd and lifting up. If the break is clean, the milk is properly clabbered. But if the curd is the consistency of yogurt, it is not ready and must sit longer. Be careful not to jiggle the pot, as this may break the curd and affect the cheese.

Cutting the Curd

When the milk has properly clabbered, much of the whey, a thin watery liquid, will have risen to the top, and the curd, a white substance with a consistency similar to soft cream cheese, will have settled to the bottom. Now it is necessary to cut the curd to allow more whey to separate out. If you are using skim milk, cut the curd into 2-inch cubes. Do not make them much smaller than this, because if you do, too much whey may separate out, making the resulting cheese dry and leathery. If you are working with whole milk, the cubes may be cut smaller. To cube the curd, cut into 2-inch strips with a spatula or knife. Then slice the curd again crosswise so that you have 2-inch squares. If the curd is more than 2 inches deep, bring your spatula under the curd and cut across horizontally. It is important to cut the curd carefully so that just enough—but not too much—of the whey can separate out.

Heating the Curd

Pour a few inches of water into another large pan or pot, set the pot or crock with the cubed curd in it, and place it over low heat. Insert the dairy thermometer in the curd and heat very gently until the thermometer reads 115°F. Hold it at this temperature for about 30 minutes, stirring occasionally so that the heat will be distributed evenly throughout the curd. Stir gently so as not to break the curd.

Straining the Curd

After about 30 minutes, the curds will have settled to the bottom of the pot or crock. Line a colander with cheesecloth. Gently pour the curds and whey into the colander. Whey is an important source of minerals and B vitamins, so you may want to place the colander in a bowl so you can save the whey for adding to soups, beverages, or casseroles, cook rice in it, or feed it to your pets or livestock. Allow most of the whey to drain off and then take up the four corners of the cheesecloth and hang the curds in the cheesecloth over the bowl so as to catch the remaining whey that drips out. Let the curds hang this way until no more whey drips out. Figure it will take 3 to 5 hours for the cheese to drain sufficiently. The curds may be rinsed at this time with clean, cold water if you wish to minimize the acid flavor, although rinsing is not necessary.

Storing Cottage Cheese

Cottage cheese keeps well in a covered container for up to a week in the refrigerator. It does not freeze well.

Goat's Milk Cottage Cheese

Unless you've made cottage cheese before, read the directions for cottage cheese made from cow's milk that precede this.

½ gallon goat's milk
¼ cup cultured buttermilk
¼ rennet tablet
1 tablespoon water

In a large stainless steel pot or large crock, bring goat's milk to 85°F. Stir in the buttermilk and let it sit overnight at room temperature (70 to 80°F).

Crush the rennet and add to water. Combine it with the milk and let it sit 3 hours at room temperature.

Fill a medium-size pot with water and heat until almost boiling. Place cheesecloth in a colander and set it in another pot.

With a fine mesh strainer, scoop out some of the curds and let them drain for several seconds. Plunge them into the almost-boiling water for 5 seconds, then dump them into the colander. Repeat as many times as necessary until all the curds are treated.

Let the curds drain for 1 hour. Wrap and refrigerate for 1 week.

Yield: 10 ounces

RICOTTA

Ricotta means "cooked once again" and is literally just that. The economical Italian country wife looked for a use for the whey left over from making her famous hard cheeses and found that with high heat and acid she could precipitate the albumin (protein) in the whey and thereby obtain a delicious fresh cheese.

Other cheese-producing countries have created similar types of whey cheese, such as the Swiss Hudelziger; the Italian Mascarpone, from goat's milk whey; and the French Gran de Montagne, made from whey and enriched with cream. Other exotic names for ricotta-type cheese include Recuit, Broccio, Brocotte, Serac, Ceracee, and Mejette.

Ricotta is most often sold fresh. It is rather sweet as opposed to the slightly tangy flavor of cottage cheese; it is creamy and melts beautifully without separating in baked dishes like lasagna. A less well-known product is dried ricotta, available only in specialized cheese shops, or your own home dairy. This is a piquant grating cheese and does not require the refrigeration mandatory for fresh ricotta. So if you make too much to consume within a few days, you can press and dry it.

To prepare authentic old-world ricotta, you need whey. This is the nutritious liquid left over from curdled milk when you have removed the curd. It contains the water-soluble proteins, vitamins, and minerals in the milk, such as the soluble calcium. Most people do not realize that one-third of the calcium in milk is lost in the whey in the cheesemaking process, even more when the cheese is made by the acid-coagulation method such as in tangy, small-curd cottage cheese, rather than the renneted method. Liquid whey also contains most of the milk sugar, or lactose. However, in the finished whole milk ricotta cheese only 3 percent lactose remains, so those on a low carbohydrate diet can enjoy it also.

You will need at least 2 to 3 gallons of whey plus a few cups of whole milk to make only 1 to 2 cups of cheese. This is a lot of whey and not very practical for home cheesemaking, especially if you must collect whey from the milk of one or two goats. If you do have the whey, however, here is how to prepare it. We suggest that you read the directions for making cottage cheese starting on page 371 before you proceed with these recipes since many steps are similar.

Old-World Ricotta
(Ricotone)

2½ gallons liquid whey
1 pint fresh whole milk
⅓ cup cider vinegar

Heat whey until the cream rises to the surface. Add milk and continue heating to just below the boiling point (about 200°F). Stir in vinegar and remove immediately from heat. Dip out whey into a cheesecloth-lined colander and drain. Then hang up the cheesecloth to drain further.

1 to 2 cups

Modern ricotta, developed in the early nineteenth century, is made from whole milk. It's easily made at home. The whole or part-skim milk is acidified to a carefully controlled level, then subjected to high temperatures. For most of us who do not have equipment for measuring or controlling pH and heat, the following method works very well.

New-World Ricotta

These easy-to-handle proportions are adaptable to small quantity cheese-making. Dried whey is available in natural food stores and is well known for its beneficial action on friendly intestinal flora. This is one of the reasons ricotta is such a highly digestible food. Whey contains about 13 percent protein, has five times the calcium of liquid milk, and is a good source of riboflavin and iron.

¼ cup whey powder
1 quart fresh whole or part-
   skim milk
2 tablespoons cultured
   buttermilk

Stir whey powder into milk with a whip to dissolve well. Stir in the buttermilk. Let sit at room temperature (70° to 80°F) for 24 hours.

Over very low heat, bring to scalding temperature (200°F). This will take about 1½ hours. It will separate into curds and whey. Gently drain through cheesecloth; hang to drip 1 to 2 hours.

This cheese has a drier consistency than store-bought ricotta.

Store fresh ricotta in moisture-proof containers, well closed, in the refrigerator. It will keep about 4 to 7 days.

Yield: about 1 cup

CREAM CHEESE

A simple, soft cream cheese can be made with either cream or milk. Be sure that the milk or cream is fresh and at room temperature. It may be either raw or pasteurized. We suggest you read the directions for making cottage cheese (see page 371) before you proceed with the following recipe since many steps are similar.

Cream Cheese

½ cup cultured buttermilk
1 gallon milk or cream
½ rennet tablet
¼ cup cold water

Add the cultured buttermilk to the milk or cream, mixing well. Dissolve rennet in water, and stir it well into the milk or cream.

Stir for about 10 minutes, or until the milk just begins to clabber. Stop stirring when you feel a slight thickening. Then cover and keep it at 70° to 80°F until it has completely clabbered. This clabbering may take 12 to 15 hours or a little more. Do not jiggle or jostle the mixture during clabbering.

When the whey has separated out and the curds have formed one soft but solid mass on the bottom of the bowl, the milk has clabbered. Now take several layers of new, clean cheesecloth and wet it in clean water. Several layers are necessary or cheese will ooze through. Wring it out and line a colander with it. Place the colander in a large bowl to catch the whey. With a clean knife slice through the clabbered milk so that the curds are cut into about 1-inch cubes. Then pour the clabbered milk cubes and its whey into the colander and let it drip for a minute or so. Pick up the cheesecloth by its four corners, being careful not to pour out any of the curds, and tie the corners together to form a bag.

Suspend this bag over a bowl and let it drip until all the whey has drained off and a gelatinous solid mass remains. You should let it drip at least overnight. If the weather is warm, put the bag in a colander, place the colander in a bowl, and put the whole thing in the refrigerator. You can speed up the process by gently squeezing the bag every so often and by changing the cheesecloth once or twice when it gets plugged up with the cream cheese.

When the consistency of the cheese is to your liking, take it out of the cheesecloth and place it in a clean bowl. Salt it if you wish. Start with a small amount of salt (¼ teaspoon) and add more to taste. The salt is not necessary, and some people will prefer not to add any. It will, however, help the cheese to keep a little longer.

Then pack the cheese into rigid containers and keep in the refrigerator. Unsalted cream cheese will keep 3 to 4 days, and if salted, about 4 to 5 days.

Yield: 3 cups

PLAIN SEMIHARD CHEESE

David Page is an amateur cheesemaker who turns out some great-tasting cheeses. Here are his directions for making what he calls a "nondescript, semihard, mild-to-sharp, pleasant-tasting, unadulterated cheese."

After you understand the process, you might like to try the cheese recipes that follow these directions.

Ripening the Milk

Your cheese is doomed to failure if your milk is not ripened properly. The idea is to inoculate the milk with a lactobacillus culture in order that other strains of bacteria don't get a chance to grow during aging and thus ruin the cheese. Obtaining a culture is simple—just use cultured buttermilk from the store. Take 1 quart fresh cultured buttermilk and add about ¼ cup to each of 4 clean, scalded quart jars. Fill the jars with fresh pasteurized milk. Seal with clean caps, shake, and allow to stand for 24 hours at room temperature. This gives you 4 quarts of fresh buttermilk, which you can also use for other things. You can put your culture in the refrigerator and use as needed. The culture can be perpetuated merely by repeating the foregoing process with your last jar of buttermilk at any given time. This is known as better living through bacteriology.

Get the biggest canning kettle you can find. David uses a 36-quart kettle, which is pretty heavy when it is full. A 24-quart canning kettle is all right. The kettle must be enamel or stainless steel. Aluminum is a no-no and so is cast iron. Add the contents of 1 quart cultured buttermilk to your kettle. Pour in sufficient milk to fill your kettle to within 2 inches of the top, and mix with a clean spoon. David uses raw milk for making cheese, but pasteurized milk is okay, too. The milk should not be more than 2 days old (having been refrigerated, of course) and may be skimmed if desired. Warm the milk up to 86° to 90°F over low heat and allow to ripen for 1 to 2 hours. That is, set it aside; go and do something; when you're done—it's done.

Forming the Curd

For each 2 gallons milk, dissolve ¼ rennet tablet in about ½ cup cool water. (A bit too much rennet is better than a bit too little.) Make sure the ripened milk is at about 86° to 90°F. (Check its temperature with a dairy thermometer.) Add the rennet solution to the milk with plenty of stirring. Cover and let stand for about 1 hour. The way to tell if it's done is to stick your finger (washed, of course) into the curd at an angle and lift up slowly. If the curd makes a clean break over your finger, it's done. If it's still the consistency of tired yogurt—be patient.

Cutting the Curd

When the milk has curdled sufficiently, get a long knife and slice the curd into cubes about ½-inch square—don't worry about getting nice-looking cubes. Holding the knife vertically, slice in a parallel fashion in lines about ½ inch apart in one direction and then slice in the same manner in a direction perpendicular to the original slicings. Then slice at a sharp angle across one way following the original lines as best you can in order to undercut the curd and make it into cubes. Do this undercutting in several directions until you think you have the curd pretty well cut up.

Heating the Curd

Place the whole works on a very low fire. (David uses the low setting on an electric stove for 8 gallons; smaller amounts require a lower setting.) Using a clean spoon, stir constantly in order not to burn the curd at the bottom. As you stir with one hand, have your knife ready in the other hand to hack up any large pieces of curd that escaped the blade previously. Besides, hacking the curd helps to relieve the tedium of standing over the pot and stirring. As you stir, the contents will warm up—slowly. It should take about 45 minutes to 1 hour to get from 86°F to 105°F. You will note that the big lumps will get smaller and a yellowish, cloudy fluid called whey separates. Keep the curds in motion during heating.

When you've reached 105°F, take the pot off the stove and let stand for 1 hour. That should allow sufficient time for the curd to harden. What you will have is something resembling a white rubber bath mat at the bottom of a pot full of whey. Pour or scoop off the whey. (Save it to feed to chickens or pigs if you have them, or dump it on the garden or compost pile.) Leave the curds in the pot—it is easier to salt them if you do.

For 8 gallons' worth of curds, add about 3 tablespoons salt. The amount you add is purely a matter of taste. Using a spatula (pancake turner), slice into the matted curd and mix in the salt. At this point, the curd is quite well held together. A commercial cheesemaking establishment would have a machine to chop up the curd—something like a compost shredder. Some whey will go sloshing around with the curds which will help to disperse the salt throughout the curds.

Pressing the Curd

Go to the hardware store and buy 10 or 20 yards of cheesecloth. The stuff you seem to be able to get these days is pretty cheesy so you must use a double thickness of cloth about a yard square. Place the double layer of cloth over a clean pail or bowl which is at least the same volume as the curd you have. Dump the curd (the spatula really comes in handy here) into the cheesecloth, pick up the corners and form the curd into a ball by twisting the cheesecloth and squeezing the curd in the appropriate places. Hang up and let drain for about 15 minutes.

Now you should have a ball of curd of varying size depending on how much milk you started with. You could now press your cheese in a cheese press at 40 to 60 pounds pressure or you could do what David does—improvise.

To improvise, fold a clean dish towel which is about 2 feet long into a multilayered band about 4 inches wide by the length of the towel. Wrap this band around the side of the ball of curd as tightly as you can and fasten the end of the band with safety pins. What you have now is a ball of curd in a cloth girdle. Place the ball on a towel which is laid in the bottom of an 8-inch-diameter shallow bowl or deep plate. This will form the shape of the bottom of your wheel of cheese. Where the twisty part of the original cheesecloth is on the top of the ball, rearrange the cloth so that when the top is compressed, the folds of the cheesecloth do not unduly indent the final wheel of cheese. Place a similar bowl over the top of the ball of curd and pile about 40 to 60 pounds of books on top of everything and let stand overnight. Smaller cheeses need less weight. The idea is to press the individual curd granules into a solid wheel of cheese. There are various appliances one can make to do the pressing job, but you may not have the time to make one.

Using the erudite method given above, you have to watch out for several things. First, if your bowls are too deep, they will just come together under pressure and the curd won't get pressed. Also, if the books slip off at an angle, your final wheel of cheese will be lopsided—so be sure to distribute your weights above the curd evenly. A bit of intelligence and ingenuity could come up with a much better way of pressing the curd.

After 12 hours, you will have a nice, compact wheel of cheese. Strip off the cheesecloth and wind a fresh band of cloth around where the old girdle was. Fasten again with safety pins. The reason for doing this is that the cheese at this point is quite plastic, and if the sides of the wheel are not supported, the cheese will tend to flatten as it forms a rind.

Turn the cheese several times a day for 5 or 6 days, or until a good, even rind has formed over the surface. Some directions say to dry for 1 to 2 days—don't believe them! Some mold may form on the outside, which is of no consequence.

Aging the Cheese

By this time you are probably wondering if you will ever get to taste your fledgling cheese. Have patience, for you must wait for at least 60 days more. Wipe off the outside of the wheel of cheese and wrap tightly with 1 or 2 layers of cheesecloth. Heat 1 to 2 pounds of paraffin in a pot until it is good and hot, and brush the hot wax over the cheese or dunk portions of the wheel into the wax. Be careful of hot wax. It is important to paraffin the entire cheese or it will dry out. The cheesecloth helps to keep the paraffin coating from cracking. Write the date on a piece of paper and glue it to the outside of the cheese with hot paraffin so you will know when the cheese is ready to eat. Place the finished cheese in a cool place on a clean surface and turn once every few days.

If there is mold growth under the paraffin, don't worry; it won't invade the cheese. If the cheese starts to swell, you've got troubles. Such behavior indicates that your milk was not properly ripened and that a "bad" microorganism is enjoying your cheese. Other than bad bacteria, the other big enemy of ripening cheese is most notably small animals. If you have no cats, then worry about mice and rats eating your cheeses. If your wheels survive, they will taste pretty good after 60 to 90 days. The cheese will become sharper the older it gets.

This completes the basics of making a good homemade semihard cheese. One can add various herbs and natural coloring agents to the milk after it has ripened in order to obtain a "different" cheese.

Now that you've had lesson number 1, here are a few semihard cheese recipes tested by the Rodale Food Center.

■ In order to enjoy the full flavor of cheese, bring it to room temperature before you serve it. But don't go overboard and expose the cheese to high temperatures which cause the cheese to sweat and lose some of the fat captured in the curd.

Easy White Cheese

Great for breading and frying, stir-frying with vegetables, or by itself, this mild cheese will keep refrigerated for 1 week.

1 gallon whole milk
3 tablespoons white vinegar
2 tablespoons lemon juice

Pour milk into a large stainless steel or enamel pot. Slowly bring the temperature up to 180°F. (This may take an hour.) Use a dairy thermometer to check the temperature.

Stir frequently to prevent scorching, and hold the temperature at 180°F for 4 minutes.

Combine vinegar and lemon juice and add to the milk, stirring gently, until the curds separate from the whey.

Line a colander with cheesecloth, and pour in the contents of the pot. Tie the corners of the cheesecloth together to form a bag and let it hang to drain for 3 hours.

The cheese will be solid when it's ready. Wrap and refrigerate. Use the whey for making a whey cheese like ricotta (see page 375), or for an extra-nutritious soup broth.

Yield: 1 pound

Variation

Herbed Easy White Cheese—Add 1½ teaspoons dried chives and ½ tablespoon dillweed to the curds in the cheesecloth before hanging.

"Instarella" Mozzarella

Mozzarella gives the highest cheese-from-milk yield of any cheese. This method of making mozzarella is so quick and simple we call it "Instarella." This recipe was given to us by Erie Cheesemaking Supply, Erie, Pennsylvania.

2 gallons milk*
2½ teaspoons citric acid powder
¼ cup cool water
½ teaspoon liquid rennet or ¼
   rennet tablet
¼ cup cold water
½ cup coarse canning or kosher
   salt
1 gallon cold water

Place milk in a large stainless steel or enamel pot. Dissolve the citric acid powder in water. Mix it into the cool milk for 2 minutes, until dissolved completely.

Heat the milk to 88°F. Dilute the liquid rennet or ¼ rennet tablet in ¼ cup cold water. Stir rennet into milk for 15 to 20 seconds. Then allow the milk to remain still for 12 to 15 minutes while it coagulates.

Cut curd into ½- to ⅜-inch cubes, using a long-handled knife. After cutting, let curds remain undisturbed for 5 minutes; then place over low heat and stir gently so as to keep curds separated. The curds will shrink somewhat as the whey is expelled from them. Slowly heat curds to 108°F. This should take 15 minutes. Use a dairy thermometer to check the temperature. Shut off the heat and continue to stir for an additional 20 minutes.

Separate the curds from the whey, either by dipping or pouring them into a colander for 15 minutes.

Cut the curd into strips about 1 × 1 inch each. Lay strips in crisscross fashion in a bowl.

Mix canning or kosher salt in 1 gallon cold water and heat to 170°F. Add the salt water to the bowl of curd strips so that they are covered by the water.

Using a wooden spoon, begin to stretch curd in an upward motion, much like pulling taffy. The curd will begin to get stringy and will become plastic and shiny. Stretch for about 10 minutes, then place the curd on a board and knead as you would with bread, shaping it into a ball, or place cheese in a mold (any food-grade plastic containers, such as cottage cheese containers, make excellent molds). Then place cheese, in or out of mold, into cold water until it is cold and firm textured. It is now ready to eat. To store, dry with a paper towel, wrap in plastic wrap, and refrigerate.

Yield: 1½ to 2 pounds

Variation

Salt-Free Cheese—If you want a salt-free cheese, you can stretch it in 170°F water without salt.

*Nonhomogenized cow's milk will stretch the best. Since goat's and sheep's milk are by nature homogenized, they won't stretch as well and must be molded with your hands; however, their taste is excellent. They fry well and can be used on pizza. If store-bought milk is used, purchase 2 percent milk.

Chèvre
(French goat cheese)

½ gallon goat's milk
¼ cup cultured buttermilk
1 drop rennet
5 tablespoons cold water

In a stainless steel or enamel pot, heat goat's milk to 85°F. Use a dairy thermometer to check the temperature. Stir in the buttermilk.

Add rennet to water and mix well. Add 1 tablespoon of this mixture to the milk and let it sit overnight. Scoop the curd into small goat cheese molds or make your own molds by punching tiny holes into plastic cups. Place filled molds to drain on a baking rack over a large pan. Let them drain for 2 days. Cheese will then be ready to eat.

Yield: 3 to 5 ounces

Variation

Herbed Chèvre—Add ½ teaspoon finely chopped herbs to each mold. Garlic, basil, or hot peppers are tasty.

Gouda Cheese

This lovely Gouda recipe is adapted from *Cheesemaking Made Easy* by Ricki and Robert Carroll (see the Appendix).

2 gallons whole milk
½ cup cultured buttermilk
1 teaspoon liquid rennet
¼ cup cold water
3 cups coarse canning or kosher
    salt
½ gallon cold water

Place milk in a large stainless steel or enamel pot. Heat milk to 90°F over low heat, stirring occasionally. This will take 30 to 40 minutes. Turn off heat.

Stir in buttermilk. Dissolve rennet in cold water. Add to milk. Stir vigorously for 1 minute, then gently stir for 3 minutes. Cover pot and let stand 1 hour so curds can form.

Cut the curds into ½-inch squares using a long-handled knife (and spoon to reach the bottom of the pot). With a dairy thermometer, check the temperature of the curds. If the temperature is less than 100°F, slowly raise the temperature 2° every 5 minutes until it reaches 100°F.

When the curd reaches 100°F, keep the curd this temperature for another 30 minutes. Every 10 minutes replace 8 cups of whey with 8 cups of water. Remove whey with a ladle and just pour in the water. Stir continuously during the remaining time.

Pour contents of pot into a strainer to remove the whey. Let the curds clump together. Line a 2-pound cheese mold with cheesecloth. Carefully place the clump of curds into the mold, taking care not to break the clump. Cover with a piece of cheesecloth.

Press in a cheese press for 20 minutes with 20 pounds pressure. Flip the cheese and press 20 minutes with 30 pounds pressure. Flip again and press for 2½ hours with 40 pounds pressure.

Prepare a brine by dissolving canning or kosher salt in ½ gallon cold water. Soak the cheese in the brine for 3 hours, flipping every half hour.

Set the cheese on a cheese mat and allow to air-dry at 50°F for 3 weeks, flipping every day. Wipe off mold with a piece of cheesecloth dipped in vinegar.

After drying, wax the cheese. (See page 368 for waxing information.) Red wax is the traditional color for Gouda. If a longer aging is desired, store at 50°F and 85 percent relative humidity. Turn frequently.

Yield: 2 pounds

Mysost Cheese

This richly aromatic, pale-brown cheese is adapted from *Cheesemaking Made Easy* by Ricki and Robert Carroll (see the Appendix).

8 quarts water
2 cups whey powder
1 cup heavy cream

Place 1 quart water in an 8- to 10-quart stainless steel or enamel saucepan. Gradually mix in whey powder. (Add slowly to avoid lumping.) Gradually stir in remaining 7 quarts water. Mix in heavy cream.

Heat mixture to boiling over medium-high heat, stirring occasionally. Boil for 7 to 10 hours, until mixture is reduced to 25 percent of the original volume. You can stop, refrigerate overnight, and continue boiling the next day. When mixture is reduced to 25 percent of volume, remove from heat, and process in 3 batches in a blender until smooth.

Return mixture to saucepan. Return to a boil. Boil until the mixture thickens like fudge. This could take 2 to 3 more hours. Place in a sink of cold water and stir until very cool. This will take about 20 to 25 minutes. Pour into plastic containers. Refrigerate.

The longer the whey is boiled initially, the firmer the cheese will be, ranging from a spreadable consistency to a cheese that can be sliced.

Yield: 2 cups

CHEDDAR CHEESE

"Cheddaring" is a step in cheesemaking that involves removing whey with dry heat from previously heated and drained curd. In commercial production, cheddaring is accomplished by placing drained curd in a heated chamber. When the steady, gentle heat causes the curd to mat together, it is cut into slabs that are turned for even drainage. Before pressing, the slabs of curd are shredded in a special machine.

The moisture content of cheeses made in this way is around 40 percent on a scale where cottage cheese stands at 80 percent and Parmesan cheese at 30 percent. Many cheeses are cheddared besides the ones called "cheddar" cheese. Monterey Jack and longhorn are examples.

Because cheddared cheeses have a lower moisture content than the fresh or semisoft types, they can usually be aged for a longer time. It is largely the bacterial action during the aging of the cheese that leads to a fuller taste, and generally, the older the cheese, the sharper the flavor. Cheddared cheeses usually have a higher butterfat content than fresh cheeses, and this creaminess prevents them from developing a dry or crumbly texture as they age.

To add cheddaring to your repertoire requires no specialized equipment aside from a cheese press and dairy thermometer. Think of the heat chamber for drying the curd as a kind of "sauna" for your curd. Then you will be able to devise any number of arrangements depending upon what colanders, strainers, racks, and kettles are on hand.

Here are step-by-step illustrations and directions for making cheddar cheese with a cheese press. See also recipe on page 388.

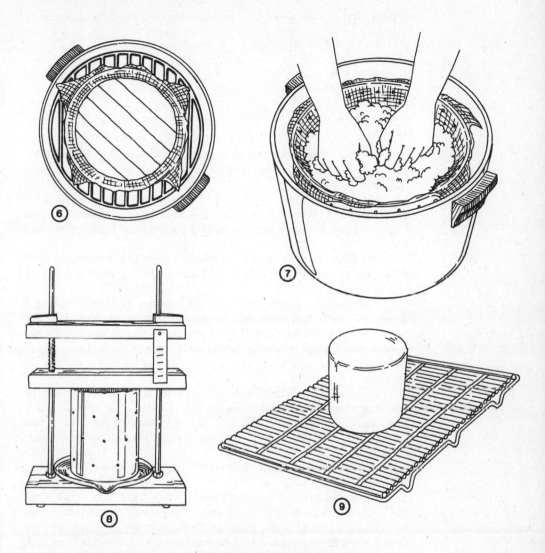

To make cheddar cheese, (1) add milk fermented with buttermilk to 4
gallons of heated milk. (2) Add rennet to the milk, cover the pot with
cheesecloth, and let it stand off the heat for 1 hour. (3) When the milk
has clabbered, cut the curd into 1-inch cubes. (4) Heat the curds, then
drain in a cheesecloth-lined colander. (5) Place the colander in a
"sauna"—on a rack over water in a large kettle. (6) With the colander
still in the kettle, slice the curd into 1-inch-wide slabs. (7) Shred the curd
by hand, then (8) pack into a cheesecloth-lined press. (9) After the
cheese has been pressed, dry it on a cheese mat on a rack.

Cheddar Cheese

¼ cup cultured buttermilk
3¾ cups milk
4 gallons milk
1 teaspoon liquid rennet
1 cup cold water
¼ cup coarse canning or kosher
  salt

Combine buttermilk and 3¾ cups milk in a clean, scalded quart jar. Seal with a clean cap, shake, and allow to stand for 24 hours at room temperature.

Heat 4 gallons milk to 86° to 90°F, over very low heat. Use a dairy thermometer to check the temperature. Add the quart of buttermilk and allow to ripen 2 hours. Keep milk at a temperature between 86° and 90°F.

Put rennet in water and mix well. Be sure milk is between 86° and 90°F. Add rennet mixture to milk and stir well. Cover with cheesecloth and let stand 1 hour.

Cut curd into 1-inch cubes, using a long-handled knife. Heat very slowly to 100°F. Stir frequently to prevent matting of the curds. The temperature should only rise 2° per 5 minutes. Curd should be firm and look something like popcorn when ready.

Drain curd in a cheesecloth-lined colander and let stand for 30 minutes.

Make a "sauna" by placing the colander with the curd on a rack in a larger kettle with a small amount of hot water in the bottom. Leave kettle over low heat for 2 hours. The temperature of the curd should remain between 100° and 110°F. Turn the curds 1 to 2 times to insure even heating.

After 1 hour, slice the mass into 5 or 6 slabs about 1-inch wide. Turn slabs occasionally.

Keep curd over the hot water and shred by hand. Mix in salt. Pack hot curds into a cheesecloth-lined press. Cover with cheesecloth.

Using a cheese press, press at 10 pounds for 15 minutes. Turn cheese. Press at 40 pounds for 18 hours. Turn cheese. Press at 50 pounds for 24 hours.

Remove cheese from press. Let it air-dry on a cheese mat on a rack for 4 days. Then wax cheese with several thin coats. (See page 368 for waxing information.)

Yield: 5 pounds

Homemade Yogurt and Other Fermented Milk Products

Yogurt is milk that has been fermented by special strains of beneficial bacteria. Kefir and piima are fermented milks, too, but differ in taste and texture because of the different bacteria that culture them. Kefir is thick like buttermilk and often has a bit of a fizz to it, similar to a carbonated drink. It is usually stirred and drunk, rather than eaten like yogurt. Piima is sweeter than kefir and is often eaten like a custard, although it can be stirred to a liquid and used in any recipe that calls for milk.

YOGURT

Yogurt can be made out of any kind of milk: raw or pasteurized, cow's or goat's milk, skim or whole. Even dry powdered milk or soy milk (made from soybeans) can be used. The starter bacteria that you introduce into the milk may be commercially prepared yogurt, your own homemade yogurt, or a pure culture, such as *Lactobacillus acidophilus*, from a natural food store.

If you buy yogurt to use as your starter, buy fresh yogurt. That means you should buy a carton with an expiration date as far in the future as possible—a week and a half or two weeks distant, or more. Also, be sure that you are buying real yogurt. Some yogurtlike substances come in similar cartons and masquerade as yogurt, but don't be fooled— read the ingredients and see what you're buying. It is best to buy plain yogurt or a kind that has the preserves on the bottom of the carton so that you can skim enough yogurt off the top of the carton to use as a starter. The kinds of yogurt that have the preserves and flavoring blended through the product can also be used, but even a small amount of the flavoring can permeate the final product to a surprising degree, which is

389

fine if you want a whole quart of yogurt that is reminiscent of strawberries or apricots. About one-half of a half-pint carton of yogurt is enough to start 1 quart of homemade yogurt.

Since there are several ways to encourage fermentation, you might like to experiment with a few methods first and then choose the way that works best for you. Your choice will depend upon how much equipment you want to use and how much time you want to spend in yogurt making. Whatever equipment you do use, make sure that it is thoroughly clean. Remember, you want to encourage the growth of beneficial, not harmful, bacteria. An unclean bowl or spoon might give an off-taste to your finished yogurt.

Basic Yogurt

The directions that follow are for your basic, all-purpose yogurt. If you want a thicker kind, see the box below.

To make yogurt with raw or pasteurized milk, begin by heating 1 quart milk to the boiling point (212°F); this destroys any bacteria already present in the milk and provides a sterile medium for your yogurt culture. Allow the milk to cool to lukewarm (about 115°F). To test, drop a little on your wrist; if the milk feels hot, allow it to cool some more. When it no longer feels hot, add about 3 tablespoons to ½ cup yogurt or the amount of *Lactobacillus acidophilus* culture suggested on the envelope. Stir well with a whisk or wooden spoon, making sure the culture is thoroughly mixed into the milk. Pour the mixture through a strainer into whatever you're incubating your yogurt in to make sure there are no lumps of yogurt or starter culture.

After 4 hours, lift the lid of one of the containers and tilt it *gently*. If the yogurt is thick, about the consistency of heavy cream, it is ready. Refrigerate the containers. If the yogurt is still rather watery, allow it to

---

A THICKER YOGURT

4 cups warm water (110° to 115°F)
2⅓ cups instant nonfat dry milk
¼ cup fresh, unflavored yogurt or 1
    package yogurt starter

Combine water and dry milk in a medium-size bowl and mix thoroughly. Stir in the yogurt or starter. Incubate using any method you like.

incubate for another hour, then check again. The longer the mixture incubates, the stronger and more sour the final result will be.

To use powdered milk instead of regular milk in the above directions, simply mix up 1 quart of powdered milk, using warm water to reconstitute it. Stir in yogurt culture, pour into containers, and incubate. There is no need to sterilize powdered milk.

You can also use soy milk in the above recipe if you are a lacto-vegetarian or simply allergic to other types of milk. Substitute 1 quart of soy milk per quart of whole milk, stir in the yogurt culture, and incubate.

Using a Yogurt Maker

A yogurt maker consists of a constant-temperature, electrically heated base, and a set of plastic or glass containers with lids. Most yogurt makers make 4 or 5 individual pints at a time. They are foolproof, inexpensive, and are available in most natural food, department, and kitchen equipment stores.

With a yogurt maker such as this one, you can make yogurt easily, without worrying if you've got the temperature right.

YOGURT MAKER

Prepare your yogurt mixture and pour it into the containers in the yogurt maker. Cover the yogurt maker with the cover that came with it or with a towel. Leave undisturbed for about 4 hours. At the end of this time, remove the lid from one container and gently tilt the glass. The yogurt should be about the consistency of heavy cream. If it's still thin, let it incubate longer and check again. When the yogurt thickens, remove gently so as not to jar it, or it will separate and get lumpy. Then refrigerate. Don't serve until thoroughly cooled.

Making Yogurt in the Oven

One way to get around using a yogurt maker is to incubate the milk-and-yogurt mixture in an earthenware bowl (because it retains heat well) which is kept warm in an oven. You'll need an accurate oven thermometer because the gauges on most ovens don't keep ovens at the low temperatures right for yogurt making. In some gas ovens the pilot light alone is enough heat to maintain the right temperature. We know quite a few people who use their ovens to make wonderful yogurt, foregoing the need for a special yogurt maker.

Make up a batch of milk and yogurt starter, as described above, and pour the lukewarm mixture into your bowl, cover, and set the bowl in the oven; heat slowly to 120°F. Turn off oven and let it cool gradually to 90°F. Try to maintain temperature between 90° and 105°F by reheating oven if necessary (after about 2 to 3 hours) until milk becomes the right consistency. Check frequently during the last 30 minutes. Chill immediately after the milk thickens. Be careful not to shake the warm yogurt.

In our Food Center it took our oven 6 hours to make yogurt with a good consistency and flavor. The yogurt was quite good, although we had to stay near the kitchen the whole time and give it lots of attention to keep the oven within the proper temperature range.

A Covered Casserole and a Warm Place

Prepare the milk and starter mixture as described above. Then warm a casserole dish by running hot water over it or heating it for a few seconds in a very low temperature oven. Pour the mixture into the warm dish and cover. Wrap the casserole dish in a large towel and set it in a quiet, warm spot in the kitchen, as on a warm radiator or the warming shelf of a cookstove. Leave undisturbed for at least 6 hours, or let it sit overnight. At the end of this time, check the consistency of the yogurt by unwrapping the towel carefully and tilting *gently*. Do not jar it. If it is solid enough for your liking, refrigerate immediately. Otherwise wrap it up again and let it sit. After you make it this way a few times, you'll know how long it will need to incubate. This method took us 24 hours. Serve only when thoroughly chilled.

This method is simple, but not as foolproof as when using a yogurt maker, since it is difficult to maintain a constant temperature in the milk mixture. The warmer the spot where the mixture sits, the quicker it will thicken and be ready, providing the area is not over 115°F. If you're not successful using this method the first time, try it again until you find just the right spot in your kitchen and until you know how long to let it sit.

Yogurt in a Thermos

If you want to try yet another way, here's an extremely simple one that is quite reliable. We found the thermos bottle method to be the best way to make yogurt without a yogurt maker because a thermos is an excellent heat retainer. Once the starter has been stirred into the lukewarm milk, pour it into a wide-mouth thermos, put on the lid, and let it sit 4 to 6 hours before refrigerating. This is practically foolproof, since the temperature is controlled for you.

The Finished Yogurt

Properly made yogurt should be rich and custardlike and have a creamy, slightly tart taste. Homemade yogurt will usually be sweeter than any unflavored store-bought variety. If, after refrigeration, there is a little water (whey) on top of the yogurt, don't worry, you haven't done anything wrong. This is natural, especially after it has been in the refrigerator for a few days. Open a commercial yogurt and you'll find water on top, too. Either mix it in or pour it off, or save it for using instead of water in other recipes, since the whey is high in vitamin B_{12} and minerals.

What Can Go Wrong

If you have trouble making yogurt the first time, check for the following problems:

1. Perhaps the milk mixture was disturbed while incubating. Even a few tilts or knocks can cause the whey to separate from the curd (as it does in cottage cheese). Instead of being a thick and smooth yogurt, it may be watery and lumpy and resemble cottage cheese. It's okay to eat, but not as good tasting as one with a smooth consistency.

2. Perhaps your mixture was too hot or too cool. If the mixture is too cool, the growth of bacteria will be retarded. If it's too hot, the bacteria may be killed. Add more starter, incubate longer, and adjust temperature to correct.

3. Perhaps the milk or yogurt starter was not too fresh. The older either is, the longer it will take to incubate and the more starter you should use. For best results, neither should be more than 5 days old.

4. Perhaps you used a pure yogurt culture which takes longer to thicken than prepared yogurt.

Storage

Yogurt will keep well for about 8 days under refrigeration if it is kept in an airtight container. It can also be frozen for several months, although it may separate and lose its smooth consistency upon thawing. Thawed yogurt is best used in cooking, rather than eating fresh. Make sure you save some to start your next batch. The new starter should be used before it is 5 days old.

Yogurt Cream Cheese

This simple-to-make yogurt product can be used just like regular cream cheese: on crackers for hors d'oeuvres, for sandwiches, and in cookies, pies, and other pastries.

To make yogurt cream cheese, make your yogurt by following one set of instructions discussed in this section. (Of course, you may also use commercial yogurt.) Instead of refrigerating the yogurt once it has formed, pour it into a colander lined with a triple thickness of cheesecloth. Catch the whey by placing a bowl under the colander. Allow the whey to drip for 1 minute so the yogurt in the cheesecloth is more manageable. Then lift up the four corners of the cheesecloth and tie them together. Hang the cheesecloth bag over the sink by suspending the bag from the faucet. Let the yogurt drip for 12 to 24 hours, then remove it from the bag and store in the refrigerator.

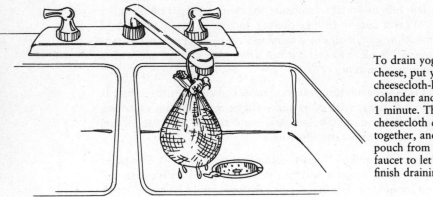

To drain yogurt for cheese, put yogurt in a cheesecloth-lined colander and drain for 1 minute. Then tie the cheesecloth corners together, and hang the pouch from the kitchen faucet to let the whey finish draining.

KEFIR

Traditionally, kefir is made in a sealed goatskin pouch kept hanging in a warm place, where it is shaken every so often. As some kefir is taken out, more milk is added to keep the fermentation process going. But you don't need a goatskin pouch to make kefir. Clean glass jars will do just fine, maybe even better.

Making Your Own Kefir

There are two types of kefir cultures—alcoholo-lactic and lactic—and your preparation method will depend upon which culture you use.

Alcoholo-lactic kefir culture is used to make a carbonated beverage that is popular in eastern Europe, the Middle East, and Russia. Alcoholo-lactic kefir contains about 1 percent lactic acid and 1 percent alcohol and is made by culturing moist kefir grains in whole or skim milk. (If you like a thick kefir, fortify your milk with nonfat dry milk before adding the grains.) A source for active kefir grains can be found in the Appendix.

Put the milk and grains in a jar, then cover loosely and leave at room temperature (ideally above 72°F) for 12 to 24 hours, depending upon the temperature of the milk and the room.

To determine if the kefir is ready, shake the jar well, then strain the milk through a medium strainer. If it is as thick as cultured buttermilk and tastes tangy, it's ready. Promptly refrigerate the kefir. If it's not ready, stir the grains back into the milk and let it stand a few more hours.

Lactic kefir culture is freeze-dried and packaged in an envelope. It is available at natural food stores or can be ordered from the source in the Appendix. This culture produces a kefir that resembles yogurt in consistency, but has a sweeter taste. To make lactic kefir, heat the milk to 180°F, cool to room temperature, and add the culture. Then follow the same procedure as for alcoholo-lactic kefir.

If you find that your kefir cultures too fast and too thick, you have too many grains in your milk. Approximately ⅓ cup of grains cultures 1 quart of milk. As you culture, the number of grains will multiply. The increase takes place most rapidly when kefir grains are cultured in skim or low-fat milk (less than 1 percent butterfat) held at room temperatures of 68° to 70°F. If you want to slow down the multiplication of kefir grains, hold the culturing milk at a lower temperature, around 55° to 60°F. This way you'll only have to make batches of kefir weekly instead of every second or third day.

You have some control over the flavor and consistency of your kefir. For tart kefir, culture for a longer period of time. For a thicker kefir, allow a larger quantity of grains to remain in the culture.

Storing the Kefir Grains

The kefir grains you strain out of your kefir can be used for your next batch. You can make it right away, or you can store the grains for using later. They can be stored in one of three ways: wet, dry, or frozen. To store them wet, wash them thoroughly in cold running water and drain well. Place them in a clean jar and cover them with cold, unchlorinated water. (To eliminate the chlorine in your water, whirl it in a blender for about 15 minutes or allow a bowl of water to sit uncovered overnight. The gas will evaporate into the air.) Store the grains in the refrigerator. They will keep for about 1 week. Kefir grains stored wet may be slower in their culturing action. To restore them to full activity, leave them in fresh milk a bit longer than usual, or culture them at a slightly higher temperature than usual.

To dry kefir grains, rinse and drain as for wet storage. Then place them on 2 layers of clean cheesecloth and air-dry them at room temperature for 36 to 48 hours. If the room doesn't have good air circulation, use a fan, but don't direct it right at the grains; you'll have them all over the room! When dry, place the grains in an envelope or wrap them in aluminum foil. Kept in a cool, dry place, dried grains will remain active for 12 to 18 months.

To freeze kefir grains, rinse and drain as for wet storage. Then place them in a small, dark bottle to keep light out. Seal the bottle tightly and place it in a larger dark container. Seal the lid with masking tape to prevent air from entering, then freeze.

To restore dried or frozen grains, soak them overnight or for 12 hours in unchlorinated water at room temperature. Drain and transfer the grains to *only 1 cup* milk. Let this stand at room temperature for 24 hours or until the milk thickens. Stir occasionally. Drain the grains from the milk, rinse, and put them in a fresh cup of milk. The grains should now be fairly active. They can be rinsed, drained, and transferred to 2 cups of milk. Continue to gradually increase the amount of milk used each time as the grains multiply, until you're back to using 1 quart.

PIIMA

Long ago it was found that when a northern European herb called butterwort was at its peak growth, the milk of the cows grazing on it clabbered at room temperature. Piima was carefully cultured from this starter. Just as with kefir, once the first batch of piima is made, you can continue to make new batches with a spoonful of the previous batch.

Piima is milder than kefir and can be used in any recipe that calls for milk. It can also be eaten like yogurt. And whipped cream can be made from light cream that has been cultured into piima.

Piima can be made with skim or whole, raw or pasteurized milk. If you prefer piima with a more yogurtlike flavor, add 1½ tablespoons yogurt along with 1 teaspoon piima for each pint of milk when starting a culture.

In hot weather piima may easily "over culture." It can still be used, even if it has an off-taste. Just use 1 teaspoon of it to make a new batch before discarding the bad one. If you freeze piima, it won't work as a starter again.

Making Your Own Piima

A source for freeze-dried piima culture can be found in the Appendix. To make your first jar of piima, carefully follow the directions on the packet. After you have your first batch, here's how to make more:

Put 1 teaspoon of prepared piima in a wide-mouth pint jar. Stir to make it smooth before adding a little milk to make a paste. Then fill the jar to the top with milk, mix well, cover, and leave in a dark place for 12 to 24 hours, depending on the temperature of the milk and the room. (In warm weather the piima will culture in less time.) A kitchen cupboard is a good place to culture piima because the temperature needed (70° to 74°F) is more evenly maintained and the darkness will prevent riboflavin destruction. You can leave the jars on the countertop if you cover them with a towel to keep them in the dark.

The piima is set when it looks as if it is gelled when the jar is tilted slightly. At this point it should be refrigerated. It will set further as it cools. Like yogurt, piima will separate if you shake or stir it, so if you want to preserve its firm, custardlike texture, move it gently.

Absolute cleanliness is essential when making piima. Scald every utensil and jar with very hot water to rid them of possible detergent and other contaminants.

The first batch of piima that you make from the freeze-dried culture may seem very liquid and ropy in consistency. This is because the organisms undergo a shock during the process of freeze-drying and require repeated culturings to produce a good-quality piima. Just take 1 teaspoon of the reactivated piima and add 2 cups milk to it, as you did the first time. When you first start making piima, this should be done every day for a week, or as often as possible, until you have a thick piima with a gelled consistency.

Homemade Ice Creams

In the mid-eighteenth century, when it was introduced to this country, ice cream was a homemade luxury. As the nineteenth century passed, America became known as a nation of ice cream lovers, and small shops serving ice cream blossomed throughout the country. The first ice cream factory in the United States was opened in Baltimore in the early 1850s and was so successful that its owner opened another in Washington, D.C., in 1856. At the same time, advances in domestic technology made it easier for people to make their ice cream at home, and several cookbooks of that time included ice cream recipes. American ice cream fanciers began to argue about which recipe produced the best ice cream and whether Philadelphia ice cream (made from sugar, cream, and scraped vanilla beans) was superior to French ice cream (based on an egg custard).

As good as homemade ice cream is, however, it passed the way of many other homemade treats when cheap commercial brands became available. Based on synthetic products, low in butterfat, and with a high overrun (meaning that lots of air is whipped into the finished product), the cheap ice creams proliferated during the 1950s and 1960s.

As it's been said many times, history has a way of repeating itself, and quality ice creams are back—in droves. We've got a virtual ice cream bonanza on our hands now, with two, three, sometimes half a dozen "designer brands" to choose from in the supermarket freezers, all boasting rich, creamy taste and all-natural flavorings. Most of these ice creams are really wonderful, and they should be, considering their high butterfat content and equally high prices.

We can no longer argue that homemade ice cream is going to be better than most store-bought kinds, when we compare them to these new quality ice creams. Nor can we argue that they're going to be cheaper to make, unless you have milk and cream from your own animals or have access to an inexpensive supply. We can say, however, that making ice cream is plain good nostalgic fun. Ice cream festivals and family gatherings that finish up with hand-cranked ice cream are vignettes securely enshrined in the tradition of American life. And you can let your creativity go wild when you make your own. It can be eggier, fruitier, richer, or less sweet than commercial ice creams. You can use honey instead of sugar, and add any flavorings you wish. Since you're putting everything together, you can be absolutely sure that there is no artificial anything.

All homemade ice cream has a slight graininess. It never achieves the perfectly uniform texture of commercial brands, but then it doesn't have the emulsifiers and stabilizers that keep store-bought kinds smooth as shaving cream. Air is whipped into commercial ice cream, although federal standards limit the amount by saying a gallon of ice cream must weigh at least 4.5 pounds. Cheaper commercial brands don't weigh much more than that. However, homemade ice creams are much denser, weighing 6 to 8 pounds per gallon, depending upon the ingredients. Federal standards also require that commercial ice creams contain at least 10 percent butterfat, and the cheaper brands don't have much more. The rich taste of homemade ice creams comes in part from the higher butterfat content, often 12 percent and up.

METHODS FOR MAKING ICE CREAM

There are several ways to make ice cream. Perhaps the most familiar is the freezer method, using a mechanical ice cream freezer fitted with a metal can and revolving dasher. Modern freezers come in both hand-cranked and electrically powered models. A less satisfactory ice cream can be made by freezing the ice cream mix in the freezer compartment of a refrigerator or in the home freezer.

Hand-Cranked Ice Cream

While not the easiest way to make ice cream, hand-cranked freezers are the *only* way to make ice cream, if you're the romantic sort. And we mean the big wooden buckets fitted with a metal can and revolving dasher.

Manually cranked freezers are a lot more appealing to most people than electrically powered models, especially if they intend making ice cream only occasionally. For one thing, the machines are cheaper initially and don't require electricity—a big plus if you want to make ice cream at your favorite isolated picnic spot (somewhere where the salt runoff

won't kill any vegetation, please). Hand churning also produces a better ice cream, many aficionados believe, and our own experiments with different ice cream makers at our Food Center proved the point. We much preferred the ice creams we cranked by hand to any made in electric machines. And in our research we noted that some of the better recipes for making commercial ice creams call for hand finishing.

Another plus for real ice cream lovers is that manual freezers are available in many sizes. White Mountain, one of the most popular makers of manual freezers, makes one that turns out a whopping 20 quarts of ice cream at a time!

Electrically Cranked Ice Cream

Some of these look very much like the hand-cranked machines and use rock salt and ice to freeze the mix as well, but they have a motor mounted on top to power the dasher and can. Others look quite different because they are designed to fit inside the freezing compartment of your refrigerator or in your freezer. These machines have heavy woven wire cords so that you can close the freezer door without damaging the cord. A motor turns the dasher while cold air from the freezer freezes the mix. The classiest and most expensive type of electric maker is a self-contained unit that provides its own freezer.

One problem with these machines is that they have small capacities. However, if you plan on making ice cream frequently, you might decide that using an electric machine will be worth the higher initial cash outlay and the higher operating costs. If you opt for one of these machines, look for a well-made one with a heavy-duty motor and a fairly large capacity.

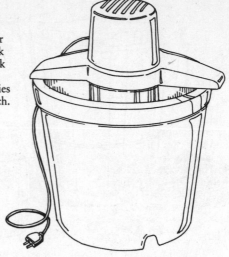

If you don't have the time or the inclination to hand-crank your ice cream, electric-crank models do the job nicely, though their smaller capacities mean less ice cream per batch.

Freezer Ice Cream

There is one method of making ice cream at home that calls for little equipment—and produces a product that is not as smooth and creamy as other ice creams, but is passable. In this method, the mix is frozen in ice cube trays in the freezer compartment of a refrigerator or in the home freezer. Better recipes for this type of ice cream usually call for whipping the product at some point. Sometimes the mix is whipped when partially frozen and returned to the freezer for finishing. Often the mix is frozen

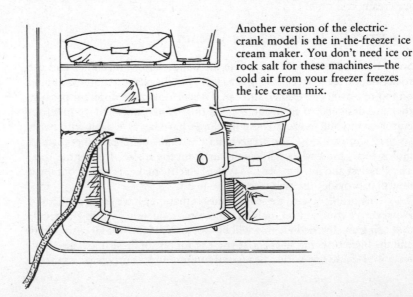

Another version of the electric-crank model is the in-the-freezer ice cream maker. You don't need ice or rock salt for these machines—the cold air from your freezer freezes the ice cream mix.

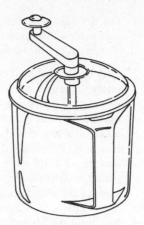

This self-contained ice cream maker has a removable interior unit that's designed to be put in the freezer overnight. Once it's freezing cold, the ice cream mix is poured in and the cold unit is put back into its plastic housing. It's now ready to crank. The ice cream will be thick and cold in 15 to 20 minutes.

completely and, just before serving, is thawed slightly in the refrigerator and then whipped before being dished up. If you're planning to use this method of freezing ice cream, it's best to buy several ice cube trays just for the ice cream, since the dairy products and flavorings tend to impart a taste to the trays which may come out in the ice cubes if the trays are also used for making ice.

CRANKED ICE CREAM HOW-TO'S

There's really only one standard method for making turned ice cream. You should be able to use these directions for any ice cream recipe even if you're using an electrically powered freezer with a bucket. (If you've purchased one of the freezers that fits inside your refrigerator freezer or one that has its own freezer, follow the directions that came with your machine.)

1. Prepare the ice cream mix according to directions and cool it in the refrigerator for several hours. (If the mix you're using does not call for cooking, you can mix it in the freezer can to save bowls, but be sure all ingredients are cold when you mix them. Also be sure that the can is clean, which leads us to Step 2.)

2. Wash the can, cover, and dasher well and scald with boiling water. Drain and cool. (Since dairy products and eggs are both ideal mediums for bacterial growth and since many recipes are entirely uncooked, it's best not to take chances.)

3. Pour the cooled mix into the can. Never fill the can more than two-thirds full. For example, never put more than 4 quarts (1 gallon) of mix in a 6-quart can. Ice cream expands as it freezes.

4. Put the dasher in the can (be sure it's seated properly), cover, and place in the freezer bucket. Place the cranking mechanism on top; make sure it fits tightly and is securely wedged in place.

5. Pack the freezer bucket with ice and salt. Salt lowers the freezing point of ice and forms a salt-water brine that is good and cold—just right for freezing ice cream. The 4-quart models we tested needed 15 to 20 pounds of crushed ice and 2½ to 3 cups of salt when all was said and done. Use only *crushed* ice. You can freeze lots of ice cubes ahead of time, then place them in a burlap bag, and smash them with a hammer. Crush them into small pieces; pieces of ice that are too large leave too many open air spaces around them and are a common cause of ice cream failures (as is too little salt). Layer the ice and salt in the bucket, beginning by filling the bucket one-third full with ice. Cover with a thin layer of rock salt or ice cream salt, then another, thinner layer

SHERBET AND SORBET

Sherbets and sorbets (ices) are low-calorie cousins of ice cream. While ice cream is rich with cream, milk, sweeteners, and flavoring, sherbet and sorbet are water-based desserts consisting of fruit or fruit juices and sweetener, with gelatin added for smoothness. But there are some crucial differences between sherbet and sorbet. Sherbet is made with milk or other dairy products, such as eggs, which gives it a creamy, smooth texture. Sorbet is the French version of sherbet, similar to American-style ice. Sorbets never contain dairy products and, as a result, are more coarse in texture. Both sherbet and sorbet can easily be made in the freezer with just occasional stirring, though you can use an ice cream maker if you want your dessert to have a creamier texture.

Nutritionally speaking, ice cream has more of everything—fat, carbohydrates, calcium, phosphorus, iron, potassium, vitamin A, thiamine, riboflavin, and niacin—than does sherbet or sorbet because of ice cream's higher milk and cream content. Sherbet usually contains less than 2 percent butterfat, while plain, fruit, and nut ice creams have about 10 to 14 percent butterfat. "Deluxe" ice creams may contain anywhere from 16 to 20 percent butterfat. As for calories, ice cream runs the gamut from 167 calories per ⅔-cup serving to 251 calories and beyond. Frozen custards, with their extra egg yolk, and ice creams with quantities of fruits and nuts are even higher in calories. Sherbets, on the other hand, contain approximately 181 to 253 calories, while sorbets contain 96 to 253. Of course, caloric content varies according to ingredients used, and one way you can control the calories in your sherbet is to use a recipe calling for less milk or cream. But some sherbets and sorbets may be higher in calories than ice cream despite a lower butterfat content. That's because the sugar content of some sherbets and sorbets is twice that of ice cream, so look for recipes with a minimum of sweetener.

of ice. Continue until the bucket is full and the can is covered by the ice/salt mixture. You can add some water—1 cup for small freezers and 2 cups for larger models—to hasten freezing.

6. Begin cranking the mixture (or plug in the motor on your electric machine). If you're using a manually cranked model, start cranking slowly, then faster as the mix begins to freeze. Throughout the whole cranking process, water should be flowing from the drain hole in the side of the bucket (keep the hole free from ice). Add more ice and salt as needed so that the can is always covered with ice and salt. When the cranking becomes difficult—or the motor begins to labor—this step is done.

7. Remove the crank (or motor), and take out the dasher. Be careful not to get salty ice or ice water in the can. Scrape what you can from the dasher (then give the dasher to the kids to clean off). Cover the mix with aluminum foil or plastic wrap, plug the hole in the cover with a cork or clean toweling, and put the cover back on the can.

8. Now comes the hardest part of all—waiting. Freeze the ice cream for 2 or 3 hours by wrapping the can in a towel and placing it in your home freezer. Alternatively, you can empty the bucket, place the can in the bucket, and repack with ice and salt, foregoing the home freezer altogether. This step is called packing, and it's essential if you want a solid, nicely textured product. However, ice cream does not *have* to be packed—it can be eaten right after churning, even though it's very soft at this stage and will melt pretty quickly.

Adding Fruits and Nuts

Fruits and nuts should be added to the mix when it is just beginning to harden in the can—and is just beginning to get hard to turn. To flavor a gallon of ice cream, add 5 cups of fruit to the mix. Use crushed or puréed fruits or cut the fruits into *small* pieces—ice crystals tend to form around large pieces of fruit. A small amount of lemon juice often enhances the flavor of fruits and keeps them from darkening, but don't add too much. Swirled ice creams can be made by swirling a small amount of fruit into the finished ice cream, rather than mixing it into the ice cream mixture before it's frozen.

If you are using fresh fruit, you may want to dribble honey over the fruit and let it sit a few hours to bring out the juice. Or, juice or blend some of the fruit to make a syrup and then mix the syrup with the rest of the whole fruit. If using nuts in your ice cream, roast them lightly first.

STORING ICE CREAM

Unfortunately, ice cream is not a good keeper. It should be stored at 0°F, and not for more than a month at a time. Store homemade ice cream in plastic freezer containers (not ones you've stored strongly flavored foods in before) or glass jars with tight-fitting lids. Allow the ice cream to soften slightly before serving.

ICE CREAMS

Philadelphia Vanilla Ice Cream

The flecks of scraped vanilla beans give this ice cream its characteristic look and definite vanilla taste.

5 cups light cream
1 vanilla bean
¾ cup mild-flavor honey

     In a small saucepan, combine 2 cups light cream and the vanilla bean. Heat over medium heat, stirring constantly, until the cream is scalded, about 10 minutes. Remove from heat. Scrape the seeds and pulp from the bean and discard the pod. Add the seeds and pulp to the scalded cream. Combine vanilla cream with remaining 3 cups light cream and stir in honey. Chill. Process in an ice cream maker.

Yield: 2 quarts

French Vanilla Ice Cream

The eggs make this a richer vanilla ice cream.

3 eggs, separated
½ cup mild-flavor honey
4 cups light cream
2 teaspoons vanilla extract

     In a medium-size bowl beat the yolks until smooth. Gradually add honey, beating until well blended and thick. In a separate bowl, beat the egg whites until stiff. Stir beaten egg whites into the yolk-and-honey mixture. In a heavy-bottom saucepan, combine cream and egg mixture. Cook, stirring constantly, over medium heat until the mixture thickens, about 15 minutes. Stir in vanilla extract. Chill. Process in an ice cream maker.

Yield: 2 quarts

Old-Fashioned Vanilla Ice Cream

This is a lighter ice cream than the previous vanillas because it uses half milk and half cream, rather than all cream.

2¼ cups milk
3 tablespoons cornstarch
¾ cup mild-flavor honey
3 eggs
2¼ teaspoons vanilla extract
2 cups light or heavy cream

Scald 2 cups milk in the top of a double boiler over boiling water. Mix the cornstarch with remaining ¼ cup milk to make a smooth paste, and stir into the rest of the milk. Add honey and stir constantly and cook until thick. In a small bowl, beat eggs lightly. Take ½ cup of the cooked milk mixture and add a very small amount of it to the eggs, stirring constantly, until the entire ½ cup is added. Then stir the egg mixture back into the milk mixture; cook for 3 minutes longer. If mixture becomes curdled, pour through a strainer. Refrigerate until cold. Stir in vanilla extract and heavy cream. Process in an ice cream maker.

Yield: 2 quarts

Blackberry Ice Cream

5 cups fresh blackberries,
    washed
¾ cup mild-flavor honey
2 envelopes unflavored gelatin
⅓ cup cold water
1 tablespoon lemon juice
2 cups light or heavy cream, or
    a mixture of both
2 egg whites

Set aside 2 cups blackberries. Drizzle honey over the remaining 3 cups.

In a small saucepan, sprinkle gelatin over water and set aside for 5 minutes to soften. Heat slowly, stirring constantly, to dissolve gelatin.

Purée honeyed blackberries in a blender. Put through a strainer to remove most of the seeds. Add dissolved gelatin to purée, then the reserved 2 cups blackberries, the lemon juice, and the cream. Process in an ice cream maker until soft.

Beat egg whites with electric mixer until stiff. Add to soft ice cream and process until ice cream is firm.

Yield: 2 quarts

Carob Ice Cream

Because carob powder doesn't dissolve easily, make a carob syrup first and add it to the milk-and-cream mixture.

Carob Syrup
¾ cup sifted carob powder
1 cup hot water
1 teaspoon vanilla extract

Ice Cream
2 cups milk
1 cup heavy cream
5 egg yolks
5 tablespoons mild-flavor
    honey
1¼ teaspoons vanilla extract

To make the carob syrup, put carob powder in a small saucepan. Slowly add water, stirring constantly until smooth. Bring to a boil over very low heat, stirring constantly. Cook for 5 to 8 minutes or until thickened and smooth. Remove from heat. Stir in vanilla extract. Let cool. Store in refrigerator until you are ready to make ice cream. Stir before using.

To make the ice cream, scald milk and cream in a heavy-bottom saucepan. Let cool slightly.

In a medium-size bowl, beat yolks and gradually add honey, beating until thick and mixture forms ribbons when beaters are lifted. Gradually stir in milk mixture. Pour back into saucepan, place over medium heat and cook, stirring constantly, until thick and mixture coats a spoon (about 12 minutes). Cool, stirring occasionally. Add ½ cup carob syrup and 1¼ teaspoons vanilla extract. Chill thoroughly. Process in an ice cream maker.

Yield: about 1 quart

Variations

1. Add ¾ cup raisins or chopped roasted nuts (walnuts, pecans, or filberts) to the churned ice cream. Or add ¾ cup carob chips. You can also add any combination of these to equal ¾ cup.

2. Mix together ½ cup smooth or chunky peanut butter and ½ cup milk until soft and very smooth. Fold into the churned ice cream to marbleize.

3. Mix 3 tablespoons orange juice and 2 teaspoons grated orange rind into the churned ice cream.

Peach Ice Cream

⅓ cup mild-flavor honey
1 tablespoon lemon juice
3 cups peaches, finely chopped
½ teaspoon unflavored gelatin
1 cup heavy cream

Drizzle honey and lemon juice over peaches. Stir to coat them. Set aside, covered, for 2 to 3 hours. Strain. There should be about ¾ cup juice.

Soften gelatin in peach juice for 5 minutes. Then heat it just enough to dissolve the gelatin. Set aside to cool slightly. Combine with peaches and refrigerate until mixture begins to set.

Whip cream until stiff and fold into peach mixture. Process in an ice cream maker.

Yield: 3 cups

Strawberry Ice Cream

1 pint fresh strawberries,
    washed and hulled
½ teaspoon lemon juice
2 eggs
6 tablespoons mild-flavor honey
3 cups light cream

Slice and purée strawberries with lemon juice in a blender or food processor. If you do not want strawberry seeds in the ice cream, pour the purée through a strainer and discard the seeds. Set purée aside.

Beat eggs until light. Add honey and beat until thick and lemon colored. Beat in cream. Stir in puréed strawberries. Process in an ice cream maker.

Yield: 1½ quarts

Variations

Super Strawberry—Fold 1 cup additional chopped strawberries into the ice cream after it is processed but while it is still soft to give it even more strawberry flavor.

Strawberry Almond—Add 1 cup chopped roasted almonds and a dash of almond extract to ice cream when processing is almost finished.

Strawberry Tangerine—Add 1 teaspoon grated tangerine peel and ⅓ cup tangerine juice to mixture before chilling.

Strawberry Raspberry—Cook 1 cup raspberries with ¼ cup water and 2 tablespoons honey until soft. Mash and cool. Swirl through ice cream after processing but while it is still soft.

Butter Pecan Ice Cream

4 tablespoons butter
⅔ cup coarsely chopped pecans
1½ teaspoons unflavored gelatin
¼ cup cold water
⅓ cup mild-flavor honey
1¼ cups half-and-half
1 cup heavy cream
½ teaspoon vanilla extract

In a small skillet, melt 2 tablespoons butter over low heat. Sauté pecans until golden brown. Set aside.

In a small bowl sprinkle gelatin over cold water. Let stand 12 to 15 minutes to soften.

In a heavy saucepan combine honey, ¼ cup half-and-half, and remaining 2 tablespoons butter. Heat over low heat, stirring occasionally, until honey is dissolved. Add gelatin mixture and stir until gelatin is dissolved (do not let boil). Pour into a bowl and let cool to room temperature. Add remaining 1 cup half-and-half, the cream, and the vanilla extract. Chill thoroughly. Process in an ice cream maker, adding pecans when almost done, or stir in pecans when processing is finished.

Yield: 1 quart

Variations

Peach—Purée 4 medium-size peeled peaches until almost smooth. Add to mixture before chilling. Substitute ⅛ teaspoon almond extract for vanilla extract. Add to mixture before chilling.

Apricot—Add 1 cup apricot purée (about ¾ pound apricots) to mixture before chilling.

Maple Walnut Ice Cream

¾ cup chopped walnuts
2 egg yolks
⅔ cup maple syrup
1 tablespoon cornstarch
2 cups cold milk
2 cups heavy cream
1 teaspoon vanilla extract

Preheat oven to 325°F. Roast walnuts 5 to 8 minutes, stirring occasionally. Set aside.

In a small bowl, beat egg yolks well.

In a medium-size heavy-bottom saucepan, combine maple syrup and cornstarch. Stir in milk and continue stirring until smooth. Cook over medium heat until mixture begins to simmer.

Stir 1 cup milk mixture a little at a time into beaten egg yolks. Stir egg yolk mixture into remaining milk mixture. Cook over low heat until slightly thickened, about 5 to 8 minutes. Cover and cool to room temperature. Chill.

In a medium-size bowl, whip cream with vanilla extract until soft peaks form. Add to milk mixture. Stir in nuts. Process in an ice cream maker.

Yield: 2 quarts

Variations

Pumpkin—Add 1 cup canned or puréed fresh pumpkin, $\frac{1}{4}$ teaspoon ground cinnamon, $\frac{1}{8}$ teaspoon ground nutmeg, and a dash of ground ginger to mixture before processing.

Cherry—After processing, but while ice cream is still soft, stir in $1\frac{1}{2}$ cups chopped, pitted, fresh cherries.

Apple—Add $\frac{1}{2}$ teaspoon ground cinnamon, $\frac{1}{4}$ teaspoon ground nutmeg, and 1 cup chunky applesauce to mixture before processing.

Banana Ice Cream

2 ripe medium-size bananas
2 teaspoons lemon juice
$\frac{1}{2}$ cup mild-flavor honey
1 teaspoon vanilla extract
2 cups half-and-half
2 cups heavy cream

Purée bananas, lemon juice, honey, vanilla extract, and half-and-half in a blender or food processor until smooth. In a large bowl thoroughly combine the banana mixture and the cream. Process in an ice cream maker.

Yield: $1\frac{1}{2}$ quarts

Variations

1. Add $\frac{1}{2}$ cup flaked coconut or 1 8-ounce can well-drained unsweetened crushed pineapple to mixture before processing. Both can be added together if desired.

2. Purée 1 cup fresh or frozen blueberries, pour through a fine strainer, and press with the back of a spoon to remove seeds and peels. Add to banana mixture.

Ice Cream Pie

coconut or nut crust (see
  below)
1½ pints ice cream (flavor of
  your choice)

Soften ice cream in refrigerator. Fill pie shell and store in freezer.
This pie is particularly nice if garnished with fresh berries or other fruit,
nuts, or toasted coconut.

Yield: 8 servings

Coconut Crust for Ice Cream Pie

1 cup unsweetened flaked
  coconut
3 tablespoons butter
½ teaspoon vanilla extract
¼ teaspoon almond extract
  (optional)
¼ teaspoon ground cinnamon
  (optional)

Preheat oven to 350°F. Toast coconut in a shallow baking pan for
approximately 5 minutes or until lightly browned, stirring frequently.
Or toast in a 10-inch skillet on top of the stove on low heat, stirring
frequently. Set aside to cool.

In a small saucepan, melt butter. Remove from heat. Add vanilla
extract, almond extract, and cinnamon. Add coconut and toss to blend
thoroughly. Press onto bottom and sides of a buttered 9-inch pie pan.
Chill thoroughly.

1 9-inch pie shell

Nut Crust for Ice Cream Pie

1½ cups finely chopped walnuts
3 tablespoons butter, softened
1 tablespoon mild-flavor honey

In a small bowl, mix all ingredients thoroughly. Press firmly onto
bottom and sides of a 9-inch pie pan. Bake in a preheated 375°F oven
for 7 to 10 minutes or until golden. Cool on a wire rack.

1 9-inch pie shell

Frozen Yogurt Pops

2 cups chopped ripe bananas,
   cherries, raspberries, or
   strawberries
2 cups yogurt
1 tablespoon mild-flavor honey
   (or to taste)
2 teaspoons vanilla extract
1 6-ounce can unsweetened
   frozen juice concentrate
   (pineapple, orange, or
   apple)

Place fruit in a blender. Add yogurt, honey, vanilla extract, and juice concentrate; blend until smooth. Pour into Popsicle molds and freeze until firm.

Yield: 4½ cups (18 2-ounce Popsicles)

SHERBETS AND ICES (SORBETS)

Rich Frozen Sherbet

10 ounces fresh or frozen
   unsweetened fruit of your
   choice
1 12-ounce can frozen apple
   juice concentrate
1 13-ounce can evaporated
   milk, cold

Wash and clean fruit. Purée fruit in a blender. Add juice concentrate to puréed fruit and blend. Pour the mixture into an ice cream maker.

Pour the cold evaporated milk into a large mixing bowl. With an electric mixer, beat milk until it is fluffy and like the consistency of whipped cream (3 to 5 minutes). Then pour the whipped milk into the ice cream can with the puréed fruit. Stir all ingredients together well before processing.

Yield: 2 quarts

Fruit Sherbet

4 cups milk
½ cup mild-flavor honey
2 tablespoons lemon juice
2½ cups fruit juice and/or purée
    or pulp

In a medium-size bowl thoroughly combine milk, honey, lemon juice, and fruit juice and/or purée or pulp. Some curdling may occur, but this will not affect the sherbet. Pour into an ice cream maker and process.

Yield: 2 quarts

Strawberry Sorbet

½ cup mild-flavor honey
3 cups fresh or frozen
    strawberries, halved
    white grape juice (optional)
1 envelope unflavored gelatin
¼ small lemon, washed and
    seeded
2 egg whites, beaten until stiff

Drizzle honey over strawberries and set aside at least 2 hours. Drain strawberries, reserving juice. Set strawberries aside. There should be ¾ cup juice. If not, add white grape juice to make this amount. In small saucepan sprinkle gelatin over strawberry juice and allow it to soften for 5 minutes. Heat slowly to melt, stirring constantly.

Place lemon quarter into the blender along with gelatin-and-juice mixture and blend until smooth. Add half the strawberries and blend until smooth. Mash the remaining strawberries and fold into puréed mixture.

Process in an ice cream maker until slightly thickened. Add beaten egg whites and process until thick. Freeze until ready to serve.

Yield: 1½ pints

Berry Ice

4 cups berries
1 cup water or unsweetened
   orange juice
¼ to ½ cup mild-flavor honey, to
   taste
1 egg white
   mint leaves (garnish)

Purée berries, then whirl in a blender or food processor with water or orange juice and honey. Pour into a metal bowl and freeze until mushy.

Return to blender or food processor, add egg white, and process again until light and completely smooth. Pour into a covered mold or container and freeze until firm (4 hours or more, depending on the shape of the container).

Remove from freezer 15 minutes before serving to soften slightly. Serve garnished with fresh mint.

Yield: 4 servings

Cantaloupe Ice

This light, refreshing ice could be used as a palate cleanser before the entrée, in the French and Italian manner.

2 cups cantaloupe purée (1
   small melon)
1 cup water
¼ cup mild-flavor honey
1 tablespoon lime juice
⅛ teaspoon ground cinnamon

Place cantaloupe, water, honey, lime juice, and cinnamon in a blender and process until thoroughly combined. Pour mixture into 2 ice cube trays. Place in freezer and freeze for at least 4 hours.

When ready to serve, pop cantaloupe cubes out of ice cube trays and place in a food processor or blender. Process until smooth and serve immediately.

Yield: 3 cups

Grape Ice

¼ cup unsweetened grape juice
    concentrate
¼ cup white grape juice
½ cup unsweetened apple juice
    concentrate
2 teaspoons lemon juice
1½ cups ice cubes

In a blender or food processor combine grape juice concentrate, white grape juice, apple juice concentrate, and lemon juice. Blend until thoroughly mixed. Add ice cubes and whirl at high speed in the blender, or process with short on/off turns in the processor, until mixture has a snowy consistency. Serve at once.

Yield: 4 servings

Dairy Recipes

EGG DISHES

Broccoli-Cheese Quiche

Quiches make very good freezer foods. Make several at a time so that you have an easy and convenient brunch, lunch, or light dinner when you need it. If you're going to freeze this quiche, follow baking instructions but bake about 10 minutes less than recipe calls for. Thaw before reheating. Then bake in a 350°F oven for 15 minutes. It can be frozen for up to 3 months.

2 cups broccoli florets
½ cup chopped onions
1 cup cottage or ricotta cheese
¼ cup buttermilk or yogurt
3 eggs, beaten
¼ cup shredded Swiss cheese
dash of freshly grated nutmeg
pastry for 1 Basic Rolled Piecrust, unbaked (see page
   594)

Preheat oven to 400°F.

Steam broccoli and onions separately for 3 to 4 minutes, just until crisp-tender. Rinse with cold water, drain, and set aside.

Combine the cottage or ricotta cheese and buttermilk or yogurt in a blender on low speed. (To make a smooth mixture without a blender, the cheese can be pressed through a sieve.) Place the cheese mixture in a mixing bowl and add the beaten eggs, Swiss cheese, and a dash of nutmeg.

Place onions in bottom of unbaked pie shell and pour cheese mixture over them. Arrange broccoli florets on top, pressing down into the cheese mixture.

Bake at 400°F for 20 minutes. Reduce heat to 350°F and continue baking 10 to 15 minutes more. The quiche should be puffed and browned. Serve hot or cold.

Yield: 6 servings

Mystery Quiche

This favorite of the late-for-dinner cook very obligingly makes its own crust. Just how it does this is, well, a mystery! Use a glass pie pan, though, or the the crust will not be crispy enough. If you're going to freeze this quiche, follow baking instructions but bake about 10 minutes less than recipe calls for. Thaw before reheating. Then bake in a 350°F oven for 15 minutes. It can be frozen for up to 3 months.

1 cup shredded Swiss or
     cheddar cheese
½ cup finely chopped onions
½ cup sliced mushrooms
2 cups milk
4 eggs
½ teaspoon cayenne pepper
½ cup whole wheat pastry flour
2 teaspoons baking powder
   paprika

Preheat oven to 350°F.

Lightly butter a 9- or 10-inch glass pie plate. Distribute cheese, onions, and mushrooms evenly over bottom of pie plate. Beat the milk, eggs, cayenne, flour, and baking powder until well blended. Pour over the ingredients in the pie plate. Sprinkle top with paprika. Bake for 50 minutes or until top is tinged with gold and knife inserted in center comes out clean.

Cool on wire rack for 5 minutes to allow custard to set.

Yield: 6 servings

Potato Quiche

The versatile potato contributes to the filling in this quiche. If you're going to freeze this quiche, follow baking instructions but bake about 10 minutes less than recipe calls for. Thaw before reheating. Then bake in a 350°F oven for 15 minutes. It can be frozen for up to 3 months.

½ cup chopped onions
½ cup chopped green or red
   sweet peppers
1 large potato, unpeeled, thinly
   sliced
   pastry for 1 Basic Rolled Piecrust, prebaked (see page
   594)

1 cup shredded Swiss or sharp
   cheddar cheese
3 eggs, slightly beaten
1½ cups milk
¼ teaspoon freshly ground
   pepper
½ teaspoon soy sauce

Preheat oven to 375°F.

Spread onions, green or red peppers, and potatoes over the bottom of the pie shell. Spread cheese over this mixture. Combine eggs, milk, ground pepper, and soy sauce, blending well, and pour over the cheese. Bake for 35 minutes or until set and golden.

Yield: 6 servings

Onion Quiche without Cheese

Even when the cheese cupboard is bare, you can enjoy this hearty quiche, provided you have some yogurt. If you're going to freeze this quiche, follow baking instructions but bake about 10 minutes less than recipe calls for. Thaw before reheating. Then bake in a 350°F oven for 15 minutes. It can be frozen for up to 3 months.

2 tablespoons butter
2 cups chopped onions
3 eggs
1 cup yogurt
½ cup milk
¼ teaspoon freshly ground
   pepper

pastry for 1 Basic Rolled Piecrust, prebaked (see page
   594)
paprika
freshly grated nutmeg

Preheat oven to 350°F.

In a large 10-inch skillet, heat butter. Add onions. Cook gently until limp. Set aside to cool slightly.

Beat the eggs; add the cooled onions, yogurt, milk, and pepper. Pour into prepared pie shell. Dust with paprika and a few gratings of nutmeg. Bake for 25 minutes or until center is firm.

Yield: 6 servings

Broccoli-Potato Frittata

This is a good way to enjoy frozen broccoli.

3 tablespoons butter or olive oil
1 cup diced cooked potatoes
1 package (10 ounces) frozen
    chopped broccoli, thawed
    and drained (or 1¾ cups
    chopped broccoli)
¼ cup chopped scallions

1 small clove garlic, minced
6 eggs
3 tablespoons water
1 tablespoon minced parsley
3 tablespoons grated cheddar or
    Parmesan cheese

Melt butter in a large ovenproof skillet. Add potatoes, broccoli, scallions, and garlic. Cover and cook 7 to 10 minutes, stirring occasionally. Preheat broiler.

Beat eggs with water; add parsley. Pour into skillet. Cook over low heat until bottom is set and lightly browned (run a spatula around the edge of the frittata to let the uncooked egg run to bottom). Slip pan under broiler and cook until top is puffed and golden. Sprinkle with grated cheese and broil to melt cheese.

Yield: 4 servings

CHEESE DISHES

Skillet Corn Bread

This light, moist bread is easily made on the top of a wood stove or range. If you're cooking with wood, it is important to place the batter over a warm, not hot, area of the stove to prevent burning.

4 tablespoons melted butter
1 egg
¾ cup milk
1 tablespoon honey
1 cup shredded cheddar cheese
1 small can hot chili peppers,
    chopped (optional)

¾ cup cornmeal
¾ cup whole wheat pastry flour
    or unbleached white flour
1 tablespoon baking powder
paprika

Pour 1 tablespoon butter into a 10-inch skillet.

In a medium-size bowl, whisk together egg, milk, honey, and remaining 3 tablespoons butter. Stir in cheese and peppers.

In a small bowl combine the cornmeal, flour, and baking powder. Stir dry ingredients into wet mixture.

Pour batter into buttered skillet, spreading evenly. Sprinkle with paprika. Cover with foil and cook over low temperature (set range on medium-low) until firm, about 20 to 25 minutes. Watch carefully.

Cut into wedges and serve.

Yield: 10 wedges

Spicy Cheesecake Appetizer

Not all cheesecakes are desserts. This one, seasoned with savory herbs, can start a meal or accompany it.

Crust
¼ cup butter
1¼ cups whole wheat pastry
   flour
5 to 6 tablespoons yogurt

Filling
2 pounds farmer cheese
⅓ cup milk
3 tablespoons whole wheat
   flour
¼ teaspoon cayenne pepper
4 teaspoons grated onions

½ teaspoon dried oregano
3 tablespoons lemon juice
5 eggs
½ cup grated Parmesan cheese
¼ cup minced parsley

To make the crust, cut butter into flour until mixture forms coarse lumps. Add a little yogurt at a time, using only enough to hold the dough together. Chill for 30 minutes.

Preheat oven to 400°F.

On a lightly floured board, roll out one-third of the dough until it's about ⅛ inch thick. Roll dough up on a rolling pin and transfer to the bottom of a 9-inch springform pan. Trim off excess.

Roll out remaining dough to the same thickness. Cut into strips to cover the sides of the pan three-quarters of the way up, sealing edges of dough together at the bottom and sides.

To make the filling, combine farmer cheese, milk, flour, cayenne, onions, oregano, and lemon juice in a food processor or large mixing bowl. Mix until smooth and creamy. Add the eggs one at a time, blending at medium speed. Add Parmesan cheese and parsley and blend. Pour the filling into the crust.

Bake at 400°F for 10 minutes. Reduce heat to 325°F and bake 50 minutes longer. Cheesecake is done when a knife inserted in the center comes out clean. Let cool 15 minutes before serving.

Yield: 20 servings as an appetizer or 10 as a side dish

Baked Macaroni and Cheese

The unusual addition of yogurt adds a nice flavor to this supper dish.

3 tablespoons butter
¼ cup minced onions
2 tablespoons minced green peppers
¼ cup whole wheat pastry flour
1¼ cups low-fat milk
1 teaspoon dry mustard
⅛ teaspoon ground white pepper
½ teaspoon paprika

1 teaspoon Worcestershire sauce (optional)
2 cups shredded sharp cheddar cheese
1½ cups whole wheat elbow macaroni, cooked and drained
¼ cup yogurt
paprika

Preheat oven to 325°F.

In a medium-size saucepan, melt butter. Add onions and green peppers and sauté over medium heat until soft, about 4 minutes. Gradually stir in flour. Cook about 1 minute, stirring constantly. Remove from heat. Add milk gradually, stirring. Return to low heat. Cook until thickened, stirring constantly. Add mustard, white pepper, paprika, Worcestershire sauce, and 1¾ cups of the cheese. Stir until cheese is melted.

In a medium-size bowl, combine macaroni and yogurt. Add sauce and mix thoroughly. Pour into a greased 1-quart casserole dish. Sprinkle with paprika and remaining ¼ cup cheese. Bake for 30 minutes or until heated through and top is lightly browned.

Yield: 4 to 6 servings

Spinach and Raisin Sauce for Pasta

Spinach and pasta have a great affinity for each other. Raisins and spinach provide a specially good contrast of flavors and textures. Serve this as a first course or for a light lunch.

½ pound whole wheat spaghetti
1 medium onion, chopped
2 cloves garlic, minced
1 tablespoon olive oil
8 mushrooms, thickly sliced
4 leaves fresh basil, chopped, or ½ teaspoon dried basil

¾ pound spinach, coarsely chopped
¼ cup golden raisins
2 tablespoons butter
¾ cup shredded mozzarella cheese
freshly ground black pepper

This cooks quickly; you can begin boiling the water for the spaghetti before making the sauce.

Over medium heat, in a 4- to 6-quart saucepan, cook onion and garlic in oil. When the onion begins to soften, add mushrooms and basil. Cook for a few minutes until mushrooms become limp.

Stir in spinach and raisins. Cover pot and lower heat. Simmer until the spinach is tender, about 5 to 7 minutes.

When the spaghetti is cooked, drain it quickly but thoroughly. Toss with the spinach sauce, then with butter and shredded cheese. Grind pepper over all and serve hot.

Yield: 4 first-course or light lunch servings

Homemade Frozen Pizza

bread dough for Crusty
   Loaves (see page 588)
2 teaspoons olive oil
1 cup tomato sauce (or 5 whole
   tomatoes, peeled and
   chopped)
1 teaspoon dried oregano
1 teaspoon dried basil
$\frac{1}{8}$ teaspoon freshly ground black
   pepper
8 ounces mozzarella cheese,
   grated

Prepare bread dough recipe (1 recipe yields 4 thick-crust or 6 thin-crust pizzas) and allow to rise until double.

Punch dough down and divide into desired number of pieces. Preheat oven to 450°F.

Press or roll 1 piece of dough into a 14-inch round, turning up the edge ½ inch, and place on a 14-inch pizza pan. Brush the dough's surface with olive oil. (Remaining pieces may be frozen whole or rolled out and frozen for future use.)

Bake crust at 450°F for 7 to 9 minutes. Do not let the crust become brown or it will burn when thawed and baked. Let the crust cool.

Spread sauce or tomatoes evenly over the surface of the dough and sprinkle with oregano, basil, and pepper. Spread grated cheese over the surface of the pizza.

Cover the cheese with wax paper. Wrap the entire pizza and pan in aluminum foil. Label, date, and freeze. It will keep in the freezer for 3 months.

When ready to serve remove from freezer, preheat oven to 475°F. and let thaw for 20 minutes. Garnish with green peppers, mushrooms, cooked ground beef, and/or onions, if desired.

Remove the pizza from the pan and place pizza directly on the oven rack. Place the pan underneath the rack to catch drippings. Bake 20 minutes until cheese is melted and crust is golden.

Yield: 1 14-inch pizza

Broccoli-Tofu Pizza

A quick, nutritious meal.

bread dough for Crusty
Loaves (see page 588)
2 cups fresh chopped broccoli
1 cup pizza sauce

1 purple onion, sliced
1 cup tofu, drained and cut into
½-inch chunks
2 cups shredded cheddar cheese

Prepare bread dough recipe (1 recipe yields 4 thick-crust or 6 thin-crust pizzas) and allow to rise until double.

Punch dough down and divide into desired number of pieces.

Press or roll 1 piece of dough into a 14-inch round, turning up the edge ½ inch. (Remaining pieces may be frozen whole or rolled out and frozen for future use.)

Steam broccoli for 2 minutes. Drain well and cool. Spread pizza sauce on shell. Top with onion, tofu, cheese, and broccoli.

Preheat oven to 475°F.

Place pizza directly on the oven rack. Place a pan underneath the rack to catch drippings. Bake 20 minutes until cheese is melted and crust is golden.

Yield: 1 14-inch pizza

Pizza Mexicali

bread dough for Crusty
Loaves (see page 588)
½ pound ground beef
¼ teaspoon ground cumin
½ teaspoon dried oregano
1 clove garlic, minced
5 teaspoons chili powder

1 cup Mexican Tomato Salsa
(see page 325)
1 small onion, sliced
½ cup minced fresh or frozen
green peppers
2 cups shredded cheddar cheese

Prepare bread dough recipe (1 recipe yields 4 thick-crust or 6 thin-crust pizzas) and allow to rise until double.

Punch dough down and divide into desired number of pieces.

Press or roll 1 piece of dough into a 14-inch round, turning up the edge ½ inch. (Remaining pieces may be frozen whole or rolled out and frozen for future use.)

In a medium-size skillet, brown beef. Add cumin, oregano, garlic, and chili powder. Drain well and cool. Spread salsa on shell. Top with meat mixture, onions, peppers, and cheese.

Preheat oven to 475°F.

Place pizza directly on the oven rack. Place a pan underneath the rack to catch drippings. Bake 20 minutes until cheese is melted and crust is golden.

Yield: 1 14-inch pizza

Pizza Primavera

bread dough for Crusty
    Loaves (see page 588)
2 cups shredded zucchini
⅔ cup sliced carrots
1 cup bite-size pieces
    cauliflower
1 small clove garlic, minced
2 scallions, including tops,
    finely chopped

2 teaspoons minced mint leaves
    or 1 teaspoon dried mint
1 tablespoon grated Parmesan
    cheese
¾ cup pizza sauce
2 cups shredded mozzarella
    cheese

Prepare bread dough recipe (1 recipe yields 4 thick-crust or 6 thin-crust pizzas) and allow to rise until double.

Punch dough down and divide into desired number of pieces.

Press or roll 1 piece of dough into a 14-inch round, turning up the edge ½ inch. (Remaining pieces may be frozen whole or rolled out and frozen for future use.)

Blanch zucchini, carrots, and cauliflower separately for 2 minutes each. Make certain all vegetables are drained well and cooled. Lightly toss with garlic, scallions, mint, and Parmesan cheese. Spread sauce on shell. Top with vegetable mixture and mozzarella cheese.

Preheat oven to 475°F.

Place pizza directly on the oven rack. Place a pan underneath the rack to catch drippings. Bake 20 minutes until cheese is melted and crust is golden.

Yield: 1 14-inch pizza

Whole Wheat Cheese Pancakes

1 cup cottage cheese or Easy
    White Cheese (see page
    381)
2 eggs, well beaten
¼ cup milk or yogurt
1 cup whole wheat pastry flour
¼ cup vegetable oil or 2
    tablespoons butter and 2
    tablespoons oil

Combine cheese with eggs. Stir in milk or yogurt. Add flour to cheese mixture, stirring gently. Heat oil or butter and oil in a skillet and drop cheese mixture by the tablespoonful into the hot fat. Cook until delicately browned on both sides.

Yield: 12 pancakes

Fruited Cheese Ball

8 ounces longhorn cheese
8 ounces cream cheese
½ cup puréed pineapple
¼ teaspoon soy sauce
¾ cup ground almonds

Shred longhorn cheese into a medium-size bowl. Stir in the cream cheese until well combined. Stir in pineapple and soy sauce. Shape into a ball and roll in ground almonds so that they cover the entire surface.

Chill 1 hour and serve, or wrap in wax paper, place in a freezer bag, and freeze. It will keep for 3 months.

Yield: 1½-pound cheese ball

Herbed Goat Cheese

8 ounces goat cheese
2 tablespoons skim milk
1 tablespoon finely chopped
   Roasted Sweet Peppers (see
   page 321)
2 teaspoons snipped chives
2 teaspoons minced parsley
½ teaspoon lemon juice
¼ teaspoon paprika
½ teaspoon dry mustard

In a small mixing bowl, combine cheese and milk until smooth. Add peppers, chives, parsley, lemon juice, paprika, and mustard. Mix thoroughly. Chill.

Yield: about 1 cup

Creamy Spread for Muffins

½ cup cream cheese, at room
   temperature
2 teaspoons honey
1 teaspoon grated orange peel

Combine cream cheese, honey, and orange peel with fork until well blended and fluffy. Serve on muffins. Refrigerate leftover spread.

Yield: 4 servings

Rosy Cheddar Cheese Spread

It's easiest to make this spread in a food processor, but an electric mixer will also work, with somewhat chunkier results. It will keep for about 2 weeks in the refrigerator.

1 small sweet red pepper, minced
1 small onion, minced
2 cloves garlic, minced
2 tablespoons butter or margarine

1 pound cream cheese
2 cups shredded sharp cheddar cheese
1 tablespoon paprika
3 tablespoons red wine vinegar

Over medium-low heat, in a small saucepan, cook peppers, onions, and garlic in butter until tender, about 8 minutes. Set aside. Blend cream cheese, cheddar cheese, paprika, and vinegar in a food processor until fairly smooth. Stir into the pepper mixture. Pack into crocks or jars and refrigerate.

Yield: 3½ cups

Herbed-Garlic Cheese Spread

This creamy spread is best when made with homemade cheese, but a store-bought jack or mozzarella will work well. If using an unherbed cheese, add 1 teaspoon snipped chives and ½ teaspoon minced fresh dill to ingredients.

1 cup Herbed Easy White Cheese (see page 382), mozzarella, or Monterey Jack cheese, pressed through a sieve with the back of a spoon

½ cup cottage cheese
2 to 3 cloves garlic, finely minced
1 teaspoon Dijon-style mustard
2 tablespoons milk

Combine all ingredients in a blender or food processor. Blend until smooth. Store in the refrigerator in a tightly covered jar.

Yield: ¾ cup

Vegetable Lasagna

½ pound lasagna noodles
1 small eggplant, peeled and
   sliced into ¼-inch rounds
2 tablespoons olive oil
¼ pound zucchini, sliced into
   ¼-inch rounds
3½ cups tomato sauce

2 teaspoons dried oregano
1 teaspoon dried basil
1 clove garlic, minced
1½ cups ricotta cheese
¼ cup grated Parmesan or
   dried ricotta cheese

Cook and drain noodles. Spread them out in single layers so that they will not stick together while you prepare remainder of recipe.

Preheat oven to 350°F.

Broil eggplant slices, brushed with oil, until they are light brown and dry. Simmer zucchini slices in tomato sauce 5 minutes. Combine tomato sauce with oregano, basil, and garlic.

Oil an 8 × 8-inch baking dish with 1 tablespoon olive oil and place a layer of noodles in the bottom. Add a layer of eggplant, then ¾ cup ricotta. Pour 1 cup tomato sauce over all. Repeat layers in the same order. End with a layer of noodles, then 1½ cups tomato sauce. Dribble the remaining 1 tablespoon olive oil over top, and sprinkle with grated cheese.

Bake for 30 minutes or until bubbly. Let stand 10 minutes. Cut into squares.

Yield: 6 to 9 servings

Ricotta Icing

1 cup ricotta cheese
¼ cup non-instant dry milk
   powder
2 tablespoons honey
1 teaspoon vanilla extract
   orange juice (optional)

In electric mixer, blend ricotta, milk powder, honey, and vanilla extract. For a thinner icing add orange juice, blending in until icing is of desired consistency. Spread on cake and refrigerate.

Yield: icing for 1 8- or 9-inch cake

Thin Ricotta Omelets

For each omelet you'll need:
1 egg
2 teaspoons milk
   freshly ground pepper, to
   taste
1 tablespoon ricotta cheese

Beat egg with milk and add pepper. Heat an oiled 6- or 7-inch fry pan and pour in egg mixture, tilting to cover bottom rather thinly. Cook until brown on bottom. Place dabs of ricotta on omelet. Roll up like a cigar and brown slightly. Remove and keep warm until ready to serve.

For a light suppers, serve 2 per person with whole-grain bread and a salad.

Butternut Cheesecake with Pecan Shortbread Crust

Crust

¼ cup cold butter
⅓ cup whole wheat pastry flour
1½ cups finely chopped pecans or walnuts

1 tablespoon honey
½ teaspoon vanilla extract

Filling

8 ounces cream cheese, at room temperature
2 eggs
1 egg yolk
1½ cups cool butternut squash purée (or any orange-colored squash)

½ cup maple syrup
2 teaspoons vanilla extract
¼ teaspoon almond extract

Topping

½ cup sour cream

To make the crust, cut butter into flour with a pastry blender until the mixture is in small crumbs. Stir in nuts. Drizzle with honey and vanilla extract. Stir to form a soft dough. Pat dough evenly over the bottom of an ungreased 9-inch springform pan. If dough is sticky, sprinkle lightly with flour. Refrigerate, covered, while preparing filling.

Preheat oven to 400°F.

To make the filling, beat cream cheese until light and fluffy. Beat in eggs and egg yolk one at a time. Stir in the squash purée, maple syrup, vanilla extract, and almond extract.

Bake pecan crust until it begins to brown, 10 to 12 minutes. Pour in squash mixture, bake 10 minutes, then reduce heat to 325°F. Bake an additional 30 minutes until center of cake is barely set. Turn oven off, open door, and let cake cool in oven for 1 hour; then cool to room temperature on a counter.

Spread sour cream over cake. Chill thoroughly before cutting.

Yield: 1 shallow 9-inch cheesecake

Cheesecake Mousse

A light mixture, served cold, that offers a refreshing dessert for warm-weather meals without the calories of traditional cheesecake.

½ cup skim milk
1 envelope unflavored gelatin
1 tablespoon lemon juice
1 teaspoon finely grated lemon
   rind
¼ cup honey
1 cup crushed ice
2 eggs
1 cup creamed cottage cheese
1 cup yogurt
½ teaspoon vanilla extract
½ cup wheat germ
   thin lemon slices (garnish)

Place the milk in a small saucepan over low heat and bring just to a boil. Place the gelatin in a blender and add the boiling milk. Process 30 seconds, or until the gelatin is completely dissolved. Scrape down the sides of the container if necessary.

Add lemon juice, lemon rind, and honey. Process until the honey is dissolved into the mixture.

Add ice and blend until ice is melted. Add eggs, cottage cheese, yogurt, and vanilla extract. Process until smooth.

Oil a 9-inch springform pan. Sprinkle the pan with wheat germ on bottom and sides.

Gently pour the blended cheese mixture into the springform pan. Cover pan with plastic wrap. Chill the cheesecake in a refrigerator 6 to 8 hours, or overnight.

To serve, carefully remove the band from the springform pan. Garnish with a border of thin lemon slices on top of the cheesecake.

Yield: 10 servings

Coeurs à la Crème
(Hearts of Cream)

These pristine little white cream hearts are like little white clouds over which fresh fruit sauce is poured. Cream hearts should be prepared in individual coeur à la creme china or wicker molds a day ahead to set.

2 cups iced water
1 tablespoon lemon juice
1 teaspoon baking soda
8 ounces cream cheese
¼ cup light honey
  scraping of ½ vanilla bean or
    1 teaspoon vanilla extract
1 cup heavy cream, whipped

3 cups fresh strawberries,
    raspberries, or peaches
2 teaspoons lemon juice
2 teaspoons grated lemon rind
1½ tablespoons honey (or to
    taste)
6 large fresh grape leaves, for
    serving (optional)

To prepare molds, cut 6 squares from length of 4 thicknesses of cheesecloth, each square large enough to line a mold with a 2-inch overhang all around. Mix water with lemon juice and baking soda. Soak cheesecloth squares in this solution while preparing cream cheese mixture.

Beat cream cheese in mixer until smooth and creamy. Add honey and vanilla and beat thoroughly. Add whipped cream and fold together lightly and evenly, using rubber scraper.

Wring cheesecloth squares damp-dry and line molds, leaving 2-inch overhang all around sides. Fill molds with cream cheese mixture and fold cheesecloth overhang over the tops. Place molds on rack on jelly roll pan and chill in refrigerator at least 8 hours or overnight.

When ready to serve, combine fruit, lemon juice, lemon rind, and honey. Unmold and unwrap each cream heart onto a fresh grape leaf on individual dessert plates (or plain dessert plate). Serve with separate bowl of the fresh fruit sauce.

Yield: 6 servings

YOGURT DISHES

Cucumber Salad

3 medium-size cucumbers
2 scallions, sliced
½ cup yogurt
1 tablespoon minced sweet red
    peppers or shredded carrots
1 tablespoon minced parsley
2 teaspoons minced fresh dill
½ teaspoon dry mustard

Peel, cut lengthwise, seed, and slice cucumbers. Place cucumbers in a medium-size serving bowl. Add scallions, yogurt, peppers or carrots, parsley, dill, and mustard and toss to combine. Refrigerate until serving time.

Yield: 4 servings

Fruit Dressing

1 cup yogurt
1 teaspoon grated orange rind
½ teaspoon grated lemon rind
2 tablespoons orange juice
1 teaspoon lemon juice
1 tablespoon honey
¼ teaspoon grated or ground
    nutmeg
⅛ teaspoon ground mace

Blend all ingredients together in order given. Pour into a container with cover and place in refrigerator. Serve with fruit salads or gelatin salads.

Yield: 1⅓ cups

Honey-Yogurt Fruit Salad Dressing

1 cup yogurt
1 tablespoon lemon juice
¼ cup honey
¼ teaspoon ground cinnamon,
    nutmeg, or mace

Blend yogurt, lemon juice, and honey together well. Stir in cinnamon, nutmeg, or mace, and use on fruit salads.

Yield: 1¼ cups

Green Onion Dressing

½ cup thinly sliced scallions,
    including tops
1 cup yogurt
1 cup mayonnaise
1 tablespoon lemon juice

Combine scallions, yogurt, mayonnaise, and lemon juice in a medium-size bowl. Mix thoroughly.

Yield: 2 cups

Russian Dressing

1 cup yogurt
1 cup mayonnaise
1 cup catsup
2 tablespoons horseradish

In a medium-size bowl combine yogurt, mayonnaise, catsup, and horseradish and stir. Refrigerate.

Yield: 3 cups

Yogurt Dip

½ cup yogurt
1 scallion, finely chopped, or 1
    onion, grated
½ teaspoon paprika
1 clove garlic, minced

Combine all ingredients in a small bowl. Serve with vegetables or crackers.

Yield: ⅔ cup

Dilly Yogurt Spread

½ cup low-fat cottage cheese
½ cup Yogurt Cream Cheese
    (see page 394)
1 teaspoon minced scallions
2 teaspoons minced fresh dill
    dash of garlic powder
½ teaspoon Dijon-style mustard

In a blender or food processor, blend cottage cheese until smooth. Add yogurt cheese and blend until smooth. Stir in scallions, dill, garlic, and mustard. Mix well. Chill.

Yield: 1 cup

Yogurt-Fruit Freeze

2 cups yogurt
2 tablespoons lemon juice
1 cup unsweetened pineapple or
  orange juice

½ cup stewed dried apricots or
  peaches
3 tablespoons honey
2 egg whites, beaten

Mix the yogurt, lemon juice, pineapple or orange juice, stewed fruit, and honey together until blended.

Process in ice cream maker for 15 minutes. Stir in beaten egg whites and continue processing for another 10 minutes or until fruit freeze appears frozen.

Yield: 1 quart

Frozen Blueberry Yogurt

Most commercial frozen yogurt is oversweetened and full of various additives and stabilizers. Fortunately, hardly anything is simpler to make, tastier, or more nutritious than the homemade version.

2 cups blueberries
⅓ cup mild-flavor honey
2 cups yogurt

Cook blueberries and honey together for about 4 minutes. Let them cool completely.

Place blueberry mixture in a food processor and process for a few seconds, or until thoroughly blended. Fold in yogurt. Freeze, then process again if smoother texture is desired. Refreeze.

Yield: 4 to 6 servings

Strawberry Yogurt Ice Cream

Almost any kind of ice-cream—even the commercial variety—is delicious, as well as being more nutritious and less fattening, when a portion of yogurt is whipped into it.

1 cup heavy cream
2 cups sliced strawberries
1 cup yogurt
⅓ cup mild-flavor honey

Whip cream and set aside. Mix strawberries, yogurt, and honey in a food processor until smooth. Fold into the whipped cream and freeze. Reprocess for smoother texture and to recombine ingredients that may have separated.

Yield: 6 servings

Lite Apricot Yogurt Pie

1 9-inch coconut or nut crust
   (see page 412)
½ cup chopped dried apricots
½ cup unsweetened apple juice
   concentrate
1 cup water
1 envelope unflavored gelatin
½ teaspoon vanilla extract
2 teaspoons honey
2 cups Yogurt Cream Cheese
   (see page 394)
2 egg whites
⅛ teaspoon cream of tartar
4 dried apricot halves, slivered

Prepare desired crust and set aside.

In a 1-quart saucepan combine apricots, apple juice concentrate, and water. Bring to a boil, reduce heat, and simmer uncovered for 10 minutes. Add gelatin and stir to dissolve. Return to heat and cook 2 minutes. Set aside to cool, about 10 to 15 minutes.

Stir vanilla extract, honey, and yogurt cheese into apricot mixture until thoroughly combined.

In a small bowl beat egg whites until foamy. Add cream of tartar and continue beating until peaks form.

Fold egg whites gently into apricot mixture. Pour into prepared crust. Let chill for at least 2 hours. Garnish attractively with dried apricot pieces.

Yield: 8 servings

Meats, Poultry, and Fish

Preparing Meats
and Poultry for Storage

Butchering chicken and other fowl is fairly easy, but getting meat on the hoof slaughtered, dressed, and cut before it can be wrapped and frozen or canned, or eaten, is a different story. A butcher can do all this work for you, or, if you have the proper equipment and the know-how, you can do the whole job yourself.

BUTCHERING YOUR OWN MEAT

If you're going to butcher meat yourself, you have a lot of things to consider. First, do you have a place in which to butcher? It must be clean, cool, dry, and well ventilated, with a ready source of water and a stove for heating water. A garage, basement, or outbuilding can be converted for this purpose, providing there is enough head room to hoist the carcass. Many farmers do their slaughtering and dressing outdoors, then bring the carcass inside to cut. If they do work outdoors, they usually choose a dry, cool fall day on which to do the job. If you are working indoors and the temperature of the room you are using is higher than 38°F, a large cooler will be needed in which to chill the meat, and in the case of beef and lamb, also to age it.

Equipment

The equipment to have on hand for butchering includes something to hoist and suspend the carcass, like strong hooks, a brace extending from an outbuilding or tree (if you're working outdoors), or a heavy rod suspended from the ceiling. A block and tackle, windlass, or chain hoist

439

would be very helpful in hoisting the carcass, especially if you're butchering steer. Rope, buckets, a thermometer to measure the temperature of water, a meat thermometer, a stunning instrument, cleaver, meat saw, hand hooks, whetstone, steel, and a good set of sharp knives are necessary. You also may want to have access to a meat grinder. If you're butchering hogs, you'll need a scalding vat or watertight barrel, and a hog scraper; and for slaughtering lambs, a low bench or box.

Slaughtering and dressing animals is an exacting job, and space doesn't allow us to explain the specifics of butchering in this book. For good, detailed information, we refer you to the booklets published by the U.S. Department of Agriculture on the subject. These booklets, which contain lists of equipment, diagrams, and easy-to-follow directions, can be obtained for a small charge from your State or County Extension Office or the Superintendent of Documents at the U.S. Government Printing Office in Washington, D.C. There are also some good books on

PREPARING WILD MEATS

If you have a hunter in your family, you know what a treat it is to have fresh game meats properly prepared and stored to enjoy throughout the year. Proper handling from field to freezer or canning jar will ensure you have high-quality meats. We don't have the room here to go into the steps involved in field dressing and skinning big-game animals, or to describe butchering techniques for big- and smaller-game animals; see the books listed in the Appendix for more information on these procedures. But here are a few things to keep in mind when preparing small-game animals for food:

- Clean small-game animals thoroughly and immediately to avoid tainted or excessively gamey meat. When you're through, wash your hands with disinfectant to ensure against contracting tularemia or parasites.

- Completely remove and discard the fat from small-game animals. It turns ran-

cid very quickly and should never be preserved or used for cooking.

- Note that many game animals have small glands under their front legs, along the small of the back, or both. The contents of these glands will ruin any meat they touch and must be removed. After you remove them, be sure to clean your knife thoroughly, or else it will contaminate any meat it touches.

Once your wild meats are cleaned, they must be hung in an open area of cool, circulating air (about 38°F). Hanging improves the flavor and texture of red meat because it enables enzymes to break down some of the meat fibers. Animals larger than rabbits should be hung for 4 or 5 days, while smaller animals should be prepared without hanging, or hung for 1 or 2 days only. The meat of elk or deer should be hung for at least 10 days, or as long as 4 weeks. This is essential if you plan to eat the meat fairly soon after slaughter. If

butchering meat and wild game that you might want to consult. You'll find a list of some books and booklets in the Appendix.

■ Game meats are lower in fat and calories than meats of domestic, grain-fed animals. Uncooked, a pound of venison has only 18 grams of fat and 572 calories, while a pound of sirloin steak has 95 grams of fat and 1,175 calories. A pound of wild rabbit meat has 18 grams of fat and 490 calories; compare that to domestic rabbit, with 29 grams of fat and 581 calories.

Chilling Meat

After the animal has been slaughtered and dressed, the carcass must be chilled promptly to rid it of its animal heat. If not chilled, the meat will spoil more rapidly because destructive bacteria thrive at normal body

you plan to freeze the meat and keep it for 6 months before eating, you may skip the hanging. Freezing will tenderize and age meat in the same way as hanging—it just takes a lot longer.

To hang small game, simply suspend it by one leg from a hook or string it from a nail. Be sure to protect the area from scavengers, insects, sunlight, and rain. Alternate the hanging leg on rabbits and larger animals. It's okay to freeze small game without hanging it; just be sure it's well bled and then freeze it as soon as the body heat is gone. If you cook or can your small game immediately after slaughter, it will be tender even without hanging.

Large game takes a bit more preparation between hanging and eating. After the meat has been hanging for about 10 days, it is ready to process for the freezer or canning jar. If you've peppered your meat in the field and in hanging, remove the pepper with the rind before freezing the meat, or else your meat may age more than you'd wish. For

large-game animals, you may want to prepare and freeze only one-quarter to one-half of the meat at a time, while the remainder ages.

Wrap and freeze it just as you would other meats (see the chapter Freezing Meats and Poultry). The size of your family and the type of animal you're processing will determine the cuts you make and their size. While small packages freeze more easily, large cuts keep better with less chance of drying.

Cuts of meat from big-game animals are much the same as those from beef. (See the beef chart on page 444.) Rabbit is usually cut up into 7 or 8 pieces, much like chicken. Separate cuts are made from the front legs, the thighs and lower parts of the hind legs, the shoulders, the rear portion of the back (called the saddle or loin), the upper back, and the ribs.

Obviously, you'll need to cut the meat into small pieces if you're planning to can it. For canning (and for drying) game meats, see the chapter Canning and Drying Meats and Poultry.

temperatures. Chilling also makes the meat easier to cut. To hasten chilling, cut off excess fat in the crotch and split the carcass. You may also want to separate the ribs and cut out the leaf fat there to speed up the chilling. Hang the carcass to chill in a well-ventilated, cold area with a temperature between 32° and 40°F. Never hang carcasses close together and certainly not touching; in either case chilling will be slowed down and spoilage could occur. A lamb or veal carcass kept in an area with a temperature between 32° and 40°F should be chilled to 40°F within 24 hours. A beef carcass may require 40 or more hours to chill to this temperature. A meat thermometer inserted into the thickest part of the carcass will show you when the meat is properly chilled.

Slaughtering on the farm is best done on a fall or early spring afternoon so that the carcass can begin to cool down during the night when temperatures just above freezing prevail. (If you will be curing and smoking your meat, it is better to slaughter in the fall. Cold winter temperatures help to retard growth of bacteria responsible for spoilage.) If night temperatures should rise above 40°F, cut the carcass in half and then into a few big pieces and immerse them in clean barrels filled with water, ice, and about 3 pounds of common salt. This solution, which is colder than ice water but warmer than solid ice, will help chill meat, but will not bring it down to freezing temperatures.

Never try to chill a carcass quickly by exposing it to freezing temperatures or by packing it in solid ice. A carcass should never hang in a cool, wet breeze because the thin layer of ice that could form on the meat surface would prevent the proper escape of animal heat from the center of the meat. If a carcass should freeze, thaw it slowly at temperatures no greater than 40°F.

Aging Beef and Lamb

Beef and lamb are aged after chilling. This means holding the meat at a temperature of from 32° to 38°F for a few days to a few weeks to increase tenderness, and in some meats, to bring out the flavor. Aging is best done in a refrigerated area where the temperature does not vary a great deal. If a cooler is not available, aging may be done in a clean, cool, and well-ventilated place, free from animals and insects. Humidity should be low; 70 percent is ideal.

The length of the time meat should be aged varies. Lamb can be held for 1 to 3 days, while older sheep (mutton) can be aged 5 to 7 days. Beef with little external fat should not be held for more than 5 days after slaughter. Beef with a good amount of external fat can be aged 5 to 18 days. Fat acts as a protection against bacteria in the air that would grow on the meat surface if it were left exposed.

If you're planning to store much of your lamb or beef in a freezer for more than 6 months, limit the aging period. Experiments at Pennsylvania State University have shown that the length of the aging period has a direct bearing on the storage life of meat because it permits oxygen absorption by the exposed fat. As we have mentioned previously, the more oxygen absorbed by the fat, the quicker the rate of rancidity. Aged meat shows higher peroxide values and shorter storage life than 48-hour chilled meat. In addition, the experiments at Penn State showed that aging does not influence the tenderness of meat that is frozen more than a month. Experimenters found that although aged meat is slightly more tender during the first month of storage, this advantage disappears in subsequent months, when the aged and the 48-hour chilled meat are on a par for tenderness. Pork and veal should never be aged, but frozen, canned, or cooked as soon as the animal heat is gone.

Cutting Meat

Whether you are cutting your own meat or having a butcher cut to order, you'll want to get those cuts that best suit your family's needs. Ask yourself these questions before the cutting begins: Do I want more steaks or chops than roasts, or would I prefer to have more roasts? Do I want some meat left around the bones for meaty soup bones, or would I prefer it removed and ground? Do I want some meat cut into stewing chunks or do I want to have it ground for hamburger meat? You do have these choices because there are several different ways certain parts of the carcass can be divided.

The size of the roasts, the thickness and number of steaks and chops, and the amount of ground beef and stewing beef are determined by the size and preferences of your family as well as your method of storage.

For freezing, you'll want your cuts as regularly square-shaped as possible for easy wrapping and packing. Canning requires smaller pieces of well-trimmed meat. If you're canning your meat or freezer space is limited, you should consider boning as much meat as is practical. Boned cuts fit into jars and cans easily. They also wrap better for the freezer and can be packed tighter, with less chance of the wrap's tearing when no large bones are protruding. Depending upon the cut, boned meat can be rolled and tied, ground for hamburger meat or sausages, cut for boneless steaks and easy-to-carve roasts, or prepared as stewing meat or bacon.

Have the larger bones cracked for making stocks. You may wish to make very concentrated soup stock from the bones and freeze this stock instead of wrapping and freezing awkwardly shaped, clumsy bones

continued on page 449

BEEF CHART

RETAIL CUTS OF BEEF —

WHERE THEY COME FROM AND HOW TO COOK THEM

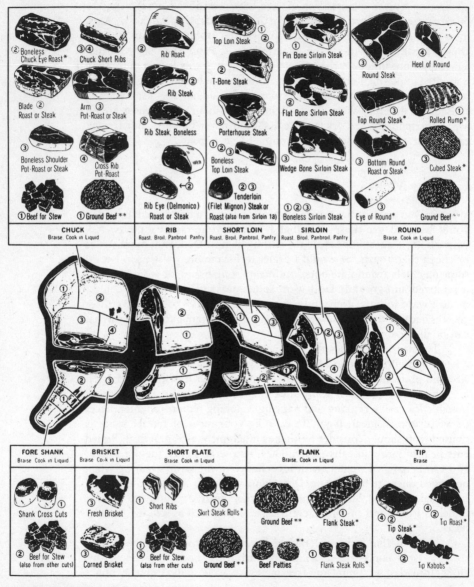

*May be Roasted, Broiled, Panbroiled, or Panfried from high quality beef
**May be Roasted (Baked), Broiled, Panbroiled, or Panfried

Courtesy of National Live Stock and Meat Board

VEAL CHART

RETAIL CUTS OF VEAL —

WHERE THEY COME FROM AND HOW TO COOK THEM

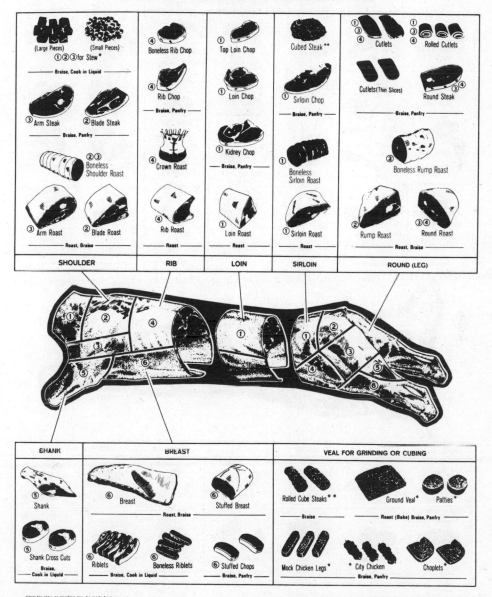

SHOULDER — (Large Pieces) (Small Pieces) ①②③ for Stew* — Braise, Cook in Liquid — ③ Arm Steak ② Blade Steak — Braise, Panfry — ②③ Boneless Shoulder Roast ③ Arm Roast ② Blade Roast — Roast, Braise

RIB — ④ Boneless Rib Chop ④ Rib Chop — Braise, Panfry — ④ Crown Roast ④ Rib Roast — Roast

LOIN — ① Top Loin Chop ① Loin Chop — Braise, Panfry — ① Kidney Chop — Braise, Panfry — ① Loin Roast — Roast

SIRLOIN — Cubed Steak** ① Sirloin Chop — Braise, Panfry — ① Boneless Sirloin Roast ① Sirloin Roast — Roast

ROUND (LEG) — ①③④ Cutlets ①③④ Rolled Cutlets Cutlets (Thin Slices) ③④ Round Steak — Braise, Panfry — ② Boneless Rump Roast ② Rump Roast ③④ Round Roast — Roast, Braise

SHANK — ⑤ Shank ⑤ Shank Cross Cuts — Braise, Cook in Liquid —

BREAST — ⑥ Breast ⑥ Stuffed Breast — Roast, Braise — ⑥ Riblets ⑥ Boneless Riblets — Braise, Cook in Liquid — ⑥ Stuffed Chops — Braise, Panfry —

VEAL FOR GRINDING OR CUBING — Rolled Cube Steaks** — Braise — Ground Veal* Patties* — Roast (Bake) Braise, Panfry — Mock Chicken Legs* * City Chicken Choplets* — Braise, Panfry —

*Veal for stew or grinding may be made from any cut
**Cube steaks may be made from any thick solid piece of boneless veal

Courtesy of National Live Stock and Meat Board

LAMB CHART

RETAIL CUTS OF LAMB —

WHERE THEY COME FROM AND HOW TO COOK THEM

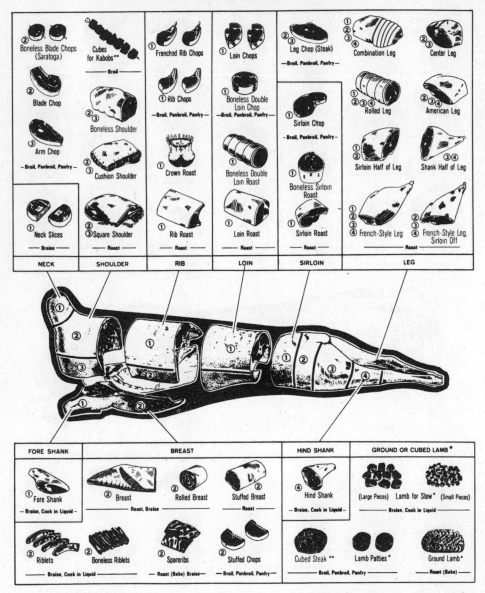

NECK	SHOULDER	RIB	LOIN	SIRLOIN	LEG

② Boneless Blade Chops (Saratoga)   Cubes for Kabobs**

② Blade Chop

③ Arm Chop

— Broil, Panbroil, Panfry —

① Neck Slices — Braise —

— Broil —

②③ Boneless Shoulder

②③ Cushion Shoulder

②③ Square Shoulder

— Roast —

① Frenched Rib Chops

① Rib Chops — Broil, Panbroil, Panfry —

① Crown Roast

① Rib Roast — Roast —

① Loin Chops

① Boneless Double Loin Chop — Broil, Panbroil, Panfry —

① Boneless Double Loin Roast

① Loin Roast — Roast —

②③ Leg Chop (Steak) — Broil, Panbroil, Panfry —

① Sirloin Chop — Broil, Panbroil, Panfry —

① Boneless Sirloin Roast

① Sirloin Roast — Roast —

②③ Combination Leg

①②③④ Rolled Leg

①② Sirloin Half of Leg

②③④ French-Style Leg

②③ Center Leg

②③④ American Leg

③④ Shank Half of Leg

②③④ French-Style Leg, Sirloin Off — Roast —

FORE SHANK	BREAST			HIND SHANK	GROUND OR CUBED LAMB*

① Fore Shank — Braise, Cook in Liquid —

① Riblets — Braise, Cook in Liquid —

② Breast   ② Rolled Breast   ② Stuffed Breast — Roast, Braise —   — Roast —

② Boneless Riblets   ② Spareribs   ② Stuffed Chops — Roast (Bake) Braise —   — Broil, Panbroil, Panfry —

④ Hind Shank — Braise, Cook in Liquid —

(Large Pieces) Lamb for Stew* (Small Pieces) — Braise, Cook in Liquid —

Cubed Steak**   Lamb Patties*   Ground Lamb* — Broil, Panbroil, Panfry —   — Roast (Bake) —

*Lamb for stew or grinding may be made from any cut
**Kabobs or cube steaks may be made from any thick solid piece of boneless Lamb

Courtesy of National Live Stock and Meat Board

PORK CHART

RETAIL CUTS OF PORK —

WHERE THEY COME FROM AND HOW TO COOK THEM

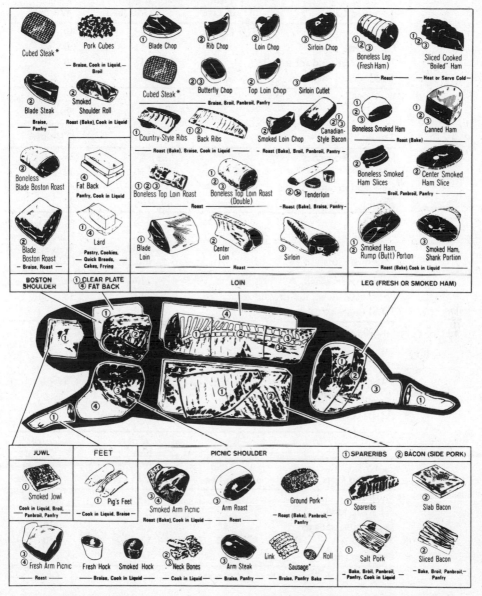

Courtesy of National Live Stock and Meat Board

*May be made from Boston Shoulder, Picnic Shoulder, Loin, or Leg

Approximate Yields of Trimmed Beef Cuts

Trimmed Cuts	Yield in Lbs.	% of Live Weight (750 lbs.)	% of Carcass Weight (420 lbs.)
Steaks, oven roasts	172	23	40
Pot roasts	83	11	20
Stew and ground meat	83	11	20
Total	338	45	80

Trimmed Cuts	Yield in Lbs.	% of Dressed Forequarters Weight (218 lbs.)
Steaks, oven roasts	55	25
Pot roasts	70	32
Stew and ground meat	59	37
Total	184	94

Trimmed Cuts	Yield in Lbs.	% of Dressed Hindquarters Weight (202 lbs.)
Steaks, oven roasts	117	58
Pot roasts, stew, and ground meat	37	18
Total	154	76

Courtesy of U.S. Department of Agriculture.

Approximate Yields of Trimmed Pork Cuts

Trimmed Cuts	Yield in Lbs.	% of Live Weight (225 lbs.)	% of Carcass Weight (176 lbs.)
Fresh hams, shoulders, bacon, jowls	90	40	50
Loins, ribs, sausage	34	15	20
Total	124	55	70
Lard rendered	12	15	27

Courtesy of U.S. Department of Agriculture.

Approximate Yields of Trimmed Lamb Cuts

Trimmed Cuts	Yield in Lbs.	% of Live Weight (85 lbs.)	% of Carcass Weight (41 lbs.)
Legs, chops, shoulders	31	37	75
Breast and stew meat	7	8	15
Total	38	45	90

Courtesy of U.S. Department of Agriculture.

that take up much space. If you are canning your meat, the only practical way to save the juices and gelatinous extracts from the bones is to make soup stock and can it.

Good information on various ways to cut beef, veal, lamb, and pork can be obtained from your State or County Extension Office or the Superintendent of Documents. This information can also be found in some of the books and booklets in the Appendix.

IF YOU'RE HAVING YOUR MEAT BUTCHERED

Not too many people who raise a few meat animals a year for family use do their own butchering anymore. Instead, they hire a butcher to do all or part of the work for them.

You can arrange for a local butcher to come for the animal and take it back to his shop in a truck to slaughter, dress, and cut. You usually have the choice of having the butcher wrap the meat for you, or of wrapping it yourself. Wrapping the cut meat from a 900-pound dressed steer is more than an all-day job for one person, and it may be enough of a savings, money-wise, to justify all the work. If you can solicit the help of family or friends, the job will go much quicker and be more fun. As a matter of fact, it can be downright festive, if there's plenty of good company and good eating to accompany the work.

Choosing a butcher that you know and like is important, especially the first time you have meat slaughtered. It's very helpful to have a butcher who will take the time to explain the different cuts of meat to you and give you tips for wrapping and freezing at home. You may find it a good idea to find a butcher who'll let you stick around when he is cutting the meat so that you can tell him how you want the cuts: how thick to make the steaks, what size roasts you want, how much fat to trim off, and so

BEEF

Name _____

Address _____

Cost of Hauling _____ Slaughtering_____

Live Weight _____

Cutting Date _____ Cut by _____

Whole Carcass _____ Wrapped by _____

Front _____ Hind _____ Side _____

Weight _____ Price _____

Number of People in Family _____

You Want:

Round _____ Soup Bones _____

Rib _____ Beef Cubes _____

Roasts _____ Hamburger _____

Steaks _____ Variety Meats _____

Pickup Date _____

Phone _____

We Wrap & Freeze? _____

on. It is against the policy of most larger meat companies to permit customers in the cutting room. Rather, they cut the meat according to order sheets customers fill out when their animals are brought in for slaughter. Typical order sheets might look like the ones here.

Although filling out such order forms will allow you to choose pretty much how you want your meat cut, you have more of a say in the matter when you're standing next to the butcher during the whole process.

For practical purposes, most large meat operations collect the beef to be ground from all the steers butchered that day and put it together in a large meat grinder. What comes out is a mixture of meat from all

PORK

Name _____

Address _____

Date _____ Hogs _____

Weight _____Live _____ Dressed _____

Backbone _____ Pork Chops _____

Number of People in Family _____

You Want:

Shoulders _____ Pudding _____

Hams _____ Casings _____

   Cure: Us _____ Dishes _____

       You _____ Variety Meats _____

Bacon _____ Lbs. of Lard _____

Knuckles _____ Our Cans _____

Stomachs _____ Your Cans _____

Sausage _____ Lbs. of Sausage _____

Scrapple _____ Beef for Sausage _____

   Our Dishes _____

   Your Dishes _____

Pickup Date _____

Phone _____

We Wrap & Freeze?_____

the carcasses. The butcher makes note of the amount of ground meat belonging to each customer so that each gets his fair share, but certainly the ground meat that each customer gets is not all from his own steer. This doesn't matter to most farmers because the beef from one steer is almost the same as that from the next, but it does make a difference to the farmer who raises his steers organically.

HEADCHEESE AND OTHER PRESSED MEATS

Early homesteaders couldn't afford to waste any part of their hog and were ingenious at finding ways to use "everything but the squeak." They ate some of the pork fresh; cured hams, shoulders; made bacon and salt pork out of the fattier pieces; and turned the lean scraps into sausage. The feet were pickled, the tails were used for stew, the remaining fat was cut off and made into lard, and the heads, skin, organs, and bones were boiled to make dishes like headcheese, liver sausage, and scrapple.

Headcheese

Prepare the hogs' heads for boiling by removing any hairs or bristles that remain. Cut out the eyes and quarter the heads. Let the cut-up heads soak in a pot of fresh water at least 7 hours to remove the remaining blood. Then rinse the head thoroughly in running water. Put the heads in a large, heavy pot and add any other scraps you wish, like bones, hearts, and skins. Before putting the skins in the pot, put them in a sack made of a double thickness of cheesecloth so that they can be easily pierced with your fingers. Cover the head and scraps with water and simmer until meat slips from the bones. Drain and reserve broth.

Remove the skins and grind them using a ⅛-inch-hole plate. Pick the meat from the bones and grind it with a ½-inch-hole plate. Mix the ground meat and ground skin together with enough broth to make the mixture the consistency of a soft cake batter (the remaining broth may be saved to make liver sausage or scrapple). Return the mixture to the pot and add your spices. For each hog's head add the following:

1 tablespoon ground mixed
    spices (this may include
    garlic, savory, and onion
    powder, or sweet marjoram
    and ground cloves)
¼ teaspoon red pepper
    (optional)
2 tablespoons freshly ground
    black pepper
1 bay leaf, crushed
2 tablespoons salt

Bring the mixture to a boil and then remove from heat. Now you're ready to form the loaves. Minnesota homesteader Joan Allard shares with us her tips for making a loaf easily:

Line a container with damp cheesecloth large enough to be tied over the top after it is filled. The bottom layer should be made up of the fattest pieces and skin, with the leaner pieces in the center of the loaf. When the bowl is full, strain boiling broth to the top, gather the edges of the cloth to the center, and tie securely. Set this container in a larger one. Place a saucer or lid on the meat and weight it down heavily with cans of food, filled jars, or a cleanly wrapped brick. The excess juices will be pressed out into the larger bowl and can be used in soups or as stock. After unwrapping the pressed meat, rewrap it in aluminum foil or another nonporous material and keep it refrigerated.

Headcheese seems to get firmer with time—but it does not keep well beyond a few weeks. One way you can preserve it longer than usual is to soak it in a salt brine for 48 hours after it is formed. Keep it in the cheesecloth to do this, and weight it down under the liquid at all times.

To best preserve headcheese (or any other sausage or loaf meat), can it at 10 pounds pressure for 75 minutes for pints and 90 minutes for quarts. Ladle the meat mixture into the jars no more than 1 inch from the top before adjusting seals and pressure canning. (See the chapter Canning and Drying Meats and Poultry for complete canning instructions.) Store it in a cool, dark place as you would for any other canned food. When you are ready to use the canned meat, bring it to a boil and simmer it for at least 20 minutes before you serve it.

Pressed meats similar to headcheese are made using cuts and types of meat other than a hog's head. All are similar in that they are loaves of chopped and cooked meat jellied with their broth and chilled before slicing. The following recipes were also given to us by Joan Allard.

Sylte
(Swedish veal and pork loaf)

4 pounds pork shoulder or
    similar cut
3 pounds veal shoulder
1 teaspoon ground allspice
2 bay leaves
¼ teaspoon pepper
    several peppercorns
1 onion, diced

Use just enough water to cover the pork and veal and cook with allspice, bay leaves, pepper, peppercorns, and onions until meat is tender and falls from the bone. Bone the meat and chop it coarsely. Then boil the stock down to 2 to 3 cups and reserve for pouring over the loaf later.

Shape, cook, and store the loaf as the directions for Headcheese explain.

Potted Hough
(Scottish all-beef loaf)

3 pounds beef shank with bones
    and marrow
1 veal knuckle
1 bay leaf
8 to 10 peppercorns

Follow the directions for cooking the meat as for Sylte on page 453, and then shape, cook, and store the loaf as the directions for Head-cheese explain.

Souse
(pressed meat with tang of vinegar)

3   pigs' feet
5   pigs' hocks
1   pound beef
1½ pounds veal
1   teaspoon salt
4   onions
1   teaspoon pepper
1   teaspoon ground allspice
2   cups vinegar

Barely cover meat with water, add salt, and boil until meat is tender and falls off the bone. Bone the meat and chop coarsely. Strain the stock and return it to the pot, along with the onions, pepper, and allspice. Let it come to a good rolling boil. Turn off the heat, add the vinegar, and reserve for pouring over the loaf later.

Shape, cook, and store the loaf as the directions for Headcheese explain.

Zolca
(jellied pigs' feet)

4 pigs' feet, cut long and   1 teaspoon salt
   cleaned   ½ teaspoon sage
1 veal knuckle   1 bay leaf
1 small onion, chopped   5 peppercorns
1 clove garlic, minced   2 tablespoons vinegar

Simmer pigs' feet, veal, onions, garlic, salt, sage, bay leaf, and peppercorns in a pot with water just to cover. Cook until meat is tender and falls from the bone; then remove and chop coarsely. Strain the stock, skim off any fat, and add the vinegar. Reserve this stock for pouring over the loaf later.

Shape, cook, and store the loaf as the directions for Headcheese explain.

Liver Sausage

Liver sausage is a variation of headcheese that is made by adding cooked pork livers to the cooked heads, tongues, skins, boned meat scraps, and broth. The livers should not make up more than about 20 percent of the ingredients by weight.

3   pounds pork liver
12 pounds cooked meat scraps
2   tablespoons salt
3   tablespoons pepper
2   tablespoons ground sage
      (optional)
1   teaspoon ground red pepper
      (optional)
1   tablespoon ground allspice
      (optional)

Cook pork liver in water to cover for 15 minutes. Do not let it overcook or it will get crumbly. Drain and reserve broth. Cool the liver and grind it moderately fine with the meat scraps. Add enough broth to make a soft but not runny mixture. Season to taste using some of the suggestions above.

Shape, cook, and store this mixture as the directions for Headcheese explain.

Scrapple

Scrapple or *Pann Haas* is a Pennsylvania Dutch breakfast meat made popular in Philadelphia. It's made by combining pork scraps with broth (which can be made from that remaining from making liver sausage or headcheese) and thickening it with cornmeal or other cereal. It's cooked in a loaf and cut when cold, and then fried in thin slices. Pork scraps are suggested here, but you can use some chicken and beef or veal scraps to make up some of this. The weight is the meat without bones, so add extra if bones are included.

continued

8 pounds pork meat scraps
2 pounds cereal (cornmeal, or
   1½ pounds cornmeal and ½
   pound buckwheat)
1 crushed bay leaf
1 tablespoon sage (optional)
1 tablespoon salt
1 tablespoon sweet marjoram

2 tablespoons pepper
½ tablespoon ground nutmeg
   (optional)
1 teaspoon ground red pepper
   (optional)
2 teaspoons onion powder
   (optional)

Cover meat scraps with water and cook until meat is tender and falls from the bone. Remove the meat and grind finely. Strain the stock and return it to the pot with the meat. Bring to a boil and slowly add the cereal, stirring to avoid lumps. Boil the mixture for 30 minutes, stirring all the while to prevent scorching. A few minutes before you take this mixture off the heat, add the seasonings.

You know that the mixture is done when it's thick enough to leave the sides of the pot as it's being stirred. Pour it into loaf pans and chill quickly. You can slice and fry it when it's cold, or you can freeze it for up to 2 months. To cook, fry quickly, as you would bacon, until sides are crisp.

RENDERING LARD

A 225-pound hog will yield about 30 pounds of fat that can be rendered into fine shortening for pastries, biscuits, and frying. The sheet of fat lying just inside the ribs makes the best quality snowy-white lard. This "leaf" fat renders most easily, too—and is 90 percent fat. The "back" fat, a thick layer just under the skin, is almost as good, giving about 80 percent of its weight in lard. Far inferior is the visceral fat around the organs, which is often dark and off-flavor; it's best used for making soap. Since these various types of fats render at different rates, melt them separately. You can blend them just before storing if you wish.

A slow fire and a heavy pot that conducts heat evenly are most important in making lard. Put ¼ inch of water in the pot to keep the fat from scorching at first. Remove any fibers, lean meat, and bloody spots from the fat and cut it into very small pieces. It's not necessary to remove pieces of skin, but many people prefer to. Put a shallow layer of fat in the pot. Add absolutely no salt or other spices. When the first layer of fat has started to melt, add more. Do not fill the kettle to the top—it can boil over too easily. Stir frequently and keep the fire low.

The temperature of the lard will be 212°F at first, but as the water evaporates the temperature will rise. The lard is ready for putting up at 255°F. Be forewarned that this will take a long time at low heat, and that you must stir the lard frequently to prevent scorching. As the lard renders, the cracklings (brown bits of crispy fried fat that do not render) will float to the surface. When the lard is almost done and the cracklings have lost the rest of their moisture, they will sink to the bottom.

At this point, turn off the heat and allow the lard to settle and cool slightly. Then carefully dip the liquid off the top into clean containers. Strain the cracklings and residual liquid through cheesecloth or a fine metal sieve. Fill the containers to the top—the lard will contract quite a bit while cooling. Chill as quickly as possible for a fine-grained shortening.

Air, light, and moisture can make lard rancid and sour. So after it has been thoroughly cooled, cover the containers tightly and store them in a dark, cool area. If the water was completely removed in rendering and the lard was chilled thoroughly before capping, there will be no souring.

The residual of cracklings are a favorite country treat. Drain them, add salt, and eat the crispy bits as they are. Or make a spread by chopping them finely with onion, pepper, and other seasonings and simmering them in ½ cup broth until they are thick and bubbly.

Cracklings can be used like bacon bits to season eggs and vegetables. You can also add ½ cup cracklings to your favorite recipe to make "cracklings" biscuits, cornbread, or other quick breads.

SAUSAGE

Making sausage is much like making meat loaf; both are a thoroughly mixed combination of meat and seasonings. But sausage also has curing agents and is aged before cooking to bring out its full flavor. Even "fresh" sausage has salt and spices added to it as curing agents and is given a few days' refrigeration to heighten its taste. The word cure not only refers to the variety of spices added to the meat for flavor and preservation, but also to the passage of time that gives those ingredients a chance to do their work.

The Meat Itself

For sausage, choose meat scraps with no skin, gristle, blood clots, or pieces of bone remaining. Using two parts of lean meat to each part fat is imperative in getting tender, juicy sausage. Too much fat makes a heavy, greasy sausage that shrinks a great deal during cooking. But do not yield to the temptation of decreasing the amount of fat, thinking you will get a leaner sausage that way; you may be disappointed with the dry, tough, surprisingly stringy texture of the finished product. Happily, the most inexpensive cuts of meat, like pork shoulder or beef chuck, have this ideal lean/fat ratio.

Grinding the Meat

The coarser the grind, the more slowly the flavors of the cure will develop and permeate the meat. Therefore most highly spiced sausages, like kielbasa, are usually coarsely ground to keep the flavor from becoming overpowering. Mild sausages, like bockwurst, are usually finely ground to be compatible with the delicate flavor of light spicing. Most manual and electric grinders come with blades that chop the meat into ⅛- to ¾-inch pieces. For a finer grind than ⅛ inch, grind once, add ¼ cup water per pound of meat and separate partially, regrinding and repeating the process until you get the texture you desire. You'll get a better texture if you grind meat when it's cold. For a dice coarser than ¾ inch, cut up partially frozen meat with a sharp knife.

Curing the Meat

Meat is cured for preservation and flavor. The oldest, simplest, and safest cure to use is salt, but even it must be used cautiously. Too little will cause spoilage, too much will dry out and harden the meat. Most recipes call for 1 to 2 teaspoons per pound of meat, and you should be careful in varying this amount.

The primary role of peppers, herbs, and spices is to add flavor, but they also improve the keeping qualities of sausage once the cure has been completed. Use them carefully, too, since a few days' curing will intensify their flavor. We suggest you underseason the mixture, then sauté and taste a bit before adding more.

If you are making a large quantity of sausage, it is a good idea to add seasonings sparingly. More spices can always be added if the meat is too mild, but none can be removed if the meat is too hot. Add your spices, mix them in well, and test the sausage meat by shaping some into a patty and cooking it. Taste the sausage and correct the seasonings. If the sausages are to be smoked, use a little less seasoning, as smoking will slightly dry out the meat and bring out the flavor of the spices. If you plan to freeze your fresh sausage meat, it is a good idea to add the seasoning after the meat has thawed, rather than before you store it in the freezer. Spices shorten the freezer life of meats. Fresh sausage meats keep safely at freezer temperatures for 2 to 3 months.

You will find that the ideal temperature for curing many sausages is the temperature inside your refrigerator: 36° to 45°F. Warmer, and the meat might spoil; cooler, and the salt penetration will be slowed.

Casings

For professional-looking results and the real fun of sausage making, you will want to try using animal casings. Alternatives to them are cheesecloth and the new plastic cooking wraps. There is a different technique for using each.

Animal Casings. Natural sheep or hog casings are best for ½- to 1-inch sausages. A pound (or cup) of casings will make 30 yards or more of sausage. You can order them in some supermarkets, and they are commonly sold around the holidays when many people use them to make traditional recipes. What you usually get is a tangle of long casings packed in salt. Cut off the lengths you need and soak them in water at least 2 or 3 hours to make them pliable. Whatever you don't use you can repack in the salt, where they keep well for a year or more.

Cheesecloth. Cheesecloth or a similar loosely woven material is a more traditional wrapper. It's often used as a substitute for the big 2- and 3-inch natural casings that are costly and hard to find. You will need a length of cloth about twice the diameter of the sausage to be wrapped. There is a trick to tying large sausages so that they hold together well while cooking: Use an extra-long piece of string to tie off each end, then spiral it down the sides to the opposite end and tie it off again. You've probably seen salami or summer sausage wrapped this way. Cheesecloth-wrapped sausages can't be fried or roasted, but should be covered with water and simmered for about 30 minutes. Remove the cloth before serving.

Plastic. Plastic cooking wraps are easy to find and store, and they can be used to make all sizes of sausages. Some people may object to using them, though, because of the chance that with exposure to heat some of the compounds in the plastic may permeate the meat. If you do wish to use them, be sure to get the type of plastic wrap meant for *cooking* and not the type used for wrapping and storing food. These "oven" wraps are easy to use: Tear off a length about eight times the diameter of the sausage you are making. Spoon a strip of the sausage mixture along one end and roll it up tightly. Tie off one of the ends, twist the roll into links of any desired length, and tie with strong string.

Sausages wrapped like this can be baked at 325°F for about 1 hour or simmered in water for about 25 minutes. Cooking time will vary with the size of the sausage. Don't forget to prick several small holes in the film of each link to let steam escape while cooking. And of course, remove the plastic film before serving. Voilá!—homemade skinless sausage!

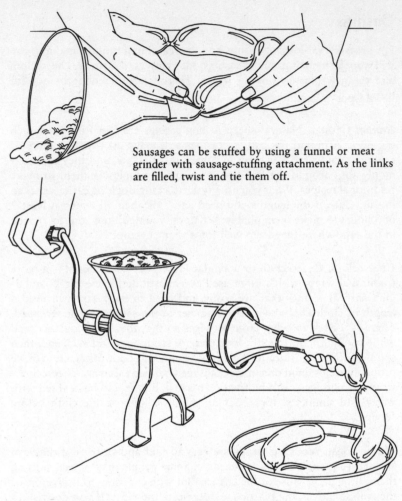

Sausages can be stuffed by using a funnel or meat grinder with sausage-stuffing attachment. As the links are filled, twist and tie them off.

The apparatus you use to get the meat into the casing may be as simple as a funnel or as complex as an electric meat grinder with a sausage-stuffing attachment. A sausage horn is a specially designed funnel found in gourmet cooking shops. They are all used similarly: Ease the casing onto the narrow end of the funnel, leaving enough "tail" to tie off securely with a string. Push the meat mixture through the funnel, using your fingers, a spoon, or a wooden mallet. The gathered casing will unravel as it fills. Hold the casing back a little so that there are as few air bubbles as possible in the compact coil. Then twist and tie off links and tie off the other, open end. Natural casings are most versatile: You can boil, roast, fry, or grill sausages made with them, and eat them casing and all.

Mild Sausage

This is a good breakfast sausage.

5 pounds medium-ground pork
2½ teaspoons pepper
2 teaspoons ground thyme
3 cloves garlic, minced

Place pork, pepper, thyme, and garlic in a large bowl and mix together thoroughly. Sausage meat may be packed loose for freezer storage, or it may be stuffed into natural casings, plastic, or cheesecloth and stored in the freezer for up to 3 months.

Yield: 5 pounds

Italian Sausage

1 pound medium-ground pork
1 medium onion, finely chopped
2 small cloves garlic, crushed
½ teaspoon fennel seeds
¼ teaspoon paprika
⅛ teaspoon cayenne pepper
1 teaspoon oregano

Follow same directions as for Mild Sausage.

Yield: 1 pound

Savory Sausage

Use this sausage to make meatballs, add to meat loaf, to top pizza, or to just fry and enjoy.

10 pounds medium-ground
    pork
1 large onion, finely chopped
4 cloves garlic, minced
2 tablespoons paprika
2 tablespoons ground sage
2 teaspoons mustard seeds,
    ground
1 teaspoon ground cloves
1 teaspoon ground allspice

Follow same directions as for Mild Sausage.

Yield: 10 pounds

Sweet and Spicy Sausage

Like Savory Sausage, this is good for meatballs, meat loaf, and for pizza.

5 pounds medium-ground pork
5 pounds medium-ground beef
1 large onion, finely chopped
4 cloves garlic, finely minced
2 tablespoons honey
1 tablespoon ground ginger

1 tablespoon freshly grated
   nutmeg
1 tablespoon mustard seeds,
   ground
1 tablespoon ground allspice

Follow same directions as for Mild Sausage.

Yield: 10 pounds

Chorizo

This is a spicy Spanish sausage used in paella and other traditional dishes of Spain. It's good in rice and bean dishes, too.

1 pound medium-ground pork
1½ teaspoons chili powder
1 teaspoon ground cumin
3 large cloves garlic, crushed
2 teaspoons vinegar
1 tablespoon water

Follow same directions as for Mild Sausage.

Yield: 1 pound

Hot Dogs

You can make your own hot dogs much as you'd make sausage. Kids enjoy making these as much as they do eating them, but they should be forewarned that their creations won't be the pink color of store-bought hot dogs because these contain no nitrates. They will be the color of boiled meat. For a variation on this recipe that's sure to please the grown-ups, grind the meat coarsely with lots of onion and garlic to make bratwurst, a German-type sausage.

1 pound finely ground pork
½ pound finely ground beef
½ teaspoon ground marjoram
½ teaspoon mustard seeds,
   ground
1 teaspoon black pepper
½ cup water
1 tablespoon vinegar

Mix the ground meats thoroughly. Combine the other ingredients separately and then mix them thoroughly into the ground meats. Sauté a bit, taste, and correct seasonings. Stuff into casings, forming 4- to 6-inch links. Refrigerate 2 to 3 days to cure and blend flavors.

To cook, simmer in water for 20 to 30 minutes.

Yield: 1½ pounds or 12 hot dogs

CURING AND SMOKING MEATS

In the last edition of *Stocking Up,* we devoted a whole chapter to the curing and smoking of meats, but in this edition we're hardly giving it mention. Let us explain, lest you accuse us of a gross oversight.

When we prepared the last edition, we had reason to believe that saltpeter was an optional ingredient in cured meats, used mainly as a color fixative. We thought that salt alone was sufficient for preserving meats that were then to be cooked, or smoked first and then cooked. Well, new studies have been done since then that suggest salt alone may be unreliable as a preservative for meats. Experts now say saltpeter is a must.

We don't dispute the need for great caution when storing meats, but when we got this news, we were faced with a major dilemma: Do we make *Stocking Up* as complete as possible on all methods of food preservation, even though it means telling readers to use an ingredient highly suspect of being a carcinogen ... or do we steer our readers clear of a health hazard and in the process neglect tradition and completeness?

We opted for caution. For after all, just because something is traditional doesn't mean that it's good. Consider these points:

Curing meat means salting it so much that it will resist the bacteria that would otherwise cause the meat to spoil. If you've tasted bacon or country ham, you know that a lot of salt has been absorbed. And salt doesn't do us any good; it's been linked to high blood pressure problems.

Saltpeter, also thought to be necessary for preservation, has been shown to present health risks as well. It's commonly known that the nitrate in saltpeter combines easily with amines in food, drugs, alcohol, and tobacco smoke to produce nitrosamines, and these compounds have been found to cause cancer in laboratory animals.

To make matters even worse, meats that go through the traditional long smoking process actually absorb smoke from burning hardwoods. Smoke is a coal-tar derivative and has long been known as a cancer-causing substance.

Enough said.

P.S. If you crave bacon now and then, let us suggest you treat yourself to the store-bought, nitrate-free kind. Most supermarkets don't carry it, but we know that some natural food stores do, and even some butchers can get it for you. It doesn't depend upon saltpeter for good keeping; it must be kept frozen. Unfortunately, nitrate-free bacon is not something that you can duplicate at home because "quick-freezing" is critical, and you can't quick-freeze in a home freezer; it just doesn't get cold enough quickly enough. To ensure there'll be no spoilage, all possible air must be kept away from the meat, something best done by shrink-wrapping with commercial equipment.

POULTRY

Dressing poultry and wild birds is a far less complicated operation than dressing meat and is commonly done on the farm. No specific area is needed to slaughter and clean birds, unless you have a lot of chickens, turkeys, geese, or ducks to process. You can slaughter your birds as you need them or do many at a time for freezing or canning. With just a little improvisation, you can do the entire job outside, in a basement, garage, or outbuilding. Naturally, when dressing poultry, your prime concern should be to end up with a bird that is attractive and free from contamination. This means working carefully and quickly, with equipment that is clean and in good working condition. Your processing area, whatever it may be, should be a place that is clean and free from flies, with a ready source of water and a stove for boiling water. It should also provide enough clean space where birds may be placed between processing steps.

Equipment

Equipment should be clean and ready to use before you choose your birds for slaughter. Like larger animals, birds also require a device to hoist and suspend them for dressing. There are instruments designed just for this purpose. A killing cone is like a funnel with the pointed end removed. The bird is placed inside this device, with its neck through the narrow opening. Killing cones come in various sizes, and it is important that you have one that fits the bird snugly. Shackles are a metal device that suspends birds by their feet. They may be used in place of the killing cone. If neither of these is available, you can suspend poultry by their feet with rope. Tie a short piece of rope to a convenient ceiling beam or support, ceiling hook, or, if you're working outside, to a tree limb. Attach a 2-inch-square block of wood on the free end of this piece of rope so that you can make an adjustable loop to hold the bird's foot. Suspend the bird by inserting each foot in one of these loops.

For slaughtering and dressing you will need a number of different tools, including at least one boning knife, small rounded knives without cutting edges for scraping pinfeathers, shears for cleaning giblets, and a lung scraper to remove the lungs. Knives and shears should be kept sharp during the operation with a whetstone and steel.

You will also need a few containers. A watertight container that is big enough to hold birds for scalding is necessary. A clean, galvanized 10- or 20-gallon garbage pail is ideal for the job. A container will be needed to hold feathers and inedible viscera until they can be disposed of. A paper-lined cardboard box or plastic-lined bucket, at least 2 feet square, will work well. You will also need a container to hold the giblets, as they should be kept separate from the rest of the bird during processing. Any clean pot, pail, or bucket will be sufficient. A clean pail or bucket big enough to hold dressed birds, ice, and water will be needed for chilling. A worktable, big enough to allow you to work freely, is also necessary. Pick one that is of a convenient height for you so that you can work comfortably, without having to stoop over unnecessarily. It should be sturdy, with a clean work surface. Have on hand a durable thermometer that will register temperatures between 120° and 212°F to measure the temperature of the water for scalding.

Slaughtering the Bird

Twenty-four to 34 hours before slaughter, pen those birds to be slaughtered and discontinue feeding them. The cage should be clean, so that the birds' feathers will not get soiled. It should have a wire bottom so that birds cannot touch the ground to pick up feathers and litter. Fasting reduces the chance of contamination of the carcass because it cleans the digestive tract of feed and ingested matter. Birds should be given water during this fasting period, however, so that they will not dehydrate. The skin of dehydrated birds is unattractive when the feathers are removed; it appears dark, dry, and scaly.

Cutting off the bird's head is the most common way of killing chickens at home. For step-by-step information on the actual slaughtering and dressing of poultry, we refer you to the books and pamphlets listed in the Appendix.

Removing the Feathers

Old-timers argue that the best way to defeather a bird is to dry-pluck it, and indeed it is if you have the skill, because it gives you a good-looking carcass when you're through. Game birds like ducks and pheasants should always be dry-plucked. Never scald them. Chill the bird for 24 to 48 hours before plucking. If you pull the feathers down and out, rather than up and out, you won't be as likely to tear the delicate skin.

As far as we can tell, most folks who butcher their own chickens dry-pluck their birds. If you have tried dry-plucking and aren't happy with the way it turned out, you have two alternatives: scalding or waxing.

To scald a bird, immerse it in hot water (150° to 190°F) for a few seconds. Any hotter or any longer and you'll actually start to cook the bird. Only use this method if you plan to eat the chicken fresh; birds don't keep well after they've been scalded.

For waxing, you can buy special wax designed for the purpose, or use paraffin. Dry-pluck the bird first, removing the main feathers on the tail and body, and all the feathers on the wings. Heat the wax to about 125°F and dip the chicken into it. Let the bird sit for 20 minutes, and then dip it into a bucket of cold water to harden the wax. Once stiff, remove the wax in strips, taking the feathers with it as you do.

Chilling the Bird

As with beef, veal, lamb, and pork, poultry must be chilled after it is dressed to remove normal animal heat. Chilling reduces the temperature of the carcass enough to retard growth of bacteria that would otherwise lead to spoilage of the meat while allowing the natural enzymes in the bird to tenderize it. Chilling also makes the carcass easier to cut and handle. To prechill the carcass, put the bird in a stopped-up sink or in a clean, watertight container filled with water that is safe for drinking. Allow this water to run slowly so that there is a constant overflow. If this is not possible, change the water periodically. This prechilling has two purposes: It helps to cool the bird, and it further cleans the animal. If you are dressing more than one bird at a time, add each to this water as it is cleaned.

Once the bird is sufficiently prechilled (it should be cooled down to water temperature), it must be chilled to 40°F before further processing.

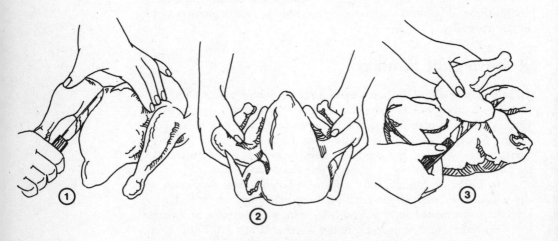

To cut up poultry, (1) place the bird breast-side up and cut the skin between the thighs and body. (2) Lift the bird by the legs and bend the legs back until the bones break at the hip joints. (3) Turn the bird to one side and remove the leg and thigh by cutting from tail to shoulder. Repeat on the other side.

This is done by placing the bird in a container filled with ice and water. Large capons will require 3 or more hours to chill to 40°F. Turkeys that are to be frozen should be held in 40°F chilled water for 18 to 24 hours before wrapping and freezing. Do not let birds freeze during chilling by packing them in ice only or exposing them to freezing temperatures. If birds should freeze, thaw them slowly in water no warmer than 40°F. Sudden changes in temperature will lower the quality of the dressed poultry. Once the carcass has reached 40°F, remove it from the ice water, hang it by the wing and let it drain 10 to 30 minutes before wrapping for freezing or refrigeration, or for canning.

Cutting the Bird

If you are canning your poultry, you will want to cut up the bird. The breast should be split and then cut along each side of the backbone so that this bone can be removed. The breast may then be cut to fit your glass jars or tin cans. Thighs should be separated from the drumsticks. Thighs may be boned, if you wish. Wings should not be canned; there is not enough meat on them to make canning them worthwhile. Rather, add the wings to other bones and simmer in water for broth or soup stock. (For more information on canning poultry, see the chapter Canning and Drying Meats and Poultry.)

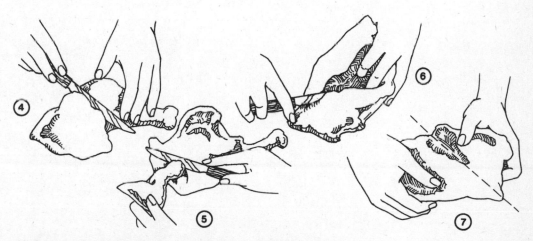

(4) Separate the thighs and legs by cutting through the knee joints. (5) With the bird on its back, remove the wings by cutting inside the wing from the top down. (6) Cut through the joints on either side of the rib cage to separate the breast from the back. (7) Split the breast by cutting the wishbone at the V.

It is advisable to cut up poultry for freezing. You'll save much freezer space if you do, because you won't have the wasted space of the body cavity. You may bone or split the breast in half and leave the other pieces whole, or bone the whole bird for compactness. Roasters that are to be frozen whole should be trimmed of excess fat. Oxygen, which causes rancidity, is absorbed by fat, and by cutting off unnecessary fat you are retarding rancidity. To save space when freezing whole roasters, tie the legs and wings tightly around the body of the bird. (For more information on freezing poultry, see the next chapter, Freezing Meats and Poultry.)

Freezing Meats and Poultry

Most meats freeze successfully, with the exceptions of processed and spiced meats, canned hams, and cured and smoked products. Luncheon meats, like salami, bologna, and spiced ham, should not be frozen, but stored in the refrigerator and used within a week. Some canned hams will get watery once frozen.

Cured meats become rancid more quickly than fresh meats because of their high fat content and because the ingredients used in curing increase the meat's ability to absorb oxygen. While we generally don't recommend that you freeze bacon, ham, cured sausage, and other such products, some people do freeze them. This is especially true of cured meats that don't contain sodium nitrite and sodium nitrate, because they will spoil more readily in the refrigerator than those with nitrates in them. If you want to freeze these foods, do so for no more than 1 to 2 months.

You can extend the period homemade *fresh* sausage may be safely stored in the freezer if you add the spices after the meat is thawed. And add seasonings and fillings for meat loaves, meatballs, and the like after, not before, freezing and thawing ground meat for extended storage life. Seasonings limit freezer life.

FREEZING IN BULK

Freezing a few extra steaks and pork chops that were on sale at the supermarket is simple enough, so long as you bide by our suggestions below for wrapping them well. But freezing your own dressed and cut-up steer or the half of lamb you bought from a neighbor who raises sheep is something else again. Buying in bulk like this from a good, reliable source can save you money and ensure quality meat. Or it can wind up

469

being more than you bargained for. It may turn out to be too much of a good thing if you find you've now got more ground meat in your freezer than you'll eat in 4 months, or if you end up with some strange cuts of meat you're not quite sure how to cook. We suggest you read the preceding chapter, Preparing Meats and Poultry for Storage, if you haven't already, and take a good look at the section Cutting Meat on page 443 so that you'll have a sense of how many pounds of what you'd be buying. Then review the Recommended Freezer Storage Time for Meats and Poultry chart on page 472 to get a sense of how long you'll be able to safely keep that meat.

Fresh-bought meats should be frozen as soon as possible; don't let them sit in the refrigerator for a few days first. But if you're freezing fresh-butchered meats, let them chill at 40°F before you freeze them. Beef, veal, lamb, and pork should be chilled for 48 hours to allow the natural enzymes time to tenderize the meat. Enzymes are not killed but only slowed down by freezing temperatures. They will still work to age and tenderize the meat once it's in the freezer, even though you only chilled it for 2 days before you froze it. Fresh-killed and dressed poultry should be chilled for no more than 12 hours before freezing.

WHAT WRAPS TO USE

There are a number of wraps on the market suitable to use for freezer storage. Heavy-duty plastic, heavy-duty aluminum foil, and freezer paper will protect frozen meats. Be certain that the wrap you use is moisture-proof. The air in freezers is relatively dry. If the wrapper is porous or poorly sealed, dry air will get in and draw moisture from the meat, dehydrating the surface and causing what is commonly referred to as freezer burn. Although these burns are not harmful to meat, the dried area will have an unappetizing color and be tough and tasteless when cooked. This is particularly detrimental to foods with high moisture contents, like meats.

Your freezer wrap should be pliable so that it will mold itself to irregularly shaped meats and eliminate as much air as possible. Oxygen from the air which is absorbed by the meat will hasten the rate of rancidity.

The wrap must also be strong. Wraps not made for freezer storage, like regular aluminum foil, thin plastic wrap, and wax paper, are often too weak to use. These weaker wraps are more likely to tear and allow oxygen and dry air to enter when meat is put in, taken out, or shuffled around inside the freezer. Take special care with cuts of meat that have sharp corners or protruding bones. These may be protected from tearing by placing a plastic bag, stockinette, or clean, old nylon stocking over the freezer wrap.

Use either of these methods to wrap meats for the freezer. To make a delicatessen wrap, grab two ends of the freezer paper, press them together, and fold them over several times. Then press the fold against the meat to squeeze out all the air and make a compact package. Now fold up the two loose ends of the paper and seal the paper securely with freezer tape. Masking tape may seal your wrap, but it has a tendency to lose its adhering ability once it is exposed to freezing temperatures or moisture. Remember to label your package.

Delicatessen Wrap

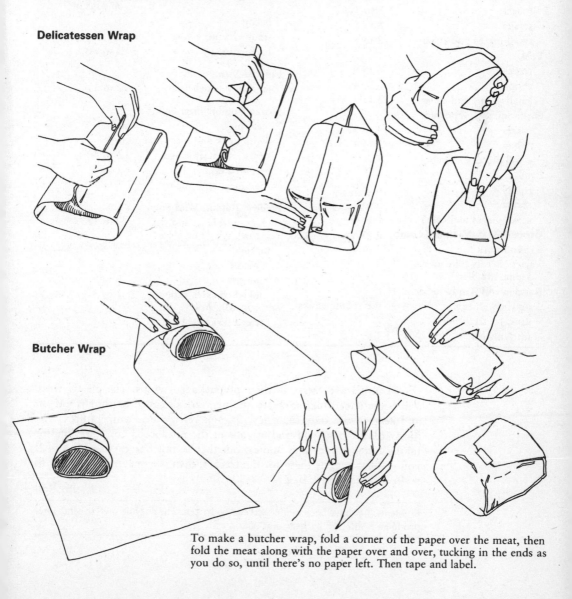

Butcher Wrap

To make a butcher wrap, fold a corner of the paper over the meat, then fold the meat along with the paper over and over, tucking in the ends as you do so, until there's no paper left. Then tape and label.

Recommended Freezer Storage Time for Meats and Poultry
(freezer temperature 0°F or colder)

Meat	Maximum Storage Time (months)	Meat	Maximum Storage Time (months)
Beef, Venison, Bear		**Cured, Cured and Smoked**	see warning on page 469
roasts	8 to 12	bacon	1
steaks	8 to 12	smoked ham, whole or slices	2
small pieces and cubes	2 to 3	beef, corned	2 weeks
Veal		**Cooked Meat**	
roasts	6 to 9	leftover cooked meat	2 to 3
chops	3 to 4		
small pieces and cubes	3 to 4	**Frozen Combination Foods**	
Pork, Squirrel, Opossum		meat pies	3
roasts	4 to 8	Swiss steak and meat loaf	3
chops	3 to 4	stews and meat sauces	3 to 4
small pieces and cubes	1 to 3	prepared dinners	2 to 6
Lamb		fried meat and poultry	1 to 3
roasts	6 to 9		
chops	3 to 4	**Poultry, Rabbit, Wild Fowl**	
small pieces and cubes	3 to 4	chicken, rabbit, and wild fowl, whole or pieces	9 to 12
Ground Beef, Veal, and Lamb	3 to 4	turkey	
Ground Pork	1 to 3	whole	12
Variety Meats (like liver, kidneys, giblets)	3	pieces	6 to 9
Sausage and Ready-to-Serve		cooked chicken, rabbit, and wild fowl	2 to 3
luncheon meats	not recommended	cooked turkey	2 to 3
sausage, fresh pork	2		
frankfurters	1		

Don't leave meats in their prepackaged wraps. The plastic wrap and Styrofoam supermarket containers are designed to show food off and keep it safe only for a few days at refrigerator temperatures. The flimsy plastic bags you find in rolls at the produce counter are fine for taking home lettuce and apples, but they're not fine for freezer use. If you want to recycle them for the freezer, then use one inside another to make a double-thick bag.

■ Meats that have been tenderized can be frozen. The enzyme used in tenderizer products is affected by heat, not cold.

Meats that are highly perishable, like pork and cured meats, should be wrapped in a double thickness of wrap if they are to be kept longer than 5 months. Beef, veal, and lamb need only be wrapped in a single thickness if they are to be used within 1 year's time. If they are to be kept longer, it is advisable to cover them in wrap of double thickness. It is a good idea to place wax paper or plastic wrap between hamburgers, sausage patties, chops, and steaks so that individual frozen pieces may be removed and cooked separately. Some people wrap their meats in plastic before they wrap them in freezer paper. This ensures an airtight, waterproof seal. All bloody cuts, like the organ meats, should always be wrapped first in plastic and then in freezer paper.

■ When making hamburger patties for the freezer, shape them on plastic lids from 1-pound coffee cans. Stack the lids with the patties in them in plastic bags and tie closed. You'll find that removing a patty at a time is easy because the plastic lid doesn't stick to the meat as does wax paper or aluminum foil.

■ Cut-up birds are fairly easy to wrap well, making sure there are no air pockets inside the wrap, but whole birds are not. To make the job easier when bagging whole birds, tie the legs together, close to the body. Then put the bird in the bag neck first and lower the bag into a pot of water, being careful not to get any water inside the bag. This will allow you to press out extra air in the bag more easily. Once you've got the bag pressed tightly against the bird, seal it with a wire twist.

After wrapping, every cut should be weighed (a kitchen scale is handy), and the weight, type of cut, and date frozen should be marked on the wrapper. With proper labeling, you'll be able to go to your freezer a few weeks or months later and choose the size and cut you want at a glance. As with any frozen food, use it in the order in which it was frozen, which means that cuts labeled with the earliest freezing dates should be used first.

■ Never stuff chickens, turkeys, or other birds with filling before freezing them. The stuffing takes a long time to cool, possibly giving spoilage organisms a chance to grow. And the bigger the bird, the stronger the possibility this will happen.

■ Remove giblets and wrap them separately from the bird before freezing. If you know you'll be cooking the bird within 3 months, it's safe to tuck the wrapped giblets inside the bird's cavity. Otherwise, freeze separately.

For information about organizing your freezer, turn back to page 46, and for advice on what to do should your freezer stop working, see pages 74 and 476.

FREEZING COMBINATION MEAT DISHES

What a convenience to have prepared dishes tucked away in your freezer, waiting to be cooked and eaten on a night when there's little time for the kitchen. Most casseroles freeze well, and so do meat pies and meat loaves. Watch out for those that contain cream or cheese sauces, cornstarch thickening, sour cream, yogurt, or cottage cheese. These ingredients may separate during freezer storage, making thawed food somewhat watery. They'll usually keep quite well for at least 3 months. And so long as you don't keep them frozen too long, some combination foods like chili and stews actually get better in the freezer because the ingredients have a chance to blend and mellow, and the meat actually marinates in the sauce. This is particularly true of stews, soups, and meat sauces. The last chapter in this section of the book is devoted just to meat and poultry dishes, and many are noted as good for freezing.

■ Mochiko rice flour is one thickener that doesn't separate in casseroles and sauces at freezing temperatures. We use it in some recipes in this book in place of cornstarch. You won't find it in supermarkets, but many Asian food stores carry it.

■ Choose your rigid storage containers carefully, making sure that you've left a little headspace, but not more than 1 inch. Extra space means extra oxygen, and oxygen affects food flavor and appearance.

■ No need to tie up useful casserole dishes in the freezer. Rather, freeze the food in the dish, and when frozen, remove it and put it in a freezer bag. (You may have to turn it upside down and run a little hot water on the bottom of the dish to loosen it first. Do this only with a dish you know won't crack with the temperature change.) When you're ready to cook it, hunt up the original casserole dish, slip the food out of the freezer bag into its original dish, and cook.

QUICK FREEZING

For best quality, meat should be frozen quickly. Slow freezing gives water within the meat tissues time to separate out and form large ice crystals, which stretch and rupture surrounding tissues. Meat frozen rapidly results in little water separation and smaller ice crystals that do little damage. Butchers have a special freezer that maintains a very low temperature to flash-freeze meat, and some home freezers have quick-freeze compartments to freeze fresh meat solid. Once the meat is completely frozen in this quick-freeze section, you ought to transfer it to the regular freezing compartment, which will keep it frozen at about 0°F. If your home freezer

FREEZING SOUP STOCK

Soup stock in the freezer, ready any time, is a busy cook's delight. Simmer it on a back burner when you're in the kitchen cooking something else. Bones for soup stock should first be cracked or crushed to free juices and gelatinous matter. Marrow bones make for a better stock, but if too many are used the stock will be too gelatinous and have a thick, gluey consistency. Reserve such stock for sauces and gravies.

Make a concentrated stock by adding just enough water to cover the bones and vegetable trimmings. Add spices, if you like, and simmer the stock in a heavy pot with the lid tilted at an angle so that the pot is practically covered. Cool the stock and skim off the fat with a ladle. To speed up cooling, let it cool a bit on the kitchen counter and then stick it in the refrigerator or freezer for a while. (If you place it in the freezer, be careful not to have it touch a frozen food, as the heat it gives off may be just enough to slightly thaw something there already, creating large ice crystals in this food as it refreezes.) Fat remaining in the stock will hasten rancidity. Once skimmed, strain the stock through a double layer of cheesecloth and pour into plastic containers or heavy glass jars, leaving $\frac{1}{2}$-inch headspace for expansion. Cover tightly and freeze.

When you are ready to make soup from your frozen stock, thaw the stock and water it down to desired strength. If you are adding meat, simmer it in the stock until almost tender, and then add your vegetables. Simmer again just until meat is tender and vegetables are chewy, neither hard nor soft.

doesn't have this special compartment, but it does have a temperature control, turn it to the coldest position and wait 24 hours after the fresh meat has been placed in the freezer before turning the control back to storage position. If you are freezing a large quantity of meat at a time— for instance, if you've just picked up half a steer cut and wrapped for freezing—put the meat in and don't plan on opening the freezer for the next 48 hours; this will ensure that no warm air gets inside.

When adding fresh meat to your freezer, put it in the coldest parts; this is usually along the bottom and walls of the freezer unit. To aid your freezer in freezing meat quickly, pack wrapped fresh meat loosely so that the cold air can circulate freely around your cuts and freeze the meat rapidly. After the meat is frozen solid, you can repack it tightly to make the most of your freezer space.

The freezer compartment of your refrigerator does not maintain the steady low temperatures of a home freezer. It's opened and closed more, on the average, than a stand-alone freezer, meaning it has more of a chance to lose its cool, so to speak, more readily. And it's not as well insulated, so it doesn't get as cold to start with. Knowing this, you can see it's not a good idea to overburden your refrigerator freezer by putting a large amount of fresh meat into it at any one time. Keep it to 2 to 3 pounds of fresh meat per cubic foot of freezer space in each 24-hour period. More than this amount raises the temperature and slows the freezing process.

■ In an emergency, like when your power is out and you're afraid all that meat in your freezer is going to thaw and spoil before you can eat it, you can salvage it by canning it. Thaw it first in the refrigerator so that it doesn't thaw too quickly. (Thawing it in a freezer that's shut down is tricky because you can't control the temperature and be certain that all the meat is kept below 40°F as it thaws.) Then can it promptly, just as you would if it were fresh meat. Do not can meats that have thawed out at room temperature or have been sitting around defrosted for some time in the refrigerator, though. You'll only be inviting trouble. And to play it safe, use hot-pack canning only (see page 484).

THAWING AND COOKING FROZEN MEATS AND POULTRY

Many meats need not be thawed before cooking. We recommend that you thaw good-size roasts before you cook them, although we do know of some cooks who roast them frozen and swear that they're juicier this way. They set the oven about 30 degrees lower than the normal roasting temperature so that the frozen roasts cook through without overbrowning the outside, and they figure half again as long for the cooking time. Stewing meat is best thawed first because it won't brown properly prior to stewing if still frozen. And meats to be breaded should be thawed first, too.

Frozen chicken need not be thawed first. Place the frozen pieces under running water for a few minutes to help you separate them from each other and their wrappings, and then cook as usual, adding 5 minutes to their cooking times. Other meats also take more cooking time if they're

Timetable for Thawing Frozen Meats and Poultry

Meat	In Refrigerator
Large roast	4 to 7 hr. per lb.
Small roast	3 to 5 hr. per lb.
1-inch steak	12 to 14 hr.
Poultry, Rabbit, Wild fowl	2 hr. per lb.

frozen. While thin steaks take about the same time to broil or panbroil whether frozen or thawed, larger cuts like roasts take half again as long to cook.

Thaw meat in its original freezer wrapper. In order to ensure uniform defrosting throughout your piece of meat, defrost it at low temperatures—in the refrigerator, if possible. You can also thaw meat in cold water, provided it is in a watertight wrapping. If you must thaw poultry at room temperature, take special precautions to keep the surface of the bird cool during thawing. Place the bird, still in its original wrapper, in a closed double bag until it is pliable. Don't let frozen meats, especially poultry or pork, thaw on surfaces or trays where other foods are kept.

Thawed meats that have been kept at 45°F or below for 2 days or less can be refrozen, although each time meat is refrozen there is some deterioration of quality; the ice crystals tend to rupture the fibers, breaking down the texture and letting more juices escape. Thawed meat will keep in the refrigerator as long as fresh meat.

Canning and Drying
Meats and Poultry

Home freezers have had their greatest impact on home-canned meats and poultry. Jarred soups, stews, and other meats have been left to the stout-hearted. Because meat is much more vulnerable to destructive enzymes and toxic bacteria than are fruits and vegetables, great care must be taken during its preparation and processing. Before considering canning meat, please read the chapter Preparing Meats and Poultry for Storage.

Can only fresh-bought or fresh-butchered meat, not something you've had sitting around in the refrigerator for a few days. Meat should be chilled to 40°F after butchering and held there briefly to give the natural enzymes time to do their tenderizing work. But beef, veal, lamb, and pork should not be aged more than 48 hours, and chicken not more than 12. If meat cannot be processed right after it has aged for these recommended times, freeze it until canning time. Meat may be processed for canning while it is still frozen, but be sure to allow extra time for the meat to cook sufficiently. If you wish to thaw meat before processing, it is best done gradually at low temperatures until most of the ice crystals have disappeared. Poultry should be rinsed and drained before it is canned.

EQUIPMENT FOR CANNING

Equipment needed for canning includes a cutting board or other smooth, clean surface, sharp knives, a kettle for boiling water, thermometer, tongs, pot holders, glass jars with lids and bands, and a pressure canner. If you're using tin cans and lids, you'll also need a sealer. All equipment should be scrupulously clean. Wash metal utensils in hot, soapy water and scald with boiling water. Scrub surfaces of wooden equipment with hot, soapy water and a stiff brush, and scald with boiling water.

For further protection against bacteria, use the new, very hard acrylic cutting boards that cannot be cut or marred with a knife, or use wooden equipment but disinfect it with a home disinfectant or household bleach. Prepare the disinfectant following the directions on the container, or dilute ¼ cup bleach with 4 cups water. Then soak wooden boards and utensils for half an hour. Scald them well with boiling water. If you use this wooden equipment in daily food preparation, it should be scrubbed well and scalded with boiling water before it is put away so that no particles of meat remain to attract bacterial growth.

Like other low-acid foods, meat may contain toxic bacteria that cause botulism, a severe form of food poisoning. There is no danger of botulism if canned meats are processed at 240°F for the required length of time. Only a pressure canner can reach this temperature. No other method of cooking—including use of an open or covered pot or steamer without pressure—is safe to use with meat and foods containing meat, such as stews, soups, and gravies. Oven canning is impossible with tin cans and is hazardous with glass jars. A temperature of 240°F inside the container cannot be reached, and there is a chance that jars in the oven may burst, blowing out the oven door and causing considerable damage to the kitchen and to anybody standing nearby.

Before canning, make sure that your pressure canner is clean and is working properly. Remove the lid and wash the kettle in hot, soapy water. Do not wash the lid, but wipe it with a damp cloth. Your canner will probably have a weighted gauge, although some canners have dial gauges. Weighted gauges have three markings: 5 pounds, 10 pounds, and 15 pounds pressure. They are usually more reliable for indicating the correct pressure than dial gauges, which have markings to indicate pounds of pressure from 5 to 15 pounds, and all pounds in between. The advantage of the dial gauge is most appreciated by those who live in high-altitude areas, where it's necessary to increase the pressure by ½ pound for each 1,000 feet above sea level. With a weighted gauge all that you can do is increase the pressure by the next mark, which means that if your food requires 5 pounds of pressure at sea level (which is how most charts are figured) and you live high in the mountains, process at 10 pounds instead; if it calls for 10 pounds, process at 15 pounds, and if it calls for 15 pounds, then increase the pressure a bit so that the marker goes past the 15-pound point. Whether yours has a dial gauge or weighted gauge, check it each year for accuracy. Instructions for checking should come with the canner. And if not, the home economist at your County Extension Office should be able to help you find a place to get your gauge checked. A weighted gauge needs only to be thoroughly cleaned.

Jars

Pint and quart jars are good for canning meats, but half-gallon jars take too long to process and are not recommended. We much prefer straight-sided, wide-mouth jars because they make getting the meat in and out much easier. There's a lengthy explanation of the different types of canning jars you can use back in the chapter Canning Vegetables and Fruits, and we repeat that information here, since you may use any of them for canning meats as well:

Ask for canning jars today, and you'll get the ones with the common 2-piece closure—a flat metal disk lined with a ring of rubber that fits snugly against the rim of the jar when processing is done right, and a metal screw band that holds the lid down during processing and that is usually removed once the jar is processed and cooled.

But there are other kinds of jars with different closures still around, left over from the days when freezers hadn't yet captured the fancy of so many people who canned. You can't buy these other types of jars and closures anymore, but you might have some good ones sitting around, perfectly fine and ready to be used. Go ahead and use them, so long as they really are perfectly fine, and so long as you get new rubber rings to use with them. Luckily, rubber rings are still for sale. They come in both narrow and wide-mouth sizes.

Be sure that all jars, lids, and bands are in perfect condition. Discard any with cracks, nicks, or chips. Even slight imperfections may prevent proper sealing. Last year's metal rings are fine to use again, so long as they are in perfect shape and have no rust on them. Use new metal lids each time you can. Jars need not be sterilized, but they should be washed in hot soapy water and scalded well with boiling water. Closures must also be washed in hot soapy water and rinsed well. Place lids and screw bands in water and bring to a simmer. Remove from heat and leave in hot water until ready to use. Porcelain-lined zinc caps that have previously been used must be boiled in water for 15 minutes. Wash rubber rings in hot soapy water and rinse well. Keep rings in hot water until ready to use. When using rubber rings, place them on jars while they are still wet, stretching only enough to fit over the shoulder of the jar.

Two-Piece Caps. When people speak about canning jars today, these are the ones they mean. Use the metal lid only once; buy new ones for next season's canning. The metal screw band can be used over and over again, so long as it's not rusted. It is needed only during processing and cooling. Screw this band on snugly over the lid before processing, and do not tighten it after taking the jar from the canner, for it provides no seal itself; its only purpose is to hold the lid down in place. When processing is successful, a vacuum in the jar will seal the lid. Remove the band after the contents of the jar are cold, usually after 24 hours. (But don't force the band off; you might just break the seal if you do.) If it doesn't come off easily, store it with the band in place but be sure to check the food carefully before you're ready to use it. (See the box Signs of Spoilage— Throw It Out on page 488.) If you leave the screw bands on during storage, there is a good chance that they will rust. The only reason you'd want to leave them on is if you have to move the sealed jars and want extra protection for the seals.

Porcelain-Lined Zinc Caps. These aren't being made anymore, but you might be able to find some usable ones at a flea market or in grandma's attic. Chances are, the jars themselves are okay; it's the caps you need to check out carefully. If the porcelain lining is cracked, broken, or loose, or if there is even a slight dent at the seal edge, discard the cap. Opening these jars by thrusting a knife blade into the rubber and prying ruins many good covers. The caps are reusable, but the rubber rings are not. Use new ones each time. If the jars are in good shape, but the caps aren't, you can probably replace the caps with the 2-piece caps; jar sizes are pretty standard.

Unlike the 2-piece caps, these zinc caps should not be screwed on snugly before processing, since there must be some room for the air to exhaust itself to form the vacuum. After filling the jars, begin by screwing these caps on all the way, just so you know how tight is tight. Then unscrew them slightly, just a fraction of an inch. Then can. As you're taking them out of the canner, while they are still hot, screw down the caps all the way. Do this slowly, so as not to disturb the rubber ring, and hence the seal. This tightening is what is meant when it says to complete the seals in the directions for canning that come later.

Bailed Wire Caps. These are the oldest of them all. Unless they have been stored carefully in a dry place, there is a very good chance that the wire bail is either rusted or bent and therefore quite unreliable. Again, check both the jar rims and the lids for cracks or nicks, and give the wire bail close scrutiny. Don't try to bend the wire back into shape, or wedge anything between it and the glass to create a tight seal. If in doubt, don't use for canning; save for storing grains, nuts, and other dry foods in your cupboard.

If you do have some perfectly good bailed wire jars, get yourself some new rubber rings. Fill the jar, put on the wet rubber ring, and then the glass lid. Clamp the longer wire over the glass lid, leaving the short piece up and loose; then can. As you remove the jars from the canner, snap the short wire down against the shoulder of the jar so the wire bail is tight. Again, this tightening is what we mean when we say complete the seals in the directions that come later.

Tin Cans

Tin cans come in two sizes: No. 2, which hold about 2½ cups, and No. 2½, which hold about 3½ cups of food. And they come in two types: plain tin and tin coated inside with a protective enamel. Meats, vegetables, and many fruits are processed in plain tin cans, with the protective enamel cans used for those fruits that react with the metal.

Even though you won't be using recycled tin cans or lids, it's still a good idea to check your new ones for damage. There's a small chance they were banged around in transport and have some dents or scratches. Or that they sat too long in a damp place and developed some rust. Throw out any that are not perfect. And test your sealer before you use it each year. You can do this simply enough by filling a can halfway with water and then sealing it. Now drop it in a pot of boiling water. Wait a few seconds and then look for air bubbles rising out of the can; if you see any, you know that the seal wasn't tight enough. Check the instructions that came with your sealer and follow them for adjusting it so that you have a tight seal at the seam where lid meets can.

STEP-BY-STEP DIRECTIONS FOR PRESSURE CANNING

1. If you are using jars, wash, rinse, and scald well with boiling water. Then put them into hot water until needed. Place lids and screw bands in water and bring to a simmer. Remove from heat and leave in hot water until ready to use. If you are using closures that have rubber rings, wash rings in hot water and rinse well. Keep rings in hot water until ready to use.

   If you are using tin cans and lids, have new ones ready and have a sealer at hand.

2. To prepare meat, trim off fat and bone to save space and make packing easier. Cut tender meats, like roasts, steaks, and chops, into pieces the length of the can or jar with the grain of the meat running lengthwise. Tougher pieces of meat should be ground or cut into chunks for stewing meat. Bony pieces may be used to make broth or stock for canning.

   Cut poultry into container-size pieces. Remove the bones from the meaty parts, like the breast. Separate the thighs from the drumsticks. Keep the giblets to process separately.

3. Make broth, if desired, to cover meat. Place meat bones in lidded pot with water and simmer until meat is tender. Skim off fat and save broth for packing.

4. Pack meat loosely. Containers may overflow if contents are packed too tightly or too full.

Hot Pack. Precook meat until medium done, which means to at least 170°F. (For more specific directions, see the chart on page 489.) Then pack it in hot, scalded glass jars or cans and pour boiling water or broth over it, leaving 1¼-inch headspace for jars or ½ inch for cans. Salt may be added to taste, if desired, but it is not necessary. If you do want to salt the meat, use nothing but table salt, since salt substitutes and salted herb blends leave an aftertaste. Wipe the rim of the jar carefully and adjust closure.

If you are using a canning jar with a 2-piece metal cap, put the lid on so that the sealing compound is next to the glass rim. Screw the metal band on tightly by hand. This lid now has enough give to let air escape during processing.

If you are using a canning jar with a porcelain-lined zinc cap or a bailed wire cap, fit the wet ring on the jar shoulder, but don't stretch it more than necessary. Screw the cap down

HOT VERSUS RAW PACKING OF MEATS

While traditionally meats have been packed both raw and hot for canning, caution now suggests that meats only be packed hot into hot, scalded canning jars. This extra cooking gives added assurance that the meat is free from active spoilage organisms. (And cooking softens the meat's tissues, making it more pliable and, hence, easier to pack into the jars.) It is our feeling that raw packing is still acceptable, so long as you are very careful and follow all directions and processing times. We give directions for both hot packing and raw packing so that you can make your own choice about which way to go.

Approximate Pounds of Meat Used per Canning Jar

This chart, which was adapted from the U.S. Department of Agriculture bulletin "Home Canning of Meat and Poultry," will give you an idea of the number of jars you'll need for canning your meat.

Cut of Meat	Pints	Quarts
Beef		
round	$1\frac{1}{2}$ to $1\frac{3}{4}$	3 to $3\frac{1}{2}$
rump	$2\frac{1}{2}$ to $2\frac{3}{4}$	5 to $5\frac{1}{2}$
Pork loin	$2\frac{1}{2}$ to $2\frac{3}{4}$	5 to $5\frac{1}{2}$
Chicken		
canned with bone	$1\frac{3}{4}$ to 2	$3\frac{1}{2}$ to $4\frac{1}{4}$
canned without bone	$2\frac{3}{4}$ to 3	$5\frac{1}{2}$ to $6\frac{1}{4}$

tightly and then turn it back just a fraction of an inch before processing.

If you are using tin cans, put a clean lid on each can and seal cans with a sealer immediately.

Raw Pack. Fill jars or cans with raw meat, leaving 1-inch headspace in jars and *no headspace in cans.* Set open, filled containers on a rack in a pan of boiling water. Keep the water level 2 inches below the tops of the containers. Heat the meat slowly to 170°F, or for 70 minutes, if a meat thermometer is not available. Remove jars or cans from the pan and add salt to the meat, if desired. Do not use a salt substitute. Wipe the rim of the container clean and adjust closure, according to directions above, under Hot Pack.

5. Process by putting 2 inches of hot water in the canner. Set filled closed jars or sealed cans on a rack in the canner. Pack them into the canner loosely, allowing room around each one for steam to circulate freely. If there is room for 2 layers of jars, place a rack between the 2 levels and stagger the containers so that none are directly over any of those below. Cans may be staggered without a rack between layers.

6. Fasten canner cover securely so that no steam escapes except through the petcock or weighted gauge opening. Allow steam to escape from the opening for 10 minutes so all the air is driven out of the canner. Then close the petcock or put on the weighted gauge. Let pressure reach 10 pounds (which is 240°F). Note the time as soon as the gauge reads 10 pounds and start counting processing time. Varying pressure may cause containers to overflow and lose some of their liquid.

To can chicken using the hot pack method, first cut the meat into container-size pieces and cook it in a pot or skillet or in the oven until medium done. Loosely pack the meat into jars and add boiling water or broth, leaving 1-inch headspace. Process in a canner at 10 pounds pressure.

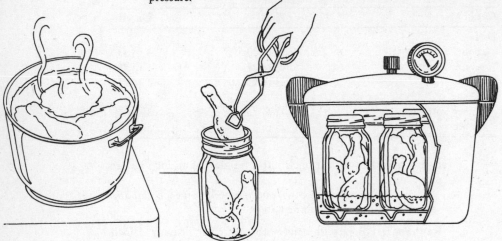

7. When processing time is up, gently remove the canner from the heat immediately. If you are using jars, do not pour cold water over the canner to reduce pressure quickly, but let the canner stand until pressure returns to zero. Wait a few minutes after pressure returns to zero and then slowly open petcock (if your canner has a dial gauge) or take off weighted gauge. Wait 2 minutes, then unfasten the cover and tilt it so that steam can escape without rising in your face. When all the steam is gone, remove the jars.

   If you are using cans, remove the canner from the heat as soon as pressure returns to zero and open petcock or remove weighted gauge to release steam. Unfasten cover and tilt it so that steam can escape without rising in your face. Remove cans.

8. Cool containers. As soon as glass jars are taken from the canner, complete seals, if necessary. Jars with porcelain-lined zinc caps or bailed wire caps need to be sealed. Do this by quickly screwing the cap down tightly or snapping down the short wire. Jars with 2-piece metal caps are self-sealing; you'll hear a reassuring high-pitched sound of the metal lid snapping down on the glass rim when the vacuum is complete and the jar seals itself. Cool the jars right side up on a wooden rack or folded cloth. Don't cover them, and don't cool them on a cold surface

or in a drafty place; you stand the risk of cracking the jars if they cool too quickly.

Put tin cans in cold water as soon as they are removed from the canner. Change the water frequently for rapid cooling. Remove the cans from water while they are still warm and allow them to dry in the air. If the cans are stacked, stagger them so that the air can circulate freely around them.

9. When containers are thoroughly cool, examine each carefully for leaks, as we explained in the chapter Canning Vegetables and Fruits and as we repeat here:

Two-Piece Caps. Press down on the center of the lids. If they do not "give" when you press on them, the jar is sealed properly.

Bailed Wire Caps. Tilt the jar so that the food in it is up against the rim. If bubbles don't appear there or in the contents as you tilt it and no liquid leaks out, you have a good seal.

Porcelain-Lined Zinc Caps. Follow the procedure above for bailed wire jars; no bubbles and no leaking mean a good seal.

Tin Cans. Examine all seams and seals. Properly sealed cans should have flat, not bulging, ends, and the seams should be smooth with no buckling.

If you suspect a container of having a faulty seal, either discard the food or open the container and process the food over again for the required time, store in the refrigerator and use in a few days, or freeze. Jars that have lost liquid during canning should not be opened and reprocessed. Although the meat inside such jars may darken during storage, the meat is not spoiled. If you suspect a faulty seal after the food has been in storage for a while, check the box Signs of Spoilage—Throw It Out, page 488. If you're still suspicious, throw the food out where no person or animal can get at it.

10. Mark containers and store them. Once satisfactorily sealed, you can put the food in storage. Remove the metal rings on 2-piece caps. The lid, not the ring, now holds the seal. Also, the ring can rust in storage, which would not only make it difficult to get off when you want to eat the meat, but also impossible to use again next time you can.

Write directly on the top of the lids, or use adhesive tape, freezer tape, or special labels for jars and cans. Label each container with the type of food canned and date of canning. Canned foods should be used in the order they were canned.

Storage

Jars and cans that contain meat should be stored in a cool, dry place. Do not subject the canned foods to warm temperatures or direct sunlight, as they will lose quality. Freezing does not cause canned meat to spoil, but it may damage the seal so that spoilage begins. To protect against freezing in an unheated area like a cellar or garage, cover the jars and cans with a clean blanket or wrap them separately in newspapers. A damp storage area invites rust which corrodes cans and metal jar lids and causes leakage.

Meat that has been processed, sealed, and stored properly will not spoil. If you suspect meat of being spoiled, don't test it by tasting. Destroy it by burning or dispose of it where it cannot be eaten by animals or humans. It is a good idea to boil all home-canned meat 20 minutes in a covered pot before tasting or serving it. Twenty minutes of rapid boiling will destroy any dangerous toxins that remain in foods that were im-

continued on page 492

SIGNS OF SPOILAGE—THROW IT OUT

Glass Jars

- A jar that is soiled or moldy on the outside indicates that food has seeped out during storage, which means that air and bacteria, yeasts, and molds could have seeped in. (Jars right out of the canner might be a bit soiled from some of the liquid that was exhausted out with the air; this is okay, so long as half the contents of the jars aren't floating outside in the canning water! If you've wiped the jars as you should have done, the jars would have gone clean into storage and any food on the outside of the jars now is *not* okay.)

- A significant change in color, most notably a much darker color, can mean spoilage. Some brown, black, or gray discoloring may be due to minerals in the water or in the cooking utensils; while it may detract from the looks of the food, there is no harm done otherwise.

- A change in texture, especially if the food feels slimy, is a sure sign that the food isn't fit to eat.

- Mold in the food or inside the lid— sometimes nothing more than little flecks—is not a good sign.

- Small bubbles in the liquid or a release of gas, however slight, when you open the can means foul play. Sometimes you get a strong message: Liquid actually spurts out when you release the seal; other times the gas is more subtle.

Tin Cans

- Bulging ends or liquid leaking from the seam, where the lid meets the can, spells trouble.

Directions for Processing Meats

Type and Cut	Preparation and Processing	Processing Time
Cut-up beef, veal, lamb, or pork	Use tender cuts for canning in strips. Making sure that grain of meat runs lengthwise, cut meat the length of the can or jar. Cut less-tender cuts into cubes for stewing or soups.	
	Glass jars:	
	HOT PACK. Precook meat in skillet or saucepan in just enough water to keep meat from scorching. Stir occasionally so that all pieces heat evenly. Cook until medium done. Pack hot meat loosely, leaving 1-inch headspace. Cover meat with boiling water or juice from meat, leaving 1-inch headspace. Adjust lids and process in pressure canner at 10 pounds for required time.	Quarts 90 min. Pints 75 min.
	RAW PACK. Pack cold, raw meat loosely, leaving 1-inch headspace in jar. Exhaust air by heating meat-filled jars in a pot of hot water. Cook at a slow boil until meat is medium done, or reaches 170°F, about 70 minutes. Adjust lids and process in pressure canner at 10 pounds for required time.	Quarts 90 min. Pints 75 min.
	Tin cans:	
	HOT PACK. Precook meat in skillet or saucepan in small amount of water until meat is medium done, stirring occasionally so that meat heats evenly. Pack cooked meat in cans, leaving ½-inch headspace. Fill cans to top with boiling water or juice from meat. Seal. Process in pressure canner at 10 pounds for required time.	No. 2 65 min. No. 2½ 90 min.
	RAW PACK. Pack cans with cold, raw meat to top. To exhaust air, cook meat in cans in a pot of hot water. Cook at a slow boil until meat is medium done, or reaches 170°F, about 70 minutes. Seal. Process in pressure canner at 10 pounds for required time.	No. 2 65 min. No. 2½ 90 min.
Ground meat	Glass jars:	
	HOT PACK. If you are making patties, press the meat tightly into patties that will fit into your jars without breaking. Meat may also be left loose although it is harder to remove from jars. Precook patties in a 300°F oven or over low heat in a skillet until medium done. Pour off all fat; do not use any fat in canning. Pack patties or loose meat in jars, leaving 1-inch headspace. Cover with boiling water or broth, leaving 1-inch headspace. Adjust lids and process in pressure canner at 10 pounds for required time.	Quarts 90 min. Pints 75 min.
	RAW PACK. Pack raw ground meat into jars, leaving 1-inch headspace. Cook meat-filled jars in a pot of hot water at a slow boil until meat is medium done, or reaches 170°F, about 70 minutes. Adjust lids and process in a pressure canner at 10 pounds for required time.	Quarts 90 min. Pints 75 min.
	Tin cans:	
	HOT PACK. If you are making patties, press the meat tightly into patties that will fit into your cans without breaking. Meat may also be packed loose. Precook patties in 300°F oven or over low heat in a skillet until medium done. Pour off all fat. Pack patties or loose meat into cans	No. 2 65 min. No. 2½ 90 min.

continued

Directions for Processing Meats—*continued*

Type and Cut	Preparation and Processing	Processing Time
Ground meat —*continued*	Tin cans, *continued:* within ½ inch of top. Cover with boiling water or juice from meat to the top of the cans. Seal and process in pressure canner at 10 pounds for required time.	
	RAW PACK. Pack raw ground meat solidly to the top of the can. Cook meat in pot of hot water at a slow boil until meat is medium done, or reaches 170°F, about 70 minutes. Seal. Process in pressure canner at 10 pounds for required time.	No. 2 100 min. No. 2½ 135 min.
Sausage and headcheese	Sausage may be packed and processed just as ground meat. Use your own recipe or one of those starting on page 461. Use seasonings sparingly in sausage intended for canning, as spices change flavor in storage. If you normally use sage, omit it; it makes canned sausage bitter.	
Poultry, small game, and rabbit	Sort meat into meaty and bony parts and can separately. Glass jars:	
	HOT PACK, WITH BONE. Bone the breast and cut bony parts into jar-size pieces. Trim off excess fat. Heat pieces in pan with broth or water. Stir occasionally until meat is medium done, when only slight pink color remains. Pack meat loosely, with thighs and drumsticks on the outside of the jar and boned pieces in the center. Leave 1-inch headspace. Cover meat with boiling water or broth, leaving 1-inch headspace. Adjust lids and process in pressure canner at 10 pounds for required time.	Quarts 75 min. Pints 65 min.
	HOT PACK, WITHOUT BONE. Remove bones, but leave skin on meaty parts. Cook meat as for hot pack, with bone. Pack jars loosely, leaving 1-inch headspace. Pour in boiling broth or water, leaving 1-inch headspace. Adjust lids and process in pressure canner at 10 pounds for required time.	Quarts 90 min. Pints 75 min.
	RAW PACK, WITH BONE. Bone the breast and cut other pieces, with bone in, into jar-size pieces. Trim off excess fat. Pack raw meat loosely by placing thighs and drumsticks on the outside and breasts in the center of the jar. Leave 1-inch headspace. Place filled jars in a pan of hot water and cook at a slow boil about 70 minutes, or until meat is medium done, or reaches 170°F. Adjust lids and process in pressure canner at 10 pounds for required time.	Quarts 75 min. Pints 65 min.
	RAW PACK, WITHOUT BONE. Remove bones, but not skin, from meaty pieces. Pack loosely, leaving 1-inch headspace. Place filled jars in pan of hot water and cook at a slow boil until meat is medium done, about 70 minutes, or until thermometer reads 170°F. Adjust lids, and process in pressure canner at 10 pounds for required time.	Quarts 90 min. Pints 75 min.
	Tin cans:	
	HOT PACK, WITH BONE. Bone the breast and cut bony parts into can-size pieces. Trim off excess fat. Heat pieces in a pan with broth or water. Stir occasionally until meat is medium done, when only slight pink color remains. Pack cans, leaving ½-inch headspace. Fill cans to top	No. 2 55 min. No. 2½ 75 min.

Type and Cut	Preparation and Processing	Processing Time
Poultry, small game, and rabbit —*continued*	Tin cans, *continued:* with boiling broth. Seal and process in pressure canner at 10 pounds for required time.	
	HOT PACK, WITHOUT BONE. Remove bones, but not skin, from meaty pieces. Cook as for hot pack, with bone. Pack loosely, leaving ½-inch headspace. Fill cans to top with boiling broth and seal. Process in pressure canner at 10 pounds for required time.	No. 2 65 min. No. 2½ 90 min.
	RAW PACK, WITH BONE. Bone the breast and cut thighs and drumsticks into can-size pieces. Trim off excess fat. Pack meat loosely, with thighs and drumsticks on the outside and breasts in the center. Pack to top of cans. Place filled cans in a pan of hot water and boil slowly until meat is medium done, or until thermometer reads 170°F, about 70 minutes. Seal and process in a pressure canner at 10 pounds for required time.	No. 2 65 min. No. 2½ 90 min.
	RAW PACK, WITHOUT BONE. Cut meat and remove bone, but not skin. Pack raw meat to top of cans. Place filled cans in a pan of hot water and slowly boil until meat is medium done, about 70 minutes, or until thermometer reads 170°F. Seal and process in a pressure canner at 10 pounds for required time.	No. 2 65 min. No. 2½ 90 min.
Giblets	Because of their delicate texture, we recommend freezing these, but they can be canned in pint jars or No. 2 cans. Cook giblets in a pan with water or broth until medium done. Stir occasionally so that meat heats evenly.	
	GLASS JARS. Pack meat, leaving 1-inch headspace. Add boiling water or broth just to cover giblets. Adjust lids and process in a pressure canner at 10 pounds for required time.	Pints 75 min.
	TIN CANS. Pack giblets, leaving ½-inch headspace. Fill cans to top with boiling broth or water. Seal and process in a pressure canner at 10 pounds for required time.	No. 2 65 min.
Liver	Wash, remove skin and membranes. Slice into container-size pieces. Organ meats are hot packed. Drop into boiling water for 5 minutes. Follow hot-pack directions for cut-up meat.	
Heart	Wash and remove thick connective tissue. Cut into container-size strips or 1-inch cubes. Put in a pan and cover with boiling water. Cook at a slow boil until medium done. Follow hot-pack directions for cut-up meat.	
Corned beef	Wash and drain corned beef. Cut it into container-size strips. Cover the meat with cold water and bring to a boil. Taste broth; if it is very salty, drain and boil meat in fresh water. Pack while hot.	
	GLASS JARS. Pack meat loosely, leaving 1-inch headspace. Cover meat with boiling water or broth, leaving 1-inch headspace. Adjust lids and process in a pressure canner at 10 pounds for required time.	Quarts 90 min. Pints 75 min.

continued

Directions for Processing Meats—*continued*

Type and Cut	Preparation and Processing	Processing Time
Corned beef —*continued*	TIN CANS. Pack meat loosely, leaving ½-inch headspace. Fill cans to top with boiling water or broth. Seal and process in a pressure canner at 10 pounds for required time.	No. 2 65 min. No. 2½ 90 min.
Tongue	Wash, put in pan, and cover with boiling water. Cook for about 45 minutes, until skin can be removed easily. Skin and slice into container-size pieces or into 1-inch cubes. Reheat to simmering in the same boiling water. Follow hot-pack directions for cut-up meat.	
Soup stock or broth	Crack or saw bones. Simmer in water until meat is tender. To save work and storage space, make a concentrated stock which can be diluted before reheating. Simmer bones in just enough water to cover. Strain stock and skim off fat. Cut up meat and return it to stock, if desired. Reheat to boiling and pack into glass jars. Adjust lids and process in a pressure canner at 10 pounds for required time.	Quarts 25 min. Pints 20 min.

properly processed. This precaution should certainly be followed by anyone who is canning for the first time or is not certain that his or her gauge is accurate. Boiling is the best way to find out if meat is safe to eat, because heat intensifies the characteristic odor of spoiled meat. If your meat develops an objectionable odor, dispose of it without tasting.

We discussed other signs of spoilage in the chapters Canning Vegetables and Fruits, and Pickles and Relishes, but we repeat the box on page 488. If you notice any of these conditions in your meat, *do not eat the food; destroy it.* Be particularly careful about sterilizing jars, screw bands, and any other equipment that might have come in contact with the food. Wash your hands with soap and hot water and rinse well.

DRYING MEATS

Jerky, best made from beef, is the most popular kind of dried meat, mainly because of its usefulness as a portable snack. It is tough, leathery, and chewy and needs no further preparation after drying.

When drying meats (and fish), you'll have to exercise more care than when drying fruits and vegetables. Pretreatment, temperature, and storage are all more crucial because they can easily spoil or get contaminated. *Game meats should be frozen for 2 months at 0°F before drying, to kill off any possibly dangerous microorganisms in the meat. And pork and poultry should never be dried because they may contain trichinae, small worms that cause the disease trichinosis in humans.* As we said, beef is the best meat for drying. Cuts of meat with more than a 10 percent fat content aren't good for drying, because fat becomes rancid, and it will only serve to encase the meat during drying, thereby slowing down the process. The leaner the meat, the better. The leanest cuts are flank, rump, brisket, and round cuts.

We can only recommend drying any meats if they are first marinated in a salt brine or in soy sauce. Salt is traditionally used, but we prefer the soy sauce because it imparts a nice flavor to meats. Soy sauce, although it provides sufficient salt to help break down the tissues, releases moisture and helps preserve the dried meat, and does not make it taste as salty as meats kept in a salt brine.

Beef Jerky

The recipe here for beef jerky can be used for veal, lamb, and game meats.

1   teaspoon pepper
½   cup soy sauce
16   cloves garlic, crushed
2   tablespoons cider vinegar
1   teaspoon snipped chives

Prepare lean meat for jerky by cutting away all fat and gristle. Cut it into strips about ½ inch thick and 2 inches wide. Cutting across the grain will result in a more tender jerky. And to make slicing easier, partially freeze the meat beforehand. Make the strips as long as you like, but 4 or 5 inches is convenient. The smaller the strips, the quicker the meat will dry.

Mix together pepper, soy sauce, garlic, vinegar, and chives. Add the meat, and then enough water to cover. Let the meat marinate for 12 hours in the refrigerator. Then blot with paper towels and dry in a food dryer. Blot again several times while drying because the soy sauce doesn't dry off as salt does.

Salt Brine for Dried Meats

Should you wish to use a salt brine instead, follow these directions.

1½   cups pickling salt
1   gallon water

Make a brine by mixing the salt and water together. Cut the meat as in the recipe above, and let it marinate in the brine 1 to 2 days in the refrigerator. Then wipe dry and proceed to dry it in your food dryer.

Drying in a Food Dryer

Meats and fish should be dried only in dryers that maintain a reliably high temperature of 140° to 150°F. If it is lower, the meat will dry too slowly and possibly spoil. And if the temperature is higher, your meats might just cook instead of dry. Electric dryers are your best bet, although we have been able to dry meats and fish in Rodale's solar food dryer (see page 143), occasionally needing to use the backup light tray for extra heat. The meat will feel leathery and tough when it's dry.

Dried meat and fish generally do not keep as long as dried fruits and vegetables. They should keep well for 2 months. If you plan on keeping them longer than this, freeze them.

SALT ALERT

Some words to the wise about salt—again. All salt, be it table salt, pickling salt, kosher salt, sea salt, or soy sauce (which is heavy in salt), contains lots of sodium. And sodium has become a nasty word in health circles, for good reason, the main one being that it increases one's risk for heart-related problems. So eat an occasional piece of dried fish or meat, but for your health's sake, don't make a habit of it.

Preparing and Storing Fish

We've stressed many times before that freshness is the key to a good stored product, and this quality is especially important for fish. Fish is the most perishable of all foods, and it must be dealt with properly very soon after it is caught to prevent rapid deterioration.

Fresh-Caught Fish

Kill the fish (except shellfish) as soon as you take it from the water. If the fish is allowed to flop around until it suffocates, the flesh may become bruised, inviting quicker deterioration. Keep shellfish alive by putting it in clean, salted water if you can.

If you can't eat or process your fish right away, pack it in ice (crushed ice is the best because it packs more tightly than does ice cubes or a large chunk of ice) and keep it well packed until you can dress and store it properly. Drain off water from melting ice often so that the fish doesn't become "water-logged" and lose some of its flavor to the melting ice.

Better yet, clean the fish immediately after killing it and wash the body cavity clean with fresh water. Spoilage will not set in as quickly if the entrails and body wastes have been removed. Then pack the body cavity with crushed ice and cover the fish with more ice.

If for some reason ice is not available, wrap the fish in damp moss, ferns, wet newspapers, or burlap and keep it out of the sun. This will not keep fish as well as ice, but it will do for a short period of time in an emergency.

■ Shrimp should be packed in ice with their shells intact and their heads cut off.

495

Fish may also be kept in the coldest part of a refrigerator until you can clean and properly store it. Keep it wrapped or in a covered container to prevent any fish odor from permeating other foods.

■ If you're traveling with your ice-packed fish, don't stash it in your trunk, because it's probably the warmest part of your car.

Fresh-Bought Fish

You can tell if whole fish is fresh by its bulging eyes and the reddish tint of its gills. The scales are shiny and are firmly attached to the skin, and the flesh is taut. Determining the freshness of fish fillets is more difficult because they don't have eyes or scales to check. Be suspicious if the fish looks soft, limp, or slimy. One of the easiest ways to tell a fresh fish—be it a whole fish or fillet—is by its odor. If it's fresh, it won't have a fishy smell. For a whole fish, smell especially around the gills and belly.

CLEANING AND DRESSING FIN FISH

Fish to be filleted need not be scaled and cleaned—skip this first section and jump to the section about filleting on page 498.

Scaling

If you're cooking your fish whole, it will need to be scaled first. Begin by filling the sink or a basin with water. Hold the fish under water as you scrape the fish, so the scales will stay in the water and not cling to the fish. Scrape against the direction of the scales, which means from tail to head. Use the dull edge of a knife or a fish scaler. Hold the knife or scaler slightly diagonally so that you raise the scales as you scrape against them.

Cleaning

It's easier to clean fish with the head on because it gives you something to hold on to; fish can be pretty slippery! To clean a fin fish, make a cut the entire length of the belly by inserting the knife just behind the bottom of the gills and drawing toward the tail. Remove the entrails. If you're careful not to cut through the entrail membrane, you can remove the entire "pouch" easily and in one piece.

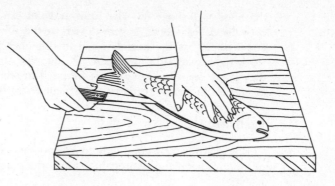

To clean a fish, slice down the belly from just below the gills to the tail and remove the entrails.

Pan Dressing

After you've cleaned the fish, pan dress it in the following manner: Cut off the head by inserting a sharp knife right behind the gills. Now cut off the dorsal and ventral fins with your knife. Cut about ½ inch into the flesh along both sides of the fins to make sure that you remove all the small bones around the fins. Then remove the tail by slicing right through

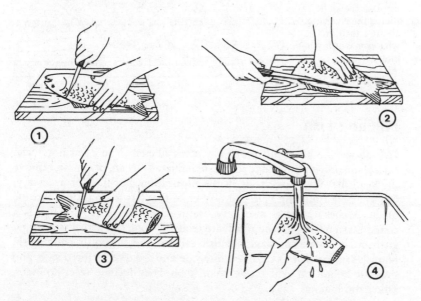

To pan dress a fish after you've cleaned it, (1) cut off the head behind the gills. (2) Cut off the fins, then (3) cut off the tail. (4) Clean off the fish by rinsing it under running water.

the body just above it. (The head and tail can be used to make fish chowder or fish stock. Be sure to remove the gills from the head first. If you wish to use the trimmings in this manner, make the chowder or stock right away—do not freeze or otherwise store them for use later; they don't keep well.) Wash the fish well to remove any scales, blood, or entrails. It is now ready to cook plain or stuffed, or to freeze or can.

Fish Steaks

This is a particularly good way to prepare large fish weighing 3 pounds or more. Salmon and swordfish, among others, are often prepared in this manner.

Clean the fish as described on page 496. Then, beginning at the head end, cut cross-sectionally into about 1-inch-thick slices.

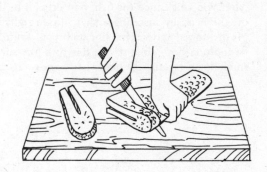

An easy way to prepare large fish is to cut them into steaks. Simply clean the fish (cut off the head and remove the entrails), then cut through the spine, slicing the steaks to about 1 inch or whatever width you'd like.

Filleting Fish

Fish about 1 pound and more are often filleted. You need not scale, eviscerate, or trim a fish that you plan to fillet. You can, of course, remove the head first if you wish, as in the illustration, but it's not necessary. Get yourself a filleting knife, or any knife that has a long, slim, flexible blade. A chef's knife is also very useful. Then decide if your fish is a roundfish or a flatfish. Roundfish are relatively long fish with a semiround girth and include trout, bass, bluefish, salmon, cod, weakfish, and tilefish. Flatfish are flat. They've got a white side and a darker-colored side, and they are round or oval rather than long. They include sole, flounder, fluke, and halibut.

Roundfish. If you're not familiar with fish anatomy—and even if you are—check the illustration as you read along.

Start by making a slanted cut from the nape to the tail along the back on both sides of the fish. With the fish on one side, make a ½-inch cut from the nape to the tail along the back next to the dorsal fin, separating the flesh from the bone structure. Peel back the flesh as you go, until you have separated one whole fillet from the backbone and rib cage. Then turn the fish over and repeat this step exactly on the other side. Now you've got 2 fillets, one from each side of the fish.

To remove the skin from the fillets, place them skin-side down on a cutting board with their tail ends closest to you. Grasp the tail end tightly with your thumb and forefinger. With your chef's knife cut through

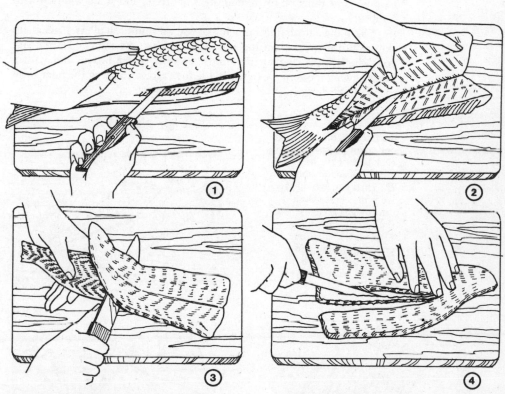

To fillet a roundfish, (1) cut from nape to tail along the back on both sides. (2) Following the plane of the backbone, continue to cut while peeling back the flesh from the bone until a fillet is separated. Then repeat on the other side.

(3) Skin the fillet by grasping the tail and separating the flesh from the skin with your knife. (4) For a boneless fillet, remove the small row of bones that runs down the center of the fillet.

the tail flesh to the skin, then flatten out the knife blade so that it's almost parallel to the cutting board. With a slight sawing motion, move the blade forward, separating the fillet from the skin as you go.

If you want all bones out of the fillets, with your fingers feel the small row of bones that runs halfway down the center line of the fillet and cut them out.

Flatfish. You can use the technique just described for roundfish, giving you 2 fillets. But we prefer to "quarter-cut" a flatfish.

Make a cut down the middle of each side along the center bone. Slide the blade between the flesh and bone and cut the fillets away from the center bone by drawing the knife out toward the edges of the fish. Do this same thing on the remaining 3 quarters, and you'll wind up with 4 fillets.

Skin the flatfish fillets much like you do roundfish fillets. Place them skin-side down on a cutting board. Grasp an end tightly. Flatten out your chef's knife so that it's almost parallel to the board, and with a slight sawing motion, move the blade forward, separating the fillet from the skin as you go.

To fillet a flatfish, (1) cut down the middle of each side of the fish along the center bone. (2) Then cut two fillets from the center bone out toward the edges of the fish on each side. (3) Skin the fillets by grasping the tail and separating the flesh from the skin with your knife.

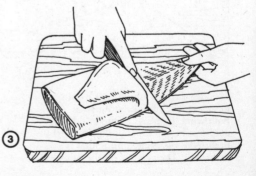

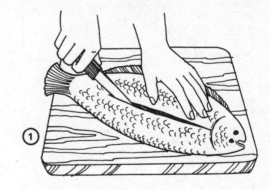

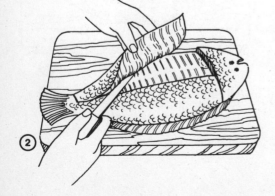

CLAMS, OYSTERS, MUSSELS, AND SCALLOPS

These shellfish should be kept alive, if possible, until you are ready to eat or preserve them in some way, like canning or freezing. Keep them covered in clean water for 1 to 2 hours in the refrigerator to allow them to clean themselves of any sand inside the shells.

Before you're ready to shuck them, wash them well in fresh water. Then, rest the shellfish on ice for an hour or put them in the freezer 30 minutes before shucking. Chill them well and don't disturb the fish until you pick them up, gently, to shuck them. They will open much more easily if they are not jostled.

Shuck them by inserting a *blunt* knife between the two shells and scraping along the top inside of each shell, cutting the muscles which hold the shells closed. Do not use a sharp knife, as a good edge is not necessary to sever the muscles, and you could quite easily cut yourself badly in the process. Wearing padded gloves to protect your hands is a good idea, especially if you're opening several shells.

If you will be freezing or canning the fish or making soup, shuck them over a bowl so that you can catch all their liquid.

These shellfish can also be steamed open. The heat will kill the fish and loosen their muscles so that the shells will open. To steam, rinse

To shuck clams, (1) grasp the clam firmly with its hinge toward your palm and insert the knife blade. Push in firmly, with the blade extending past the hinge. (2) Draw the blade back in and bend the handle down to angle the blade up. Scrape along the inside of the top shell—do not cut straight across. (3) Continue scraping along the top shell until you reach the other side of the clam. (4) Put your thumb down on the top shell and twist it off. Keep the clam in the same position in your palm at all times.

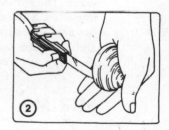
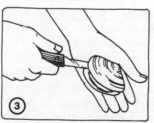
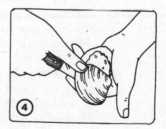

them off and place them in a steam basket or wire rack over boiling water. Cover the pot and reduce to a slow boil. Steam them 10 minutes and check to see if their shells have opened slightly. If not, continue to steam until they do. If you find a couple of shellfish that don't open, throw them away.

CRABS, LOBSTERS, AND CRAYFISH

Crabs, lobsters, and crayfish should be alive and frisky when you get them. Keep them alive by putting them in clean, salted water, if you can, until you cook them for eating or processing.

Boiling Hard-Shell Crabs

Place crabs one at a time in rapidly boiling fresh or lightly salted water. Do this slowly so as not to reduce the water temperature too much as you add them. Make sure the crabs are entirely covered with water. Reduce the heat to simmering and cook the crabs about 10 to 15 minutes. Remove. If they are to be shelled or eaten cold, plunge into cold water.

Boiling Lobsters and Crayfish

Plunge live lobsters or crayfish headfirst into a large pot of boiling fresh water. The pot should be big enough so that the fish will be completely immersed. Bring the water to a boil again, reduce heat, and simmer the fish until the entire shell is bright red: about 8 minutes for the first pound and 3 minutes for each additional pound. Remove. If the fish is to be shelled or eaten cold, plunge into cold water.

SHRIMP

To clean shrimp, cut off the heads and peel the shell from one side to the other with your thumb, pulling off the entire shell in one piece. Leave the tail intact. Make an incision the length of the back and cut or pull out the black vein (which is the colon). To make sure all the vein is removed, hold the shrimp under cold running water as you take it out.

Shrimp may be cooked before or after cleaning. To cook shrimp, bring water to a boil. Add shrimp slowly to the boiling water so as not to reduce its temperature too much. Reduce heat to simmering. Shrimp need only cook 3 to 5 minutes, until they lose their transparency. Do not overcook them or they will become tough.

To cool them for eating cold or shelling, remove them from the hot water and plunge into very cold water.

EXTENDING THE REFRIGERATOR LIFE OF FISH

To improve the keeping quality of fish for the refrigerator, use the technique described below. This technique has been adapted for home use from *A Thermal Treatment for the Extension of Fresh Fish* by Stephen D. Kelleher and Robert R. Zall, Department of Food Science, Cornell University, Ithaca, New York.

Use fillets or whole, gutted fish, but start with the freshest fish possible; fish more than 2 days out of the water is too old for this procedure.

Bring a large pot of water to a simmer (190°F). With a slotted spoon or spatula, or even some cheesecloth, hold each piece of fish in the water for 2 seconds. Then put the fish one layer deep on a tray and cover loosely with wax paper. Refrigerate.

Fish blanched quickly like this should last 6 or 7 days in the refrigerator, which is 4 or 5 days longer than you'd want to keep unblanched fish there.

FREEZING FRESH-CAUGHT FISH

Because of the minimal amount of processing involved and the excellent preservation qualities of freezing, this is the recommended method for keeping fish. However, you should only freeze fish that are very fresh and that have not already been frozen. The best fish for freezing is that which has just been caught. Fresh fish you buy will never be as fresh, unless you buy it right off the boat. And quite a bit of supermarket fish sold these days is not fresh, but thawed fish that was frozen at one time. We've noticed that such fish is sometimes sold under the mystifying label "fresh frozen fish," and sometimes there is no label at all that suggests it has been frozen before. If you're not sure that it is really fresh, only buy as much of this fish as you can eat in a few days; don't plan on freezing the extras.

Freeze fish within 24 hours after it is caught, and freeze it at temperatures at or below 0°F, which usually means keeping it in a separate home freezer, not in the freezer compartment of a refrigerator, which hardly ever maintains a temperature of 0°F.

Fin Fish

Fish weighing up to around 2 pounds can be frozen whole, but it is best to fillet fish weighing more than 1 pound and cut fish larger than 3 pounds into steaks before freezing. Fresh fish may be frozen as is, wrapped well in freezer paper or in a heavy-duty plastic bag that you've pressed closely against the fish to squeeze out all of the air. But if you give the fish a

Recommended Freezer Storage Time for Fish
(freezer temperature 0°F or colder)

Fish	Maximum Storage Time (months)	Fish	Maximum Storage Time (months)
Bass	2 to 3	Ocean perch	4 to 5
Blowfish	2 to 3	Oyster	3 to 4
Bluefish	2 to 3	Pickerel	2 to 3
Bonito	4 to 5	Pike	2 to 3
Carp	4 to 5	Pompano	4 to 5
Catfish	4 to 5	Porgy	2 to 3
Clam	3 to 4	Red snapper	2 to 3
Cod	4 to 5	Salmon (pink and chum)	4 to 5
Crab	2	Scallop	3 to 4
Eel	4 to 5	Shad	2 to 3
Flounder	4 to 5	Shrimp	2
Fluke	4 to 5	Smelts	2 to 3
Freshwater herring	2 to 3	Sole	4 to 5
Haddock	4 to 5	Squid	4 to 5
Halibut	2 to 3	Striped bass	4 to 5
Herring	4 to 5	Swordfish	2 to 3
Lake trout	4 to 5	Tuna	4 to 5
Lobster	2	Whitefish	4 to 5
Mackerel	2 to 3	Whiting	2 to 3
Mullet	4 to 5	Yellow perch	2 to 3
Mussel	3 to 4	Yellow pike	2 to 3

little extra attention, by freezing it in a thin layer of ice or a block of ice before freezing it, it'll keep even better. This ice keeps air off the surface of the fish and prevents excessive oxidation which would otherwise deteriorate its quality.

Ice Glaze #1. In this method, fish can be glazed in milk, half lemon and half water, or plain water.

Prefreeze fresh fish by single layering them on a baking sheet and putting them in the freezer for 30 minutes. This prefreezing helps the glazing liquid freeze immediately to the fish.

Then pour whatever glazing liquid you've chosen in an oblong pan and dip each piece of fish into the glaze. Freeze the fish briefly on a baking sheet so that this layer of glaze freezes. Then dip the fish in the glaze 2 more times, again briefly freezing between dips, so that you end up with

3 layers of glazing in all. Wrap the fish in heavy-duty plastic bags or in freezer wrap, and freeze.

Ice Glaze #2. Make a glaze from lemon juice, water, and gelatin in the following manner: Pour $\frac{1}{4}$ cup lemon juice into 2 cups water. Reserve $\frac{1}{2}$ cup of this mixture and pour the rest into a pot and bring it to a boil. Dissolve 1 envelope of unflavored gelatin into the reserved $\frac{1}{2}$ cup of the lemon-water mixture, and then stir it into the boiling lemon-water mixture. Cool the glaze before you use it.

Pour the glaze into an oblong pan and dip each piece of fish separately into the glaze and then place each on a rack to drain. Be particularly fussy about glazing steaks and fillets because they are not protected by skin. Freeze briefly on a baking sheet so that the glaze freezes. Then wrap in heavy-duty plastic bags or in freezer paper, and freeze.

Ice Block. Another way to prevent oxidation is to pack fish in an ice block. Ice blocks do the job admirably, but they take up more room than an ice glaze. To make an ice block, fill a loaf pan, a recycled coffee tin or milk carton, or large freezer container with several small fish, fish steaks, or fillets to within a few inches of the top. Fill with water to cover the fish, making sure you leave a 1-inch headspace to prevent spillage and to allow for expansion as the water freezes. Run a knife around the inside edges of the container to make sure there are no air bubbles and the water completely surrounds the fish. You can leave the block in its container once frozen solid, or you can remove it from the container and wrap in freezer paper. Then store again in the freezer.

Clams, Oysters, Mussels, and Scallops

None of these shellfish should be cooked before freezing, as the heat would toughen them. Merely wash them well in cold water to clean all the sand out and then shell them. Save their liquid. Scallops can be rinsed again after shelling, but don't rewash clams, oysters, or mussels.

All should be packed in liquid to cover for freezing. Their liquid may be used, but if there is not enough of this liquid (and this will be the case with scallops, as they have little liquid), cover with cold, fresh water. Do not use seawater. Pack in rigid freezer containers, leaving $\frac{1}{2}$-inch headspace, and seal.

Crabs, Lobsters, and Crayfish

Cook the fish as described on page 502. Cool them quickly in cold water, crack the shells, and remove the meat. Pack lightly in plastic bags or airtight containers, leaving no headspace. Seal and freeze.

Shrimp

Shrimp may be frozen shelled or unshelled, cooked or uncooked, but we prefer that shrimp be frozen uncooked because they tend to get tough if cooked first. Shrimp that have been shelled and have had their heads removed and the black vein running under the surface of their backs cut out will keep longer. For cooking and cleaning directions, see page 502.

Freeze shrimp by laying out on a baking sheet and putting them in the freezer. When shrimp are solid, pack in plastic bags or rigid freezer containers, leaving no headspace. Seal, label, and return to freezer.

Use raw, frozen shrimp straight from the freezer, but thaw cooked, frozen shrimp in the refrigerator for 6 to 8 hours.

THAWING AND COOKING FROZEN FISH

Frozen fish need not be thawed before cooking unless you plan to stuff it or bread it; then thawing is necessary. Allow extra time for cooking unthawed fish, about $1\frac{1}{4}$ times as long as unfrozen fish.

If you wish to thaw fish, do it slowly so that it loses little of its own juice and delicate texture. Don't thaw completely or its delicate texture will break down and flavorful juices will leak out. There still should be some ice crystals remaining. Thaw in the refrigerator, keeping the fish in its freezer wrapping. Never thaw at room temperature. Fish that is completely thawed should be cooked as soon as possible. Do not refreeze thawed fish.

CANNING FISH

Because of the delicate nature and high perishability of fish, canning is a tedious task; you will have to prepare several brine solutions to prevent the fish's protein from coagulating. In addition, it is necessary to first cook fish-filled jars to exhaust air and then process for a relatively long time. You can imagine what all this does to the fish. Freezing is by far a better choice.

We tested lots of canned fish, and most of it left us very tired and very disappointed. Standard procedures for canning fin fish were hardly worth the trouble, and canned shellfish lost all its flavor and texture. We did, however, find a few recipes we worked on to be particularly good.

Because you can substitute any fin fish for the tuna in the Canned Tuna recipe on page 507, this is sort of an all-purpose recipe. We've included a recipe for Canned Mussels because we discovered that they can well when blanched in citric acid first. Unfortunately, this recipe cannot be used for other shellfish. We didn't like the way the chowders we tried canned, but we found out that you can make up bases for fish and clam chowders ahead of time and can (or freeze) them and then add the rest of the ingredients later, before you serve them. The bases involve all the hard work anyway, so making them in large batches ahead of time can be a real convenience, not to mention a good way to can or freeze the fish you're using.

Canned Tuna

While most of us think only of tuna and salmon when it comes to canned fish, this process is applicable to any freshly caught fin fish. This recipe was adapted from one created by Linda Gilbert, director of the Rodale Food Consultants at the Rodale Food Center and a deep-sea fishing enthusiast. Canned fish is, of course, good in salads, but it's also nice in a white sauce over spaghetti, in casseroles, or on an antipasto tray.

5   pounds fresh bonito or
    albacore tuna or other fresh
    fin fish
½   cup salt (optional)
1   gallon water
    (optional)
30 tablespoons water
10 ½ teaspoons olive oil
    (optional)

Cut fish into 1-inch chunks. Marinate tuna for at least 4 hours (in a nonmetal container) with salt and a gallon of water. (Omit this step if you choose not to use salt.)

Rinse fish well. Fill clean half-pint jars and add 3 tablespoons water and ½ teaspoon olive oil to each jar, leaving 1-inch headspace.

Seal and process in a pressure canner for 90 minutes at 10 pounds pressure.

Yield: 10 half-pints

Canned Mussels

4 dozen fresh mussels
1 gallon water
1½ teaspoons citric acid

Clean mussels. Discard any that gape and do not close when tapped, or those whose shells slide easily across each other. Remove "beards" by clipping with scissors.

In a large pot with 2 inches of water at the bottom, steam mussels until shells open. (Discard any mussels that don't open.) Remove mussels from shells and set aside while you bring 1 gallon water to a boil. Add citric acid.

Place mussels in cheesecloth or in a strainer and blanch in the citric acid solution. (This helps keep the mussels from turning dark during the canning process.)

Fill hot, scalded half-pint jars with mussels and then cover with water, leaving 1-inch headspace. Seal and process in a pressure canner for 70 minutes at 10 pounds pressure.

Yield: 4 half-pints

Fin Fish Chowder Base
(to can or freeze)

Fish Stock
2 pounds fish bones
6 cups water
1 onion, quartered
1 stalk celery
2 sprigs parsley
1 bay leaf

Chowder
3 tablespoons vegetable oil
1½ cups chopped onions
½ cup chopped green peppers
½ cup chopped celery
2 cups water
2 cups diced potatoes
2 to 2½ pounds cod or
    haddock fillets, cut into
    1-inch pieces
    dash of ground thyme
2 tablespoons lemon juice

To make the fish stock, combine fish bones, water, onion, celery, parsley, and bay leaf in a kettle or large saucepan. Bring to a boil, skimming off foam as it rises to the surface. Lower heat. Cover partially and simmer 45 minutes. Remove bones. Strain stock through cheesecloth and reserve.

In a large saucepan, heat oil. Add onions, peppers, and celery. Sauté for 2 to 3 minutes. Add 4 cups fish stock and 2 cups water. Bring to a boil. Add potatoes and fish. Boil 5 to 7 minutes. Add thyme and lemon juice. Cool and freeze, if desired, or can.

To can: With a slotted spoon, put solid mixture into hot, scalded pint jars, filling each jar half full. Add liquid from vegetable-fish mixture to fill jars, leaving 1-inch headspace. Seal and process in a pressure canner at 10 pounds pressure for 60 minutes.

Yield: 6 pints

Fisherman's Chowder

3 pints Fin Fish Chowder Base
  (see page 508)
3 cups chopped canned or
  cooked tomatoes
⅛ teaspoon ground thyme
4 tablespoons chopped parsley

Heat chowder base over low heat. Add tomatoes, thyme, and 2 tablespoons parsley. Simmer 10 minutes. Serve with remaining parsley sprinkled on top.

Yield: 10 to 12 servings

Creamy Fish Chowder

3 pints Fin Fish Chowder Base
  (see page 508)
3½ cups milk
½ cup light or heavy cream
2 tablespoons butter, cut into
  bits
⅛ teaspoon ground thyme
  finely chopped parsley

Heat chowder base to simmering point. Add milk, cream, butter, and thyme. Simmer until heated through. Do not let boil. Serve with a sprinkling of parsley.

Yield: 10 to 12 servings
continued

Variation

For a thicker chowder, melt 1 tablespoon butter in a small saucepan. Stir in 1 tablespoon whole wheat flour. Remove from heat. Whisk in 1 cup milk. Cook over low heat, stirring constantly until thickened. Add to fish chowder base with 2 cups milk, 1 cup heavy or light cream, and ⅛ teaspoon thyme. Heat through.

Clam Chowder Base
(to can or freeze)

2   dozen chowder clams
3   tablespoons vegetable oil or
      butter
1   cup finely chopped onions
½   cup chopped celery
1   bay leaf
2   sprigs parsley
2½ cups diced potatoes
½   cup chopped carrots
      dash of ground thyme
2   tablespoons lemon juice

Steam clams open. (Discard any clams that don't open.) Reserve clam broth. Chop clams.

In a kettle or large saucepan, heat oil or butter. Add onions and celery and sauté 3 to 4 minutes. Add enough water to clam broth to measure 6 cups and add to onion mixture along with bay leaf and parsley. Bring to a boil. Reduce heat. Add clams and simmer 15 minutes. Add potatoes and carrots. Boil gently 5 minutes. Remove bay leaf and parsley. Add thyme and lemon juice. Cool and freeze, if desired, or can.

To can: Into hot, scalded pint jars, ladle solid mixture until jars are half full. Add liquid from vegetable-clam mixture to fill jars, leaving 1-inch headspace. Seal and process in a pressure canner at 10 pounds pressure for 100 minutes.

Yield: 6 pints

New England Clam Chowder

3 pints Clam Chowder Base
   (see page 510)
3 cups milk
1 cup light cream
1 tablespoon butter
⅛ teaspoon ground thyme
   paprika

     Heat chowder base slowly to a simmer. Add milk, cream, butter, and thyme. Heat through but do not let boil. Serve with a sprinkling of paprika.

Yield: 10 to 12 servings

Variation

For a thicker chowder, melt 1 tablespoon butter in a small saucepan. Stir in 1 tablespoon whole wheat flour. Remove from heat. Whisk in 1 cup milk and ½ cup light cream. Cook over low heat, stirring constantly, until thickened. Add to chowder base with 2 cups milk, ½ cup cream, and ⅛ teaspoon thyme. Heat through.

Manhattan Clam Chowder

3 pints Clam Chowder Base
   (see page 510)
3 cups chopped canned or
   cooked tomatoes
⅛ teaspoon ground thyme
3 tablespoons chopped parsley

     Heat chowder base slowly to a simmer. Add tomatoes and thyme and simmer 5 to 7 minutes. Serve with a sprinkling of parsley.

Yield: 10 to 12 servings

Variation

Other vegetables, such as cooked corn or peas, may be added.

Spicy Shellfish Boil

1   tablespoon coriander seeds
1   tablespoon mustard seeds
2½   teaspoons whole allspice
1   teaspoon whole cloves
½   teaspoon peppercorns
¼   teaspoon crushed red pepper
¼   teaspoon ground ginger
3   bay leaves, crumbled
2 to 3 quarts water
1   large onion, sliced
1   lime, sliced
1   stalk celery, chopped
2   pounds shrimp, crab legs, or
      hard-shell crab

In a jar, combine coriander seeds, mustard seeds, allspice, cloves, peppercorns, red pepper, ginger, and bay leaves. Store, tightly covered, at room temperature.

When ready to use, boil spice mixture in water for 10 minutes in a large pot with onions, lime, and celery. Add shrimp or crab. Cook shrimp 5 minutes and crab 12 minutes.

Yield: about ¼ cup spice mix, enough
to cook 2 pounds shrimp or crab

Mussels Jambalaya

1½   dozen mussels (if using
      canned mussels, use 2 half-
      pints and ½ cup clam juice)
3   tablespoons butter
¼   cup finely chopped onions
¼   cup finely chopped scallions
½   cup finely chopped celery
⅓   cup finely chopped green
      peppers
1   teaspoon minced garlic

1   tablespoon finely chopped
      parsley
1   cup uncooked brown rice
1½   cups water or chicken broth
¼   teaspoon cayenne pepper
¼   cup paprika
⅛   teaspoon ground thyme
1   tomato, seeded and finely
      chopped

Clean mussels. Discard any that gape and do not close when tapped, or those whose shells slide easily across each other. Remove "beards" by clipping with scissors.

Steam mussels open. (Discard any that don't open.) Remove mussels from shells and set aside. Reserve broth.

In a 3-quart saucepan, melt butter over medium-low heat. Add onions, scallions, celery, green peppers, garlic, and parsley. Sauté for 5 minutes or until vegetables are soft but not brown. Add rice and stir 1 to 2 minutes, until rice is coated with butter. Add water or broth, cayenne, paprika, thyme, and ½ cup reserved mussel broth. Bring to a boil. Reduce heat to low. Cover and simmer 35 to 40 minutes or until liquid is almost all absorbed. Add tomato and mussels. Cover and cook 5 to 10 minutes longer until rice is tender and mixture is heated through.

Yield: 4 to 5 servings

Variation

Substitute 1½ pounds shrimp for mussels. Use ½ cup clam juice for broth.

Scallop Stew

1 pound frozen sea scallops
3 tablespoons olive oil
1 cup chopped onions
½ cup finely chopped celery
1 clove garlic, minced
¼ cup sliced mushrooms
1 bay leaf
½ teaspoon ground marjoram
½ teaspoon paprika
  dash of cayenne pepper
1 sprig parsley
¼ cup water
½ cup chopped seeded tomato
  chopped fresh parsley

Place container of scallops in warm water for 10 minutes. Slide frozen block into medium saucepan. Heat gently over low heat just until thawed. Do not cook. Drain scallops, reserving liquid.

In a large saucepan, heat oil over medium heat. Add onions, celery, and garlic. Sauté about 5 minutes until vegetables are soft, stirring frequently. Add mushrooms and cook 2 minutes. Add bay leaf, marjoram, paprika, cayenne, parsley, water, and ½ cup reserved scallop liquid. Bring to a boil, stirring occasionally. Lower heat and simmer, covered, 15 minutes. Add tomatoes and cook 5 minutes. Add scallops and cook over low heat until scallops are done (when they are no longer transparent),

3 to 4 minutes. Discard bay leaf and parsley. Serve with a sprinkling of chopped parsley.

Yield: 4 servings

Note: Fresh scallops may be used by substituting ½ cup clam juice for the ½ cup reserved liquid that comes from defrosting frozen ones.

DRYING FISH

Any kind of lean, white-meat fish can be dried. As with meat, the fattier it is, the more chance it will get rancid during the drying. Cod is a good, lean fish and is the fish that most usually comes to mind when one thinks of drying. For other lean and fatty fish, see the chart below. Much of what was said about meat applies to fish, too. The speed with which you do the job is of the utmost importance when drying fish, because fish begins to spoil if not used or preserved soon after it is caught. Don't attempt to dry fish that you have bought unless you know that it is very fresh. It should be processed as soon as you get it home from the market or your fishing trip. Fillet the fish (see page 498), then slice it in the same way you would when drying meat, in ¼-inch strips. Small fish can be dried whole after it's been cleaned.

Unlike meat, fish must be layered with salt and must sit in the brine

Lean and Fatty Fish

Lean		Fatty
Black drum	Pollack	Bluefish
Blackfish (tautog)	Red snapper	Butterfish
Black sea bass	Rockfish	Carp
Blowfish tails	Scrod	Catfish
(sea squab)	Shark	Eel
Cod	Skate	Hake (whiting)
Croaker	Squid	Herring
Cusk	Tilefish	Kingfish
Flounder	Weakfish	Mackerel
Gray sole	(sea trout)	Mullet
Haddock	Yellow perch	Salmon
Halibut	Yellow pike	Shad
Lemon sole		Smelts
Monkfish		Swordfish
Ocean perch		Trout (freshwater)
Pickerel		Tuna
Pike		Whitefish

that forms for several days to remove a good deal of the moisture before it's put in the food dryer. The fish, needless to say, is going to be very salty, even though it's been rinsed off afterward. So, before using the dried fish, it should be soaked in water or water and milk to remove more of the salt (see last paragraph this chapter). For a salt brine, follow the directions here.

Salt Brine for Fish

1 cup pickling salt
1 gallon water
  more pickling salt

Make a brine by mixing together 1 cup salt and 1 gallon water and rinse the fish in this. As you do so, check the fish carefully to make sure there are no traces of dirt, blood, or insects.

Then weigh the fish and rub pickling salt into each piece, using 1 pound of salt for each 4 pounds of fish. Finely grained pickling salt is best for this because it more easily penetrates the pores of the fish. Stack the fish skin-side down in a long, flat container. A wooden box with holes in the bottom for drainage of the fish juices and the brine that forms is ideal. Stagger the layers of fish, sprinkling salt generously between the layers, using a second pound of salt for each 4 pounds of fish.

Keep the fish in the refrigerator for 4 to 12 days. The more layers, the thicker the slices of fish, and the more humid the air, the longer the fish should stay in the brine for this first phase of drying.

Then rinse the fish well in a half vinegar-half water solution to remove as much salt as possible before you place it in the food dryer.

Dry your fish at a constant 140° to 150°F. An electric dryer will be the least risky because it's the most reliable, although we have been able to dry fish and meats in Rodale's solar food dryer (see page 143), occasionally needing to use the backup light tray for extra heat. When the fish is dry, it should spring back when you press it, and it should be firm and dry to the touch.

Dried fish can be kept for 2 months, so long as you keep it in moisture-proof, airtight containers or plastic bags. For longer keeping, freeze it.

Because it's very salty, dried fish needs to be soaked in water, or water and then milk, for 24 hours before it's used. Place the pieces of dried fish in a large bowl, cover with cool, clean water, seal with a lid or plastic wrap, and refrigerate, changing the soaking water at least 4 times in that period. After the 24 hours of soaking in water, you may wish to soak it for another couple of hours in cool milk to further condition and to remove more salt.

Meat and Poultry Recipes

MEAT DISHES

Appetizer Meatballs
(to freeze)

Meatballs
1¼ pounds lean ground beef
1 egg
½ cup chopped walnuts
2 cloves garlic, minced

Sauce
½ pint grape jelly
1 cup tomato purée
1 small onion, minced
1 tablespoon chili powder

¼ cup cider vinegar
1 teaspoon soy sauce
2 tablespoons Worcestershire sauce

Preheat oven to 350°F.

To make the meatballs: Combine beef, egg, walnuts, and garlic. Roll into 1-inch balls and bake for 20 minutes. Drain fat.

To make the sauce: In a medium-size saucepan, combine jelly, tomato purée, onions, chili powder, vinegar, soy sauce, and Worcestershire sauce. Add meatballs. Slowly bring to a boil, then reduce heat and simmer for 20 minutes until flavors are combined. Freeze.

To serve, defrost in refrigerator overnight, then reheat gently. Serve on small plates with cocktail forks or toothpicks.

Yield: 6 to 8 appetizer servings (50 1-inch balls)

Beef Stew
(to can or freeze)

This classic beef stew may be canned or frozen, but we prefer freezing, because there is a texture and flavor loss in the canned version. In commercially canned foods like this, chemicals and salt are added to help preserve the texture and flavor. To minimize these losses in canning, follow the recipe, leaving out the vegetables and cooking the stew for only 45 minutes. Then add the vegetables and cook for only about 3 minutes instead of the time recommended here. Let the vegetables do their real cooking in the canner.

1½ pounds lean beef stew meat, cut into 1-inch cubes
1 tablespoon vegetable oil
4 cups beef stock
2 teaspoons lemon juice
1 clove garlic, minced
2 bay leaves
½ teaspoon freshly ground pepper
¼ teaspoon ground allspice
½ teaspoon paprika
1 small onion, finely chopped
1 tablespoon Worcestershire sauce

10 pearl onions, peeled and left whole, or 3 small yellow onions, quartered
6 carrots, sliced into 1-inch pieces
4 medium-size potatoes, cut into 1-inch cubes
2 tablespoons whole wheat flour
¼ cup milk
1 cup beef stock (optional)
2 cups frozen or fresh peas

Brown meat in oil slowly for about 15 minutes. Add beef stock, lemon juice, garlic, bay leaves, pepper, allspice, paprika, chopped onions, and Worcestershire sauce. Simmer for 1½ hours. Add pearl or yellow onions, carrots, and potatoes and cook for 20 minutes. Whisk flour and milk until well blended. Add flour mixture to the broth. Add beef stock, if necessary. Stir until thick and then add peas. Cook until heated through. Remove bay leaves.

Can or freeze. To can, pack hot into hot, scalded pint or quart jars, leaving 1-inch headspace. Adjust seals and process in a pressure canner, 75 minutes for pints and 90 minutes for quarts.

Yield: 6 pints or 3 quarts

Variations

1. Add 1 pint canned tomatoes with beef stock.
2. Add ⅓ cup tomato paste when you add flour mixture to broth.

Goulash
(to can or freeze)

To minimize texture and flavor losses during canning, follow the recipe, leaving out the vegetables and cooking the meat and spices for 1 hour. Add the vegetables at the end and cook for 3 minutes. Then can.

½ cup whole wheat flour
1 tablespoon soy sauce
3 tablespoons paprika
3 teaspoons dry mustard
6 pounds boned chuck, cut into 1-inch pieces
3 tablespoons vegetable oil
1¾ cups water
½ cup cider vinegar

4 bay leaves
20 peppercorns
2½ teaspoons caraway seeds
6 medium-size onions, cut into 1-inch pieces
6 large carrots, cut into 1-inch pieces
10 stalks celery, cut into 1-inch pieces

Combine flour, soy sauce, paprika, and mustard. Roll meat in flour mixture. Brown slowly in oil. Sprinkle remaining flour mixture over meat; add water, vinegar, bay leaves, peppercorns, and caraway seeds. Cover and simmer for 1 hour. Then add onions, carrots, and celery and simmer for 30 minutes or until tender. Remove bay leaves.

When ready to serve, reheat and serve with boiled potatoes or whole wheat pasta.

Can or freeze. To can, pour hot into hot, scalded pint or quart jars, leaving 1-inch headspace, and seal. Process in a pressure canner, 75 minutes for pints and 90 minutes for quarts.

Yield: about 6 pints or 3 quarts

Beef Stroganoff
(to can or freeze)

To minimize the texture and flavor losses in canning, follow the recipe but add the mushrooms and cook them for only about 3 minutes instead of the time recommended here; let them do their real cooking in the canner. For both canning and freezing: Don't add the sour cream now, but rather when you heat up the stroganoff for serving.

2 tablespoons butter
3 cloves garlic, minced
1 medium-size onion, halved and sliced into ½-inch pieces
1½ pounds boneless sirloin, cubed or thinly sliced

½ teaspoon freshly ground pepper
1 tablespoon soy sauce
2 cups mushrooms, whole or sliced
1 cup sour cream or more

continued

Melt butter in a pan. Add garlic and onions and sauté until onions are tender. Add meat, pepper, and 2 teaspoons soy sauce. Cook until juice is almost gone, about 10 minutes. Add mushrooms and cook for 5 minutes. Add the remaining 1 teaspoon soy sauce and, if serving now and not canning or freezing, the sour cream. Cook over low heat until heated through, 5 to 7 minutes.

Can or freeze. To can, pack hot into hot, scalded pint jars, leaving 1-inch headspace. Adjust seals and process in a pressure canner for 75 minutes. Remember to add sour cream to canned or frozen stroganoff when heating.

Yield: 3 pints

Hamburger Stroganoff
(to can or freeze)

Make the same adjustments when canning or freezing this ground meat version of stroganoff as recommended for the Beef Stroganoff recipe on page 519.

1½ pounds lean ground beef
3   cloves garlic, minced
1   medium-size onion, sliced
½   teaspoon freshly ground
    pepper
1   tablespoon soy sauce (you
    can add more)
2   cups mushrooms, sliced
1½ cups sour cream

In a medium skillet, cook beef for 10 minutes, or until done. Drain off fat. Add garlic, onions, pepper, and 2 teaspoons soy sauce, and cook until onions are tender. Add mushrooms and cook for 5 minutes. Add the remaining 1 teaspoon soy sauce and, if serving now and not canning or freezing, the sour cream. Let sauce just heat through, 5 to 7 minutes.

Can or freeze. To can, pack hot into hot, scalded pint or quart jars, leaving 1-inch headspace. Adjust seals and process in a pressure canner, 75 minutes for pints and 90 minutes for quarts. Remember to add sour cream to canned or frozen stroganoff when heating.

Yield: 6 servings

Texas Chili
(to freeze)

This is the real stuff. It's a very good dish for the freezer because it needs "resting time"—time for the spices to blend together. If you don't want to freeze it, at least refrigerate it overnight before serving.

3 to 5 dried red chili peppers,
    2 inches long (3 makes it
    medium-hot, 5 makes it
    hot-hot)
2 teaspoons cumin seeds
1 teaspoon coriander seeds
2 cloves garlic
½ cup water
2 tablespoons vegetable oil
3 pounds beef stew meat, cut
    into 1-inch chunks
3 tablespoons whole wheat
    flour
1 tablespoon chili powder
6 to 7 cups beef stock
1½ teaspoons dried oregano
1 tablespoon cornmeal
    (optional)

Combine peppers, cumin seeds, coriander seeds, and garlic in a small saucepan. Cover with ½ cup water and bring to a boil. Simmer for 15 minutes, or until chilies are soft, adding more water if needed.

Strain and reserve liquid. Using a mortar and pestle, mash chili mixture into a paste, using reserved liquid if necessary. (You can also combine spices and ½ cup water in a blender and blend on high speed until paste is formed.) Set aside while you warm the oil in a 6- or 8-quart saucepan. Add beef and brown over medium-high heat. Drain fat if necessary.

In a small bowl, combine flour and chili powder. Add to meat and stir to combine. Add chili paste and reserved liquid. Add stock and oregano and simmer gently for 2 to 3 hours. Let cool and freeze. When reheating, do so slowly, adding cornmeal to thicken if necessary.

Yield: 6 servings

Fruited Meat Loaf
(to freeze)

The flavors in this recipe are best after freezing, because they have a chance to mingle.

1¼ pounds lean ground beef
1 cup rolled oats
1 onion, chopped
1 egg, beaten
½ cup chopped raisins

½ cup grated apple, with water squeezed out (1 large apple)
1½ tablespoons Worcestershire sauce

In a medium-size bowl mix all ingredients until well combined.

Oil a 9 × 5-inch metal loaf pan and press mixture in firmly. Smooth top, wrap in plastic, and freeze.

To serve, defrost in refrigerator overnight. Bake at 350°F for 1 hour. Serve with warm applesauce or warm cranberry sauce.

Yield: 8 servings

Shepherd's Pie
(to freeze)

1¾ pounds potatoes
¼ cup milk, scalded
1 egg, slightly beaten
3 tablespoons softened butter
⅛ teaspoon nutmeg
1 tablespoon vegetable oil
1 pound boneless lamb, diced into 1-inch cubes
⅔ cup minced onions
½ cup minced celery
½ cup minced carrots
1 clove garlic, minced
2 tablespoons whole wheat flour

1¾ cups chicken or beef stock or water
¼ teaspoon ground thyme
¼ teaspoon ground basil
½ bay leaf
2 tablespoons tomato paste
½ cup frozen peas
3 tablespoons minced parsley
1 egg white
1 tablespoon grated Parmesan cheese

Halve potatoes. Put them in a medium-size saucepan and cover with cold water. Bring to a boil. Reduce heat and cook until tender. Drain and peel. Mash with milk, egg, 2 tablespoons butter, and nutmeg. Cover and set aside.

In a medium-size skillet, heat oil and cook lamb until browned. Set aside.

In a medium-size saucepan, melt 1 tablespoon butter. Add onions, celery, carrots, and garlic. Cook over medium heat 10 minutes or until vegetables are soft. Add flour and cook, stirring, 1 minute. Add ½ cup stock or water. Cook gently 1 minute.

Add remaining 1¼ cups stock or water, thyme, basil, bay leaf, and tomato paste. Bring to a boil. Reduce heat. Simmer 15 minutes. Add lamb and peas. Cook 10 minutes. Add parsley and cook for 5 more minutes. Discard bay leaf.

Line the sides of an oiled 2-quart casserole with two-thirds of the potato mixture. Brush with egg white. Pour lamb mixture into center. Spoon or pipe remaining potato mixture on top. Sprinkle with Parmesan cheese. Freeze now or bake for serving.

Bake just-made or thawed pie in a preheated 350°F oven for 30 minutes or until heated through.

Yield: 4 to 5 servings

Lamb-Stuffed Eggplant
(to freeze)

This delicious dish is an excellent way to use your garden eggplant.

2 medium-size eggplants	1 teaspoon dried oregano
2 tablespoons olive oil	¼ teaspoon ground red pepper
1 pound lean ground lamb	¼ teaspoon ground thyme
⅔ cup minced onions	⅛ teaspoon ground cumin
2 cloves garlic, minced	⅓ cup minced parsley
1 cup canned tomatoes, chopped, with liquid	1 cup cooked brown rice
1 cup beef stock	¼ cup shredded mozzarella cheese
2 tablespoons tomato paste	

Cut eggplants in half lengthwise. Scoop out pulp, leaving a ¼-inch shell. Chop pulp. Place shells in a baking dish.

In a large skillet heat olive oil. Add lamb, onions, and garlic. Sauté 3 to 5 minutes, stirring, until lamb is no longer pink. Add eggplant pulp and cook until tender, about 10 minutes, stirring frequently.

Add tomatoes, ¾ cup stock, tomato paste, oregano, pepper, thyme, and cumin. Bring to a boil. Lower heat. Simmer, partially covered, stirring occasionally, for 35 to 40 minutes. Add parsley and simmer 10 minutes. Remove from heat. Stir in rice.

Fill eggplant shells with lamb-rice mixture. Pour remaining ¼ cup stock into dish. Cover dish with foil. It can then be frozen if you'd like.

Bake in a preheated 375°F oven for 45 minutes or until eggplant is tender. Remove foil. Sprinkle with cheese. Bake uncovered about 2 minutes or until cheese melts. If frozen, partially thaw before baking, then bake at 375°F for 60 minutes. Continue as for unfrozen eggplant.

Yield: 4 servings

Variation

You may substitute ground beef, ground pork, or a combination for the lamb.

Sausage-Stuffed Apples
(to freeze)

6 large baking apples
¾ pound country-style bulk
    sausage
¾ cup finely chopped celery
¼ cup finely chopped onions
2 cups soft whole wheat bread
    crumbs
⅔ cup chicken stock or water
¼ teaspoon ground sage
⅛ teaspoon ground cinnamon
    dash of nutmeg

Slice ½ inch off top of apples and core. Scoop out pulp and chop finely. Reserve ½ cup pulp. Remaining pulp may be used in salads, muffins, and so on.

In a medium-size skillet, brown sausage over medium heat, breaking it up with a wooden spoon. Remove with a slotted spoon. Place celery and onions in skillet, and sauté for 5 minutes or until vegetables are tender. Stir in reserved chopped apple pulp and cook, stirring, for 2 to 3 minutes. Drain off any fat. Return sausage to skillet. Add bread crumbs, stock or water, sage, cinnamon, and nutmeg. Mix well. Stuff apples with this mixture. Freeze now if you wish.

Place apples in a baking dish that has been coated with vegetable spray. Bake in a preheated 350°F oven for 35 to 40 minutes or until apples are tender. If frozen, defrost slightly and bake for 50 minutes or until apples are tender.

Yield: 6 servings

Variations

1. Add ¼ cup finely chopped prunes to sausage mixture.
2. For a moister stuffing, combine 1 egg, slightly beaten, and ½ cup sour cream and add to sausage mixture.

Stuffed Green Peppers
(to freeze)

These freeze well, and if you freeze them individually, as described below, you've got hearty, 1-serving meals ready any time.

24	large green peppers	1	pound pork sausage
2	cups minced onions	1	pound ground beef
1	pound mushrooms, diced	6	cups cooked brown rice
3	cloves garlic, minced	4	eggs, beaten
3	tablespoons butter	1	cup grated Parmesan cheese

Cut off tops of green peppers, and remove seeds and membranes. Blanch peppers for 5 minutes.

Sauté onions, mushrooms, and garlic in butter until soft.

Brown sausage and beef in a separate skillet. Drain off excess fat. Add sausage-beef mixture, rice, eggs, and cheese to the sautéed vegetables. Combine. Stuff peppers.

To freeze, set peppers on a tray in the freezer. When completely frozen, wrap individually or in family-size portions in plastic bags or heavy-duty foil.

When ready to serve, preheat oven to 375°F. Place peppers upright in a covered casserole dish. Bake, covered, for approximately 1 hour.

Yield: 24 stuffed peppers

Italian Meat Sauce
(to can or freeze)

4	pounds ground beef	$2\frac{2}{3}$	cups tomato paste (4 6-ounce cans)
1	pound ground pork or sausage meat	1	tablespoon soy sauce
2	cups chopped onions	$\frac{1}{4}$	cup minced parsley
1	cup chopped green peppers	1	tablespoon dried oregano
9	cups whole tomatoes, chopped, with juice	2	tablespoons minced basil
		2	tablespoons vinegar

Brown beef and pork; add onions and green peppers and cook slowly until tender. Skim off excess fat. Add remaining ingredients and simmer several hours until thick.

Serve over pasta or use in casseroles or as base for lasagna.

Can or freeze. To can, pour hot into hot, scalded pint or quart jars, leaving 1-inch headspace. Adjust seals and process in a pressure canner 75 minutes for pints and 90 minutes for quarts.

Yield: about 6 pints or 3 quarts

Stuffed Pork Chops
(to freeze)

Have your butcher cut a pocket in each double pork chop.

¾ cup bulgur	¾ cup finely chopped celery
vegetable oil	½ teaspoon ground thyme
1½ cups water or stock	⅓ cup chopped parsley
1½ cups chopped onions	3 eggs, slightly beaten
¼ pound butter	12 double pork chops
1 cup chopped mushrooms	1 tablespoon soy sauce

To prepare bulgur, brown the grains lightly in a little oil in a heavy skillet. Add water or stock, bring to a boil, lower heat, cover, and simmer for 20 to 25 mintues until grains are light and fluffy.

Sauté onions in the butter until limp. Then add the mushrooms, celery, thyme, and parsley. Cook for another 5 minutes. Remove from heat and add bulgur and eggs.

Fill chop pockets with this mixture. Skewer with toothpicks to hold in stuffing.

To freeze, wrap in a package enough stuffed pork chops for a single meal, inserting a double thickness of freezer paper between the chops.

When ready to serve: While chops are still frozen, brush them with soy sauce, and broil until lightly browned on both sides. Bake, uncovered, in a 325°F oven for about 30 minutes, and then covered for about 1 hour.

Yield: 12 stuffed pork chops

Roast Venison

Venison benefits in texture from long marinating. If you have the time, marinate the meat in the refrigerator for 48 hours or more.

2 cups cider vinegar	2 cloves garlic, sliced
1 cup water	1 bay leaf
¼ cup Worcestershire sauce	3 peppercorns
2 slices peeled ginger root	1 venison roast (2 pounds)

In a large bowl, combine vinegar, water, Worcestershire sauce, ginger, garlic, bay leaf, and peppercorns. Add venison, cover, and let marinate in the refrigerator overnight, turning once.

Preheat oven to 350°F.

Set venison in pan and cover with marinade. Set pan in a larger pan that's filled with water. Cover venison loosely with a tent of foil. Bake 1½ hours for medium rare or 2½ hours for medium well.

Yield: 4 servings

Venison Stew
(to freeze)

The long, slow cooking results in tender meat in a rich gravy.

1 pound venison, cut coarsely
    into 2-inch cubes
¼ cup whole wheat flour
3 tablespoons vegetable oil
1 to 2 onions, coarsely chopped
2 cloves garlic, minced
3 to 4 carrots, coarsely chopped
3 pounds tomatoes, chopped
1 bay leaf
1 tablespoon celery seed

    Toss venison with flour. In a large stew pot, heat oil. Brown venison and then add onions, garlic, carrots, tomatoes, bay leaf, and celery seeds. Bring to a boil and then reduce heat to low. Cover and continue to cook for 3 hours. Remove bay leaf.

    If frozen, thaw and reheat in double boiler, or thaw, cover, and reheat in a 350°F oven for 30 minutes.

Yield: 8 servings

Hearty Beef Soup
(to can or freeze)

This stock may be canned or frozen, and so may the soup itself, if made from fresh, not previously canned or frozen, stock. We prefer freezing the soup because there is a texture and flavor loss in the canned version. In commercially canned foods like this, chemicals and salt are added to help preserve the texture and flavor. To minimize these losses in canning, follow the recipe for the stock as it is here, then prepare the soup as directed, leaving out the vegetables. Cook the soup for only 1 hour. After that time, add the vegetables and cook about 3 minutes; let them do their real cooking in the canner.

Beef Stock
2½ pounds beef bones
3 bay leaves
3 carrots, cut into chunks
3 peppercorns
3 tablespoons cider vinegar
1 onion, quartered
¼ cup parsley
3 quarts water

continued

In an 8-quart stockpot, combine all ingredients. Bring to a boil, cover, and then simmer for 3 hours. Let cool, skim fat, strain, and can or freeze. To can, pour hot into hot, scalded pint or quart jars, leaving 1-inch headspace. Adjust seals and process in a pressure canner 20 minutes for pints and 25 minutes for quarts.

Yield: 4 pints or 2 quarts

Hearty Beef Soup

2 quarts beef stock
3 tablespoons tomato paste
1 tablespoon soy sauce
2 teaspoons Worcestershire
    sauce
1 tablespoon cider vinegar
2 cups chopped potatoes
1 cup chopped carrots
1 cup chopped sweet red
    peppers
1 cup chopped green beans
2 pounds lean beef stew meat,
    cut into 1-inch cubes
¼ cup uncooked barley
1 teaspoon dried basil
1 teaspoon ground thyme
1 cup minced spinach or
    romaine lettuce

In a large stockpot, combine stock, tomato paste, soy sauce, Worcestershire sauce, and vinegar and bring to a boil.

Reduce heat and add potatoes, carrots, peppers, beans, meat, and barley. Cover and simmer for 2 hours.

Add basil, thyme, and spinach or romaine and simmer for 5 minutes more.

Can or freeze. To can, pack hot into hot, scalded pint or quart jars, leaving 1-inch headspace. Adjust seals and process in a pressure canner, 60 minutes for pints and 75 minutes for quarts.

Yield: 6 pints or 3 quarts

POULTRY DISHES

Turkey Chop Suey
(to freeze)

If you wish to freeze this, add the bean sprouts after thawing.

5 cups celery, cut diagonally into ½-inch strips	¼ cup vegetable oil
½ cup sliced onions	1½ cups mung bean sprouts
1 tablespoon soy sauce	1½ cups sliced water chestnuts or diced kohlrabi
¼ teaspoon pepper	½ cup cornstarch
1 tablespoon honey	½ cup cold water
2 quarts turkey stock	
2 quarts cooked turkey, in pieces	

Simmer celery, onions, soy sauce, pepper, and honey in stock for 20 minutes. Heat turkey in oil, and add turkey, bean sprouts, and water chestnuts or kohlrabi to the vegetable mixture. Blend cornstarch with cold water, and stir into the mixture. Simmer for 15 minutes, stirring frequently.

If frozen, thaw and reheat in double boiler. Add sprouts.

Yield: about 3 quarts

Sautéed Chicken with Egg Noodles
(to freeze)

If you wish to freeze this, add the broccoli and noodles after thawing.

1 tablespoon butter	1 teaspoon ground thyme
⅓ cup minced onions	1 tablespoon whole wheat flour
3 cloves garlic, minced	¾ cup chicken stock
1 pound boneless chicken, cut into 1½-inch squares	2 cups blanched broccoli florets
1 teaspoon ground basil	½ pound cooked Egg Noodles (see page 592)

Melt butter in a large skillet and sauté onions and garlic for about 3 minutes. Add chicken, basil, and thyme and cook for 10 minutes more.

Sprinkle chicken with flour. Add stock, stir, and cook gently until thick, 5 to 7 minutes. Add broccoli and noodles and toss to combine well.

Yield: 4 to 6 servings

Chicken Casserole
(to freeze)

1   10-ounce package frozen broccoli spears
1½ cups sliced cooked chicken
¼   cup butter (or substitute 2 tablespoons butter and 2 tablespoons vegetable oil)
2   cups sliced mushrooms
2   tablespoons whole wheat flour

½   cup milk
½   cup mayonnaise
½   cup shredded sharp cheese
1   teaspoon lemon juice
½   teaspoon freshly ground pepper
1   cup whole wheat bread crumbs

Preheat oven to 350°F. Steam broccoli for 5 minutes. Place spears in a greased 1½-quart baking dish. Lay chicken over top. In a medium-size skillet, melt 1 tablespoon butter. Add mushrooms and cook over low heat until tender. Strain off the juices. Remove mushrooms from pan and set aside. Melt 2 tablespoons butter in the same skillet over low heat. Add flour and whisk until mixture forms smooth paste. Add milk, reserved mushrooms, and mayonnaise, cooking on low heat until thickened. Add cheese, lemon juice, and pepper to the sauce. Pour over chicken.

Melt the remaining tablespoon of butter. Add bread crumbs, and stir until they are well coated with the melted butter. Then sprinkle them over the top of the casserole. Bake uncovered for 30 minutes.

Yield: 6 servings

Chicken Pot Pie
(to freeze)

This recipe will accommodate frozen, canned, or fresh cooked chicken. The casserole itself may also be frozen. But do not freeze if it contains meat that has once been frozen or canned.

Sour Cream Pastry
¼   cup butter, cut into ½-inch pieces
1¼ cups whole wheat pastry flour
4 to 5 tablespoons sour cream

Filling

½ pound potatoes, peeled and
    cut into ½-inch cubes
4 medium-size carrots, peeled
    and sliced diagonally ½ inch
    thick
2 to 3 cups chicken stock
¼ pound green beans, trimmed
    and cut into ½-inch lengths
¼ cup butter
¼ cup finely chopped celery
½ cup minced onions
½ cup whole wheat flour
⅛ teaspoon paprika
4 cups diced cooked chicken
    dash of lemon juice
1 egg
1 tablespoon milk

To make the pastry: In a small bowl, cut butter into flour. Add enough sour cream to hold dough together. Chill 30 minutes.

To make the filling: In a medium-size saucepan combine potatoes and carrots. Add enough stock to cover. Bring to a boil. Simmer 5 to 7 minutes or until barely tender. Remove vegetables with a slotted spoon. Add green beans and cook until barely tender. Drain, reserving stock.

Melt butter in a medium-size saucepan over medium-low heat. Add celery and onions and sauté 5 minutes or until vegetables are soft. Stir in flour and paprika and cook 2 minutes, stirring constantly. Remove from heat. Measure reserved stock and add additional stock to make 3 cups. Gradually add stock to saucepan and cook, stirring constantly, until mixture is smooth and thickened. Add chicken, lemon juice, and vegetables. Pour into a 2-quart ovenproof casserole dish.

Beat egg with milk.

Roll out pastry to fit casserole with a 2-inch overhang. Trim with shears. Crimp edges. Brush with beaten egg and then cut vents in top crust.

Bake in a preheated 375°F oven 35 to 40 minutes or until heated through and crust is golden brown. Frozen pot pie should not be thawed first, but should be baked 10 to 15 minutes longer.

Yield: 6 to 8 servings

Chicken Stock
(to can or freeze)

This rich stock cans and freezes well. You'll be glad you've got some frozen when you want to make gravy, chicken-based sauce, or soup. You can substitute turkey for the chicken.

12 cups water
2 chickens, 3½ pounds each
2 large celery stalks, sliced into 3-inch pieces
2 large carrots, sliced into 3-inch pieces
2 medium-size onions, halved

1 teaspoon freshly ground pepper
2 large cloves garlic, minced
1 tablespoon minced parsley, or 1½ teaspoons dried parsley

Put water, chickens, celery, carrots, onions, pepper, garlic, and parsley into a large stockpot. Bring to a boil and then reduce heat to a simmer. Cover and cook for 2 hours or until chicken is tender and falls off the bones. Strain and save the stock. You may chill the stock until the fat comes to the top, or just freeze in meal-size portions and remove the fat upon defrosting; it will have risen to the top and be quite easy to scoop off.

Clean chicken meat off the bones and freeze or can it for later use.

Can or freeze. To can, pour hot stock into hot, scalded pint or quart jars, leaving 1-inch headspace. Adjust seals and process in a pressure canner 20 minutes for pints and 25 minutes for quarts.

Yield: 8 pints or 4 quarts

Note: To make a double-rich chicken stock, substitute already-made chicken stock for the water.

Chicken Noodle Soup
(to freeze)

Leftover turkey is a fine substitute for the chicken.

8 cups chicken stock
2 large cloves garlic, minced
2 cups sliced carrots
1 cup diced celery
2 small onions, cut in half and sliced

1 pound cooked chicken, cubed
¼ pound thin whole wheat noodles
2 tablespoons soy sauce
1 tablespoon chopped parsley

Put chicken stock in a large saucepan and add garlic, carrots, celery, and onions. Simmer on low heat in a covered saucepan for about 45 minutes. Add chicken cubes and simmer for about 5 minutes. Add noodles, soy sauce, and parsley. Cook for about 10 minutes or until the noodles are tender.

Yield: 6 to 8 servings

Cream of Chicken and Rice Soup

¼ cup butter
¼ cup finely chopped onions
¼ cup finely chopped scallions
¼ cup finely chopped carrots
⅓ cup finely chopped celery
1 tablespoon minced parsley
1 clove garlic, minced
¼ cup whole wheat flour
4 cups chicken stock
¾ cup milk
4 ounces cream cheese, cut into
    bits and softened
1 egg yolk
2 cups shredded cooked chicken
1 cup cooked brown rice
    dash of ground nutmeg
⅛ teaspoon white pepper
    chopped parsley or scallions

Melt butter in a 3- or 4-quart saucepan. Add onions, scallions, carrots, celery, parsley, and garlic and sauté over low heat for 5 minutes. Cover and cook, stirring occasionally, for 10 minutes or until vegetables are soft.

Stir flour into mixture and cook for several minutes, stirring constantly (do not let brown). Remove pan from heat and gradually whisk in stock. Return to medium heat. Bring to a boil, whisking constantly, then reduce heat and simmer 5 minutes.

Purée the mixture in 2 batches, using a food processor or blender. Return purée to saucepan.

In a blender or food processor, blend together milk, cream cheese, and egg yolk. Slowly add to puréed soup along with chicken, rice, nutmeg, and white pepper. Heat through but do not boil.

Garnish with parsley or scallions.

Yield: 6 servings

Savory Chicken Vegetable Soup

8 cups chicken stock
1 clove garlic, minced
½ teaspoon dried basil
½ teaspoon celery seeds
¼ teaspoon ground ginger
1 teaspoon ground savory
½ teaspoon freshly ground
    pepper (fine)
1 cup cubed carrots
1 cup cubed potatoes
1 medium-size onion, cut in
    half and sliced
2 cups cubed cooked chicken
1 large tomato, seeded and
    chopped
1 cup corn
1 cup peas
1 cup string beans, cut in half
    lengthwise

Bring stock to a boil. Reduce heat and simmer with garlic, basil, celery seeds, ginger, savory, and pepper for about 20 minutes. Add carrots and potatoes and cook for about 10 minutes. Then add onions and cook until just tender, about 5 minutes. Add chicken, tomatoes, corn, peas, and string beans. Cook, covered, for about 15 minutes or until vegetables are tender.

Yield: 2½ quarts

Nuts, Seeds, Grains, and Sprouts

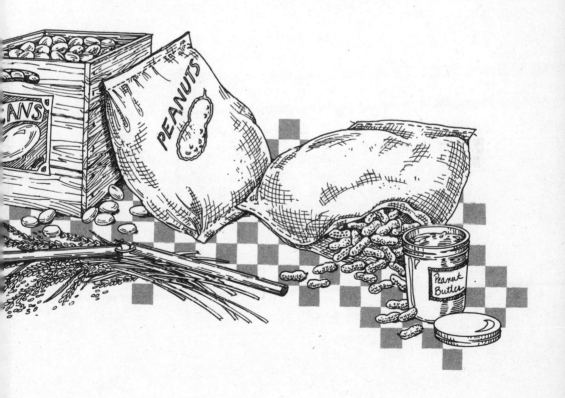

Nuts and Seeds

Nuts and seeds are food powerhouses. Despite their compact size, they are loaded with lots of good things: protein, vitamins, and minerals. And they are rich in fiber, too, but you pay a price for all these goodies in terms of fats and calories, so don't go overboard.

NUTS

Harvesting Tree Nuts

Nuts should be allowed to fully mature and fall from the tree naturally. Some growers, because they are impatient or want to make the harvesting easier, shake the trees to get the nuts to fall. Shake the tree if you wish, but shake gently. Harsh jolts may cause immature nuts to fall, and rough handling can damage the branches. Whatever method you use to get the nuts to the ground, be sure to gather them as soon as possible. Nuts left on the ground mold quickly, especially in damp weather. This is particularly true with English walnuts (also known as Persian or Chinese walnuts) and chestnuts. If you don't gather and hull the nuts of the black walnut promptly, the bitter fluid secreted in their hulls penetrates to the kernels and this discolors them and impairs their flavor. The nuts of the English walnut, if infested with husk maggots, will not open on the tree. Rather, the nuts will fall to the ground with the hulls still on them. In such cases, English walnuts should be picked from the ground soon after they fall and hulled like black walnuts (see page 540) before the dark, bitter fluid of the hulls penetrates the nutmeats.

Hulling Nuts

To get a light-colored, high-quality nut, black walnuts should be hulled before the hull turns black. The importance of hulling was proven to Spencer B. Chase of the Northern Nut Growers Association after the experiment he performed one year at harvesttime. Nuts from ten trees were collected, and the first batch was hulled within a few weeks after maturity. The remainder was hulled at weekly intervals. These hulled nuts were then stored and cured, and subsequently cracked open for inspection from the following January through March. "Without exception," says Mr. Chase, "the first batch of nuts, which had been hulled within a week after maturity, was light in color, mild in flavor, and could be eaten out of the hand like peanuts." This was not the case with the nuts hulled later at weekly intervals. These nuts produced "darker kernels and suffered considerably in flavor and overall quality." Most commercial walnut operations dip their nuts in a bleaching solution to get the light color which can be obtained naturally just by hulling the nuts as soon as they are mature.

There are several different ways of getting the tough but porous hulls off black walnuts. The old-fashioned corn sheller does a first-rate job when it is equipped with a flywheel and pulley and is driven by a ¼-horsepower motor. For small quantities of nuts—a few bushels or so—you can spread the nuts on a hard dirt or concrete road and drive over them with a car or truck until all the hulls are mashed. The trouble with this method is that the nuts tend to shoot out from under the wheels

It's not easy getting the hulls off black walnuts, but you can let your car do a lot of the work with a wooden hulling trough. Leave the trough open-ended so your car wheel can roll in and out. Drive slowly back and forth a few times, and the hulls will be cracked for easy removal. One word of advice: Wear gloves when you remove the hulls to prevent staining your skin.

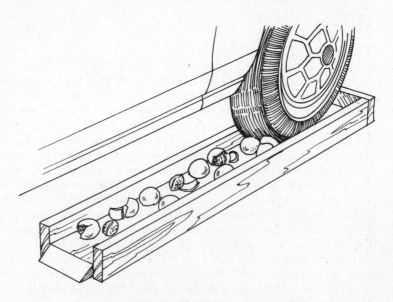

when the car rolls forward to crush them. Be ready to hunt for stray nuts and line them up again under the wheels. You can prevent the nuts from shooting out from under the wheels by placing a small quantity of nuts in a wooden trough that is just the width of the wheel. Leave off the crosspiece from one end of the trough and bevel the bottom board as in the illustration so that the wheel can roll in and out of it. Roll the wheel only slightly when crushing the nuts so that you don't drive right over the other end of the trough.

We learned the hard way that you really should wear thick rubber gloves to protect your hands when you're removing the hulls. The acrid fluid secreted from the hulls will leave persistent stains on your skin; no matter how hard you clean them, your hands will look dirty for weeks. It is this staining agent that also penetrates the hulls and stains the delicate kernels and otherwise impairs their quality and flavor. After hulling, wash the nuts, which are still in their inner shells, with a hose or put them in a tub and scrub them.

Not all nut varieties, however, will give you as much trouble as the black walnuts. The hulls of pecans, hickory nuts, English walnuts (if not infested with husk maggot), filberts, and chestnuts obligingly open on the tree and let the nuts fall to the ground, so harvesting is merely a matter of picking the nuts off the ground.

Drying Nuts

Once gathered (and hulled and washed, if need be), put the nuts in water, and discard the rotten and diseased nuts which float to the top. The nuts must then be dried or cured. Green, uncured nuts are bitter and unpalatable. To dry the nuts, spread them out rather thinly on a dry, clean surface and allow them to dry gradually by exposure to a gentle, but steady, movement of air. A clean, cool, darkened, well-ventilated attic or porch is ideal. Nuts dried this way will not be attacked by fungus or mildew. When done properly, such drying will make for light-flavored, light-colored nut kernels. The nuts may also be spread thinly on wire trays or window screens. Nuts should not be spread more than two deep on such trays and screens. Some growers use deep wire baskets, but they are careful to pour the nuts every 4 days from one basket into another to prevent mildew from forming.

Drying time varies with nut variety. All nuts except chestnuts contain a great amount of oil. This oil prevents nuts from drying out completely and from becoming hard and brittle. Chestnuts contain little oil, but they do contain much water and many carbohydrates. Because of their high water and carbohydrate content, chestnuts dry out easily and become hard and inedible. Dry chestnuts only for 3 to 7 days. All other nuts need several weeks to dry properly.

Walnuts, pecans, filberts, and hickory nuts are dry enough to be stored when the kernels shake freely in their shells, or when the kernels break with a sharp snap when bent between the fingers or bitten with the teeth. Avoid excessive drying, which will cause the nut shells to crack.

After drying, nuts still in their shells may be stored in attics for up to a year, but cool underground cellars are preferable for longer storage. Storage containers for nuts may be made from large plastic bags with ventilation holes punched in them to allow air to circulate and excess moisture to escape. Then put these bags in tin cans lined with paper. Keep them tightly closed, but punch a small hole in the can below the lid. Store the nuts at 34° to 40°F and check regularly for mold and mildew.

Some nut growers store their unshelled nuts in peat moss and other moisture-absorbing materials. By so doing, there is no need to allow for ventilation because the peat moss takes care of excess moisture that would cause mildew. Prepare peat moss for nut storage by moistening it with just enough water to prevent its being dusty. It should be damp, but not wet. Add about one-third as much peat moss as nuts by volume when packing nuts in lidded cans or plastic bags.

Nuts may also be packed in clean, dry sand and then stored in a cool area. Stored this way, nuts will retain their germinating powers (should you wish to plant them to start new trees), but may lose some of their flavor.

Cracking Nuts

You can crack a nut with almost anything that does the job. You can use a hammer with a block of wood or metal. Or you can swing a heavy iron like the one your grandmother used to iron shirts. There are other ways as well. Take wild foods gourmet Euell Gibbons, for example. Here are his instructions for shelling black walnuts, especially hard nuts to crack:

"If you stand the nut—pointed end up—on a solid surface and hit it with a sharp blow with a hammer, it will crack into two halves. Stand each half, again pointed end up, and strike it again, which will break it into quarters. Strike each quarter again on the pointed end, and it will break into eighths—at which point the nutmeats fall out. When the nuts are well dried, you should be able to completely empty shell after shell without resorting to a nutpick with this method."

And his secret for shelling hickory nuts:

"Put the unshelled nuts in the deep-freeze for a day, then remove a few handfuls at a time and shell them while they are still frozen and brittle. The nuts are narrower one way than the other, so hold them up edgewise and strike each a sharp blow with the hammer, just hard enough to crack the shell but not smash the kernel. Cracked this way, many entire halves can be removed while the others usually have to come out in quarters."

Hard-shelled nuts are more easily shelled if the shells are softened first. You can do this by pouring boiling water over the nuts and allowing them to stand for 15 to 20 minutes before shelling. Another method of softening the nuts is to place them in a container, sprinkle them with water, and cover them first with a damp cloth and then the container cover. Let them stand this way for 12 to 24 hours. The shells will be easier to crack, and the nutmeats will not splinter when the shells are cracked.

You can peel off the shells of soft-shelled nuts like chestnuts with a knife. To do so, first cut across the base of the nut to allow steam to escape so that the nut won't explode, and then place the nut in boiling water for 3 to 4 minutes. The shell will then pull off easily.

Harvesting and Curing Peanuts

One sign that peanut plants are ready to harvest is when the leaves begin to yellow. To make sure they're ready at this time, dig up a plant or two from different rows and check the nuts, especially those under the main part of the plant, because this is where your big harvest is. If the nuts are fully developed, the skins are light pink and papery thin, and the veins inside the pods have begun to darken in color. Harvest when about 80 percent of your crop is ready. You can wait until after frost to dig up if you must, but don't allow any dug-up peanuts to sit out during freezing temperatures; frost gives them an unpleasant taste.

When harvesttime arrives, lift each bush carefully out of the soil with a garden fork, and shake it free of all dirt. You might want to run your fingers through the dirt left in the hole to rescue any peanuts that have broken off.

Peanuts need to be cured in the sun. You can do this by making small "haystacks" of them right in the garden and leaving them there for a few weeks, or by laying them one layer deep up off the ground in a sunny place for several days. A picnic table is good, although not big enough for a sizable harvest; the tin roof of a shed works well for at least one of *Rodale's Organic Gardening* writers. If you have a small crop, you can remove them from the vines and lay them out on boards for a few days. When the vines dry, you can remove the pods and then put them in a burlap sack and hang the sack in a dry place for a few weeks. Do not cover the peanuts with anything that doesn't let air pass through it because they'll most likely get moldy without good ventilation. Never store in a cool, damp basement, as the moisture still in the uncured pods will cause them to mildew and rot. Two months of curing time will make the peanuts fit for roasting (see below) or for storing more permanently.

Storing Shelled Nuts

Shelled nuts don't store as well as those with their shells intact. Without their protective shells, nutmeats are exposed to light, heat, moisture, and air—all of which cause rancidity in the nut. If you plan to keep your nuts for a while, crack them as you need them. Nutmeats can be stored safely for a few months under refrigeration if they are placed in tight-closing jars or sealed plastic bags. They may also be frozen.

In the last edition of *Stocking Up* we gave directions for canning nutmeats, but we no longer advise it. In our most recent taste tests we found that canned nuts lose much of their good flavor—so much so that the work involved in canning is simply not worth it. The Agricultural Extension people at Pennsylvania State University agree with us, and home economists at Ball Canning Company have told us that Ball no longer includes canning nuts in their *Blue Book*.

Nutmeats will keep well at freezer temperatures for up to 2 years or so, as long as they are stored in airtight containers or sealed plastic freezer bags.

Savory Roasted Peanuts

2 cups peanuts
2 teaspoons soy sauce

Preheat oven to 300°F.

Skin the nuts, if you wish. Place the nuts in a bowl, and pour the soy sauce over them. Mix the nuts so that they're coated with the soy sauce.

Spread them on a baking sheet and bake for about 20 minutes, stirring once or twice, until the nuts are lightly roasted. Watch the nuts carefully in the last few minutes of roasting so that they don't become too dark.

Roasted peanuts are best kept in the refrigerator or freezer.

Yield: 2 cups

SUNFLOWER SEEDS

The back of a thoroughly ripe sunflower head is brown and dry, with no trace of green left in it. But the trouble with leaving it in the field until that point is that the birds may have harvested the crop for you, or the head may have shattered and dropped many of its seeds to the ground.

Harvesting the Seeds

In the home garden, sunflower seeds may be covered with cheesecloth to keep away birds. Or the heads may be cut off when the seeds are large enough and allowed to dry elsewhere. If cut with a foot or two of stem attached, they may be hung in a dry, well-ventilated place to finish drying. They may also be cut and spread on boards on the ground—protected with a wire screening from rodents—to dry in the sun for a couple of weeks. Heads should not be piled on top of each other, as seeds may rot or become moldy. If you've only got a small amount, you can dry them in a low-temperature oven or food dryer.

The heads are dry and ready to have their seeds removed when the rough stalks are brittle and the seeds separate from the head easily as you run your thumb lightly over the surface of the head. You can brush the seeds out with a stiff brush, a fish-scaler, or a currycomb; or you can remove them by rubbing the heads over a screen of $\frac{1}{2}$-inch hardware cloth stretched over a box or barrel. If some seeds are still moist, they may be spread out to complete drying after being removed from the head.

Hulling the Seeds

Hand hulling is a very tedious task and not recommended for more than a handful of seeds. To make the hand-hulling job easier, put the seeds in boiling water for a short time. You can also crack the shells with pliers or a clothespin. Lay the seed between the prongs as you would between your teeth, so that it will be cracked lengthwise.

To hull larger quantities, a hand-cranked or motorized grain mill does a serviceable job. You may need to run the seeds through the mill twice. Grade the seeds first so that you remove small and cracked ones. To do this, just sift your seeds through a $\frac{3}{16}$-inch mesh screen. Throw out those seeds and scraps that fall through, and hull those that remain on top of the screen.

You can also use any small farm hammermill. A 10-inch size is adequate. Remove screens and set the mill to run at 350 revolutions per minute. You can use a tachometer (which measures the speed of rotation) to judge so no hulled seeds go up the dust collector. Slowly pour in about 2 gallons of seeds, then speed up the mill to 1,200 to 1,500 revolutions per minute. This clears the mill so that it won't clog at the bottom. Such a mill will hull out about 80 percent or more of the seeds.

Local feed mills may be willing to shell sunflower seeds in amounts too large for hand hulling if you haven't a hammermill or a quantity large enough to make purchasing one practical.

After hulling you'll want to remove the hulls from the loose seeds, a process called winnowing. About the simplest way to do this is to toss seeds and hulls into a shallow pan of water and swirl them around a bit. The lighter hulls will rise to the surface, where they can be skimmed off. Then remove the seeds and dry them well.

Storing the Seeds

Dried seeds should be stored in a cool, dry place in small containers and should be stirred once or twice a week to prevent mustiness. You can also freeze them. If packed in freezer containers or freezer bags, sunflower seeds will keep for a year at freezer temperatures.

Savory Sunflower Seeds

3 tablespoons vegetable oil
3 tablespoons soy sauce
1 pound sunflower seeds

Preheat oven to 250°F.

In a shallow pan combine the oil and soy sauce and mix well. Then add the seeds and toss so that they are all coated with the oil-and-soy-sauce mixture.

Bake for 20 to 25 minutes, stirring occasionally. When done, the seeds should be dry and rich brown in color.

Cool before eating or storing. For storing, place in a plastic bag or jar and store in the refrigerator or freezer for best keeping.

Yield: about 3 cups

PUMPKIN SEEDS

If you're planning to grow pumpkins for the seeds as well as the flesh, choose a variety that is hull-less, like Lady Godiva, or partially hulled, like Triple Treat. Don't store the pumpkins long after harvest; seed them and freeze the meat instead, if you want to keep it.

To remove the seeds break the pumpkin by smashing it against the ground and then pulling it apart with your hands, rather than cutting it with a knife; a knife will probably cut through some of the seeds. Then just scoop out the seeds with your fingers and put them in a bucket with some warm water. Leave them in this water for a few days until the fiber attached to the seeds weakens, and the seeds sink to the bottom. The fiber will float to the top where it can be skimmed off. Then strain out the seeds and dry them.

You can dry them in the sun between clean screens, or dry small quantities in a very-low-temperature oven or a food dryer set at 90°F.

Storing the Seeds

Like sunflower seeds, pumpkin seeds can be stored in plastic bags or jars with lids in a cool, dry place. Stir them once in a while and check over them to make sure the seeds are really dry. You can also freeze them for up to a year.

NUT AND SEED BUTTERS

The peanut butter and jelly sandwich is practically an American tradition; it's part of every kid's diet. But peanut butter need not be paired only with jelly (try it with sliced bananas or honey), nor must it be relegated only to sandwiches (it's good as an ingredient in many breads and muffins, and in sauces for meats, fish, rice, and vegetables). While peanuts make a very good nut butter, cashews, almonds, pecans, and seeds like sesame, sunflower, and pumpkin seeds, also make good butters. Pumpkin seeds are best blended with other seeds and/or nuts to make butter. Sesame butter, also called tahini, has a strong flavor and is not good as a spread by itself. But it is wonderful as an ingredient in certain soups and sauces. Middle Eastern cookbooks will give you several ideas for using it.

If you have a blender or a food processor, you can make nut and seed butters at home easily. Here's how:

To make about 1 cup of butter, put 1½ cups nuts or seeds into your blender or food processor (use the metal blade). If you want to make more than 1 cup of butter, do it in batches. A blender or food processor can only handle about 1½ cups of nuts at a time; the dense consistency puts a strain on the machine. You can use roasted or unroasted nuts and seeds. If you leave the skins on, you'll have a butter richer in fiber and nutrition.

Blend or process for 1 minute, turning the machine off every 10 seconds, until you've got a thick paste. Then add oil or boiling water slowly, starting with just 1 tablespoon, to get the clumping action started. Add more only if you need it to smooth and thin the butter. Be careful not to go overboard with the oil or water. The heat of the blending or processing releases oils in the nuts or seeds so you may need less than you first think. And different kinds of nuts and seeds need different amounts of oil or water.

Turn the machine off every 30 seconds during this final stage, which may take about 3 minutes in a food processor and 5 minutes in a blender.

If you want a chunky butter, make a smooth butter first and then add whole nuts or seeds and process for 15 to 30 seconds more.

We found that the blender makes a smoother butter than a food processor, but they're both good—richer and fresher-tasting than most butters you can buy.

Grains

We're starting this chapter not at the real beginning, but somewhere in the middle, under the assumption that most of you who are reading this are more interested in storing the flour or the baked goods, rather than the grains. If, however, you want to harvest and store homegrown grains, we have not forgotten you; just skip to page 554.

REALLY FRESH FLOUR

The freshest flour comes from grain you've just ground yourself. Real bread-baking enthusiasts say there's no comparison. Grind it just before you need it, for grinding will expose the germ, which will turn rancid in the presence of oxygen and warm temperatures. Rancidity destroys vitamins E, A, and K and has been found to destroy several of the B vitamins. If you have ground extra, or have bought fresh-ground flour, store it in the refrigerator, or, better yet, in the freezer.

■ Do not use cold flour when you're baking with yeast. Leave the cold flour at room temperature for a few hours before you use it for baking so that the yeast will not be chilled and become inactivated.

If flour stored in a pantry becomes infested, it can still be used, provided the infestation is not severe. Follow the directions on page 559 for killing grain-loving insects. Then clean the flour by straining it through a sieve.

STORING BREAD

Before the time of factory-made bread, all bread was made at home and one day a week was set aside as bread-baking day. On that day, the baker of the household would rise before dawn and build a roaring fire in the brick oven. By mid-morning, when the oven's inner walls were thoroughly heated, the glowing embers would be shoveled out. Then the bread, which had been mixed, kneaded, left to rise, shaped into loaves, and left to rise again, would be placed in the oven. The heavy iron oven door would be closed and sealed tightly with clay so that no heat could escape, and the bread would be left to bake for the rest of the morning and afternoon. The farmhouse soon would be filled with the sweet yeasty smell of baking bread, and by early evening there would be enough loaves cooling in the kitchen to last a family of 10 or 12 for a week, until the next bread-baking day came around.

It made good sense then—and still does today—to bake a number of loaves at one time. Although we're spared the chore of building a fire in the brick oven, we still must mix and knead the dough, let it rise twice, and bake it. It takes just about as long to prepare and bake a double or triple bread batter as it does a single one. Once you have the kneading board out, the bread pans lined up, and your hands covered with flour, you might as well go ahead and bake 4 loaves instead of 2.

What do you do with all those loaves after they're baked? Farm wives used to put them in a wooden box especially made for keeping bread, cover them with a clean towel, and store them in a cool place. The bread tasted just great for the first few days, but as the week wore on the bread started to get a little stale—no preservatives to keep bread "tasting" fresh forever, then.

Freezing Baked Bread

Today we're more fortunate. We have a way of keeping bread fresh for months, not by adding sodium or calcium propionate or another bread freshener to our breads, but by using the freezer.

Baked yeast breads retain their just-baked quality at freezer temperatures for 6 to 8 months. Prepare and bake your loaves according to the recipe. Allow them to cool in a draft-free place (drafts tend to shrink baked goods) thoroughly before wrapping for the freezer. Warm or hot breads which are wrapped tightly will emit water vapor while they cool, and this water vapor will condense on the inside of their wrappings. This moisture can lead to the growth of mold even under the most sanitary of conditions. Cool breads first and then wrap in aluminum foil or heavy-duty plastic bags. Then freeze them.

Freezing Breads

Food	Preparation	Approximate Storage Time	Thawing and Using
Quick Breads			
Biscuits and muffins	Cool completely; wrap individually in foil or place in plastic bags.	3 to 6 months	Thaw at room temperature for 1 hour, or heat frozen, in foil, at 300°F for 20 minutes.
Fruit and nut breads	Cool completely; wrap in plastic wrap or foil, or place in plastic bags.	3 to 6 months	Thaw in package at room temperature for 45 minutes. Or warm in foil, when thawed, at 400°F for 10 minutes.
Waffles	Bake to light brown, cool, and wrap individually in foil or place in plastic bags.	1 to 2 months	Remove from package and heat in toaster.
Yeast Breads			
Baked	Cool completely; wrap in foil or place in plastic bags.	6 to 8 months	Thaw at room temperature for 45 to 60 minutes, or heat in foil in a 250°F oven for 30 minutes. Reheat in foil at 400°F for 10 minutes.
Unbaked	Wrap in plastic wrap.	3 to 4 weeks	Thaw at room temperature before rising and baking.

Excerpted from *Rodale's Basic Natural Foods Cookbook*, Rodale Press, 1984.

Thawing Bread

Frozen breads should be thawed in a low oven or at room temperature while still in their wrappers. If you like to thaw your breads in a low oven, your freezer wrap should be aluminum foil. Slice bread while still fresh, but cool, and then freeze the whole loaf, so you can easily take out frozen slices as you need them. The slices will thaw and toast at the same time and taste just as good as fresh toasted bread.

Start with Moist Breads

Bread should be eaten soon after it has thawed, for thawed bread dries out quickly. To keep your bread from becoming stale too rapidly after thawing, begin with a recipe that makes a moist bread. One that calls

MAKING BREADS MOISTER

- Use cottage cheese, yogurt, or butter-milk as the liquid in recipes.

- Use vegetable oil instead of butter. Add fruits and vegetables (crushed, stewed, blended, grated, raw, dried, or juiced).

- Use potato water in place of any water called for.

- Substitute ½ cup cooked cereal or rice for ½ cup of the unbleached or whole wheat flour called for.

- Add fresh corn to quick bread recipes.

- Use honey or barley malt as your sweetener instead of sugar.

- Add ½ cup mashed potatoes to your recipe.

- Add peanut butter or cashew butter to your recipe.

- Add the minimum amount of flour; too much will create a dry, heavy loaf.

- Don't let your bread rise longer than necessary; too long a rising period can dry out the dough.

- Watch the baking time; don't over-bake.

- Watch your oven temperature and check to see that the thermometer reads true; low oven temperatures will dry out bread because it must bake longer than necessary.

for honey will make a moister loaf than one that uses sugar, corn syrup, cane syrup, maple sugar, or molasses as a sweetener. The more honey you use, the moister your bread will be and the longer it will keep. Honey is hygroscopic. It absorbs moisture from the air and holds this moisture in bread. Recipes that call for a good amount of oil will also make a moist bread that will keep for a longer time because shortening doesn't dry out. See the above box for other ideas.

Don't freeze French and Italian breads unless you know that you're going to finish off the entire loaf soon after it is thawed, or unless you have a use for stale, dried-out bread. French and Italian breads do not contain oil or butter, so they dry out very quickly.

■ If your thawed bread starts to dry out and get stale, do what the farm wives used to do with their 6-day-old bread: Rejuvenate it by sprinkling a little water on it and putting it in the oven for a few minutes. You can also lay a flat strainer above a pot of boiling water or cooking vegetables or soup or anything you've got on the stove, and place slices of bread in the strainer. Put the lid over the bread. The steam rising from the pot below will moisten and warm your dry pieces of bread.

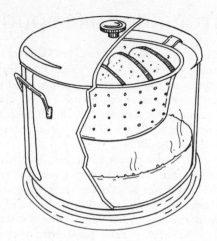

Don't throw away dried-out bread—steam it back to life. Boil some water in a large pot and hook a strainer with your bread in it onto the lip of the pot. Put the lid on the pot, allow the water to simmer, and in a minute or two you'll have moist, warm bread.

Freezing Unbaked Bread Dough

If you're the kind of person who goes crazy over the taste and smell of bread right from the oven and would rather take the time to bake every day just so that you can enjoy just-baked bread all the time, don't despair; here's a shortcut for you. Just freeze your bread *before* it's baked, and then when you're ready for a loaf, let it thaw and rise, and bake it as you would freshly risen dough. Your kitchen can smell like it's bread-baking day every day even though you only get your hands and the kneading board floury once a week.

Unbaked yeast dough can only be stored in the freezer for 3 to 4 weeks. Use twice the amount of yeast the recipe calls for; all the other ingredients stay the same. Mix and knead it the way you usually do, then allow it to rise once. When it's risen to double its bulk, punch it down, shape it into loaves, and freeze it. Your loaves should be thinner than usual—no more than 2 inches deep—so that they will thaw quickly when taken from the freezer. When you're ready for a fresh loaf, thaw the dough at room temperature then bake as usual.

■ Dry yeast sold in foil packets will keep for months in the refrigerator, but yeast cakes are much more perishable. The expiration date for both packets and cakes is marked on the outside of the package. Yeast cakes may be frozen for up to 6 months. To use, thaw at room temperature and use immediately. To tell if your yeast cake is still active, rub a small amount between your fingers. If it crumbles, it is still usable; if it is pasty, it should be discarded.

STORING STORE-BOUGHT GRAINS

Whole rice, wheat berries, buckwheat, oats, rye, barley, and all other kinds of grains that you might have for cooking store fine for several months at room temperature, provided that you keep them in airtight containers, like closed plastic bags or glass jars with screw lids. This is assuming that they are well cured, which they should be if you bought them (but might not be if you dried them yourself and are unsure of how dry they should be).

Partially processed grains, like oatmeal and oat flakes, couscous, kasha, and, of course, flours, will not keep quite so well this way, but will be fine for several weeks, so long as you keep them in a place that doesn't get too warm and that is out of direct sun. If you plan to keep them any longer, freezing is your best bet.

Sometimes grains are infested with insects when you get them, and no matter how well you store them, you'll notice little grain moths or other insects in your kitchen. Check your jars and bags for bugs, and if you don't find any, the infestation probably isn't too heavy. You can kill off what bugs you do have by putting all your grains (and nuts and dried fruits, which could also be harboring the culprits) in your freezer for about 3 days or more. The freezing temperatures will do in any insects, and your grains will be salvaged. For more exotic extermination methods, see page 560.

HARVESTING AND STORING YOUR OWN GRAINS

Baking your own breads is one thing; making them from grain you grew yourself is something else again. Granted, not everyone has such commitment to do-it-yourselfism, but if you're so inclined, find yourself a copy of *Small-Scale Grain Raising* by Gene Logsdon (Rodale Press, 1977— now out-of-print, but probably available in some libraries) and read about how to do it. Growing it isn't difficult at all; what little hard work there is comes at the end, when you must harvest, grind, and store the grains.

If you were a big operator, you would wait until your grain was dead ripe and had dried down to a moisture content of about 14 to 14½ percent, and then get out the combine that would do the whole job of harvesting: cutting the stems, beating the grain loose from the hulls, and separating the straw and chaff from the grains. Then you would run the grain through a mechanical fan seed cleaner to remove the wild plants and seeds that were harvested with the grain. After the grain was cleaned you might machine dry it to prevent it from heating up and spoiling and to retard mold and fungus growth during storage. Then you would pour the cleaned, dry grain into 100-pound sacks and store them in an atmospherically controlled warehouse.

Harvesting by Hand

A combine costs several thousand dollars, and unless a neighbor has one that can be borrowed, a grower with only a small amount of grain to harvest will have to do it the old-fashioned way and harvest the grains by hand. (The cutting can be done with a sickle-bar on a garden tractor, but the machine running over the heads may cause the grain to shatter onto the ground.)

Harvesting by hand involves cutting the grain before it is completely ripe (contrary to combine harvesting), then binding the stalks into sheaves, arranging the bundles into shocks, and allowing the grain to remain drying in the field until it is ripe. The best way to tell if the wheat is ready to cut is to pull a few heads and shell out the grain in the palms of your hands with a rubbing motion. The wheat should come free from its husks fairly easily, but not too easily. Blow the chaff out of your cupped hand and chew a few grains. They should feel hard when you bite into them. If the grain is still milky, wait a few more days. If the grains are very hard and shatter out of the husks very easily, you've waited too long. The stalks should be nearly all yellow, with only a few green streaks remaining. When wheat is dead ripe, there is no more green in the stalk.

Rye should be harvested in the almost-ripe stage, which it usually reaches about a week before the wheat does. Oats are hand harvested when the kernels can be dented by the thumbnail—not too hard and not too soft—when the heads are yellow and some leaves are still green. Buckwheat, which takes longer to mature, should be harvested after the first seeds mature. Ideally, this is after one or two frosts have made the grains easier to separate from the plants.

Cradling

To harvest by hand, cut the stems near the ground after the dew is off, on a dry day. To do this properly, you need a grain cradle. A grain cradle is a scythe equipped with 3 or 4 long wooden tines arranged about 6 inches apart above the scythe blade. When you swing the cradle, the cut stalks of grain gather against the wooden tines as you make your stroke through the standing grain. The cut stalks then fall in a neat little pile to the left of the swath you are cutting as you complete your stroke. These little piles are then easily tied into bundles.

It takes practice to develop the proper rhythm for cradling. But if

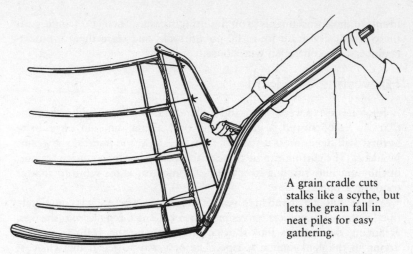

A grain cradle cuts stalks like a scythe, but lets the grain fall in neat piles for easy gathering.

you've ever done scything, you can catch on to it in a hurry. The trick of scything is to cut a rather narrow strip, letting the scythe blade slice through the standing stalks at a sidewise, 45-degree angle. Don't try to whack off the stalks with the blade at right angles to the stalks. The blade should be very sharp and always be held parallel to the ground. Don't let the point dip down to catch the ground.

If a grain cradle isn't available, an ordinary scythe will do. This cuts the stalks, but instead of letting the grain fall in convenient piles, it lets the stalks fall where they are cut. This means that you have to gather the stalks in bundles, which could become a laborious job if you've got a big area to harvest. A hedge trimmer could conceivably be used to cut down the grain, too. Like a scythe, a hedge trimmer would let the stalks fall haphazardly, making gathering difficult. It wouldn't give you the aching arm and back a manually operated cradle or scythe would, but you would have to consider the practicality of using a power tool in the field. You would have to have an extra-long extension cord for an electrically powered trimmer or get one that runs on gasoline.

After the stalks are cut, tie them into bundles with ordinary binder twine, available from farm stores. A bundle should measure about 8 inches in diameter at the tie. The bundles are then set up in shocks.

Building the Shocks

To build a shock, grab a bundle in each hand, set the butt ends firmly down on the ground, and then lean the tops against each other. Two more bundles are set the same way on either side of the first ones. Sometimes your beginning shocks will fall over until you get the knack of it. With the first 4 bundles in place, you can then stand about 6 or 8 more evenly around them. When you have a fairly sturdy shock of 12 bundles or so, you can tie a piece of twine around the whole shock to make it stand more solidly. After the shocks dry in the sun for about 10 days (a few days longer for oats), put the bundles in an airy shelter where no rain will fall on them to finish ripening.

Threshing

Before the advent of the combine, a steam-powered threshing machine would make the rounds and farmers would take their sheaves down out of the mow and feed it to the roaring, hungry monster. Before that—for thousands of years, and it's still done this way in many parts of the world—people beat the grain out of the hulls with flails.

You can make a simple flail by taking an old broom handle and drilling a $\frac{1}{4}$-inch hole near one end. Then similarly drill a $\frac{3}{4}$-inch stick about 1 foot long and attach it loosely to the broom handle with a leather or wire loop through the drilled hole. Throw a sheaf of wheat on the threshing floor—a clean garage or cellar floor or a hard-packed piece of ground free of growth or debris. Then beat the heck out of the sheaf with the loose end of the flail; the grain will easily fall out.

A flail isn't the only instrument you can use for this job, though. Gene Logsdon, who raises the grain his family uses each year, uses a flail he made himself, but he recommends trying a plastic baseball bat instead. His son used it and found that it worked better than the flail because it was firm enough to knock the kernels out, but flexible enough not to crack the grains. David Criner in Arkansas uses a compost shredder to thresh his grain. He places a tarpaulin under the shredder to catch the grain and feeds the bundles of wheat—one at a time, head first—into the shredder chute. You could also wham a handful of stems against the inside of a barrel. The grain falls neatly into the barrel instead of flying around and landing in a wide area on the floor.

Removing the Chaff

Once the straw bundles are relieved of their grain and removed, there still remain lots of chaff with the grain. Traditionally, grain was winnowed simply by slowly pouring it from a height of a couple of feet into a bucket on a day when there was a brisk breeze. The wind blew away the light husks, and the heavier grain fell directly to the bucket. (If the day you pick is windless, use an electric fan to generate a winnowing wind; it works like a charm. But if the day you choose is quite windy, wait for another day. A strong wind could blow both the grain and chaff away.) Repeat this process until the grain is clean, or nearly so. A few grains may not hull out completely, but this will not affect the flour.

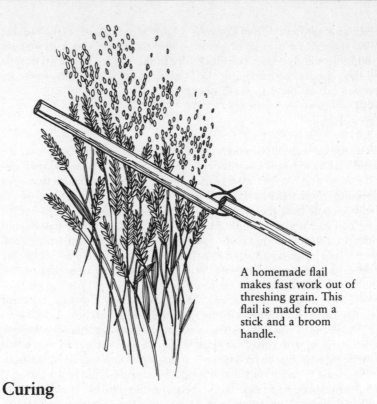

A homemade flail makes fast work out of threshing grain. This flail is made from a stick and a broom handle.

Curing

If you harvested your grain when it was almost ripe and allowed it to dry in the field for at least a week or so, the moisture content of your grain is probably somewhere between 12 and 15 percent. If this is the case, your grain is dry enough to store as is, although it should be cured for at least 1 month before you try to mill it for flour. Green grain heats up and gums up a flour mill, and the flour is difficult to work with. Grain makes much better bread if it is allowed to cure longer than a month.

If the weather should be damp when you harvest the grain, and it rains while the grain is curing in the field, there is a good chance that its moisture content is somewhere above 15 percent. If you store high-moisture grain you are inviting all kinds of trouble. Mold, fungi, beetles, and mites thrive in moist grain. Wet grain should be dried before it is stored. The drier the grain, the less susceptible it is to damage by bacteria, fungi, and insects.

A small quantity of wet grain may be dried by putting it into a box that is enclosed with screen wire on all 6 sides. Ordinary house screen wire should be reinforced with ½-inch wire mesh to support the weight of the grain. The wet grain may also be poured into bags and placed on end on slats in a dry place, preferably not on a concrete or earth floor.

After a few days the boxes or bags should be inverted and the grain stirred to permit air to get to all the kernels. Invert again in a week or so and allow it to cure at least 1 month before attempting to store or mill it.

Keeping Rats Out of Your Grain

Dry grain keeps best when stored in a cool, dry place. It may be stored in bags on slats, so long as precautions are taken against rat infestation. Rats are capable of doing severe damage to stored foods. Not only can they consume many pounds of food in a year, they can also contaminate foods by carrying into the storage area insects and bacteria. You'll know you have a rat problem when you see droppings, tracks, and grease marks. In dusty locations you may notice tracks left by the trail of a tail and the four-toed rear paws. Storing bags of grains in a cellar or outbuilding that has double walls and space between floors and ceilings invites rat problems because such structures provide ideal homes for these rodents. Choose a storage area that is rat-tight and provides no hidden areas in which rats can nest.

Many commercial warehouses take care of rat problems by using rodenticides. These poisons are not only toxic to rats, but to domestic animals and humans as well. At home, rat infestation can be prevented by making sure the storage area is clean and rodent-proof. Having a couple of good-working felines around to patrol the area is also a good idea. Perhaps the simplest and most logical way to protect your grain is to store it in metal drums in a dry place—not in the cellar, if possible, although this is all right, too, if the cellar is dry and the drums are kept a couple of feet above the floor in case of flooding. Small quantities of cured grains may be kept in glass jars; light helps to inhibit mold.

Preventing Insect Infestation

Weevils, moths, beetles, and the other insects that feed on grain are unlikely to cause you any trouble if your grains and storage containers are clean and dry and kept cool. If your grain should become infested, examine all of your grain products to determine the extent of the infestation. If the infestation is severe, remove and destroy that grain which is infested. If, after examining your grains, you find that little damage has been done, you may kill the insects by putting the grain on trays and heating it in a 140° to 160°F oven for 30 minutes. Or for 3 or 4 days you may put your grain in a freezer that maintains a 0°F temperature. Such temperature extremes will destroy insects. Carefully clean out your storage containers, making sure that you have not overlooked any place where insects may be hiding. Pour the cleaned grain back into the containers and check frequently for future infestations.

Even packaged flours, nuts, cereals, grains, and other dried foods can contain some insect eggs when you get them. Should you notice a problem with them, follow the hot or cold treatment. It'll do the trick.

■ If you store rather large quantities of grain, like 5 to 10 gallons, you might like to try this dry ice method for killing insects. As dry ice evaporates it forms carbon dioxide, which kills insects. *Dry ice can burn; wear insulated gloves when working with it. Don't stick your mouth and nose too close to it, especially as you lift the lid of the can in which you've put the ice.* Spread 2 ounces of crushed dry ice over the bottom of a 5-gallon can and put your grain right over the top of the ice. Allow about 30 minutes for the dry ice to evaporate before you put the lid on the can. If pressure develops within the can you'll see some bulging. Remove the lid carefully if this occurs, and leave if off for 2 minutes; then put it back on.

■ You can also use diatomaceous earth to kill insects in grains. It is a natural product known for its abrasiveness that won't harm animals or humans, but will destroy insects that ingest it. You can buy it in some gardening shops, especially those that feature organic gardening products. To 25 pounds of grain add 1 cup of diatomaceous earth and mix thoroughly. And we mean thoroughly. Each grain kernel should be covered with a light coating of the powder. For best effectiveness, the grain should be quite dry, with a moisture content of 12 percent or lower.

Refrigerating Grains

Refrigeration of grains is a good idea, especially if you want to hold grain over the summer, when the cool weather is gone. Insects that attack grains multiply at temperatures greater than 70°F. Insect infestations of this type are controlled at the commercial level with fumigants like methyl bromide and methyl parathion, both deadly poisons that are pumped into airtight sealed bins. Experiments are being done with carbon dioxide fumigation, which, while deadly to insects and rodents, will leave no toxic residues. But, like all fumigants, carbon dioxide requires sealed storage bins, and these are not very practical for the grower with small grain acreage because they are usually too big and too expensive to construct. The same insects that multiply at 70°F lie dormant at 35°F and will eventually be killed by extended periods of low temperatures. Refrigeration also aids in controlling fungus attack: Fungus grows very slowly at temperatures of 45°F and below.

Sprouts

Sprouting is not actually a means of preserving any food, but we include it here because we think it's a wonderful way to turn stored grains, seeds, and even beans into vitamin-rich vegetables that you can have fresh whenever you want—any day of the year. Sprouting is fast, simple, and requires no special equipment.

■ When you sprout beans, seeds, and grains, you're unleashing their full nutritional potential. Wheat and millet sprouts, for instance, contain more than 5 times the vitamin C of their unsprouted counterparts. The amount of vitamin B grows substantially as bean sprouts grow, and most sprouts double their original protein content.

Many grains, beans, and vegetable and herb seeds can be sprouted, but we recommend that you stick to those contained in our lists. There's enough there to keep you satisfied. Others are, at best, disappointing—and, at worst, dangerous. For instance, potato and tomato seeds are members of the nightshade family and grow sprouts that are toxic. Seeds from tree fruits, sorghum, and Sudan grass are also poisonous when sprouted.

The best seeds to use are those that you've grown yourself or have gotten from a natural food store that sells special seeds for sprouting. Packaged beans for eating, sold in regular food stores, are fine, too. Some mail-order seed companies sell seeds for sprouting and will advertise them as such in their catalogs. Be sure that seeds you use have not been treated with chemicals or dyes. *Such seeds should not be sprouted.*

If you want to use some of the grains, seeds, or beans that you grow for sprouting, harvest and prepare them as you do for drying, but

561

continued on page 565

Sprouts: Vital Statistics

Seed	Rinses per Day	Recommended Length of Sprout	Sprouting Time (days)	Approximate Yield of Sprouts from Seed	Comments
Alfalfa	2	1 to 2 inches (place in sun last day and let tiny green leaves appear)	3 to 5	3 tablespoons = 4 cups	Easy to sprout. Pleasant, light taste.
Almond	2 to 3	¼ inch	3 to 5	1 cup = 1½ cups	Similar to unsprouted nuts. Crunchy, nutty flavor.
Amaranth	3	¼ inch	2 to 3	3 tablespoons = 1 cup	Mild taste. Sprouts smell like corn silk.
Anise	6	1 inch	2	3 tablespoons = 1 cup	A strong anise flavor. Good if used sparingly.
Barley	2 to 3	length of the seed	3 to 4	½ cup = 1 cup	A chewy texture and pleasant taste. Not sweet. Toasting enhances flavor.
Beans (all kinds except those listed individually in chart)	3 to 4	1 inch (the bigger the bean, the smaller the sprout should be so that it remains tender)	3 to 5	1 cup = 4 cups	Taste like unsprouted beans. For tender sprouts, limit germination time to 3 days. Most beans, especially the larger and tougher ones, are better cooked before eating.
Buckwheat	1	½ inch	2 to 3	1 cup = 3 cups	Simple to sprout. Buy raw, hulled groats for sprouting.
Chia	4 to 6	¼ inch	1 to 4	2 tablespoons = 3 to 4 cups	Hard to sprout because of their tendency to become gelatinous. Sprinkling rather than thorough rinsing can help prevent this problem. Their strong flavor adds zip to any dish.
Chick-pea (garbanzo)	4	½ inch	3	1 cup = 3 cups	These are best cooked before eating.

Seed	Rinses per Day	Recommended Length of Sprout	Sprouting Time (days)	Approximate Yield of Sprouts from Seed	Comments
Clover (red)	2	1 to 2 inches	3 to 5	1½ tablespoons = 4 cups	Similar to alfalfa sprouts.
Corn	2 to 3	½ inch	2 to 3	1 cup = 2 cups	Sweet corn taste, with chewy texture. Difficult to find untreated kernels for sprouting.
Cress	4 to 6	1 to 1½ inches	3 to 5	1 tablespoon = 1½ cups	A gelatinous seed. Sprinkle rather than rinse. A strong, peppery taste.
Fenugreek	1 to 2	1 to 3 inches	3 to 5	¼ cup = 1 cup	Spicy taste, good in curry dishes. Bitter if sprouts get too long.
Flax	4 to 6	1 to 2 inches (nice to place in sun and let leaves appear)	4	2 tablespoons = 1½ to 2 cups	Tend to become gelatinous when wet. Sprinkle rather than rinse. Sprouts have a mild flavor.
Lentil	2 to 4	¼ to ½ inch	3 to 4	1 cup = 6 cups	Chewy bean texture. Can be eaten raw or steamed lightly.
Millet	2 to 3	¼ inch	3 to 4	1 cup = 2 cups	Similar to barley sprouts.
Mung bean	3 to 4	1 to 2 inches or longer	3 to 5	1 cup = 4 to 5 cups	Easy to sprout. Popular in Asian dishes. Sprouts begin to lose their crispness after 4 days of storage.
Mustard	2	1 to 1½ inches	3 to 4	2 tablespoons = 3 cups	Spicy, tangy taste, not unlike fresh English mustard.
Oat	1	length of the seed	3 to 4	1 cup = 2 cups	Only unhulled oats will sprout. Water sparingly; too much water makes sprouts sour.
Pea	2 to 3	length of the seed	3	1½ cups = 2 cups	Taste like fresh peas. Best when steamed lightly.

continued

Sprouts: Vital Statistics—*continued*

Seed	Rinses per Day	Recommended Length of Sprout	Sprouting Time (days)	Approximate Yield of Sprouts from Seed	Comments
Pumpkin	2 to 3	¼ inch	3	1 cup = 2 cups	Hulled seeds make best sprouts. Light toasting improves flavor.
Radish	2	½ to 1½ inches (nice to place in sun last day and let tiny leaves appear—these are remarkably sweet when they are long)	2 to 6	1 tablespoon = 1 cup	Sprouts taste just like the vegetable.
Rice	2 to 3	length of the seed	3 to 4	1 cup = 2½ cups	Similar to other sprouted grains. Only whole-grain brown rice will sprout.
Rye	2 to 3	length of the seed	3 to 4	1 cup = 3½ cups	Easy to sprout. Very sweet taste, with crunchy texture.
Sesame	4	length of the seed	3	1 cup = 1½ cups	Only unhulled seeds will sprout. Delicious flavor when young; sprouts over $\frac{1}{16}$ inch turn bitter.
Soybean	4 to 6	1 to 2 inches	4 to 6	1 cup = 4 to 5 cups	Difficult to sprout because they ferment easily. Need frequent, thorough rinses. Cook before eating for optimum protein availability.
Sunflower	2	⅛ inch or less	1 to 3	½ cup = 1½ cups	Good snacks, especially if lightly roasted. Become bitter if grown too long.
Triticale	2 to 3	length of the seed	2 to 3	1 cup = 2 cups	Similar to wheat sprouts.
Vegetable seeds	2	1 to 2 inches	3 to 5	1 tablespoon = 1 to 2 cups	Usually easy to sprout. Best eaten raw.
Wheat	2 to 3	length of the seed	2 to 4	1 cup = 3½ to 4 cups	Simple to sprout. Very sweet taste.

do not use an oven or dryer that gets above 175°F. Do not pasteurize food that you plan to sprout. Store in airtight containers in a cool, dry place.

Many long-time sprouters stick to just alfalfa seeds and mung beans because they are the easiest and most reliable to sprout, but many other foods can be sprouted, as the chart shows you.

THE HOW-TO'S OF SPROUTING

Begin sprouting by soaking your beans, seeds, or grains overnight to soften the seed case and make sprouting easier. You'll only need a small quantity of seeds, as they increase their volume many times over as they sprout. Two tablespoons of the smallest seeds (like alfalfa, cress, flax, and radish), or about $\frac{1}{4}$ cup of the medium seeds (the grains), or $\frac{1}{2}$ cup of the larger ones (the beans) should be sufficient.

Place them in a small bowl, cover with tepid water, and let them sit overnight. (Chia, cress, and flax seeds tend to stick together when moistened, so they should not be soaked like the others. Rather, sprinkle the seeds over a saucer of water, being careful not to clump them together. After soaking, pour the seeds through a strainer or your sprouter. With a good stream of water, remove any that stick to the saucer. Then follow the regular sprouting procedure, but rinse them at least 4 times daily and 6 times if you can.)

After soaking, drain this water off the seeds and put them into something that will allow them to continue to drain now and every time that you rinse them. You can place them in a strainer and prop the

Good Sprout Combinations

Seeds to Mix	Rinses per Day	Sprouting Time (days)
Mung bean, Mustard, and Rye	3	4
Sesame, Cress, and Rice	2	4
Lentil, Alfalfa, and Almond	3	4
Mung bean, Clover (red), and Mustard	3	4
Chick-pea and Pea	3	3
Barley and Sunflower	2	3
Barley and Pumpkin	2	3
Lentil, Sesame, and Buckwheat	4	3
Amaranth, Anise, and Wheat	5	3
Radish and Wheat	3	4
Oat and Flax	2	4

A commercial sprouter such as this allows you to sprout several different types of seeds at one time.

strainer over a bowl. Or you can put the seeds in a glass jar and cover the jar with cheesecloth or nylon netting which is held in place with a string or rubber band. Or you can buy a plastic sprouting lid that screws on like any other lid, but it is made of a plastic mesh so that water can drain out of the jar. (If you use this jar and cheesecloth or netting or plastic lid setup you can forgo the bowl and strainer mentioned above and soak your seeds right in the jar.) Tilt the jar on an angle upside down so moisture can run out into a bowl. There are commercially made sprouting containers that work quite well, too.

Once in their container, rinse the seeds again and let them drain. Put the container in a nearby cabinet, closet, or other place that is out of bright light and that stays at about 70°F. Bright light or direct sunlight will make the seeds dry out too quickly, too high a temperature will promote mold, and too low a temperature will discourage sprouting. Make sure the place is convenient, because you have to rinse most sprouts at least 2 times and preferably 3 times a day for the entire sprouting

A homemade seed sprouter can be easily made out of a jar covered with cheesecloth that's held in place by a rubber band. This sprouter can also be used to soak seeds in before sprouting.

time. This rinsing prevents fungus from growing on the sprouting seeds. Never eat any sprouts that have even a trace of mold on them, as it could prove to be toxic.

■ Kitchens in winter may be too cold for growing sprouts, since they need an environment around 70°F to grow. Gas ovens with pilot lights on and doors open a crack, the tops of refrigerators, or cabinets that get warmed by sun through windows may be cozy and warm places, even if the thermostat reads 65°F.

When the sprouts are a good size you can rinse them once more and leave them in a sunny window for a day so they grow tiny leaves. These leaves make the sprouts look pretty and also add chlorophyll to your diet. Sprouts that are particularly nice with little leaves include alfalfa, flax, and radish.

STORING AND USING SPROUTS

All sprouts but bean sprouts (other than lentils and mung beans) can be and are best eaten fresh—on salads, sandwiches, or any other food. The

DIASTATIC MALT

Made from sprouted and roasted grain, diastatic malt is the European bread bakers' secret ingredient. The enzymes in the malt mellow and soften the gluten in flour by converting some of the flour's starch into sugar. The result is a bread that has a delicately nutty flavor and an improved texture. You can buy it in liquid or powdered form; it's called malt extract. But you can also make it from your sprouted grains. It's very simple.

Diastatic malt is most often made from sprouted barley, but you can use sprouted rye or wheat as well. Make your sprouts and then rinse and dry them on towels. Spread them out one layer thick on baking sheets or drying trays and dry in either a very-low temperature oven or in a food dryer until dry. The pilot light in your gas oven may be warm

enough; in that case, leaving the sprouts to dry overnight will probably be about right. (Don't let the temperature get over 170°F, because if you do, you'll kill off all the diastatic enzymes. You'll still have a malt which will give your bread a deep color and nutty flavor, but it won't do anything to improve its texture.) The sprouts will be dry, crisp, and dark brown. Grind up the sprouts in your blender or in a grain mill until you have a powder. It lasts just about forever in the freezer or refrigerator.

Use about 1 teaspoon for each bread batter, assuming that the batter makes 2 to 4 loaves of bread. A little is good, but more is not better: too much malt makes bread dark and sticky, sometimes too sweet and sometimes bitter.

other bean sprouts are more palatable and digestible if they're cooked before they're eaten. To cook the sprouted beans, drop them into boiling water slowly (so as to keep the water boiling), then turn down the heat and simmer, covered, for 30 to 45 minutes, or until they are as tender as you like them. Kidney and marrow beans take almost an hour to cook. The others take about 30 minutes.

You could freeze extra sprouts by first blanching them over steam for 3 minutes, then cooling and drying them before packing them in freezer bags or containers, but why bother? They are much better fresh, and they're so easy to make that you can sprout a new batch twice weekly and always have a fresh supply.

There are so many ways you can use or cook sprouted beans. Add them to stock, vegetables, and seasonings for soup; cool and marinate them for a 3-bean salad; or put them in a Boston baked bean pot, in a cassoulet, or in a lima bean bake. Or you may want to stir-fry some vegetables Chinese style, adding uncooked sprouts and steaming them at the end until tender.

Nut, Seed, Grain, and Sprout Recipes

ENTRÉES

Almond Loaf

1 cup hot stock or potato
  water (approximately)
1 cup oatmeal
2 eggs, beaten
1½ cups ground almonds
½ cup ground sunflower seeds
1 medium-size onion, chopped
½ cup diced celery and tops
½ green pepper or pimiento,
  chopped
1 teaspoon fresh or dried
  marjoram
1 tablespoon vegetable oil
  sweet red pepper (garnish)
  parsley (garnish)

Pour 1 cup stock or potato water over oatmeal, blend together, cover, and let stand until cool.

Preheat oven to 350°F.

To the oatmeal add eggs, almonds, sunflower seeds, onions, celery, green pepper or pimiento, marjoram, and oil. Mix together well and add more stock or potato water as needed for loaf consistency. Pour into an oiled 8½ × 4½-inch loaf pan and bake for 55 minutes. Turn out on a meat platter and garnish with red pepper and parsley. Serve hot or cold.

Yield: 4 servings

Nutty-Rice Loaf

2 onions, chopped
½ cup chopped green peppers
¼ cup chopped celery and tops
2 tablespoons vegetable oil or
    butter
1 cup chopped nuts
1 cup cooked brown rice
1 cup wheat germ
2 eggs, beaten
1 cup water
¼ cup soy or wheat flour
    freshly ground pepper
1 teaspoon ground marjoram
¼ teaspoon dry mustard

Preheat oven to 350°F. Sauté onions, green peppers, and celery in oil or butter until transparent. To the vegetables add nuts, rice, wheat germ, eggs, water, flour, pepper, marjoram, and mustard. Blend and turn into a greased 9 × 5-inch loaf pan. Place pan in pan of water. Bake for 55 minutes. Serve with tomato sauce or your favorite sauce.

Yield: 6 servings

Nutty Burgers

These are a very flavorful meat substitute.

1 cup walnuts
½ cup sunflower seeds
½ cup chopped carrots
1 stalk celery, sliced
1 small onion, chopped
½ green pepper, chopped
1 sprig parsley, chopped

1 tomato
½ cup vegetable broth or stock
2 eggs, beaten
    pinch of sage or marjoram
6 slices whole wheat bread,
    made into crumbs

Put half the nuts, seeds, carrots, celery, onions, peppers, parsley, tomato, and stock through the food grinder or the blender. Repeat procedure with remaining half of ingredients.

Add the eggs, sage or marjoram, and bread crumbs. Blend the ingredients, and if they are too dry, add more broth or tomato pulp; if too moist, add whole wheat bread crumbs. Shape into patties and broil on a baking sheet until browned on each side.

Yield: 8 patties or 4 servings

Sunburgers

Sunburgers are good served with sautéed mushrooms or shredded cheese, which melts if burgers are hot when you sprinkle it over them.

1 cup ground sunflower seeds
½ cup finely chopped celery
2 tablespoons chopped onions
    or snipped chives
1 egg, beaten
1 tablespoon chopped green
    peppers
1 tablespoon chopped fresh
    parsley
½ cup grated carrots
1 tablespoon vegetable oil
¼ cup tomato juice
    pinch of basil

Preheat oven to 350°F.

Mix all ingredients together well. Add more tomato juice if necessary so that the patties hold a good formed shape. Arrange in an oiled shallow baking dish and bake until browned, about 10 minutes, then turn and brown on the other side for 10 minutes. They can also be broiled if coated with oil on both sides before cooking.

Yield: 5 3-inch patties

Sunflower Goulash

A moist, unusual variation that's delicious.

2 onions, sliced
1 clove garlic, minced
2 tablespoons vegetable oil
1 cup chopped sunflower seeds
2 cups mushrooms, halved
1 cup fresh sprouts
1 cup cooked and cooled millet
2 cups fresh or home-canned
    tomatoes
1 cup lima beans
1 tablespoon chili powder
1 teaspoon soy sauce

Preheat oven to 350°F. Sauté onions and garlic in oil until tender and slightly browned. Add all other ingredients, and pour in casserole dish. Bake about 30 minutes, and serve.

Yield: 4 servings

Bean Sprout, Pepper, and Tomato Stir-Fry

This combination of colors and textures is nice over pasta or brown rice.

1 green pepper
2 tablespoons soy sauce
¼ teaspoon honey
2 tablespoons vegetable oil
1 pound mung bean sprouts (or
    other bean sprouts)
2 medium-size tomatoes,
    chopped
¼ teaspoon sesame oil (optional)

Cut pepper into thin slivers. Thoroughly blend soy sauce and honey in a cup.

Heat oil until hot in a wok or large, heavy skillet. Add bean sprouts. Stir-fry for 1 minute. Add peppers and stir-fry for 2 minutes. Pour in soy sauce-honey mixture. Mix well. Add chopped tomatoes and stir until heated through. Serve immediately. If desired, sprinkle with sesame oil and toss for a rich, nuttier flavor.

Yield: 4 to 6 servings

Egg Foo Yong with Mung Bean Sprouts

2 onions, finely chopped
2 cups mung bean sprouts (or
    other bean sprouts)
6 eggs, slightly beaten
1 teaspoon soy sauce

In a medium-size bowl combine onions, bean sprouts, eggs, and soy sauce. Fry 2 tablespoons of egg mixture at a time in a non-stick skillet or lightly oiled skillet. Do not stir, but cook until the pancake is lightly browned on both sides. Continue frying pancakes.

Yield: 12 3-inch pancakes

Meat Loaf with Sprouts

The sprouts add texture and help to extend the meat in this otherwise traditional meat loaf.

1½ cups mung bean sprouts,
    minced
1½ pounds ground chuck
¼ cup minced celery
1 medium-size onion, minced
½ cup whole wheat bread
    crumbs
1 egg, well beaten
2 teaspoons soy sauce
1 clove garlic, minced
¼ teaspoon pepper

Preheat oven to 350°F. In a large bowl combine sprouts, chuck, celery, onions, bread crumbs, egg, soy sauce, garlic, and pepper. Form into a loaf and place in a shallow baking pan, or pack mixture into a 9 × 5-inch loaf pan.

Bake for 45 to 55 minutes.

Yield: 6 to 8 servings

Meat and Sprout Patties

¾ pound ground chuck
½ cup fresh sprouts (soy or
    mung), chopped
1 teaspoon Worcestershire
    sauce
1 clove garlic, minced
1 tablespoon chopped onion
2 tablespoons grated carrot
    pepper, to taste

In a medium-size mixing bowl, combine chuck, sprouts, Worcestershire sauce, garlic, onions, carrots, and pepper. Form into 4 patties and broil or fry according to preference.

Yield: 4 large patties

SALADS

Sprouted Lentil, Bean, and Rice Salad

Salad
1 pound fresh green beans,
    cooked
½ pound pinto beans or kidney
    beans, cooked
2 cups cooked brown rice
1 cup diced celery
½ green pepper, diced
¼ cup chopped pimiento
¼ cup lentils, sprouted (or ⅓ cup
    mung beans, sprouted or 2
    tablespoons alfalfa,
    sprouted)

Dressing
½ cup vegetable oil
½ cup wine vinegar
1 tablespoon honey
1 teaspoon pepper

1 medium-size red onion, thinly
    sliced (garnish)

To make the salad, combine green beans and pinto or kidney beans, rice, celery, peppers, pimiento, and sprouts.

To make the dressing, combine oil, vinegar, honey, and pepper. Toss salad in dressing. Garnish with onion slices.

Yield: 10 servings

Sprout Salad

This is a lovely way to dress up plain cottage cheese.

1 cup cottage cheese
2 tomatoes, cubed
1 cucumber, sliced or diced
¼ cup mung bean sprouts
½ cup alfalfa sprouts
¼ cup sesame seeds
    herb dressing

Put cottage cheese in center of serving bowl. Arrange tomatoes, cucumbers, and mung bean sprouts around it. Top with alfalfa sprouts and sesame seeds. Serve with your favorite herb dressing.

Yield: 2 servings

SOUPS

Bean Sprout Soup

4½ teaspoons cornstarch
¼ cup water
6 cups chicken stock
2 cups mung bean sprouts (or
    other bean sprouts)
1 teaspoon soy sauce or more,
    to taste
2 eggs, beaten
1 scallion, minced (garnish)

Mix cornstarch and water. In a large saucepan heat chicken stock to boiling and add bean sprouts. Reduce heat and simmer for 3 minutes. Add soy sauce.

Stir the cornstarch mixture well and pour it into hot soup. Stir until slightly thickened. Slowly pour in beaten eggs, stirring with a fork. Remove soup from heat immediately and serve garnished with scallions.

Yield: 5 to 6 servings

Potato and Alfalfa Sprout Soup

½ cup chopped celery
1 small onion, chopped
1 medium-size carrot, shredded
1 tablespoon butter
5 cups diced peeled potatoes
8 cups milk
⅛ teaspoon white pepper
1 cup alfalfa sprouts
¼ cup minced parsley

In a 3- to 4-quart pot, sauté celery, onions, and carrots in butter until slightly tender, about 5 minutes. Add potatoes and milk; cook over medium heat, partially covered, for 30 minutes or until vegetables are tender. Season with white pepper.

Add alfalfa sprouts and parsley just before serving.

Yield: 9 cups

QUICK BREADS

Pumpkin Bread

4   eggs, beaten
2   cups honey
2   cups cooked pumpkin, fresh
    or canned
⅔   cup water
1   cup vegetable oil
3½ cups whole wheat flour
2   teaspoons baking soda
1   teaspoon ground cinnamon
1   teaspoon ground nutmeg

Preheat oven to 350°F.

Beat eggs, honey, pumpkin, water, and oil together well. In a separate bowl mix flour, baking soda, cinnamon, and nutmeg. Then pour the dry mixture into the wet one and mix thoroughly. Pour the mixture into 2 oiled 9 × 5-inch loaf pans. Bake 1 hour and 10 minutes.

Yield: 2 loaves

Susquehanna Loaf

The molasses and dates make this steamed bread moist and rich.

1   cup yellow cornmeal
1   cup whole wheat flour
1   cup whole wheat pastry flour
½   teaspoon ground cinnamon
1   teaspoon baking soda
1   cup pitted dates, quartered
¼   cup vegetable oil
½   cup molasses
½   cup honey
1½ cups milk

Combine cornmeal, flours, cinnamon, and baking soda in a medium-size mixing bowl. Add dates and mix until dates are coated with flour. In a small bowl combine oil, molasses, honey, and milk; mix thoroughly. Combine the two mixtures and pour into 2 buttered 1-pound coffee cans. Cover tightly with foil. Place cans on rack in a pot with water halfway up coffee cans. Bring water to a boil, lower heat, cover pot, and steam for 2½ hours. Remove immediately from steamer and cool slightly before unmolding.

Yield: 2 loaves

Split Pea Bread

Don't be put off by the unusual combination of ingredients here; they work together beautifully.

2 cups dried split peas	¾ cup honey
2½ cups whole wheat flour	3 eggs, beaten
1 teaspoon ground cinnamon	1 cup pecans or walnuts, chopped
½ teaspoon ground nutmeg	
½ teaspoon ground cloves	1 cup dried fruit (dates and raisins or other combination), chopped
2 teaspoons baking soda	
½ teaspoon baking powder	
⅔ cup butter	

Cover 2 cups of dried split peas with water. Bring to a boil and simmer for about 1 hour or until peas are soft. Drain off excess liquid. Mash peas and measure out 2 cups of pea purée. The purée should be thick enough to mound on a spoon (like applesauce). Freeze remaining purée for soup.

Preheat oven to 325°F. In a medium-size bowl combine flour, cinnamon, nutmeg, cloves, baking soda, and baking powder. Cream butter and honey until fluffy. Add eggs and pea purée. Mix well. Add flour mixture to creamed mixture and stir to combine. Fold in nuts and fruit.

Pour into 2 oiled 8½ × 4½-inch loaf pans. Bake 40 to 45 minutes or until cake tester comes out clean.

Yield: 2 loaves

Wheat-Free Bread Squares

2 cups brown rice flour
½ cup oat bran
½ cup chopped raisins
½ teaspoon ground cinnamon
½ teaspoon ground cardamom
3 eggs
½ cup honey
1 teaspoon vanilla extract
2 teaspoons baking soda

Preheat oven to 375°F.

In a medium-size bowl, combine flour, bran, raisins, cinnamon, and cardamom. In another medium-size bowl, combine eggs, honey, vanilla extract, and baking soda. Add wet ingredients to dry and mix well.

Oil an 8 × 8-inch glass pan and scoop in batter, smoothing top with your hand. Bake 20 to 25 minutes.

Yield: 16 2-inch squares

Corn Bread

1 cup cornmeal
¾ cup whole wheat flour
2 tablespoons baking powder
1 egg, well beaten
1 cup milk
⅓ cup honey
3 tablespoons vegetable oil

Preheat oven to 425°F. Mix cornmeal, whole wheat flour, and baking powder together. Add egg, milk, honey, and oil. Stir just enough to mix. Bake in 2 greased 8-inch round pans for 15 minutes.

Yield: 2 8-inch rounds

Sunflower Corn Bread

This is a good keeper.

1 cup sunflower seed flour
1 cup cornmeal
2 teaspoons baking powder
½ teaspoon baking soda
2 egg yolks, beaten
⅓ cup sour cream or yogurt
2 tablespoons honey
⅓ cup buttermilk
2 egg whites, beaten until stiff

Preheat oven to 375°F.
In a medium-size bowl, mix sunflower seed flour, cornmeal, baking powder, and baking soda together. Combine egg yolks, sour cream or yogurt, honey, and buttermilk. Pour liquid ingredients into dry and mix until just combined. Fold in egg whites. Bake in a greased and floured 8 × 8-inch pan 5 minutes at 375°F, then turn down to 325°F and bake 10 minutes more.
Serve hot with butter.

Yield: 1 8 × 8-inch pan

Multi-Grain Carrot Bread

This rich, high-fiber loaf freezes well.

1¼ cups whole wheat pastry
   flour
½ cup whole wheat flour
¼ cup brown rice flour
¼ cup cornmeal
2½ teaspoons baking powder
2 tablespoons nonfat dry milk
½ cup wheat germ
¼ cup butter, softened

2 tablespoons honey
2 tablespoons molasses
2 eggs
1¼ cups water
½ cup shredded carrots
2 tablespoons chopped roasted
   sunflower seeds
3 tablespoons chopped roasted
   peanuts

Preheat oven to 375°F.

Sift whole wheat flours, brown rice flour, cornmeal, baking powder, and nonfat dry milk into a medium-size bowl. Stir in wheat germ.

In another medium-size bowl, cream butter with honey and molasses until light. Add eggs. Mix together water and carrots. Add to creamed mixture alternately with dry ingredients, stirring to mix. Stir in sunflower seeds and nuts. Pour into a greased 8½ × 4½-inch loaf pan. Bake for 45 to 60 minutes or until bread tests done. Cool in pan 5 minutes. Remove from pan and cool completely on a wire rack.

Yield: 1 loaf

Honey-Glazed Nut Bread

3 cups whole wheat flour
3 teaspoons baking soda
¼ teaspoon ground nutmeg
1 cup chopped nuts
2 eggs
⅔ cup and 1 tablespoon honey
1¼ cups buttermilk or yogurt
1 tablespoon melted butter
  chopped nuts

Preheat oven to 350°F.

Combine flour, baking soda, nutmeg, and 1 cup chopped nuts. Beat eggs until lemon colored. Beat in ⅔ cup honey and buttermilk or yogurt. Mix into dry ingredients. Pour into well-greased 9 × 5-inch loaf pan. Bake for 45 minutes.

Remove from oven and glaze top of loaf with the remaining 1 tablespoon honey mixed with melted butter. Sprinkle with more chopped nuts. Return to oven and let glaze for additional 5 minutes.

Yield: 1 loaf

Soda Bread

3 cups whole wheat flour	2 tablespoons wheat germ
1 cup unbleached white flour	¾ cup currants or raisins
1 tablespoon baking powder	1 tablespoon caraway seeds
¼ teaspoon salt	2 eggs
2 tablespoons butter, cut into bits	1¾ cups buttermilk
	¾ teaspoon baking soda

Preheat oven to 350°F.

In a large bowl, combine flours, baking powder, and salt. With fingertips, blend in butter until mixture is mealy. Add wheat germ, currants or raisins, and caraway seeds.

In a small bowl, beat eggs slightly. Add buttermilk and baking soda and whisk to combine. Pour into flour mixture and stir well with a wooden spoon. The dough should be soft but not sticky (add a little more flour if too sticky or more buttermilk if mixture does not hold together). Turn dough onto a lightly floured board and knead gently for 1 minute. Shape dough into a ball. Flatten slightly. Turn into a well-greased round casserole dish. With a sharp knife, cut a shallow cross in the center. Bake for about 50 to 60 minutes or until bread tests done. Cool 10 minutes in pan. Remove from pan and cool on a wire rack. Serve warm or cold.

Yield: 1 loaf

Variation

Substitute ½ cup cornmeal for ½ cup whole wheat flour.

YEAST BREADS AND ROLLS

Banana Corn Bread

The moistness of the fruit balances the dryness of the cornmeal.

1 tablespoon dry yeast
2 tablespoons warm water
1¼ cups cornmeal
¼ cup wheat germ
¼ cup potato flour
½ cup soy flour
2 eggs
½ cup mashed banana
½ cup honey
2 tablespoons corn oil

Soften yeast in warm water. Combine cornmeal, wheat germ, potato flour, soy flour, and softened yeast in a bowl. In another bowl, beat eggs, banana, honey, and corn oil. Add the dry ingredients to the moist mixture and mix well.

Place in a greased 9 × 5-inch loaf pan and let rise about 1 hour. Preheat oven to 325°F. Bake for 40 to 50 minutes.

Yield: 1 loaf

Seven Grain Bread

Seven Grain Flour:
- 6 cups whole wheat flour
- ¼ cup cornmeal
- ¼ cup rye flour
- ¼ cup buckwheat flour
- ¼ cup soy flour
- ¼ cup oat flour
- ¼ cup barley flour
- 1 tablespoon dry yeast
- 2 cups warm water
- ⅓ cup molasses
- 3 tablespoons vegetable oil
- ½ teaspoon salt

Combine the seven flours in a large bowl.

In a large bowl soften yeast in warm water. When it is dissolved, add the molasses, oil, salt, and enough Seven Grain Flour to make a stiff dough. Turn out onto a floured board and knead. If necessary, add plain whole wheat flour if you use all the Seven Grain Flour and the dough is still sticky. Form into a ball, place in an oiled bowl, turn once to oil top, and cover with a cloth. Let rise until double in bulk, about 1 hour.

Punch down, divide into 2 loaves, and place in greased 8½ × 4½-inch loaf pans. Cover and allow to rise only until the dough just reaches the top of the pans. Do not allow to rise too long (more than 1 hour) in a warm place or the bread will fall.

Preheat oven to 375°F. Bake for 40 minutes.

Yield: 2 loaves

Plymouth Bread

1   tablespoon dry yeast
½   cup warm water
½   cup yellow cornmeal
2   cups boiling water
2   tablespoons butter
½   cup molasses
½   teaspoon salt
4¾ cups unbleached white flour

Soften yeast in warm water. Stir cornmeal very slowly into boiling water, stirring constantly to prevent lumps. Boil 5 minutes, and add butter, molasses, and salt. Cool. When lukewarm, add softened yeast. Add flour until dough is stiff. Turn out onto a floured board and knead well. Place in an oiled bowl and turn to oil top. Cover and let rise in a warm place until double in bulk.

Punch down and shape into 2 loaves. Place in well-greased 8½ × 4½-inch pans, cover, and let rise again until double in bulk.

Preheat oven to 350°F. Bake 1 hour.

Yield: 2 loaves

Granola Bread

Here's a sweet bread that's perfect for breakfast.

2   tablespoons dry yeast
2   cups warm water
1   cup milk, warmed
1   teaspoon salt
½   cup vegetable oil
⅓   cup honey
8   cups whole wheat flour
1   cup granola
½   cup sunflower seeds
1   cup raisins
2   tablespoons freshly grated
      orange peel
1   egg, lightly beaten
1   tablespoon milk

In a large bowl, combine yeast, water, milk, salt, oil, honey, and 4 cups flour. Cover with plastic wrap and let proof for 5 minutes. Stir in granola, sunflower seeds, raisins, orange peel, and the remaining 4 cups flour. Knead for 8 to 10 minutes or until smooth. Place in an oiled bowl, turn to oil top, cover, and let rise until double in bulk—about 30 to 45 minutes. Turn out onto a floured board, punch down, return to bowl, cover, and let rise until double in bulk again (about 1 hour).

After second rise, turn out onto floured board, punch down, and knead for just a couple of minutes. Divide into 3 equal loaves and place in greased 8½ × 4½-inch loaf pans.

Place the pans in a warm spot in the kitchen, cover, and let rise until double in bulk (about 45 minutes to 1 hour).

When loaves are doubled in size, slash tops with a sharp floured knife. Combine egg and milk, and use to brush tops.

Preheat oven to 350°F. Bake for 45 to 50 minutes or until they test done. Turn out and cool on wire racks.

Yield: 3 loaves

Raisin Bread

1   medium-size potato
4   cups water
2   tablespoons butter
2   teaspoons salt
2   tablespoons dry yeast
1   cup warm water
½   cup honey
6   cups whole wheat flour
5½ cups unbleached white flour
1   pound raisins (4 cups)
½   teaspoon ground cloves
2   teaspoons ground cinnamon

Peel potato and cut into pieces. Cook until tender in water. Mash potato, return it to the water in which it was cooked, add butter and salt, and combine. Cool until lukewarm.

Dissolve yeast in 1 cup warm water. Let stand 5 to 10 minutes. Add honey.

Add whole wheat flour to potato mixture, beating until smooth. Mix in the yeast. Beat thoroughly. Cover and let rise for about 1 hour.

Work in unbleached flour to make a soft dough. Stir in raisins, cloves, and cinnamon. Knead until smooth on floured board. Put dough in an oiled bowl and turn to oil top. Cover and let rise until double in bulk (about 1 to 1½ hours).

Punch down dough, and divide into 3 portions. Place each in an 8½ × 4½-inch oiled loaf pan. Cover and let rise again until double.

Preheat oven to 375°F. Bake for 40 minutes.

Yield: 3 loaves

Oat Bread

1 tablespoon dry yeast	1 egg, beaten
2 cups warm milk	1 teaspoon salt
½ cup honey	4 cups whole wheat flour
½ cup oil	2 cups oat flour

In large bowl sprinkle yeast into warm milk, add honey, and mix together well. Allow to proof for 5 minutes. Then add oil, egg, and salt. Stir in whole wheat flour and add oat flour so that the dough is dry enough to leave sides of bowl.

Turn out onto a floured board and knead until dough is smooth and elastic, about 10 minutes. Place dough in a large, oiled bowl, and turn to oil top. Cover and allow to rise until double in bulk.

Punch down and cut into 3 pieces. Shape into loaves and place in greased 8½ × 4½-inch loaf pans. Cover and let rise until double in bulk.

Preheat oven to 375°F. Bake for about 45 minutes.

Yield: 3 loaves

Sprouted Wheat Bread

1½ tablespoons dry yeast	2 cups warm water
1 cup warm potato water or other liquid	½ cup sprouted wheat
1 tablespoon maple syrup or honey	½ cup raisins, chopped black figs, or currants
½ teaspoon salt	½ cup chopped nuts
2 tablespoons molasses	½ cup rolled oats
2 tablespoons vegetable oil	½ cup soy flour (or other grain)
	5 to 6 cups whole wheat flour

In large bowl dissolve yeast in potato water with maple syrup or honey and let proof. Then add salt, molasses, oil, water, sprouted wheat, raisins, figs, or currants, and nuts. Stir in rolled oats and soy flour or other grain. Add the whole wheat flour a cup at a time until dough is stiff enough to knead. Turn dough onto a floured surface and knead about 8 to 10 minutes using more flour if necessary.

Place dough in a large, lightly oiled bowl and turn to oil top. Cover dough and let rise in a warm draft-free place for 1 to 1½ hours or until double in bulk.

Punch down dough. Divide dough in half and place in 2 8½ × 4½-inch lightly oiled loaf pans. Cover and allow to rise until double in bulk, about 1 hour.

Preheat oven to 350°F. Bake for 35 to 45 minutes, or until loaves sound hollow when tapped.

Yield: 2 loaves

Sprouted Wheat and Rye Bread

2 tablespoons dry yeast
½ cup warm water
4 tablespoons molasses
4 to 6 cups whole wheat flour
¾ cup rye flour
½ teaspoon salt
2 cups sprouts, finely chopped
    (wheat, rye, or triticale)
1 teaspoon caraway seeds,
    coarsely chopped
1 tablespoon vegetable oil
1½ cups buttermilk

In a medium-size glass bowl, combine yeast, water, 1 tablespoon molasses, and ¼ cup whole wheat flour. Cover with plastic wrap and let proof for 10 minutes.

In a large bowl, combine 4 of the remaining cups whole wheat flour, rye flour, salt, sprouts, and seeds. Add the yeast mixture, remaining 3 tablespoons molasses, oil, and buttermilk, beating until smooth. Beat in enough of the remaining whole wheat flour to make a stiff dough that can be kneaded.

Turn dough out onto a floured surface and knead for 10 minutes. Place into a lightly oiled bowl and turn dough to oil top. Cover with plastic wrap and let rise in a draft-free place until double in bulk—45 minutes to 1 hour. Punch down, divide dough in half, and shape into loaves. Set into 2 oiled 8½ × 4½-inch loaf pans, cover, and let rise again until not quite double in bulk—about 30 minutes.

Preheat oven to 375°F. Bake for about 20 minutes; cover bread with foil if brown. Continue baking for 20 to 25 minutes. Let bread cool for 10 minutes, remove from pans, and cool on wire racks.

Yield: 2 loaves

Variation

Substitute 1¾ cups alfalfa and ¼ cup mung bean sprouts for the wheat, rye, or triticale sprouts.

Peanut Bread

This bread freezes particularly well because the peanut butter makes it moist.

2 tablespoons dry yeast
1¾ cups warm water
3 tablespoons honey
½ teaspoon salt
¼ cup nonfat dry milk
½ cup peanut butter
4 to 4½ cups whole wheat flour

In a large bowl, dissolve yeast in water. Stir in honey. Let proof for 5 minutes.

Mix in salt, nonfat dry milk, peanut butter, and enough flour to make a stiff dough. Knead on a floured surface until dough is smooth and elastic, about 10 minutes. Place dough in an oiled bowl, and turn to oil top. Cover with a clean towel and let rise until double in bulk, about 1 hour.

Punch down dough and form into a loaf. Place formed loaf into a greased 9 × 5-inch loaf pan. Cover with towel and let rise until double in bulk, about 30 minutes.

Preheat oven to 350°F. Bake loaf for 40 minutes.

Yield: 1 loaf

Veggie Bread

1 tablespoon dry yeast
¼ cup warm water
1 teaspoon honey
1½ to 2 cups whole wheat flour
2 tablespoons stock or water
¾ cup finely minced onions
¾ cup finely minced green peppers
¾ cup finely minced sweet red peppers
½ cup mashed potatoes
½ cup milk
1 tablespoon vegetable oil
1½ cups unbleached white flour
½ teaspoon salt
1 tablespoon ground marjoram

In a large bowl dissolve yeast in water. Add honey and 2 tablespoons whole wheat flour and combine well. Cover with plastic wrap and allow to proof for 5 minutes.

In a saucepan heat stock or water and sauté onions, green peppers, and red peppers until tender. Add vegetables, mashed potatoes, milk, and oil to yeast mixture. Add remaining whole wheat flour, unbleached white flour, salt, and marjoram and combine well. Knead about 10 minutes. The dough should be quite soft.

Place dough in an oiled bowl and turn to oil top. Cover the dough and let rise in a warm place until double in bulk, about 1 hour. Punch down and shape into a smooth round ball or 2 smooth loaf shapes. Place in a well-greased 2-quart casserole dish or 2 8½ × 4½-inch loaf pans. Cover and let rise again until double in bulk.

Preheat oven to 350°F. Bake for about 40 minutes or until bottom sounds hollow when thumped.

Yield: 1 or 2 loaves

Dill Bread

This is a wonderful bread that comes out of the oven smelling fantastic, thanks to the dill seeds.

1 tablespoon dry yeast
¼ cup warm water
1 cup cottage cheese
2 tablespoons honey
1 tablespoon minced onions
1 tablespoon butter
2 teaspoons dill seeds
¼ teaspoon baking soda
1 egg
2¼ to 2½ cups whole wheat flour
1 teaspoon butter

Soften yeast in warm water in a large bowl. Warm the cottage cheese to lukewarm, and add to yeast mixture with the honey, onions, butter, dill seeds, baking soda, and egg. Add flour until a stiff dough is formed. Beat well.

Place dough in an oiled bowl and turn to oil top. Cover and let rise in a warm place until double in bulk—about 1½ hours. Punch down, turn into a well-oiled 1½-quart round casserole, and cover. Let dough rise in a warm place for 40 minutes.

Preheat oven to 350°F. Bake for 35 to 45 minutes. Spread butter on top of loaf after removing from oven.

Yield: 1 loaf

Crusty Loaves
(to freeze)

This dough also makes delicious crusts for homemade pizzas (see pages 423–25).

6¼ to 6¾ cups flour (whole wheat, unbleached white, or a combination)
¼ cup honey
2 teaspoons salt

⅓ cup instant nonfat dry milk
2 tablespoons dry yeast
2 tablespoons vegetable oil
2 cups very warm water (120° to 130°F)

In a large bowl thoroughly mix 4 cups flour, honey, salt, nonfat dry milk, and undissolved yeast. Add oil.

Gradually add water and mix well. Stir in enough additional flour to make a stiff dough. Turn out onto lightly floured board; knead until smooth and elastic, about 15 minutes. Cover with a towel; let rest 15 minutes.

Divide dough into 2 equal pieces. Form each piece into a smooth ball. Flatten each into a mound 6 inches in diameter. Place on oiled baking sheets. Cover sheets tightly with plastic wrap. Freeze until firm. Transfer to plastic bags. Keep frozen up to 4 weeks.

Remove from freezer; unwrap and place on ungreased baking sheets. Cover; let stand at room temperature until fully thawed, about 4 hours. Roll each mound to a 12 × 8-inch rectangle. Beginning at an 8-inch end, roll dough as for jelly roll. Pinch seam to seal. With seam side down, press down ends with heel of hand. Fold underneath. Place each, seam side down, in an oiled 8½ × 4½-inch loaf pan. Cover; let rise in warm place, free from draft, until double in bulk, about 1½ hours.

Bake in a preheated 350°F oven 30 to 35 minutes, or until done. Remove from pans and cool on wire racks.

To make round loaves: Place thawed mounds on oiled baking sheets. Cover and let rise in warm place, free from draft, until double in bulk, about 1 hour. Bake as for loaves.

Yield: 2 loaves

Green Onion Crescent Rolls

1 tablespoon dry yeast
¼ cup warm water
2 tablespoons honey
1¼ cups water
¼ cup nonfat dry milk
½ teaspoon salt

2 tablespoons wheat germ
3 to 3½ cups whole wheat flour
2 tablespoons butter, melted
⅓ cup chopped scallions (green onions)
4 teaspoons sesame seeds

In a small bowl dissolve yeast in warm water. Add honey. Set aside to proof.

In a large bowl mix water, nonfat dry milk, salt, and wheat germ. Add yeast mixture. Gradually add flour, mixing well. Knead on a floured surface until dough is smooth and elastic, about 10 minutes. Place dough in an oiled bowl, turning to oil top. Cover with a clean towel and let rise until double in bulk, about 1 hour.

Lightly oil 2 baking sheets.

Punch down dough and divide in half. Roll each half into a large circle. Brush each circle with 2 teaspoons melted butter and sprinkle with one half of the chopped scallions. Divide each circle into 12 wedges. Roll each wedge toward the center, shape into crescents, and place seam side down on prepared sheets. Brush tops with remaining butter and sprinkle with sesame seeds.

Preheat oven to 400°F. Bake crescents for 10 to 15 minutes.

Yield: 2 dozen rolls

Whole Wheat Dinner Rolls

1   tablespoon dry yeast
½   cup warm water
1   tablespoon honey
3¼ cups whole wheat flour
½   cup buttermilk
2   eggs
    pinch of salt
2   tablespoons sesame seeds

In a large glass bowl, combine yeast, water, honey, and ¼ cup whole wheat flour. Cover with plastic wrap and let proof for 15 minutes.

Add buttermilk and 1 egg and mix well. Add salt and rest of flour, combining until dough is a proper consistency for kneading. On a lightly floured surface, knead dough for 10 minutes.

Lightly oil a glass bowl and place dough in it. Turn once to oil top. Cover with plastic wrap and let rise for 45 minutes.

Punch dough down and divide into 12 equal portions. Form portions into round balls and place 1 inch apart on a lightly oiled baking sheet. Cover and let rise for 45 minutes.

Glaze rolls with 1 beaten egg and sprinkle with sesame seeds. Bake in a *non-preheated* oven at 350°F for 25 minutes.

Yield: 1 dozen rolls

MUFFINS, WAFFLES, CRACKERS, AND PASTA

Sunflower Sour Cream Muffins

¾ cup sunflower seed flour
1 cup whole wheat or oat flour
2½ teaspoons baking powder
½ teaspoon salt
½ teaspoon baking soda
¼ cup currants
1 egg, beaten
2 tablespoons honey
¾ cup sour cream
⅓ cup buttermilk
(approximately)

Preheat oven to 375°F.

Mix flours, baking powder, salt, baking soda, and currants, then combine with egg, honey, and sour cream, stirring as little as possible. Add buttermilk last, as needed, to make a soft dough. Bake in a greased muffin tin for 5 minutes at 375°F, then 10 to 13 minutes more at 325°F.

Yield: 9 muffins

Caraway Onion Biscuits

These flavorful biscuits are good with a hearty soup.

3 medium-size onions, grated
   or finely blended (1⅓ cups)
2 eggs
½ cup vegetable oil
2½ cups whole wheat flour
2 teaspoons baking powder
2 tablespoons caraway seeds

Preheat oven to 425°F.

Beat onions, eggs, and oil together. Combine flour, baking powder, and caraway seeds. Combine dry and wet mixtures.

Take a heaping tablespoonful of the batter and place on buttered baking sheet. For a better-looking biscuit, roll out dough and cut with a biscuit cutter.

Bake for 10 to 15 minutes.

Yield: 1 dozen biscuits

Nutty Waffles

1¾ cups whole wheat pastry
    flour
2 teaspoons baking powder
3 egg yolks
1 tablespoon honey
4 tablespoons melted butter or
    vegetable oil
1½ cups milk
½ cup chopped nuts
3 egg whites

Mix together flour and baking powder. In another bowl beat together egg yolks, honey, butter or oil, and milk.

Make a well in the dry ingredients and pour in the milk mixture. Combine them with a few swift strokes. Mix in the nuts.

Beat egg whites until stiff and fold them into the batter briefly. Pour the batter ½ cup at a time onto a hot waffle iron and cook for about 4 minutes or until brown and crispy, when the waffle iron stops steaming.

Yield: 6 waffles

Poppy Seed Crackers

½ cup whole wheat flour
½ cup unbleached white flour
2 tablespoons poppy seeds
½ cup freshly grated Parmesan
    cheese
⅓ cup vegetable oil
1 teaspoon soy sauce
2 to 3 tablespoons ice water

In a medium-size bowl, combine flours, seeds, and cheese. Add oil and soy sauce and stir to blend. Add water and mix until dough forms a ball. Wrap and chill for 30 minutes.

Set ball in middle of an oiled baking sheet and roll into a 9 × 12-inch rectangle, ⅛ inch thick.

With a sharp knife or pizza cutter, cut into 1½ × 2-inch rectangles.

Preheat oven to 325°F. Bake about 15 to 18 minutes or until firm to the touch.

Yield: 3 dozen crackers

Egg Noodles

1 cup whole wheat pastry flour
1 cup unbleached white flour
1 egg
6 egg yolks
1 tablespoon vegetable oil
3 tablespoons cold water

Mix flours in a large mixing bowl. Mound flour and make a deep well in the center of the mound. Mix egg and egg yolks lightly with fork. Drop the beaten eggs into the center of the dry ingredients. Blend eggs into flour with a fork until well mixed. Add oil and water.

Knead on a lightly floured board until firm, shiny, and elastic. Cover with plastic and let rest for at least 1 hour or up to 24 hours in the refrigerator.

When ready to use, divide dough into quarters. Roll dough ¼ inch thick and cut by hand or machine into linguine noodles. Cook fresh noodles for 3 minutes in boiling water, or dry noodles on rack and when ready to cook, drop in boiling water for 10 to 12 minutes.

Yield: 1 pound

Note: After the noodles are cut, they may be frozen. Dust with cornmeal and separate layers with wax paper (see last paragraph on page 593). To use, just plunge into boiling water without defrosting and cook about 5 minutes.

Spinach Pasta

The spinach doesn't add much flavor, but it does make the pasta a lovely green, which looks particularly striking with a white sauce.

1 cup fresh spinach
2 to 2½ cups whole wheat flour
2 eggs
3 teaspoons olive oil
1 to 3 tablespoons warm water

Steam spinach for 3 minutes and dry it well on towels to remove as much moisture as you can. Squeeze it gently as you dry it. Then finely mince it (you should have about ¼ cup).

On a work surface or in a medium-size bowl, mound flour and make a well in the center. In this well, break open eggs and beat lightly with a fork. Place minced spinach and 1 teaspoon olive oil on top of eggs and stir until all is well mixed. Then, with a circular motion, begin to draw flour into spinach-egg mixture from all sides. Add 1 tablespoon water and continue mixing. Add more water if necessary to moisten all flour. When the dough becomes too stiff to mix with a fork, use your hands. Pat into a ball.

Clean and lightly flour work surface. Knead dough 5 to 8 minutes or until it is no longer sticky and is smooth and elastic. Sprinkle with a little more flour if necessary. Let dough rest 20 minutes, covered. If it's a hot, sticky day, let it rest in the refrigerator instead of on the counter; it'll cool more easily if it's in a cool place. Divide dough into 4 parts.

With pasta machine or by hand, roll out one-quarter of the dough at a time to desired thickness. This pasta should be rolled slightly thicker than white flour dough, about ¼ inch. If you are using a pasta machine, roll the 4 pieces of dough beginning at the first setting on your machine, then the second, and the third, and finally the fourth, if you like a thinner noodle, so that the dough gets progressively thinner. The fourth setting is about as thick as you'll want to make this pasta. When all the dough is rolled, let it rest for about 5 minutes to dry slightly; it'll be easier to cut. Then cut the dough into noodles by machine or by hand.

Cook fresh pasta in a large kettle of boiling water to which the remaining 2 teaspoons olive oil have been added, until al dente, 3 to 4 minutes. Drain and place in a serving bowl.

Pasta can also be stored dry or in the freezer. Dry noodles on racks or clean towels—anywhere you can find room. (Finding room is often the hardest part of the whole project!) Allow to dry at least 8 hours and then place in shirt boxes or shoe boxes for storage. Dry pasta will keep well for about 6 months. When ready to cook dry pasta, place it in boiling water to which 2 teaspoons olive oil have been added and cook for 10 to 12 minutes.

To freeze pasta, don't dry it, but lay it one layer deep on a sheet of wax paper and dust it with cornmeal; separate the noodles as best you can so that the cornmeal gets around each strand. Cover with another sheet of wax paper and lay down more noodles. Top last layer with wax paper, roll up neatly, and wrap in freezer paper or a plastic bag, forcing as much air out as you can. Then freeze for up to 3 months. To cook frozen pasta, thaw just until it's flexible—about 10 minutes—then drop into boiling water and cook for about 5 minutes.

Yield: about 1 pound

SWEET THINGS

Chewy Squares

2 eggs, separated
½ cup honey
⅓ cup whole wheat pastry flour
1 cup nuts, chopped
½ cup ground sunflower seeds
⅓ cup coconut

Preheat oven to 350°F.

Beat egg yolks until thick. Blend in honey. Combine with flour, nuts, seeds, and coconut. Beat egg whites until stiff and then fold into flour mixture. Turn into oiled 8 × 8-inch pan. Bake for 20 to 25 minutes, until light brown. Cool. Cut into squares.

Yield: 9 squares

Basic Rolled Piecrust

1¼ cups whole wheat pastry
    flour
3 tablespoons butter
2 to 3 tablespoons vegetable
    oil
2 to 3 tablespoons ice water

Measure flour into a medium-size bowl. Cut butter into flour with a fork or pastry blender. Add oil slowly and continue to cut or mix until dough looks crumbly. Slowly add ice water, while mixing, until you can gather dough into a ball.

Place dough on a piece of floured wax paper on a flat surface. Flatten dough with your hand, sprinkle a little flour over it, cover with another piece of wax paper and roll out to form a circle about 12 inches in diameter, ⅛ to ¼ inch thick.

Remove top piece of wax paper; invert a buttered 9-inch pie plate over dough; turn plate, dough, and remaining piece of wax paper right-side up; remove wax paper; and line plate with dough. Flute edges or simply trim away excess dough with a knife.

If recipe calls for a baked crust, prick dough with a fork and bake for 12 to 15 minutes at 425°F. Cool on a wire rack.

Yield: 1 9-inch piecrust

No-Bake Nut-Coconut Pie Shell

This is a wonderful recipe for people who are all thumbs when it comes to rolling out a pastry shell. This one can be used for any pie that does not get baked, such as a frozen mousse pie or fresh custard pie.

1 cup nuts, ground
1 cup shredded coconut
2 tablespoons vegetable oil
2 tablespoons honey

Blend all ingredients. Press into 9-inch pie pan. Chill and fill with a filling that needs no cooking.

Yield: 1 9-inch pie shell

Sprouted Wheat Flour Cookies

1   cup butter, softened
⅓   cup honey
2   eggs
1   teaspoon vanilla extract
1⅓ cups whole wheat flour,
      sifted
⅔   cup Sprouted Wheat Flour
      (see below)
1   egg white, beaten
½   cup ground nuts

In a medium-size bowl, beat butter, honey, eggs, and vanilla extract until fluffy light. Stir in flours, blending well. Wrap in plastic wrap and refrigerate 1 hour.
Preheat oven to 350°F.
Roll dough into 1-inch balls. Roll balls in beaten egg white. Then roll balls in ground nuts. Place on ungreased baking sheets. Flatten slightly with the back of a spoon. Bake until lightly browned, 12 to 15 minutes. Remove from baking sheets and cool on wire racks.

Yield: about 4 dozen cookies

Sprouted Wheat Flour

3½ to 4 cups wheat sprouts

Grind up sprouts in a grain mill or blender.

Yield: 1 cup

Walnut Torte

An impressive dessert when you've got someone to impress.

Cake
6 eggs, separated
¾ cup honey
½ cup powdered skim milk
½ cup wheat germ
2 cups finely ground walnuts*
1 teaspoon vanilla extract

Custard Filling
⅓ cup cornstarch
¼ cup instant nonfat dry milk
1¾ cups water
¼ cup honey
4 egg yolks, slightly beaten
   (use 2 reserved from cake,
   above)
1 teaspoon vanilla extract

Frosting
2 egg whites
½ cup honey
½ teaspoon vanilla extract

Prepare two 9-inch layer cake pans by oiling bottoms of pans with pastry brush. Cut two circles from heavy brown paper. Place a circle of heavy brown paper on the bottom of each pan. Brush paper thoroughly with oil.

Preheat oven to 325°F.

To make the cake, put egg whites into a large bowl and yolks into a smaller bowl, *reserving 2 of the yolks for filling.*

Beat whites until stiff peaks form when beater is slowly raised. Set to one side. With same beater, beat 4 yolks until thick and lemon colored. Gradually blend honey into yolks. Stir into the beaten yolks the powdered milk, wheat germ, and ground walnuts. Blend together. Add vanilla extract.

With wire whisk or rubber scraper, gently fold yolk mixture into beaten egg whites, using an under-and-over motion, until well combined. Pour the batter into the prepared pans, spreading evenly to edge.

Bake 25 to 30 minutes.

Remove from oven and loosen sides with a spatula to ease the cake out of the pan. Invert pans on a wire rack and carefully remove paper immediately. Cool cakes completely before frosting.

To make the custard filling, combine cornstarch and nonfat dry milk in medium-size saucepan. Add ¼ cup of the water gradually, stirring with wooden spoon until mixture is smooth and free of lumps. Add remaining 1½ cups of water, mixing thoroughly.

Add honey to mixture and place over medium heat, stirring constantly until custard thickens; this should take from 10 to 12 minutes.

Remove custard from heat. Add 3 tablespoons of hot mixture to beaten egg yolks. Mix well. Gradually pour yolk mixture into custard, blending well. Return to medium heat and cook 3 minutes, stirring constantly. Remove from heat. Add vanilla extract. Cool custard completely before using to fill cake.

To make the frosting, combine egg whites and honey in top of double boiler. Beat 1 minute with rotary beater (hand or electric type) to combine ingredients.

Cook over rapidly boiling water (water in bottom should not touch top of double boiler), beating constantly until soft peaks form when beater is slowly raised. Allow about 8 minutes of beating to get proper consistency.

Remove from boiling water. Add vanilla extract. Continue beating until frosting is thick enough to spread—about 2 minutes.

Put layers together with filling. Frost top and sides with frosting.

Yield: 10 to 12 servings

*Ground pecans or ground almonds may be substituted for the walnuts. When using ground almonds, use ½ teaspoon almond extract in cake and frosting in place of the vanilla extract.

OTHER GOOD FOODS

Chestnut Stuffing

3 cups chestnuts
3 cups diced celery
2 tablespoons butter
3 cups whole wheat bread
    crumbs
⅓ cup light cream
¼ teaspoon ground mace

Make an X through the shells on the flat sides of the chestnuts, and then boil for 20 minutes. Let cool; then peel and break into small pieces.

Brown celery in butter, add chestnuts and bread crumbs, and mix. Moisten with cream, sprinkle with mace, and stuff loosely into turkey or chicken.

Yield: 6 cups—enough to stuff a 12-pound bird

Sunflower Seed Loaf

This loaf is an unusual appetizer. It may be served warm or cold.

1 cup finely ground sunflower
    seeds
½ cup finely ground walnuts
1 cup cooked lentils
2 tablespoons minced onions
2 eggs
1 tablespoon vegetable oil
½ cup whole wheat bread
    crumbs

½ cup grated carrots
½ cup chopped green peppers
½ teaspoon ground oregano
½ teaspoon paprika
¼ teaspoon ground thyme
2 teaspoons lemon juice

Preheat oven to 350°F.

Mix together all ingredients and press into a greased 1-quart soufflé dish.

Bake for 45 minutes or until firm in the center. Let set for 5 minutes. Turn out onto a serving plate and cut into wedges.

Yield: 16 appetizer wedges

Sweet Party Mix

2 tablespoons orange juice
    concentrate, undiluted
2 tablespoons water
1 egg white
½ cup honey
¼ teaspoon ground cinnamon
    dash of nutmeg
3 cups mixed shelled nuts (such
    as peanuts, cashews,
    pecans, and almonds)

Preheat oven to 275°F.

In a medium-size bowl, combine orange juice concentrate, water, egg white, honey, cinnamon, and nutmeg. Add nuts ½ cup at a time, stirring until well coated. With a slotted spoon, remove nuts, draining off excess liquid. Spread nuts on a lightly greased baking sheet. Bake, stirring occasionally, for 30 minutes or until nuts are fairly dry and golden. Cool immediately on wax paper. Store in a tightly covered container.

Yield: 3 cups

Savory Party Mix

1 egg white
2 tablespoons Worcestershire
    sauce
1 tablespoon soy sauce
½ teaspoon ground red pepper
    or chili powder
1 clove garlic, minced

1 pound mixed shelled nuts
    (such as walnuts, pecans,
    Brazil halves, and whole
    almonds)
4 tablespoons butter or
    vegetable oil

In a blender container, combine egg white, Worcestershire sauce, soy sauce, red pepper or chili powder, and garlic. Process until garlic is puréed. Pour over nuts in medium-size bowl and toss to coat nuts. Let stand 15 minutes.

In a large fry pan over low heat, melt butter or heat oil. Cook nuts and sauce mixture 10 to 15 minutes or until golden, stirring constantly. Remove nuts with a slotted spoon. Drain on paper towels. Cool. Store in a tightly covered container.

Yield: 4 cups

Granola

3½ cups rolled oats
1 cup wheat or rye flakes or a
    combination of both
¾ cup bran
½ cup wheat germ
¼ cup soy flour
¾ cup sunflower seeds
¼ cup unhulled sesame seeds
½ cup shredded coconut
1 cup coarsely chopped nuts
    (peanuts, cashews, almonds,
    hazelnuts or walnuts, or
    any combination)

¼ cup safflower oil
½ cup honey
⅔ cup apple juice or water
1 teaspoon vanilla extract
½ teaspoon ground cinnamon
    dash of nutmeg
1 cup raisins

Preheat oven to 250°F.

In a large bowl, combine oats, wheat or rye flakes, bran, wheat germ, soy flour, sunflower and sesame seeds, coconut, and nuts. Mix well.

In a small saucepan, combine oil and honey. Add apple juice or water. Heat over low heat just until warmed. Add vanilla extract. Add to dry ingredients with cinnamon and nutmeg. Mix 1 to 2 minutes or until dry ingredients are moistened. Spread mixture onto 2 lightly greased jelly roll pans. Bake for 50 to 60 minutes or until lightly roasted and dry. Stir frequently (about every 10 minutes), so cereal doesn't burn. Transfer to a large bowl, add raisins, and let cool completely. Store in plastic airtight bag.

Yield: 8 to 10 cups

Variations

1. Diced dried fruit (apricots, pears, peaches, apples) may be used in combination with or in place of the raisins.

2. For added nutrition, add 2 tablespoons nonfat dry milk or brewer's yeast.

3. Other seeds and nuts, such as pumpkin seeds or pine nuts, can be used.

4. Use molasses as a sweetener instead of honey.

Malted Milk

1 cup milk
2 teaspoons Sprouted Wheat
   Flour (see page 595)
1 teaspoon honey
¼ teaspoon vanilla extract

Combine all ingredients in a blender and process until smooth.

Yield: 1 serving

Variation

Add 1 teaspoon sifted carob powder and process.

Appendix

GOOD, GENERAL INFORMATION
Rodale Books

At the risk of sounding biased, let us mention some other Rodale books that go into detail on one or several methods of storing foods. You might like to take a look at these to supplement the information in *Stocking Up*. Check your local library for the titles that are out-of-print.

The Complete Dairy Foods Cookbook by E. Annie Proulx and Lew Nichols, 1982 (out-of-print). Especially good for its recipes that show you what to do with all the terrific cheese you make. Plus, there's a very good appendix for information and supplies.

Home Food Systems edited by Roger B. Yepsen, Jr., 1981 (out-of-print). This is, as its subtitle says, "Rodale's catalog of methods and tools for producing, processing, and preserving naturally good foods." The book is a virtual goldmine of very good information on all sorts of kitchen techniques that involve food preservation. The chapters on grains, beans, sprouts, and drying foods are especially strong.

The Pantry Gourmet by Jane Doerfer, 1984. The specialties here are mustards, relishes, vinegars, cheeses, sausages, pâtés, and preserves. There's also a wonderful section on making pastas and another on preserving herbs.

Rodale's Complete Book of Home Freezing by Marilyn Hodges and the Rodale Test Kitchen staff, 1984. This volume contains many good recipes for freezing all sorts of combination dishes, and it provides some specialized information not found in *Stocking Up*.

Root Cellaring by Mike and Nancy Bubel, 1979. You'll find detailed information on underground storage for almost every fruit and vegetable you can imagine, as well as illustrations of many storage ideas and stories of homeowners' experiences with root cellaring.

The Wild Palate by Nancy and Walter Hall, 1980 (out-of-print). This book specializes in otherwise-hard-to-find material on venison, rabbit, and other game meats.

The Ball Corporation's Canning and Freezing "Bible"

The Ball Blue Book: The Guide to Home Canning and Freezing by the Ball Corporation, Muncie, Indiana, 1985. We had to include this book; it's reliable, updated frequently, and inexpensive. Many bookstores now carry copies, and you can often find it where Ball canning products are sold.

Government Publications

The government has been publishing bulletins and fact sheets on preserving foods longer than just about anyone, and it's still a good, cheap source of information. The step-by-step photographs and illustrations are often excellent. The United States Department of Agriculture (USDA) is the biggest publisher of such material, but some State Extension Services have awfully good information, too.

There's no way we could list all such sources here, and we see no need to do so, since a lot of what these government publications have to say is already in *Stocking Up*. Moreover, many of the publications duplicate one another.

Your County Extension Service will either have these in stock to send you or tell you the easiest way to get them.

A word of caution first: Besides sometimes being a bit old-fashioned in their presentation of material, these bulletins may also be a bit dated. This may be especially true if they haven't been revised lately, although the most popular bulletins are revised every several years. (What immediately comes to our minds is a popular bulletin that contains recommended processing times and techniques for canning. While the directions are for the most part just fine, some canning times and raw versus hot pack suggestions are not as up to date as they should be.) To play it safe, if the publication date on the bulletin you're consulting is older than that of *Stocking Up,* go with the recommendations in this book. On the other hand, you may find a more recent edition of a specific bulletin available when you go looking for it, since a revision may have been made since we researched this material.

After all that has been said, here are some of the USDA classics:

- H&G (House and Garden) Bulletin #8: *Home Canning Fruits and Vegetables,* 1972.

- H&G Bulletin #10: *Home Freezing Fruits and Vegetables,* 1971.

- H&G Bulletin #40: *Freezing Combination Dishes,* 1973.

- H&G Bulletin #56: *How to Make Jams and Jellies at Home,* 1971.

- H&G Bulletin #70: *Home Freezing of Poultry,* 1970.

- H&G Bulletin #78: *Storing Perishable Foods in the Home,* 1976.

- H&G Bulletin #92: *Making Pickles and Relishes at Home,* 1970.

- H&G Bulletin #93: *Freezing Meat and Fish in the Home,* 1973.

- H&G Bulletin #106: *Home Canning Meat and Poultry,* 1972.

- H&G Bulletin #119: *Storing Vegetables and Fruits in Basements, Cellars, Outbuildings, and Pits,* 1973.

- H&G Bulletin #129: *Making Cottage Cheese at Home,* 1975.

- H&G Bulletin #162: *Keeping Food Safe to Eat,* 1971.

- H&G Bulletin #217: *Drying Food at Home,* 1977.

- Farmers' Bulletin #2125: *Making and Preserving Apple Cider,* 1971.

And for information on slaughtering and butchering meats, see these USDA Farmers' Bulletins:

- Farmers' Bulletin #2152: *Slaughtering, Cutting, and Processing Lamb on the Farm,* 1967.

- Farmers' Bulletin #2209: *Slaughtering, Cutting, and Processing Beef on the Farm,* 1973.

- Farmers' Bulletin #2265: *Pork: Slaughtering, Cutting, Preserving, and Cooking on the Farm,* 1983.

COMMUNITY CANNING CENTERS

If you want to find out if there is a center near you, how much it charges, and what you must bring with you, contact the two companies that run community canning centers in the United States:

- Dixie Canner Equipment Co.
  NEFCO Centers
  Box 1384
  Athens, GA 30603

- Food Preservation Systems
  Joel Jackson
  1604 Old New Windsor Rd.
  New Windsor, MD 21776

SPECIAL PECTINS AND GELLING AGENTS FOR JAMS AND JELLIES

Low-methoxyl (LM) pectin is available on some supermarket shelves under the brand name Mrs. Wages Light Home Jell. As we write this, we have learned that Slim Set pectin is converting its product to a low-methoxyl pectin, too, and it can be bought at many supermarkets. LM pectins can also be mail-ordered, along with the dicalcium phosphate powder you need to make the pectin gel, from the following mail-order house:

- Walnut Acres
  Penns Creek, PA 17862

Agar flakes, a gelling agent used in some freezer jams, is sold in some natural food stores and some Asian markets (it's used in Japanese jellied fruit desserts). You can get it through the mail from the following:

- Erewhon, Inc.
  5 Waltham St.
  Wilmington, MA 01887

- Walnut Acres
  Penns Creek, PA 17862

INFORMATION AND SUPPLIES FOR HOMEMADE CHEESES

The chapter on cheesemaking in *Stocking Up* only scratches the surface when it comes to the cheese you can make. For more recipes, see any of these books:

Cheese Making at Home: The Complete Illustrated Guide by Don Radke. New York: Doubleday & Co., 1974.

Cheesemaking Made Easy by Ricki and Robert Carroll. Charlotte, Vt.: Garden Way Publishing, 1982.

The Little Cheesemaking Workbook by Carroll and Potter. Ashfield, Mass.: The Cheese Press, 1981.

Making Cheeses at Home by Susan Ogilvy. New York: Crown Publishers, 1976.

Also see the heading Good, General Information on page 601.

And cheesemaking supplies and the *Cheesemaker's Journal*, a newsletter that provides a forum for exchange between cheesemakers and small dairies, as well as recipes and valuable bits of information, can be ordered from:

- New England Cheesemaking Supply Co.
  P.O. Box 85
  Ashfield, MA 01330

Cheesemaking equipment and supplies can also be ordered from the companies below. Send for their catalogs to see what they've got.

- Cheesemaking Supply Outlet
  260 Moore Rd.
  Butler, PA 16001

- Homecraft
  111 Stratford Center
  Winston-Salem, NC 27104

- Nasco Farm and Ranch
  901 Janesville Ave.
  Fort Atkinson, WI 53538

CULTURES FOR YOGURT
AND OTHER FERMENTED MILKS

Cultures for yogurts are common enough in natural food stores that there's no need to make a long list of mail-order suppliers here, but we will mention just two that we know of:

- The International Yogurt Co.
  628 N. Doheny Dr.
  Los Angeles, CA 90069

- Walnut Acres
  Penns Creek, PA 17862

The International Yogurt Company also mail-orders a culture that produces a soft, cream-cheeselike cheese, sour cream, or buttermilk, depending upon the type of milk you add to it.

Grains for making alcoholo-lactic kefir, a carbonated fermented milk beverage, can be ordered from:

- RAJ Laboratory
  35 Park Ave.
  Blue Point, NY 11715

You can find the freeze-dried culture for making lactic kefir, a sweet, yogurtlike fermented milk, in many natural food stores. It can also be mail-ordered from The International Yogurt Company, listed above.

And freeze-dried piima culture can be gotten from:

- Piima
  P.O. Box 2614
  La Mesa, CA 92041

MORE INFORMATION ON
PREPARING MEATS AND POULTRY
FOR STORAGE

Stocking Up does not go into much detail on butchering and cutting up meats, but some other, more specialized books do. Your County Extension Service might be able to send you some pamphlets, and you ought to consider U.S. government publications, listed earlier in this appendix. You can also look for these books:

Butchering, Processing, and Preservation of Meat by Frank B. Ashbrook. New York: Van Nostrand Co., 1955.

The Complete Book of Meat by Phyllis Reynolds. New York: M. Barrows and Co., 1963.

How to Be Your Own Butcher by Leon Stanley and Evan Lobel. New York: Putnam Publishing Group, 1983.

The Meat Handbook by Albert Levie. Westport, Conn.: The Avi Publishing Co., 1979.

Also see the heading Good, General Information on page 601.

MOCHIKO FOR FREEZER SAUCES AND BINDERS

Mochiko is a sweet rice flour that can be used in place of cornstarch in dishes intended for the freezer; it doesn't separate the way cornstarch does. It's sold in some Asian markets. You can also write to either of the following distributors to see who might carry their brand of mochiko in your area:

- Koda Farms, Inc.
  Dos Palos, CA 93665

- Pacific National Rice Mills, Inc.
  848 Kentucky Ave.
  Woodland, CA 95695

Index

Page numbers in **boldface** indicate entries for charts, tables, boxes, and hints.

juice extraction for, 242-43
Lemon Honey Jelly, 277
natural sweeteners in, 241
Paradise Jelly, 278-79
and pectin
  LM, 253, 255, **258-61**, 262
  special, **604**
Persimmon Jelly, 279
pigs' feet, 454-55
Raspberry Jelly with Homemade
  Pectin, 280
sealing containers, 262
storing, 266
tests for, **248-49**
uncooked, **240**, 251-52, 254
Wild Berry Jelly, 278
jelly tests, **248-49**
jerky, 492
juicers
  centrifuge, 291
  choice of, 289
  citrus, 293
  liquefier, 291
  mechanical, 291, 293
  pulverizer, 291
  steam, 290
juices. *See also* apple cider
  Apricot Nectar, 304
  Berry and Currant Juices, 302
  boiling-water-bath timetable for,
    107
  and bulk, 287
  canning, 288-89, 291
  Cherry Juice, 303
  Cranberry Juice, 303
  equipment for making, 287
  and fiber, 287
  freezing, 288-89, 291
  Fresh Fruit Salad Popsicles, 336
  fruit, 287-88
  Grape Juice, 303
  juicers for, 289-91, 293
  Nectarine Nectar, 304
  orange
    freezing fruit in, **67**
  Peach Nectar, 304
  Plum Juice, 304
  procedure for making, 288
  Spiced Tomato Juice, 306
  Spicy Hot Tomato Juice, 306
  storing, 288-89
  Syrup for Lemonade, 304

Tomato Juice, 305-6
Tomato Juice Cocktail, 305
vegetable, 287-88

K
kale
  dried, using, 155
  drying, 125
  freezing, preparing for, 63
  harvesting, 32
  varieties of, **10-11**
kefir
  alcoholo-lactic, 606
  homemade, 395
  making, 394
  storing, 395-96
killing cone, 464
Kim Chee, **194**, 226
kiwi fruits, preparing for freezing,
  70
kohlrabi
  freezing, preparing for, 61
  harvesting, 32
  in storage, underground, 175
  varieties of, **11**
Korean Pickled Vegetables. *See*
  Kim Chee

L
lactic acid, **194**, 203
Lactobacillus acidophilus, 389-90
lamb. *See also* meats
  aging, 442-43
  cuts of, **446**
    yields of trimmed, **449**
  Lamb-Stuffed Eggplant, 523
  processing, **489**
lard, 456-57. *See also* butters
lasagna
  Vegetable Lasagna, 428
leathers. *See* fruit leathers
leeks
  dried, using, 154
  drying, 123
  freezing, preparing for, 61
  harvesting, 32
  varieties of, **11**
legumes. *See* beans
lemons
  Dried Lemon Zest, 131
  freezing, preparing for, 70
  harvesting, 38

Lemon Honey Jelly, 277
Lemon Vinaigrette, 322
Syrup for Lemonade, 304
lentil sprouts
  Sprouted Lentil, Bean, and Rice
    Salad, 579
  statistics on, **563**
lettuce. *See also* salads
  drying, 123
  freezing, preparing for, 63
  harvesting, 32
lids. *See* closures
lima beans. *See* beans
lime, for pickling, **213**
limes
  freezing, preparing for, 70
  harvesting, 38
liver, processing, **491**. *See also*
  meats
LM pectin. *See* pectin, low-
  methoxyl
lobsters
  boiling, 502
  freezing, 505
lovage, preparing for freezing, 75
low-methoxyl pectin. *See* pectin
lychees, preparing for freezing, 70

M
Mango Chutney, 235
marinade
  from Marinated Artichokes, 307
  for peppers, roasted, 322
marmalades. *See also* conserves;
    jams; jellies; preserves
  Bitter Orange Marmalade, 286
  definition of, **240**
  Quince Marmalade, 285
Mason jars. *See* jars
meats. *See also specific types of*
  aging, 442-43
  and butcher, 449-51
  butchering, 439-41
  canning
    equipment for, 479-83
    pounds per jar, **485**
    pressure canning, steps for,
      483-87
    processing for, 479
    spoiling of, **488**
    storing after, 487, 492
    timetable for, **489-92**

ventilation
    for drying, 132
    for storage, underground, 181
vinaigrettes, 322
vinegars. *See also* pickling
    from apple cider, 297-99
    Basil and Garlic Wine Vinegar,
        300-301
    cider, 196
    Cucumber Vinegar, 300
    Dill and Nasturtium Bud
        Vinegar, 300
    distilled, 196
    herb, 299-300
    homemade, 196
    Horseradish in Vinegar, 222-23
    Hot Pepper Vinegar, 301
    Peach Vinegar, 302
    and pickling, 196
    pickling with, **298**
    Ruby Vinegar, 301
vitamins. *See also* nutrients
    A, 51, 118, 549
    B, 51, 193, 393, 549
    C
        and blanching, 49-51
        in broccoli, 30
        in cabbage, 30
        and canning, 92
        in cauliflower, 30
        and drying, 118
        and freezing, 43
        in fruits, 27
        and harvesting, 41, 43
        loss of, 51
        and pickling, 193
        and sauerkraut, 209
        in vegetables, 49-50
    E, 549
    K, 549

W

waffles. *See also* pancakes
    freezing, 551
    Nutty Waffles, 591

walnuts. *See* nuts
watermelons
    Gingered Watermelon Rind, 233
    harvesting, 40-41
waxing, 262, 368-69, 465-66
wheat sprouts
    Sprouted Wheat and Rye Bread,
        585
    Sprouted Wheat Bread, 584
    Sprouted Wheat Flour, 595
    statistics on, **464**
whey, 373-75
window wells, for storage, 182
wraps, freezer, 470, 472-73

Y

yams. *See* sweet potatoes
yeast. *See also* yeast breads and
        rolls
    and cold flour, **549**
    freezing, 553
yeast breads and rolls. *See also*
        breads
    Crusty Loaves, 588
    Dill Bread, 587
    freezing, 551
    Granola Bread, 582-83
    Green Onion Crescent Rolls,
        588-89
    Oat Bread, 584
    Peanut Bread, 586
    Plymouth Bread, 582
    Raisin Bread, 583
    Seven Grain Bread, 581
    Sprouted Wheat and Rye Bread,
        585
    Sprouted Wheat Bread, 584
    Veggie Bread, 586-87
    Whole Wheat Dinner Rolls,
        589
yellow beans. *See* beans
yogurt
    and bacteria, 389-90
    buying, 389-90
    and cheeses, homemade, 368

cream cheese, 394
Cucumber Salad, 431
cultures for, 606
Dilly Yogurt Spread, 433
Frozen Blueberry Yogurt,
    434
Frozen Yogurt Pops, 413
Fruit Dressing, 432
and fruit purée, 158
Green Onion Dressing, 432
Honey-Yogurt Fruit Salad
    Dressing, 432
Lite Apricot Yogurt Pie, 435
making
    basic, 390-91
    in casserole dish, 392
    failure of, 393
    ingredients for, 389
    in oven, 391-92
    in thermos, 392-93
    with yogurt maker, 391
Russian Dressing, 433
storing, 393-94
Strawberry Yogurt Ice Cream,
    434
thicker, **390**
Yogurt Dip, 433
Yogurt-Fruit Freeze, 434
yogurt maker, 391
yolks. *See* eggs

Z

Zolca, 454-55
zucchini
    dried, using, 155
    drying, 125
    freezing, preparing for, 65
    Giant Stuffed Squash, 318
    harvesting, 36
    pressure canning timetable for,
        116
    Refrigerator Zucchini Pickles,
        217
    Tomato-Zucchini Sauce, 329
    varieties of, 19